THE BOOK

Suzuki GSX600F, GSX750F & GSX750
Service and Repair Manual

by Matthew Coombs

Models covered

(3987-288)

GSX600F. 600cc. 1998 to 2002
GSX750F. 750cc. 1998 to 2002
GSX750. 750cc. 1998 to 2001

© Haynes Publishing 2003

A book in the **Haynes Service and Repair Manual Series**

ABCDE
FGHIJ
KLMNO
PQRS

Printed in the USA

Haynes Publishing
Sparkford, Yeovil, Somerset BA22 7JJ, England

Haynes North America, Inc
861 Lawrence Drive, Newbury Park, California 91320, USA

Editions Haynes
4, Rue de l'Abreuvoir
92415 COURBEVOIE CEDEX, France

Haynes Publishing Nordiska AB
Box 1504, 751 45 UPPSALA, Sweden

ISBN **1 85960 987 2**

British Library Cataloguing in Publication Data
A catalogue record for this book is available from the British Library.

Library of Congress Catalogue Card Number 2003101251

Contents

LIVING WITH YOUR SUZUKI

Introduction

Suzuki – Every which way	Page	0•4
Acknowledgements	Page	0•8
About this manual	Page	0•8
Model development	Page	0•9
Performance data	Page	0•9
Bike spec	Page	0•10
Safety first!	Page	0•12
Identification numbers	Page	0•13
Buying spare parts	Page	0•13

Daily (pre-ride) checks

Engine/transmission oil level check	Page	0•14
Suspension, steering and drive chain checks	Page	0•14
Brake checks	Page	0•15
Tyre checks	Page	0•16
Legal and safety checks	Page	0•16

MAINTENANCE

Routine maintenance and servicing

Specifications	Page	1•1
Recommended lubricants and fluids	Page	1•2
Maintenance schedule	Page	1•3
Component locations	Page	1•4
Maintenance procedures	Page	1•6

Contents

REPAIRS AND OVERHAUL

Engine, transmission and associated systems

Engine, clutch and transmission   Page **2•1**

Fuel and exhaust systems   Page **3•1**

Ignition system   Page **4•1**

Chassis components

Frame, suspension and final drive   Page **5•1**

Brakes, wheels and tyres   Page **6•1**

Fairing and bodywork   Page **7•1**

Electrical system

Page **8•1**

Wiring diagrams

Page **8•31**

REFERENCE

Tools and Workshop Tips   Page **REF•2**

Security   Page **REF•20**

Lubricants and fluids   Page **REF•23**

Conversion Factors   Page **REF•26**

MOT test checks   Page **REF•27**

Storage   Page **REF•32**

Fault finding   Page **REF•35**

Fault finding equipment   Page **REF•44**

Technical terms explained   Page **REF•48**

Index

Page **REF•52**

Suzuki
Every Which Way

by Julian Ryder

From Textile Machinery to Motorcycles

Suzuki were the second of Japan's Big Four motorcycle manufacturers to enter the business, and like Honda they started by bolting small two-stroke motors to bicycles. Unlike Honda, they had manufactured other products before turning to transportation in the aftermath of World War II.

In fact Suzuki has been in business since the first decade of the 20th-Century when Michio Suzuki manufactured textile machinery.

The desperate need for transport in post-war Japan saw Suzuki make their first motorised bicycle in 1952, and the fact that by 1954 the company had changed its name to Suzuki Motor Company shows how quickly the sideline took over the whole company's activities. In their first full manufacturing year,

Suzuki made nearly 4500 bikes and rapidly expanded into the world markets with a range of two-strokes.

Suzuki didn't make a four-stroke until 1977 when the GS750 double-overhead-cam across-the-frame four arrived. This was several years after Honda and Kawasaki had established the air-cooled four as the industry standard, but no motorcycle epitomises the era of what came to be known as the Universal

The T500 two-stroke twin

50 cc racer won six of the eight world titles chalked up by Suzuki during the 1960s as well as providing Mitsuo Itoh with the distinction of being the only Japanese rider to win an Isle of Man TT. Mr Itoh still works for Suzuki, he's in charge of their racing program.

Europe got the benefit of Suzuki's two-stroke expertise in a succession of air-cooled twins, the six-speed 250 cc Super Six being the most memorable, but the arrival in 1968 of the first of a series of 500 cc twins which were good looking, robust and versatile marked the start of mainstream success.

So confident were Suzuki of their two-stroke expertise that they even applied it to the burgeoning Superbike sector. The GT750 water-cooled triple arrived in 1972. It was big, fast and comfortable although the handling and stopping power did draw some comment. Whatever the drawbacks of the road bike, the engine was immensely successful in Superbike and Formula 750 racing. The roadster has its devotees, though, and is now a sought-after bike on the classic Japanese scene. Do not refer to it as the Water Buffalo in such company. Joking aside, the later disc-braked versions were quite civilised, but the audacious idea of using a big two-stroke motor in what was essentially a touring bike was a surprising success until the fuel crisis of the mid-'70s effectively killed off big strokers.

The same could be said of Suzuki's only real lemon, the RE5. This is still the only mass-produced bike to use the rotary (or Wankel) engine but never sold well. Fuel consumption in the mid-teens allied to frightening complexity and excess weight meant the RE5 was a non-starter in the sales race.

One of the later GT750 'kettle' models with front disc brakes

Japanese motorcycle better than the GS. So well engineered were the original fours that you can clearly see their genes in the GS500 twins that are still going strong in the mid-1990s. Suzuki's ability to prolong the life of their products this way means that they are often thought of as a conservative company. This is hardly fair if you look at some of their landmark designs, most of which have been commercial as well as critical successes.

Two-stroke Success

Early racing efforts were bolstered by the arrival of Ernst Degner who defected from the East German MZ team at the Swedish GP of 1961, bringing with him the rotary-valve secrets of design genius Walter Kaaden. The new Suzuki 50 cc racer won its first GP on the Isle of Man the following year and winning the title easily. Only Honda and Ralph Bryans interrupted Suzuki's run of 50 cc titles from 1962 to 1968.

The arrival of the twin-cylinder 125 racer in 1963 enabled Hugh Anderson to win both 50 and 125 world titles. You may not think 50 cc racing would be exciting - until you learn that the final incarnation of the thing had 14 gears and could do well over 100 mph on fast circuits. Before pulling out of GPs in 1967 the

Suzuki's GT250X7 was an instant hit in the popular 250 cc 'learner' sector

The GS400 was the first in a line of four-stroke twins

Development of the Four-stroke range

When Suzuki got round to building a four-stroke they did a very good job of it. The GS fours were built in 550, 650, 750, 850, 1000 and 1100 cc sizes in sports, custom, roadster and even shaft-driven touring forms over many years. The GS1000 was in on the start of Superbike racing in the early 1970s and the GS850 shaft-driven tourer was around nearly 15 years later. The fours spawned a line of 400, 425, 450 and 500 cc GS twins that were essentially the middle half of the four with all their reliability. If there was ever a criticism of the GS models it was that with the exception of the GS1000S of 1980, colloquially known as the ice-cream van, the range was visually uninspiring.

They nearly made the same mistake when they launched the four-valve-head GSX750 in 1979. Fortunately, the original twin-shock version was soon replaced by the 'E'-model with Full-Floater rear suspension and a full set of all the gadgets the Japanese industry was then keen on and has since forgotten about, like 16-inch front wheels and anti-dive forks. The air-cooled GSX was like the GS built in 550, 750 and 1100 cc versions with a variety of half, full and touring fairings, but the GSX that is best remembered is the Katana that first appeared in 1981. The power was provided by an 1000 or 1100 cc GSX motor, but wrapped around it was the most outrageous styling package to come out of Japan. Designed by Hans Muth of Target

Design, the Katana looked like nothing seen before or since. At the time there was as much anti feeling as praise, but now it is rightly regarded as a classic, a true milestone in motorcycle design. The factory have even started making 250 and 400 cc fours for the home market with the same styling as the 1981 bike.

Just to remind us that they'd still been building two-strokes for the likes of Barry Sheene, in 1986 Suzuki marketed a road-going version of their RG500 square-four racer which had put an end to the era of the four-stroke in 500 GPs when it appeared in 1974. In 1976 Suzuki not only won their first 500 title with Sheene, they sold RG500s over the counter and won every GP with them - with the exception of the Isle of Man TT which the works riders boycotted. Ten years on, the RG500 Gamma gave road riders the nearest experience they'd ever get to riding a GP bike. The fearsome beast could top 140 mph and only weighed 340 lb - the other alleged GP replicas were pussy cats compared to the Gamma's man-eating tiger.

The RG only lasted a few years and is already firmly in the category of collector's item; its four-stroke equivalent, the GSX-R, is still with us and looks like being so for many years. You have to look back to 1985 and its launch to realise just what a revolutionary step the GSX-R750 was: quite simply it was the first race replica. Not a bike dressed up to look like a race bike, but a genuine racer with lights on, a bike that could be taken straight to the track and win.

The first GSX-R, the 750, had a completely new motor cooled by oil rather than water and an aluminium cradle frame. It was sparse, a little twitchy and very, very fast. This time Suzuki got the looks right, blue and white bodywork based on the factory's racing colours and endurance-racer lookalike twin headlights. And then came the 1100 - the big GSX-R got progressively more brutal as it chased the Yamaha EXUP for the heavyweight championship.

The GS750 led the way for a series of four cylinder models

Later four-stroke models, like this GSX1100, were fitted with 16v engines

motorcycle of the type everyone had thought was becoming extinct. And it was still cheap compared to the state-of-the-art sportsters. Suzuki liked it so much they restored the venerable power plant to its original dimensions and produced the GSX750F, to all intents and purposes an identical motorcycle to the 600 cc version.

The result was another very able motorcycle. But in a sportster obsessed market, who would buy them? There were several answers: those who couldn't afford to insure a top-of-the-range machine, those who were looking for an affordable first bike after getting their licence, and those diehards who will not be led by fashion. In the case of the 600 and 750 GSXs, they have a point. For sensible money you can ride all day in comfort with a pillion for company (try that on a GSX-R), carry a reasonable mount of luggage and – on the bigger bike – enjoy torque from low down and genuine top-gear flexibility. In short, Suzuki retained all the old Teapot's usability but thankfully improved on the looks immeasurably with swoopy new bodywork.

The GSX750 (note the lack of an 'F') is an entirely different – um, pot of tea... although it does share with its brothers the distinction of being an awful lot of motorcycle for very little money. The GSX750 is a retro, a bike styled like bikes were styled before the first GSX-R750 was a twinkle in its daddy's eye. No GSX-R ever had twin shocks, a tubular steel frame or non-adjustable front forks. This is a styling exercise harking back to the days of the UJM, the Universal Japanese Motorcycle, a phrase coined, I believe by Cycle magazine editor Cook Neilsen to describe the proliferation of air-cooled across-the-frame four cylinder bikes coming out of Japan.

Not surprisingly, the retro GSX attracted its fair share of riders returning to motorcycling after a long time out of the saddle. Here was a

And alongside all these mould-breaking designs, Suzuki were also making the best looking custom bikes to come out of Japan, the Intruders; the first race replica trail bike, the DR350; the sharpest 250 Supersports, the RGV250; and a bargain-basement 600, the Bandit. The Bandit proved so popular they went on to build 1200 and 750 cc versions of it. I suppose that's predictable, a range of four-stroke fours just like the GS and GSXs. It's just like the company really, sometimes predictable, admittedly - but never boring.

The GSXF and GSX models

The story really starts with the first GSX-R750, which revolutionised our view of what a sports motorcycle should be when it appeared back in 1985 with its 70 x 48.7 mm air/oil-cooled motor. The lightweight GSX-R was the first real race replica – actually, not so much of a replica more an out-and-out racer with lights on.

Fast forward ten years and Suzuki are looking for ways to make a budget machine; not a boring ride-to-work hack but a fun machine that would be fun to own and ride. Enter the 600 Bandit, featuring a sleeved down version of the very same motor that powered the first GSX-R750. Wrapped in a steel frame with noticeable lack of bodywork, the Bandit delivered more thrills for your money than anything else you could buy.

Time to move the time machine a little

further forward, to 1998, and Suzuki decide to reinvent the GSX600F sports tourer, an idea that's been around since 1988 when the first F-model's unlovely lines earned the nickname 'teapot'. This time Suzuki wrapped a bit of swoopy bodywork around the 600 Bandit motor and fitted a few more parts from the spare-parts bin and et voila! – produced a very practical and useable all-round

Suzuki's GSX-R range represented their cutting edge sports bikes

The GSX600F-K1 model

machine that was comfortably familiar. It deserves more than just an audience of 'born-again bikers' though, its another good choice for a relative novice and if a fair amount of your mileage is in town it makes a great commuter. And like the Fs it is perfectly capable of carrying a pillion in comfort.

Acknowledgements

Our thanks are due to GT Motorcycles and V & J Motorcycles who supplied the machines featured in the illustrations throughout this manual. We would also like to thank NGK Spark Plugs (UK) Ltd for supplying the colour spark plug condition photographs, the Avon Rubber Company for supplying information on tyre fitting and Draper Tools Ltd for some of the workshop tools shown.

Thanks are also due to Julian Ryder who wrote the introduction 'Every Which Way' and to Suzuki (GB) Ltd who supplied some of the model photographs used on the cover.

About this Manual

The aim of this manual is to help you get the best value from your motorcycle. It can do so in several ways. It can help you decide what work must be done, even if you choose to have it done by a dealer; it provides information and procedures for routine maintenance and servicing; and it offers diagnostic and repair procedures to follow when trouble occurs.

We hope you use the manual to tackle the work yourself. For many simpler jobs, doing it yourself may be quicker than arranging an appointment to get the motorcycle into a dealer and making the trips to leave it and pick it up. More importantly, a lot of money can be saved by avoiding the expense the shop must pass on to you to cover its labour and overhead costs. An added benefit is the sense of satisfaction and accomplishment that you feel after doing the job yourself.

References to the left or right side of the motorcycle assume you are sitting on the seat, facing forward.

We take great pride in the accuracy of information given in this manual, but motorcycle manufacturers make alterations and design changes during the production run of a particular motorcycle of which they do not inform us. No liability can be accepted by the authors or publishers for loss, damage or injury caused by any errors in, or omissions from, the information given.

The GSX750-Y model

GSX600F (1998 to 2002)

The GSX600F was introduced in 1998 as a fully faired 'sports-tourer'. It superseded the original GSX600F which had been discontinued in 1995.

The GSX600F used the air/oil-cooled engine from the GSF600 Bandit models, this being a sleeved down version of the original GSX-R750 engine. This four cylinder engine had chain drive to its double overhead camshafts which operated four valves per cylinder. Power was transmitted via a conventional wet multi-plate clutch to the 6-speed constant mesh gearbox, and then to the rear wheel by chain and sprockets. The engine was fed by four 32 mm Mikuni CV carburettors, with ignition by a transistorized electronic system.

The engine was mounted in a box-section steel cradle frame. Suspension was provided by 41 mm oil-damped telescopic forks at the front, and a box-section aluminium swingarm acting on a single shock absorber via a three-way linkage at the rear. The forks were adjustable for rebound damping. The shock absorber was adjustable for spring pre-load and rebound damping. Braking was by twin disc and twin-piston sliding calipers at the front and by a disc and single opposed-piston caliper at the rear.

The GSX600F has remained virtually unchanged during its production history.

GSX750F (1998 to 2002)

The GSX750F used virtually the same chassis as the 600 models, but was powered by the 749 cc air/oil-cooled engine fitted to the original GSX-R750. It superseded the original GSX750F which had been discontinued in 1996.

Differences between the GSX600 and 750F models were few; the 750 had larger carburettors, and used different handlebars and a different rear shock absorber.

The GSX750F has remained virtually unchanged during its production history.

GSX750 (1998 to 2001)

The GSX750 used the same engine as the GSX750F, but in a retro-style chassis. The engine was mounted in a tubular section frame, with conventional non-adjustable front forks and twin rear shocks. In keeping with the naked retro image, it had one-piece handlebars, a single chromed headlight and chromed instrument pods.

The GSX750 has remained virtually unchanged during its production history.

Performance Data

Maximum power
GSX600F . . . . 73 bhp (54 kW) @ 10,350 rpm
GSX750F . . . . 92 bhp (69 kW) @ 10,500 rpm
GSX750 . . . . 86 bhp (64 kW) @ 9500 rpm

Maximum torque
GSX600F . . . . 39 lbf ft (53 Nm) @ 7950 rpm
GSX750F . . . . 49 lbf ft (66 Nm) @ 9500 rpm
GSX750 . . . . 49 lbf ft (66 Nm) @ 8500 rpm

Top speed
GSX600F . . . . 135 mph (216 km/h)
GSX750F . . . . 150 mph (240 km/h)
GSX750 . . . . 131 mph (211 km/h)

Acceleration
GSX600F
Time taken to cover a 1/4 mile from a standing start . . . . 12.2 secs
Terminal speed after 1/4 mile . . . . 110 mph (176 km/h)
GSX750F
Time taken to cover a 1/4 mile from a standing start . . . . 11.8 secs
Terminal speed after 1/4 mile (estimated) . . . . 117 mph (188 km/h)
GSX750
Time taken to cover a 1/4 mile from a standing start . . . . 12.3 secs
Terminal speed after 1/4 mile (estimated) . . . . 112 mph (180 km/h)

Average fuel consumption
Miles per Imp gal, miles per litre, litres per 100 km
GSX600F . . . . 52 mpg, 11.44 mpl, 5.4 l/100 km
GSX750F . . . . 42 mpg, 9.24 mpl, 6.7 l/100 km
GSX750 . . . . 38 mpg, 8.36 mpl, 7.4 l/100 km

Fuel tank range
Based on average fuel consumption rate
GSX600F . . . . 228 miles (365 km)
GSX750F . . . . 184 miles (288 km)
GSX750 . . . . 150 miles (241 km)

Power/torque curves

Performance data sourced from Motor Cycle News road test features. See the MCN website for up-to-date biking news. **MCN www.motorcyclenews.com**

Dimensions and weights

GSX600F

Overall length
  Austria, Germany, Switzerland,
    and Scandinavia models .....2175 mm
  UK and all other models ....2135 mm
Overall width ....745 mm
Overall height ....1195 mm
Wheelbase ....1470 mm
Seat height ....785 mm
Ground clearance ....120 mm
Weight (dry)
  Austria, Switzerland and
    California models ....209 kg
  UK and all other models ....208 kg

GSX750F

Overall length
  Austria, Germany, Switzerland,
    and Scandinavia models .....2175 mm
  UK and all other models ....2135 mm
Overall width ....750 mm
Overall height ....1190 mm
Wheelbase ....1465 mm
Seat height ....790 mm
Ground clearance ....120 mm
Weight (dry)
  Austria and Switzerland models ....212 kg
  California models ....213 kg
  UK and all other models ....211 kg

GSX750

Overall length
  Austria, Germany, Switzerland,
    and Scandinavia models .....2175 mm
  UK and all other models ....2145 mm
Overall width ....750 mm
Overall height ....1095 mm
Wheelbase ....1470 mm
Seat height ....785 mm
Ground clearance ....130 mm
Weight (dry) ....201 kg

Engine

Type .... Four stroke in-line four cylinder, air/oil-cooled, four valves per cylinder
Capacity
  GSX600F .... 600 cc
  GSX750F and GSX750 .... 750 cc
Bore and stroke
  GSX600F .... 62.6 x 48.7 mm
  GSX750F and GSX750 .... 70.0 x 48.7 mm
Compression ratio
  GSX600F 11.3:1
  GSX750F and GSX750 .... 10.7:1
Camshafts .... DOHC, chain-driven
Lubrication .... Wet sump

Engine (continued)

Carburettors
 GSX600F . . . .   4 x 32 mm Mikuni, CV type
 GSX750F . . . .   4 x 36 mm Mikuni, CV type
 GSX750 . . . .   4 x 32.5 mm Keihin, CV type
Starter . . . .   Electric
Ignition system . . . .   Transistorized with electronic advance
Clutch . . . .   Wet multi-plate, cable-operated
Gearbox . . . .   6-speed constant mesh
Final drive . . . .   Chain and sprockets

Chassis – GSX600F and GSX750F

Frame type . . . .   Box-section steel cradle
Rake
 GSX600F . . . .   25.0° 30′
 GSX750F . . . .   25.0° 18′
Trail . . . .   99.5 mm
Fuel tank capacity (including reserve) . . . .   20 litres
Front suspension
 Type . . . .   41 mm oil-damped telescopic forks
 Travel . . . .   130 mm
 Adjustment . . . .   Rebound damping
Rear suspension
 Type
  GSX600F . . . .   Single shock absorber with spring pre-load and rebound damping adjustment, rising rate linkage, box section aluminium swingarm
  GSX750F . . . .   Single shock absorber with remote reservoir providing spring pre-load, rebound damping and compression damping adjustment, rising rate linkage, box section aluminium swingarm
 Travel . . . .   142 mm (at rear wheel)
Wheels
 Front . . . .   17 inch cast aluminium-alloy
 Rear . . . .   17 inch cast aluminium-alloy
Tyres
 Front . . . .   120/70ZR17 (58W) tubeless
 Rear . . . .   150/70ZR17 (69W) tubeless
Front brake
 Discs . . . .   2 x 290 mm discs
 Calipers . . . .   2 x twin piston sliding calipers
Rear brake
 Discs . . . .   1 x 240 mm disc
 Caliper . . . .   1 x twin opposed-piston caliper

Chassis – GSX750

Frame type . . . .   Tubular-section steel cradle
Rake . . . .   25.0° 30′
Trail . . . .   101 mm
Fuel tank capacity (including reserve) . . . .   18 litres
Front suspension
 Type . . . .   43 mm oil-damped telescopic forks, non-adjustable
 Travel . . . .   130 mm
Rear suspension
 Type . . . .   Twin shock absorbers with remote reservoir and pre-load adjustment, box section aluminium swingarm
 Travel . . . .   120 mm (at rear wheel)
Wheels . . . .   17 inch cast aluminium-alloy
Tyres
 Front . . . .   120/70ZR17 (58W) tubeless
 Rear . . . .   170/60ZR17 (72W) tubeless
Front brake
 Discs . . . .   2 x 300 mm discs
 Calipers . . . .   2 x twin piston sliding calipers
Rear brake
 Discs . . . .   1 x 240 mm disc
 Caliper . . . .   1 x opposed-piston caliper

Professional mechanics are trained in safe working procedures. However enthusiastic you may be about getting on with the job at hand, take the time to ensure that your safety is not put at risk. A moment's lack of attention can result in an accident, as can failure to observe simple precautions.

There will always be new ways of having accidents, and the following is not a comprehensive list of all dangers; it is intended rather to make you aware of the risks and to encourage a safe approach to all work you carry out on your bike.

Asbestos

● Certain friction, insulating, sealing and other products - such as brake pads, clutch linings, gaskets, etc. - contain asbestos. Extreme care must be taken to avoid inhalation of dust from such products since it is hazardous to health. If in doubt, assume that they do contain asbestos.

Fire

● Remember at all times that petrol is highly flammable. Never smoke or have any kind of naked flame around, when working on the vehicle. But the risk does not end there - a spark caused by an electrical short-circuit, by two metal surfaces contacting each other, by careless use of tools, or even by static electricity built up in your body under certain conditions, can ignite petrol vapour, which in a confined space is highly explosive. Never use petrol as a cleaning solvent. Use an approved safety solvent.

● Always disconnect the battery earth terminal before working on any part of the fuel or electrical system, and never risk spilling fuel on to a hot engine or exhaust.

● It is recommended that a fire extinguisher of a type suitable for fuel and electrical fires is kept handy in the garage or workplace at all times. Never try to extinguish a fuel or electrical fire with water.

Fumes

● Certain fumes are highly toxic and can quickly cause unconsciousness and even death if inhaled to any extent. Petrol vapour comes into this category, as do the vapours from certain solvents such as trichloroethylene. Any draining or pouring of such volatile fluids should be done in a well ventilated area.

● When using cleaning fluids and solvents, read the instructions carefully. Never use materials from unmarked containers - they may give off poisonous vapours.

● Never run the engine of a motor vehicle in an enclosed space such as a garage. Exhaust fumes contain carbon monoxide which is extremely poisonous; if you need to run the engine, always do so in the open air or at least have the rear of the vehicle outside the workplace.

The battery

● Never cause a spark, or allow a naked light near the vehicle's battery. It will normally be giving off a certain amount of hydrogen gas, which is highly explosive.

● Always disconnect the battery ground (earth) terminal before working on the fuel or electrical systems (except where noted).

● If possible, loosen the filler plugs or cover when charging the battery from an external source. Do not charge at an excessive rate or the battery may burst.

● Take care when topping up, cleaning or carrying the battery. The acid electrolyte, evenwhen diluted, is very corrosive and should not be allowed to contact the eyes or skin. Always wear rubber gloves and goggles or a face shield. If you ever need to prepare electrolyte yourself, always add the acid slowly to the water; never add the water to the acid.

Electricity

● When using an electric power tool, inspection light etc., always ensure that the appliance is correctly connected to its plug and that, where necessary, it is properly grounded (earthed). Do not use such appliances in damp conditions and, again, beware of creating a spark or applying excessive heat in the vicinity of fuel or fuel vapour. Also ensure that the appliances meet national safety standards.

● A severe electric shock can result from touching certain parts of the electrical system, such as the spark plug wires (HT leads), when the engine is running or being cranked, particularly if components are damp or the insulation is defective. Where an electronic ignition system is used, the secondary (HT) voltage is much higher and could prove fatal.

Remember...

✗ **Don't** start the engine without first ascertaining that the transmission is in neutral.

✗ **Don't** suddenly remove the pressure cap from a hot cooling system - cover it with a cloth and release the pressure gradually first, or you may get scalded by escaping coolant.

✗ **Don't** attempt to drain oil until you are sure it has cooled sufficiently to avoid scalding you.

✗ **Don't** grasp any part of the engine or exhaust system without first ascertaining that it is cool enough not to burn you.

✗ **Don't** allow brake fluid or antifreeze to contact the machine's paintwork or plastic components.

✗ **Don't** siphon toxic liquids such as fuel, hydraulic fluid or antifreeze by mouth, or allow them to remain on your skin.

✗ **Don't** inhale dust - it may be injurious to health (see Asbestos heading).

✗ **Don't** allow any spilled oil or grease to remain on the floor - wipe it up right away, before someone slips on it.

✗ **Don't** use ill-fitting spanners or other tools which may slip and cause injury.

✗ **Don't** lift a heavy component which may be beyond your capability - get assistance.

✗ **Don't** rush to finish a job or take unverified short cuts.

✗ **Don't** allow children or animals in or around an unattended vehicle.

✗ **Don't** inflate a tyre above the recommended pressure. Apart from overstressing the carcass, in extreme cases the tyre may blow off forcibly.

✔ **Do** ensure that the machine is supported securely at all times. This is especially important when the machine is blocked up to aid wheel or fork removal.

✔ **Do** take care when attempting to loosen a stubborn nut or bolt. It is generally better to pull on a spanner, rather than push, so that if you slip, you fall away from the machine rather than onto it.

✔ **Do** wear eye protection when using power tools such as drill, sander, bench grinder etc.

✔ **Do** use a barrier cream on your hands prior to undertaking dirty jobs - it will protect your skin from infection as well as making the dirt easier to remove afterwards; but make sure your hands aren't left slippery. Note that long-term contact with used engine oil can be a health hazard.

✔ **Do** keep loose clothing (cuffs, ties etc. and long hair) well out of the way of moving mechanical parts.

✔ **Do** remove rings, wristwatch etc., before working on the vehicle - especially the electrical system.

✔ **Do** keep your work area tidy - it is only too easy to fall over articles left lying around.

✔ **Do** exercise caution when compressing springs for removal or installation. Ensure that the tension is applied and released in a controlled manner, using suitable tools which preclude the possibility of the spring escaping violently.

✔ **Do** ensure that any lifting tackle used has a safe working load rating adequate for the job.

✔ **Do** get someone to check periodically that all is well, when working alone on the vehicle.

✔ **Do** carry out work in a logical sequence and check that everything is correctly assembled and tightened afterwards.

✔ **Do** remember that your vehicle's safety affects that of yourself and others. If in doubt on any point, get professional advice.

● If in spite of following these precautions, you are unfortunate enough to injure yourself, seek medical attention as soon as possible.

Frame and engine numbers

The frame serial number is stamped into the right-hand side of the steering head. The engine number is stamped into the crankcase on the right-hand side of the engine. Both of these numbers should be recorded and kept in a safe place so they can be furnished to law enforcement officials in the event of a theft. The carburettors also have an ID number stamped into them.

The frame serial number, engine serial number, colour code and carburettor ID should also be kept in a handy place (such as with your driver's licence) so they are always available when purchasing or ordering parts for your machine.

Procedures in this manual identify bikes by model code and production year, e.g. GSX750F-X (1999). If not known, the model code can be determined from the initial frame numbers given below on UK and US market machines.

UK models

Model	Year	Initial frame no.
GSX600F-W	1998	JS1AJ111100100001
GSX600F-X	1999	JS1AJ111100100867
GSX600F-Y	2000	JS1AJ111100101623
GSX600F-K1	2001	JS1AJ111100102227
GSX600F-K2	2002	JS1AJ111100102327
GSX750F-W	1998	JS1AK111100100001
GSX750F-X	1999	JS1AK111100100781
GSX750F-Y	2000	JS1AK111100101251
GSX750F-K1	2001	JS1AK111100101712
GSX750F-K2	2002	JS1AK111100101892
GSX750-W	1998	JS1AE111200100001
GSX750-X	1999	JS1AE111200100480
GSX750-Y	2000	JS1AE111200100777
GSX750-K1	2001	JS1AE111200100914

US models

Model	Year	Initial frame no.
GSX600F-W	1998	JS1GN79A W2100001
GSX600F-X	1999	JS1GN79A X2100001
GSX600F-Y	2000	JS1GN79A Y2100001
GSX600F-K1	2001	JS1GN79A 122100001
GSX600F-K2	2002	JS1GN79A 222100001
GSX750F-W	1998	JS1GR7GA W2100001
GSX750F-X	1999	JS1GR7GA X2100001
GSX750F-Y	2000	JS1GR7GA Y2100001
GSX750F-K1	2001	JS1GR7GA 12100001
GSX750F-K2	2002	JS1GR7GA 22100001

The frame number is stamped into the right-hand side of the steering head

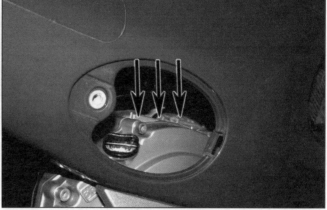

The engine number is stamped into the crankcase on the right-hand side of the engine. On F models remove the oil filler cap access panel to see it

Buying spare parts

Once you have found all the identification numbers, record them for reference when buying parts. Since the manufacturers change specifications, parts and vendors (companies that manufacture various components on the machine), providing the ID numbers is the only way to be reasonably sure that you are buying the correct parts.

Whenever possible, take the worn part to the dealer so direct comparison with the new component can be made. Along the trail from the manufacturer to the parts shelf, there are numerous places that the part can end up with the wrong number or be listed incorrectly.

The two places to purchase new parts for your motorcycle – the franchised or main dealer and the parts/accessories store – differ in the type of parts they carry. While dealers can obtain every single genuine part for your motorcycle, the accessory store is usually limited to normal high wear items such as chains and sprockets, brake pads, spark plugs and cables, and to tune-up parts and various engine gaskets, etc. Rarely will an accessory outlet have major suspension components, camshafts, transmission gears, or engine cases.

Used parts can be obtained from breakers yards for roughly half the price of new ones, but you can't always be sure of what you're getting. Once again, take your worn part to the breaker for direct comparison, or when ordering by mail order make sure that you can return it if you are not happy.

Whether buying new, used or rebuilt parts, the best course is to deal directly with someone who specialises in your particular make.

Note: *The daily (pre-ride) checks outlined in the owner's manual covers those items which should be inspected on a daily basis.*

Engine/transmission oil level

Before you start:
✔ Take the motorcycle on a short run to allow it to reach normal operating temperature.

 Caution: Do not run the engine in an enclosed space such as a garage or workshop.

✔ Stop the engine and support the motorcycle on its centrestand. Allow it to rest undisturbed for a few minutes to allow the oil level to stabilise. Make sure the motorcycle is on level ground.

Bike care:
● If you have to add oil frequently, check whether you have any oil leaks from the engine joints, seals and gaskets. If not, the engine could be burning oil, in which case there will be white smoke coming out of the exhaust – (see *Fault Finding* in the Reference section).

The correct oil
● Modern, high-revving engines place great demands on their oil. It is very important that the correct oil for your bike is used.
● Always top up with a good quality motorcycle oil of the specified type and viscosity and do not overfill the engine.

Oil type	API grade SF or SG	Oil viscosity	SAE 10W40

1 Wipe the oil level inspection window so that it is clean – it is located on the right-hand side of the engine.

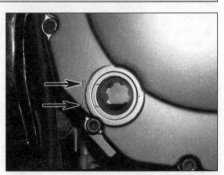

2 With the motorcycle upright and level, the oil level should lie between the F (full) and L (low) level lines on the window (arrowed).

3 On GSX600/750F models, if the level is below the L line, undo the oil filler cap access panel screw and remove the panel.

4 Unscrew the oil filler cap from the top of the clutch cover.

5 Top up with the recommended grade and type of oil to bring the level up to the F line on the inspection window. Do not overfill. On completion, make sure the filler cap is secure in the cover. Fit the access panel on GSX600/750F models, ensuring its tab locates correctly.

Suspension, steering and drive chain

Suspension and steering:
● Check that the front and rear suspension operates smoothly without binding (see Chapter 1).
● Check that the suspension is adjusted as required, where applicable (see Chapter 5).

● Check that the steering moves smoothly from lock-to-lock, and that there is no freeplay.

Drive chain:
● Check that the chain isn't too loose or too tight, and adjust it if necessary (see Chapter 1).
● If the chain looks dry, lubricate it (see Chapter 1).

Brake fluid levels

> ⚠️ **Warning: Brake hydraulic fluid can harm your eyes and damage painted surfaces, so use extreme caution when handling and pouring it and cover surrounding surfaces with rag. Do not use fluid that has been standing open for some time, as it is hygroscopic (absorbs moisture from the air) which can cause a dangerous loss of braking effectiveness.**

Before you start:

✔ The front master cylinder reservoir is on the right-hand handlebar. The rear master cylinder reservoir is located on the right-hand side of the frame, just below the seat.
✔ Make sure you have the correct hydraulic fluid. DOT 4 is recommended.
✔ Wrap a rag around the reservoir being worked on to ensure that any spillage does not come into contact with painted surfaces.
✔ Support the motorcycle upright using an auxiliary stand so that the reservoir being worked on is level – you may have to turn the handlebars to achieve this when working on the front reservoir.

Bike care:

● The fluid in the front and rear brake master cylinder reservoirs will drop slightly as the brake pads wear down (refer to Chapter 1 to check the amount of wear in the pads if required).
● If either fluid reservoir requires repeated topping-up there could be a leak somewhere in the hydraulic system, which must be investigated immediately.
● Check for signs of hydraulic fluid leakage from the hoses and brake components – if found, rectify immediately (see Chapter 6).
● Check the operation of both brakes before taking the machine on the road; if there is evidence of air in the system (a spongy feel to lever or pedal), the system must be bled (see Chapter 6).

1 The front brake fluid level, visible through the window in the reservoir body, must be above the LOWER level line (arrowed).

3 Top up with new DOT 4 fluid until the level is up to the ridge along the inside of the front wall of the reservoir (arrowed). Do not overfill.

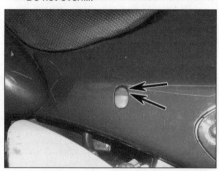

5 On GSX600/750F models, the rear brake fluid level can be viewed via the aperture in the seat panel. The fluid must lie between the UPPER and LOWER level lines (arrowed).

2 If the level is below the LOWER line, undo the two reservoir cover screws and remove the cover, diaphragm plate and diaphragm.

4 Ensure that the diaphragm is correctly seated before installing the plate and cover. Secure the cover with the two screws.

6 If the level is below the LOWER level line, remove the fairing right-hand side panel (see Chapter 7), then unscrew the reservoir cap (arrowed) and remove the diaphragm plate and diaphragm.

7 Top up with new DOT 4 fluid until the level is up to the UPPER level line. Do not overfill.

8 Ensure that the diaphragm is correctly seated before installing the plate and cap.

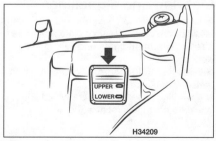

H34209

9 On GSX750 models, remove the seat to view the rear brake fluid level, which must be between the UPPER and LOWER level lines. To access the reservoir cover for topping up, remove the document tray.

Tyres

The correct pressures:

● The tyres must be checked when cold, not immediately after riding. Note that low tyre pressures may cause the tyre to slip on the rim or come off. High tyre pressures will cause abnormal tread wear and unsafe handling. The pressures listed are for both solo riding and carrying a pillion.

● Use an accurate pressure gauge. Many forecourt gauges are wildly inaccurate. If you buy your own, spend as much as you can justify on a quality gauge.

● Proper air pressure will increase tyre life and provide maximum stability and ride comfort.

Tyre care:

● Check the tyres carefully for cuts, tears, embedded nails or other sharp objects and excessive wear. Operation of the motorcycle with excessively worn tyres is extremely hazardous, as traction and handling are directly affected.

● Check the condition of the tyre valve and ensure the dust cap is in place.

● Pick out any stones or nails which may have become embedded in the tyre tread. If left, they will eventually penetrate through the casing and cause a puncture.

● If tyre damage is apparent, or unexplained loss of pressure is experienced, seek the advice of a tyre fitting specialist without delay.

Tyre tread depth:

● At the time of writing UK law requires that tread depth must be at least 1 mm over 3/4 of the tread breadth all the way around the tyre, with no bald patches. Many riders, however, consider 2 mm tread depth minimum to be a safer limit. Suzuki recommend a minimum of 1.6 mm on the front and 2 mm on the rear.

● Many tyres now incorporate wear indicators in the tread. Identify the location marking on the tyre sidewall to locate the indicator bar and renew the tyre if the tread has worn down to the bar – some tyres have wear bars near the edge as well as in the centre.

1 Remove the dust cap from the valve. Check the tyre pressures when cold. Do not forget to fit the cap after checking the pressure.

2 Measure tread depth at the centre of the tyre using a depth gauge.

3 Tyre tread wear indicator bar (A) and its location marking (usually either an arrow, a triangle, a logo or the letters TWI) on the sidewall (B).

Model	Front	Rear
GSX600F and GSX750F models	33 psi (2.25 Bar)	36 psi (2.50 Bar)
GSX750 model	36 psi (2.50 Bar)	36 psi (2.50 Bar)

Legal and safety checks

Lighting and signalling:

● Take a minute to check that the headlight, tail light, brake light, licence plate light (where fitted), instrument lights and turn signals all work correctly.

● Check that the horn sounds when the button is pressed.

● A working speedometer, graduated in mph, is a statutory requirement in the UK.

Safety:

● Check that the throttle grip rotates smoothly when opened and snaps shut when released, in all steering positions. Also check for the correct amount of freeplay in the cable (see Chapter 1).

● Check that the clutch operates smoothly in all steering positions. Also check for the correct amount of freeplay in the cable (see Chapter 1).

● Check that the engine shuts off when the kill switch is operated.

● Check that the stand return springs hold the stands up securely when retracted.

● Check the operation of the starter interlock system. It should only be possible to start the engine if the transmission is in neutral and the clutch lever is pulled in, or if the transmission is in gear with the clutch lever pulled in and the sidestand up.

Fuel:

● This may seem obvious, but check that you have enough fuel to complete your journey. If you notice signs of fuel leakage, rectify the cause immediately.

● Ensure you use the correct grade fuel – see Chapter 3 Specifications.

Chapter 1
Routine maintenance and servicing

Contents

Air filter – check and clean 2
Air filter – renewal 21
Battery – charging ....see Chapter 8
Battery – check 33
Battery – removal, installation, inspection and
    maintenance ....see Chapter 8
Brake master cylinders and calipers – seal renewal 31
Brake fluid – change 23
Brake hoses – renewal 24
Brake pads – check 10
Brake system – check 11
Carburettors – synchronisation 17
Clutch – check and adjustment 8
Cylinder compression – check 26
Drive chain and sprockets – check, adjustment, cleaning
    and lubrication 1
Drive chain – wear and stretch check 9
Engine oil pressure – check 27
Engine/transmission – oil change 5
Engine/transmission – oil and filter change 22

Front forks – oil change 32
Fuel filter – renewal (GSX600/750F) 18
Fuel hoses – renewal 25
Fuel system – check 4
Headlight aim – check and adjustment 35
Idle speed – check and adjustment 6
Nuts and bolts – tightness check 13
Sidestand and centrestand – check 34
Spark plugs – check and adjustment 3
Spark plugs – renewal 15
Stand pivots, lever pivots and cables – lubrication 14
Steering head bearings – check and adjustment 19
Steering head bearings – re-greasing 29
Suspension – check 20
Swingarm and suspension linkage bearings – re-greasing 30
Throttle and choke cables – check and adjustment 7
Tyres and wheels – general check 12
Valve clearances – check and adjustment 16
Wheel bearings – check 28

Degrees of difficulty

Easy, suitable for novice with little experience	**Fairly easy,** suitable for beginner with some experience	**Fairly difficult,** suitable for competent DIY mechanic	**Difficult,** suitable for experienced DIY mechanic	**Very difficult,** suitable for expert DIY or professional

Specifications

Engine

Engine idle speed
  GSX600F
    Austria and Switzerland models .... 1200 ± 50 rpm
    California models .... 1300 ± 100 rpm
    All other models .... 1200 ± 100 rpm
  GSX750F
    Austria and Switzerland models .... 1100 ± 50 rpm
    All other models .... 1200 ± 100 rpm
  GSX750
    Austria and Switzerland models .... 1200 ± 50 rpm
    All other models .... 1200 ± 100 rpm
Spark plugs
  Type
    Standard .... NGK CR9EK or Denso U27ETR
    For constant slow speed riding or cold countries (see text) ..... NGK CR8EK or Denso U24ETR
    For extended high speed riding or hot countries (see text) ...... NGK CR10EK or Denso U31ETR
  Electrode gap .... 0.6 to 0.7 mm

1

Engine (continued)

Valve clearances (COLD engine)
Intake valves	0.10 to 0.15 mm
Exhaust valves	0.18 to 0.23 mm
Carburettor synchronisation – max. difference between readings	20 mm Hg

Cylinder compression
Standard	142 to 213 psi (10.0 to 15.0 Bar)
Service limit	114 psi (8.0 Bar)
Max. difference between cylinders	28 psi (2.0 Bar)
Oil pressure (at main oil gallery plug, with engine warm)	43 to 85 psi (3.0 to 6.0 Bar) @ 3000 rpm, oil @ 60°C

Miscellaneous

Drive chain
Freeplay	20 to 30 mm with motorcycle on centrestand
Stretch limit (21 pin length – see text)	319.4 mm

Throttle twistgrip freeplay
Opening (front) cable	2.0 to 4.0 mm
Closing (rear) cable	zero (no freeplay)
Clutch lever freeplay	10 to 15 mm
Clutch release mechanism screw	¼ turn out
Tyre pressures (cold)	see *Daily (pre-ride) checks*

Rear brake pedal height
GSX600F	54 mm
GSX750F	55 mm
GSX750	50 mm

Gearchange lever height
GSX600F	54 mm
GSX750F	55 mm
GSX750	45 mm

Recommended lubricants and fluids

Fuel grade
European models	Unleaded, minimum 91 RON (Research Octane Number)
US models	Unleaded, minimum 87 ((R+M) /2 method)
Engine/transmission oil type	API grade SF or SG motor oil
Engine/transmission oil viscosity	SAE 10W40

Engine/transmission oil capacity
Oil change	3.3 litres
Oil and filter change	3.5 litres
Following engine overhaul – dry engine, new filter	4.7 litres
Brake fluid	DOT 4
Drive chain	Heavy motor oil (such as gear oil) or chain lubricant suitable for O-ring and X-ring chains
Steering head bearings	Multi-purpose grease
Swingarm pivot bearings	Multi-purpose grease
Suspension linkage bearings	Multi-purpose grease
Bearing seal lips	Multi-purpose grease
Gearchange lever/rear brake pedal/footrest pivots	Multi-purpose grease
Brake and clutch lever pivots	Multi-purpose grease
Sidestand and centrestand pivots	Multi-purpose grease
Throttle grip	Multi-purpose grease or dry film lubricant
Front brake lever piston tip	Silicone grease
Cables	Engine oil or cable lubricant

Torque settings

Bottom yoke fork clamp bolts	23 Nm
Engine/transmission oil drain plug	23 Nm
Main oil gallery plug	40 Nm

Rear brake torque arm nut
GSX600F	32 Nm
GSX750F and GSX750	35 Nm

Rear wheel axle nut
GSX600F and GSX750F	65 Nm
GSX750	100 Nm
Spark plugs	11 Nm
Steering stem nut	65 Nm

Note: *The daily (pre-ride) checks outlined in the owner's manual covers those items which should be inspected on a daily basis. Always perform the pre-ride inspection at every maintenance interval (in addition to the procedures listed). The intervals listed below are the intervals recommended by the manufacturer for each particular operation during the model years covered in this manual. Your owner's manual may have different intervals for your model.*

Daily (pre-ride)

See *'Daily (pre-ride) checks'* at the beginning of this manual.

After the initial 600 miles (1000 km)

Note: *This check is usually performed by a Suzuki dealer after the first 600 miles (1000 km) from new. Thereafter, maintenance is carried out according to the following intervals of the schedule.*

Every 600 miles (1000 km)

☐ Check, adjust, clean and lubricate the drive chain (Section 1)

Every 4000 miles (6000 km) or 6 months

Carry out all the items under the Daily (pre-ride) checks and the 600 mile (1000 km) check, plus the following:
☐ Check and clean the air filter element (Section 2)
☐ Check the spark plugs (Section 3)
☐ Check the fuel hoses and fuel system components (Section 4)
☐ Change the engine/transmission oil (Section 5)
☐ Check and adjust the engine idle speed (Section 6)
☐ Check throttle/choke cable operation and freeplay (Section 7)
☐ Check the operation of the clutch (Section 8)
☐ Check for drive chain wear and stretch (Section 9)
☐ Check the brake pads for wear (Section 10)
☐ Check the operation of the brake system (Section 11)
☐ Check the tyre and wheel condition, and the tyre tread depth (*Daily (pre-ride) checks* and Section 12)
☐ Check the tightness of all nuts and bolts (Section 13)
☐ Check and lubricate the stand pivots, lever pivots and cables (Section 14)

Every 7500 miles (12,000 km) or 12 months

Carry out all the items under the 4000 mile (6000 km) check, plus the following:
☐ Renew the spark plugs (Section 15)
☐ Check the valve clearances (Section 16)
☐ Check carburettor synchronisation (Section 17)
☐ Renew the in-line fuel filter – GSX600/750F (Section 18)
☐ Check the steering head bearings (Section 19)
☐ Check the front and rear suspension (Section 20)

Every 11,000 miles (18,000 km) or 18 months

Carry out all the items under the 4000 mile (6000 km) check, plus the following:
☐ Renew the air filter element (Section 21)
☐ Change the engine/transmission oil and renew the oil filter (Section 22)

Every two years

☐ Change the brake fluid (Section 23)

Every four years

☐ Renew the brake hoses (Section 24)
☐ Renew the fuel hoses, and on Austria, Switzerland and California models renew the EVAP system hoses (Section 25)

Non-scheduled maintenance

☐ Check the cylinder compression (Section 26)
☐ Check the engine oil pressure (Section 27)
☐ Check the wheel bearings (Section 28)
☐ Re-grease the steering head bearings (Section 29)
☐ Re-grease the swingarm and suspension linkage bearings (Section 30)
☐ Renew the brake master cylinder and caliper seals (Section 31)
☐ Change the front fork oil (Section 32)
☐ Check the battery (Section 33)
☐ Check the stands and the starter interlock circuit operation (Section 34)
☐ Check and adjust the headlight aim (Section 35)

1

Component locations – right-hand side

1 Rear brake fluid reservoir
2 Engine oil filler cap
3 Front brake fluid reservoir

4 Throttle cable adjusters
5 Fork seals
6 Engine oil filter

7 Engine oil level inspection window
8 Rear brake pedal height adjuster
9 Drive chain adjuster

Component locations – left-hand side

1 Clutch cable upper adjuster
2 Steering head bearing
   adjuster
3 In-line fuel filter

4 Fuel tap fuel filter
5 Idle speed adjuster
6 Air filter
7 Battery

8 Engine oil drain plug
9 Clutch cable lower adjuster
10 Clutch release mechanism
   adjuster

1

1 This Chapter is designed to help the home mechanic maintain his/her motorcycle for safety, economy, long life and peak performance.

2 Deciding where to start or plug into the routine maintenance schedule depends on several factors. If your motorcycle has been maintained according to the warranty standards and has just come out of warranty, start routine maintenance as it coincides with the next mileage or calendar interval. If you have owned the machine for some time but have never performed any maintenance on it, start at the nearest interval and include some additional procedures to ensure that nothing important is overlooked. If you have just had a major engine overhaul, then start the maintenance routine from the beginning. If you have a used machine and have no knowledge of its history or maintenance record, combine all the checks into one large service initially and then settle into the specified maintenance schedule.

3 Before beginning any maintenance or repair, the machine should be cleaned thoroughly, especially around the oil filter, spark plugs, valve covers, body panels, carburettors, etc. Cleaning will help ensure that dirt does not contaminate the engine and will allow you to detect wear and damage that could otherwise easily go unnoticed.

4 Certain maintenance information is sometimes printed on labels attached to the motorcycle. If the information on the labels differs from that included here, use the information on the label.

Every 600 miles (1000 km)

1 Drive chain and sprockets – check, adjustment, cleaning and lubrication

Check

1 A neglected drive chain won't last long and will quickly damage the sprockets. Routine chain adjustment and lubrication isn't difficult and will ensure maximum chain and sprocket life.

2 To check the chain, place the bike on its centrestand and shift the transmission into neutral. Make sure the ignition switch is OFF.

3 Push up on the bottom run of the chain midway between the two sprockets and measure the total up and down amount of freeplay, then compare your measurement to that listed in this Chapter's Specifications **(see illustration)**. As the chain stretches with wear, adjustment will periodically be necessary (see below). Since the chain will rarely wear evenly, rotate the wheel so that another section of chain can be checked; do this several times to check the entire length of chain, and mark the tightest spot.

4 In some cases where lubrication has been neglected, corrosion and galling may cause the links to bind and kink, which effectively shortens the chain's length. Such links should be thoroughly cleaned and worked free. If the chain is tight between the sprockets, rusty or kinked, it's time to fit a new one. If you find a tight area, mark it with felt pen or paint, and repeat the measurement after the bike has been ridden. If the chain is still tight in the same area, it may be damaged or worn. Because a tight or kinked chain can damage the transmission bearings, it's a good idea to fit a new one.

5 Check the entire length of the chain for damaged rollers, loose links and pins, and missing O-rings, and fit a new one if damage is found. **Note:** *Never fit a new chain on old sprockets, and never use the old chain if you fit new sprockets – renew the chain and sprockets as a set.*

6 Remove front sprocket cover (see Chapter 5). Check the teeth on the front sprocket and the rear sprocket for wear **(see illustration)**.

7 Inspect the drive chain slider on the front of the swingarm for excessive wear and damage and fit a new one if necessary (see Chapter 5, Sections 14 and 15).

Adjustment

8 Position the bike on it centrestand. Rotate the rear wheel so that the chain is positioned with the tightest point at the centre of its bottom run.

9 On US and Canada models, remove the split pin from the end of the axle. Discard it as a new one must be used. On Germany F models remove the protective cap from the end of each chain adjuster stud.

10 Slacken the rear axle nut **(see illustration)**. Also slacken the nut on the bolt securing the torque arm to the rear brake caliper **(see illustration)**.

11 Turn the adjuster nut (GSX600/750F models) or bolt (GSX750 models) on each side

1.3 Push up on the chain and measure the freeplay

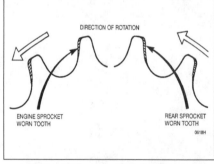

DIRECTION OF ROTATION

ENGINE SPROCKET WORN TOOTH

REAR SPROCKET WORN TOOTH

0618H

1.6 Check the sprockets in the areas indicated to see if they are worn excessively

1.10a Slacken the axle nut (arrowed) . . .

1.10b . . . and the torque arm nut/bolt (arrowed)

1.11a Turn the adjusters as required until the slack is correct

1.11b Make sure each adjustment marker is aligned with the same notch on each side of the swingarm (GSX600/750F shown)

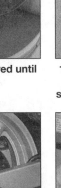

1.12 Tighten the axle nut to the specified torque

1.15 Use only the correct lubricant and apply it as described

Cleaning and lubrication

14 If required, wash the chain in paraffin (kerosene) or a suitable non-flammable or high flash-point solvent that will not damage the O-rings, using a soft brush to work any dirt out if necessary. Wipe the cleaner off the chain and allow it to dry. If the chain is excessively dirty it should be removed from the machine and allowed to soak in the paraffin or solvent (see Chapter 5).

Caution: Don't use petrol (gasoline), an unsuitable solvent or other cleaning fluids which might damage the internal sealing properties of the chain. Don't use high-pressure water to clean the chain. The entire process shouldn't take longer than ten minutes, otherwise the O-rings could be damaged.

15 For routine lubrication, the best time to lubricate the chain is after the motorcycle has been ridden. When the chain is warm, the lubricant will penetrate the joints between the sideplates better than when cold. **Note:** *Suzuki specifies a heavy motor oil (such as gear oil) or an aerosol chain lube that it is suitable for O-ring and X-ring (sealed) chains; do not use any other chain lubricants – the solvents could damage the chain's sealing rings.* Apply the oil to the area where the sideplates overlap – not the middle of the rollers **(see illustration)**.

> **HAYNES HiNT**
>
> *Apply the lubricant to the top of the lower chain run, so centrifugal force will work the oil into the chain when the bike is moving. After applying the lubricant, let it soak in a few minutes before wiping off any excess.*

> ⚠ *Warning: Take care not to get any lubricant on the tyres or brake system components. If any of the lubricant inadvertently contacts them, clean it off thoroughly using a suitable solvent or dedicated brake cleaner before riding the machine.*

evenly until the amount of freeplay specified at the beginning of the Chapter is obtained at the centre of the bottom run of the chain **(see illustration)**. Following adjustment, check that the notch in the top (GSX600/750F models) or the rear edge (GSX750) of each chain adjustment marker is in the same position in relation to the index lines on the swingarm **(see illustration)**. It is important the same index line on each side aligns with the notch or rear edge otherwise the rear wheel will be out of alignment with the front. If there is a discrepancy in the marker positions, adjust one of them so that its position is exactly the

same as the other. Check the chain freeplay as described above and readjust if necessary.
12 Counter-hold the axle head and tighten the nut to the torque setting specified at the beginning of the Chapter **(see illustration)**. Recheck the adjustment as above, then check that the wheel runs freely. Tighten the brake torque arm nut to the specified torque setting.
13 On US and Canada models, fit a new split pin through the nut slots and hole in the end of the axle; bend the split ends securely to lock it in place. On Germany models, fit the caps to the ends of the chain adjuster studs on GSX600/750F models.

Every 4000 miles (6000 km) or 6 months

2 Air filter – check and clean

Caution: If the machine is constantly used in dirty or dusty conditions the filter should be cleaned and renewed at more frequent intervals than specified.

1 On GSX600/750F models remove the fuel tank (see Chapter 3). Where fitted, release the wiring from the tie(s) on the tank mounting bracket **(see illustration)**. Unscrew the fuel tank bracket bolts and remove the bracket, noting how it fits **(see illustration)**. Release

2.1a Release the wiring from the tie(s) . . .

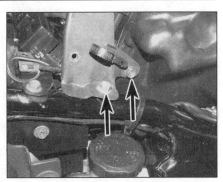

2.1b . . . then unscrew the bolts (arrowed) on each side and remove the bracket

1

2.1c Free the hoses from their clips

2.3a Undo the screws (arrowed) . . .

2.3b . . . and withdraw the filter from the housing

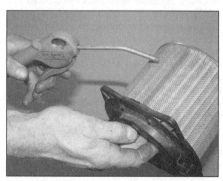

2.4 Direct the air in the opposite direction of normal flow

the air vent hoses from their clips on the air filter cover **(see illustration)**.

2 On GSX750 models remove the seat (see Chapter 7). Remove the document tray, noting how it fits.

3 Undo the screws securing the air filter and withdraw it from the housing, noting how it fits **(see illustrations)**.

4 To clean the filter, tap it on a hard surface to dislodge any dirt, and use compressed air if available, directing the air in the opposite way to normal flow, i.e. from the outside in **(see illustration)**. Do not use any solvents or cleaning agents on the element. Check the element for tears and excessive oil contamination and renew it if necessary.

5 Install the filter in the housing with the arrow

on the cover pointing up. Make sure it is correctly seated, then secure it with its screws.

6 On GSX600/750F models release the clamp and remove the plug from the air filter housing drain hose located below the oil level inspection window on the right-hand side, and allow any residue to drain. On GSX750 models release the clamp and remove the blanking cap from the drain stub located just below the left-hand side panel. Refit the plug or cap and secure it with the clamp.

7 On GSX600/750F models fit the air vent hoses into their clips on the air filter cover. Install the fuel tank bracket and tighten its bolts. Secure the wiring in the tie(s) on the bracket. Install the fuel tank (see Chapter 3).

8 On GSX750 models install the document tray and seat (see Chapter 7).

3 Spark plugs – check and adjustment

1 Make sure your spark plug socket is the correct size before attempting to remove the plugs – a suitable one is supplied in the motorcycle's tool kit which is stored under the seat.

2 Remove the fuel tank (see Chapter 3).

3 Work on one plug at a time. Clean the area around the plug cap seal on the valve cover

before removing the cap to prevent any dirt falling into the spark plug channel. Pull the cap off the spark plug **(see illustration)**. Using either the plug removing tool supplied in the bike's toolkit or a deep socket type wrench with an extension bar, unscrew and remove the plug from the cylinder head **(see illustrations)**.

4 Inspect the electrodes for wear. Both the centre and side electrodes should have square edges and the side electrodes should be of uniform thickness – if not, they are worn. Look for excessive deposits and evidence of a cracked or chipped insulator around the centre electrode. Compare your spark plugs to the colour spark plug reading chart at the end of this manual. Check the threads, the washer and the ceramic insulator body for cracks and other damage.

5 If the electrodes are not excessively worn, if no cracks or chips are visible in the insulator, and if the deposits can be easily removed with a wire brush, the plugs can be re-gapped and re-used. If in doubt concerning the condition of the plugs, renew them.

6 Cleaning spark plugs by sandblasting is permitted, provided you blow out the plugs with compressed air and clean them with a high flash-point solvent afterwards.

7 Before installing the plugs, make sure they are the correct type and heat range and check the gap between the electrodes **(see illustrations)**. Compare the gap to that

3.3a Pull the cap off the plug . . .

3.3b . . . then unscrew the plug . . .

3.3c . . . and withdraw it from the head

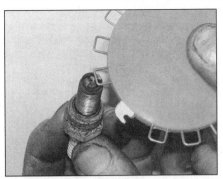

3.7a Using a wire type gauge to measure the spark plug electrode gap

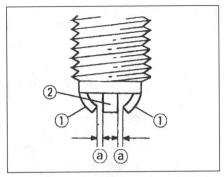

3.7b The gap (a) between the two earth electrodes (1) and the centre electrode (2) must be equal and as specified

3.7c Adjust the electrode gap by bending the side electrode only

specified and adjust as necessary. If the gap must be adjusted, bend the side electrodes only and be very careful not to chip or crack the insulator nose **(see illustration)**. Make sure the washer is in place before installing each plug.

8 Fit the plug into the end of the tool, then use the tool to insert the plug. Since the cylinder head is made of aluminium, which is soft and easily damaged, thread the plug as far as possible into the head turning the tool by hand. Once the plug is finger-tight, the job can be finished with a spanner on the tool supplied or a socket drive. If a torque wrench can be applied, tighten the spark plugs to the torque setting specified at the beginning of the Chapter. Otherwise, tighten them according the instructions on the box – generally if new plugs are being used, tighten them by 1/2 a turn after the washer has seated, and if the old plugs are being reused, tighten them by 1/8 to 1/4 turn after they have seated. Do not over-tighten them.

> **HAYNES HINT**
> *You can slip a short length of hose over the end of the plug to use as a tool to thread it into place. The hose will grip the plug well enough to turn it, but will start to slip if the plug begins to cross-thread in the hole – this will prevent damaged threads.*

9 Fit the spark plug cap, making sure it locates correctly onto the plug.
10 Install the fuel tank (see Chapter 3).

> **HAYNES HINT**
> *Stripped plug threads in the cylinder head can be repaired with a Heli-Coil insert – see 'Tools and Workshop Tips' in the Reference section.*

4 Fuel system – check

> ⚠ *Warning: Petrol (gasoline) is extremely flammable, so take extra precautions when you work on any part of the fuel system. Don't smoke or allow open flames or bare light bulbs near the work area, and don't work in a garage where a natural gas-type appliance is present. If you spill any fuel on your skin, rinse it off immediately with soap and water. When you perform any kind of work on the fuel system, wear safety glasses and have a fire extinguisher suitable for a Class B type fire (flammable liquids) on hand.*

Check

1 On GSX600/750F models remove the fairing side panels (see Chapter 7).

2 Check the tank, the fuel tap, the carburettors and the fuel and vacuum hoses for signs of leakage, deterioration or damage. Replace any hoses that are cracked or deteriorated with new ones **(see illustration)**. On Austria, Switzerland and California models also check the PAIR system hoses, and on California models the EVAP system hoses (refer to Chapter 3 for details of these systems).

3 If the fuel tap is leaking, tighten the mounting bolts and/or assembly screws, according to the source of the leak **(see illustrations)**. Slacken the screws a little first, then tighten them evenly and a little at a time to ensure a good seat. If leakage persists remove and disassemble the tap, noting how the components fit (see Chapter 3). Inspect and clean all components and rebuild the tap. If leakage persists, renew the whole tap - individual components are not available. If the carburettor gaskets are leaking, disassemble the carburettors and rebuild them using new gaskets and seals (see Chapter 3). Refer to Chapter 3 for checks on the condition and operation of the vacuum diaphragm in the fuel tap.

Fuel strainer cleaning

4 On GSX600/750F models an in-line filter is fitted in the fuel hose between the tap and the carburettors. Renew the filter after the specified mileage has been covered or if it is the suspected cause of fuel starvation (see Section 18).

1

4.2 Check the fuel hose and fuel tap vacuum hose as described

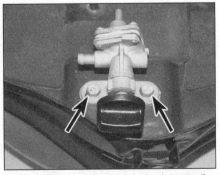

4.3a Fuel tap mounting bolts (arrowed)

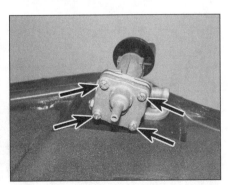

4.3b Fuel tap assembly screws (arrowed)

4.5 Check the strainer (arrowed) as described

5.3 Undo the screw and remove the access panel

5.4 Unscrew the oil filler cap to act as a vent . . .

5 A fuel strainer is incorporated in the fuel tap. Cleaning or renewal of the strainer is advised after a particularly high mileage has been covered. It is also necessary if it is the suspected cause of fuel starvation, or if it looks clogged or dirty. Remove the fuel tap (see Chapter 3). Clean all traces of dirt and fuel sediment off the gauze strainer **(see illustration)**. Check the gauze for holes. If any are found, a new tap must be fitted. Install the tap (see Chapter 3).

6 Check the condition of the inside of the tank – if it is old and there is evidence of rust, remove, drain and clean the tank (see Chapter 3).

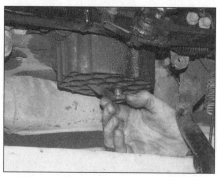

5.5a . . . then unscrew the oil drain plug (arrowed) . . .

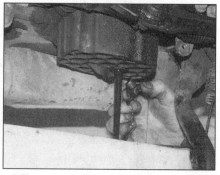

5.5b . . . and allow the oil to completely drain

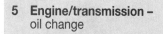

5 Engine/transmission – oil change

> *Warning: Be careful when draining the oil, as the exhaust pipes, the engine, and the oil itself can cause severe burns.*

1 Consistent routine oil and filter changes are the single most important maintenance procedure you can perform on a motorcycle. The oil not only lubricates the internal parts of the engine, transmission and clutch, but it also acts as a coolant, a cleaner, a sealant, and a protector. Because of these demands, the oil takes a terrific amount of abuse and should be changed often with new oil of the recommended grade and type. Saving a little

money on the difference in cost between good oil and cheap oil won't pay off if the engine is damaged. The oil filter should be changed with every third oil change (see Section 22).

2 Before changing the oil, warm up the engine so the oil will drain easily. Place the bike on its centrestand on level ground.

3 On GSX600/750F models remove the lower fairing (see Chapter 7). Also undo the oil filler cap access panel screw and remove the panel **(see illustration)**.

4 Position a clean drain tray below the engine. Unscrew the oil filler cap from the clutch cover to vent the crankcase and to act as a reminder that there is no oil in the engine **(see illustration)**.

5 Unscrew the oil drain plug from the bottom

of the engine and allow the oil to flow into the drain tray **(see illustrations)**. Check the condition of the sealing washer on the drain plug and fit a new one if it is damaged or worn – it is advisable to use a new one whatever the condition of the old one.

6 When the oil has completely drained, fit the plug to the sump, using a new sealing washer if necessary, and tighten it to the torque setting specified at the beginning of the Chapter **(see illustrations)**. Avoid overtightening, as it is quite easy to damage the threads in the sump.

7 Refill the engine using the recommended type of oil (see the Specifications at the beginning of this chapter) until the level is up to the F line on the inspection window (see *Daily (pre-ride) checks)* **(see illustration)** – the

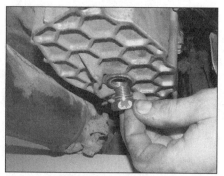

5.6a Install the drain plug, using a new sealing washer if necessary . . .

5.6b . . . and tighten it to the specified torque setting

5.7 Always use the correct grade of oil

5.9 Make sure the tab at the front of the panel locates correctly in the fairing

amount of oil required may not be quite as much as that specified because not all the old oil will have drained out (some will be trapped in pockets). Do not overfill. Install the filler cap. Start the engine and let it run for two or three minutes (make sure that the oil pressure light extinguishes after a few seconds). Shut it off, wait a few minutes, then re-check the oil level. If necessary, add more oil to bring the level back to the F line on the inspection window.

> **HAYNES HiNT**
> *Saving a little money on the difference between good and cheap oils won't pay off if the engine is damaged as a result.*

8 Check that there are no leaks from around the drain plug and the oil filter. A leak around the drain plug probably means a new washer is needed.
9 On GSX600/750F models install the lower fairing (see Chapter 7). Also fit the oil filler cap access panel and secure it with the screw **(see illustration)**.
10 The old oil drained from the engine cannot be re-used and should be disposed of properly. Check with your local refuse disposal company, disposal facility or environmental agency to see whether they will accept the used oil for recycling. Don't pour used oil into drains or onto the ground.

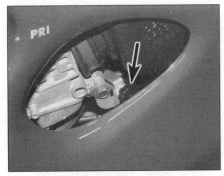

6.3 Idle speed adjuster (arrowed) – GSX600/750F model shown

Note: It is antisocial and illegal to dump oil down the drain. To find the location of your local oil recycling bank, call this number free.

OIL BANK LINE
0800 66 33 66
www.oilbankline.org.uk

In the US note that any oil supplier must accept used oil for recycling.

> **HAYNES HiNT**
> *Check the old oil carefully – if it is very metallic coloured, then the engine is experiencing wear from break-in (new engine) or from insufficient lubrication. If there are flakes or chips of metal in the oil, then something is drastically wrong internally and the engine will have to be disassembled for inspection and repair. If there are pieces of fibre-like material in the oil, the clutch is experiencing excessive wear and should be checked.*

6 Idle speed – check and adjustment

1 The idle speed should be checked and adjusted before and after the carburettors are synchronised (balanced), and when it is obviously too high or too low. Before adjusting the idle speed, turn the handlebars from side-to-side and check the idle speed does not change as you do. If it does, the throttle cables may not be adjusted or routed correctly, or may be worn out. This is a dangerous condition that can cause loss of control of the bike. Be sure to correct this problem before proceeding.
2 The engine should be at normal operating temperature, which is usually reached after 10 to 15 minutes of stop-and-go riding. Place the motorcycle on its centrestand, and make sure the transmission is in neutral.
3 The idle speed adjuster is a knurled knob located on the left-hand end of the carburettors; on GSX600/750F models it is accessed via the aperture in the left-hand fairing side panel **(see illustration)**. With the engine idling, adjust the speed by turning the knob until the idle speed listed in this Chapter's Specifications is obtained. Turn the knob clockwise to increase idle speed, and anti-clockwise to decrease it.
4 Snap the throttle open and shut a few times, then recheck the idle speed. If necessary, repeat the adjustment procedure.

5 If a smooth, steady idle can't be achieved, the fuel/air mixture may be incorrect (see Chapter 3) or the carburettors may need synchronising (see Section 17). Also check the intake manifold rubbers for cracks or a loose clamp that will cause an air leak, resulting in a weak mixture.

7 Throttle and choke cables – check and adjustment

Throttle cables

1 Make sure the throttle grip rotates smoothly and freely from fully closed to fully open with the front wheel turned at various angles. The grip should return automatically from fully open to fully closed when released.
2 If the throttle sticks, this is probably due to a cable fault. Remove the cables (see Chapter 3) and lubricate them (see Section 14). Check that the inner cables slide freely and easily in the outer cables. If not, renew the cables. With the cables removed, make sure the throttle twistgrip rotates freely on the handlebar. Install the cables, making sure they are correctly routed. If this fails to improve the operation of the throttle, new cables must be installed. Note that in very rare cases the fault could lie in the carburettors rather than the cables, necessitating their removal and inspection (see Chapter 3).
3 With the throttle operating smoothly, check for a small amount of freeplay in the cables, measured in terms of the amount of free twistgrip rotation before the throttle opens, and compare the amount to that listed in this Chapter's Specifications **(see illustration)**. If it's incorrect, adjust the cables to correct it as follows.
4 Freeplay adjustments can be made using the adjusters in the cables where they leave the throttle/switch housing on the handlebar. The front cable in the housing is the opening cable, and the rear is the closing cable. Loosen the lockring on the closing cable adjuster and turn the adjuster fully in **(see**

1

7.3 Throttle cable freeplay is measured in terms of twistgrip rotation

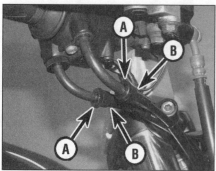

7.4 Slacken the lockrings (A), then turn the adjusters (B) as described

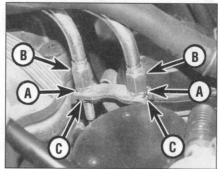

7.5 Slacken the locknuts (A), then turn the adjusters (B) as required, keeping the captive nuts (C) locked by the bracket

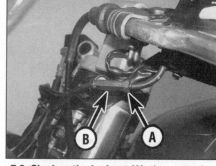

7.8 Slacken the locknut (A), then turn the adjuster (B) as required

illustration). Now loosen the lockring on the opening cable adjuster and turn the adjuster until the specified amount of freeplay is obtained (see this Chapter's Specifications), then retighten the lockring. Now turn the closing cable adjuster out until a resistance can just be felt – at this point all the freeplay has been taken up. Do not turn the adjuster out any further than the point at which the resistance is felt. Tighten the lockring.

5 If the adjusters have reached their limit, or if major adjustment is required, reset them so that the freeplay is at a maximum (i.e. the adjusters are fully turned in), then remove the fuel tank (see Chapter 3), and adjust the cables at the carburettor end. Slacken the adjuster locknuts, then turn the adjusters until the specified amount of freeplay is obtained (see Step 3), then tighten the locknuts **(see illustration)**. Further adjustments can now be made at the throttle end. If the cables cannot be adjusted as specified, install new ones (see Chapter 3).

6 Check that the throttle twistgrip operates smoothly and snaps shut quickly when released.

 Warning: Turn the handlebars all the way through their travel with the engine idling. The idle speed should not change. If it does, the cables may be routed incorrectly. Correct this condition before riding the bike.

Choke cable

7 If the choke does not operate smoothly this is probably due to a cable fault. Remove the cable (see Chapter 3) and lubricate it (see Section 14). Check that the inner cable slides freely and easily in the outer cable. If not, renew the cable. With the cable removed, make sure the choke lever is able to move freely. Install the cable, making sure it is correctly routed.

8 Check for a small amount of freeplay in the cable before the choke opens and adjust it if necessary using the adjuster at the lever end of the cable. Slacken the locknut, then turn the adjuster as required until a small amount of freeplay is evident, then retighten the

locknut **(see illustration)**. If this fails to improve the operation of the choke, the cable must be renewed.

9 Note that the fault could lie in the choke plungers and their bores in the carburettors rather than the cable (see Chapter 3).

8 Clutch – check and adjustment

Check

1 Check that the clutch lever operates smoothly and easily.

2 If the lever operation is heavy or stiff, remove the cable (see Chapter 2) and lubricate it (see Section 14). Check that the inner cable slides smoothly and freely in the outer cable. If the cable is still stiff, renew it. Install the lubricated or new cable (see Chapter 2). If the cable is good, remove the lever (see Chapter 5) and check the lever, bracket and pivot for wear and damage, and clean and grease all components before reassembling them. If this fails to cure the problem, disassemble the release mechanism on the engine and check it for dirt, wear and damage (see Chapter 2).

Adjustment

3 With the cable operating smoothly, check that it is correctly adjusted. Periodic

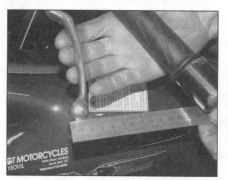

8.3 Measuring clutch cable freeplay

adjustment is necessary to compensate for wear in the clutch plates and stretch of the cable. Check that the amount of freeplay in the cable, measured in terms of the amount of free movement at the clutch lever end, is within the specifications listed at the beginning of the Chapter **(see illustration)**. If adjustment is required, it can be made both at the lever end of the cable and at the clutch end, but start the procedure at the lever end.

4 To adjust the freeplay at the lever, pull back the rubber boot covering the adjuster, then loosen the adjuster lockring and turn the adjuster in or out until the required amount of freeplay is obtained **(see illustration)**. To increase freeplay, thread the adjuster into the lever bracket. To reduce freeplay, thread the adjuster out of the bracket. Tighten the lockring. When adjusting the cable make sure that the slots in the adjuster and lockring are not aligned with each other and the slot in the lever bracket – these slots are to allow removal of the cable. Fit the rubber boot over the adjuster.

5 If all the adjustment has been taken up at the lever, reset the adjuster to give the maximum amount of freeplay (i.e. thread it all the way into the bracket), then set the correct amount of freeplay using the adjusters on the clutch end of cable.

6 On GSX600/750F models remove the fairing left-hand side panel (see Chapter 7).

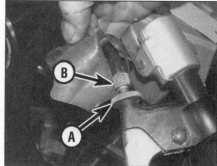

8.4 Slacken the lockring (A) and turn the adjuster (B) in or out as required

8.7 Remove the release mechanism cap

8.8 Slacken the locknut and turn the adjuster screw as described

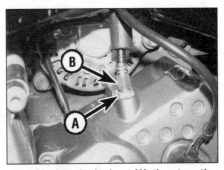

8.10 Slacken the locknut (A), then turn the adjuster (B) as required

7 Remove the release mechanism cap **(see illustration)**.

8 Slacken the locknut on the release mechanism adjuster screw, then undo the adjuster screw a few turns **(see illustration)**.

9 Now turn the release mechanism adjuster screw in until resistance is felt, then back it off 1/4 turn. When doing this, counter-hold the locknut as shown to prevent it from tightening and locking the adjuster. Now counter-hold the adjuster screw to prevent it turning and tighten the locknut.

10 Pull up the rubber boot on the cable adjuster on the top of the sprocket cover, then slacken the locknut **(see illustration)**. Turn the adjuster as required until the freeplay in the lever is correct (see Step 3), then tighten the locknut. Now check the freeplay at the lever and if necessary adjust it as described in Step 4.

11 On completion, fit the release mechanism

cap. On GSX600/750F models install the fairing left-hand side panel (see Chapter 7).

9 Drive chain – wear and stretch check

1 Place the bike on its centrestand. Rotate the rear wheel and check the entire length of the chain for damaged rollers, loose links and pins, and missing O-rings. Fit a new chain if damage is found. **Note:** *Never install a new chain on old sprockets, and never use the old chain if you install new sprockets – renew the chain and sprockets as a set.*

2 Chain stretch is assessed by measuring several sections of the chain with the chain held taut. On US and Canada models, remove the split pin from the rear axle nut, then on all models slacken the axle nut **(see illustration 1.10a)**. Also slacken the nut on the bolt securing the torque arm to the rear brake caliper **(see illustration 1.10b)**. Turn the adjuster nuts or bolts in evenly until all slack in the chain is taken up **(see illustration 1.11a)**. Measure along the bottom run the length of 21 pins (from the centre of the 1st pin to the centre of the 21st pin) and compare the result with the service limit specified at the beginning of the Chapter **(see illustration)**. Rotate the rear wheel so that several sections of the chain are measured, then calculate the average. If the chain stretch measurement exceeds the service limit it must be renewed (see Chapter 5).

3 If the chain is good, reset the adjusters so that there is the correct amount of freeplay

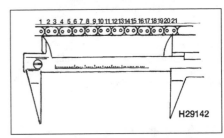

9.2 Measure the distance between 21 pins as shown to determine the amount of stretch in the chain

(see Section 1), then tighten the axle nut and the brake torque arm nut to the specified torque settings.

10 Brake pads – check

1 Each brake pad has wear indicators in the friction material that should be plainly visible, but note that an accumulation of road dirt and brake dust could make them difficult to see. The wear indicators will be in the form of a cutout or groove in the friction material. On the front brake look at the leading or trailing edge of the pad from above or below the caliper, and on the rear brake look at the lower edge of the pad from below the caliper, having removed the pad cover **(see illustrations)**.

1

10.1a Brake pad wear indicator (arrowed) – front pads in situ

10.1b To view the rear pads remove the cover

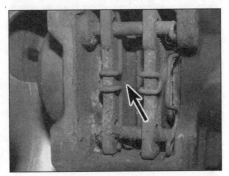

10.1c Brake pad wear indicator (arrowed) – rear pads in situ

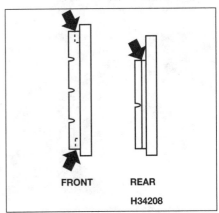

10.1d Brake pad wear indicators

2 If the indicators aren't visible, then the amount of friction material remaining should be, and it will be obvious when the pads need renewing. **Note:** *Some after-market pads may use different indicators to those on the original equipment.*

3 If the pads are worn to or beyond the wear indicator or there is little friction material remaining, new ones must be installed, although it is advisable to renew the pads before they become this worn. If the pads are dirty or if you are in doubt as to the amount of friction material remaining, remove them for inspection and measure the thickness of the material (see Chapter 6). Suzuki do not specify a minimum thickness, but anything less than 1 mm is worn. If the pads are excessively worn, check the brake discs (see Chapter 6).

4 Refer to Chapter 6 for details of pad renewal. **Note:** *Always renew the pads in both front brake calipers at the same time.*

11 Brake system – check

1 A routine general check of the brake system will ensure that any problems are discovered and remedied before the rider's safety is jeopardised.

11.3 Flex the hoses and check for cracks, bulges and leaking fluid. Also check all hose connections for leaks

11.6 Adjusting the front brake lever span

2 Check the brake lever and pedal for loose mountings, improper or rough action, excessive play, bends, and other damage. Renew any damaged parts (see Chapter 6).

3 Make sure all brake component fasteners are tight. Check the brake pads for wear (see Section 10) and make sure the fluid level in the reservoirs is correct (see *Daily (pre-ride) checks*). Look for leaks at the hose connections and check for cracks in the hoses **(see illustration)**. If the lever or pedal is spongy, bleed the brakes (see Chapter 6).

4 Make sure the brake light operates when the front brake lever is pulled in. The front brake light switch, mounted on the underside of the master cylinder, is not adjustable. If it fails to operate properly, check it (see Chapter 8).

5 Make sure the brake light is activated just before the rear brake takes effect. If adjustment is necessary, hold the switch body and turn the adjuster nut until the brake light is activated when required **(see illustration)**. The switch is mounted on the inside of the frame, near the brake pedal. If the brake light comes on too late, turn the nut clockwise. If the brake light comes on too soon or is permanently on, turn the nut anti-clockwise. If the switch doesn't operate the brake light, check it (see Chapter 8).

6 The front brake lever has a span adjuster that alters the distance of the lever from the

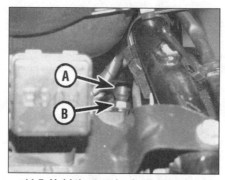
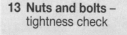

11.5 Hold the rear brake light switch body (A) and turn the adjuster ring (B) as required

11.7a Measure the rear brake pedal height and adjust if required

handlebar **(see illustration)**. Each setting is identified by a number on the adjuster. Pull the lever away from the handlebar and turn the adjuster ring until the setting that best suits the rider is obtained.

7 Measure the height of the rear brake pedal in relation to the top of the rider's footrest and compare it to that specified at the beginning of the Chapter **(see illustration)**. To adjust the height, slacken the clevis locknut, then turn the pushrod using a spanner on the hex at the top of the rod until the pedal is at the correct or desired height **(see illustration)**. On completion tighten the locknut. Adjust the rear brake light switch after adjusting the pedal height (see Step 5).

12 Tyres and wheels – general check

Tyres

1 Check the tyre condition and tread depth thoroughly – see *Daily (pre-ride) checks*.

Wheels

2 Cast wheels are virtually maintenance free, but they should be kept clean and checked periodically for cracks and other damage. Also check the wheel runout and alignment (see Chapter 6). You should never attempt to repair damaged cast wheels, even though there are specialists who claim to be able to do so; they should be replaced with new ones. Check the valve rubber for signs of damage or deterioration and have it renewed if necessary. Also, make sure the valve stem cap is in place and tight.

13 Nuts and bolts – tightness check

1 Since vibration of the machine tends to loosen fasteners, all nuts, bolts, screws, etc.

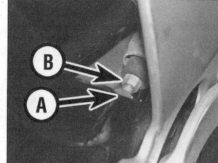

11.7b Slacken the locknut (A) and turn the pushrod using the hex (B) to adjust pedal height

should be periodically checked for proper tightness.

2 Pay particular attention to the following:

Spark plugs
Engine oil drain plug
Lever and pedal bolts
Footrest and stand bolts
Engine mounting bolts
Shock absorber bolts and nuts; suspension linkage bolts and nuts (GSX600/750F models); swingarm pivot bolt nut
Handlebar bolts
Front fork clamp bolts (top and bottom yoke) and fork top bolts
Steering stem nut
Front axle nut or bolt (according to model) and axle clamp bolt(s)
Rear axle nut
Brake caliper and master cylinder mounting bolts, brake caliper body bolts (rear caliper)
Brake hose banjo bolts and caliper bleed valves
Rear brake torque arm nuts
Brake disc bolts
Rear sprocket nuts
Exhaust system bolts/nuts

3 If a torque wrench is available, use it along with the torque specifications at the beginning of this and other Chapters.

14 Stand pivots, lever pivots and cables – lubrication

1 Since the controls, cables and various other components of a motorcycle are exposed to the elements, they should be checked and

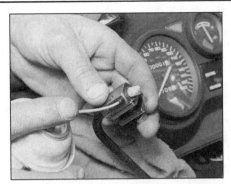

14.3a Lubricating a cable with a pressure lubricator. Make sure the tool seals around the inner cable

lubricated periodically to ensure safe and trouble-free operation.

2 The footrests, clutch and brake levers, brake pedal, gearchange lever and linkage, and stand pivots should be lubricated frequently. In order for the lubricant to be applied where it will do the most good, the component should be disassembled. The lubricant recommended by Suzuki for each application is listed at the beginning of the Chapter. If chain or cable lubricant is being used, it can be applied to the pivot joint gaps and will usually work its way into the areas where friction occurs, so less disassembly of the component is needed (however it is always better to do so and clean off all corrosion, dirt and old lubricant first). If motor oil or light grease is being used, apply it sparingly as it may attract dirt (which could cause the controls to bind or wear at an accelerated rate). **Note:** *One of the best lubricants for the control lever pivots is a dry-*

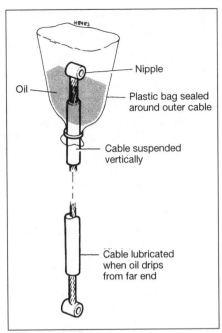

14.3b Lubricating a cable with a makeshift funnel and motor oil

film lubricant (available from many sources by different names).

3 To lubricate the cables, disconnect the relevant cable at its upper end, then lubricate it with a pressure adapter and aerosol lubricant, or if one is not available, using the set-up shown **(see illustrations)**. See Chapter 3 for the choke and throttle cable removal procedures, and Chapter 2 for the clutch cable.

1

Every 7500 miles (12,000 km) or 12 months

Carry out all the items under the 4000 mile (6000 km) check, plus the following:

15 Spark plugs – renewal

1 Remove the old spark plugs as described in Section 3 and install new ones.

16 Valve clearances – check and adjustment

1 The engine must be completely cool for this

maintenance procedure, so let the machine sit overnight before beginning. Place the motorcycle on its centrestand. On GSX600/750F models remove the right-hand fairing side panel (see Chapter 7).

2 Remove the spark plugs (see Section 3).

3 Remove the valve cover (see Chapter 2).

4 Unscrew the five bolts securing the pulse generator coil cover to the right-hand side of the engine **(see illustration)**.

5 Rotate the engine using a 19 mm socket or ring spanner on the large hex on the timing rotor, turning it in a **clockwise** direction only, until the line next to the T mark on the rotor aligns with the sensor on the pulse generator

16.4 Unscrew the bolts (arrowed) and remove the cover

16.5a Turn the engine in a clockwise direction . . .

16.5b . . . until the scribe line aligns with the sensor on the coil . . .

coil **(see illustrations)**. Alternatively, the engine can be turned by selecting a high gear and rotating the rear wheel by hand in its normal direction of rotation. At this point make sure that the notches in the ends of the camshafts are pointing away from each other and are aligned with the gasket mating surface on the cylinder head **(see illustration)**. If not, turn the engine clockwise through one full turn (360°) until the line next to the T mark again aligns with the sensor. The camshafts will now be correctly positioned.

Caution: DO NOT use the timing rotor Allen bolt to turn the crankshaft – it may

snap or strip out. Also be sure to turn the engine clockwise (its normal direction of rotation).

6 With the engine in this position the clearance for the following valves can be checked:

● No. 1 cylinder intake and exhaust valves
● No. 2 cylinder exhaust valves
● No. 3 cylinder intake valves

7 Start with the No. 1 intake valve clearances. Insert a feeler gauge of the thickness listed in this Chapter's Specifications between each valve stem and clearance adjuster screw **(see illustration)**. Pull the feeler gauge out slowly – you should feel a slight drag. If there's no drag,

the clearance is too loose. If there's a heavy drag, or the gauge will not fit, the clearance is too tight.

8 If the clearance is incorrect on either valve, loosen the adjuster screw locknut with a spanner and turn the adjuster screw in or out as needed until the specified clearance is obtained **(see illustration)**.

9 Hold the adjuster screw (to keep it from turning) and tighten the locknut. Recheck the clearance.

10 Now adjust the remaining valves listed in Step 6, following the same procedure. Make sure you use a feeler gauge of the specified thickness - intake and exhaust valve clearances differ.

11 Rotate the crankshaft one full turn (360°) until the line next to the T mark again aligns with the sensor **(see illustrations 16.5a and b)**. The notches in the ends of the camshafts should now point toward each other **(see illustration)**.

12 Check and adjust the following valves as described in Steps 7, 8 and 9 **(see illustrations 16.7 and 16.8)**:

● No. 2 cylinder intake valves
● No. 3 cylinder exhaust valves
● No. 4 cylinder intake and exhaust valves

13 Install all disturbed components in a reverse of the removal sequence. Install the pulse generator cover using a new gasket and a suitable non-permanent thread lock

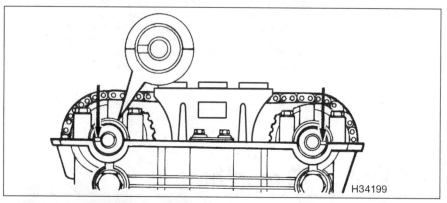

16.5c . . . and the notches (arrowed) in the camshaft ends face away from each other

16.7 Slip the feeler gauge between the top of the valve stem end and the bottom of the adjuster screw

16.8 Adjust the clearance by slackening the locknut and turning the adjuster screw as required

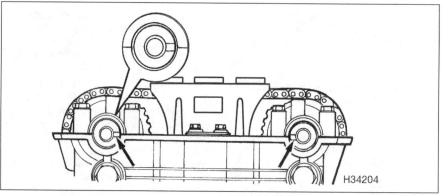

16.11 The notches (arrowed) should now point towards each other

16.13a Fit the cover using a new gasket . . .

16.13b . . . and do not forget the sealing washer with the top bolt

17.5a Detach the vacuum hose from its union . . .

on the bolts, and make sure the sealing washer is installed with the top bolt (see illustrations).

17 Carburettors – synchronisation

 Warning: Petrol (gasoline) is extremely flammable, so take extra precautions when you work on any part of the fuel system. Don't smoke or allow open flames or bare light bulbs near the work area, and don't work in a garage where a natural gas-type appliance is present. If you spill any fuel on your skin, rinse it off immediately with soap and water. When you perform any kind of work on the fuel system, wear safety glasses and have a fire extinguisher suitable for a Class B type fire (flammable liquids) on hand.

Warning: Take great care not to burn your hand on the hot engine unit when accessing the gauge take-off points on the intake ducts. Do not allow exhaust gases to build up in the work area; either perform the check outside or use an exhaust gas extraction system.

1 Carburettor synchronisation is simply the process of adjusting the carburettors so they pass the same amount of fuel/air mixture to each cylinder. This is achieved by measuring the vacuum produced in each intake duct. Carburettors that are out of synchronisation will result in increased fuel consumption, increased engine temperature, less than ideal throttle response and higher vibration levels.

2 To properly synchronise the carburettors, you will need a set of vacuum gauges or calibrated tubes to indicate engine vacuum. The equipment used should be suitable for a four cylinder engine and come complete with the necessary hoses to fit the take-off points. **Note:** *Because of the nature of the synchronisation procedure and the need for special instruments, most owners leave the task to a Suzuki dealer.*

3 Start the engine and let it run until it reaches normal operating temperature, then set the idle speed to 1750 rpm (see Section 6) and switch off the engine.

4 Remove the fuel tank (see Chapter 3).

5 Detach the fuel tap vacuum hose from the take-off point on either the No. 1 or 4 cylinder carburettor (according to model) (see illustration). Remove the blanking caps from the take-off points on the remaining carburettors (see illustration).

6 Connect the gauge hoses to the vacuum take-off points (see illustrations). Make sure they are a good fit because any air leaks will result in false readings.

7 Arrange a temporary fuel supply, either by using a small temporary tank (see *Tool Tip*) or by using an extra long fuel hose to the now remote fuel tank. Alternatively, position the tank on a suitable base on the motorcycle, taking care not to scratch any paintwork, and making sure that the tank is safely and securely supported. If using the motorcycle's fuel tank, turn the fuel tap to the PRI position.

8 Start the engine. If using vacuum gauges fitted with damping adjustment, set this so that the needle flutter is just eliminated but so that they can still respond to small changes in pressure.

9 The vacuum readings for the cylinders should be the same, or at least within the maximum difference specified at the beginning

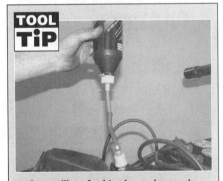

An auxiliary fuel tank can be made using an empty gear oil container (or any container of a suitable material that has a nozzle cap to which a hose can be attached). Simply fill it with fuel, attach one end of a suitable hose to the cap nozzle and the other to the fuel hose on the bike, then invert the container and hang or support it so that it is safe.

Alternatively obtain a two-stroke motorcycle oil tank from a breaker and attach a hose between the outlet union on its base and the fuel hose.

17.5b . . . and remove the blanking caps from the other unions on the carburettors

17.6 Connect the gauge hoses to the unions

1

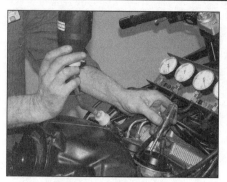
17.9a Check carburettor synchronisation . . .

17.9b . . . and adjust if necessary using the synchronisation screw (arrowed) between each carburettor pair

18.1 In-line fuel filter (arrowed)

of the Chapter **(see illustration)**. If the vacuum readings vary, adjust the carburettors by turning the synchronising screws situated in-between each carburettor, in the throttle linkage **(see illustration). Note:** *Do not press down on the screws whilst adjusting them, otherwise a false reading will be obtained.* First synchronise No. 3 carburettor to No. 4 using the right-hand screw until the readings are the same. Then synchronise No. 1 carburettor to No. 2 using the left-hand screw. Finally synchronise Nos. 1 and 2 carburettors to Nos. 3 and 4 using the centre synchronising screw.

10 When the carburettors are synchronised, open and close the throttle quickly to settle the linkage, and recheck the gauge readings, readjusting if necessary.

11 When the adjustment is complete, reset the idle speed to its normal level (see Section 6). Stop the engine.

12 Remove the gauges and hoses, then fit the fuel tap vacuum hose and the blanking caps back onto the relevant take-off points.

13 Detach the temporary fuel supply and install the fuel tank (see Chapter 3). Turn the fuel tap back to the ON position.

18 Fuel filter – renewal (GSX600/750F)

⚠️ *Warning: Petrol (gasoline) is extremely flammable, so take extra precautions when you work on any part of the fuel system. Don't smoke or allow open flames or bare light bulbs near the work area, and don't work in a garage where a natural gas-type appliance is present. If you spill any fuel on your skin, rinse it off immediately with soap and water. When you perform any kind of work on the fuel system, wear safety glasses and have a fire extinguisher suitable for a Class B type fire (flammable liquids) on hand.*

1 The in-line filter is fitted in the fuel hose between the tap and the carburettors **(see illustration)**. Raise or remove the fuel tank to access it (see Chapter 3). Note which way round the filter fits.

2 Release the clamps securing the hoses to the filter and detach them, having a rag handy to soak up any residual fuel that will flow out. Fit the new filter, noting that the directional arrow on the body must point in the direction of fuel flow (i.e. towards the carburettors). Make sure the clamps are in good condition and are secure.

19 Steering head bearings – check and adjustment

1 Steering head bearings can become dented, rough or loose during normal use of the machine. In extreme cases, worn or loose steering head bearings can cause steering wobble – a condition that is potentially dangerous.

Check

2 Support the motorcycle on its centrestand. On GSX600/750F models remove the lower fairing (see Chapter 7). Raise the front wheel off the ground using a jack and block of wood under the engine.

3 Point the front wheel straight-ahead and slowly move the handlebars from side-to-side. Any dents or roughness in the bearing races will be felt and the bars will not move smoothly and freely.

4 Grasp the bottom of the forks and gently pull and push them forward and backward **(see illustration)**. Any looseness or freeplay in

the steering head bearings will be felt as front-to-rear movement of the forks. If play is felt, adjust the bearings as described below.

> **HAYNES HINT** *Make sure you are not mistaking any movement between the bike and stand, or between the stand and the ground, for freeplay in the bearings. Do not pull and push the forks too hard – a gentle movement is all that is needed. Freeplay in the forks themselves due to worn bushes can also be misinterpreted as steering head bearing play – do not confuse the two.*

Adjustment

5 As a precaution, remove the fuel tank (see Chapter 3). Though not actually necessary, this will prevent the possibility of damage should a tool slip.

6 On GSX750 models displace the handlebars from the top yoke (see Chapter 5). Support them so the brake master cylinder is upright to prevent the possibility of fluid leakage. There is no need to remove assemblies from the handlebars, or to disconnect any cables, hoses or wiring. Note that if you do not have a socket or torque wrench, and are using a spanner to slacken and tighten the steering stem nut, the handlebars can remain in place.

7 Slacken the steering stem nut and the fork clamp bolts in the bottom yoke **(see illustrations)**.

19.4 Checking for play in the steering head bearings

19.7a Slacken the steering stem nut (arrowed) . . .

19.7b ... and the bottom yoke fork clamp bolts (arrowed) on each side

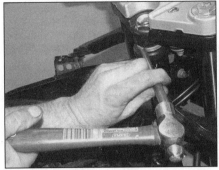

19.8a Adjust the bearings as described using either a drift ...

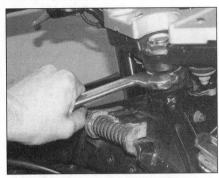

19.8b ... or a C-spanner

8 Using a suitable C-spanner (or a drift) located in one of the notches of the adjuster nut, slacken the nut slightly until pressure is just released, then tighten it until all freeplay is removed, yet the steering is able to move freely as described in Steps 3 and 4 **(see illustrations)**. The object is to set the adjuster nut so that the bearings are under a very light loading, just enough to remove any freeplay, but not so much that the steering does not move freely from side to side.

Caution: Take great care not to apply excessive pressure because this will cause premature failure of the bearings.

9 If the bearings cannot be correctly adjusted, disassemble the steering head and check the bearings and races (see Chapter 5).

10 Tighten the steering stem nut to the torque setting specified at the beginning of the Chapter. Now tighten the fork clamp bolts in the bottom yoke to the specified torque. On GSX750 models install the handlebars if displaced (see Chapter 5).

11 Check the bearing adjustment as described is Steps 3 and 4 and re-adjust if necessary. If available, the bearing loading can be checked with a spring balance. Attach one end of a spring balance (graduated 100 to 600 grams) to the outer end of the rubber grip on the handlebars. With the steering straight-ahead, pull on the balance and check the

reading at which the handlebars start to turn **(see illustration)**. If the reading is below 200 grams, the steering head is too loose, if the reading is above 500 grams the steering head is too tight. Connect the balance to the other handlebar and check the loading again – the result should be the same. Check that the steering movement is uninhibited by the resistance of cables or hoses when making this check.

12 Install the fuel tank (see Chapter 3).

20 Suspension – check

1 The suspension components must be maintained in top operating condition to ensure rider safety. Loose, worn or damaged suspension parts decrease the motorcycle's stability and control.

Front suspension

2 While standing alongside the motorcycle, apply the front brake and push on the handlebars to compress the forks several times. Check that they move up-and-down smoothly without binding. If binding is felt, the forks should be disassembled and inspected (see Chapter 5).

3 Inspect the area around the dust seal for signs of oil leakage, then carefully lever up the dust seal using a flat-bladed screwdriver and inspect the area above the fork seal **(see**

illustration)**. If leakage is evident, new seals must be installed (see Chapter 5).

4 Check the tightness of all suspension nuts and bolts to be sure none have worked loose, applying the torque settings at the beginning of Chapter 5.

Rear suspension

5 Inspect the rear shock absorber(s) for fluid leakage and tightness of the mountings. If leakage is found, a new shock must be installed (see Chapter 5). On GSX750 models, both shocks must be renewed as a pair if they are faulty.

6 With the aid of an assistant to support the bike, compress the rear suspension several times. It should move up and down freely without binding. If any binding is felt, the worn or faulty component must be identified and checked (see Chapter 5). The problem could be due to either the shock absorber(s), the suspension linkage components (GSX600/750F models), or the swingarm components.

7 Support the motorcycle on its centrestand so that the rear wheel is off the ground. Grab the swingarm ends and rock it from side to side – there should be no discernible movement at the rear **(see illustration)**. If there's a little movement or a slight clicking can be heard, inspect the tightness of all the swingarm and rear suspension mounting bolts and nuts, referring to the torque settings specified at the beginning of Chapter 5, and re-check for movement.

1

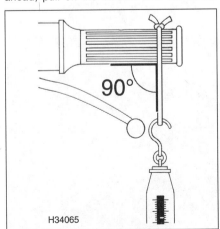

19.11 Using a spring balance to check bearing loading

20.3 Check above and below the dust seal for signs of oil leakage

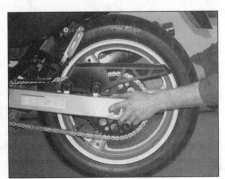

20.7 Checking for play in the swingarm bearings

8 Next, grasp the top of the rear wheel and pull it upwards – there should be no discernible freeplay before the shock absorber(s) begins to compress **(see illustration)**. Any freeplay felt in either check indicates worn bearings in the swingarm, or worn suspension linkage bearings (GSX600/750F models), or worn shock absorber mountings. The worn components must be identified and renewed (see Chapter 5).

9 To make an accurate assessment of the swingarm bearings, remove the rear wheel (see Chapter 6) and the bolt(s) securing the suspension linkage assembly (GSX600/750F models) or the shock absorbers (GSX750 models) to the swingarm (see Chapter 5). On GSX750 models pivot the shock absorbers back so they are clear of their mounts.

10 Grasp the rear of the swingarm with one hand and place your other hand at the junction of the swingarm and the frame. Try to move the rear of the swingarm from side-to-side. Any wear (play) in the bearings should be felt as movement between the swingarm and the frame at the front. If there is any play the swingarm will be felt to move forward and backward at the front (not from side-to-side). Next, move the swingarm up and down through its full travel. It should move freely, without any binding or rough spots. If there is any play in the swingarm or if it does not move freely, remove the swingarm for closer inspection of the bearings (see Chapter 5).

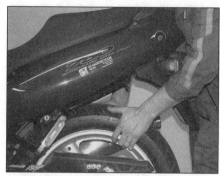

20.8 Checking for play in the rear shock mountings and suspension linkage bearings

Every 11,000 miles (18,000 km) or 18 months

Carry out all the items under the 4000 mile (6000 km) check, plus the following:

21 Air filter – renewal

Caution: If the machine is continually ridden in wet or dusty conditions, the filter should be renewed more frequently.

1 Refer to the procedure in Section 2 and renew the air filter.

22 Engine/transmission – oil and filter change

 Warning: Be careful when draining the oil and when removing and installing the filter as the exhaust pipes, the engine, and the oil itself can cause severe burns.

1 Refer to Section 5, Steps 2 to 6 and drain the engine oil.

2 Now place the drain tray below the oil filter, located on the front of the engine. Unscrew the filter using a filter socket adaptor, either an aftermarket type **(see illustration)** or the Suzuki special tool (Pt. No. 09915-40610).

Alternatively a filter removing strap or a chain-wrench can be used. Tip any residual oil into the drain tray **(see illustration)**. Discard the filter, noting that it should be taken to the disposal site along with the used oil.

3 Smear clean engine oil onto the rubber seal on the new filter. Thread the filter onto the engine until the seal just contacts its mating surface **(see illustrations)**. Now tighten the filter by two full turns – make a reference mark between the filter and crankcase as a guide to how far the filter has turned if necessary. On

22.2a Unscrew the filter using a filter removing tool . . .

the model photographed we found that the filter became tight enough after about one and a half turns, so some discretion may be required. **Note:** *Do not use a strap or chain filter removing tool to tighten the filter as you will damage it. If you do not have a filter socket you can tighten the filter by hand, but make sure it is tightened by the number of turns specified or it will probably leak.*

4 Refer to Section 5, Steps 7 to 10 and refill the engine to the proper level using the recommended type and amount of oil.

22.2b . . . and allow the oil to drain

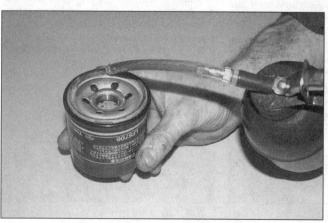

22.3a Smear clean oil onto the seal . . .

22.3b . . . then install the filter and tighten it as described

Every two years

23 Brake fluid – change

1 The brake fluid should be changed at the prescribed interval or whenever a master cylinder or caliper overhaul is carried out. Refer to the brake fluid renewal section in Chapter 6, noting that all old fluid must be pumped from the fluid reservoir and hydraulic hoses before filling with new fluid.

Every four years

24 Brake hoses – renewal

1 The brake hoses will deteriorate with age and should be renewed regardless of their apparent condition. Refer to Chapter 6 and disconnect the brake hoses from the master cylinders and calipers. Always renew the banjo union sealing washers.

25 Fuel hoses – renewal

 Warning: Petrol (gasoline) is extremely flammable, so take extra precautions when you

work on any part of the fuel system. Don't smoke or allow open flames or bare light bulbs near the work area, and don't work in a garage where a natural gas-type appliance is present. If you spill any fuel on your skin, rinse it off immediately with soap and water. When you perform any kind of work on the fuel system, wear safety glasses and have a fire extinguisher suitable for a Class B type fire (flammable liquids) on hand.

1 The fuel system hoses should be renewed at this interval or before if signs of cracking or hardening are noticed. This includes all the vent and drain hoses, and the vacuum hoses. On Austria, Switzerland and California models you should also renew the PAIR system hoses, and on California models the EVAP system hoses (refer to Chapter 3 for more information on these systems).
2 Remove the fuel tank (see Chapter 3). It is advisable to make a sketch of the various hoses before removing them to ensure they can be correctly installed.
3 Release the clamp and detach the fuel hose from the carburettors. On GSX600/750F models remove the in-line fuel filter from between the hose sections (see Section 18). Detach the fuel tap vacuum hose from the take-off point on either the No. 1 or 4 cylinder carburettor (according to model) **(see illustration 17.5a)**. Note the routing of each hose.
4 Secure each new hose to its unions using new clamps where fitted. Run the engine and check that there are no leaks before taking the machine out on the road.

Non-scheduled maintenance

26 Cylinder compression – check

1 Poor engine performance can be caused by many things, including leaking valves, incorrect valve clearances, a leaking head gasket, loose cylinder head nuts or worn pistons, rings and/or cylinder walls. A cylinder compression check will help pinpoint these conditions and can also indicate the presence of excessive carbon deposits in the cylinder head.
2 The only tools required are a compression gauge and a spark plug wrench. A

compression gauge with a threaded end for the spark plug hole is required. Depending on the outcome of the initial test, a squirt-type oil can may also be needed.
3 Make sure the valve clearances are correctly set (see Section 16).
4 Refer to *Fault Finding Equipment* in the Reference section for details of the compression test. Refer to the specifications at the beginning of the Chapter for compression figures.

27 Engine oil pressure – check

1 The oil pressure warning light should come on when the ignition (main) switch is turned ON and extinguish a few seconds after the engine is started – this serves as a check that the warning light bulb is sound. If the oil pressure light comes on whilst the engine is running, low oil pressure is indicated – stop the engine immediately and check the oil level (see *Daily (pre-ride) checks*).
2 An oil pressure check must be carried out if the warning light comes on when the engine is running yet the oil level is good (Step 1). It can also provide useful information about the condition of the engine's lubrication system.

3 To check the oil pressure, a suitable gauge and adapter (which screws into the crankcase) will be needed. Suzuki provide the components (Pt. Nos. 09915-74510, 74540 and 77330) for this purpose, or they can be obtained commercially. You will also need a container and some rags to catch and mop up any residual oil that gets lost in between removing the main oil gallery plug and installing the gauge. Place the motorcycle on its sidestand when installing the gauge to minimise oil loss, but have it on the centrestand when running the engine to check the pressure. Check the oil level after installing the gauge and replenish if necessary (see *Daily (pre-ride) checks*).
4 On GSX600/750F models remove the lower fairing (see Chapter 7).
5 Unscrew the main oil gallery plug, located on the right-hand side of the engine below the pulse generator coil cover, and swiftly screw the gauge assembly in its place **(see illustration)**.
6 Warm the engine up to normal operating temperature – Suzuki specify 10 mins at 2000 rpm in the summer, and 20 mins at 2000 rpm in the winter.
7 Increase the engine speed to 3000 rpm whilst watching the gauge reading. The oil pressure should be similar to that given in the Specifications at the start of this Chapter. Stop the engine.

1

27.5 Main oil gallery plug (arrowed)

8 If the pressure is significantly lower than the standard, either the pressure relief valve is stuck open, the oil pump or its drive mechanism is faulty, the oil strainer or filter is blocked, or there is other engine damage. Also make sure the correct grade oil is being used. Begin diagnosis by checking the oil filter, strainer and relief valve, then the oil pump (see Chapter 2). If those items check out okay, chances are the bearing oil clearances are excessive and the engine needs to be overhauled.

9 If the pressure is too high, either an oil passage is clogged, the relief valve is stuck closed or the wrong grade of oil is being used.

10 Unscrew the gauge assembly and immediately install the oil gallery plug, tightening it to the torque setting specified at the beginning of the Chapter.

11 Check the oil level and replenish if necessary (see *Daily (pre-ride) checks*).

28 Wheel bearings – check

1 Wheel bearings will wear over a period of time and result in handling problems.

2 Place the motorcycle on its centrestand. On GSX600/750F models remove the lower fairing (see Chapter 7). When checking the front wheel raise the wheel off the ground using a jack and block of wood under the engine.

3 Check for any play in the bearings by pushing and pulling the wheel against the axle – turn the steering to full lock to keep it steady when checking the front wheel **(see illustration)**. Also spin the wheel and check that it rotates smoothly.

4 If any play is detected in the hub, or if the wheel does not rotate smoothly (and this is not due to brake or transmission drag), remove the wheel and check the bearings for wear or damage (see Chapter 6). If in doubt renew the bearings.

29 Steering head bearings – re-greasing

1 Over a period of time the grease will harden or may be washed out of the bearings by incorrect use of jet washes.

2 Disassemble the steering head for re-greasing of the bearings. Refer to Chapter 5 for details.

30 Swingarm and suspension linkage bearings – re-greasing

1 Over a period of time the grease will harden or dirt will penetrate the bearings due to failed seals.

28.3 Checking for play in the wheel bearings

2 The suspension is not equipped with grease nipples. Remove the swingarm and suspension linkage as described in Chapter 5 for greasing of the bearings.

31 Brake master cylinders and calipers – seal renewal

1 Brake seals will deteriorate over a period of time and lose their effectiveness, leading to sticking operation or fluid loss, or allowing the ingress of air and dirt. Refer to Chapter 6 and dismantle the components for seal renewal.

32 Front forks – oil change

1 Fork oil degrades over a period of time and loses its damping qualities. Refer to the fork oil change procedure in Chapter 5. The forks do not need to be completely disassembled.

33 Battery – check

1 All models are fitted with a sealed MF (maintenance free) battery. **Note:** *Do not attempt to remove the battery caps to check the electrolyte level or battery specific gravity. Removal will damage the caps, resulting in electrolyte leakage and battery damage.* All that should be done is to check that the terminals are clean and tight and that the casing is not damaged or leaking. See Chapter 8 for further details.

2 If the machine is not in regular use, remove the battery and give it a refresher charge every month to six weeks (see Chapter 8).

34 Sidestand and centrestand – check

1 Check the stand springs for damage and distortion. The springs must be capable of

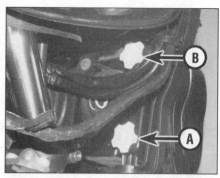

35.2 Vertical adjustment screw (A), horizontal adjustment screw (B) – GSX600/750F

retracting the stands fully and holding them retracted when the motorcycle is in use. If a spring is sagged or broken it must be renewed.

2 Lubricate the stand pivots regularly (see Section 14).

3 Check the stands and their mounting brackets for bends and cracks, and that the bolts and nuts are tight.

4 Check the operation of the sidestand switch by shifting the transmission into neutral, retracting the stand, pulling in the clutch lever and starting the engine. With the clutch lever still held in, select a gear. Extend the sidestand. The engine should stop as the sidestand is extended. If the sidestand switch does not operate as described, check its circuit (see Chapter 8).

35 Headlight aim – check and adjustment

Note: *An improperly adjusted headlight may cause problems for oncoming traffic or provide poor, unsafe illumination of the road ahead. Before adjusting the headlight aim, be sure to consult with local traffic laws and regulations – for UK models refer to MOT Test Checks in the Reference section.*

1 The headlight beam(s) can adjusted both horizontally and vertically. Before making any adjustment, check that the tyre pressures are correct and the suspension is adjusted as required. Make any adjustments to the headlight aim with the machine on level ground, with the fuel tank half full and with an assistant sitting in the normal solo riding position. If the bike is usually ridden with a passenger on the back, have a second assistant to do this.

2 On GSX600/750F models, vertical adjustment is made by turning the bottom adjuster on each headlight unit **(see illustration)**. Horizontal adjustment is made by turning the top adjuster on the each headlight unit.

3 On GSX750 models, vertical adjustment is made by slackening the adjuster clamp bolt, then tilting the headlight up or down in the bracket as required. Tighten the clamp bolt on completion. Horizontal adjustment is made by turning the adjuster screw on the left-hand side of the headlight rim.

Chapter 2
Engine, clutch and transmission

Contents

Alternator – removal and installation . . . . .see Chapter 8
Cam chain and tensioner blade – removal,
   inspection and installation 10
Cam chain tensioner and cam chain guides –
   removal and installation 9
Camshafts and rocker arms – removal, inspection
   and installation 11
Clutch – removal, inspection and installation 18
Clutch cable – removal and installation 19
Clutch check . . . . .see Chapter 1
Connecting rods – removal, inspection and installation 28
Crankcase – inspection and servicing 25
Crankcase – separation and reassembly 24
Crankshaft and main bearings – removal, inspection and installation . . . 27
Cylinder block – removal, inspection and installation 15
Cylinder compression check . . . . .see Chapter 1
Cylinder head – removal and installation 12
Cylinder head and valves – disassembly, inspection
   and reassembly 14
Engine – removal and installation 5
Engine disassembly and reassembly – general information 6
Gearchange mechanism – removal, inspection and installation 20
General information 1
Idle speed check . . . . .see Chapter 1
Ignition pulse generator coil – removal and installation . .see Chapter 4
Ignition timing rotor – removal and installation 22
Initial start-up after overhaul 33
Main and connecting rod bearings – general information 26
Major engine repair – general information 4
Oil cooler and hoses – removal and installation 7
Oil and filter change . . . . .see Chapter 1
Oil level check . . . . .see *Daily (pre-ride) checks*
Oil pressure check . . . . .see Chapter 1
Oil pressure switch – check, removal and installation . . .see Chapter 8
Oil pump – removal, inspection and installation 32
Oil sump, pressure regulator and strainer – removal,
   inspection and installation 23
Operations possible with the engine in the frame 2
Operations requiring engine removal 3
Pistons – removal, inspection and installation 16
Piston rings – inspection and installation 17
Recommended running-in procedure 34
Selector drum and forks – removal, inspection and installation 29
Spark plug checks . . . . .see Chapter 1
Starter clutch and idle/reduction gear – check, removal,
   inspection and installation 21
Starter motor – removal and installation . . . . .see Chapter 8
Transmission shafts – disassembly, inspection and reassembly . . . 31
Transmission shafts – removal and installation 30
Valve clearance check . . . . .see Chapter 1
Valve cover – removal and installation 8
Valves/valve seats/valve guides – servicing 13

Degrees of difficulty

Easy, suitable for novice with little experience		**Fairly easy,** suitable for beginner with some experience		**Fairly difficult,** suitable for competent DIY mechanic		**Difficult,** suitable for experienced DIY mechanic		**Very difficult,** suitable for expert DIY or professional	

Specifications – GSX600F models

General

Type	Four-stroke in-line four
Capacity	600 cc
Bore	62.6 mm
Stroke	48.7 mm
Compression ratio	11.3 to 1
Clutch	Wet multi-plate
Transmission	Six-speed constant mesh
Final drive	Chain

Camshafts and rocker arms
Camshaft
  Intake lobe height
    Austria and Switzerland models
      Standard .... 32.38 to 32.42 mm
      Service limit (min) .... 32.08 mm
    All other models
      Standard .... 33.13 to 33.17 mm
      Service limit (min) .... 32.83 mm
  Exhaust lobe height
    Austria and Switzerland models
      Standard .... 32.10 to 32.14 mm
      Service limit (min) .... 31.80 mm
    All other models
      Standard .... 32.85 to 32.89 mm
      Service limit (min) .... 32.55 mm
  Journal diameter .... 21.959 to 21.980 mm
  Journal bore diameter .... 22.012 to 22.025 mm
  Journal oil clearance
    Standard .... 0.032 to 0.066 mm
    Service limit (max) .... 0.15 mm
  Runout (max) .... 0.10 mm
Rocker arm bore ID .... 12.000 to 12.018 mm
Rocker arm shaft OD .... 11.973 to 11.984 mm

Cylinder head
Warpage (max) .... 0.20 mm

Cylinder block
Bore
  Standard .... 62.600 to 62.615 mm
  Service limit (max) .... 62.690 mm
Warpage (max) .... 0.20 mm
Cylinder compression .... see Chapter 1

Valves, guides and springs
Valve clearances .... see Chapter 1
Intake valve
  Head diameter .... 23 mm
  Stem diameter .... 4.965 to 4.980 mm
  Guide bore diameter .... 5.000 to 5.012 mm
  Stem-to-guide clearance .... 0.020 to 0.047 mm
  Stem deflection (max) – see text .... 0.35 mm
  Face thickness (min) .... 0.5 mm
  Seat width .... 0.9 to 1.1 mm
  Head runout (max) .... 0.03 mm
  Stem runout (max) .... 0.05 mm
  Stem length above collet groove (min) .... 2.5 mm
Exhaust valve
  Head diameter .... 20 mm
  Stem diameter .... 4.955 to 4.970 mm
  Guide bore diameter .... 5.000 to 5.012 mm
  Stem-to-guide clearance .... 0.030 to 0.057 mm
  Stem deflection (max) – see text .... 0.35 mm
  Face thickness (min) .... 0.5 mm
  Seat width .... 0.9 to 1.1 mm
  Head runout (max) .... 0.03 mm
  Stem runout (max) .... 0.05 mm
  Stem length above collet groove (min) .... 2.5 mm
Valve springs (intake and exhaust)
  Free length limit (min)
    Inner spring .... 35.0 mm
    Outer spring .... 38.4 mm
  Spring tension
    Inner spring .... 28.0 mm with 5.6 to 6.6 kg load
    Outer spring .... 31.5 mm with 12.8 to 15.0 kg load

Pistons

Piston diameter (measured 15.0 mm up from skirt, at 90° to piston pin axis)
Standard	62.555 to 62.570 mm
Service limit (min)	62.480 mm
1st oversize	+0.5 mm
2nd oversize	+1.0 mm

Piston-to-bore clearance
Standard	0.040 to 0.050 mm
Service limit (max)	0.120 mm

Piston pin diameter
Standard	17.996 to 18.000 mm
Service limit (min)	17.98 mm

Piston pin bore diameter in piston
Standard	18.002 to 18.008 mm
Service limit (max)	18.03 mm

Piston rings

Ring end gap (free)
Top ring	
Standard	6.70 mm
Service limit (min)	5.40 mm
2nd ring	
Standard	7.00 mm
Service limit (min)	5.60 mm

Ring end gap (installed)
Top ring	
Standard	0.10 to 0.30 mm
Service limit (max)	0.50 mm
2nd ring	
Standard	0.30 to 0.50 mm
Service limit (max)	0.70 mm

Ring thickness
Top ring	0.97 to 0.99 mm
2nd ring	0.77 to 0.79 mm

Ring groove width in piston
Top ring	1.02 to 1.04 mm
2nd ring	0.81 to 0.83 mm
Oil ring	1.51 to 1.53 mm

Ring-to-groove clearance
Top ring (max)	0.18 mm
2nd ring (max)	0.15 mm

Ring identification
Top ring	R
2nd ring	RN
Oil ring	none

Oversize ring identification
Top and second rings	
1st oversize (+0.5 mm)	50
2nd oversize (+1.0 mm)	100
Oil ring (standard uncoloured)	
1st oversize (+0.5 mm)	Red
2nd oversize (+1.0 mm)	Yellow

Clutch

Friction plates
Quantity	8
Thickness – outer (type A) plates	
Standard	2.92 to 3.08 mm
Service limit (min)	2.62 mm
Thickness – inner (type B) plate	
Standard	3.42 to 3.58 mm
Service limit (min)	3.12 mm
Tab width – all plates	
Standard	15.9 to 16.0 mm
Service limit (min)	15.1 mm

Plain plates
Quantity	7
Warpage (max)	0.1 mm
Spring free length (min)	47.6 mm
Release mechanism screw	1/4 turn out

2

Crankshaft and bearings

Journal diameter . . . . 31.976 to 32.000 mm
Journal width . . . . 24.000 to 24.050 mm
Main bearing oil clearance
    Standard . . . . 0.020 to 0.044 mm
    Service limit (max) . . . . 0.08 mm
Runout (max) . . . . 0.05 mm
Thrust bearing clearance . . . . 0.04 to 0.09 mm
Right-hand (inner) thrust bearing thickness . . . . 2.425 to 2.450 mm
Left-hand (outer) thrust bearing thickness . . . . Selective fit, see Section 27

Connecting rods

Small-end internal diameter
    Standard . . . . 18.010 to 18.018 mm
    Service limit (max) . . . . 18.040 mm
Big-end side clearance
    Standard . . . . 0.1 to 0.2 mm
    Service limit (max) . . . . 0.3 mm
Big-end width . . . . 20.95 to 21.00 mm
Crankpin width . . . . 21.10 to 21.15 mm
Crankpin diameter . . . . 33.976 to 34.000 mm
Big-end oil clearance
    Standard . . . . 0.032 to 0.056 mm
    Service limit (max) . . . . 0.08 mm

Transmission

Gear ratios (no. of teeth)
    Primary reduction . . . . 1.744 to 1 (75/43T)
    Final reduction . . . . 3.133 to 1 (47/15T)
    1st gear . . . . 3.083 to 1 (37/12T)
    2nd gear . . . . 2.062 to 1 (33/16T)
    3rd gear . . . . 1.647 to 1 (28/17T)
    4th gear . . . . 1.400 to 1 (28/20T)
    5th gear . . . . 1.227 to 1 (27/22T)
    6th gear . . . . 1.095 to 1 (23/21T)

Selector drum and forks

Selector fork-to-groove clearance
    Standard . . . . 0.1 to 0.3 mm
    Service limit (max) . . . . 0.5 mm
Selector fork end thickness
    Nos. 1 and 3 forks . . . . 4.6 to 4.7 mm
    No. 2 fork . . . . 4.8 to 4.9 mm
Selector fork groove width
    Nos. 1 and 3 fork grooves . . . . 4.8 to 4.9 mm
    No. 2 fork groove . . . . 5.0 to 5.1 mm

Lubrication system

Oil pressure . . . . see Chapter 1

Torque wrench settings

Cam chain tensioner mounting bolts . . . . 7 Nm
Cam chain tensioner spring cap bolt . . . . 35 Nm
Cam chain top guide bolts . . . . 10 Nm
Camshaft holder bolts . . . . 10 Nm
Camshaft sprocket bolts . . . . 25 Nm
Clutch nut . . . . 95 Nm
Clutch pressure plate bolts . . . . 12 Nm
Connecting rod cap nuts
    Initial setting (see text) . . . . 34 Nm
    Final setting . . . . 66 Nm
Crankcase 6 mm bolts and nuts . . . . 11 Nm
Crankcase 8 mm bolts . . . . 23 Nm
Cylinder block nut . . . . 9 Nm
Cylinder head 6 mm bolt . . . . 10 Nm
Cylinder head 10 mm nuts . . . . 38 Nm

Torque wrench settings (continued)

Cylinder studs	15 Nm
Engine mounting bolts	
Rear mounting bolts (upper and lower)	75 Nm
Cradle-to-frame bolts (front and rear)	32 Nm
Cradle-to-engine bolts (middle)	55 Nm
Cradle-to-engine bracket bolts (front)	32 Nm
Front mounting bolt nuts (if undone)	55 Nm
Frame cross-member bolts	32 Nm
Ignition timing rotor bolt	25 Nm
Main oil gallery plug	40 Nm
Oil cooler mounting bolts	10 Nm
Oil hose banjo bolts	23 Nm
Oil hose union bolts	10 Nm
Oil pressure regulator	28 Nm
Oil pump mounting bolts	10 Nm
Oil sump bolts	14 Nm
Rocker shaft locking bolt	9 Nm
Rocker shaft plug	28 Nm
Starter clutch bolt	150 Nm
Valve cover banjo bolts	
GSX600F-W (1998) models	16 Nm
All later models	20 Nm
Valve cover standard bolts	14 Nm

Specifications – GSX750F and GSX750 models

General

Type	Four-stroke in-line four
Capacity	750 cc
Bore	70.0 mm
Stroke	48.7 mm
Compression ratio	10.7 to 1
Clutch	Wet multi-plate
Transmission	Six-speed constant mesh
Final drive	Chain

Camshafts and rocker arms

Camshaft	
Intake lobe height	
Standard	32.66 to 32.71 mm
Service limit (min)	32.36 mm
Exhaust lobe height	
Standard	32.65 to 32.70 mm
Service limit (min)	32.35 mm
Journal diameter	21.959 to 21.980 mm
Journal bore diameter	22.012 to 22.025 mm
Journal oil clearance	
Standard	0.032 to 0.066 mm
Service limit (max)	0.15 mm
Runout (max)	0.10 mm
Rocker arm bore ID	12.000 to 12.018 mm
Rocker arm shaft OD	11.973 to 11.984 mm

Cylinder head

Warpage (max)	0.20 mm

Cylinder block

Bore	
Standard	70.000 to 70.015 mm
Service limit (max)	70.075 mm
Warpage (max)	0.20 mm
Cylinder compression	see Chapter 1

2

Valves, guides and springs

Valve clearances	see Chapter 1
Intake valves	
Head diameter	27 mm
Stem diameter	4.965 to 4.980 mm
Guide bore diameter	5.000 to 5.012 mm
Stem-to-guide clearance	0.020 to 0.047 mm
Stem deflection (max) – see text	0.35 mm
Face thickness (min)	0.5 mm
Seat width	0.9 to 1.1 mm
Head runout (max)	0.03 mm
Stem runout (max)	0.05 mm
Stem length above collet groove (min)	2.3 mm
Exhaust valves	
Head diameter	24 mm
Stem diameter	4.945 to 4.960 mm
Guide bore diameter	5.000 to 5.012 mm
Stem-to-guide clearance	0.040 to 0.067 mm
Stem deflection (max) – see text	0.35 mm
Face thickness (min)	0.5 mm
Seat width	0.9 to 1.1 mm
Head runout (max)	0.03 mm
Stem runout (max)	0.05 mm
Stem length above collet groove (min)	2.3 mm
Valve springs (intake and exhaust)	
Free length limit (min)	
Inner spring	33.9 mm
Outer spring	37.3 mm
Spring tension	
Inner spring	28.0 mm with 6.0 to 6.8 kg load
Outer spring	31.5 mm with 15.4 to 17.8 kg load

Pistons

Piston diameter (measured 15.0 mm up from skirt, at 90° to piston pin axis)	
Standard	69.940 to 69.955 mm
Service limit (min)	69.880 mm
1st oversize	+ 0.5 mm
2nd oversize	+ 1.0 mm
Piston-to-bore clearance	
Standard	0.055 to 0.065 mm
Service limit (max)	0.120 mm
Piston pin diameter	
Standard	17.992 to 18.000 mm
Service limit (min)	17.98 mm
Piston pin bore diameter in piston	
Standard	18.002 to 18.008 mm
Service limit (max)	18.03 mm

Piston rings

Ring end gap (free)	
GSX750F models	
Top ring	
Standard	7.00 mm
Service limit (min)	5.60 mm
2nd ring	
Standard	10.50 mm
Service limit (min)	8.40 mm
GSX750 models	
Top ring	
Standard	8.20 mm
Service limit (min)	6.60 mm
2nd ring	
Standard	7.70 mm
Service limit (min)	6.20 mm

Piston rings (continued)
Ring end gap (installed)
  GSX750F models
    Top ring
      Standard .... 0.10 to 0.25 mm
      Service limit (max) .... 0.50 mm
    2nd ring
      Standard .... 0.25 to 0.40 mm
      Service limit (max) .... 0.70 mm
  GSX750 models
    Top ring
      Standard .... 0.20 to 0.30 mm
      Service limit (max) .... 0.50 mm
    2nd ring
      Standard .... 0.20 to 0.35 mm
      Service limit (max) .... 0.50 mm
Ring thickness
  Top ring .... 0.97 to 0.99 mm
  2nd ring .... 0.97 to 0.99 mm
Ring groove width in piston
  Top ring .... 1.01 to 1.04 mm
  2nd ring .... 1.004 to 1.027 mm
  Oil ring .... 1.51 to 1.53 mm
Ring-to-groove clearance
  Top ring (max) .... 0.18 mm
  2nd ring (max) .... 0.15 mm
Ring identification
  Top ring .... N
  2nd ring 2N
  Oil ring .... none
Oversize ring identification
  Top and second rings
    1st oversize (+0.50 mm) N50
    2nd oversize (+1.00 mm) N100
  Oil ring (standard uncoloured)
    1st oversize (+0.50 mm) .... Blue
    2nd oversize (+1.00 mm) .... Yellow

Clutch
Friction plates
  Quantity 8
  Thickness – outer (type A) plates
    Standard .... 2.92 to 3.08 mm
    Service limit (min) .... 2.62 mm
  Thickness – inner (type B) plate
    Standard .... 3.42 to 3.58 mm
    Service limit (min) .... 3.12 mm
  Tab width – all plates
    Standard .... 15.9 to 16.0 mm
    Service limit (min) .... 15.1 mm
Plain plates
  Quantity 7
  Warpage (max) .... 0.1 mm
Spring free length (min) .... 47.6 mm
Release mechanism screw .... 1/4 turn out

Crankshaft and bearings
Journal diameter .... 31.976 to 32.000 mm
Journal width .... 24.000 to 24.050 mm
Main bearing oil clearance
  Standard .... 0.020 to 0.044 mm
  Service limit (max) .... 0.08 mm
Runout (max) .... 0.05 mm
Thrust bearing clearance .... 0.06 to 0.11 mm
Right-hand (inner) thrust bearing thickness .... 2.425 to 2.450 mm
Left-hand (outer) thrust bearing thickness .... Selective fit, see Section 27

Connecting rods
Small-end internal diameter
    Standard . . . . 18.010 to 18.018 mm
    Service limit (max) . . . . 18.040 mm
Big-end side clearance
    Standard . . . . 0.1 to 0.2 mm
    Service limit (max) . . . . 0.3 mm
Big-end width . . . . 20.95 to 21.00 mm
Crankpin width . . . . 21.10 to 21.15 mm
Crankpin diameter . . . . 33.976 to 34.000 mm
Big-end oil clearance
    Standard . . . . 0.032 to 0.056 mm
    Service limit (max) . . . . 0.08 mm

Transmission
Gear ratios (no. of teeth)
    Primary reduction . . . . 1.744 to 1 (75/43T)
    Final reduction
      GSX750F models . . . . 3.000 to 1 (45/15T)
      GSX750 models . . . . 2.800 to 1 (42/15T)
    1st gear . . . . 3.083 to 1 (37/12T)
    2nd gear . . . . 2.062 to 1 (33/16T)
    3rd gear . . . . 1.647 to 1 (28/17T)
    4th gear . . . . 1.400 to 1 (28/20T)
    5th gear . . . . 1.227 to 1 (27/22T)
    6th gear . . . . 1.095 to 1 (23/21T)

Selector drum and forks
Selector fork-to-groove clearance
    Standard . . . . 0.1 to 0.3 mm
    Service limit (max) . . . . 0.5 mm
Selector fork end thickness
    Nos. 1 and 3 forks . . . . 4.6 to 4.7 mm
    No. 2 fork . . . . 4.8 to 4.9 mm
Selector fork groove width
    Nos. 1 and 3 fork grooves . . . . 4.8 to 4.9 mm
    No. 2 fork groove . . . . 5.0 to 5.1 mm

Lubrication system
Oil pressure . . . . see Chapter 1

Torque wrench settings
Cam chain tensioner mounting bolts . . . . 7 Nm
Cam chain tensioner spring cap bolt . . . . 35 Nm
Cam chain top guide bolts . . . . 10 Nm
Camshaft holder bolts . . . . 10 Nm
Camshaft sprocket bolts . . . . 25 Nm
Clutch nut . . . . 95 Nm
Clutch pressure plate bolts . . . . 12 Nm
Connecting rod cap bolts
    Initial setting (see text) . . . . 34 Nm
    Final setting . . . . 66 Nm
Crankcase 6 mm bolts and nuts . . . . 11 Nm
Crankcase 8 mm bolts . . . . 23 Nm
Cylinder block nut . . . . 9 Nm
Cylinder head 6 mm bolt . . . . 10 Nm
Cylinder head 10 mm nuts . . . . 38 Nm
Cylinder studs . . . . 15 Nm
Engine mounting bolts – GSX750F
    Rear mounting bolt nuts (upper and lower) . . . . 75 Nm
    Cradle-to-frame bolts (front and rear) . . . . 32 Nm
    Cradle-to-engine bolts (middle) . . . . 55 Nm
    Cradle-to-engine bracket bolts (front) . . . . 32 Nm
    Front mounting bolt nuts (if undone) . . . . 55 Nm
Engine mounting bolts – GSX750
    Rear mounting bolt nuts (upper and lower) . . . . 75 Nm
    Cradle-to-frame bolts . . . . 50 Nm
    Cradle/frame-to-engine bolts (middle) . . . . 55 Nm
    Cradle/frame-to-engine bracket bolts (front) . . . . 23 Nm
    Front mounting bolt nuts (if undone) . . . . 55 Nm

Torque wrench settings (continued)

Frame cross-member bolts	32 Nm
Ignition timing rotor bolt	25 Nm
Main oil gallery plug	40 Nm
Oil cooler mounting bolts	10 Nm
Oil hose banjo bolts	23 Nm
Oil hose union bolts	10 Nm
Oil pressure regulator	28 Nm
Oil pump mounting bolts	10 Nm
Oil sump bolts	14 Nm
Rocker shaft locking bolt	9 Nm
Rocker shaft plug	28 Nm
Starter clutch bolt	150 Nm
Valve cover banjo bolts	
GSX750F-W and GSX750-W (1998) models	16 Nm
All later models	20 Nm
Valve cover standard bolts	14 Nm

1 General information

The engine/transmission unit is an air/oil-cooled in-line four. The valves are operated by double overhead camshafts which are chain driven off the crankshaft. The engine/transmission assembly is constructed from aluminium alloy. The crankcase is divided horizontally.

The crankcase incorporates a wet sump, pressure-fed lubrication system which uses a gear-driven, dual-rotor oil pump with pressure relief valve, an oil filter with by-pass valve assembly, a pressure regulator and an oil pressure switch. The oil is cooled by a radiator matrix mounted on the frame downtubes.

Power from the crankshaft is routed to the transmission via the clutch, which is of the wet, multi-plate type and is gear-driven off the crankshaft. All models have a conventional cable-operated clutch. The transmission is a six-speed constant-mesh unit. Final drive to the rear wheel is by chain and sprockets.

2 Operations possible with the engine in the frame

The components and assemblies listed below can be removed without having to remove the engine/transmission assembly from the frame. If however, a number of areas require attention at the same time, removal of the engine is recommended.

Oil hoses and cooler
Valve cover
Cam chain tensioner and cam chain guides
Camshafts and rocker arms
Cylinder head, block, pistons and rings (see Note in Section 12)
Ignition timing rotor and pulse generator coil assembly
Oil pressure switch
Clutch
Gearchange mechanism
Neutral switch
Engine sprocket
Alternator
Starter motor
Starter clutch and idle/reduction gear
Oil sump, oil strainer and oil pressure regulator

3 Operations requiring engine removal

It is necessary to remove the engine/transmission assembly from the frame and separate the crankcase halves to gain access to the following components:

Connecting rod big-ends and bearings
Crankshaft and bearings
Cam chain and tensioner blade
Transmission shafts
Oil pump
Selector drum and forks (see Note in Section 29)

4 Major engine repair – general note

1 It is not always easy to determine when or if an engine should be completely overhauled, as a number of factors must be considered.
2 High mileage is not necessarily an indication that an overhaul is needed, while low mileage, on the other hand, does not preclude the need for an overhaul. Frequency of servicing is probably the single most important consideration. An engine that has regular and frequent oil and filter changes, as well as other required maintenance, will most likely give many miles of reliable service. Conversely, a neglected engine, or one which has not been run in properly, may require an overhaul very early in its life.
3 Exhaust smoke and excessive oil consumption are both indications that piston rings and/or valve guides are in need of attention, although make sure that the fault is not due to oil leakage.
4 If the engine is making obvious knocking or rumbling noises, the connecting rods and/or main bearings are probably at fault.
5 Loss of power, rough running, excessive valve train noise and high fuel consumption may also point to the need for an overhaul, especially if they are all present at the same time. If a complete tune-up does not remedy the situation, major mechanical work is the only solution.
6 An engine overhaul generally involves restoring the internal parts to the specifications of a new engine. The piston rings and main and connecting rod bearings are usually renewed and the cylinder walls honed or, if necessary, re-bored (oversize pistons are available), during a major overhaul. Generally the valve seats are re-ground, since they are usually in less than perfect condition at this point. The end result should be a like new engine that will give as many trouble-free miles as the original.
7 Before beginning the engine overhaul, read through the related procedures to familiarise yourself with the scope and requirements of the job. Overhauling an engine is not all that difficult, but it is time consuming. Plan on the motorcycle being tied up for a minimum of two weeks. Check on the availability of parts and make sure that any necessary special tools, equipment and supplies are obtained in advance.
8 Most work can be done with typical workshop hand tools, although a number of precision measuring tools are required for inspecting parts to determine if they must be renewed. Often a dealer will handle the inspection of parts and offer advice concerning reconditioning and renewal. As a general rule, time is the primary cost of an overhaul so it does not pay to install worn or substandard parts.
9 As a final note, to ensure maximum life and minimum trouble from a rebuilt engine, everything must be assembled with care in a spotlessly clean environment.

2

5 Engine – removal and installation

Caution: *The engine is very heavy. Engine removal and installation should be carried out with the aid of at least one assistant; personal injury or damage could occur if the engine falls or is dropped. An hydraulic or mechanical floor jack should be used to support and lower or raise the engine if available.*

Removal

1 Position the motorcycle on its centrestand. Work can be made easier by raising the machine to a suitable working height on an hydraulic ramp or other suitable platform. Make sure the motorcycle is secure and will not topple over (also see *Tools and Workshop Tips* in the Reference section).

2 If the engine is dirty, particularly around its mountings, wash it thoroughly before starting any major dismantling work. This makes working on the engine much easier and rules out the possibility of caked on lumps of dirt falling into some vital component.

3 Remove the seat (see Chapter 7). On GSX750 models remove the document tray. Disconnect the negative (-ve) lead from the battery (see Chapter 8). Either unscrew the crankcase bolt that secures the lead to the engine, or disconnect the earth wire connector close to the battery terminal, then feed the lead through to the engine and coil it on the crankcase, noting its routing **(see illustrations)**.

4 On GSX600/750F models remove the lower fairing and fairing side panels (see Chapter 7). On GSX750 models remove the side panels (see Chapter 7).

5 Drain the engine oil and remove the oil filter (see Chapter 1).

6 Remove the fuel tank (see Chapter 3). On GSX600/750F models remove the air filter housing (see Chapter 3).

7 Remove the carburettors (see Chapter 3). Plug the engine intake manifolds with clean rag.

8 Pull the spark plug caps off the plugs and secure them clear of the engine **(see illustration)**.

9 Remove the exhaust system (Chapter 3).

10 Remove the oil cooler (see Section 7).

11 Remove the front sprocket (see Chapter 5).

12 Trace the neutral switch and sidestand switch wiring back from the left-hand side of the crankcase and disconnect it at the connectors **(see illustration)**. Release the wiring from any guides, clips or ties, noting its routing. Coil the neutral switch wiring on top of the crankcase.

13 Trace the ignition pulse generator and oil pressure switch wiring back from its exit hole in the crankcase behind the cylinder block and disconnect it at the connectors **(see illustration 5.12)**. Release the wiring from any

clips or ties, noting its routing, and coil it on top of the crankcase.

14 Pull back the rubber boot covering the alternator lead terminal, then unscrew the nut and detach the lead **(see illustration)**. Also disconnect the wiring connector. Secure the wiring clear of the engine. Remove the alternator now if required (see Chapter 8), or do so after the engine has been removed.

15 Pull back the rubber boot covering the starter motor lead terminal, then unscrew the bolt (GSX600/750F models) or nut (GSX750 models) and detach the lead **(see illustration)**. Release the lead from any ties and secure it clear of the engine. Remove the starter motor now if required (see Chapter 8), or do so after the engine has been removed.

16 On Austria, Switzerland and California

models, detach the PAIR system hoses from the pipes on the front of the engine and secure them clear (see Chapter 3). Remove the pipes if required, in which case discard the gaskets as new ones must be used.

17 At this point, position an hydraulic or mechanical jack under the engine with a block of wood between them. Make sure the jack is centrally positioned so the engine will not topple in any direction when the last mounting bolt is removed. Raise the jack to support the weight of the engine, but make sure it is not lifting the bike and taking the weight of that as well. The idea is to support the engine so that there is no pressure on any of the mounting bolts once they have been slackened, so they can be easily withdrawn. Note that it may be necessary to adjust the jack as some of the

5.3a **Either unscrew the bolt (arrowed) and detach the earth lead . . .**

5.3b **. . . or disconnect the wiring connector (arrowed) and remove the lead with the engine**

5.8 **Pull the caps off the spark plugs and secure them clear**

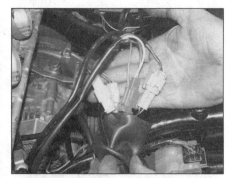

5.12 **Disconnect the wiring connectors – GSX600/750F model shown**

5.14 **Detach the alternator lead and wiring connector (arrowed) . . .**

5.15 **. . . and the starter motor lead**

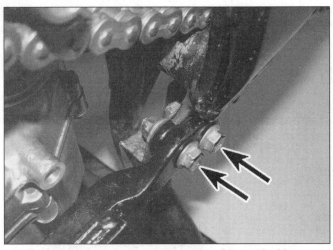

5.18 Remove the rear bolts (arrowed) on each side

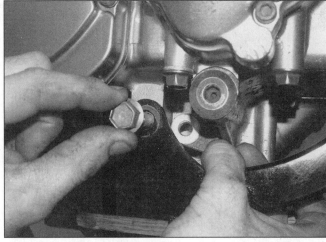

5.19 Unscrew the middle bolt on each side, noting the tabbed nut

bolts are removed to relieve the stress transferred to the other bolts.

GSX600/750F models

18 Before removing the engine, it is advisable to remove the breather cover from the top of the valve cover (disconnect the hose, then unscrew the four bolts) – this provides better clearance. To remove the engine, the cradle section of the frame must be separated from the main frame and engine, then removed.

Unscrew the nuts and remove the bolts securing each side of the cradle to the frame at the rear, noting the bracket on the left-hand side, and the hose clamp on the right **(see illustration)**.
19 Unscrew the bolts securing the cradle to the engine in the middle, noting the tabbed nuts which locate against the engine **(see illustration)**.
20 Unscrew the bolts securing the front of the cradle to the main frame **(see illustration)**.

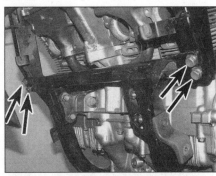

5.20 Unscrew the front bolts (arrowed) on each side

21 Support the cradle, then unscrew the bolts securing the front mounting brackets to it and manoeuvre the cradle away **(see illustrations)**. Withdraw the front mounts from the engine if they are loose **(see illustration)**.
22 Unscrew the nuts on the upper and lower rear mounting bolts **(see illustration)**.
23 Check that the engine is properly supported by the jack. Withdraw the upper rear mounting bolt and remove the spacer

5.21a Unscrew the bolts (arrowed) on each side . . .

5.21b . . . and remove the cradle

5.21c Remove the front mounts if they are loose

5.22 Unscrew the two nuts (arrowed)

2

5.23a Withdraw the upper bolt and remove the spacer

5.23b Slip the chain off the end of the shaft when possible . . .

5.23c . . . and carefully manoeuvre the engine out

(see illustration). Withdraw the lower rear mounting bolt. Check that all wiring, cables and hoses are well clear, then carefully lower the jack and manoeuvre the engine so the drive chain can be slipped off the end of the output shaft (see illustration). Fully lower the jack, then lift the engine, remove the jack, and manoeuvre the engine out of the frame (see illustration).

24 Suzuki recommend that where self-locking nuts are fitted they are only used once, so discard them and use new ones on installation. If this is impractical, apply a suitable thread locking compound to the nut threads on installation as an interim measure.

25 Check the condition of the damping rubbers on the front mounts and renew them if they are damaged, deformed or deteriorated (see illustration 5.21c). Note that the nuts are likely to be seized on the bolts.

GSX750 models

26 To remove the engine, the cradle section of the frame on the right-hand side must be separated from the main frame. Unscrew the nuts and bolts securing the cradle to the frame at the rear, noting the hose clamp on the right, to the engine in the middle, noting the tabbed nuts which locate against the engine, and to the frame and engine at the front, and remove it. Withdraw the front right-hand mount from the engine if it is loose.

27 Unscrew the bolts on the left-hand front engine mounting bracket.

28 Unscrew the bolt securing the frame to the engine in the middle on the left-hand side, noting the tabbed nut which locates against the engine.

29 Unscrew the nuts on the upper and lower rear mounting bolts.

30 Check that the engine is properly supported by the jack. Withdraw the upper rear mounting bolt and remove the spacer. Withdraw the lower rear mounting bolt. Check that all wiring, cables and hoses are well clear, then carefully lower the jack and manoeuvre the engine so the drive chain can be slipped off the end of the output shaft. Fully lower the jack, then lift the engine, remove the jack, and manoeuvre the engine out of the frame.

31 Suzuki recommend that where self-locking nuts are fitted they are only used once, so discard them and use new ones on installation. If this is impractical, apply a suitable thread locking compound to the nut threads on installation as an interim measure.

32 Check the condition of the damping rubbers on the front mounts and renew them if they are damaged, deformed or deteriorated. Note that the nuts are likely to be seized on the bolts.

Installation

33 Manoeuvre the engine into position under the frame and lift it onto the jack (see illustration 5.23c). Raise the engine, taking care not to catch any part on the frame, and loop the drive chain around the output shaft as early as possible (see illustration 5.23b). Raise and move the engine as required to align the rear mounting bolt holes. Note that it may be necessary to adjust the jack as the bolts are installed.

34 Slide the rear bolts through from the left-hand side, not forgetting to fit the spacer with the upper bolt (see illustration 5.23a). Thread the nuts onto the ends of the bolts, either using new ones or applying a thread locking compound, but do not yet fully tighten them.

35 If removed fit the front mounts into the engine (see illustration 5.21c). Manoeuvre the engine cradle into position and install all its bolts and nuts finger-tight only at this stage (see illustration 5.21b). Do not forget the bracket (GSX600/750F models) and hose

5.35 On GSX600/750F models do not forget the bracket and make sure it is the correct way round

clamp with the rear bolts on the left-hand and right-hand sides respectively (see illustration). Apply a suitable non-permanent thread locking compound to the middle bolts that thread into the obelisk-shaped nuts (see illustration 5.19).

36 Tighten the nuts on the rear mounting bolts to the torque setting specified at the beginning of the Chapter.

37 Tighten all the cradle-to frame bolts to the specified torque setting.

38 Tighten the cradle-to-engine bolts to the specified torque setting.

39 The remainder of the installation procedure is the reverse of removal, noting the following points:

● Use new gaskets on the exhaust pipe connections.
● When fitting the gearchange linkage arm onto the gearchange shaft, align the slit in the arm with punch mark on the shaft, and tighten the pinch bolt.
● Make sure all wires, cables and hoses are correctly routed and connected, and secured by any clips or ties.
● Refill the engine with oil to correct level (see Chapter 1).
● Adjust the throttle and clutch cable freeplay.
● Adjust the drive chain (see Chapter 1).
● Start the engine and check that there are no oil leaks. Adjust the idle speed (see Chapter 1).

6 Engine disassembly and reassembly – general information

Disassembly

1 Before disassembling the engine, thoroughly clean and degrease its external surfaces. This will prevent contamination of the engine internals, and will also make working a lot easier and cleaner. A high flash-point solvent, such as paraffin (kerosene) can be used, or better still, a proprietary engine degreaser such as Gunk. Use old paintbrushes and toothbrushes to work the solvent into the various recesses of the casings. Take care to exclude solvent or water

6.4 A typical engine support made from pieces of 2 x 4 inch wood – adjust the dimensions as required to suit the engine

7.2a Unscrew the banjo bolts (arrowed) and detach the pipes

7.2b Unscrew the bolts (arrowed) and separate the pipes from the cooler if required

from the electrical components and intake and exhaust ports.

 Warning: The use of petrol (gasoline) as a cleaning agent should be avoided because of the risk of fire.

2 When clean and dry, position the engine on the workbench, leaving suitable clear area for working. Gather a selection of small containers, plastic bags and some labels so that parts can be grouped together in an easily identifiable manner. Also get some paper and a pen so that notes can be taken. You will also need a supply of clean rag, which should be as absorbent as possible.

3 Before commencing work, read through the appropriate section so that some idea of the necessary procedure can be gained. When removing components note that great force is seldom required, unless specified (checking the specified torque setting of the particular bolt being removed will indicate how tight it is, and therefore how much force should be needed). In many cases, a component's reluctance to be removed is indicative of an incorrect approach or removal method – if in any doubt, re-check with the text.

4 An engine support stand made from short lengths of 2 x 4 inch wood bolted together into a rectangle will help support the engine **(see illustration)**. The perimeter of the mount should be just big enough to accommodate the lower part of the crankcase. Alternatively place individual blocks under the crankcase as required to ensure the engine is stable.

5 When disassembling the engine, keep 'mated' parts together (including gears, cylinder bores, pistons, connecting rods, valves, etc. that have been in contact with each other during engine operation). These 'mated' parts must be reused or renewed as an assembly.

6 A complete engine/transmission disassembly should be done in the following general order with reference to the appropriate Sections.

Remove the valve cover
Remove the camshafts and cam chain tensioner
Remove the cylinder head
Remove the cylinder block
Remove the pistons
Remove the timing rotor and pulse generator coil
Remove the clutch
Remove the gearchange mechanism
Remove the alternator (see Chapter 8)
Remove the starter motor (see Chapter 8)
Remove the starter clutch and idle/reduction gear
Separate the crankcase halves
Remove the crankshaft and the connecting rods
Remove the transmission shafts/gears
Remove the oil pump
Remove the selector drum and forks

Reassembly

7 Reassembly is accomplished by reversing the general disassembly sequence.

7 Oil cooler and hoses – removal and installation

Note: *The oil cooler and its hoses can be removed with the engine in the frame.*

Removal

1 Drain the engine oil (see Chapter 1) and on GSX600/750F models remove the fairing side panels (see Chapter 7). For best access to the banjo bolts on the sump remove the exhaust system (see Chapter 3). Note that removing the exhaust is the only way to get a torque wrench onto the bolts for correct tightening on installation, unless a crows-foot adapter is available.

2 Unscrew the banjo bolt securing each pipe to the sump **(see illustration)**. Discard the sealing washers as new ones must be used. Release any ties holding the pipes against the frame. If required, unscrew the two bolts securing each pipe union to the top of the cooler and detach the hoses **(see illustration)**. Discard the O-rings as new ones must be used.

3 Unscrew the two bolts securing the top of the cooler to the frame, then carefully lift the cooler out of its bottom mounting lugs on the frame downtubes and free the rubber shield from around the pipes and mounting lugs **(see illustrations)**. Take care not to lose the U-shaped rubber mounts from the lugs, and

2

7.3a Unscrew the bolts (arrowed) . . .

7.3b . . . then lift the cooler out of its mounts . . .

7.3c . . . and free the rubber shield from around the mounts and unions

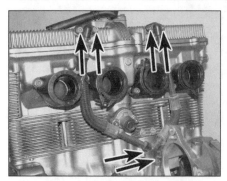

7.4 Unscrew the bolts (arrowed) and remove the hose

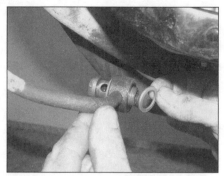

7.5 Always use new sealing washers on the banjo connections

renew them if they are damaged, deformed or deteriorated. Note the collar inside the rubber mounting bush. Renew the bushes if necessary.

4 To remove the oil hose between the valve cover and the crankcase (behind the cylinder block), first remove the carburettors (see Chapter 3). Unscrew the two bolts securing the union to the crankcase behind the cylinder block, then unscrew the two bolts securing each union to the valve cover **(see illustration)**. Discard the O-rings as new ones must be used.

Installation

5 Installation is the reverse of removal. Always use new sealing washers and O-rings when installing the hoses **(see illustration)**. Tighten the cooler mounting bolts, the banjo bolts and the union bolts to the torque settings specified at the beginning of the Chapter.

---

8 Valve cover –
removal and installation

Note: *The valve cover can be removed with the engine in the frame. If the engine has been removed, ignore the steps which do not apply.*

Removal

1 Remove the fuel tank (see Chapter 3).
2 Disconnect the breather hose from the top of the valve cover.
3 Release the ties securing any cables, hoses or leads to the frame cross-member above the valve cover. Unscrew the bolts securing the cross-member and remove it.
4 Remove the ignition HT coils (see Chapter 4).
5 Unscrew the two bolts securing each oil hose union and displace the hoses **(see illustration)**. Discard the O-rings as new ones must be used. If the engine is being

8.5a Unscrew the bolts (arrowed) and detach the hoses

completely disassembled, also unscrew the two bolts securing the hose to the crankcase behind the cylinder block **(see illustration)**.
6 The valve cover is secured by fourteen bolts, the four running along the middle of the cover, adjacent to the spark plug holes, being of the banjo type. Unscrew the bolts and remove them along with their sealing washers where fitted, noting the positions of the different types of bolt and washer **(see illustration)**. Check the condition of the sealing washers and replace them with new ones if necessary. It is a good idea to fit new ones as a matter of course.
7 Lift the valve cover off the cylinder head **(see illustration)**. If it is stuck, do not try to lever it off with a screwdriver. Tap it gently around the sides with a rubber hammer or block of wood to dislodge it. Take care not to strain the throttle and choke cables as you remove the cover – displace the carburettors from the cylinder head to improve clearance if required (see Chapter 3). Note the two locating dowels and remove them if they are loose **(see illustration 8.9)**.

Installation

8 Examine the valve cover gasket and the plug hole gaskets for signs of damage or deterioration and replace them with new ones if necessary.

8.5b Unscrew the bolts (arrowed) and remove the hose if required

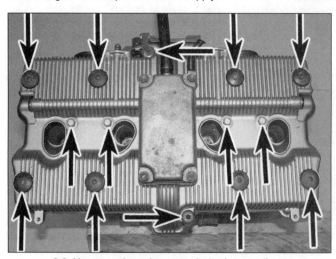

8.6 Unscrew the valve cover bolts (arrowed) . . .

8.7 . . . and remove the cover

8.9 Make sure the dowels are installed

8.10 Make sure the gaskets locate in their grooves

8.11 Install the bolts in their correct location and tighten them to the specified torque

9 Clean the mating surfaces of the cylinder head and the valve cover with solvent. Make sure the cover dowels are installed (see illustration).

10 If new gaskets are being used, apply a smear of a suitable adhesive (such as Suzuki Bond no. 1207B) into the grooves in the valve cover. Fit the gaskets onto the cover, making sure they fit correctly into the groove (see illustration). Apply a sealant to the cut-outs in the cylinder head where the gasket half-circles fit.

11 Position the cover on the head, making sure the gaskets stay in place and the cover locates correctly onto the dowels. Install the cover bolts, using new sealing washers if required (you should use new ones on the banjo bolts as a matter of course) (see illustration). On X (1999) models onward apply clean engine oil to the sealing washers on the banjo bolts. Tighten the bolts to the torque settings specified at the beginning of the Chapter, noting the difference between the standard bolts and the banjo bolts.

12 Fit the oil hose unions onto the valve cover, and onto the crankcase if detached, using new O-rings (see illustration). Tighten the union bolts to the specified torque setting.

13 Install the remaining components in the reverse order of removal. Apply a suitable non-permanent thread locking compound to the frame cross-member bolts and tighten them to the specified torque setting.

9 Cam chain tensioner and cam chain guide blades – removal, inspection and installation

Note: The cam chain tensioner and guide blades can be removed with the engine in the frame.

Cam chain tensioner

Caution: Once you start to remove the tensioner bolts, you must remove the tensioner all the way and reset it before tightening the bolts. The tensioner extends itself and locks in place, so if you loosen the bolts partway and then retighten them, the tensioner or cam chain will be damaged.

Removal

1 For best access remove the carburettors (see Chapter 3).
2 Remove the valve cover (see Section 8), then align the valve timing marks as described in Step 3 of Section 11.
3 Unscrew the tensioner spring cap bolt and withdraw the spring from the tensioner body (see illustration).
4 Unscrew the two tensioner mounting bolts and withdraw the tensioner from the back of the cylinder block (see illustration). Remove the gasket from the base of the tensioner or from the cylinder block and discard it as a new one must be used.

8.12 Use a new O-ring on each hose union

Inspection

5 Examine the tensioner components for signs of wear or damage.
6 Release the ratchet mechanism from the tensioner plunger and check that the plunger moves freely in and out of the body (see illustration).
7 If the tensioner or any of its components are worn or damaged, or if the plunger is seized in the body, they must be replaced with new ones.

Installation

8 Turn the crankshaft in a **clockwise** direction using a 19 mm spanner or socket on the large hex on the timing rotor (see illustration 11.3b). Alternatively, place the motorcycle on its centrestand, then select a high gear and rotate

9.3 Unscrew the bolt (arrowed) and remove the spring

9.4 Unscrew the bolts (arrowed) and remove the tensioner

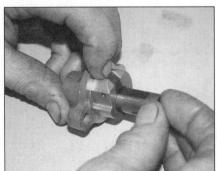

9.6 Release the ratchet and check the movement of the plunger in the body

9.10 Install the tensioner using a new gasket

9.11 Fit the spring into the tensioner and the cap bolt into the spring, then tighten it to the specified torque

9.15 Unscrew the bolts (arrowed) and remove the top guide

the rear wheel by hand in its normal direction of rotation. This removes all the slack between the crankshaft and the camshaft in the front run of the chain and transfers it to the back run where it will be taken up by the tensioner. *Caution: DO NOT use the timing rotor Allen bolt to turn the crankshaft – it may snap or strip out. Also be sure to turn the engine in its normal direction of rotation.*

9 Release the ratchet mechanism and press the tensioner plunger all the way into the tensioner body **(see illustration 9.6)**.

10 Place a new gasket on the tensioner body, then install it in the engine **(see illustration)**. Tighten the mounting bolts to the torque setting specified at the beginning of the Chapter.

11 Fit a new sealing washer on the spring cap bolt. Install the spring and cap bolt and tighten the bolt to the torque setting specified at the beginning of the Chapter – as you install and tighten the bolt you should hear the plunger being pushed out by the spring pressure **(see illustration)**. Turn the crankshaft through two full turns as in Step 8.

12 Check that the cam chain is tensioned. If it is slack, the ratchet did not release the plunger. Check that the valve timing marks are still in alignment (see Step 3 of Section 11).

13 Install the pulse generator cover using a new gasket and a suitable non-permanent thread lock on the bolts, and make sure the sealing washer is installed with the top bolt **(see illustrations 11.35b and c)**. Install the valve cover (see Section 8), the carburettors (see Chapter 3), and the spark plugs (see Chapter 1).

Cam chain guide blades

Removal

14 Remove the valve cover (see Section 8).

15 To remove the top guide unscrew the four bolts securing it to the cylinder head. Note which way round the top guide fits – look for the arrow on its top surface **(see illustration)**.

16 To remove the front guide blade first remove the exhaust camshaft (see Section 11). Lift the blade out of the front of the cam chain tunnel, noting which way round it fits and how it locates in the cut-outs in the cylinder head **(see illustration)**.

Inspection

17 Examine the sliding surface of the guides for signs of wear or damage, and replace them with new ones if necessary.

Installation

18 Fit the front guide blade into the front of the cam chain tunnel, making sure it locates correctly in its seat and its lugs locate in their cut-outs in the cylinder head **(see illustration)**. Install the exhaust camshaft (see Section 11).

19 Fit the top guide onto the cylinder head, making sure the arrow on its top faces the front of the engine **(see illustrations)**. Tighten the mounting bolts to the torque setting specified at the beginning of the Chapter.

20 Install the valve cover (see Section 8).

9.16 Lift the front guide blade out of the cam chain tunnel

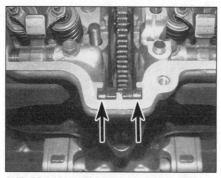

9.18 Make sure the lugs locate correctly in the cut-outs (arrowed)

10 Cam chain and cam chain tensioner blade – removal, inspection and installation

Note: *To remove the cam chain and the cam chain tensioner blade the engine must be removed from the frame and the crankcases separated.*

Cam chain

Removal

1 Separate the crankcase halves (see Section 24) and remove the crankshaft (see Section 27).

2 Slip the cam chain off the crankshaft.

9.19a Install the top guide . . .

9.19b . . . with the arrow pointing to the front

10.6a Lift out the rubber cushions . . .

10.6b . . . then remove the tensioner blade

10.8 Make sure the cushions are installed the correct way round as described

Installation

3 Slip the cam chain onto its sprocket on the crankshaft, making sure it is properly engaged.
4 Install the crankshaft (see Section 27) and reassemble the crankcase halves (see Section 24)

Cam chain tensioner blade

Removal

5 Separate the crankcase halves (see Section 24) and remove the crankshaft (see Section 27).
6 Remove the two rubber cushions from the upper crankcase half, noting which way up and round they fit, then lift the cam chain tensioner blade out of its cut-outs in the crankcase, noting which way round it fits **(see illustrations)**. Take care not to lose the pivot pin which fits into the bottom of the blade.

Inspection

7 Examine the sliding surface of the tensioner blade for signs of wear or damage, and replace it with a new one if necessary. Check the condition of the rubber cushions and renew them if they are damaged or deteriorated.

Installation

8 If removed, fit the pivot pin into the bottom of the blade. Fit the tensioner blade into the upper crankcase half, making sure it is the correct way round and its pin locates correctly in the cut-outs. Fit the rubber cushions into the cut-outs with their rounded ends facing away from the tensioner blade pin and with the arrows facing front and back, not side to side **(see illustration)**.
9 Install the crankshaft (see Section 27) and reassemble the crankcase halves (see Section 24).

---

11 Camshafts and rocker arms
– removal, inspection and installation

Note: *The camshafts and rocker arms can be removed with the engine in the frame. The*

camshaft holder bolts are of the high tensile type and must not be substituted with a weaker bolt. The bolts are identified by a 9 on the head. If new bolts are required, make sure you obtain the correct ones from a Suzuki dealer.

Camshafts

Removal

1 Remove the spark plugs (see Chapter 1).
2 Remove the valve cover (see Section 8).
3 Unscrew the five bolts securing the pulse generator coil cover to the right-hand side of the engine **(see illustration)**. Note the sealing washer with the top bolt – discard the washer

as a new one should be used. To turn the engine use a 19 mm spanner or socket on the large hex on the timing rotor and turn it in a clockwise direction only **(see illustration)**. Alternatively, place the motorcycle on its centrestand, then select a high gear and rotate the rear wheel by hand in its normal direction of rotation. Rotate the engine until the line next to the T mark on the rotor aligns with the pick-up in the centre of the pulse generator coil **(see illustration)**, and the notches in the right-hand end of each camshaft face towards each other **(see illustration)** and the number 1 arrow on the exhaust camshaft sprocket points at the valve cover gasket mating surface on the cylinder

11.3a Unscrew the bolts (arrowed) and remove the cover

11.3b Turn the engine in a clockwise direction . . .

11.3c . . . until the scribe line aligns with the sensor on the coil . . .

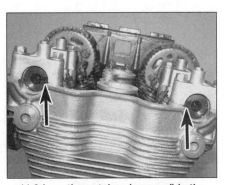

11.3d . . . the notches (arrowed) in the camshaft ends face towards each other

2

11.3e . . . and the No. 1 arrow points forwards flush with the head

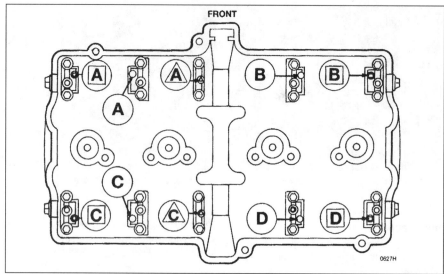

11.5 Cam journal cap positions – the caps must be installed in their original locations or the camshafts may seize

head **(see illustration)**. Check the positions of all the marks on the timing rotor and the exhaust and intake sprockets **(see illustration 11.27)**. This is how they should be positioned for installation later.

Caution: DO NOT use the timing rotor Allen bolt to turn the crankshaft – it may snap or strip out. Also be sure to turn the engine in its normal direction of rotation.

4 Remove the cam chain tensioner and the cam chain top guide (see Section 9).

5 Before disturbing the camshaft holders, check for identification markings, which should be the letters A, B, C or D, one for each holder, cast into their top surface, on its own or inside either a square or a triangle, and corresponding to the mark on the cylinder head **(see illustration)**. These markings ensure that the holders can be matched to their original location on installation. If no markings are visible, mark your own using a felt pen.

6 Remove the intake camshaft first. Unscrew the bolts securing the holders, slackening them **evenly and a little at a time** in a criss-cross pattern, then remove them **(see illustration)**. Retrieve the dowels from either the holders or the cylinder head if they are loose.

Caution: If the bearing holder bolts aren't loosened evenly, the camshaft could break.

7 Pull up on the cam chain and carefully guide the intake camshaft out, disengaging the cam chain from the sprocket as you do

(see illustration). The camshafts are marked for identification – IN (intake camshaft), and EX (exhaust camshaft) but if these marks are unclear make your own so they do not get muddled **(see illustration 11.26a)**. **Note:** *Don't remove the sprockets from the camshafts unless absolutely necessary.*

8 Repeat Steps 6 and 7 for the exhaust camshaft. On completion cover the top of the cylinder head with a rag to prevent anything falling into the engine.

9 While the camshafts are out, don't allow the chain to go slack – the chain may drop down and bind between the crankshaft and case, which could damage these components. Wire the chain to another component to prevent it from dropping. Also, cover the top of the cylinder head with a rag to prevent foreign objects from falling into the engine.

10 Remove the cam chain front guide (see Section 9).

Inspection

Note: *Before renewing the camshafts or the cylinder head and camshaft holders because of damage, check with local machine shops*

specialising in motorcycle engineering work. In the case of the camshafts, it may be possible for cam lobes to be welded, reground and hardened, at a cost far lower than that of a new camshaft. If the bearing surfaces in the cylinder head are damaged, it may be possible for them to be bored out to accept bearing inserts. Due to the cost of a new cylinder head, it is recommended that all options be explored.

11 Inspect the bearing surfaces of the camshaft holders and cylinder head and the corresponding journals on the camshafts. Look for score marks, deep scratches and evidence of spalling (a pitted appearance). Check the oil passages for clogging.

12 Check the camshaft lobes for heat discoloration (blue appearance), score marks, chipped areas, flat spots and spalling. Also check the lobe contact surfaces on the rocker arms. Measure the height of each lobe with a micrometer and compare the results to the minimum height listed in this Chapter's Specifications **(see illustration)**. If damage is noted or wear is excessive, the camshaft must be renewed.

11.6 Unscrew the bolts as described and lift the holders off the camshaft . . .

11.7 . . . then remove the camshaft

11.12 Measure the height of each lobe with a micrometer

11.18 Measure the diameter of each journal with a micrometer

13 Check for any camshaft runout by supporting each end on V-blocks, and measuring the runout using a dial gauge. If the runout exceeds the specified limit the camshaft must be renewed.

14 Next, check each camshaft journal oil clearance. Work on one camshaft at a time when doing this. Clean the camshaft and the bearing surfaces in the cylinder head and camshaft holders with a clean lint-free cloth, then lay the camshaft in its correct location in the head (see Step 7), positioning it correctly to prevent the valves contacting the piston (see Step 3).

 Refer to Tools and Workshop Tips in the Reference section for details of how to read a micrometer and dial gauge.

15 Cut strips of Plastigauge and lay one piece on each bearing journal parallel with the camshaft centreline. Make sure the camshaft holder dowels are installed then fit the holders, making sure they are in their correct location (see Step 5), and that the camshaft does not rotate at all **(see illustrations 11.5 and 11.29)**. Install the holder bolts and tighten them **evenly and a little at a time** in a criss-

cross sequence, to the torque setting specified at the beginning of the Chapter.

16 Now unscrew the bolts, slackening them **evenly and a little at a time** in a criss-cross pattern, then remove the holders, again making sure the camshaft does not turn.

17 To determine the oil clearance, compare the crushed Plastigauge (at its widest point) on each journal to the scale printed on the Plastigauge container. Compare the results to this Chapter's Specifications.

18 If the oil clearance is greater than specified, measure the diameter of each camshaft journal with a micrometer. Renew the camshaft if any journal is worn beyond the service limit specified at the beginning of the Chapter **(see illustration)**. If the camshaft journals are not worn, check the head and holders (see Step 19). If a new camshaft is fitted, check the oil clearance again with the new one in place. If the clearance is still too great, check the head and holders (see Step 19).

19 Measure the journal bores formed by the cylinder head and the camshaft holders as follows: make sure the camshaft holder dowels are installed then fit the holders, making sure they are in their correct location (see Step 5) **(see illustrations 11.5 and 11.29)**. Tighten the holder bolts evenly and a little at a time to the torque setting specified at the beginning of the Chapter. Using telescoping gauges and a micrometer (see *Tools and Workshop Tips*), measure each journal bore diameter. If any is greater than specified, the cylinder head and holders must be renewed.

20 Except in cases of oil starvation, a cam chain wears very little. If a chain has stretched excessively, which makes it difficult to maintain proper tension, it must be replaced with a new one (see Section 10).

21 Check each sprocket for cracks and other damage, replacing them with new ones if necessary – the sprockets are available separately. If the sprocket teeth are worn, the cam chain is also worn, as will be the drive sprocket on the crankshaft. If wear this severe

is apparent, the entire engine should be disassembled for inspection.

Installation

22 If removed, fit each sprocket onto its camshaft, making sure they are installed with the numbered side facing the notched end of the camshaft and so that the numbers align as shown **(see illustration 11.27)** when the notches are facing each other. Apply a smear of a suitable non-permanent thread locking compound to the sprocket bolts before installing them, and tighten them to the torque setting specified at the beginning of the Chapter.

23 Install the cam chain front guide (see Section 9).

24 Make sure all bearing surfaces in the cylinder head, holders and camshafts are clean, then lubricate the journals and lobes with molybdenum disulphide oil (a mixture of 50% molybdenum disulphide grease and 50% engine oil).

25 Check that the cam chain is engaged around the lower sprocket teeth on the crankshaft and that the crankshaft is positioned as described in Step 3.

26 Install the exhaust camshaft (identified by EX) first **(see illustration)**. Fit the camshaft through the cam chain, with the notch in its right-hand end facing the right-hand side of the engine, aligning it so that the notch points backwards, and so that the arrow marked 1 on the sprocket points forwards and is flush with the top of the cylinder head mating surface **(see illustration 11.3e)**, and the arrow marked 2 points vertically upwards. Keeping the front run of the chain taut engage the chain on the sprocket teeth **(see illustration)**. Check that the chain is tight at the front so that there is no slack between the crankshaft sprocket and the exhaust camshaft sprocket – move the chain around the sprocket so that the slack is taken up if required, then check that all marks are still correctly aligned.

27 Starting with and including the cam chain

2

11.26a The intake camshaft is marked IN, the exhaust camshaft is marked EX

11.26b Make sure the front run of the chain is taut before laying it on the sprocket

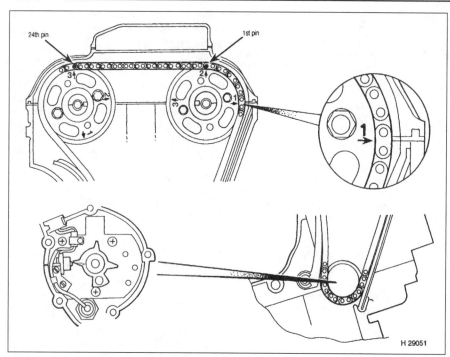

11.29 Make sure the dowels (arrowed) are installed then fit the holders

11.27 Valve timing marks

pin that is directly above the arrow marked 2 on the exhaust camshaft sprocket, count twenty-four pins along the chain towards the intake side. Fit the intake camshaft (identified by IN) through the cam chain with the notch in its right-hand end facing the right-hand side of the engine and pointing forwards, then engage the sprocket with the chain so that the arrow marked 3 on the sprocket aligns with the twenty-fourth pin **(see illustration)**. Again check that the chain is tight at the front and between the sprockets – any slack in the chain must lie in the portion of the chain in the back of the cylinder so that it can be taken up by the tensioner.

28 Before proceeding further, check that everything aligns as described in Steps 3, 26 and 27. If it doesn't, the valve timing will be inaccurate and the valves will contact the pistons when the engine is turned over.

29 Ensure the camshaft holder dowels are installed then fit the holders **(see illustration)**,

making sure they are in their proper positions as noted on removal (Step 5). Tighten the cap bolts on one camshaft **evenly and a little at a time** in a criss-cross sequence, until the specified torque setting is reached. Repeat for the other camshaft. **Note**: *The journal cap bolts are of the high tensile type, indicated by a 9 mark on the bolt head. Don't use any other type of bolt.*

30 With all holders tightened down, check that the valve timing marks still align (see Steps 3, 26 and 27). If they don't, unscrew the sprocket bolts, slip the sprocket off its mount on the shaft, then disengage it from the chain and move it round the required number of teeth in the correct direction, then realign the camshaft so that the bolt holes align and fit the sprocket back onto the shaft. Apply a smear of a suitable non-permanent thread locking compound to the sprocket bolts before installing them, and tighten them to the torque setting specified at the beginning of

the Chapter. Assuming that the previous pin-count described in Step 27 was correct you will now have to perform the same procedure on the other camshaft to bring that into alignment and re-instate the correct pin count. If the pin count was initially incorrect you will only have to adjust one camshaft to re-instate it. On completion check the alignment of all marks again, and make sure the chain pin-count is correct.

31 When you are sure that all marks are correctly aligned and that all slack in the chain is between the intake camshaft and the crankshaft, install the cam chain tensioner (see Section 9).

32 Turn the engine clockwise through two full turns (720°) using a 19 mm spanner on the timing rotor hex, then check the marks and the pin-count again.

Caution: If the marks are not aligned exactly as described, the valve timing will be incorrect and the valves may strike the pistons, causing extensive damage to the engine.

33 Install the cam chain top guide (see Section 9).

34 Check the valve clearances and adjust them if necessary (see Chapter 1).

35 Smear sealant over the crankcase joint areas **(see illustration)**. Install the pulse generator cover using a new gasket and a suitable non-permanent thread lock on the bolts, and make sure the sealing washer is installed with the top bolt **(see illustrations)**.

11.35a Apply the sealant to the crankcase joints (arrows)

11.35b Fit the cover using a new gasket . . .

11.35c . . . and do not forget the sealing washer with the top bolt

11.37 Remove the rocker shaft plug (arrowed)

11.38 Thread an M8 bolt into the end of the rocker shaft and use it to withdraw the shaft

11.39 Remove the rocker shaft locking bolt (arrowed)

Install the valve cover (see Section 8) and the spark plugs (see Chapter 1).

Rocker arms

Removal

36 Remove the camshafts (see above).

37 Unscrew the rocker shaft plug from the cylinder head **(see illustration)**. Discard the sealing washer as a new one must be used.

38 Thread an M8 bolt (8 mm, such as one of the valve cover banjo bolts) into the end of the rocker shaft to use as a tool to pull the shaft out **(see illustration)**.

39 Unscrew the rocker shaft locking bolt **(see illustration)**.

40 Grasp the bolt in the end of the shaft, withdraw the shaft and remove the rocker arms and springs, noting how they fit **(see illustrations 11.44c, b and a)**.

41 Repeat the above Steps to remove the other shafts and rocker arms. Keep all of the parts in order so they can be reinstalled in their original locations.

Inspection

42 Clean all of the components with solvent and dry them off. Blow through the oil passages with compressed air, if available. Inspect the rocker arm faces for pits, spalling, score marks and rough spots. If any are found

also check the camshaft lobes. Check the rocker arm-to-shaft contact areas for wear and damage. Check the clearance adjusting screw ends and the tops of the valve stems. Look for cracks in each rocker arm. If the rocker arms or shafts are damaged or worn, they should be renewed as a set.

43 Measure the diameter of the rocker shafts, in the area where the rocker arms ride, and compare the results with this Chapter's Specifications **(see illustration)**. Also measure the inside diameter of the rocker arm bores and compare the results with this Chapter's Specifications **(see illustration)**. If either the shaft or the rocker arms are worn

beyond the specified limits, renew them as a set.

Installation

44 Lubricate the rocker shaft with molybdenum disulphide oil (a mixture of 50% molybdenum disulphide grease and 50% engine oil). Position each spring and rocker arm in the cylinder head in turn, making sure that each spring is on the outside of its rocker, then slide the shaft into the cylinder head and through the rocker arms and springs **(see illustrations)**.

45 Install the rocker shaft locking bolt and tighten it to the torque setting specified at the beginning of the Chapter **(see**

11.43a Measure the external diameter of the rocker arm shaft . . .

11.43b . . . and the internal diameter of the rocker arm

11.44a Install the spring on the outside . . .

11.44b . . . followed by the rocker arm, then slide the shaft part-way through . . .

11.44c . . . and install the second spring and rocker arm

2

11.45 Install the rocker shaft locking bolt with its washer

11.46 Install the plug with a new sealing washer

12.5a Remove the cylinder head front bolt

illustration). Remove the 8 mm bolt from the end of the rocker shaft, if not already done.
46 Install the rocker shaft plug with a new sealing washer and tighten it to the specified torque setting **(see illustration)**.
47 Install the other rocker assemblies. Install the camshafts (see above).

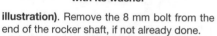

12 Cylinder head –
removal and installation

Note: *The cylinder head can be removed with the engine in the frame, although on*

GSX600/750F models it may be necessary to detach the engine mountings, except for the rear upper mounting bolt, and pivot the engine about this bolt to provide sufficient clearance for removal of the cylinder head. In this instance, refer to Section 5, noting that you do not need to drain the engine oil or disconnect the neutral switch, ignition pulse generator and oil pressure switch wiring connectors, and you can leave the front sprocket on the shaft, though you must still remove the sprocket cover. You can also leave the starter motor and alternator wiring connected, but keep an eye on it when pivoting the engine down to make sure it is not strained, and disconnect it

if necessary. Also slacken the nut on the upper rear engine mounting bolt to allow the engine to pivot. On installation, reverse the removal procedure, again referring to Section 5, and tightening all engine mounting bolts as described therein to the specified torque settings. In the author's opinion, however, it is advisable to remove the engine completely to make getting the head off the block easier, and to negate the possibility of damaging either the engine or frame should the head be stuck on the block.
Caution: The engine must be completely cool before beginning this procedure or the cylinder head may become warped.

Removal
1 Place the motorcycle on its centrestand.
2 Remove the exhaust system and the carburettors (see Chapter 3).
3 Remove the spark plugs (see Chapter 1).
4 Remove the valve cover (see Section 8) and the camshafts (see Section 11).
5 The cylinder head is secured by four 10 mm domed nuts with copper washers, four 10 mm plain nuts with a common plate, four 10 mm plain nuts with steel washers, and one 6 mm bolt **(see illustration 12.17)**. Unscrew the bolt on the front of the cylinder head **(see illustration)**. The four domed nuts and eight plain nuts are numbered for identification **(see illustration)**. Slacken the nuts evenly and a little at a time in a **reverse** of their numerical tightening sequence until they are all slack. Remove all the nuts and their washers, taking great care not to drop any of them into the crankcase. Note which type of nut and washer fits on which stud. Also remove the plate from the centre of the cylinder head **(see illustration)**.
6 Pull the cylinder head up off the studs, pulling the oil drain tubes out of their holes as you do **(see illustration)**. If the head is stuck, tap around the joint faces of the cylinder head with a soft-faced mallet to free the head, but take care not to strike any of the cooling fins as they break easily, especially on the corners. Do not attempt to free the head by inserting a screwdriver between the head and cylinder block – you'll damage the sealing surfaces.
7 Lift the head off the block, passing the cam

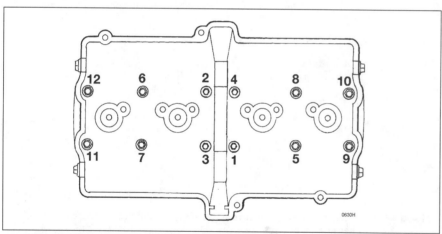

12.5b Cylinder head nut TIGHTENING sequence – slacken the bolts in reverse order

12.5c Remove the plate from the head

12.6 Free the pipes from the head as you lift it off . . .

12.7 . . . and pass the cam chain down the tunnel

chain down through the tunnel as you do **(see illustration)**. Do not let the chain fall into the block – secure it with a piece of wire or metal bar to prevent it from doing so. Remove the old cylinder head gasket and the O-rings which fit around the four end cylinder head studs and the two centre studs at the front **(see illustration 12.14)**. Stuff a clean rag into the cam chain tunnel to prevent any debris

falling into the engine. Discard the gasket and O-rings as new ones must be used.

8 If loose, remove the dowel from each end of the cylinder block **(see illustration 12.14)**. If either dowel appears to be missing it is probably stuck in the underside of the cylinder head.

9 Remove the O-ring from the top of each oil drain tube and discard them as new ones must be used **(see illustration 12.12)**.

10 Check the cylinder head gasket and the mating surfaces on the cylinder head and block for signs of leakage, which could indicate warpage. Refer to Section 14 and check the cylinder head.

11 Clean all traces of old gasket material from the cylinder head and block. If a scraper is used, take care not to scratch or gouge the soft aluminium. Be careful not to let any of the gasket material drop into the crankcase, the cylinder bore or the oil passages. Unless you are removing the cylinder block, cover it with a clean rag to prevent any debris falling into the engine.

Installation

12 Fit a new O-ring smeared with grease onto the top of each oil drain tube **(see illustration)**.

13 Lubricate the cylinder bores with clean engine oil.

14 If removed, fit the two dowels into the cylinder block **(see illustration)**. Fit new O-rings around the four end cylinder head studs and the two centre studs at the front. Make sure they are pressed into their recesses in the block and are properly seated.

15 Ensure both cylinder head and block mating surfaces are clean, then lay the new head gasket in place on the cylinder block, making sure all the holes are correctly aligned and that the UP letters stamped out of the gasket read correctly, and that it locates over the dowels **(see illustrations)**. Never re-use the old gasket.

16 Carefully lower the cylinder head over the studs and onto the block. It is helpful to have an assistant to pass the cam chain up through the tunnel and slip a piece of wire through it to prevent it falling back into the engine. Keep

12.12 Fit a new O-ring onto each oil drain tube and grease them

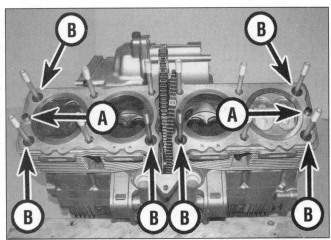

12.14 Install the dowels if removed (A). Fit new O-rings around the two front centre studs and all four end studs (B)

2

12.15a Fit the new cylinder head gasket . . .

12.15b . . . making sure the UP mark reads correctly

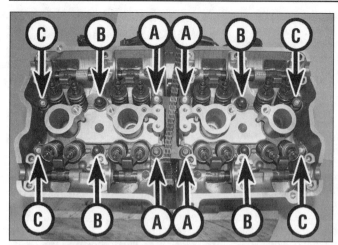

12.17 Cylinder head nuts and washers – plain nuts with plate (A), domed nuts with copper washers (B), plain nuts with steel washers (C)

14.4 Remove the intake ducts if required, noting their orientation

the chain taut to prevent it becoming disengaged from the crankshaft sprocket. Make sure the oil drain tubes locate correctly into their holes in the base of the cylinder head **(see illustration 12.6)**.

17 Install the cylinder head plate and the four 10 mm plain nuts, the four 10 mm domed nuts with their copper washers and the four 10 mm plain nuts with steel washers onto their correct studs and tighten them finger-tight **(see illustration)**. Now tighten the nuts evenly and a little at a time in their correct numerical sequence to the torque setting specified at the beginning of the Chapter **(see illustration 12.5b)**.

18 When the nuts are correctly torqued, install the bolt in the front of the cylinder head and tighten it to the specified torque setting **(see illustration 12.5a)**.

19 Install the camshafts (see Section 11) and the valve cover (see Section 8).

20 Install the spark plugs (see Chapter 1).

21 Remove the exhaust system and the carburettors (see Chapter 3).

22 If applicable on GSX600/750F models, install or re-mount the engine.

13 Valves/valve seats/valve guides – servicing

1 Because of the complex nature of this job and the special tools and equipment required, most owners leave servicing of the valves, valve seats and valve guides to a professional. However, you can make an initial assessment of whether the valves are seating correctly, and therefore sealing, by pouring a small amount of solvent into each of the valve ports. If the solvent leaks past any valve into the combustion chamber area the valve is not seating correctly and sealing.

2 You can also remove the valves from the cylinder head, clean the components, check them for wear to assess the extent of the work

needed, and, unless a valve service is required, grind in the valves (see Section 14). The head can then be reassembled.

3 A dealer service department will dismantle the valve assemblies, inspect and measure each component for wear, fit new guides and re-cut the valve seats if necessary, clean and reassemble the valve components using new components where necessary. **Note:** *Suzuki advise that the valves should not be ground in (lapped) immediately after seat re-cutting; the valve seat must be soft in order for final seating to occur when the engine is first run.*

4 After the valve service has been performed, the head will be in like-new condition. When the head is returned, be sure to clean it again very thoroughly before installation on the engine to remove any metal particles or abrasive grit that may still be present from the valve service operations. Use compressed air, if available, to blow out all the holes and passages.

14 Cylinder head and valves – disassembly, inspection and reassembly

1 As mentioned in the previous section, valve overhaul should be left to a Suzuki dealer or cylinder head specialist. However, disassembly, cleaning and inspection of the valves and related components can be done (if the necessary special tools are available) by the home mechanic. This way no expense is incurred if the inspection reveals that overhaul is not required at this time.

2 To disassemble the valve components without the risk of damaging them, a valve spring compressor is absolutely essential. Make sure it is suitable for motorcycle work and comes with the correct adapters for your valve size.

Disassembly

3 Before proceeding, arrange to label and store the valves along with their related

components in such a way that they can be returned to their original locations without getting mixed up. A good way to do this is to obtain a container which is divided into sixteen compartments, and label each compartment with the location of a valve, for example the No. 1 cylinder, intake camshaft, left-hand valve could be marked 1-I-L. If a container is not available, use labelled plastic bags (an egg carton also does very well!).

4 If not already done, remove the rocker arms (see Section 11). If required, unscrew the bolts securing the intake ducts and remove them **(see illustration)**. Discard the O-rings as new ones must be used. Check the condition of the ducts and replace them with new ones if they are damaged, deformed or deteriorated. Clean all traces of old gasket material from the cylinder head. If a scraper is used, take care not to scratch or gouge the soft aluminium.

HAYNES HiNT *Refer to Tools and Workshop Tips for details of gasket removal methods.*

5 First locate the valve spring compressor on each end of the valve assembly, making sure it is the correct size **(see illustration)**. On the

14.5a Compressing the valve springs using a valve spring compressor

14.5b Make sure the compressor is a good fit both on the top . . .

14.5c . . . and the bottom of the valve assembly

14.6a Remove the collets with needle-nose pliers, tweezers, a magnet or a screwdriver with a dab of grease on it

top of the valve the adaptor needs to be about the same size as the spring retainer – if it is too big it will not seat properly on the top of the spring retainer, and if it is too small it will be difficult to remove and install the collets **(see illustration)**. On the underside of the head make sure the plate on the compressor only contacts the valve and not the soft aluminium of the head – if the plate is too big for the valve, use a spacer between them **(see illustration)**.

6 Compress the valve springs on the first valve – do not compress the springs any more than is absolutely necessary. Remove the collets, using either needle-nose pliers, tweezers, a magnet or a screwdriver with a dab of grease on it **(see illustration)**. Carefully release the valve spring compressor and remove it. Remove the spring retainer, noting which way up it fits **(see illustration 14.30c)**. Remove the springs, noting that the closer wound coils are at the bottom **(see illustrations 14.30a and b)**. Press down on the top of the valve stem and draw the valve out from the underside of the head. If the

valve binds in the guide (won't pull through), push it back into the head and deburr the area around the collet groove with a very fine file or whetstone **(see illustration)**.

7 Once the valve has been removed and labelled, pull the valve stem oil seal off the top of the valve guide and discard it (the old seals should never be reused) **(see illustration)**. Now remove the spring seat **(see illustration 14.28)**. If the seat is difficult to grasp, either use a small magnet or turn the head upside down and tip it out, taking care not to lose it.

8 Repeat the procedure for the remaining valves. Remember to keep the parts for each valve together and in order so they can be reinstalled in the same location.

9 Next, clean the cylinder head with solvent and dry it thoroughly. Compressed air will speed the drying process and ensure that all holes and recessed areas are reached.

10 Clean all of the valve springs, collets, retainers and spring seats with solvent and dry them thoroughly. Do the parts from one valve at a time so they don't get mixed up.

11 Scrape off any deposits that may have

formed on the valve, then use a motorised wire brush to remove deposits from the valve heads and stems. Again, make sure the valves do not get mixed up.

Inspection

12 Inspect the head very carefully for cracks and other damage. If cracks are found, a new head will be required. Check the camshaft bearing surfaces for wear and evidence of seizure. Check the camshafts and holders for wear as well (see Section 11).

13 Using a precision straight-edge and a feeler gauge set to the warpage limit listed in the specifications at the beginning of the Chapter, check the head gasket mating surface for warpage. Refer to *Tools and Workshop Tips* in the Reference section for details of how to use the straight-edge.

14 Examine the valve seats in the combustion chamber. If they are pitted, cracked or burned, the head will require work beyond the scope of the home mechanic. Measure the valve seat width and compare it to this Chapter's Specifications **(see**

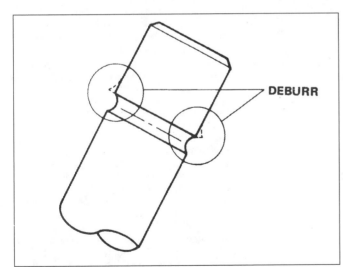

14.6b If the valve stem won't pull through the guide, deburr the area above the collet groove

14.7 Pull the seal off the top of the guide

2

14.14 Measure the valve seat width with a ruler (or for greater precision use a Vernier caliper)

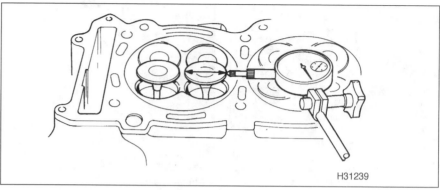

14.15a Measure the amount of wobble as shown, relocating the gauge to measure in both directions

14.15b Measure the valve stem diameter with a micrometer . . .

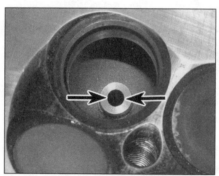

14.15c . . . then measure the guide bore using a small hole gauge, and measure the small hole gauge with a micrometer

illustration). If it exceeds the service limit, or if it varies around its circumference, overhaul is required.

15 Clean the valve guides to remove any carbon build-up, then install each valve in its guide in turn so that its face is 10 mm above the seat. Mount a dial gauge against the side of the valve face and measure the amount of stem deflection (wobble) between the valve stem and its guide – you need to measure in two perpendicular directions, so take the first measurement, then relocate the dial gauge and take a second measurement (see illustration). Make sure the gauge is solidly mounted so that any deflection recorded indicates movement in the valve and not the gauge body itself. If the deflection exceeds the limit specified, remove the valve and measure the valve stem diameter (see illustration). Also measure the inside diameter of the guide with a small hole gauge and micrometer (see illustration). Measure the guide at the ends and at the centre to determine if they are worn in a bell-mouth pattern (more wear at the ends). Subtract the stem diameter from the valve guide diameter to obtain the valve stem-to-guide clearance. If the stem-to-guide clearance is greater than listed in this Chapter's Specifications, renew whichever component is worn beyond its specifications. If the valve guide is within specifications, but is worn unevenly, it should be renewed.

16 Carefully inspect each valve face, stem and collet groove area for cracks, pits and burned spots (see illustration). Measure the thickness of the valve face and compare it to the specifications (see illustration). If it is worn below the service limit renew the valve.

17 Rotate the valve and check for any obvious indication that it is bent, in which case it must be renewed. Using V-blocks and a dial gauge, measure the valve stem runout and the valve head runout and compare the results to the specifications (see illustration). If either measurement exceeds the service limit specified, the valve must be renewed.

18 Check the end of the stem for pitting and excessive wear. The stem end can be ground down, provided that the amount of stem above the collet groove after grinding is greater than the minimum specified.

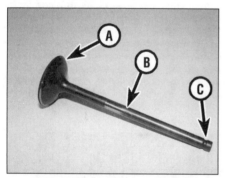

14.16a Check the valve face (A), stem (B) and collet groove (C) for signs of wear and damage

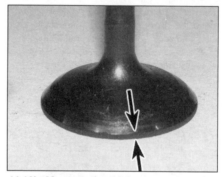

14.16b Measure the thickness of the valve face

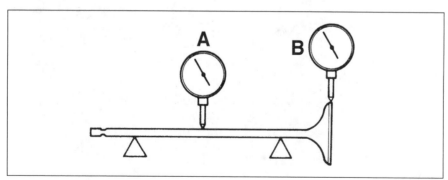

14.17 Measure the valve stem runout (A) and the valve head runout (B)

14.19a Measure the free length of the
valve springs . . .

14.19b . . . and check them for squareness

14.23a Apply the lapping compound very
sparingly, in small dabs, to the valve face only

14.23b Lubricate the stem and insert the
valve in the guide

19 Check the end of each valve spring for wear and pitting. Measure the spring free lengths and compare them to the specifications (see illustration). If any spring is shorter than specified it has sagged and must be renewed. Also place the spring upright on a flat surface and check it for bend by placing a ruler against it, or alternatively lay it against a set square (see illustration). If the bend in any spring is excessive, it must be renewed. Always new the inner and outer springs as a set, never singly.

20 Check the spring seats, retainers and collets for obvious wear and cracks. Any questionable parts should not be reused, as extensive damage will occur in the event of failure during engine operation.

21 If the inspection indicates that no overhaul work is required, the valve components can be reinstalled in the head.

Reassembly

22 Unless the valve seats have been re-cut, before installing the valves they should be ground in (lapped) to ensure a positive seal between the valves and seats. This procedure requires coarse and fine valve grinding compound and a valve grinding tool (either hand-held or drill driven). If a grinding tool is not available, a piece of rubber or plastic hose can be slipped over the valve stem (after the valve has been installed in the guide) and used to turn the valve. Note: *Suzuki advise that the valves should not be ground in*

immediately after seat re-cutting; the valve seat must be soft in order for final seating to occur when the engine is first run.

23 Apply a small amount of coarse grinding compound to the valve face, and some molybdenum disulphide oil (a 50/50 mixture of molybdenum disulphide grease and engine oil) to the valve stem, then slip the valve into the guide (see illustrations). Note: *Make sure each valve is installed in its correct guide and be careful not to get any grinding compound on the valve stem.*

24 Attach the grinding tool (or hose) to the valve and rotate the tool between the palms of your hands. Use a back-and-forth motion (as though rubbing your hands together) rather than a circular motion (i.e. so that the valve rotates alternately clockwise and anti-clockwise rather than in one direction only) (see illustration). If a motorised tool is being used, take note of the correct drive speed for it – if your drill runs too fast and is not variable, use a hand tool instead. Lift the valve off the seat and turn it at regular intervals to distribute the grinding compound properly. Continue the grinding procedure until the valve face and seat contact area is of uniform and correct width, and unbroken around the entire circumference (see illustration 14.14).

25 Carefully remove the valve from the guide and wipe off all traces of grinding compound, making sure none gets in the guide. Use solvent to clean the valve and wipe the seat area thoroughly with a solvent soaked cloth.

26 Repeat the procedure with fine valve grinding compound, then repeat the entire procedure for the remaining valves.

27 Working on one valve at a time, fit a new valve stem seal onto the guide. Usually finger pressure is sufficient to get it to clip into place, otherwise use a stem seal fitting tool or an appropriate size deep socket to push the seal over the end of the valve guide until it is felt to clip into place (see illustration). Don't twist or cock the seal, or it will not seal properly against the valve stem. Also, don't remove it again or it will be damaged.

28 Lay the spring seat in place in the cylinder head, making sure the shouldered side faces up – sliding the seat down a rod or screwdriver shaft helps to locate it around the top of the guide and prevents it getting skewed (see illustration).

2

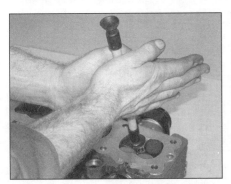

14.24 Rotate the valve grinding tool back
and forth between the palms of your hands

14.27 Fit a new valve stem seal

14.28 Fit the spring seat, making sure it is
the correct way up

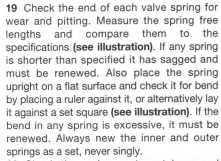

14.30a Fit the inner valve spring . . .

14.30b . . . and the outer valve spring . . .

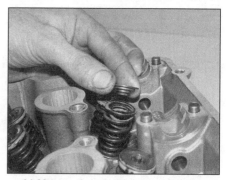

14.30c . . . then fit the spring retainer

29 Coat the valve stem with molybdenum disulphide oil (a 50/50 mixture of molybdenum disulphide grease and engine oil), then install it into its guide, rotating it slowly to avoid damaging the seal (see illustration 14.23b). Check that the valve moves up and down freely in the guide.

30 Next, install the inner and outer springs, with the closer-wound coils facing down into the cylinder head (see illustrations). Fit the spring retainer, with its shouldered side facing down so that it fits into the top of the springs (see illustration).

31 Compress the valve spring with a spring compressor, making sure it is correctly located onto each end of the valve assembly (see Step 5) (see illustrations 14.5a, b and c). Do not compress the springs any more than is necessary to slip the collets into place. Apply a small amount of grease to the collets to help hold them in place. Locate each collet in turn into the groove in the valve stem, then carefully release the compressor, making sure the collets seat and lock as you do (see illustration 14.6a). Check that the collets are locked in the retaining groove.

32 Support the cylinder head on blocks so the valves can't contact the workbench top, then very gently tap the top of the valve stem with a brass drift. This will help seat the collets in the groove.

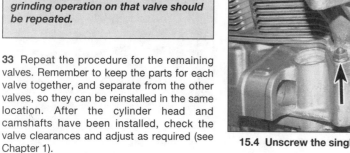

Haynes Hint: *Check for proper sealing of the valves by pouring a small amount of solvent into each of the valve ports. If the solvent leaks past any valve into the combustion chamber area the valve grinding operation on that valve should be repeated.*

33 Repeat the procedure for the remaining valves. Remember to keep the parts for each valve together, and separate from the other valves, so they can be reinstalled in the same location. After the cylinder head and camshafts have been installed, check the valve clearances and adjust as required (see Chapter 1).

34 If removed, install the intake ducts, using new ones if necessary (see illustration 14.4). Smear each new O-ring with grease and fit one into the groove in the mating surface of each duct. Each duct is coded according to its location. Ducts marked 1-08FO are for cylinders 1 and 2, ducts marked 3-08FO are for cylinders 3 and 4. Install them with the UP mark at the top and apply a suitable non-permanent thread locking compound to the bolts.

15 Cylinder block – removal, inspection and installation

Note: *The block can be removed with the engine in the frame (but see the Note at the beginning of Section 12). If the engine has been removed, ignore the steps that don't apply.*

Removal

1 Remove the cylinder head (see Section 12).
2 Clean any dirt and grit from around the base of each oil drain tube to prevent it falling in the crankcase, then pull them out of their holes (see illustration 15.28). Discard the O-rings as new ones must be used.
3 On California, Austria and Switzerland models, detach the PAIR system hose from each pipe on the front of the block. If required, unscrew the nuts securing the pipes and

15.4 Unscrew the single nut (arrowed)

remove them. Discard the gaskets as new ones must be used.
4 Unscrew the single nut which secures the front of the block to the crankcase (see illustration).
5 Hold the cam chain up and lift the cylinder block off the studs (see illustration), then pass the cam chain down through the tunnel. Do not let the chain fall into the crankcase – secure it with a piece of wire or metal bar to prevent it from doing so. If the block is stuck, tap around the joint faces of the block with a soft-faced mallet to free it from the crankcase, but take care not to strike any of the cooling fins as they break easily, especially on the corners. Don't attempt to free the block by inserting a screwdriver between it and the crankcase – you'll damage the sealing surfaces. When the block is removed, stuff clean rags around the pistons to prevent anything falling into the crankcase.
6 Note the location of the two dowels which will be either on the bottom of the block or in the crankcase (see illustration 15.19). Remove them if they are loose.
7 Check the base gasket and the mating surfaces on the cylinder head and block for signs of leakage, which could indicate warpage. Refer below and check the block.
8 Clean all traces of old gasket material from the cylinder block and crankcase. If a scraper is used, take care not to scratch or gouge the soft aluminium. Be careful not to let any of the gasket material drop into the crankcase or the oil passages.

15.5 Hold the cam chain up and lift the block off the crankcase

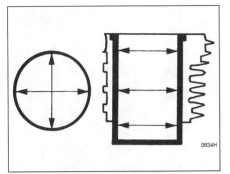

15.12a Measure the cylinder bore in the directions shown . . .

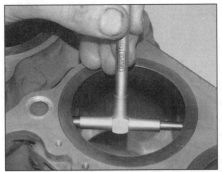

15.12b . . . with a telescoping gauge, then measure the gauge with a micrometer

15.19 Cylinder block locating dowels (arrowed)

Inspection

9 Do not attempt to separate the liners from the cylinder block.

10 Check the bore walls carefully for scratches and score marks.

11 Using a precision straight-edge and a feeler gauge set to the warpage limit listed in the specifications at the beginning of the Chapter, check the top mating surface of the cylinder for warpage. Refer to *Tools and Workshop Tips* in the Reference section for details of how to use the straight-edge. If warpage is excessive the cylinder block must be renewed.

12 Using a telescoping bore gauge and a micrometer (see *Tools and Workshop Tips*), check the dimensions of each bore to assess the amount of wear, taper and ovality. Measure near the top (but below the level of the top piston ring at TDC), centre and bottom (but above the level of the oil ring at BDC) of the bore, both parallel to and across the crankshaft axis **(see illustrations)**. Compare the results to the specifications at the beginning of the Chapter. If the bores are worn, oval or tapered beyond the service limit they can be rebored, and an oversize (+0.5 or +1.0 mm) set of pistons and rings are available from Suzuki. Note that the person carrying out the rebore must be aware of the piston-to-bore clearance for the oversize piston (see Specifications).

13 If the precision measuring tools are not available, take the cylinder block to a Suzuki

dealer or specialist motorcycle repair shop for assessment and advice.

14 If the cylinder bores are in good condition and the piston-to-bore clearance is within specifications (see Section 16), the bores should be honed (de-glazed). To perform this operation you will need the proper size flexible hone with fine stones, or a bottle-brush type hone, plenty of light oil or honing oil, some clean rags and an electric drill motor.

15 Hold the cylinder sideways (so that the bore is horizontal rather than vertical) in a vice with soft jaws or cushioned with wooden blocks. Mount the hone in the drill motor, compress the stones and insert the hone into the bore. Thoroughly lubricate the cylinder walls, then turn on the drill and move the hone up and down in the bore at a pace which produces a fine cross-hatch pattern on the cylinder wall with the lines intersecting at an angle of approximately 60°. Be sure to use plenty of lubricant and do not take off any more material than is necessary to produce the desired effect. Do not withdraw the hone from the cylinder while it is still turning. Switch off the drill and continue to move it up and down in the cylinder until it has stopped turning, then compress the stones and withdraw the hone. Wipe the oil from the cylinder and repeat the procedure on the other one. Remember, do not take too much material from the cylinder wall.

16 Wash the bores thoroughly with warm soapy water to remove all traces of the abrasive grit produced during the honing

operation. Be sure to run a brush through the stud holes and flush them with running water. After rinsing, dry the cylinders thoroughly and apply a thin coat of light, rust-preventative oil to all machined surfaces.

17 If you do not have the equipment or desire to perform the honing operation, take the cylinder block to a Suzuki dealer or specialist motorcycle repair shop.

Installation

18 Check that the mating surfaces of the cylinder block and crankcase are free from oil or pieces of old gasket.

19 If removed, fit the dowels into their correct locations in the crankcase, and push them firmly home **(see illustration)**.

20 Remove the rags from around the pistons, taking care not to let the connecting rods fall against the rim of the crankcase. Lay the new base gasket in place over the studs, making sure it locates over the dowels (if they are in the crankcase) and all the holes are correctly aligned, and the UP mark stamped out of the gasket reads the correct way round **(see illustrations)**. Never re-use the old gasket.

21 Ensure the piston ring end gaps are positioned correctly before fitting the cylinder block **(see illustration 17.13)**.

> **HAYNES HiNT** *Rotate the crankshaft until the inner pistons (2 and 3) are uppermost and feed them into the block first. Access to the lower pistons (1 and 4) is easier since they are on the outside.*

22 Rotate the crankshaft so that the inner pistons are at their highest point (top dead centre). It is useful to place a support under the pistons so that they remain at TDC while the block is fitted, otherwise the downward pressure will turn the crankshaft and the pistons will drop. Lubricate the cylinder bores, pistons and piston rings with clean engine oil.

23 Carefully lower the block onto the pistons, feeding the cam chain up the tunnel as you do, until the crowns fit into their bores. It is helpful to have an assistant to pass the chain up and slip a piece of wire through it to

2

15.20a Fit a new gasket . . .

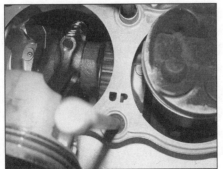

15.20b . . . making sure the UP letters stamped out of the gasket read correctly

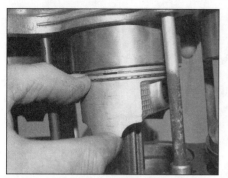

15.24 Feed the rings into the bore as you
lower the block

15.26 Install the single nut and tighten it to
the specified torque setting

15.28 Use a new O-ring on each oil drain
tube and smear them with grease

prevent it falling back into the engine. Keep
the chain taut to prevent it becoming
disengaged from the crankshaft sprocket.

24 Gently push the cylinder down, holding
the underside of the pistons if you are not
using a support to prevent them dropping,
and making sure they enter the bore squarely
and do not get cocked sideways. Carefully
compress and feed each ring into the bore as
the cylinder is lowered **(see illustration)**. Do
not use force if it appears to be stuck as the
piston and/or rings will be damaged. If
necessary, use a soft mallet to gently tap the
block down.

25 When the inner pistons are correctly
located in the cylinders, remove the support if
used then carefully press the block down with
the inserted pistons so that the crankshaft
turns and the outer piston crowns then enter
the bore. Feed the rings on the outer pistons
into their bores in the same way as before.
When all pistons are correctly located press
the block onto the base gasket, making sure it
locates on the dowels.

26 Install the single nut which secures the
front of the block to the crankcase and tighten
it to the torque setting specified at the
beginning of the Chapter **(see illustration)**.

27 On California, Austria and Switzerland
models, if removed, install the PAIR system
pipe using a new gasket and tighten the nuts.
Connect the hose to the pipe and secure it
with its clamp.

28 Fit a new O-ring smeared with grease

onto the bottom of each oil drain tube, then
press the tubes into their holes in the
crankcase **(see illustration)**.

29 Install the cylinder head (see Section 12).

16 Pistons – removal, inspection and installation

Note: *The pistons can be removed with the
engine in the frame (but see the **Note** at the
beginning of Section 12).*

Removal

1 Remove the cylinder block (see Section 15).
2 Before removing the pistons from the
connecting rods, use a sharp scriber or felt
marker pen to write the cylinder identity on
the crown of each piston (or on the inside of
the skirt if the piston is dirty and going to be
cleaned). Each piston should already have an
arrow on its crown that points to the front of
the engine, though the mark may not be
visible until the piston is cleaned **(see
illustration)**. If not already done stuff clean
rag around the connecting rod to prevent a
dropped circlip falling into the crankcase.
3 Carefully prise out the circlip on one side of
the piston using needle-nose pliers or a small
flat-bladed screwdriver inserted into the notch
(see illustration). Push the piston pin out
from the other side to free the piston from the
connecting rod **(see illustration)**. Remove the
other circlip and discard them both as new

ones must be used. When the piston has been
removed, slide its pin back into its bore so
that related parts do not get mixed up.

Inspection

4 Using your thumbs or a piston ring removal
and installation tool, carefully remove the rings
from the pistons **(see illustrations 17.12, 11b,
and 9c, b and a)** – don't use a ring removal tool
on the oil ring. Do not nick or gouge the pistons
in the process. Carefully note which way up
each ring fits and in which groove as they must
be installed in their original positions if being re-
used. On 600 cc engines the upper surface of
the top ring should be marked with the letter R
at one end, and the second (middle) ring
marked RN. On 750 cc engines the upper
surface of the top ring should be marked with
the letter N at one end, and the second (middle)
ring marked 2N. The top and middle rings can
also be identified by their different profiles and
thickness **(see illustration 17.11a)**.
5 Scrape all traces of carbon from the tops of

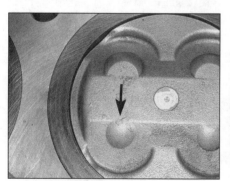

16.2 Note the arrow stamped into each
piston crown which must face forward

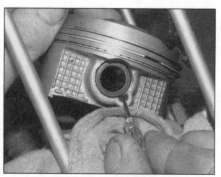

16.3a Remove the circlip using a
screwdriver inserted in the notch . . .

16.3b . . . then push the pin out from the
other side and remove the piston

16.10 Measuring the piston ring-to-groove clearance with a feeler gauge

16.11 Measure the piston diameter at the specified distance from the bottom of the skirt

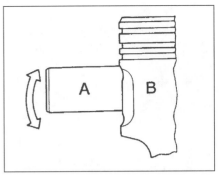

16.12a Slip the pin (A) into the piston (B) and try to rock it back and forth. If it's loose, replace the piston and pin

the pistons. A hand-held wire brush or a piece of fine emery cloth can be used once most of the deposits have been scraped away. Do not, under any circumstances, use a wire brush mounted in a drill motor to remove deposits from the pistons; the piston material is soft and will be eroded away by the wire brush.

6 Use a piston ring groove cleaning tool to remove any carbon deposits from the ring grooves. If a tool is not available, a piece broken off an old ring will do the job. Be very careful to remove only the carbon deposits. Do not remove any metal and do not nick or gouge the sides of the ring grooves.

7 Once the deposits have been removed, clean the pistons with solvent and dry them thoroughly. If the identification previously marked on the piston is cleaned off, be sure to re-mark it with the correct identity. Make sure the oil return holes below the oil ring groove are clear.

8 Carefully inspect each piston for cracks around the skirt, at the pin bosses and at the ring lands. Normal piston wear appears as even, vertical wear on the thrust surfaces of the piston and slight looseness of the top ring in its groove. If the skirt is scored or scuffed, the engine may have been suffering from overheating and/or abnormal combustion, which caused excessively high operating temperatures. The oil pump should be checked thoroughly. Also check that the circlip grooves are not damaged.

9 A hole in the piston crown, an extreme to

be sure, is an indication that abnormal combustion (pre-ignition) was occurring. Burned areas at the edge of the piston crown are usually evidence of spark knock (detonation). If any of the above problems exist, the causes must be corrected or the damage will occur again.

10 Measure the piston ring-to-groove clearance, either by laying each piston ring in its groove and slipping a feeler gauge in beside it, or by measuring the thickness of the ring and the width of the groove and subtracting one from the other (see illustration). Make sure you have the correct ring for the groove (see Step 4). Check the clearance at three or four locations around the groove. If the clearance is greater than specified, renew both the piston and rings as a set. If new rings are being used anyway, measure the clearance using the new rings. If the clearance is greater than that specified, the piston is worn and must be renewed.

11 Check the piston-to-bore clearance by measuring the bore (see Section 15) and the piston diameter. Make sure each piston is matched to its correct cylinder. Measure the piston 15.0 mm up from the bottom of the skirt and at 90° to the piston pin axis (see illustration). Subtract the piston diameter from the bore diameter to obtain the clearance. If it is greater than the specified figure, and if not already done, check the cylinder for wear (see Section 15). If the cylinder is good but the piston is worn, renew

the piston. If the cylinder is worn it can be rebored, and then oversize pistons and rings, available from Suzuki, can be fitted (see Specifications).

12 Apply clean engine oil to the piston pin, insert it into the piston and check for any freeplay between the two (see illustration). Measure the pin external diameter and the pin bore in the piston (see illustrations). Calculate the difference to obtain the piston pin-to-piston pin bore clearance. Compare the result to the specifications at the beginning of the Chapter. If the clearance is greater than specified, renew the components that are worn beyond their specified limits. If not already done, repeat the measurements between the pin and the connecting rod small-end (see Section 28).

13 Carefully pull the oil jet out of each end of the block mating surface with the crankcase using needle-nosed pliers, taking great care not to drop it into the crankcase – make sure your rag covers the hole completely (see illustration). Remove the O-rings and discard them. Clean the oil jets with solvent and blow them through with compressed air if available. Fit a new O-ring onto each jet, then press them into their passages in the crankcase, making sure the wider ends are at the top.

Installation

14 Inspect and install the piston rings (see Section 17).

15 Lubricate the piston pin, the piston pin

16.12b Measure the external diameter of the pin . . .

16.12c . . . and the internal diameter of the bore in the piston

16.13 Pull the oil jet out of its passage

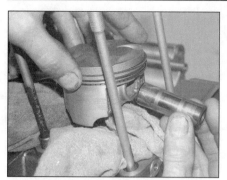

16.17a Line the piston up with the connecting rod and slide in the pin

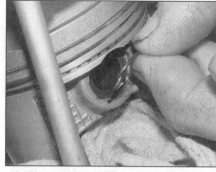

16.17b Install the circlip, making sure it is properly seated in its groove, with the open end away from the notch

bore and the connecting rod small-end bore with molybdenum disulphide oil (a 50/50 mixture of molybdenum disulphide grease and clean engine oil).

16 When installing the pistons onto the connecting rods, make sure you have the correct piston for the cylinder being worked on. Note that the arrow on the piston crown points to the front of the engine **(see illustration 16.2)**.

17 Stuff clean rag around the connecting rod to prevent a dropped circlip falling into the crankcase. Install a *new* circlip in one side of the piston (do not re-use old circlips). Line up the piston on its correct connecting rod, and insert the piston pin from the other side **(see illustration)**. Secure the pin with the other

new circlip **(see illustration)**. When installing the circlips, compress them only just enough to fit them in the piston, and make sure they are properly seated in their grooves with the open end away from the removal notch.

18 Install the cylinder block (see Section 15).

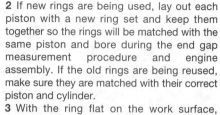

17 Piston rings – inspection and installation

1 It is good practice to renew the piston rings when an engine is being overhauled. Before installing the rings (new or old), check the free and installed end gaps of the top and second (middle) rings as follows.

2 If new rings are being used, lay out each piston with a new ring set and keep them together so the rings will be matched with the same piston and bore during the end gap measurement procedure and engine assembly. If the old rings are being reused, make sure they are matched with their correct piston and cylinder.

3 With the ring flat on the work surface, measure its end gap using a Vernier caliper **(see illustration)**. To measure the installed ring end gap, insert the ring into the top of the bore and square it up with the bore walls by pushing it in with the top of the piston **(see illustration)**. The ring should be about 20 mm below the top edge of the bore. Slip a feeler gauge between the ends of the ring and measure the gap. Compare the measurements to the specifications at the beginning of the Chapter **(see illustration)**.

4 If the gap is larger or smaller than specified, double check to make sure that you have the correct rings before proceeding.

5 If the gap is too small, the ring ends may come in contact with each other during engine operation, which can cause serious damage.

6 Excess end gap is not critical unless it exceeds the service limit. Again, double-check to make sure you have the correct rings for your engine and check that the bore is not worn (see Section 15).

7 Repeat the procedure for the other ring. Remember to keep the rings, pistons and bores matched up.

8 Once the ring end gaps have been checked, the rings can be installed on the pistons.

9 Install the oil control ring (lowest on the piston) first. It is composed of three separate components, namely the expander and the upper and lower side rails. Slip the expander into the groove, making sure the ends don't overlap, then install one side rail **(see illustrations)**. Do not use a piston ring installation tool on the side rails as they may be damaged. Instead, place one end of the side rail into the groove between the expander and the ring land. Hold it firmly in place and slide a finger around the piston while pushing the rail into the groove. Next, install the other

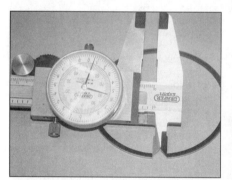

17.3a Measure the piston ring free end gap

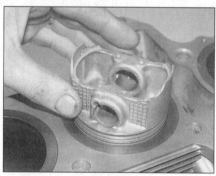

17.3b Square the ring up in the bore using the piston . . .

17.3c . . . then measure the installed end gap

17.9a Install the oil ring expander in its groove . . .

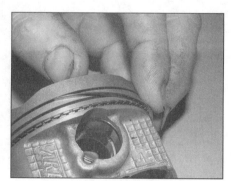

17.9b . . . then fit one side rail . . .

side rail in the same manner **(see illustration)**. Check that the ends of the expander have not overlapped.

10 After the three oil ring components have been installed, check to make sure that both the upper and lower side rails can be turned smoothly in the ring groove.

11 On 600 cc engines the upper surface of the top ring should be marked with the letter R at one end, and the second (middle) ring marked RN **(see illustration)**. On 750 cc engines the upper surface of the top ring should be marked with the letter N at one end, and the second (middle) ring marked 2N. The top and middle rings can also be identified by their different profiles and thicknesses. Install the second (middle) ring, making sure that the identification letter near the end gap is facing up, and the wider edge is at the bottom, as shown in the illustration of the profile. Fit the second (middle) ring into the middle groove in the piston **(see illustration)**. Do not expand the ring any more than is necessary to slide it into place. To avoid breaking the ring, use a piston ring installation tool.

12 Finally, install the top ring in the same manner into the top groove in the piston **(see illustration)**. Make sure the identification letter near the end gap is facing up.

13 Once the rings are correctly installed,

17.9c . . . and the other side rail

check they move freely without snagging and stagger their end gaps as shown **(see illustration)**.

18 Clutch – removal, inspection and installation

Note: *The clutch can be removed with the engine in the frame. If the engine has already been removed, ignore the preliminary steps which don't apply.*

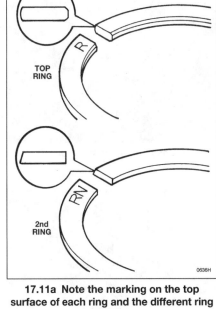

17.11a Note the marking on the top surface of each ring and the different ring profiles

Removal

1 On GSX600/750F models remove the fairing side panels (see Chapter 7). On all models, drain the engine oil (see Chapter 1).

2 Working in a criss-cross pattern, unscrew the clutch cover bolts **(see illustration)**. Note which size bolts fit where, and that the two front bolts are fitted with sealing washers. Discard these washers as new ones must be used. Lift the cover away from the engine, being prepared to catch any residual oil. Remove the gasket and discard it. Note the positions of the two locating dowels fitted to the crankcase and remove them for safe-keeping if they are loose.

3 Working in a criss-cross pattern, gradually slacken the clutch pressure plate bolts until

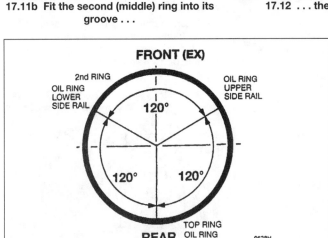

17.11b Fit the second (middle) ring into its groove . . .

17.12 . . . then fit the top ring

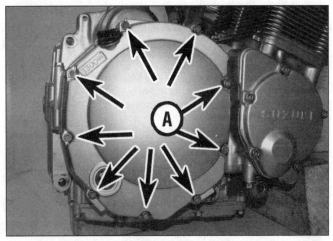

18.2 The clutch cover is secured by nine bolts (arrowed), two of which have sealing washers (A)

18.3a Unscrew the bolts (arrowed) . . .

18.3b . . . and remove the bolts, springs and the pressure plate

18.4a Remove the right-hand pushrod . . .

18.4b . . . and left-hand pushrod as described

18.5 Removing the clutch plates as a pack

spring pressure is released, then remove the bolts, springs and the pressure plate **(see illustrations)**. Counter-hold the clutch to prevent it turning while doing this – hand pressure should suffice as the bolts are not tight.

4 Withdraw the pressure plate lifter, noting the thrust washer and bearing **(see illustrations 18.30b and a)**. If the sprocket cover has been displaced from the left-hand side of the engine, push the left-hand pushrod into the input shaft and withdraw the right-hand pushrod from the right-hand end **(see illustration)**. Do not withdraw the right-hand pushrod from the left-hand side as it has a larger diameter knurled section on each end which will damage the oil seal. Withdraw the left-hand pushrod from the left-hand side if required **(see illustration)**. If the sprocket cover is in place, pull the clutch lever in to push the rods as far into the shaft as possible, then remove the right-hand rod from the right-hand end of the shaft, using a magnet or hooked piece of wire to draw it out. Remove the sprocket cover if required (see Chapter 5).

5 Grasp the complete set of clutch plates and remove them as a pack **(see illustration)**. Unless the plates are being renewed, keep them assembled in their original order. Note there are two types of friction plate, identified as A and B – the innermost (type B) plate has a larger internal diameter allowing it to locate over the anti-judder spring and its seat, and it is slightly thicker than the type A plates.

6 Remove the anti-judder spring and the spring seat **(see illustrations 18.28b and a)**.
7 To remove the clutch nut the transmission input shaft must be locked. This can be done in several ways. If the engine is in the frame, engage 6th gear and have an assistant hold the rear brake on hard with the rear tyre in firm contact with the ground. Alternatively, the Suzuki service tool (Pt. No. 09920-53740) or a

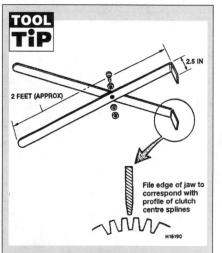

TOOL TiP

2.5 IN

2 FEET (APPROX)

File edge of jaw to correspond with profile of clutch centre splines

H16190

A clutch centre holding tool can easily be made using two strips of steel bolted together in the middle and with the ends bent and shaped as shown.

commercially available or home-made equivalent (see *Tool tip*) can be used to stop the clutch centre from turning whilst the nut is slackened **(see illustration)**. With the shaft locked, unscrew the clutch nut and remove the shaped washer, noting which way round it fits, and the washer seat **(see illustrations 18.27c, b and a)**.
8 Slide the clutch centre off the shaft **(see illustration 18.26)**.
9 Slide the outer thrust washer off the shaft **(see illustration 18.25)**.
10 Withdraw the needle roller bearing and spacer from the centre of the clutch housing **(see illustrations 18.24b and c)**. It may be necessary to pull the clutch housing part-way out and then push it back in order to expose the bearing and spacer.
11 Remove the clutch housing complete with the alternator and oil pump drive gear assembly from the shaft, then remove the inner thrust washer **(see illustration 18.24a and 18.23)**. If required, the alternator/oil pump drive gear can be separated from the clutch housing by lifting it off the back of the primary driven gear **(see illustration 18.21)**.

Inspection

12 After an extended period of service the clutch friction plates will wear and promote clutch slip. Measure the thickness of each friction plate using a Vernier caliper **(see**

18.7 Unscrew the clutch nut as described – here a commercially available holding tool is being used

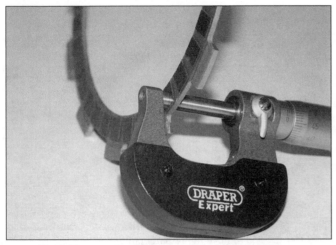

18.12 Measure the thickness of the friction plates . . .

18.13 . . . and the width of the tabs

illustration). If any plate has worn to or beyond the service limit given in the Specifications at the beginning of the Chapter, the friction plates must be renewed as a set. Also, if any of the plates smell burnt or are glazed, they must be renewed as a set. Note that the type B friction plate (the innermost plate) is thicker than the other friction plates – ensure the correct dimensions are referred to in the Specifications.

13 Also measure the width of the friction plate tabs and renew any plates that are worn beyond the service limit specified **(see illustration)**.

14 The plain plates should not show any signs of excess heating (bluing). Check for warpage using a flat surface and feeler gauges **(see illustration)**. If any plate exceeds the maximum amount of warpage, or shows signs of bluing, all plain plates must be renewed as a set.

15 Measure the free length of each clutch spring using a Vernier caliper **(see illustration 14.19a)**. If any spring is below the

service limit specified, renew all the springs as a set. Also place the spring upright on a flat surface and check it for bend by placing a ruler against it, or alternatively lay it against a set square **(see illustration 14.19b)**. If the bend in any spring is excessive, all six springs must be renewed.

16 Inspect the clutch assembly for burrs and indentations on the edges of the protruding tabs of the friction plates and/or slots in the edge of the housing with which they engage **(see illustrations)**. Similarly check for wear between the inner tongues of the plain plates and the slots in the clutch centre. Wear of this nature will cause clutch drag and slow disengagement during gear changes as the plates will snag when the pressure plate is lifted. With care a small amount of wear can be corrected by dressing with a fine file, but if this is excessive the worn components should be renewed.

17 Check the clutch housing needle bearing, the clutch housing bore and the spacer for signs of damage or scoring, and renew them if necessary.

18.14 Check the plain plates for warpage

18 Check the clutch pressure plate, the lifter, the bearing and the thrust washer for signs of roughness, wear or damage, and renew any parts necessary. If not already done, withdraw the clutch pushrods from the input shaft (see Step 4) **(see illustrations 18.4a and b)**. Check that each pushrod is straight by rolling it on a flat surface.

19 To access the pushrod oil seal, remove

2

18.16a Check the clutch housing . . .

18.16b . . . and centre as described

18.19a Bend down the tabs, then unscrew the bolts . . .

18.19b . . . and remove the retainer plate to access the oil seal (arrowed)

the front sprocket cover (see Chapter 5). Check the pushrod oil seal for signs of leakage and renew it if necessary. First remove the front sprocket (see Chapter 5). Bend down the locking tabs on the oil seal retainer plate bolts then unscrew the

bolts and remove the plate **(see illustrations)**. Lever out the old seal, then drive a new seal squarely into place. Install the retainer plate, making sure the neutral switch and sidestand wiring is correctly routed behind the long tab, and tighten its bolts.

Bend the retainer plate tabs up to lock the bolts. Install the front sprocket (see Chapter 5).

20 Inspect the clutch release mechanism whilst the sprocket cover is removed. Check the mechanism for smooth operation

18.20a Unhook the spring . . .

18.20b . . . then unscrew the bolts and remove the release mechanism . . .

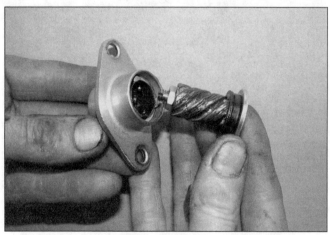

18.20c . . . then disassemble it, clean it and re-grease it

18.21 Check the teeth on the various gears on the back of the housing

18.23 Slide the inner thrust washer onto the shaft . . .

18.24a . . . then fit the clutch housing . . .

and any signs of wear or damage. Detach the clutch cable if not already done (see Section 19). Unhook the arm return spring, then unscrew the two bolts securing the mechanism to the cover and remove it for cleaning and re-greasing **(see illustrations)**. Reassemble the mechanism and fit it back onto the cover, then attach the return spring.

21 Check the teeth of the primary driven gear on the back of the clutch housing and the corresponding teeth of the primary drive gear on the crankshaft **(see illustration)**. Renew the clutch housing and/or crankshaft if worn or chipped teeth are discovered. Similarly check the alternator and oil pump drive and driven gear teeth

Installation

22 Remove all traces of old gasket from the crankcase and clutch cover surfaces.
23 Slide the inner thrust washer onto the shaft with its flat side facing out **(see illustration)**.
24 Lubricate the clutch housing needle

18.24b . . . the bearing . . .

18.24c . . . and the spacer

bearing and spacer with molybdenum disulphide oil (50% molybdenum grease and 50% engine oil). Slide the clutch housing onto the shaft, making sure it engages correctly with the teeth on the primary drive gear, the alternator driven gear and the oil pump driven gear, then support it in position and slide the bearing and spacer onto the shaft and into the middle of the housing **(see illustrations)**. To check that the housing is fully engaged with

its related gears, hold the housing and try to turn the oil pump driven gear using a screwdriver – if it turns, the gears are not engaged.
25 Slide the outer thrust washer onto the shaft **(see illustration)**.
26 Slide the clutch centre onto the shaft **(see illustration)**.
27 Slide the washer seat and shaped washer onto the shaft, making sure the raised inner rim

2

18.25 Slide the outer thrust washer onto the shaft . . .

18.26 . . . followed by the clutch centre

18.27a Fit the washer seat . . .

18.27b . . . and the shaped washer . . .

18.27c . . . then fit the clutch nut . . .

18.27d . . . and tighten it to the specified torque

of the shaped washer faces out – convex side outwards (see illustrations). Thread the clutch nut onto the shaft, then use the method employed on removal to lock the input shaft (see Step 7), and tighten the nut to the torque setting specified at the beginning of the Chapter (see illustrations). Note: *Check that the clutch centre rotates freely after tightening the clutch nut.*

28 Fit the anti-judder spring seat onto the clutch centre, then fit the spring with its outer rim raised off the spring seat – concave side outwards (see illustrations).

29 Coat each clutch plate with engine oil. Build up the plates in the housing, starting with the type B friction plate with the wider internal diameter, then a plain plate, then alternating friction plates (type A) and plain plates until all are installed (see illustrations).

18.28a Fit the spring seat . . .

18.28b . . . and the spring . . .

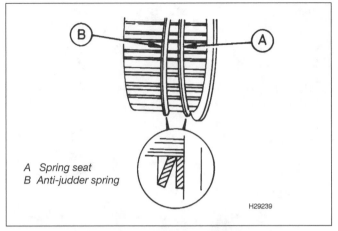

A Spring seat
B Anti-judder spring

H29239

18.28c ... fitting it as shown

18.29a Fit the friction plate with the larger internal diameter first ...

18.29b ... then alternate plain plates ...

18.29c ... and friction plates

Make sure the type B plate locates correctly over the anti-judder spring and its seat.

30 If removed, smear molybdenum grease onto each end of each pushrod and slide them into the input shaft – if the sprocket cover has been removed slide the left-hand rod with the rounded ends into the left-hand end of the shaft through the oil seal **(see illustration 18.4b)**. If the sprocket cover is in place slide the left-hand rod into the right-hand end of the input shaft, then insert the right-hand rod with the knurled ends and use it to push the left-hand rod all the way through **(see illustration 18.4a)**. Lubricate the pressure plate lifter, the bearing and thrust washer with clean oil, then slide the lifter into the input shaft and fit the bearing and washer onto it **(see illustrations)**.

2

18.30a Fit the lifter into the shaft ...

18.30b ... then fit the bearing and washer

18.31b . . . then fit the springs and bolts

18.31a Fit the pressure plate, making sure it locates as described . . .

18.32a Apply sealant around the joints (arrowed) . . .

18.32b . . . then fit the gasket onto the dowels (arrowed) . . .

34 Replenish the engine with the specified type and quantity of oil (see Chapter 1), then check the oil level (see *Daily (pre-ride) checks*).
35 Check the clutch lever freeplay and adjust if necessary (see Chapter 1).
36 Install the fairing side panels on GSX600/750F models (see Chapter 7).

19 Clutch cable –
removal and installation

Removal

1 Remove the front sprocket cover (see Chapter 5) – this procedure involves detaching the clutch cable from the release mechanism in the cover.
2 Pull back the rubber cover from the clutch adjuster at the handlebar end of the cable **(see illustration)**. Fully slacken the lockring, then screw the adjuster fully in. This resets it to the beginning of its adjustment range.

31 Fit the pressure plate into the clutch centre, making sure it seats correctly with its inner rim castellations locating in the slots in the centre – if there is any clearance between the clutch plates as you push on the pressure plate then it has not located properly **(see illustration)**. Fit the clutch springs and bolts and tighten the bolts evenly in a criss-cross sequence to the specified torque setting **(see illustration)**.
32 Apply a smear of sealant (Suzuki Bond

1215 or equivalent) to the area around the crankcase joints as shown **(see illustration)**. If removed, insert the clutch cover dowels into the crankcase, then place a new gasket onto the crankcase, making sure it locates correctly over the dowels **(see illustration)**.
33 Install the clutch cover and tighten its bolts evenly in a criss-cross sequence, making sure that two new sealing washers are used on the front two bolts **(see illustrations)**.

18.33a . . . and install the cover . . .

18.33b . . . not forgetting the sealing washers

19.2 Pull back the cover, then slacken the lockring (arrowed) and turn the adjuster in

3 Align the slots in the adjuster and lockring with that in the lever bracket, then pull the outer cable end from the socket in the adjuster and release the inner cable end from the lever **(see illustrations)**.

4 Take note of the exact routing of the cable and any guides that hold it – incorrect installation could result in poor steering movement and affect clutch action. Carefully withdraw the cable – if it gets stuck do not be tempted to pull it out using force as you will only damage something.

>
> **Before removing the cable from the bike, tape the lower end of the new cable to the upper end of the old cable. Slowly pull the lower end of the old cable out, guiding the new cable down into position. Using this method will ensure the cable is routed correctly.**

Installation

5 Installation is the reverse of removal. Apply grease to the cable ends. Make sure the cable is correctly routed. Do not forget to bend up the tab in the release arm to secure the cable end. Adjust the amount of clutch lever freeplay (see Chapter 1).

20 Gearchange mechanism – removal, inspection and installation

Note: *The gearchange mechanism can be removed with the engine in the frame. If the engine has already been removed, ignore the preliminary steps.*

Removal

1 Drain the engine oil (see Chapter 1).
2 Remove the front sprocket cover (see Chapter 5).
3 Remove the clutch (see Section 18). Place some clean rag in the opening to the sump to prevent anything dropping down.
4 Remove the circlip securing the left-hand

19.3a Align the slots and slip the cable out of the bracket . . .

end of the shaft and slide off the washer **(see illustrations)**.

5 Working on the right-hand side of the engine, note how the gearchange shaft centralising spring ends locate on each side of the pin in the crankcase, and how the teeth on the shaft arm engage with those on the pawl holder, then withdraw the gearchange shaft from the right-hand side of the engine **(see illustration)**.

6 Undo the screws securing the pawl lifter plate and holder guide plate to the crankcase and remove them **(see illustration)**. A thread locking compound is used on these screws during assembly, so you may need to use an impact driver for removal.

7 The pawls are spring-loaded in the holder. Before removing the holder, place a finger over each pawl to prevent them from

20.4a Remove the circlip . . .

20.5 Withdraw the shaft from the engine

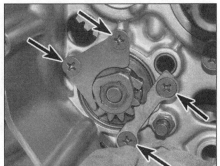

20.6 Undo the screws (arrowed) and remove the pawl lifter plate and the holder guide plate

19.3b . . . and detach it from the lever

springing out **(see illustration)**. Remove the holder along with the pawls. Place the holder on a bench and carefully release the pawls, noting how they and their pins and springs fit.

Inspection

8 Inspect the shaft centralising spring for fatigue, wear or damage **(see illustration 20.14a)**. If any is found, it must be replaced with a new one. Also check that the spring locating pin in the crankcase is tight. If it is loose, remove it and apply a non-permanent thread locking compound to its threads, then tighten it.

9 Check the gearchange shaft for straightness and damage to the splines or arm teeth. If the shaft is bent you can attempt to straighten it, but if the splines or teeth are damaged the shaft must be replaced with a

20.4b . . . and the washer

2

20.7 Hold the pawls so they won't fly out when removing the holder

20.9a Lever out the old gearchange shaft seal

20.9b Fit the new seal with the marked side facing out . . .

20.9c . . . and drive it in, setting it flush with the crankcase

new one. Also check the condition of the shaft oil seal in the left-hand side of the crankcase. If it is damaged or deteriorated it must be replaced with a new one. Lever out the old seal using a seal hook or screwdriver (see illustration). Drive the new seal squarely into place, with its marked side facing out, using a seal driver, a suitable socket, or a piece of wood as shown (see illustrations).

10 Check the pawl holder, pawls, pins and springs for wear and damage. Replace them with new ones if defects are found.

Installation

11 Fit the springs, pins and pawls into the holder (see illustrations). Make sure the rounded end of each pawl fits into the rounded cut-out in the holder, and that the pins locate correctly in the cut-outs in the pawls, with the wider edge of the cut-out facing the holder teeth. It will be necessary to hold each pawl assembly in place while the holder is installed in the end of the selector drum.

12 Fit the holder with its teeth facing forward and down so that they will align centrally with the teeth on the shaft arm when it is installed (see illustration 20.7). Apply a suitable non-permanent thread locking compound to the pawl lifter and holder guide plate screws, then install the plates and tighten the screws (see illustration 20.6).

13 Apply a smear of grease to the lips of the gearchange shaft seal in the left-hand side of the crankcase.

14 If removed, slide the centralising spring onto the gearchange shaft and locate the spring ends each side of the pin on the arm (see illustration). Smear clean engine oil over the shaft then carefully slide it into the engine, making sure the centralising spring ends locate correctly on each side of the pin on the crankcase, and engage the shaft arm teeth centrally with the teeth of the pawl holder (see illustration).

15 Slide the washer onto the left-hand end of the shaft and fit the circlip, making sure it locates in its groove (see illustrations 20.4b and a).

16 Install the clutch (see Section 18).

17 Install the front sprocket cover (see Chapter 5).

18 Replenish the engine with the specified type and quantity of oil (see Chapter 1), then check the oil level (see Daily (pre-ride) checks).

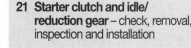

21 Starter clutch and idle/reduction gear – check, removal, inspection and installation

Note 1: The starter clutch can be removed with the engine in the frame. If the engine has been removed, ignore the steps which do not apply.

Note 2: The Suzuki service tool (Pt. No. 09930-33720) will be required to pull the starter clutch off its crankshaft taper.

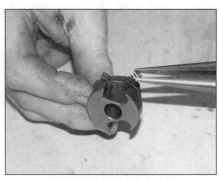

20.11a Fit the springs . . .

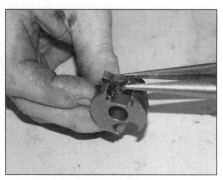

20.11b . . . the pins . . .

20.11c . . . and the pawls, with the wider edge on the side of the holder teeth

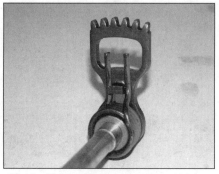

20.14a Make sure the centralising spring is correctly fitted

20.14b The installed assembly should be as shown

21.4 Unscrew the bolts (arrowed) and remove the cover

21.5 Withdraw the shaft and remove the idle/reduction gear

Check

1 The operation of the starter clutch can be checked while it is in situ. Remove the starter motor (see Chapter 8). Check that the starter idle/reduction gear is able to rotate freely clockwise as you look at it via the starter motor aperture, but locks when rotated anti-clockwise. If not, the starter clutch is faulty and should be removed for inspection.

Removal

2 On GSX600/750F models remove the left-hand fairing side panel (see Chapter 7).
3 Drain the engine oil (see Chapter 1).
4 Working in a criss-cross pattern, unscrew the starter clutch cover bolts, noting which bolt fits where as they are of different lengths and that the front top bolt has a sealing washer (see illustration). Note: *Take care when unscrewing the bottom bolt at the front as its thread bore has an open end and therefore the bolt may be corroded in place. If necessary apply some penetrating fluid to the open end, then work the bolt free if necessary by undoing it a little, then doing it back up again a little, and carrying on as such until the bolt frees up.* Lift the cover away from the engine, being prepared to catch any residual oil. Remove the gasket and discard it. Note the position of the

dowel and remove it for safe-keeping if it is loose. Note how the idle/reduction gear shaft end locates in the cover.
5 Withdraw the starter idle/reduction gear shaft, then remove the gear, noting which way round it fits (see illustration).
6 To slacken the starter clutch bolt the crankshaft must be locked. This can be done in several ways. If the engine is in the frame, engage 6th gear and have an assistant hold the rear brake on hard with the rear tyre in firm contact with the ground. Alternatively, the Suzuki service tool (Pt. No. 09920-34810) or a commercially available or home-made equivalent (see *Tool tip*) can be used to stop the shaft from turning whilst the bolt is slackened (see illustration). With the crankshaft locked, slacken the bolt by a few turns – **do not** remove the bolt as it must now be used in conjunction with a puller as described below.
7 The starter clutch locates on the crankshaft taper and must be pulled off with the Suzuki service tool (Pt. No. 09930-33720) (see illustration). Thread the service tool onto the outer threads on the starter clutch, then counter-hold the tool using a suitable spanner on its large flats, and tighten the centre bolt against the crankshaft bolt head to pull the starter clutch off the taper – note that the puller bolt has left-hand

threads and so must be tightened **anti-clockwise (see illustration)**. Once the starter clutch is dislodged, remove the tool, then unscrew the crankshaft bolt and remove the starter clutch along with the starter driven gear.

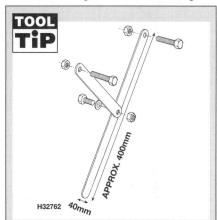

TOOL TiP

A starter clutch holding tool can easily be made using two strips of steel bolted together in the middle, and with a bolt (sized to fit in the holes in the starter clutch) through one end of each strip – lock the bolts in place using nuts.

2

21.6 Prevent the starter clutch from turning as described and slacken the starter clutch bolt

21.7a This tool is needed to remove the starter clutch

21.7b Thread the service tool onto the starter clutch, then counter-hold the tool and tighten the centre bolt until the clutch is free

21.11 Inspect the friction surface (A) and the sprags (B)

21.16a Fit the starter clutch onto the crankshaft

8 Clean all old gasket and sealant from the cover and crankcase.

Inspection

9 With the clutch face down on a workbench, check that the starter driven gear rotates freely in an anti-clockwise direction and locks against the rotor in a clockwise direction. If it doesn't, replace the starter clutch with a new one.

10 Withdraw the starter driven gear – if it appears stuck, rotate it anti-clockwise as you withdraw it to free it from the clutch.

11 Check the bearing surface of the driven gear hub and the condition of the sprags inside the clutch body **(see illustration)**. If the bearing surface shows signs of excessive wear or the sprags are damaged, marked or flattened at any point, renew the starter clutch and/or driven gear.

12 Check the bush in the starter driven gear

hub and its corresponding surface on the crankshaft. If the bush surfaces show signs of excessive wear replace the gear with a new one.

13 Examine the teeth of the starter idle/reduction gear and the corresponding teeth of the starter driven gear and starter motor drive shaft. Renew the gears and/or starter motor if worn or chipped teeth are discovered on related gears. Also check the idle/reduction gear shaft for damage, and check that the gear is not a loose fit on it. Replace the shaft with a new one if necessary.

Installation

14 Lubricate the hub of the starter driven gear with clean engine oil, then fit it into the clutch, rotating it anti-clockwise as you do so to spread the sprags and allow the hub to enter.

15 Thoroughly clean the tapered end of the crankshaft and the corresponding friction surface inside the starter clutch with solvent to remove all traces of oil.

16 Slide the starter clutch assembly onto the end of the crankshaft **(see illustration)**. Apply a suitable non-permanent thread locking compound to the bolt and thread it into the crankshaft **(see illustration)**. Using the method employed on removal to stop the crankshaft from turning, tighten the bolt to the torque setting specified at the beginning of the Chapter **(see illustration)**.

17 Lubricate the idle/reduction gear shaft with clean engine oil, then locate the gear with the smaller pinion facing outwards and fit the shaft **(see illustration 21.5)**. Make sure the gear meshes correctly with the starter driven gear and the starter motor shaft.

18 Apply a smear of sealant (Suzuki Bond 1215 or equivalent) to the area around the

21.16b Apply thread locking compound to the threads of the starter clutch bolt . . .

21.16c . . . then lock the starter clutch and tighten the bolt to the specified torque setting

21.18a Apply the sealant to the crankcase joints (arrows)

21.18b Check that the dowel (arrowed) is installed, then fit a new gasket . . .

21.18c . . . and the cover . . .

21.18d . . . making sure the sealing washer is fitted with the front top bolt

crankcase joints as shown (see illustration). If removed, insert the dowel in the crankcase, then fit the cover using a new gasket, making sure it locates correctly onto the dowel and the idle/reduction gear shaft (see illustrations). Tighten the cover bolts evenly in a criss-cross sequence, making sure the sealing washer is installed on the front top bolt (see illustration).

 HAYNES HINT *It is advisable to apply a little silicone sealant to the open end of the bore for the bottom bolt at the front to prevent corrosion.*

19 Replenish the engine with the specified type and quantity of oil (see Chapter 1), then check the oil level (see *Daily (pre-ride) checks*).
20 On GSX600/750F models install the left-hand fairing side panel (see Chapter 7).

22 Ignition timing rotor – removal and installation

Note: *The timing rotor can be removed with the engine in the frame. If the engine has been removed, ignore the steps which do not apply.*

Removal

1 On GSX600/750F models remove the fairing right-hand side panel (see Chapter 7).
2 Drain the engine oil (see Chapter 1).
3 Unscrew the five bolts securing the pulse generator coil cover to the right-hand side of the engine (see illustration 11.3a). Note the sealing washer with the top bolt – discard the washer as a new one should be used. Lift the cover away from the engine, being prepared to catch any residual oil. Remove the gasket and discard it.

4 Counter-hold the timing rotor hex using a 19 mm ring spanner, then unscrew the bolt in the centre (see illustration). Remove the rotor, noting how it locates on the pin in the end of the crankshaft. Remove the pin for

22.4 Counter-hold the hex and unscrew the Allen bolt

2

22.6a Locate the cut-out in the rotor over the pin (arrowed) . . .

22.6b . . . then install the bolt and tighten it to the specified torque

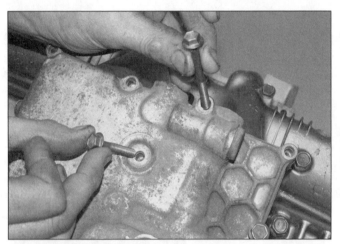

23.4a Do not forget the bolt in the middle, and note the position of the long bolt at the front . . .

23.4b . . . and the bolt with the sealing washer

safekeeping if it is loose **(see illustration 22.6a)**.

Installation

5 If removed, fit the rotor locating pin into the end of the crankshaft.

6 Fit the rotor, locating the cut-out over the pin, then install the bolt and tighten it to the torque setting specified at the beginning of the Chapter, counter-holding the rotor as on removal **(see illustrations)**.

7 Apply a suitable sealant (such as Suzuki Bond 1215) to the area around the crankcase joints **(see illustration 11.35a)**. Install the pulse generator cover using a new gasket and a suitable non-permanent thread lock on the bolts, and fit a new sealing washer with the top bolt **(see illustrations 11.35b and c)**.

8 Replenish the engine with the specified type and quantity of oil (see Chapter 1), then check the oil level (see *Daily (pre-ride) checks*).

9 On GSX600/750F models install the fairing right-hand side panel (see Chapter 7).

23 Oil sump, pressure regulator and strainer – removal, inspection and installation

Note: *The oil sump, pressure regulator and strainer can be removed with the engine in the frame.*

Removal

1 Remove the exhaust system (see Chapter 3).

2 Drain the engine oil (see Chapter 1).

3 Unscrew the banjo bolt securing each oil cooler hose to the sump just below the oil filter **(see illustration 7.2a)**. Discard the sealing washers as new ones must be used.

4 Unscrew the sump bolts, slackening them evenly in a criss-cross sequence to prevent distortion, and not forgetting the bolt in the middle **(see illustration)**. Note the position of the bolt with the sealing washer **(see illustration)**. Remove the sump and its

gasket. Discard the gasket and sealing washer as new ones must be used.

5 Unscrew the oil pressure regulator from inside the sump and remove it with its washer **(see illustration)**.

6 If required unscrew the three bolts securing the strainer cover to the body and remove it

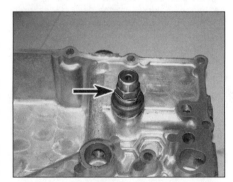

23.5 Remove the oil pressure regulator (arrowed) from the sump

23.6a Strainer cover bolts (arrowed)

23.6b Strainer body bolts (arrowed)

(see illustration). Unscrew the two bolts securing the strainer body to the underside of the crankcase (see illustration). Discard the gasket as a new one must be used.

7 Remove the oil outlet shim and its O-ring from the underside of the crankcase just ahead of the oil strainer (see illustration). Discard the O-ring as a new one must be fitted whenever the sump is removed.

8 Remove all traces of gasket from the sump and crankcase mating surfaces.

Inspection

9 Clean the sump, making sure all the oil passages are free of any debris.

10 Make sure the oil strainer is clean and remove any debris caught in the mesh. Inspect the strainer for any signs of wear or damage and replace it with a new one if necessary.

11 Clean the pressure regulator, and check that its plunger moves freely in the body (see

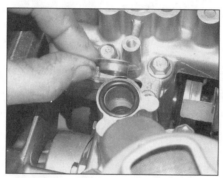

23.7 Remove the shouldered shim and the O-ring from the oil passage

illustration). Inspect it for signs of wear or damage and replace it with a new one if necessary.

Installation

12 Fit a new O-ring into the oil outlet in the underside of the crankcase, then install the shim.

23.11 Check the action of the plunger in the body by pressing down on it

13 Install the oil strainer body using a new gasket and tighten its bolts (see illustration). If removed, fit the strainer cover, making sure the arrow points to the front of the engine, and tighten its bolts (see illustration).

14 Install the oil pressure regulator using a new washer, and tighten it to the torque

23.13a Install the strainer assembly using a new gasket

23.13b Make sure the arrow on the cover points to the front

2

23.14 Fit the regulator using a new sealing washer

23.15 Fit a new gasket . . .

setting specified at the beginning of the Chapter **(see illustration)**.

15 Lay a new gasket onto the sump (if the engine is in the frame) or onto the crankcase (if the engine has been removed and is positioned upside down on the work surface) **(see illustration)**. Make sure the holes in the gasket align correctly with the bolt holes.

16 Position the sump onto the crankcase and install the sump bolts, using a new sealing washer on the rear bolt on the right-hand side of the sump **(see illustration and 23.4a and b)**. Tighten the bolts evenly in a criss-cross pattern to the torque setting specified at the beginning of the Chapter.

17 Fit the oil cooler hoses onto the sump using new sealing washers, and tighten the banjo bolts to the specified torque setting **(see illustration 7.5)**.

18 Install the exhaust system (see Chapter 3).

19 Replenish the engine with the specified type and quantity of oil (see Chapter 1), then check the oil level (see *Daily (pre-ride) checks)*. Start the engine and check that there are no leaks from around the sump.

24 Crankcase – separation and reassembly

Note: *When the engine is upside down, referrals to the right and left-hand ends or sides of the transmission shafts or components are made as though the engine is the correct way up. Therefore the right-hand end of a shaft or side of a crankcase will actually be on your left as you look down onto the underside of the crankcase assembly.*

Separation

1 To access the oil pump, crankshaft, cam chain and tensioner blade, connecting rods, transmission shafts and the selector drum and forks (although see Note in Section 29), the crankcase must be split into two parts.

2 To enable the crankcases to be separated, the engine must be removed from the frame (see Section 5). Before the crankcases can be separated the following components must be removed:

● Cam chain tensioner (Section 9).
● Camshafts (Section 11).
● Cylinder head (Section 12).
● Cylinder block (Section 15).
● Timing rotor (Section 22) and ignition pulse generator coil assembly (Chapter 4)
● Clutch (Section 18).
● Gearchange mechanism (Section 20).
● Alternator (Chapter 8).
● Starter motor (Chapter 8).
● Starter clutch and idle/reduction gear (Section 21).
● Oil filter (Chapter 1).
● Oil sump and oil strainer (Section 23).

Note: *If the crankcases are being separated to inspect or access the transmission components, or to inspect the crankshaft without removing it, the engine top-end components (cam chain tensioner, camshafts, cylinder head, cylinder block) can remain in situ. However, if removal of the crankshaft and connecting rod assemblies is intended, full disassembly of the top-end is necessary.*

3 Undo the two screws securing the transmission input shaft bearing retainer plate

23.16 . . . then install the sump

24.3 Undo the screws (arrowed) and remove the bearing retainer plate

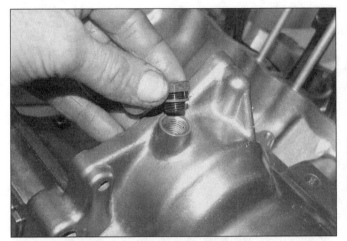

24.5a Remove the plug to access the bolt . . .

24.5b . . . and use a long socket-based hex key to unscrew it

24.6a Unscrew the six external bolts . . .

24.6b . . . and the internal bolt and nut

to the right-hand side of the crankcase and remove the plate, noting how it fits **(see illustration)**. A thread locking compound is used on these screws during assembly, so you may need to use an impact driver.

4 Bend back the tabs on the transmission output shaft bearing and the clutch pushrod oil seal retainer plate **(see illustration 18.19a)**. Unscrew the four bolts and remove the plate **(see illustration 18.19b)**.

5 Unscrew the plug located next to the alternator mounting flange in the upper crankcase half **(see illustration)**. This provides access to one of the upper crankcase bolts, but note that you will need a long and preferably socket-based hex key to unscrew the bolt – the socket-based hex is necessary in order to apply a torque setting to the bolt when tightening it on reassembly **(see illustration)**. Discard the plug's sealing washer as a new one must be used.

6 Unscrew the seven 6 mm upper crankcase bolts and the single 6 mm nut which is located inside the alternator mounting flange **(see illustrations and 24.5b)**. If the earth (ground)

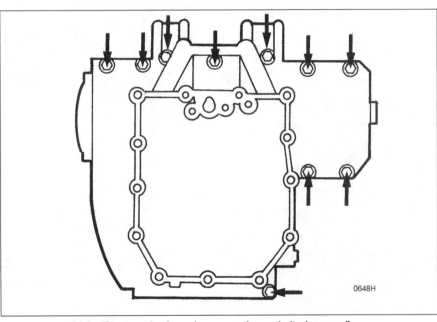

24.8a Remove the 6 mm lower crankcase bolts (arrowed) . . .

2

24.8b . . . the oil drain tube bolt and the tube . . .

24.8c . . . and the 6 mm nut (arrowed)

cable wasn't detached when removing the engine, note which bolt secures it.

7 Turn the engine upside down so that it rests on the cylinder studs and the back of the upper crankcase half. Support it on wood blocks so that no strain is placed on the cylinder studs.

8 Unscrew the ten 6 mm lower crankcase bolts as shown **(see illustration on previous page)**. Also unscrew the 6 mm bolt securing the left-hand oil drain tube, and the single 6 mm nut located just ahead of the transmission output shaft on the left-hand side of the crankcase **(see illustrations)**. Remove the oil drain tube. On K1 (2001) models onward, note the sealing washers fitted with the central front bolt and the rear bolt on the starter clutch housing – discard these as new ones should be used.

9 Unscrew the main oil gallery plug from the right-hand side of the crankcase, below the ignition pulse generator coil assembly housing **(see illustration)**. Discard the plug's O-ring as a new one must be used.

10 Working in a **reverse** of the tightening sequence shown **(see illustration)**, and noting that two of the bolts (Nos. 2 and 4) are Allen bolts, and that the No. 1 bolt also secures the right-hand oil drain tube **(see**

illustration 24.23b), slacken each 8 mm lower crankcase bolt a little a time until they are all finger-tight, then remove the bolts. **Note:** *As each bolt is removed, store it in its relative position in a cardboard template of the crankcase halves. This will ensure all bolts are installed in the correct location on reassembly.* Note that bolt Nos. 9 and 11 are fitted with copper sealing washers, and that new washers must be used on reassembly. Also remove the oil drain tube.

11 Carefully lift the lower crankcase half off the upper half, using a soft-faced hammer to tap around the joint to initially separate the

halves if necessary **(see illustration)**. **Note:** *If the halves do not separate easily, make sure all fasteners have been removed. Do not try to separate the halves by levering against the crankcase mating surfaces as they are easily scored and will leak oil. A leverage point is cast into the crankcase at the front of the engine.* The lower crankcase half will come away with the oil pump and the selector drum and forks, leaving the crankshaft, cam chain tensioner blade and transmission shafts in the upper crankcase half.

12 Remove the four locating dowels from the crankcase if they are loose (they could be in

24.9 Remove the main oil gallery plug (arrowed) for access to the crankcase bolt next to it

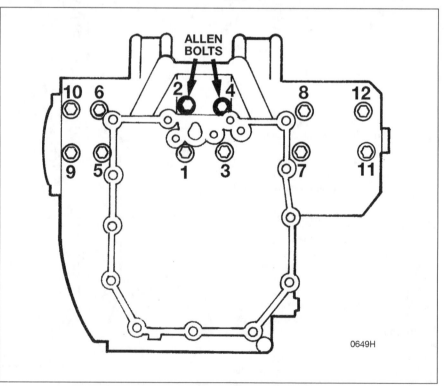

24.10 8 mm lower crankcase bolt TIGHTENING sequence

24.11 Carefully separate the lower half from the upper half and lift it away

24.12 Remove the four dowels (arrowed) if they are loose

either crankcase half), noting their locations **(see illustration)**. Also remove the three oil passage O-rings from the upper crankcase half **(see illustration 24.20)**. Discard these as new ones must be used.

13 Remove the output shaft oil seal from the left-hand end of the output shaft and the clutch pushrod oil seal from the crankcase and discard them as new ones must be used **(see illustrations)**. Refer to Sections 25 to 32 for the removal and installation of the components housed within the crankcases.

Reassembly

14 Remove all traces of old sealant from the crankcase mating surfaces.

15 Ensure that all components and their bearings are in place in the upper and lower crankcase halves. Check that the crankshaft thrust bearings and the transmission bearing locating pins and half-ring retainers are all correctly located, and that the cam chain tensioner blade, its cushions, and all oil jets have been installed, if removed. If not already done, fit a new output shaft oil seal onto the left-hand end of the output shaft and a new clutch pushrod oil seal into its cut-out in the crankcase, having first applied grease to their lips where the shaft and pushrod run.

16 Generously lubricate the transmission shafts, selector drum and forks, and the crankshaft, particularly around the bearings, with clean engine oil, then use a rag soaked in high flash-point solvent to wipe over the mating surfaces of both halves.

17 Fit the four locating dowels into one crankcase half **(see illustration 24.12)**. Make sure that the selector drum is in the neutral position (see Section 29).

18 Fit new O-rings into the oil passage holes in the upper crankcase half **(see illustration 24.20)**.

19 Apply a small amount of suitable sealant to the mating surfaces of the lower crankcase half **(see illustration)**.

24.13a Remove the output shaft oil seal . . .

Caution: Do not apply an excessive amount of sealant as it will ooze out when the case halves are assembled and may obstruct oil passages. Do not apply the sealant on or too close to any of the bearing shells or surfaces.

20 Check again that all components are in position, particularly that the bearing shells are still correctly located in the lower crankcase half. Carefully fit the lower crankcase half down onto the upper crankcase half, making sure that the selector

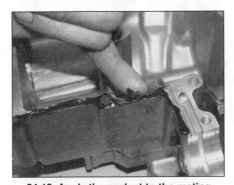

24.19 Apply the sealant to the mating surfaces

24.13b . . . and the pushrod oil seal

forks locate correctly into their grooves in the gears **(see illustration)**. Make sure the dowels all locate correctly and the O-rings stay in place.

21 Check that the lower crankcase half is correctly seated. **Note:** *The crankcase halves should fit together without being forced. If the casings are not correctly seated, remove the lower crankcase half and investigate the problem. Do not attempt to pull them together using the crankcase bolts as the casing will crack and be ruined.*

2

24.20 Carefully fit the lower half down onto the upper half. Note the crankcase O-rings (arrowed)

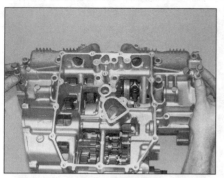

24.23a Install copper washers on bolt
Nos. 9 and 11 . . .

24.23b . . . and secure the oil drain tube
with No. 1 bolt

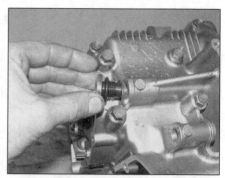

24.31 Use a new O-ring smeared with
grease on the oil gallery plug

22 Locate the oil drain tubes in the lower crankcase, but do not yet install their bolts (see illustrations 24.8b and 24.23b).
23 Clean the threads of the 8 mm lower crankcase bolts and insert them in their original locations, not forgetting to use new copper washers with bolt No. 9 and 11, and that the right-hand oil drain tube is secured by bolt No. 1 (see illustrations). Secure all bolts finger-tight at first, then tighten the bolts evenly and a little at a time in the numerical sequence shown to the torque setting specified at the beginning of the Chapter (see illustration 24.10).
25 Clean the threads of the 6 mm lower crankcase bolts and insert them in their original locations (see illustration 24.8a). On K1 (2001) models onward, fit new sealing washers with the central front bolt and the

rear bolt on the starter clutch housing. Also insert the 6 mm bolt securing the left-hand oil drain tube (see illustration 24.8b), and the single 6 mm nut located just ahead of the transmission output shaft on the left-hand side of the crankcase (see illustration 24.8c). Tighten all the bolts and the nut evenly and a little at a time to the specified torque setting.
26 Turn the engine over. Install the seven 6 mm upper crankcase bolts and the single nut which is located inside the alternator mounting flange (see illustrations 24.6a and b). If the earth (ground) cable was still attached to the engine when the engine was removed, clean the terminal and secure it with the middle rear bolt. Tighten all the bolts and the nut a little at a time to the specified torque setting, accessing the internal bolt as described and shown (see Step 5) (see

illustrations 24.5b and 24.6b). Access to the nut with a torque wrench could prove tricky depending on the tools available.
27 With all crankcase fasteners tightened, check that the crankshaft and transmission shafts rotate smoothly and easily. Check the operation of the transmission in each gear by turning the selector drum by hand as you turn the input shaft. If there are any signs of undue stiffness, tight or rough spots, or of any other problem, the fault must be rectified before proceeding further.
28 Fit the plug into its hole on the alternator mounting flange using a new sealing washer, and tighten it (see illustration 24.5a).
29 Fit the retainer plate for the transmission output shaft bearing and the clutch pushrod oil seal onto the left-hand side of the crankcase (see illustration 18.19b). Tighten the bolts, then bend up the tabs on the plate to lock them in place.
30 Install the transmission input shaft bearing retainer plate onto the right-hand side of the crankcase (see illustration 24.3). Apply a suitable non-permanent thread locking compound to the threads of the screws and tighten them.
31 Install the main oil gallery plug using a new O-ring smeared with grease and tighten it to the specified torque setting (see illustration).
32 Install all other removed assemblies in the reverse of the sequence given in Step 3.

25 Crankcase – inspection and servicing

1 After the crankcases have been separated, remove the crankshaft, bearing shells, cam chain tensioner blade, oil pressure switch, neutral switch and transmission components, referring to the relevant Sections of this Chapter and to Chapter 8 for the oil pressure and neutral switches.
2 Remove the oil jets from the bearing shell cut-outs in the upper crankcase half – pushing them out from the top using a small screwdriver is the easiest way (see illustrations). If not already done carefully pull

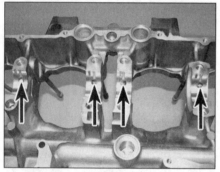

25.2a Remove the four jets (arrowed) . . .

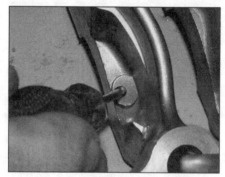

25.2b . . . by pushing them out from
the top . . .

25.2c . . . and withdrawing them with
needle-nosed pliers

25.2d Transmission shaft oil jet (arrowed)

the oil jet out of each end of the cylinder block mating surface with the crankcase using needle-nosed pliers (see illustration 16.13). Also unscrew the transmission shaft oil jets from the lower crankcase half (see illustration). Remove the O-rings and discard them. Clean the oil jets with solvent and blow them through with compressed air if available.

3 Remove all traces of old gasket sealant from the mating surfaces. Clean up minor damage to the surfaces with a fine sharpening stone or grindstone.

4 Clean the crankcases thoroughly with new solvent and dry them with compressed air. Blow through all oil passages with compressed air. *Caution: Be very careful not to nick or gouge the crankcase mating surfaces or oil leaks will result. Check both crankcase halves very carefully for cracks and other damage.*

5 Small cracks or holes in aluminium castings can be repaired with an epoxy resin adhesive as a temporary measure or using one of the low temperature welding kits. Permanent repairs can only be done by argon-arc welding, and only a specialist in this process is in a position to advise on the economy or practical aspect of such a repair. If any damage is found that can't be repaired, replace the crankcase halves as a set.

6 Damaged threads can be economically reclaimed using a diamond section wire insert, for example of the Heli-Coil type (though there are other makes), which is easily fitted after drilling and re-tapping the affected thread.

7 Sheared studs or screws can usually be removed with extractors, which consist of a tapered, left-hand thread screw of very hard steel. These are inserted into a pre-drilled hole in the stud, and usually succeed in dislodging the most stubborn stud or screw. If a stud has sheared above its bore line, it can be removed using a conventional stud extractor which avoids the need for drilling.

8 Check that all the cylinder studs are tight in the crankcase halves. If any are loose, remove them, noting which fits where as they are of different lengths and colours, then clean their threads. Apply a suitable non-permanent thread locking compound and tighten them to the torque setting specified at the beginning of the Chapter.

25.9 Press the jets into their passages

9 Apply clean engine oil to the oil jet O-rings and fit them onto the jets – make sure you fit the right O-ring on the right jet. Fit the jets for the bearing shell cut-outs in the upper crankcase half with the wider shoulder for the O-rings at the bottom (see illustration). Push them into place using needle-nosed pliers (see illustration 25.2c). Fit the jets for each end of the cylinder block mating surface with the wider ends at the top (see illustration 16.13). Thread the transmission shaft oil jets into the lower crankcase half (see illustration 25.2d). Install all other components and assemblies, referring to the relevant Sections of this Chapter and to Chapter 8, before reassembling the crankcase halves.

 HAYNES HiNT *Refer to Tools and Workshop Tips in the Reference section at the end of this manual for details of installing a thread insert, using screw extractors and removing and installing studs.*

26 Main and connecting rod bearings – general information

1 Even though main and connecting rod bearing shells are generally replaced with new ones during the engine overhaul, the old bearings should be retained for close examination as they may reveal valuable information about the condition of the engine.

2 Bearing failure occurs mainly because of lack of lubrication, the presence of dirt or other foreign particles, overloading the engine and/or corrosion. Regardless of the cause of bearing failure, it must be corrected before the engine is reassembled to prevent it from happening again.

3 When examining the bearing shells, remove them from their housings and lay them out on a clean surface in the same general position as their location on the crankshaft to enable you to match any noted bearing problems with its corresponding journal.

4 Dirt and other foreign particles get into the engine in a variety of ways. It may be left in the engine during assembly or it may pass through filters or breathers. It may get into the oil and from there into the bearings. Metal chips from machining operations and normal engine wear are often present. Abrasives are sometimes left in engine components after reconditioning operations, especially when parts are not thoroughly cleaned using the proper cleaning methods. Whatever the source, these foreign objects often end up imbedded in the soft bearing material and are easily recognised. Large particles will not imbed in the bearing and will score or gouge the bearing and journal. The best prevention for this cause of bearing failure is to clean all parts thoroughly and keep everything

spotlessly clean during engine reassembly. Frequent and regular oil and filter changes are also recommended.

5 Lack of lubrication or lubrication breakdown has a number of interrelated causes. Excessive heat (which thins the oil), overloading (which squeezes the oil from the bearing face) and oil leakage or throw off (from excessive bearing clearances, worn oil pump or high engine speeds) all contribute to lubrication breakdown. Blocked oil passages will also starve a bearing and destroy it. When lack of lubrication is the cause of bearing failure, the bearing material is wiped or extruded from the steel backing of the bearing. Temperatures may increase to the point where the steel backing and the journal turn blue from overheating.

HAYNES HiNT *Refer to Tools and Workshop Tips for bearing fault finding.*

6 Riding habits can have a definite effect on bearing life. Full throttle low speed operation, or labouring the engine, puts very high loads on bearings, which tend to squeeze out the oil film. These loads cause the bearings to flex, which produces fine cracks in the bearing face (fatigue failure). Eventually the bearing material will loosen in pieces and tear away from the steel backing. Short trip riding leads to corrosion of bearings, as insufficient engine heat is produced to drive off the condensed water and corrosive gases produced. These products collect in the engine oil, forming acid and sludge. As the oil is carried to the engine bearings, the acid attacks and corrodes the bearing material.

7 Incorrect bearing installation during engine assembly will lead to bearing failure as well. Tight fitting bearings that leave insufficient bearing oil clearances result in oil starvation. Dirt or foreign particles trapped behind a bearing insert result in high spots on the bearing that lead to failure.

8 To avoid bearing problems, clean all parts thoroughly before reassembly, double check all bearing clearance measurements and lubricate the new bearings with clean engine oil during installation.

27 Crankshaft and main bearings – removal, inspection and installation

Note: *To remove the crankshaft the engine must be removed from the frame and the crankcases separated.*

Removal

1 Separate the crankcase halves (see Section 24).

2 Before removing the crankshaft check the thrust bearing clearance. The thrust bearings are located between the crank webs and the

2

27.2 Pull the crankshaft and measure the clearance between the left-hand (outer) thrust bearing and the crank web

27.3a Carefully lift the crankshaft out of the case . . .

27.3b . . . and remove the thrust bearings

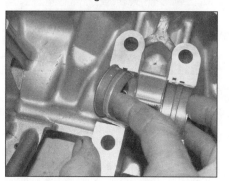

27.4 Remove the main bearing shells

27.10 Measure the thickness of the right-hand (inner) thrust bearing

main bearing housing between cylinder Nos. 1 and 2. Pull the crankshaft as far as it will go toward the starter clutch (left-hand) end – this eliminates play in the right-hand (inner) bearing. Insert a feeler gauge between the crankshaft and the left-hand (outer) thrust bearing and record the clearance **(see illustration)**. Compare the measurement with this Chapter's Specifications. If the clearance is excessive, refer to Steps 10 and 11 for selection of replacement bearings.

3 Lift the crankshaft together with the connecting rods and cam chain out of the upper crankcase half **(see illustration)**. If the crankshaft appears stuck, tap it gently using a soft faced mallet. Remove the thrust bearings, noting how and where they fit – do not get them mixed up **(see illustration)**.

4 If required remove the main bearing shells from their cut-outs by pushing their centres to the side, then lifting them out **(see illustration)**. Keep the bearing shells in order.

5 If required, separate the connecting rods from the crankshaft (see Section 28), and disengage the cam chain from its sprocket.

Inspection

6 Clean the crankshaft with solvent, using a rifle-cleaning brush to scrub out the oil passages. If available, blow the crank dry with compressed air, and also blow through the oil passages. Check the cam chain sprocket and primary drive gear for wear or damage. If any of the sprocket or gear teeth are excessively worn, chipped or broken, the crankshaft must

be replaced with a new one. Similarly check the driven sprockets on the camshafts and the primary driven gear on the clutch housing. If a new crankshaft is installed, make sure you select the correct new bearing shells to go with it (see Steps 23 and 24).

7 Refer to Section 26 and examine the main bearing shells. If they are scored, badly scuffed or appear to have been seized, new bearings must be installed. Always fit new main bearings as a set. If they are badly damaged, check the corresponding crankshaft journals. Evidence of extreme heat, such as discoloration, indicates that lubrication failure has occurred. Be sure to thoroughly check the oil pump, pressure relief valve and pressure regulator as well as all oil holes and passages before reassembling the engine.

8 Inspect the crankshaft journals, paying particular attention where damaged bearings have been discovered. If the journals are scored or pitted in any way a new crankshaft will be required. Note that undersizes are not

available, precluding the option of re-grinding the crankshaft.

9 Place the crankshaft on V-blocks and check for runout at the main bearing journals using a dial gauge. Compare the reading to the maximum specified at the beginning of the Chapter. If the runout exceeds the limit, the crankshaft must be replaced with a new one.

Thrust bearing selection

10 If the thrust bearing clearance was excessive (see Step 2), measure the thickness of the right-hand (inner) thrust bearing, and compare the result to the specifications at the beginning of the Chapter **(see illustration)**. If the thickness measured is below the service limit specified, the right-hand (inner) thrust bearing must be replaced with a new one; there is only one size of bearing, and it is colour-coded green. Install the new bearing and check the clearance again (see Step 2). If the clearance is still excessive, or if the right-hand (inner) bearing was within specifications, select a replacement left-hand (outer) bearing as follows:

11 Remove the left-hand (outer) thrust bearing. Install the right-hand (inner) bearing, then lay the crankshaft in place and push it as far as it will go toward the starter clutch end to eliminate any clearance. Insert a feeler gauge between the crankshaft and the main bearing housing where the left-hand (outer) bearing fits, and record the clearance **(see illustration 27.2)**. Using the table below, select a new left-hand (outer) thrust bearing according to the clearance measured. For example, if the clearance recorded was 2.475 mm on a 600 cc engine, the bearing colour-code required is blue. Re-check the clearance with the new bearing (see Step 2).

600 cc engine		
Left-hand (outer) bearing clearance (bearing removed)	Bearing colour-code required	Bearing thickness
2.415 to 2.440 mm	Red	2.350 to 2.375 mm
2.440 to 2.465 mm	Black	2.375 to 2.400 mm
2.465 to 2.490 mm	Blue	2.400 to 2.425 mm
2.490 to 2.515 mm	Green	2.425 to 2.450 mm
2.515 to 2.540 mm	Yellow	2.450 to 2.475 mm
2.540 to 2.565 mm	White	2.475 to 2.500 mm

750 cc engine		
Left-hand (outer) bearing clearance (bearing removed)	Bearing colour-code required	Bearing thickness
2.435 to 2.460 mm	Red	2.350 to 2.375 mm
2.460 to 2.485 mm	Black	2.375 to 2.400 mm
2.485 to 2.510 mm	Blue	2.400 to 2.425 mm
2.510 to 2.535 mm	Green	2.425 to 2.450 mm
2.535 to 2.560 mm	Yellow	2.450 to 2.475 mm
2.560 to 2.585 mm	White 2	

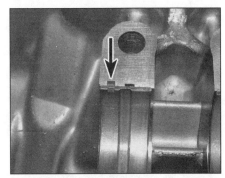

27.14 Make sure the tab on the shell locates in the cut-out in the housing (arrowed)

Main bearing oil clearance check

12 Whether new bearing shells are being fitted or the original ones are being re-used, the main bearing oil clearance should be checked before the engine is reassembled. Main bearing oil clearance is measured with a product known as Plastigauge.

13 Clean the backs of the bearing shells and the bearing housings in both crankcase halves.

14 Press the bearing shells into their cut-outs, ensuring that the tab on each shell engages in the notch in the crankcase **(see illustration)**. The shells with the oil holes locate in the lower crankcase half. Make sure the bearings are fitted in the correct locations and take care not to touch any shell's bearing surface with your fingers.

15 Ensure the shells and crankshaft are clean and dry. Lay the crankshaft in position in the upper crankcase. If removed fit the dowels into one crankcase half **(see illustration 24.12)**.

16 Cut several lengths of the appropriate size Plastigauge (they should be slightly shorter than the width of the crankshaft journals). Place a strand of Plastigauge on each (cleaned) journal. Make sure the crankshaft is not rotated.

17 Carefully fit the lower crankcase half onto the upper half. Make sure that the selector forks (if installed) engage with their respective slots in the transmission gears as the halves are joined and the dowels locate correctly. Check that the lower crankcase half is correctly seated. **Note:** *Do not tighten the*

crankcase bolts if the casing is not correctly seated. Install the lower crankcase 8 mm bolts Nos. 1 to 12 **(see illustration 24.10)** in their original locations and tighten them evenly and a little at a time in the numerical sequence shown to the torque setting specified at the beginning of the Chapter. Make sure that the crankshaft is not rotated as the bolts are tightened.

18 Slacken each bolt in reverse sequence starting at number 12 and working backwards to number 1. Slacken each bolt a little at a time until they are all finger-tight, then remove the bolts. Carefully lift off the lower crankcase half, making sure the Plastigauge is not disturbed.

19 Compare the width of the crushed Plastigauge on each crankshaft journal to the scale printed on the Plastigauge envelope to obtain the main bearing oil clearance. Compare the reading to the specifications at the beginning of the Chapter.

20 On completion carefully scrape away all traces of the Plastigauge material from the crankshaft journal and bearing shells; use a fingernail or other object which is unlikely to score them.

21 If the oil clearance falls into the specified range, no bearing shell renewal is required (provided they are in good condition). If the clearance is more than the standard range, but within the service limit, refer to the marks on the case and the marks on the crankshaft and select new bearing shells (see Steps 23 and 24). Install the new shells and check the oil clearance once again (the new shells may bring bearing clearance within the specified

range). Always renew all of the shells at the same time.

22 If the clearance is greater than the service limit listed in this Chapter's Specifications (even with new shells), measure the diameter of the crankshaft journals with a micrometer and compare your findings with this Chapter's Specifications **(see illustration)**. By measuring the diameter at a number of points around each journal's circumference, you'll be able to determine whether or not the journal is out-of-round. Also take a measurement at each end of the journal, near the crank throws, as well as in the middle, to determine if the journal is tapered. If the journals are worn replace the crankshaft with a new one, then select the appropriate shells for it.

Main bearing shell selection

23 New bearing shells are supplied on a selected fit basis. Code numbers stamped on various components are used to identify the correct replacement bearings. The crankshaft main bearing journal size letters, one letter for each journal (either an A, a B or a C), are stamped on the outside of the crankshaft left-hand web **(see illustration)**. The corresponding main bearing housing size letters (either an A or a B), are stamped into the rear of the upper crankcase half **(see illustration)**. The first letter of each set of six is for the outer left-hand journal, the second for the middle left-hand, the third for the inner

2

27.22 Measure the diameter of each crankshaft journal

27.23a Crankshaft main bearing journal size letters

27.23b Crankshaft main bearing housing size letters

left-hand, the fourth for the inner right-hand, the fifth for the middle right-hand and the sixth for the outer right-hand. **Note:** *Referrals to left- and right-hand are made as though the engine is the correct way up. Do not confuse the two if the engine is upside down.*

24 A range of bearing shells is available. To select the correct bearing for a particular journal, using the table below cross-refer the main bearing journal size letter (stamped on the crank web) with the main bearing housing size letter (stamped on the crankcase) to determine the colour code of the bearing required. For example, if the journal code is C, and the housing code is B, then the bearing required is Yellow.

27.25 Loop the cam chain around the sprocket

27.28 Smear grease onto the back of each bearing to hold them in place – the oil groove must face out

Crankcase housing code	Crankshaft journal code		
	A (31.992 to 32.000 mm)	**B** (31.984 to 31.992 mm)	**C** (31.976 to 31.984 mm)
A (35.000 to 35.008 mm)	**Green** (1.480 to 1.484 mm)	**Black** (1.484 to 1.488 mm)	**Brown** (1.488 to 1.492 mm)
B (35.008 to 35.016 mm)	**Black** (1.484 to 1.488 mm)	**Brown** (1.488 to 1.492 mm)	**Yellow** (1.492 to 1.496 mm)

Installation

25 If removed, fit the connecting rods onto the crankshaft (see Section 28), and loop the cam chain around its sprocket **(see illustration)**.

26 Clean the backs of the bearing shells and the bearing cut-outs in both crankcase halves. If new shells are being fitted, ensure that all traces of the protective grease are cleaned off

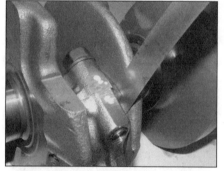

28.2 Slip a feeler gauge between the connecting rod and the crank web to check side clearance

28.3 This number indicates the connecting rod bearing size and faces to the back – make your own marks to indicate cylinder number

using paraffin (kerosene). Wipe dry the shells and crankcase halves with a lint-free cloth. Make sure all the oil passages and holes are clear, and blow them through with compressed air if it is available.

27 Lubricate each shell, preferably with molybdenum paste, or if not available then with clean engine oil. Press the bearing shells into their locations. The shells with the oil holes locate in the lower crankcase half. Make sure the tab on each shell engages in the cut-out in the casing **(see illustration 27.14)**. Make sure the bearings are fitted in the correct locations and take care not to touch any shell's bearing surface with your fingers.

28 Smear the backs of the thrust bearings with grease to hold them in place, then fit them into their correct locations (do not mix them up – the right-hand (inner) bearing is colour-coded green), making sure that the oil grooves face out **(see illustration)**. Take care not to dislodge them when installing the crankshaft.

29 Lower the crankshaft into position in the upper crankcase, feeding the cam chain down through its tunnel **(see illustration 27.3a)**.

30 Reassemble the crankcase halves (see Section 24).

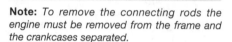

28 Connecting rods – removal, inspection and installation

Note: *To remove the connecting rods the engine must be removed from the frame and the crankcases separated.*

Removal

1 Remove the crankshaft (see Section 27).

2 Before separating the rods from the crankshaft, measure the side clearance on each rod with a feeler gauge **(see illustration)**. If the clearance on any rod is greater than the service limit listed in this Chapter's Specifications, measure the big-end and crankpin widths as described in Step 8.

3 Using paint or a felt marker pen, mark the relevant cylinder identity on each connecting rod. Mark across the join between rod and cap and take note which side of the rod faces the front of the engine to ensure they are fitted the correct way around on reassembly. Note that the number already across the rod and cap indicates bearing size grade, not cylinder number, and that this number faces the rear of the engine **(see illustration)**.

28.4a Unscrew the bolts (arrowed) on 750 cc engines or nuts (600 cc engine) . . .

28.4b . . . and separate the rods from the crankshaft

28.5 Remove the big-end shells

28.8a Measure the width of the connecting rod . . .

28.8b . . . and of the corresponding crankpin

4 Unscrew the big-end cap nuts (600 cc engine) or bolts (750 cc engine) and separate the rod and cap from the crankpin **(see illustrations)**. On the 600 cc engine do not remove the bolts from the connecting rods. Keep the rod, cap, nuts or bolts, and (if they are to be reused) the bearing shells together in their correct positions to ensure correct installation.

5 If required remove the big-end bearing shells from their cut-outs by pushing their centres to the side, then lifting them out **(see illustration)**. Keep the bearing shells in order.

Inspection

6 Check the connecting rods for cracks and other obvious damage.

7 If not already done (see Section 16), apply clean engine oil to the piston pin, insert it into the connecting rod small-end and check for any freeplay between the two. Measure the pin external diameter and the small-end bore diameter and compare the measurements to the specifications at the beginning of the Chapter **(see illustration 16.12b)**. Renew components that are worn beyond the specified limits.

8 If the side clearance measured in Step 2 exceeds the service limit specified, measure the width of the connecting rod big-end and the width of the crankpin **(see illustrations)**. Compare the results to the specifications at the beginning of the Chapter, and replace whichever component exceeds those specifications with a new one.

9 Refer to Section 26 and examine the connecting rod bearing shells. If they are scored, badly scuffed or appear to have seized, new shells must be installed. Always fit new shells in the connecting rods as a set. If they are badly damaged, check the corresponding crankpin. Evidence of extreme heat, such as discoloration, indicates that lubrication failure has occurred. Be sure to thoroughly check the oil pump, pressure relief valve and pressure regulator as well as all oil holes and passages before reassembling the engine.

10 Have the rods checked for twist and bend by a Suzuki dealer if you are in doubt about their straightness.

Oil clearance check

11 Whether new bearing shells are being fitted or the original ones are being re-used, the connecting rod bearing oil clearance should be checked prior to reassembly. Check one rod at a time.

12 Clean the backs of the bearing shells and the bearing locations in both the connecting rod and cap. Also clean the crankpin journal on the crankshaft.

13 Press the bearing shells into their locations, ensuring that the tab on each shell engages the cut-out in the connecting rod/cap **(see illustration)**. Make sure the bearings are fitted in the correct locations and take care not to touch any shell's bearing surface with your fingers.

14 Cut a length of the appropriate size Plastigauge (it should be slightly shorter than the width of the crankpin). Place a strand of Plastigauge on the crankpin journal and fit the connecting rod and cap. Make sure they are fitted the correct way around so the previously made markings align. Fit the nuts or bolts and tighten them in two stages, first to the initial torque setting specified at the beginning of the Chapter, and then to the final torque setting specified, whilst ensuring that the connecting rod does not rotate. Slacken the nuts or bolts and remove the connecting rod, again taking great care not to rotate the crankshaft.

15 Compare the width of the crushed Plastigauge on the crankpin to the scale printed on the Plastigauge envelope to obtain

the connecting rod bearing oil clearance. Compare the reading to the specifications at the beginning of the Chapter.

16 On completion carefully scrape away all traces of the Plastigauge material from the crankpin and bearing shells using a fingernail or other object which is unlikely to score the shells.

17 If the clearance is within the range listed in this Chapter's Specifications and the bearings are in perfect condition, they can be reused. If the clearance is beyond the service limit, fit new bearing shells (see Steps 21 and 22). Check the oil clearance once again (the new shells may be thick enough to bring bearing clearance within the specified range). Always renew all of the shells at the same time.

18 If the clearance is still greater than the service limit listed in this Chapter's Specifications, measure the diameter of the crankpin journal with a micrometer and compare your findings with this Chapter's Specifications **(see illustration)**. Also, by measuring the diameter at a number of points around the journal's circumference, you'll be able to determine whether or not the journal is out-of-round. Also take a measurement at each end of the journal, near the crank throws, as well as in the middle, to determine if the journal is tapered.

19 If any journal has worn down past the service limit, replace the crankshaft with a new one.

20 Repeat the bearing selection procedure for the remaining connecting rods.

28.13 Make sure the tab on the shell locates in the cut-out in the housing (arrowed)

28.18 Measure the diameter of each crankpin journal

2

28.21 Crankpin journal size numbers

28.23 Install the bolts – 750 cc engine, or nuts – 600 cc engine . . .

Bearing shell selection

21 New bearing shells are supplied on a selected fit basis. Codes stamped on various components are used to identify the correct replacement bearings. The crankpin journal size numbers are stamped on the crankshaft inner left web and will be either a 1, a 2 or a 3 (see illustration). The number coming immediately after the L is for the outer left-hand big-end (cyl No. 1), the next number is for the inner left-hand big-end (cyl No. 2), the next for the inner right-hand (cyl No. 3) and the number coming before the R is for the outer right-hand big-end cyl No. 4). The connecting rod size code is marked on the flat face of the connecting rod and cap and will be either a 1 or a 2 (see illustration 28.3).

22 A range of bearing shells is available. To select the correct bearing for a particular big-end, using the table below cross-refer the crankpin journal size number (stamped on the web) with the connecting rod size letter (stamped on the rod) to determine the colour code of the bearing required. For example, if the connecting rod size is 2, and the crankpin size is 3, then the bearing required is Yellow.

Installation

23 Fit the bearing shells in the connecting rods and caps, aligning the tab with the cut-out in the rod or cap (see illustration 28.13). Lubricate the shells, preferably with molybdenum paste, or if not available with clean engine oil, and assemble each connecting rod on its correct crankpin so that the previously made matchmarks align and the connecting rod size letter is facing the rear of the engine when the crankshaft is installed (see illustration 28.4b and 28.3). Install the nuts or bolts and tighten them finger-tight at this stage (see illustration). Check to make sure that all components have been returned to their original locations using the marks made on disassembly.

24 Tighten the bearing cap nuts or bolts in two stages, first to the initial torque setting specified at the beginning of the Chapter, and then to the final torque setting specified (see illustration).

25 Check that the rods rotate smoothly and freely on the crankpins. If there are any signs of roughness or tightness, remove the rods and re-check the bearing clearance.

Sometimes tapping the bottom of the connecting rod cap will relieve tightness, but if in doubt, recheck the clearances.

26 Install the crankshaft (see Section 27).

29 Selector drum and forks – removal, inspection and installation

Note: Access to the selector drum and forks is easiest after the crankcases have been separated, though if they are the only components you want to access you can do so with them joined. A procedure is given for both methods.

Removal

Crankcases joined

1 Remove the engine from the frame (see Section 5). Remove the gearchange mechanism (see Section 20), the sump (see Section 23), and the neutral switch (see Chapter 8).

2 Before removing the selector forks, it is best to mark them according to their location and orientation as an aid to installation.

3 Withdraw the fork shaft from the right-hand side of the crankcase – you will probably need to tease it out initially using a pair of pliers (see illustration). Pivot the forks out of their tracks in the selector drum.

4 Unhook the stopper arm return spring from its lug in the crankcase (see illustration). Remove the circlip securing the stopper arm on its shaft, then slide the arm off. If required, unscrew the stopper arm shaft from the outside of the crankcase and remove it.

5 Remove the circlip from the left-hand end of the selector drum, then slide the drum out of the right-hand side of the case, taking care not to let the stopper arm cam fall off the end

Crankcase housing code	Crankshaft journal code		
	1 (33.992 to 34.000 mm)	2 (33.984 to 33.992 mm)	3 (33.976 to 33.984 mm)
1 (37.000 to 37.008 mm)	Green (1.480 to 1.484 mm)	Black (1.484 to 1.488 mm)	Brown (1.488 to 1.492 mm)
2 (37.008 to 37.016 mm)	Black (1.484 to 1.488 mm)	Brown (1.488 to 1.492 mm)	Yellow (1.492 to 1.496 mm)

28.24 . . . and tighten them as described to the specified torque setting

29.3 Withdraw the selector fork shaft

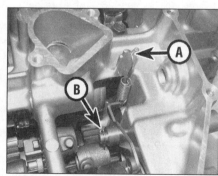

29.4 Unhook the spring (A), then remove the circlip (B) and slide the arm off the shaft

29.5a Remove the circlip . . .

29.5b . . . and slide the drum out – keep a finger on the cam to prevent it dropping off the end of the drum

29.6a Withdraw the forks from the crankcase . . .

as you do (see illustrations). If required, slide the cam off the end of the drum, noting how the slot in the plate locates over the pin in the drum (see illustration 29.21b). Take care not to lose the pin – remove it from the drum if it is loose (see illustration 29.21a).

6 Withdraw the forks, noting how they locate (see illustration). Once removed from the crankcase, slide the forks back onto the shaft in their correct order and way round (see illustration).

Crankcases separated

7 Separate the crankcase halves (see Section 24). The selector drum and forks are housed inside the lower half.

8 Before removing the selector forks, it is best to mark them according to their location and orientation as an aid to installation.

9 Supporting the selector forks, withdraw the fork shaft from the right-hand side of the crankcase – you will probably need to tease it out initially using a pair of pliers, then remove the forks (see illustrations). Once removed from the crankcase, slide the forks back onto the shaft in their correct order and way round (see illustration).

10 Remove the neutral switch (see Chapter 8).

11 Unhook the stopper arm return spring from its lug in the crankcase (see illustration). Remove the circlip securing the stopper arm on its shaft, then slide the arm off. If required, unscrew the stopper arm

shaft from the outside of the crankcase and remove it.

12 Remove the circlip from the left-hand end of the selector drum (see illustration 29.5a), then slide the drum out of the right-hand side of the case, noting that the stopper arm cam might fall off the end as you do (see illustration). If required, slide the stopper cam off the end of the drum, noting how the slot locates over the pin in the drum (see illustration 29.21b). Take care not to lose the pin – remove it from the drum if it is loose (see illustration 29.21a).

Inspection

13 Inspect the selector forks for any signs of wear or damage, especially around the fork

29.6b . . . and reassemble them on the shaft to keep them in order

29.9a Ease the shaft out . . .

29.9b . . . then withdraw it and remove the forks . . .

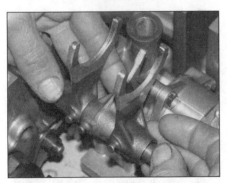

29.9c . . . and reassemble them on the shaft to keep them in order

29.11 Unhook the spring, then remove the circlip (arrowed) and slide the arm off the shaft

29.12 Remove the circlip and withdraw the selector drum

2

29.14a Measure the fork-to-groove clearance using a feeler gauge

29.14b Measure the thickness of the fork end . . .

29.14c . . . and the width of the groove

ends where they engage with the groove in the pinion. Check that each fork fits correctly in its pinion groove. Check closely to see if the forks are bent. If the forks are in any way damaged they must be replaced with new ones.

14 With the fork engaged in its pinion groove, measure the fork-to-groove clearance using a feeler gauge, and compare the result to the specifications at the beginning of the Chapter (see illustration). If the clearance exceeds the service limit specified, measure the thickness of the fork ends and the width of the groove and compare the readings to the specifications (see illustrations). Replace whichever components are worn beyond their specifications with new ones.

15 Check that the forks fit correctly on their shaft. They should move freely with a light fit but no appreciable freeplay. Check that the fork shaft holes in the crankcases are not worn or damaged.

16 The selector fork shaft can be checked for trueness by rolling it along a flat surface. A bent rod will cause difficulty in selecting gears and make the gearshift action heavy. Replace the shaft with a new one if it is bent.

17 Inspect the selector drum grooves and selector fork guide pins for signs of wear or damage. If any components shows signs of wear or damage they must be replaced with new ones.

18 Check that the selector drum bearings rotate freely and have no sign of freeplay

between them and the crankcase (refer to *Tools and Workshop Tips* in the Reference Section for information on bearing checks and removal and installation methods). Replace the bearings with new ones if necessary. To remove the ball bearing, remove the circlip and drift the bearing out of the crankcase (see illustration). To remove the needle bearing, drift it out of the crankcase, noting that once it has been removed it cannot be re-used. Draw or drive the new bearings into place, making sure they enter squarely. Secure the ball bearing with a new circlip.

19 Check the stopper arm roller and the stopper cam for signs of wear or damage and replace them with new ones if necessary. Check that the arm is a light fit on the shaft with no appreciable freeplay between them.

Installation

Crankcases joined

20 Make certain of the correct order and way round for the forks before you install them to make sure you get it right (see illustration 29.6b). Fit each selector fork in turn into the groove in its pinion, making sure they are in the correct position and the right way round (see illustrations). Pivot the forks so they will not get in the way of the drum when it is installed.

21 If removed, fit the stopper cam locating pin into the drum (see illustration). Slide the cam onto the selector drum, making sure the

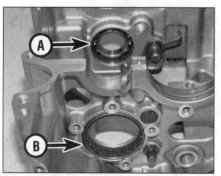

29.18 Selector drum ball bearing (A) and needle bearing (B)

29.20a Slot the right-hand fork into the output shaft . . .

29.20b . . . the centre fork into the input shaft . . .

29.20c . . . and the left-hand fork into the output shaft

29.21a Fit the pin into its hole . . .

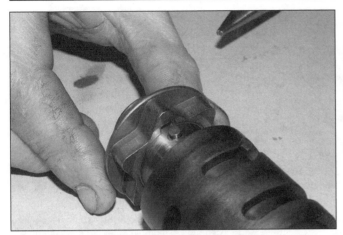

29.21b . . . then fit the cam, locating the slot over the pin

29.24a Pivot each fork so the guide pin locates in the drum track . . .

29.24b . . . and slide the shaft through

29.29 Locate the roller in the neutral detent in the cam

slot locates over the pin in the drum **(see illustration)**.

22 Slide the drum into position in the crankcase. Secure the left-hand end of the drum with a new circlip, making sure it fits properly in its groove.

23 If removed, apply a suitable non-permanent thread locking compound to the stopper arm shaft threads, then install it in the crankcase and tighten it. Lubricate the shaft, then slide the arm on and secure it with the circlip. Locate the arm roller onto the stopper cam, then hook the return spring onto its lug, making sure it is secure in the cut-out. Rotate the drum into the neutral position, so that the stopper arm locates in the neutral detent in the cam, identifiable by its shallower depth.

24 Pivot each selector fork onto the drum, locating the guide pins into the drum tracks. Lubricate the selector fork shaft with clean engine oil and slide it into its bore in the crankcase and through each fork in turn **(see illustrations)**.

25 Install the neutral switch (see Chapter 8).

26 Reassemble the crankcase halves (see Section 24).

Crankcases separated

27 If removed, fit the stopper cam locating pin into the drum. Slide the cam onto the selector drum, making sure the slot locates over the pin in the drum.

28 Slide the drum into position in the crankcase. Secure the left-hand end of the drum with the circlip, making sure it fits properly in its groove.

29 If removed, apply a suitable non-permanent thread locking compound to the stopper arm shaft threads, then install it in the crankcase and tighten it. Slide the arm onto the shaft and secure it with the circlip. Locate the arm roller onto the stopper cam, then hook the return spring onto its lug, making sure it is secure in the cut-out. Rotate the drum into the neutral position, so that the stopper arm locates in the neutral detent in the cam, identifiable by its shallower depth **(see illustration)**.

30 Lubricate the selector fork shaft with clean engine oil and slide it into its bore in the crankcase. As the shaft is installed, fit each selector fork in turn, making sure they are in the correct position and the right way round,

and that its guide pin locates in its track in the selector drum.

31 Install the neutral switch (see Chapter 8).

32 Reassemble the crankcase halves (see Section 24).

30 Transmission shafts –
removal and installation

2

Note 1: *To remove the transmission shafts the engine must be removed from the frame and the crankcases separated.*

Note 2: *Referrals to the right and left-hand ends of the transmission shafts are made as though the engine is the correct way up, even though throughout this procedure it is upside down. Therefore the right-hand end of a shaft will actually be on your left as you look down onto the underside of the upper crankcase assembly.*

Removal

1 Separate the crankcase halves (see Section 24). If not already done, remove the clutch pushrod oil seal from the crankcase

30.2a Remove the output shaft . . .

30.2b . . . and the input shaft

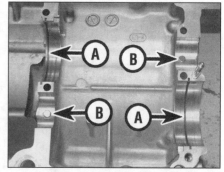

30.3 Remove the bearing retainers (A) and the dowel pins (B)

and discard it as new a one should be used **(see illustration 24.13b)**.

2 Lift the output shaft out of the crankcase, then the input shaft, noting their relative positions in the crankcase and how they fit together **(see illustrations)**. If they are stuck, use a soft-faced hammer and gently tap on the ends of the shafts to free them.

3 Remove the ball bearing half-ring retainers and the needle bearing dowel pins from the upper crankcase half, noting how they fit **(see illustration)**. If they are not in their slots or hole in the crankcase, remove them from the bearings on the shafts.

4 If not already done, remove the output shaft oil seal from the left-hand end of the output shaft and discard it as a new one should be used **(see illustration 24.13a)**. If necessary, the input shaft and output shaft can be

disassembled and inspected for wear or damage (see Section 31).

Installation

5 Fit the ball bearing half-ring retainers into their slots in the upper crankcase half, and fit the needle bearing dowels into their holes **(see illustrations)**.

6 Lower the input shaft into position in the upper crankcase, making sure the hole in the needle bearing engages correctly with the dowel, the ball bearing locating pin faces forward and locates in its recess, and the groove in the bearing engages correctly with the bearing half-ring retainer **(see illustrations)**.

7 Lower the output shaft into position in the crankcase half, making sure the hole in the needle bearing engages correctly with the

dowel **(see illustration 30.6a)**, the ball bearing locating pin faces back and locates in its recess, and the groove in the bearing engages correctly with the bearing half-ring retainer **(see illustration)**.

8 Make sure both transmission shafts are correctly seated and their related pinions are correctly engaged.

Caution: If the ball bearing locating pins and half-ring retainers or needle bearing dowel pins are not correctly engaged, the crankcase halves will not seat correctly.

9 Position the gears in the neutral position and check the shafts are free to rotate easily and independently (i.e. the input shaft can turn whilst the output shaft is held stationary) before proceeding further.

10 Fit a new output shaft oil seal onto the left-hand end of the output shaft and a new clutch pushrod oil seal into its cut-out in the crankcase, having first applied grease to their lips where the shaft and pushrod fit **(see illustrations 24.13a and b)**.

11 Reassemble the crankcase halves (see Section 24).

30.5a Fit the half-ring retainers into their slots . . .

30.5b . . . and the dowel pins into their holes

31 Transmission shafts – disassembly, inspection and reassembly

Note: *References to the right- and left-hand ends of the transmission shafts are made as*

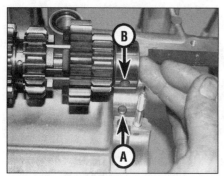

30.6a Locate the dowel (A) in the hole (B), . . .

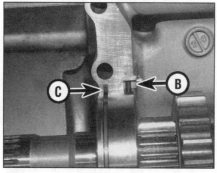

30.6b . . . the pin in its cut-out (B), and the retainer in its groove (C)

30.7 Locate the pin in its cut-out (A), and the retainer in its groove (B)

HAYNES HINT *When disassembling the transmission shafts, place the parts on a long rod or thread a wire through them to keep them in order and facing the proper direction.*

though they are installed in the engine and the engine is the correct way up.

1 Remove the transmission shafts from the crankcase (see Section 30). Always disassemble the transmission shafts separately to avoid mixing up the components **(see illustrations)**.

Input shaft disassembly

2 Remove the needle bearing and oil seal from the left-hand end of the shaft, noting which way round the seal fits **(see illustrations 31.20b and a)**.

3 Reach behind the 6th gear pinion with circlip pliers, spread the circlip and slide it

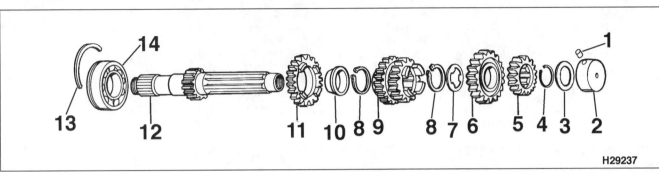

31.1a Input shaft components

1 Dowel pin	5 2nd gear pinion	9 3rd/4th gear pinion	12 Input shaft with integral 1st
2 Needle bearing	6 6th gear pinion	10 5th gear pinion	gear pinion
3 Oil seal	7 Splined washer	bush	13 Half-ring retainer
4 Snap-ring	8 Circlip	11 5th gear pinion	14 Ball bearing

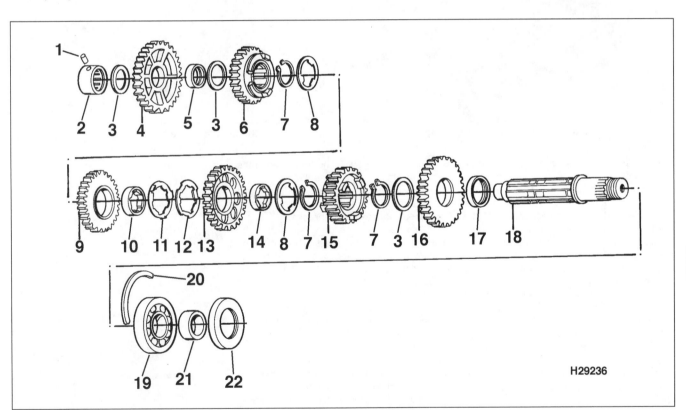

31.1b Output shaft components

1 Dowel pin	7 Circlip	12 Inner (slotted)	17 2nd gear pinion bush
2 Needle bearing	8 Splined washer	lockwasher	18 Output shaft
3 Thrust washer	9 4th gear pinion	13 3rd gear pinion	19 Ball bearing
4 1st gear pinion	10 4th gear pinion bush	14 3rd gear pinion bush	20 Half-ring retainer
5 1st gear pinion bush	11 Outer (tabbed)	15 6th gear pinion	21 Spacer
6 5th gear pinion	lockwasher	16 2nd gear pinion	22 Oil seal

2

31.3a Release the circlip from its groove . . .

31.3b . . . then slide it back along with the two end pinions . . .

31.3c . . . and remove the snap-ring

31.13a Check the ball bearings . . .

toward the 3rd/4th gear pinion **(see illustrations)**. Slide the 6th and 2nd gear pinions back to expose the snap-ring on the end of the shaft, then remove it **(see illustration)**. Slide the 2nd gear pinion off the shaft, noting which way round it fits or having marked its outer face as a guide, then slide the 6th gear pinion off the shaft, followed by the splined washer **(see illustrations 31.19a and 31.18b and a)**.

4 Remove the circlip, then slide the combined 3rd/4th gear pinion off the shaft **(see illustrations 31.17b and a)**.

5 Remove the circlip securing the 5th gear pinion, then slide the pinion and its shouldered bush off the shaft **(see illustrations 31.16d, c, b and a)**.

6 The 1st gear pinion is integral with the shaft.

Input shaft inspection

7 Wash all of the components in clean solvent and dry them off.

8 Check the gear teeth for cracking chipping, pitting and other obvious wear or damage. Any pinion that is damaged as such must be renewed.

9 Inspect the dogs and the dog holes in the gears for cracks, chips, and excessive wear especially in the form of rounded edges. Make sure mating gears engage properly. Renew the paired gears as a set if necessary.

10 Check for signs of scoring or bluing on the pinions, bushes and shaft. This could be caused by overheating due to inadequate lubrication. Check that all the oil holes and passages are clear. Renew any damaged pinions or bushes.

11 Check that each pinion moves freely on the shaft or bush but without undue freeplay. Check that each bush moves freely on the shaft but without undue freeplay.

12 The shaft is unlikely to sustain damage unless the engine has seized, placing an unusually high loading on the transmission, or the machine has covered a very high mileage. Check the surface of the shaft, especially where a pinion turns on it, and renew the shaft if it has scored or picked up, or if there are any cracks. Damage of any kind can only be cured by renewal.

13 Check that the transmission shaft bearings rotate freely and smoothly and are tight on the shaft **(see illustrations)**. Remove

the old bearings and fit new ones if necessary (see *Tools and Workshop Tips* in the Reference Section).

14 Discard all the circlips and the snap-ring as new ones must be used.

Input shaft reassembly

15 During reassembly, apply molybdenum disulphide oil (a 50/50 mixture of molybdenum disulphide paste or grease and clean engine

31.13b . . . and needle bearings as described

31.16a Slide the 5th gear pinion . . .

31.16b . . . and its bush onto the shaft . . .

31.16c . . . locating the bush as shown . . .

31.16d . . . then fit the circlip . . .

oil) to the mating surfaces of the shaft, pinions and bushes. When installing the circlips, use new ones and do not expand the ends any further than is necessary. Install the stamped circlips so that their chamfered side faces the pinion it secures, i.e. so that its sharp edge faces the direction of thrust load (see *correct*

fitting of a stamped circlip illustration in Tools and Workshop Tips of the Reference section).
16 Slide the 5th gear pinion, with its dogs facing away from the integral 1st gear, onto the left-hand end of the shaft **(see illustration)**. Slide the 5th gear bush onto the shaft so that it fits into the pinion **(see**

illustrations). Install the circlip, making sure that it locates correctly in the groove in the shaft **(see illustrations)**.
17 Slide the combined 3rd/4th gear pinion onto the shaft, so that the larger (4th gear) pinion faces the 5th gear pinion dogs **(see illustration)**. Fit the circlip onto the shaft but

31.16e . . . locating it in its groove

31.17a Slide the 3rd/4th gear pinion onto the shaft . . .

2

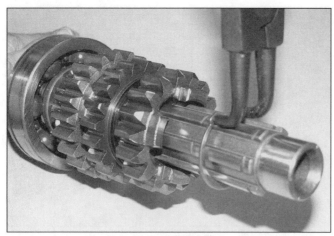

31.17b . . . then fit the circlip . . .

31.17c . . . sliding it beyond its groove

31.18a Slide the thrust washer . . .

31.18b . . . and the 6th gear pinion onto the shaft

do not locate it in its groove – slide it past the groove and as far towards the 3rd/4th gear pinion as possible (see illustrations).

18 Slide the splined thrust washer onto the shaft (see illustration). Slide the 6th gear pinion onto the shaft, with its dog holes facing the dogs on the 3rd gear pinion (see illustration).

19 Slide the 2nd gear pinion onto the shaft with the slightly shouldered side facing in and secure it with the snap-ring, making sure it is properly seated in its groove (see illustration and 31.3c); note that the pinion should have a recess in its outer face to accommodate the snap-ring. Now slide the 6th and 2nd gear pinions along to expose the groove for the 3rd/4th gear pinion circlip, then move the circlip along the shaft and fit it into the groove (see illustrations).

31.19a Slide the 2nd gear pinion onto the shaft

31.19b Slide the pinions to the end of the shaft then slide the circlip along . . .

31.19c ... locating it in its groove

31.20a Fit the oil seal as described ...

20 Slide the oil seal onto the shaft making sure it is the correct way round – the outer rim should be slightly raised away from the pinion **(see illustration)**. Lubricate the needle bearing and slide it onto the end of the shaft **(see illustration)**.
21 Check that all components have been correctly installed **(see illustration)**.

Output shaft disassembly

22 Remove the needle bearing and thrust washer from the right-hand end of the shaft **(see illustrations 31.37d and c)**.
23 Slide the 1st gear pinion and its bush off the shaft, followed by the thrust washer and the 5th gear pinion **(see illustrations 31.37b and a and 31.36b and a)**.
24 Remove the circlip securing the 4th gear pinion, then slide the thrust washer, the pinion and its splined bush off the shaft **(see illustration 31.35d, c, b and a)**.
25 Slide the tabbed lockwasher off the shaft, then turn the slotted splined washer to offset the splines and slide it off the shaft, noting how they fit together **(see illustrations 31.34c and a)**.

26 Slide the 3rd gear pinion, its bush and the splined washer off the shaft **(see illustrations 31.33c, b and a)**.
27 Remove the circlip securing the 6th gear pinion, then slide the pinion off the shaft **(see illustrations 31.32b and a)**.
28 Remove the circlip securing the 2nd gear pinion, then slide the thrust washer, the pinion and its bush off the shaft **(see illustrations 31.31d, c, b and a)**.

Output shaft inspection

29 Refer to Steps 7 to 14 above.

Output shaft reassembly

30 During reassembly, apply molybdenum disulphide oil (a 50/50 mixture of molybdenum disulphide paste or grease and clean engine oil) to the mating surfaces of the shaft, pinions and bushes. When installing the circlips, do not expand the ends any further than is necessary. Install the stamped circlips so that their chamfered side faces the pinion it secures, i.e. so that its sharp edge

31.20b ... then fit the needle bearing over the end of the shaft

faces the direction of thrust load (see *correct fitting of a stamped circlip* illustration in Tools and Workshop Tips of the Reference section).
31 Slide the 2nd gear pinion bush onto the shaft, aligning the oil holes, then slide the pinion onto the bush so that its open side faces away from the bearing **(see illustrations)**.

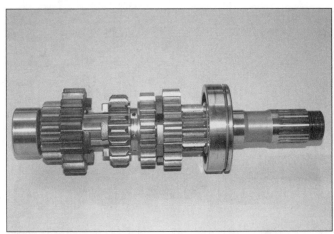

31.21 The assembled input shaft should be as shown

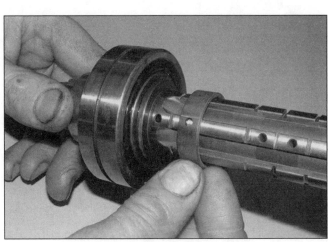

31.31a Slide the bush ...

2

31.31b . . . the pinion . . .

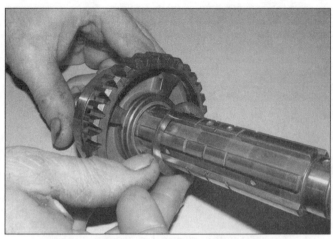

31.31c . . . and the thrust washer onto the shaft . . .

31.31d . . . then fit the circlip . . .

31.31e . . . locating it in its groove

Slide the thrust washer onto the shaft then fit the circlip, making sure it is properly seated in its groove **(see illustrations)**.

32 Slide the 6th gear pinion onto the shaft with its selector fork groove facing away from the 2nd gear pinion, and secure it in place with the circlip, making sure it is properly seated in its groove **(see illustrations)**.

33 Slide the splined thrust washer onto the shaft, followed by the 3rd gear pinion

31.32a Slide the 6th gear pinion onto the shaft . . .

31.32b . . . then fit the circlip . . .

31.32c . . . locating it in its groove

31.33a Slide the splined washer . . .

31.33b . . . and the bush onto the shaft . . .

31.33c . . . then fit the 3rd gear pinion onto the bush

splined bush, aligning the oil hole in the bush with that in the shaft (see illustrations). Slide the 3rd gear pinion onto the bush with its dog holes facing the 6th gear pinion (see illustration).

34 Slide the slotted splined washer onto the shaft and locate it in its groove, then turn it in the groove so that the splines on the washer align with the splines on the shaft and

secure the washer in the groove (see illustrations). Slide the lockwasher onto the shaft, so that the tabs on the lockwasher locate into the slots in the

2

31.34a Slide the slotted splined washer onto the shaft . . .

31.34b . . . locating it as shown . . .

31.34c ... then fit the tabbed lockwasher ...

31.34d ... locating it as shown

outer rim of the splined washer (see illustrations).

35 Slide the 4th gear pinion bush onto the shaft, aligning the oil hole in the bush with that in the shaft, then slide the 4th gear pinion onto the bush with the dog holes facing away from the 3rd gear pinion (see illustrations). Slide the splined washer onto the shaft, then secure them in place with the circlip, making sure it is properly seated in its groove (see illustrations).

31.35a Slide the bush onto the shaft ...

31.35b ... then slide the 4th gear pinion onto the bush

31.35c Slide the thrust washer on ...

31.35d ... then fit the circlip ...

31.35e ... locating it in its groove

31.36a Slide the 5th gear pinion . . .

31.36b . . . the thrust washer . . .

36 Slide the 5th gear pinion onto the shaft with its selector fork groove facing the 4th gear pinion, followed by the thrust washer **(see illustrations)**.

37 Slide the 1st gear pinion bush and pinion onto the shaft with the dog holes facing the 5th gear pinion, followed by the thrust washer **(see illustrations)**. Lubricate the needle

bearing and slide it onto the end of the shaft **(see illustration)**.

38 Check that all components have been correctly installed **(see illustration)**.

31.37a . . . the bush . . .

31.37b . . . the 1st gear pinion . . .

31.37c . . . and the thrust washer onto the shaft . . .

31.37d . . . then fit the needle bearing over the end of the shaft

31.38 The assembled output shaft should be as shown

2

32.2a Remove the circlip . . .

32.2b . . . and the outer washer . . .

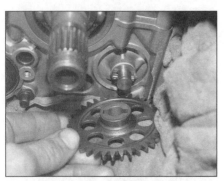

32.2c . . . then slide the gear off . . .

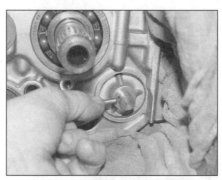

32.2d . . . and remove the drive pin . . .

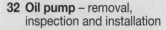

32 Oil pump – removal, inspection and installation

Note 1: *To remove the oil pump the engine must be removed from the frame and the crankcases separated.*

Note 2: *If the oil pressure check described in Chapter 1 shows that the oil pressure is lower than it should be, and all other possible causes (as listed in Chapter 1) have been eliminated, then the pump is worn or faulty and a new one must be installed. No individual components are available.*

Removal

1 Separate the crankcase halves (see Section 24). The oil pump is located inside the lower half.

2 Remove the circlip from the end of the oil pump drive shaft, then remove the outer washer and the oil pump driven gear, noting how it locates over the drive pin **(see illustrations)**. Withdraw the drive pin from the shaft, and remove the inner washer **(see illustrations)**.

3 Unscrew the three bolts securing the pump to the crankcase, then remove the pump **(see illustrations)**. Remove the O-rings from the pump and the crankcase and discard them as new ones must be used **(see illustrations)**.

32.2e . . . and the inner washer

32.3a Unscrew the bolts (arrowed) . . .

32.3b . . . and remove the oil pump

32.3c Remove the O-ring from the oil pump . . .

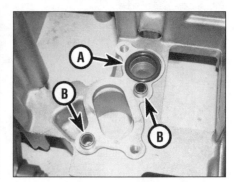

32.3d . . . and from the crankcase (A). Also remove the dowels (B) if loose

Also remove the two dowels from either the crankcase or the pump if they are loose.

Inspection

4 Inspect the pump body for any obvious damage such as cracks or distortion, and check that the shaft rotates smoothly and freely and without any side-to-side play or excessive endfloat.

5 Check the pressure relief valve in the pump for clogging and check that the plunger moves freely in the body.

6 The oil pump fitted to this machine is not serviceable and Suzuki provide no specifications for it, and even go to the extent of advising that it should not be disassembled for cleaning. If the pump is suspected of being faulty a new one must be installed.

Installation

7 Fit a new O-ring into the groove in the crankcase and fit the dowels into their holes in the crankcase, making sure they are secure.

8 Prime the pump with some clean oil and turn the shaft to distribute it **(see illustration)**. Fit a new O-ring into the groove on the pump, then install the pump, making sure it locates correctly onto the dowels. Apply a suitable non-permanent thread locking compound to the threads of the pump bolts and tighten them to the torque setting specified at the beginning of the Chapter – the longer bolt is for the hole shown **(see illustration)**.

9 Reassemble the crankcase halves (see Section 24).

33 Initial start-up after overhaul

1 Make sure the engine oil level is correct (see *Daily (pre-ride) checks*). Make sure there is fuel in the tank.

2 Turn the engine kill switch to the ON position and place the transmission in neutral. Turn the ignition ON. Set the choke enough to encourage the bike to start, but not so much as to allow it to race.

3 Pull in the clutch lever and start the engine, allowing it to run at a moderately fast idle until it reaches operating temperature.

 Warning: If the oil pressure warning light doesn't go off, or it comes on while the engine is running, stop the engine immediately.

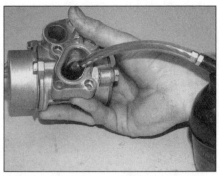

32.8a Feed some oil into the pump

4 Check carefully that there are no oil leaks and make sure the transmission and controls, especially the brakes, function properly before road testing the machine. Refer to Section 34 for the recommended running-in procedure.

5 Upon completion of the road test, and after the engine has cooled down completely, recheck the valve clearances (see Chapter 1) and check the engine oil level (see *Daily (pre-ride) checks*).

34 Recommended running-in procedure

1 Treat the machine gently for the first few miles to make sure oil has circulated throughout the engine and any new parts installed have started to seat.

2 Even greater care is necessary if the

32.8b Threadlock the bolts and fit the longer one as shown

cylinders have been rebored or a new crankshaft has been fitted. In the case of a rebore, the engine will have to be run in as when new. This means greater use of the transmission and a restraining hand on the throttle until at least 500 miles (800 km) have been covered. There's no point in keeping to any set speed limit – the main idea is to keep from labouring the engine and to gradually increase performance up to the 500 mile (800 km) mark. These recommendations can be lessened to an extent when only a new crankshaft is installed. Experience is the best guide, since it's easy to tell when an engine is running freely. The following maximum engine speed limitations, which Suzuki provide for new motorcycles, can be used as a guide.

3 If a lubrication failure is suspected, stop the engine immediately and try to find the cause. If an engine is run without oil, even for a short period of time, severe damage will occur.

GSX600F		
Up to 500 miles (800 km)	5500 rpm max	Vary throttle position/speed
500 to 1000 miles (800 to 1600 km)	8500 rpm max	Vary throttle position/speed. Use full throttle for short bursts
Over 1000 miles (1600 km)	11,000 rpm max	Do not exceed tachometer red line
GSX750F		
Up to 500 miles (800 km)	6000 rpm max	Vary throttle position/speed
500 to 1000 miles (800 to 1600 km)	9000 rpm max	Vary throttle position/speed. Use full throttle for short bursts
Over 1000 miles (1600 km)	12,000 rpm max	Do not exceed tachometer red line
GSX750		
Up to 500 miles (800 km)	6000 rpm max	Vary throttle position/speed
500 to 1000 miles (800 to 1600 km)	9000 rpm max	Vary throttle position/speed. Use full throttle for short bursts
Over 1000 miles (1600 km)	11,500 rpm max	Do not exceed tachometer red line

2

Notes

Chapter 3
Fuel and exhaust systems

Contents

Air filter check and renewal . . . . .see Chapter 1
Air filter housing – removal and installation 4
Air/fuel mixture adjustment – general information 5
Carburettor heater system (UK 750 models) – check 11
Carburettor overhaul – general information 6
Carburettor synchronisation .see Chapter 1
Carburettors – disassembly, cleaning and inspection 8
Carburettors – reassembly and float height check 10
Carburettors – removal and installation 7
Carburettors – separation and joining 9
Choke cable – removal and installation 13
EVAP system (California models) 17

Exhaust system – removal and installation 14
Fuel level sender and warning light sensor – check, removal
   and installation 15
Fuel system check . . . . .see Chapter 1
Fuel tap – check, removal, inspection and installation 3
Fuel tank – removal, installation and repair 2
General information and precautions 1
Idle speed check . . . . .see Chapter 1
PAIR system (Austria, Switzerland and California models) 16
Throttle and choke cable check . . . . .see Chapter 1
Throttle cables – removal and installation 12
Throttle position sensor – check and replacement . . . . .see Chapter 4

Degrees of difficulty

Easy, suitable for novice with little experience 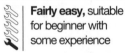	**Fairly easy,** suitable for beginner with some experience 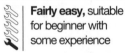	**Fairly difficult,** suitable for competent DIY mechanic	**Difficult,** suitable for experienced DIY mechanic 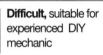	**Very difficult,** suitable for expert DIY or professional 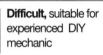

Specifications

Fuel

Fuel grade
  European models . . . . Unleaded, minimum 91 RON (Research Octane Number)
  US models . . . . Unleaded, minimum 87 ((R+M) /2 method)
Fuel tank capacity (inc. reserve)
  GSX600/750F . . . . 20 litres
  GSX750 . . . . 18 litres
Reserve capacity
  GSX600/750F . . . . approx 5 litres after switching tap to RES
  GSX750 . . . . approx 4 litres after warning light comes on

Carburettors – GSX600F

Type . . . . 4 x Mikuni BSR32SS
Pilot jet 12.5
Jet needle
  European models (clip position) 5DH29-54 (3)
  US and Canada models 5DH30-54
Needle jet P-0
Main jet
  Germany full power Y, K1 and K2 (2000 to 2002) models 115
  All other models
    Carburettors 1 and 4 115
    Carburettors 2 and 3 . . . . 112.5
Pilot screw setting (turns out)
  Austria and Switzerland models 2 5/8
  Germany restricted models 2
  Germany full power models
    W and X (1998 and 1999) models 2 1/4
    Y, K1 and K2 (2000 to 2002) models 2
  All other European models 2 1/4
  Canada models 2 5/8
  US models . . . . pre-set and non-adjustable

3

Carburettors – GSX600F (continued)

Float height	13.0 ± 0.5 mm
Idle speed	see Chapter 1
Synchronisation vacuum range	see Chapter 1

Carburettors – GSX750F

Type	4 x Mikuni BSR36SS
Pilot jet	
Austria and Switzerland models	12.5
All other European models	15
US and Canada models	12.5
Jet needle	
Austria and Switzerland models (clip position)	5DF19-53 (3)
All other European models (clip position)	5DF20-52 (3)
US and Canada models	5DF21-53
Needle jet	
European models	P-0
US and Canada models	P-0M
Main jet	
Austria and Switzerland models	
Carburettors 1 and 4	120
Carburettors 2 and 3	117.5
All other European models	117.5
US and Canada models	117.5
Pilot screw setting (turns out)	
Austria and Switzerland models	3
All other European models	
Carburettors 1 and 4	2
Carburettors 2 and 3	1 1/2
Canada models	3
US models	pre-set and non-adjustable
Float height	13.0 ± 0.5 mm
Idle speed	see Chapter 1
Synchronisation vacuum range	see Chapter 1
Heater system resistance (UK models)	12 to 18 ohms

Carburettors – GSX750

Type	4 x Keihin CVK32
Pilot jet	35
Jet needle	N2NQ
Needle jet	2.6
Main jet	105
Pilot screw setting (turns out)	
Austria and Switzerland models	1 3/4
All other European models	2 1/4
Float height	17.0 ± 1.0 mm
Idle speed	see Chapter 1
Synchronisation vacuum range	see Chapter 1
Heater system resistance (UK models)	12 to 18 ohms

Fuel level sender

Resistance – GSX600/750F	
Full position	1.0 to 5.0 ohms
Half way position	approx. 32.5 ohms
Empty position	103 to 117 ohms
Resistance – GSX750	
Full position	4.0 to 10 ohms
Half way position	approx. 51 ohms
Empty position	90 to 100 ohms

Torque settings

Carburettor heaters (UK models)	3 Nm
Exhaust system downpipe flange retaining bolts	23 Nm
Exhaust system mounting bolt/nut	29 Nm
Fuel level sender/warning light sensor bolts	3 Nm

1 General information and precautions

General information

The fuel system consists of the fuel tank, the fuel tap and strainer, an in-line fuel filter (GSX600/750F models only), the carburettors, fuel hoses and control cables.

The fuel tap has an automatic vacuum operated valve with an integral strainer inside the fuel tank. The valve opens when a vacuum taken off an intake duct acts on a diaphragm in the tap. The vacuum is created as soon as the engine is turned over by the starter motor.

On GSX600/750F models it is possible to bypass the vacuum valve by setting the fuel tap to the PRI position, but this should only be done when draining the tank, or when priming the carburettors with fuel after an overhaul. There is also a manual reserve facility (RES) in the tap, and a level sender inside the tank transmits to a gauge in the instrument cluster.

On GSX750 models there is no manual facility on the tap. There is also no reserve facility, but a level sender inside the tank transmits to a fuel gauge in the instrument cluster, and a level sensor transmits to a low fuel warning light in the gauge that lights up when there is approximately 4 litres of fuel remaining in the tank.

The carburettors (one for each cylinder) on GSX600F models are 32 mm Mikuni CV, on GSX750F models are 36 mm Mikuni CV, and on GSX750 models are 36 mm Keihin CV. For cold starting, a choke lever mounted in the left-hand handlebar switch housing and connected by a cable controls an enrichment circuit in each carburettor. The UK GSX750F-Y, K1 and K2 models and UK GSX750 models are fitted with a carburettor heater system to prevent icing.

Air is drawn into the carburettors via an air filter housed under the fuel tank.

The exhaust system on all models is a four-into-one design.

Many of the fuel system service procedures are considered routine maintenance items and for that reason are included in Chapter 1.

Precautions

⚠️ **Warning: Petrol (gasoline) is extremely flammable, so take extra precautions when you work on any part of the fuel system. Don't smoke or allow open flames or bare light bulbs near the work area, and don't work in a garage where a natural gas-type appliance is present. If you spill any fuel on your skin, rinse it off immediately with soap and water. When you perform any kind of work on the fuel system, wear safety glasses and have a fire extinguisher suitable for a class B type fire (flammable liquids) on hand.**

Always perform service procedures in a well-ventilated area to prevent a build-up of fumes.

Never work in a building containing a gas appliance with a pilot light, or any other form of naked flame. Ensure that there are no naked light bulbs or any sources of flame or sparks nearby.

Do not smoke (or allow anyone else to smoke) while in the vicinity of petrol (gasoline) or of components containing it. Remember the possible presence of vapour from these sources and move well clear before smoking.

Check all electrical equipment belonging to the house, garage or workshop where work is being undertaken (see the Safety First! section of this manual). Remember that certain electrical appliances such as drills, cutters etc create sparks in the normal course of operation and must not be used near petrol (gasoline) or any component containing it. Again, remember the possible presence of fumes before using electrical equipment.

Always mop up any spilt fuel and safely dispose of the rag used.

Any stored fuel that is drained off during servicing work must be kept in sealed containers that are suitable for holding petrol (gasoline), and clearly marked as such; the containers themselves should be kept in a safe place. Note that this last point applies equally to the fuel tank if it is removed from the machine; also remember to keep its cap closed at all times.

Note that the fuel system consists of the fuel tank and tap, with its cap and related hoses.

Read the Safety first! section of this manual carefully before starting work.

2.3 Unscrew the two bolts (arrowed)

2.4 Raise the tank using a suitable block of wood

2 Fuel tank – removal, installation and repair

⚠️ **Warning: Refer to the precautions given in Section 1 before starting work.**
Caution: If the fuel tank is full it will be heavy. It is advisable therefore to only remove the tank when it is at least half empty. If the tank is full it is best to drain it before removal. The best way to do this is to obtain a commercially available syphoning tool and a jerry can. Alternatively attach a suitable hose to the tap and feed its open end into a jerry can. On GSX600/750F models, turn the tap to the PRI position and allow the fuel to drain into the can. On GSX750 models, apply a vacuum to the tap via the vacuum hose – the fuel will now flow out.

Removal

1 Make sure the fuel cap is secure. On GSX600/750F models ensure that the fuel tap is in the ON or RES position, not PRI.
2 Remove the seat (see Chapter 8). On GSX600/750F models remove the fairing side panels (see Chapter 7).
3 Unscrew and remove the fuel tank mounting bolts, noting the washers **(see illustration)**.
4 To make access to the hoses easier, raise the tank at the rear and place a suitable block of wood between it and the tank bracket **(see illustration)**.
5 Release the fuel hose clamp and detach the hose from the tap **(see illustration)**. Detach the vacuum hose from the tap **(see illustration)**.

3

2.5a Detach the fuel hose . . .

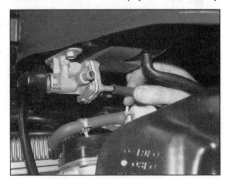

2.5b . . . the vacuum hose . . .

2.5c ... and the breather hose

2.6a Disconnect the wiring connector ...

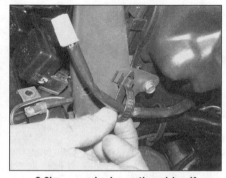

2.6b ... and release the wiring if necessary

Detach the breather hose from its union on the tank **(see illustration)**.

6 Disconnect the fuel level sender wiring connector, and on GSX600/750F models (according to model – depending on which side of the tie the connector is) release the wiring from its tie on the tank bracket **(see illustrations)**.

7 Remove the tank prop if used and lower the tank. Carefully remove the tank **(see illustration)**.

8 Check the tank mounting grommets and rubbers for damage or deterioration and renew them if necessary. Note the collars fitted with the rear mounting grommets.

Installation

9 Installation is the reverse of removal, noting the following:

● If removed, fit the tank mounting grommets and rubbers. Make sure the rubbers remain in place when installing the tank. Do not omit the collars in the grommets.

● Locate the tab at the front of the tank under the front mounting rubber **(see illustration)**. Check that the tank is properly seated and is not pinching any control cables or wires. In particular on GSX600/750F models make sure the in-line filter does not trap any other hose.

● Make sure the hoses are fully pushed onto their unions, and secure the fuel hose with its clamp.

● Start the engine and check again that there is no sign of fuel leakage, then shut if off.

Repair

10 All repairs to the fuel tank should be carried out by a professional who has experience in this critical and potentially dangerous work. Even after cleaning and flushing of the fuel system, explosive fumes can remain and ignite during repair of the tank.

11 If the fuel tank is removed from the bike, it should not be placed in an area where sparks or open flames could ignite the fumes coming out of the tank. Be especially careful inside garages where a natural gas-type appliance is located, because the pilot light could cause an explosion.

2.7 Carefully lift the tank off the bike and remove it

3 Fuel tap – check, removal, inspection and installation

Check

1 If the tap is thought to be faulty, it can be disassembled and inspected. The most likely problem is a hole or split in the diaphragm. Before removing and dismantling the tap, check that there are no splits or cracks in the vacuum hose. If in doubt, release the clamp securing the fuel hose to the tap and detach the hose **(see illustration 2.5a)**.

2 Place the end in a container suitable for holding fuel. Detach the vacuum hose from

3.4a Unscrew the bolts (arrowed) ...

2.9 Make sure the tab locates correctly

the tap **(see illustration 2.5b)**. Attach a good spare hose to the vacuum union and apply a vacuum to the hose. If fuel does not flow through the tap (and there is definitely fuel in the tank), or if fuel flows when there is no vacuum applied, remove and inspect the tap as described below.

Removal

3 Remove the fuel tank (see Section 2).

4 Unscrew the bolts securing the tap to the tank and withdraw the tap, noting its orientation **(see illustrations)**. Discard the O-ring.

Inspection

5 Undo the cover screws and remove the spring and diaphragm, noting how they fit

3.4b ... and remove the tap

3.5 Fuel tap cover screws (arrowed)

3.6 Check the strainer (arrowed) for damage

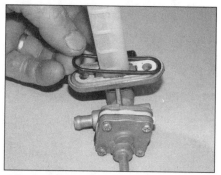

3.7a Install the tap using a new O-ring . . .

3.7b . . . and new sealing washers on the bolts

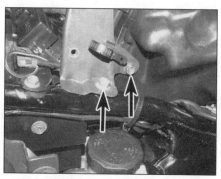

4.2a Unscrew the two bolts (arrowed) on each side . . .

4.2b . . . and remove the bracket

(see illustration). Hold the diaphragm up to a light to check for splits or holes. If any are found a new tap must be fitted – individual components are not available. If the diaphragm is good, reassemble the tap and tighten the cover screws evenly and a little at a time in a criss-cross sequence.

6 Clean the strainer to remove all traces of dirt and fuel sediment (see illustration). Check the gauze for holes. If any are found, a new tap should be fitted – the strainer is not available separately.

Installation

7 Installation is the reverse of removal. Use a new O-ring on the tap and new sealing

washers with the mounting bolts (see illustrations). Make sure the tap is pointing the correct way (see illustration 3.4a). Tighten the bolts.

---

4 Air filter housing –
removal and installation

Removal

GSX600/750F models

1 Remove the fuel tank (see Section 2).
2 Where fitted (according to model), release

the wiring from the tie(s) fitted on the tank mounting bracket (see illustration 2.6b). Unscrew the fuel tank bracket bolts (two secure the bracket to the frame, and two secure the air filter housing to the bracket) and remove the bracket, noting how it fits (see illustrations).

3 Release the carburettor air vent hoses from their guide clips on the air filter cover (see illustration). Detach the engine breather hose from the front of the air filter housing (see illustration).

4 Slacken the clamp screws securing the air filter housing to the carburettor intakes (see illustration). Draw the housing back off the

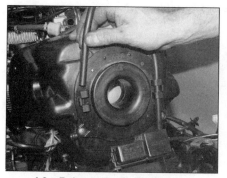

4.3a Release the vent hoses . . .

4.3b . . . then detach the breather hose

4.4a Slacken the clamp screws (arrowed) on each side . . .

3

4.4b . . . and draw the housing off the carburettors . . .

4.4c . . . and detach the drain hose

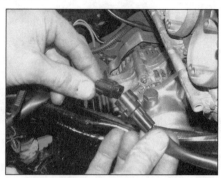

7.4 Disconnect the throttle position sensor wiring connector

carburettors, then lift the rear and detach the drain hose from its union and remove the housing **(see illustrations)**.

GSX750 models

5 Remove the carburettors (see Section 7). Detach the engine breather hose from the front of the air filter housing. Draw the housing forwards and manoeuvre it out from between the frame and the engine.

Installation

6 Installation is the reverse of removal. On GSX600/750F models, do not tighten the clamp screws on the intakes until the fuel tank bracket has been installed as you need to align the bolt holes between the bracket and filter housing. Make sure all the hoses are correctly installed and routed and secured by their clamps.

5 Air/fuel mixture adjustment – general information

Note: *Due to the increased emphasis on controlling exhaust emissions in certain world markets, regulations have been formulated which prevent adjustment of the air/fuel mixture. On such models the pilot screw positions are pre-set at the factory and in some cases have a limiter cap fitted to prevent tampering. Where adjustment is possible, it can only be made in conjunction with an exhaust gas analyser to ensure that the machine does not exceed emissions regulations.*

1 If the engine runs extremely rough at idle or continually stalls, and if a carburettor overhaul does not cure the problem (and it definitely is a carburation problem – see Section 6), the pilot screws may require adjustment. It is worth noting at this point that unless you have the experience to carry this out it is best to entrust the task to a motorcycle dealer, tuner or fuel systems specialist. The pilot screws are located underneath the carburettors, between the float bowl and the intake duct on the cylinder head **(see illustration 8.13)**, and are best accessed using a purpose-made angled screwdriver, available from any good

accessory dealer. Make sure the valve clearances are correct and the carburettors are synchronised before adjusting the pilot screws (see Chapter 1).

2 Before adjusting the pilot screws, warm the engine up to normal working temperature, then stop it. Screw in the pilot screw on all carburettors until they seat lightly, counting the number of turns as an analysis check, then back them out to the number of turns specified (see this Chapter's Specifications). This is the base position for adjustment.

3 Start the engine and reset the idle speed to the correct level (see Chapter 1). Working on one carburettor at a time, turn the pilot screw by a small amount either side of this position to find the point at which the highest consistent idle speed is obtained. When you've reached this position, reset the idle speed to the specified amount (see Chapter 1). Repeat on the other carburettors.

6 Carburettor overhaul – general information

1 Poor engine performance, hesitation, hard starting, stalling, flooding and backfiring are all signs that major carburettor maintenance may be required.

2 Keep in mind that many so-called carburettor problems are really not carburettor problems at all, but mechanical problems within the engine or ignition system or other electrical malfunctions. Try to establish for certain that the carburettors are in need of maintenance before beginning a major overhaul.

3 Check the fuel tap and strainer, the fuel and vacuum hoses, the intake duct joint clamps, the air filter, the ignition system, the spark plugs and carburettor synchronisation before assuming that a carburettor overhaul is required.

4 Most carburettor problems are caused by dirt particles, varnish and other deposits which build up in and block the fuel and air passages. Also, in time, gaskets and O-rings shrink or deteriorate and cause fuel and air leaks which lead to poor performance.

5 When overhauling the carburettors, disassemble them completely and clean the parts thoroughly with a carburettor cleaning solvent and dry them with filtered, unlubricated compressed air. Blow through the fuel and air passages with compressed air to force out any dirt that may have been loosened but not removed by the solvent. Once the cleaning process is complete, reassemble the carburettor using new gaskets and O-rings.

6 Before disassembling the carburettors, make sure you have all necessary O-rings and other parts, some carburettor cleaner, a supply of clean rags, some means of blowing out the carburettor passages and a clean place to work. It is recommended that only one carburettor be overhauled at a time to avoid mixing up parts.

7 Carburettors – removal and installation

> **Warning: Refer to the precautions given in Section 1 before starting work.**

Removal

1 Remove the fuel tank (see Section 2).

2 On GSX600/750F models remove the air filter housing (see Section 4).

3 On GSX750 models pull the side covers off the air filter housing. Remove the side panels (see Chapter 7). Unscrew the bolt securing each side of the air filter housing to the frame. Slacken the clamps securing the air filter housing to the carburettors, then draw the housing back as far as it will go. Note the orientation of the clamps.

4 Disconnect the throttle position sensor wiring connector **(see illustration)**. On UK GSX750F-Y, K1 and K2 models and UK GSX750 models, disconnect the carburettor heater wiring connector. Release the wiring from any ties.

5 Detach the choke cable from the carburettors (see Section 13).

6 Detach the throttle cables from the carburettors (see Section 12). As it is difficult

7.7a Slacken the clamp screws (arrowed) on each side . . .

7.7b . . . and ease the carburettors back out of the intake ducts

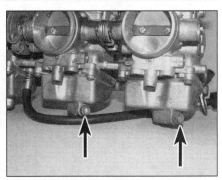

7.9 Carburettor drain screws (arrowed) – slacken each screw in turn and drain all the carburettors

7.10 Intake duct bolts (arrowed)

to detach the cable ends from the throttle cam with the carburettors in situ, just release the cable elbows from the bracket at this stage and free the ends from the cam after the carburettors have been displaced.

7 Slacken the clamps securing the carburettors to the cylinder head intake ducts, then ease the carburettors back out of the ducts **(see illustrations)**.

8 Detach the throttle cable ends (see Section 12), then remove the carburettors; on UK models, where fitted, bring the thermo sensor for the carburettor heaters with them. **Note:** *Keep the carburettors as upright as possible to prevent fuel spillage from the float chambers and the possibility of the piston diaphragms being damaged.*

9 Place a suitable container below the float chambers, then slacken the drain screws and drain all the fuel from the carburettors **(see**

illustration)**. Once all the fuel has been drained, tighten the drain screws.

10 If necessary, unscrew the bolts securing the intake ducts to the cylinder head and remove them, noting how they fit **(see illustration)**. Discard the O-rings as new ones must be used. Check for cracks or splits in the ducts and replace them with new ones if necessary.

Installation

11 Installation is the reverse of removal, noting the following.

● If removed, install the cylinder head intake ducts, using new ones if necessary. Smear each new O-ring with grease and fit one into the groove in the mating surface of each duct. Each duct is coded according to its location. Ducts marked 1-08FO are for cylinders 1 and 2, ducts marked 3-08FO are for cylinders 3 and 4. Install them with the UP mark at the top and apply a suitable non-permanent thread locking compound to the bolts **(see illustration 7.10)**.

● Connect the throttle cables before fitting the carburettors onto the intake ducts.

● Make sure the carburettors are fully engaged with the intake ducts and the clamps are tightened.

● Do not forget to connect the throttle position sensor wiring connector **(see illustration 7.4)**. On UK GSX750F-Y, K1 and K2 models and UK GSX750 models do not forget to connect the carburettor heater wiring connector.

● Make sure all hoses are correctly routed

and connected and secured, and are not trapped or kinked.

● Check the operation of the choke and throttle cables and adjust them as necessary (see Chapter 1).

● Check idle speed (see Chapter 1).

● If the carburettor bodies have been separated, synchronise the carburettors (see Chapter 1).

● If the pilot screws have been disturbed, or new pilot screws fitted, adjust them as described in Section 5.

---

8 Carburettors – disassembly, cleaning and inspection

⚠️ **Warning: Refer to the precautions given in Section 1 before starting work.**

Disassembly
GSX600/750F models

1 Remove the carburettors (see Section 7). **Note:** *Do not separate the carburettors unless absolutely necessary; each carburettor can be dismantled sufficiently for all normal cleaning and adjustments while in place on the mounting brackets. Dismantle the carburettors separately to avoid interchanging parts.*

2 Unscrew and remove the top cover retaining screws, then remove the cover and withdraw the spring from inside the piston **(see illustrations)**. On 750 models remove the air passage O-ring **(see illustration)**.

3

8.2a Undo the screws (arrowed) . . .

8.2b . . . and remove the cover and spring . . .

8.2c . . . and on 750 models the O-ring (arrowed)

8.3 Peel the diaphragm out of its groove and withdraw the diaphragm/piston assembly from the carburettor

8.4a Pull the needle retainer out . . .

8.4b . . . then push the needle up from the bottom and withdraw it, noting the washer

3 Carefully peel the diaphragm away from its sealing groove in the carburettor and withdraw the diaphragm and piston assembly **(see illustration)**. *Do not use a sharp instrument to displace the diaphragm as it is easily damaged.*

4 Carefully pull the jet needle retainer out of the piston using a pair of long-nose pliers **(see illustration)**. Note the spring on its underside – it should stay in place, but take care not to lose it and remove it if it is loose **(see illustration 10.11)**. Push the needle up from the bottom of the piston and withdraw it from the top **(see illustration)**. Note the washer,

E-clip and spacer fitted on the top of the needle. Check the condition of the O-ring on the holder and fit a new one it if it is damaged, deformed or deteriorated.

5 On UK GSX750F-Y, K1 and K2 models and all GSX750 models, disconnect the carburettor heater wiring connector(s) from the heater on the float chamber. If required, unscrew the heater from the chamber.

6 Undo the screws securing the float chamber to the base of the carburettor and remove it **(see illustration)**. Remove the rubber seal and discard it as a new one must be fitted.

7 Undo the screw retaining the float pivot pin **(see illustration)**. Remove the float assembly, noting how it fits **(see illustration)**. Withdraw the pivot pin if required. Unhook the needle valve from the tab on the float, noting how it fits **(see illustration 10.7a)**.

8 Undo the screw securing the float needle valve seat, then carefully pull the seat out, taking care not to damage its gauze filter **(see illustrations)**. Check the condition of the O-ring and renew it if it is damaged, deformed or deteriorated.

9 Unscrew and remove the main jet from the base of the emulsion tube **(see illustration)**.

8.6 Undo the screws (arrowed) and lift off the float chamber

8.7a Undo the screw (arrowed) . . .

8.7b . . . then remove the float assembly

8.8a Undo the screw . . .

8.8b . . . then remove the float needle valve seat

8.9 Remove the main jet (arrowed) . . .

8.10 . . . the emulsion tube (arrowed) . . .

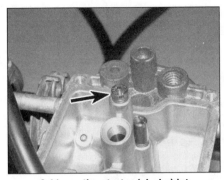

8.11 . . . the starter (choke) jet (arrowed) . . .

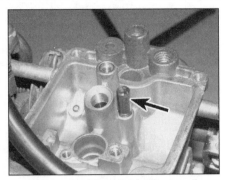

8.12 . . . and the pilot jet (arrowed)

10 Unscrew and remove the emulsion tube **(see illustration)**. With the tube removed the needle jet may come out if it is loose, or otherwise push it down from the venturi – note which way round it fits.

11 Unscrew and remove the starter (choke) jet **(see illustration)**.

12 Unscrew and remove the pilot jet **(see illustration)**.

13 The pilot screw can be removed from the carburettor, but note that its setting will be disturbed (see **Haynes Hint**). If required, unscrew and remove the pilot screw along with its spring, washer and O-ring **(see illustration)**. Note that models sold in certain markets may have a tamperproof cap fitted

HAYNES HiNT *To record the pilot screw's current setting, turn the screw in until it seats lightly, counting the number of turns necessary to achieve this, then fully unscrew it. On installation, the screw is simply screwed fully in then backed out the number of turns you've recorded.*

over the head of the pilot screw, precluding adjustment and access to the screw.

14 Undo the screws securing the choke linkage bar, noting the plastic washers **(see illustration)**. Lift the bar off the arms, noting how it locates. Unscrew the choke plunger nut, using a pair of thin nosed pliers if access is too restricted for a spanner, and withdraw the plunger assembly from the carburettor body **(see illustrations)**.

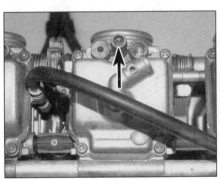

8.13 Pilot screw (arrowed)

15 A throttle position sensor is mounted on the outside of the right-hand carburettor. Do not remove the sensor unless absolutely necessary. Refer to Chapter 4 for details.

GSX750 models

16 Remove the carburettors (see Section 7). **Note:** *Do not separate the carburettors unless absolutely necessary; each carburettor can be dismantled sufficiently for all normal cleaning and adjustments while in place on the*

8.14a Undo the screws (arrowed) and remove the choke linkage bar

8.14b Unscrew the nut (arrowed) . . .

8.14c . . . and withdraw the plunger assembly

3

mounting brackets. *Dismantle the carburettors separately to avoid interchanging parts* **(see illustration).**

17 Unscrew and remove the top cover retaining screws. Lift off the cover and remove the spring from inside the piston. The spring seat may come out with the spring – if not, it will come out with the jet needle (Step 19).

18 Carefully peel the diaphragm away from its sealing groove in the carburettor and withdraw the diaphragm and piston assembly, noting which way round it fits.

Caution: Do not use a sharp instrument to displace the diaphragm as it is easily damaged.

19 Push the jet needle up from the bottom of the piston and withdraw it from the top. Take care not to lose the spring seat, if not already removed.

20 On UK models disconnect the carburettor heater wiring connector(s) from the heater on the float chamber. If required unscrew the

carburettor heater from its adapter, and the adapter from the carburettor body.

21 Remove the screws securing the float chamber to the base of the carburettor and remove the float chamber, noting how it fits. Remove the rubber seal and discard it as a new one must be used.

22 Using a pair of thin-nose pliers, carefully withdraw the float pivot pin. If necessary, carefully displace the pin using a small punch or a nail. Remove the float assembly, noting how it fits. Unhook the needle valve from the tab on the float, noting how it fits.

23 Unscrew and remove the main jet.

24 Unscrew and remove the pilot jet.

25 The pilot screw can be removed from the carburettor, but note that its setting will be disturbed (see **Haynes Hint**). If required, unscrew and remove the pilot screw along with its spring, washer and O-ring. Note that models sold in certain markets may have a tamperproof cap fitted over the head of the pilot screw, precluding adjustment and access to the screw.

 To record the pilot screw's current setting, turn the screw in until it seats lightly, counting the number of turns necessary to achieve this, then fully unscrew it. On installation, the screw is simply screwed fully in then backed out the number of turns you've recorded.

26 Detach the vacuum hose and remove the vacuum blanking caps, then unhook the choke linkage bar return spring from the vacuum take-off adapter. Remove the three screws securing the linkage bar to the carburettors, then remove the outer plastic washers. Lift off the bar, noting how it fits, and remove the inner plastic washers.

27 Unscrew the choke plunger nut, using a pair of thin nosed pliers if access is too restricted for a spanner, and withdraw the plunger assembly from the carburettor body,

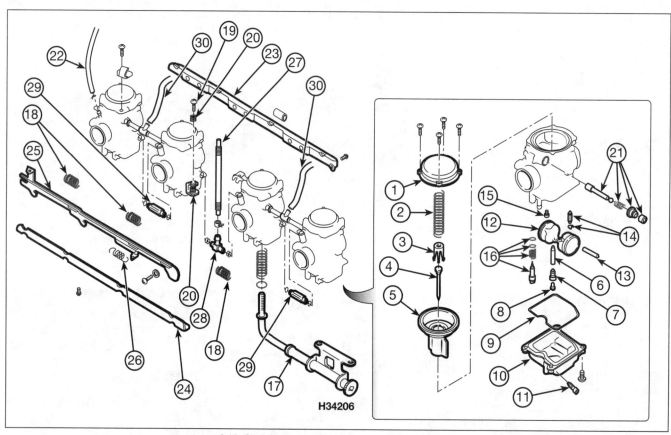

H34206

8.16 Carburettor components – GSX750 models

1 Top cover	8 Main jet	16 Pilot screw, spring, washer and O-ring	23 Upper mounting bracket
2 Spring	9 Rubber seal		24 Lower mounting bracket
3 Spring seat	10 Float chamber	17 Idle speed adjuster cable	25 Choke linkage bar
4 Jet needle	11 Drain screw	18 Spring	26 Return spring
5 Diaphragm/piston assembly	12 Float	19 Synchronisation screw	27 Fuel hose
6 Emulsion tube/needle jet	13 Float pivot pin	20 Springs	28 Fuel hose union
7 Emulsion tube/needle jet holder	14 Needle valve	21 Choke plunger assembly	29 Fuel joint pieces
	15 Pilot jet	22 Fuel tap vacuum hose	30 Air vent hose

8.31 Check the choke plunger assembly as described

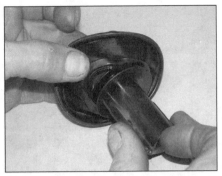

8.34 Peel the diaphragm off the piston and replace it with a new one

8.37 Check the float needle valve and its seat as described

noting how they fit. Take care not to lose the spring when removing the nut.

Cleaning

Caution: Use only a petroleum-based solvent for carburettor cleaning. Don't use caustic cleaners.

28 Submerge the metal components in the solvent for approximately thirty minutes (or longer, if the directions recommend it).

29 After the carburettor has soaked long enough for the cleaner to loosen and dissolve most of the varnish and other deposits, use a nylon-bristled brush to remove the stubborn deposits. Rinse it again, then dry it with compressed air.

30 Use a jet of compressed air to blow out all of the fuel and air passages in the main and upper body, not forgetting the air passages in the carburettor intake.

Caution: Never clean the jets or passages with a piece of wire or a drill bit, as they will be enlarged, causing the fuel and air metering rates to be upset.

Inspection

31 Inspect the choke plunger assembly for wear and damage **(see illustration)**. If the plunger needle or seat is worn or damaged, replace it with a new one.

32 If removed from the carburettor, check the tapered portion of the pilot screw and the spring and O-ring for wear or damage. Renew them if necessary.

33 Check the carburettor body, float

chamber and top cover for cracks, distorted sealing surfaces and other damage. If any defects are found, replace the faulty component with a new one, although an entire new carburettor might be necessary (check with a Suzuki dealer on the availability of separate components).

34 Check the piston diaphragm for splits, holes and general deterioration. Holding it up to a light will help to reveal problems of this nature. On GSX600/750F models, if necessary, separate the diaphragm from the piston, noting how it locates in the groove, and fit a new one **(see illustration)**. On GSX750 models the diaphragm and piston come as an assembly.

35 Insert the piston in the carburettor body and check that it moves up-and-down smoothly. Check the surface of the piston for wear. If it's worn excessively or doesn't move smoothly in the guide, replace it with a new one.

36 Check the jet needle for straightness by rolling it on a flat surface such as a piece of glass. Replace it with a new one it if it's bent or if the tip is worn.

37 Check the tip of the float needle valve and the valve seat **(see illustration)**. If either has grooves or scratches in it, or is in any way worn, they should be renewed as a set. Gently push down on the rod on the top of the needle valve then release it – if it doesn't spring back, replace the valve with a new one. Check the gauze strainer on the valve seat for holes or splits and replace the seat with a new one if necessary.

38 Operate the throttle shaft to make sure the throttle butterfly valve opens and closes smoothly. If it doesn't, cleaning the throttle linkage may help. Otherwise, renew the carburettors – spare parts are not available for the throttle linkage.

39 Check the float for damage. This will usually be apparent by the presence of fuel inside the float. If the float is damaged, replace it with a new one.

40 On UK GSX750F-Y, K1 and K2 models and UK GSX750 models, to check the carburettor heaters and circuit, refer to Section 11.

9 Carburettors – separation and joining

 Warning: Refer to the precautions given in Section 1 before proceeding

Separation

GSX600/750F models

1 The carburettors do not need to be separated for normal overhaul. If you need to separate them (to renew a carburettor body, for example), refer to the following procedure.

2 Remove the carburettors from the machine (see Section 7). Mark the body of each carburettor with its cylinder number to ensure that it is positioned correctly on reassembly.

3 On UK GSX750F-Y, K1 and K2 models disconnect the wiring connector from each carburettor heater.

4 Undo the screws securing the choke linkage bar, noting the plastic washers **(see illustration 8.14a)**. Lift the bar off the arms, noting how it locates.

5 Make a note of how the throttle return springs, linkage assembly and carburettor synchronisation springs are arranged to ensure that they are fitted correctly on reassembly **(see illustration)**. Also note the arrangement of the various hoses, unions, joint pieces and collars, and of the cable brackets **(see illustration)**. Detach the fuel hose, air vent hoses and vacuum hose from their unions if required.

3

9.5a Note arrangement of the various springs . . .

9.5b . . . and of the hoses and their unions

9.6 Unscrew the two long bolts (arrowed)

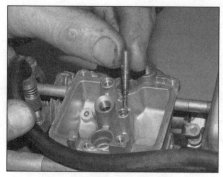

10.2 Install the pilot jet

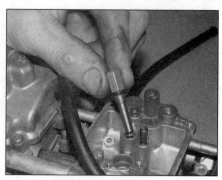

10.4 Install the emulsion tube . . .

6 Unscrew the two long bolts which join the carburettors together and withdraw them, noting how the lower one retains the idle speed adjuster **(see illustration)**. Note the spacers between each carburettor. If it is not essential to separate all the carburettors, only release those necessary and leave the others joined.

7 Mark the position of each carburettor and gently separate them, noting how the throttle linkage is connected, and being careful not to lose any spacers, springs or fuel and vent fittings that are present between the carburettors, noting any O-rings and seals fitted with them.

GSX750 models

8 The carburettors do not need to be separated for normal overhaul. If you need to separate them (to replace a carburettor body, for example), refer to the following procedure.
9 Remove the carburettors from the machine (see Section 7). Mark the body of each carburettor with its cylinder location to ensure that it is positioned correctly on reassembly **(see illustration 8.16)**.
10 On UK models disconnect the wiring connector from each carburettor heater.
11 Detach the vacuum hose and remove the vacuum blanking caps, then unhook the choke linkage bar return spring from the vacuum take-off adapter. Remove the three screws securing the linkage bar to the carburettors, then remove the outer plastic

washers. Lift off the bar, noting how it fits, and remove the inner plastic washers.
12 Make a note of how the throttle return springs, linkage assembly and carburettor synchronisation springs are arranged to ensure that they are fitted correctly on reassembly. Also note the arrangement of the various hoses, unions, joint pieces and collars, and of the cable brackets. Detach the fuel hose and air vent hoses from their unions if required.
13 Undo the screws securing the carburettors to the two mounting brackets and remove the brackets. Note that the carburettors are assembled using a thread locking compound which may make the bracket screws difficult to remove.
14 Mark the position of each carburettor and gently separate them, noting how the throttle linkage is connected, and being careful not to lose any spacers, springs or fuel and vent fittings that are present between the carburettors, noting any O-rings fitted with them.

Joining

15 Assembly is the reverse of the disassembly procedure, noting the following:
● Renew the O-rings on the fuel and vent fittings, and smear them with oil to aid installation.
● Make sure the fuel and breather hoses and elbows are correctly routed and securely connected.

● Check the operation of the throttle linkage ensuring that it operates smoothly and returns quickly under spring pressure.
● Install the carburettors (see Section 7). Check carburettor synchronisation and idle speed (see Chapter 1).

10 Carburettors – reassembly and float height check

> ⚠ **Warning: Refer to the precautions given in Section 1 before proceeding.**

GSX600/750F models

Note: *When reassembling the carburettors, be sure to use new O-rings and seals if the old ones are damaged, deformed or deteriorated. Do not overtighten the carburettor jets and screws as they are easily damaged.*

1 Install the pilot screw (if removed) along with its spring, washer and O-ring, turning it in until it seats lightly **(see illustration 8.13)**. Now turn the screw out the number of turns previously recorded, or as specified at the beginning of the Chapter. Note that where a tamperproof plug was previously fitted (and required by law in that market), the pilot screw must be set to the specified number of turns out and a new plug secured over the screw head – refer to Section 5.
2 Screw the pilot jet into the body of the carburettor **(see illustration)**.
3 Screw the starter (choke) jet into the body of the carburettor **(see illustration 8.11)**.
4 If removed, fit the needle jet into the carburettor, tapered end first. Screw the emulsion tube into the carburettor, using a new O-ring if necessary **(see illustration)**.
5 Thread the main jet into the bottom of the emulsion tube **(see illustration)**.
6 If removed, fit the O-ring onto the float needle valve seat, using a new one if necessary. Press the seat into the carburettor and secure it with the screw **(see illustration)**.
7 Hook the float needle valve onto the tab on

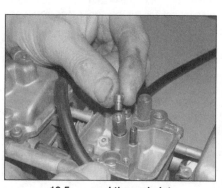

10.5 . . . and the main jet

10.6 Press the valve seat into the carburettor and secure it with its screw

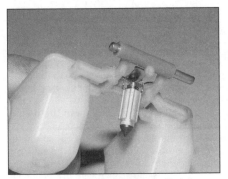

10.7a Hook the valve onto its tab

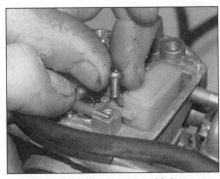

10.7b Secure the pivot pin with its screw

10.8 With the carburettor angled as shown, measure the float height (A)

the float assembly (see illustration). Insert the pivot pin into the float pivot if removed. Position the float assembly onto the carburettor, making sure the needle valve locates in the seat (see illustration 8.7b). Install the pivot pin retaining screw (see illustration).

8 To check the float height, hold the carburettor so the float hangs down, then tilt it back until the needle valve is just seated, but not so far that the needle's spring-loaded tip is compressed. Measure the distance between the base of the carburettor body and the bottom of the float with an accurate ruler (see illustration). The correct setting should be as given in the Specifications at the beginning of the Chapter. If it is incorrect, adjust the float height by carefully bending the float tab a little at a time until the correct height is obtained (see illustration 10.7a). Note: *With the float*

held the same way up as it is when installed, bending the tab up increases the float height – bending it down reduces it.

9 Fit a new seal into the groove in the float chamber, then fit the chamber onto the carburettor and secure it with the screws (see illustration).

10 On UK GSX750F-Y, K1 and K2 models, if removed, apply a smear of thermo-grease (Suzuki pt. no. 99000-59029) to the carburettor heater threads, then screw it into the float chamber and tighten it to the torque setting specified at the beginning of the Chapter. Connect the heater wiring connector(s).

11 Check that the spacer and E-clip are fitted on the jet needle, then fit the washer onto the top (see illustration). If the E-clip was removed, fit it into the 3rd groove from the top of the needle.

12 Carefully fit the needle into the piston (see illustration). If removed, fit the O-ring onto the needle retainer, using a new one if necessary (see illustration 10.11). Check that the spring is fitted to the retainer and is secure. Insert the retainer and carefully press it down until the O-ring is felt to locate (see illustration).

13 Turn the diaphragm inside out so that its rim faces down. Insert the piston/diaphragm assembly into the carburettor, ensuring the needle is correctly aligned with the needle jet (see illustration). Keep a finger on the bottom of the piston to keep it raised (inserting your finger via the air intake) so the diaphragm stays inside out – this will prevent the rim popping out of the groove. Press the diaphragm outer edge into its groove, making sure it is correctly seated (see illustration).

10.9 Fit a new sealing-ring into the groove and install the float chamber

10.11 Jet needle and retainer

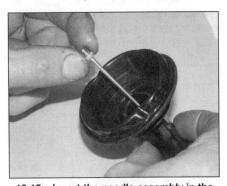

10.12a Insert the needle assembly in the piston

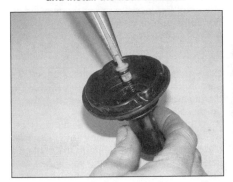

10.12b Fit the retainer onto the needle head

10.13a Fit the piston/diaphragm assembly into the carburettor

10.13b Fit the rim of the diaphragm into the groove

3

10.14 Locate the post in the top of the spring and fit the cover

10.15a Fit the linkage bar . . .

10.15b . . . locating the arms behind the plunger ends . . .

10.15c . . . then fit the screws with their plastic washers

14 On 750 models fit the air passage O-ring **(see illustration 8.2c)**. Fit the spring, locating it over the needle retainer in the piston **(see illustration 8.2b)**. Fit the top cover onto the carburettor, locating the top of the spring over the post in the cover **(see illustration)**. Make sure the diaphragm rim stays seated in its groove and does not get pinched by the cover, then install the cover screws and tighten them. Check that the piston moves up and down smoothly.

15 Fit the choke plunger assembly into the carburettor body and tighten the nut to secure it **(see illustration 8.14c)**. Check the operation of the plunger – the action should be smooth and it should return under its own spring pressure. Fit the choke linkage bar, making sure the slots in the arms locate correctly behind the nipple on the end of each plunger **(see illustrations)**. Fit the plastic washers and secure the linkage bar in place with the screws **(see illustration)**.

16 If removed, install the throttle position sensor (see Chapter 4).

17 Install the carburettors (see Section 7).

GSX750 models

Note: *When reassembling the carburettors, be sure to use new O-rings and seals. Do not overtighten the carburettor jets and screws as they are easily damaged.*

18 Install the pilot screw (if removed) along with its spring, washer and O-ring, turning it in until it seats lightly **(see illustration 8.16)**.

Now turn the screw out the number of turns previously recorded, or as specified at the beginning of the Chapter. Note that where a tamperproof plug was previously fitted (and required by law in that market), the pilot screw must be set to the specified number of turns out and a new plug secured over the screw head – refer to Section 5.

19 Screw the pilot jet into the body of the carburettor.

20 Thread the main jet into the carburettor.

21 Hook the float needle valve onto the tab on the float assembly, then position the float assembly in the carburettor and install the pin, making sure it is secure.

22 To check the float height, hold the carburettor so the float hangs down, then tilt it back until the needle valve is just seated, but not so far that the needle's spring-loaded tip is compressed. Measure the distance between the base of the carburettor body and the bottom of the float with an accurate ruler. The correct setting should be as given in the Specifications at the beginning of the Chapter. If it is incorrect, adjust the float height by carefully bending the float tab a little at a time until the correct height is obtained. **Note:** *With the float held the same way up as it is when installed, bending the tab up increases the float height – bending it down reduces it.*

23 Fit a new seal into the groove in the float chamber, then fit the chamber onto the carburettor and secure it with the screws.

24 On UK models, if removed, install the carburettor heater adapter in the carburettor body. Apply a smear of thermo-grease (Suzuki pt. no. 99000-59029) to the heater threads, then screw it into the adapter and tighten it to the torque setting specified at the beginning of the Chapter. Connect the heater wiring connector(s).

25 Carefully fit the needle into the piston. Fit the spring seat into the piston.

26 Turn the diaphragm inside out so that its rim faces down. Insert the piston/diaphragm assembly into the carburettor, ensuring the needle is correctly aligned with the needle jet. Keep a finger on the bottom of the piston to keep it raised (inserting your finger via the air intake) so the diaphragm stays inside out – this will prevent the rim popping out of the groove. Press the diaphragm outer edge into its groove, making sure it is correctly seated.

27 Fit the spring, locating it over the seat. Fit the top cover onto the carburettor, locating the top of the spring over the post in the cover. Make sure the diaphragm rim stays seated in its groove and does not get pinched by the cover, then install the cover screws and tighten them. Check that the piston moves up and down smoothly.

28 Fit the choke plunger assembly into the carburettor body and tighten the nut to secure it. Check the operation of the plunger – the action should be smooth and it should return under its own spring pressure. Fit the inner plastic washers, then fit the choke linkage bar onto the plungers, making sure the slots locate correctly behind the nipple on the end of each choke plunger. Fit the outer plastic washers and secure the linkage bar in place with the screws. Hook the return spring onto the vacuum take-off adapter, then fit the caps and the vacuum hose.

29 Install the carburettors (see Section 7).

11 Carburettor heater system (UK 750 models) – check

Note: *The heater system is only fitted on UK GSX750F-Y, K1 and K2 models and UK GSX750 models.*

Warning: Refer to the precautions given in Section 1 before starting work.

1 Each carburettor has a heater unit threaded into its float chamber. The heaters are controlled by a thermo-switch.

2 To access the heater units, remove the carburettors (see Section 7). To access the thermo switch for the heaters, remove the fuel tank (see Section 2).

3 To check a heater unit, disconnect the wiring connector(s) from the heater. Using an ohmmeter or multimeter set to the ohms x 1 scale, connect the positive (+ve) probe to the tip of the heater and the negative (-ve) probe to the spade terminal (fitted with one heater) or the float chamber itself **(see**

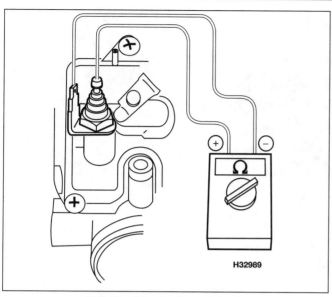

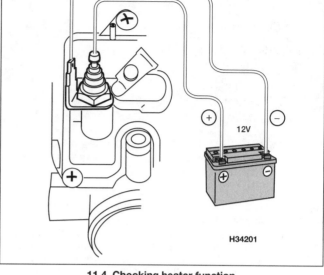

11.3 Checking heater resistance

11.4 Checking heater function

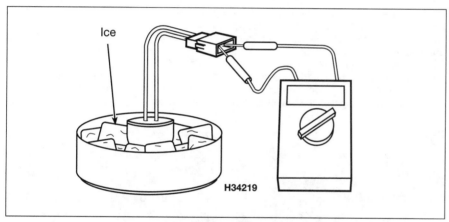

11.6 Checking the thermo-switch

refer to the wiring diagrams at the end of Chapter 8 and check the circuits for damaged or broken wiring.

12 Throttle cables –
removal and installation

 Warning: Refer to the precautions given in Section 1 before proceeding.

Removal

1 Remove the fuel tank (see Section 2).
2 Mark each cable according to its location at both ends. If new cables are being fitted, match them to the old cables to ensure they are correctly installed.
3 Slacken the cable adjuster locknuts and thread them up against the adjusters **(see illustration)**.
4 Displace the carburettors (see Section 7). Move the adjusters down in the bracket until the captive nuts clear the small lugs on the bracket and slip them out of the bracket **(see illustration)**. Hold the throttle cam open and

illustration). The resistance of each heater should be as specified at the beginning of the Chapter.
4 If a meter is not available, connect a fully charged 12 volt battery to each heater in turn, using the terminals as described above. After about five minutes, the float chamber should be felt to be warm **(see illustration)**.
5 If any heater does not perform as described, unscrew it from the carburettor. Apply a smear of thermo-grease (Suzuki pt. no. 99000-59029) to the threads on a new heater, then thread it into the carburettor and tighten it to the torque setting specified at the beginning of the Chapter.
6 To check the thermo-switch, unplug it from the wiring loom. Using a continuity tester or multimeter, insert the probes into the switch wiring connector and check for continuity. In normal or warm conditions, there should be no continuity. Now immerse the switch into a bowl of ice **(see illustration)**. After a few minutes the switch should close and

continuity should be shown. If not, the switch is faulty.
7 If the heaters and the switch are all good, turn the ignition switch ON and check for battery voltage at each heater wiring connector, and at the switch wiring connector in the loom. If battery voltage isn't shown,

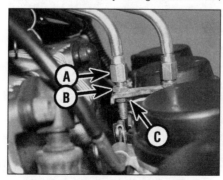

12.3 Adjuster (A), locknut (B) captive nut (C)

12.4a Slip the cables out of the bracket . . .

3

12.4b . . . and detach the cable ends from the throttle cam

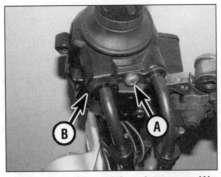

12.5a Undo the retaining plate screw (A) and the ring (B)

12.5b Remove the housing screws and separate the halves

detach the cable ends from it as they become accessible **(see illustration)**.

5 Remove the screw securing the front (throttle opening) cable retaining plate to the handlebar switch/throttle pulley housing, and unscrew the rear (throttle closing) cable retaining ring **(see illustration)**. Remove the handlebar switch/throttle pulley housing screws and separate the halves **(see illustration)**. Hook the cable ends out of the pulley and remove the cable elbows from the housing **(see illustration)**. Mark each cable to ensure it is connected correctly on installation.

6 Remove the cables from the machine noting their correct routing.

Installation

7 Install the cables making sure they are correctly routed. The cables must not interfere with any other component and should not be kinked or bent sharply.

8 Fit the cables into the throttle pulley housing, making sure the throttle opening cable is at the front and the closing cable is at the back. Secure the opening cable elbow with the retainer plate, and thread the closing cable retaining ring into the housing. Lubricate the end of each inner cable with multi-purpose grease, then locate the lower half of the housing and attach them to the pulley.

9 Assemble the housing on the handlebar, aligning its locating pin with the hole in the top

of the handlebar **(see illustration)**. Install the retaining screws and tighten them.

10 Position the carburettors in a convenient place to work on. Lubricate the cable ends with multi-purpose grease. Hold the throttle cam open and fit the rear (throttle opening) cable end down between the carburettors and into its socket **(see illustrations)**. Fit the cable adjuster into the mounting bracket and draw it up so the captive nut locates against the lug on the bracket **(see illustration)**. Tighten the locknut finger-tight against the bracket **(see illustration)**.

11 Fit the front (throttle closing) cable end into its socket **(see illustration 12.4b)**. Fit the cable adjuster into the mounting bracket and

12.5c Detach the cable ends from the pulley

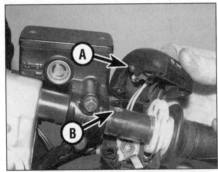

12.9 Assemble the switch on the handlebar, locating the pin (A) in the hole (B)

12.10a Locate the cable between the carburettors . . .

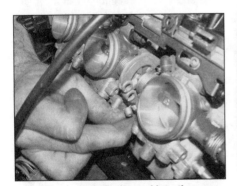

12.10b . . . then fit the end into the cam

12.10c Fit the cable adjuster into the bracket . . .

12.10d . . . and thread the locknut down

draw it up so the captive nut locates against the lug on the bracket. Tighten the locknut finger-tight against the bracket.

12 Install the carburettors (see Section 7). Operate the throttle to check that it opens and closes freely.

13 Check the amount of freeplay in the throttle cable and adjust if necessary (Chapter 1). Turn the handlebars back and forth to make they don't cause the steering to bind.

14 Install the air filter housing (see Section 4).

15 Start the engine and check that the idle speed does not rise as the handlebars are turned. If it does, the throttle cables are routed incorrectly. Correct the problem before riding the motorcycle.

13 Choke cable –
removed and installation

Removal

1 Remove the fuel tank (see Section 2).

2 On GSX600/750F models, draw the choke outer cable end out of its holder, then detach the inner cable end from its socket **(see illustrations)**.

3 On GSX750 models, slacken the choke outer cable holder screw and free the cable from the holder, then detach the inner cable end from its socket.

13.2a Draw the cable out of its holder . . .

13.2b . . . and detach the end from its socket

4 Unscrew the two handlebar switch/choke lever housing screws, one of which secures the choke cable elbow via a retainer plate, and separate the two halves **(see illustrations)**. Detach the choke lever from the housing, noting how it fits **(see illustration)**. Detach the choke lever from the cable, then withdraw the cable from the housing **(see illustrations)**.

5 Remove the cable from the machine noting its correct routing.

Installation

6 Install the cable making sure it is correctly routed. The cable must not interfere with any other component and should not be kinked or bent sharply.

7 Lubricate the cable nipples with multi-

purpose grease. Install the cable in the switch/choke lever housing and attach the nipple to the choke lever. Locate the lever in the lower half of the housing, then fit the two halves of the housing onto the handlebar, locating the pin in the upper half in the hole in the top of the handlebar **(see illustration)**. Install the screws, making sure the elbow retainer is correctly positioned, and tighten them.

8 Attach the lower end of the cable to its socket on the choke linkage arm on the carburettor. Fit the outer cable into its bracket, and on GSX750 models tighten the clamp screw.

9 Check the operation of the choke cable (see Chapter 1).

10 Install the fuel tank (see Section 2).

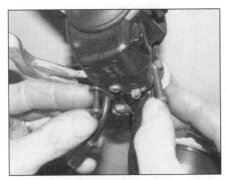
13.4a Undo the screws . . .

13.4b . . . and separate the switch halves

13.4c Detach the lever from the housing . . .

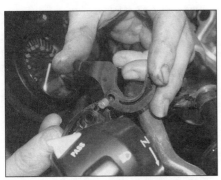
13.4d . . . and the cable from the lever . . .

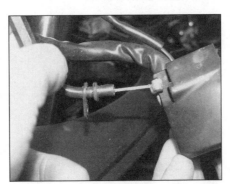
13.4e . . . then draw the cable out of the housing

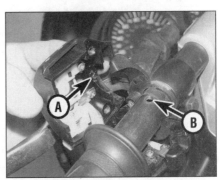
13.7 Assemble the switch on the handlebar, locating the pin (A) in the hole (B)

3

14.2 Unscrew the flange bolts and draw the flange off the studs

14.3a Unscrew the centre mounting bolt

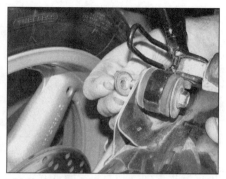

14.3b Unscrew the nut but leave the bolt in place

14.4 Manoeuvre the complete system away from the bike

14.6 Fit a new gasket into each port

- Leave all fasteners loose until the entire system has been installed, making alignment easier. Tighten the silencer mounting last.
- Tighten all nuts and bolts to the torque setting specified at the beginning of the Chapter.
- Run the engine and check that there are no exhaust gas leaks from the exhaust system joints.

15 Fuel level sender and warning light switch – check, removal and installation

> ⚠ **Warning: Refer to the precautions given in Section 1 before starting work.**

Fuel level sender

Check

1 The circuit consists of the sender mounted in the fuel tank and the gauge mounted in the instrument panel. If the system malfunctions check first that the battery is fully charged and that the bulb and fuses are good (see Chapter 8). If they are, remove the sender (see Steps 6 to 8).

2 Connect the positive (+ve) probe of an ohmmeter to the yellow/black wire terminal on the sender connector, and the negative (-ve) probe to the black/white wire terminal. Check the resistance of the sender in both the FULL, HALF and EMPTY positions and compare the readings to those specified at the beginning of the Chapter **(see illustrations)**. If the readings

14 Exhaust system – removal and installation

> ⚠ **Warning: If the engine has been running the exhaust system will be very hot. Allow the system to cool before carrying out any work.**

Removal

1 On GSX600/750F models remove the fairing side panels (see Chapter 7).
2 Unscrew the downpipe flange retaining bolts from the cylinder head **(see illustration)**.

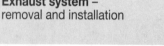

> **HAYNES HiNT**
> *Note that the downpipe flange bolts are very exposed to adverse conditions and are likely to be heavily corroded if the bike is ridden in all weather. It is advisable to apply some penetrating fluid before trying to undo them, and to allow some time for it to work its way in.*

3 Unscrew and withdraw the centre mounting bolt **(see illustration)**. Unscrew the nut on the rear mounting bolt, but leave the bolt in place **(see illustration)**.
4 Support the system, then withdraw the rear mounting bolt and manoeuvre the complete system to release the downpipes from the ports in the cylinder head **(see illustration)**. Remove the gasket from each port in the

cylinder head and discard them as new ones must be fitted **(see illustration 14.6)**.
5 If required, slacken the clamp bolt to allow the silencer to be separated from the header pipes. Hook the gasket ring out of its location.

Installation

6 Installation is the reverse of removal, noting the following:
- Use a new gasket in each cylinder head port **(see illustration)**. Renew any damaged, deformed or deteriorated mounting rubbers with new ones.
- Clean all corrosion off the bolts using a wire brush.
- If the silencer was detached from the header pipes, fit a new gasket ring and tighten the clamp bolt – fully tighten the clamp bolt when the system is in place.

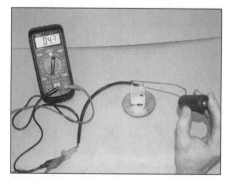

15.2a Fuel level sender test – full position

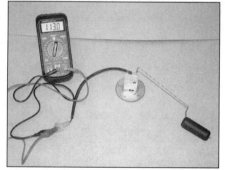

15.2b Fuel level sender test – empty position

15.8a Unscrew the bolts . . .

15.8b . . . and withdraw the sender

15.9 Always use a new gasket

are not as specified, replace the sender with a new one.

3 If the readings are as specified, connect the sender wiring connector and turn the ignition switch ON. With the sender in the FULL position, the gauge should read FULL, and with the sender in the empty position the gauge should read EMPTY (the gauge needle may not respond immediately – you may have to leave it in the position being tested for a few minutes to accurately check the system).

4 If the gauge does not respond as described, check for continuity in the yellow/black wire to the instrument cluster wiring connector, and in the black/white wire to earth, referring to the *Wiring Diagrams* at the end of Chapter 8. On GSX600/750F models remove the fairing centre panel above the headlight to access the wiring connector (See Chapter 7). On GSX750 models remove the headlight from its shell (see Chapter 8). If the wiring and connectors are good, perform the instrument cluster circuit check (see Chapter 8). If all is good, replace the gauge with a new one.

5 Check that no fuel has entered the float due

to a leak, and check that the arm moves up and down smoothly.

Removal and installation

6 To access the sender, remove the fuel tank (see Section 2).

7 If required, connect a drain hose to the fuel outlet union on the tap and insert its end in a container suitable and large enough for storing the fuel. On GSX600/750F models turn the fuel tap to the PRI position and allow the tank to drain. On GSX750 models connect an auxiliary hose to the vacuum hose union on the tap, then apply a vacuum to the hose to open the tap and allow the tank to drain – use a hand pump only, and applying a small vacuum only to avoid damaging the tap. When the tank has drained, on GSX600/750F models turn the tap to the ON or RES position, on GSX750 models release the vacuum and detach the hose.

8 Unscrew the bolts securing the sender and carefully manoeuvre it out of the tank **(see illustrations)**. Discard the gasket.

9 Fit a new gasket onto the sender then

install then sender in the tank, on GSX600/750F models with the wiring to the back and on GSX750 models with the wiring to the middle **(see illustration)**. Tighten the bolts evenly and a little at a time in a criss-cross pattern to the torque setting specified at the beginning of the Chapter.

10 Install the tank (see Section 2), and check carefully that there are no leaks around the sender gasket before using the bike.

11 See Chapter 8 for renewal of the fuel gauge.

Warning light sensor – GSX750 models

Check

12 In normal operation, the fuel level warning light will come on when the ignition is first turned on and extinguish after three seconds – this serves as a check of the warning light system. The light will come on when the volume of fuel remaining in the tank reaches approximately 4.0 litres, and then stay on until the tank is replenished.

13 If the warning light does not work as

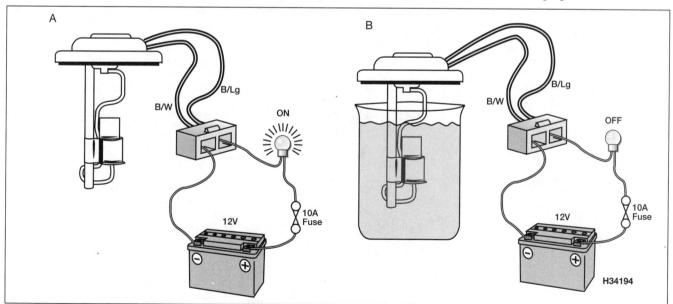

15.14 Warning light sensor test set-ups – GSX750

A With sensor open to the air   *B With sensor immersed in fuel*

described, first check the bulb (see Chapter 8). If that is good, disconnect the sensor wiring connector (trace the wiring from the switch, located in the base of the fuel tank) and check for continuity in the black/light green wire to the instrument cluster wiring connector, and in the black/white wire to earth, referring to the *Wiring Diagrams* at the end of Chapter 8. Remove the headlight from its shell to access the instrument wiring connector (see Chapter 8). If the wiring and connectors are good, check the wiring between the instrument cluster wiring connector and the instrument itself. If that is good, remove the sensor (see below).

14 Connect a test light circuit to the black/white and black/light green wire terminals in the sensor wiring connector as shown **(see illustration on previous page)**. Obtain a container suitable for holding fuel and large enough to contain the switch. Check the operation of the switch by observing the test light first with the switch open to the air, and second immersed in the fuel. Give the light a few seconds to react in each case, and stir the sensor around in the fuel when submerged. If the bulb lights up when in air and goes out when submerged, the switch is good. If the test results are not as described, install a new switch.

Removal and installation

15 The procedure for the warning light sensor is the same as for the level sender (see Steps 6 to 10).
16 See Chapter 8 for bulb renewal.

16 PAIR system (Austria, Switzerland and California models)

General information

1 When the engine is running under normal conditions, the control valve is open so whenever there is a negative pulse in the exhaust system filtered fresh air is drawn from the PAIR system air cleaner, through the control valve and reed valves and into the

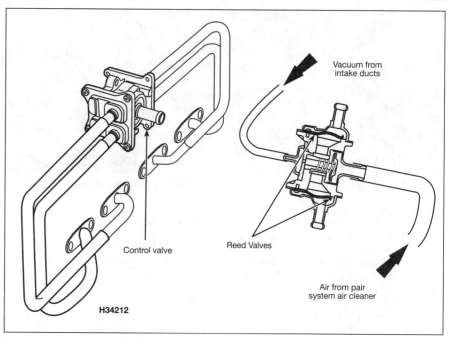

16.1 PAIR system diagram

exhaust port of each cylinder head via a flexible hose and metal pipe **(see illustration)**. This fresh air promotes the burning of any excess fuel present in the exhaust gases, so reducing the amount of harmful hydrocarbons emitted into the atmosphere via the exhaust gases. Exhaust gases are prevented from passing back into the PAIR system by the reed valves.

2 When the throttle is closed the vacuum present in the intake ducts acts on the diaphragm in the PAIR control valve, closing the valve and so cutting off the flow of air, thereby negating the tendency to backfire on overrun.

3 The system is not adjustable and requires

no maintenance, except to ensure that the hoses are in good condition and are securely connected at each end, and that there is no build-up of carbon fouling the reed valves. Renew any hoses that are cracked, split or generally deteriorated. The reed valves can be checked for any build-up of carbon by unscrewing the control valve cover screws – if any is found, clean up the valves as much as possible, though it is best to install a new control valve (no individual components are available).

4 The control valve should allow air to pass through it when no vacuum is applied to the vacuum union, and should not allow air to pass through it when a vacuum is applied.

5 To test the valve, blow into the air inlet hose union – air should flow out of the four outlet unions **(see illustration)**. Now apply the correct vacuum via the vacuum hose union, then blow into the air inlet hose union – air should not flow out of the four outlet unions **(see illustration)**. Release the vacuum and again blow through the inlet union – air should flow from the outlets. As a specific vacuum range is required (270 to 450 mmHg), it is best to have the valve tested by a Suzuki dealer. However If you have a pump and gauge, it is easy to test.

Removal and installation

6 Remove the fuel tank for access to the PAIR control valve, located above the valve cover.
7 Before disconnecting any of the components from their mountings, label the hoses to ensure correct reconnection. If the metal pipes on the cylinder head are removed, use new gaskets on installation.

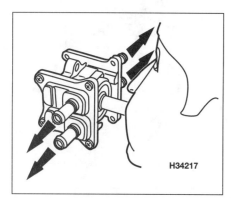

16.5a With no vacuum, air should flow through the valve

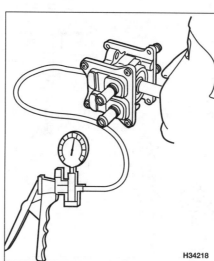

16.5b Apply a vacuum and no air should flow

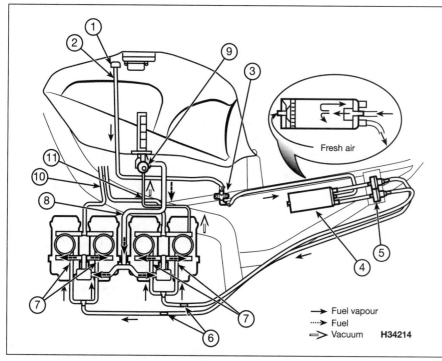

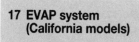

17.1 EVAP system diagram

1 Fuel vapour separator	5 Purge control valves	8 Fuel feed hose
2 Vent pipe/hose	6 Jets	9 Fuel tap
3 Shut-off valve	7 Carburettor purge	10 Air vent hoses
4 Canister	ports	11 Vacuum hose

17 EVAP system (California models)

General information

1 This system prevents the escape of fuel vapour into the atmosphere by storing it in a charcoal-filled canister located on the frame left-hand side at the rear **(see illustration)**.

2 When the engine is stopped, fuel vapour from the tank is directed into the canister where it is absorbed and stored whilst the motorcycle is standing. When the

17.5 Canister is clamped to the frame on the left-hand side

engine is started, vapours that are stored in the canister are drawn into the carburettors to be burned during the normal combustion process.

3 The vent hose from the fuel tank to the canister incorporates a shut-off valve. The tank filler cap has a one way valve which allows air into the tank as the volume of fuel decreases, but prevents any fuel vapour from escaping.

4 The system is not adjustable and should be tested only by a Suzuki dealer. However the owner can check that all the hoses are in good condition and are securely connected at each end. Renew any hoses that are cracked, split or generally deteriorated.

Removal and installation

5 To access the canister remove the seat cowling (see Chapter 7). Prior to their removal, label and disconnect the hoses, then remove the clamp screw and take the canister out **(see illustration)**. Make sure the hoses are correctly reconnected on installation.

3

Chapter 4
Ignition system

Contents

Clutch switch – check and renewal . . . . .see Chapter 8
General information 1
Ignition control unit – check, removal and installation 5
Ignition (main) switch – check, removal and installation . .see Chapter 8
Ignition HT coils – check, removal and installation 3
Ignition system – check 2
Ignition timing – general information 6

Ignition timing rotor . . . . .see Chapter 2
Neutral switch – check and renewal . . . . .see Chapter 8
Pulse generator coil – check and renewal 4
Sidestand switch – check and renewal . . . . .see Chapter 8
Spark plugs – gap check and renewal . . . . .see Chapter 1
Throttle position sensor – check, removal and installation 7

Degrees of difficulty

Easy, suitable for novice with little experience	Fairly easy, suitable for beginner with some experience	Fairly difficult, suitable for competent DIY mechanic	Difficult, suitable for experienced DIY mechanic	Very difficult, suitable for expert DIY or professional

Specifications

General information

Spark plugs	see Chapter 1
Firing order	1-2-4-3

Pulse generator coil

Resistance	135 to 200 ohms at 20°C
Minimum peak voltage (see text)	1.0 volt

Ignition HT coils

Spark performance (gap test)	8 mm
Primary winding resistance	2.0 to 4.0 ohms at 20°C
Secondary winding resistance	
With plug cap	30 to 40 K-ohms at 20°C
Without plug cap	25 to 35 K-ohms at 20°C
Plug cap resistance	approx. 5 K-ohms
Minimum peak voltage (see text)	140 volts

Throttle position sensor

Resistance – GSX600/750F	
Throttle closed	3.5 to 6.5 K-ohms
Throttle open	see Text
Resistance – GSX750	
Throttle closed	5 K-ohms
Throttle open	3.09 to 4.63 K-ohms

4

1 General information

All models are fitted with a fully transistorised electronic ignition system, which due to its lack of mechanical parts is totally maintenance free.

The system comprises the timing rotor, pulse generator coil, ignition control unit, ignition HT coils, and throttle position sensor. Each HT coil supplies two spark plugs and operates on the 'wasted spark' principle. Refer to the wiring diagrams at the end of Chapter 8 for details.

The ignition timing rotor is on the right-hand end of the crankshaft. The triggers on the rotor magnetically actuate the pulse generator coil as the crankshaft rotates. The pulse generator coil sends signals to the ignition control unit which then supplies the ignition HT coils with the power necessary to produce a spark at the plugs. The ignition control unit incorporates an electronic advance system.

The throttle position sensor supplies the ignition control unit with information on throttle position and rate of opening or closing.

The system incorporates a safety interlock circuit which will cut the ignition if the sidestand is extended whilst the engine is running and in gear, or if a gear is selected whilst the engine is running and the sidestand is down. It also prevents the engine from being started if the sidestand is down and the engine is in gear even though the clutch is held in. The engine can only be started on the sidestand with the transmission in neutral and the clutch lever pulled in, or, if the transmission is in gear, if the sidestand is up and the clutch lever is pulled in.

Because of their nature, the individual ignition system components can be checked but not repaired. If ignition system troubles occur, and the faulty component can be isolated, the only cure for the problem is to renew the part. Keep in mind that most electrical parts, once purchased, cannot be returned. To avoid unnecessary expense, make very sure the faulty component has been positively identified before buying a new part.

Note that there is no provision for adjusting the ignition timing.

2 Ignition system – check

⚠ Warning: The energy levels in electronic systems can be very high. On no account should the ignition be switched on whilst the plugs or plug caps are being held. Shocks from the HT circuit can be most unpleasant. Secondly, it is vital that the engine is not turned over or run with any of the plug caps removed, and that the

2.2 Pull the cap off the spark plug

plugs are soundly earthed (grounded) when the system is checked for sparking. The ignition system components can be seriously damaged if the HT circuit becomes isolated.

1 As no means of adjustment is available, any failure of the system can be traced to failure of a system component or a simple wiring fault. Of the two possibilities, the latter is by far the most likely. In the event of failure, check the system in a logical fashion, as described below.

2 Working on one HT lead at a time, disconnect the lead from its spark plug – to access them refer to Chapter 1, Section 3 **(see illustration)**. Connect the lead to a spare spark plug that is known to be good and lay the plug against the cylinder head with the threads contacting it. If necessary, hold the spark plug with an insulated tool.

⚠ Warning: Do not remove any of the spark plugs from the engine to perform this check – atomised fuel being pumped out of the open spark plug hole could ignite, causing severe injury! Make sure the plugs are securely held against the engine – if they are not earthed when the engine is turned over, the ignition control unit could be damaged.

3 Having observed the above precautions, check that the kill switch is in the RUN position and the transmission is in neutral, then turn the ignition switch ON, pull in the clutch lever and turn the engine over on the starter motor. If the system is in good condition a regular, fat blue spark should be evident at the plug electrode. If the spark appears thin or yellowish, or is non-existent, further investigation will be necessary. Turn the ignition OFF and repeat the check for the other leads.

4 The ignition system must be able to produce a spark which is capable of jumping an 8 mm gap at normal atmospheric pressure. A tool to test this is commercially available – set the required gap on the adjuster, then fit the tool into the spark plug cap and lay the other end against the engine. Alternatively a simple testing tool can be made to test the minimum gap across which the spark will jump (see **Tool Tip**).

5 Connect one of the spark plug HT leads from one coil to the protruding electrode on

the test tool, and clip the tool to a good earth (ground) on the engine or frame. Check that the kill switch is in the RUN position, turn the ignition switch ON, pull in the clutch lever and turn the engine over on the starter motor. If the system is in good condition a regular, fat blue spark should be seen to jump the gap between the ends. Repeat the test for the other coil. If the test results are good the entire ignition system can be considered good. If the spark appears thin or yellowish, or is non-existent, further investigation will be necessary.

6 Ignition faults can be divided into two categories, namely those where the ignition system has failed completely, and those which are due to a partial failure. The likely faults are listed below, starting with the most probable source of failure. Work through the list systematically, referring to the subsequent sections for full details of the necessary checks and tests. **Note:** *Before checking the following items ensure that the battery is fully charged and that all fuses are in good condition.*

- Loose, corroded or damaged wiring connections, broken or shorted wiring between any of the component parts of the ignition system (see *Wiring Diagrams*).
- Faulty HT lead or spark plug cap, faulty spark plug, dirty, worn or corroded plug electrodes, or incorrect gap between electrodes.
- Faulty ignition (main) switch or engine kill switch (see Chapter 8).
- Faulty neutral, clutch or sidestand switch (see Chapter 8).
- Faulty pulse generator coil or damaged trigger on timing rotor.
- Faulty ignition HT coil(s).
- Faulty throttle position sensor.
- Faulty ignition control unit.

7 If the above checks don't reveal the cause of the problem, have the ignition system tested by a Suzuki dealer.

TOOL TiP

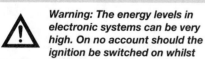

A simple spark gap testing tool can be made from a block of wood, a large alligator clip and two nails, one of which is fashioned so that a spark plug cap or bare HT lead end can be connected to its end. Make sure the gap between the two nail ends is the same as specified.

3.3 Disconnect the primary circuit wiring connectors (arrowed)

3.4 To test the coil primary resistance, connect the multimeter leads to the primary circuit terminals

3 Ignition HT coils – check, removal and installation

Check

1 Remove the fuel tank (see Chapter 3). The coils are bolted to the frame cross-member behind the cylinder head. Check the coils visually for loose or damaged terminals, cracks and other damage.
2 Disconnect the battery negative (–ve) lead (see Chapter 8).
3 Disconnect the primary circuit wiring connectors from the coil being tested, noting which fits where, and pull the relevant spark plug caps off the plugs (see illustration and 2.2).
4 To check the condition of the primary windings, set the meter to the ohms x 1 scale. Connect one meter probe to one primary circuit terminal and the other probe to the other terminal and measure the resistance (see illustration). The reading should be consistent with the value given in the Specifications at the beginning of the Chapter.
5 To check the condition of the secondary windings, set the meter to the K-ohm scale.

Connect one meter probe to one spark plug cap and the other probe to the other cap and measure the resistance (see illustration). If the reading obtained is not within the range shown in the Specifications, unscrew the caps from the ends of the HT leads and repeat the measurement. If the reading is now as specified, then the cap(s) could be faulty. To test a cap, measure the resistance between the lead socket and the plug socket, which should be around 5 K-ohms. If the caps are good, it is likely that the coil is defective, though it could only be the lead. Unfortunately the coil is supplied with an integral lead, so even if the coil itself is good, a new one will have to be fitted.
6 The coil can be tested further using a peak voltage adapter (Pt. No. 09900-25008) in conjunction with a multimeter. If this equipment is available, for the No. 1 and 4 cylinder coil connect the positive (+ve) lead of the voltmeter and peak voltage adapter arrangement to the white (GSX600/750F models) or black (GSX750 models) wire primary terminal on the coil, with the wiring connector still securely connected, and connect the negative (–ve) lead to a suitable earth (ground) point. For the No. 2 and 3 cylinder coil connect the positive (+ve) lead of the voltmeter and peak voltage adapter

arrangement to the black/yellow wire primary terminal on the coil, with the wiring connector still securely connected, and connect the negative (–ve) lead to a suitable earth (ground) point.
7 Check that the kill switch is in the RUN position and the transmission is in neutral, then turn the ignition switch ON. Pull the clutch lever in and turn the engine over on the starter motor for a few seconds. Note the ignition coil peak voltage reading on the meter. Once both readings have been noted, turn the ignition switch off and disconnect the meter.
8 If the peak voltage reading is lower than the specified minimum (and the coils have proven good when tested as above) then a fault is present somewhere else in the ignition system circuit (see Section 2); note that the peak voltage readings for each coil can be different but each one must exceed the specified minimum.
9 If the peak voltage reading is as specified and the plug does not spark, then the ignition HT coil, HT lead or plug cap are faulty (the plug caps are available separately). In order to determine conclusively that an ignition coil is defective, it should be tested by a Suzuki dealer. If the coil is confirmed to be faulty, a new one must be installed; the coil is a sealed unit and cannot therefore be repaired.

Removal and installation

10 Remove the fuel tank (see Chapter 3). Mark the locations of all wires and leads before disconnecting them.
11 Disconnect the primary circuit wiring connectors from the coils (see illustration 3.3). Pull the caps off the spark plugs (see illustration 2.2). Release the leads from any clips and note their routing.
12 Unscrew the bolts securing the coil, noting the spacers, and remove the coil (see illustration).
13 Installation is the reverse of removal. Make sure the wiring connectors and HT leads are securely connected.

4

3.5 To test the coil secondary resistance, connect the multimeter leads to the spark plug sockets

3.12 HT coil mounting bolts (arrowed)

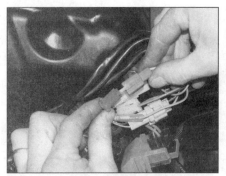

4.2 Disconnect the pulse generator coil wiring connector

4.4 Check the resistance of the pulse generator coil

4.8 Disconnect the pulse generator coil wiring connector and the oil pressure switch bullet connector

---

4 Pulse generator coil – check, removal and installation

Check

1 On GSX600/750F models remove the seat (see Chapter 7). You may be able to access the coil wiring connector from there – it is a red 2-pin connector inside the rubber boot on the left-hand end of the fuel tank mounting bracket. If you can't access it, remove the fairing left-hand side panel (see Chapter 7). On GSX750 models remove the fuel tank to access the connector.

2 Disconnect the wiring connector and perform the following check(s) **(see illustration)**.

3 Using an ohmmeter check for continuity between each of the connector terminals on the coil side of the connector and earth (ground). If there is continuity between any of the connector terminals and earth (ground) then the pulse generator coil is faulty.

4 Set the meter to the ohms x 100 scale and measure the resistance between the terminals in the wiring connector (coil side) **(see illustration)**. If the reading is widely different to that specified at the beginning of the chapter, first check the connector and the wiring between the connector and the coil itself (see below to access it). If the wiring is good, the pulse generator coil is faulty.

5 The coil can be tested further using a peak voltage adapter (Pt. No. 09900-25008) in conjunction with a multimeter. If this equipment is available, connect the positive (+ve) lead of the voltmeter and peak voltage adapter arrangement to the blue terminal of the pulse generator coil connector and the negative (–ve) lead to the yellow terminal of the connector – the test is made on the coil side of the connector. Turn the engine over on the starter motor for a few seconds and note the voltage reading obtained. If this reading is below the specified minimum, the pulse generator coil is faulty.

6 If the pulse generator coil functions correctly then the fault must be in the wiring harness or the ignition control unit (ICU). Check the wiring between the loom side of the connector and the ICU connector for continuity, and check the connectors themselves for loose or broken terminals. If the wiring is good the ICU could be faulty (see Section 5).

Removal and installation

7 On GSX600/750F models remove the fairing side panels (see Chapter 7). On GSX750 models remove the fuel tank (see Chapter 3).

8 Disconnect the pulse generator coil wiring connector and the oil pressure switch wire bullet connector, then free the wiring from any ties and feed it down to the right-hand side of the engine, noting its routing **(see illustration)**.

9 Remove the ignition timing rotor (see Chapter 2).

10 Undo the screw securing the wiring terminal to the oil pressure switch and detach it **(see illustration)**.

11 Undo the three screws securing the pulse generator coil backing plate to the crankcase **(see illustration)**. Displace the plate, then free the wiring grommet from its cut-out and carefully draw the wiring through the hole in the crankcase **(see illustration)**.

12 Installation is the reverse of removal. Apply a suitable sealant (such as Suzuki Bond 1215) to the grommet before fitting it into the cut-out. Make sure the wiring connectors are securely connected.

---

5 Ignition control unit – check, removal and installation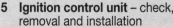

Check

1 If the tests shown in the preceding Sections have failed to isolate the cause of an ignition fault, it is possible that the ignition control unit (ICU) is faulty. No details are available with which the unit can be tested on home workshop equipment. Take the machine to a Suzuki dealer for testing. If there is a fault in the interlock circuit that cannot be traced to the neutral switch, clutch switch, sidestand switch, the sidestand relay/diode unit, or to a fault in the wiring between any of those components and the ICU, again the ICU could be faulty.

4.10 Undo the screw and detach the oil pressure switch wire

4.11a Undo the screws securing the plate . . .

4.11b . . . and free the wiring grommet from its cut-out

5.3 Ignition control unit – GSX600/750F
model shown

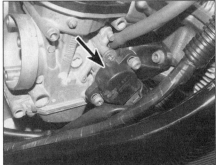

7.1 Throttle position sensor (arrowed) –
GSX750F model shown

7.2a Disconnect the wiring connector

Removal and installation

2 On GSX600/750F models remove the seat cowling (see Chapter 7). On GSX750 models remove the right-hand side panel (see Chapter 7).

3 Disconnect the wiring connector(s) from the unit (see illustration). On GSX600/750F models withdraw the unit from its holder. On GSX750 models undo the two screws and remove the unit.

4 Installation is the reverse of removal. Make sure the wiring connector(s) is/are correctly and securely connected.

6 Ignition timing –
general information

Since it is not possible to adjust the ignition timing and as no component is subject to mechanical wear, there is no provision for any checks. While in theory it is possible to check the timing dynamically (engine running) using a stroboscopic lamp, the firing point at idle is not marked on the ignition timing rotor.

7 Throttle position sensor –
check, removal and installation

Check

1 The throttle position sensor (TPS) is mounted on the right-hand side of the carburettors (see illustration). Remove the fuel tank for access (see Chapter 3).

2 Disconnect the sensor wiring connector (see illustration). Using a multimeter set to the K-ohm scale, connect the probes to the A terminals on the sensor wiring connector as shown (see illustration). If the resistance reading obtained is not within the range specified at the beginning of the Chapter, take the sensor to a Suzuki dealer for testing. If it is confirmed faulty, a new one must be installed; the sensor is a sealed unit and cannot therefore be repaired. Note that on GSX600/750F models it is worth disconnecting the TPS sub-loom from the

sensor itself and testing it again, using the top and bottom terminals on the sensor itself. If the results are now good then there is a break in the wiring in the sub-loom. You can test each individual wire by checking for continuity between the terminals at each end of the loom.

3 Check the sensor visually for cracks and other damage.

4 Using a multimeter set to resistance or a continuity tester, check for continuity between the terminals of the sensor wiring connector (main loom side) and the corresponding terminals on the ignition control unit connector. There should be continuity between each terminal. If not, this is probably due to a damaged or broken wire between the connectors; pinched or broken wires can usually be repaired.

Removal

Caution: Suzuki advise against removing the sensor from the carburettors or throttle bodies unless absolutely necessary.

5 The throttle position sensor is mounted on the right-hand side of the carburettors. Remove the fuel tank for access (see Section 2). Disconnect the sensor wiring connector.

6 Before removing the mounting screws, mark or scribe lines on the sensor to indicate the exact position of the screws in relation to it. Remove the screws and remove the sensor, noting how it fits.

Installation

7 Install the sensor, making sure it engages correctly with the throttle shaft. Thread the two screws into position, but only secure them finger-tight at this stage. If the original sensor is being reinstalled, realign the marks made prior to removal. Before the sensor screws are tightened, the position of the sensor body must be set as follows.

8 On GSX600/750F models, Suzuki advise that with the throttle fully open the resistance value across the B terminals should be 76% of the resistance value measured across the A terminals in Step 2 (see illustration 7.2b). For example, if reading A was 5 K-ohm, when the throttle is opened, the reading B should be 3.8

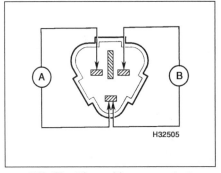

7.2b Throttle position sensor test
connections

K-ohm. If necessary, move the sensor body to bring the readings into line according to the graph (see illustration), then tighten the sensor screws, making sure the position of the sensor is not disturbed. Note that on GSX600F models the B terminals on the triangular sub-loom connector correspond to the top and middle terminals on the sensor itself (sub-loom disconnected from it), and on GSX750F models they correspond to the middle and bottom terminals on the sensor.

9 On GSX750 models, measure the resistance value across the B terminals with the throttle fully open. If necessary, move the sensor body to bring the reading into line, then tighten the sensor screws, making sure the position of the sensor is not disturbed.

10 Connect the sensor wiring connector and install the fuel tank.

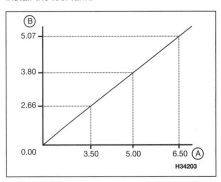

7.8 Throttle position sensor set-up values
– GSX600/750F models

Notes

Chapter 5
Frame, suspension and final drive

Contents

Drive chain – removal, cleaning and installation 16
Drive chain and sprockets – check, adjustment
   and lubrication . . . . .see Chapter 1
Footrests, brake pedal and gearchange lever – removal
   and installation 3
Forks – disassembly, inspection and reassembly 8
Forks – oil change 7
Forks – removal and installation 6
Frame – inspection and repair 2
Front sprocket cover – removal and installation 17
General information 1
Handlebars and levers – removal and installation 5
Handlebar switches – check .see Chapter 8
Handlebar switches – removal and installation . . . . . . .see Chapter 8
Rear shock absorber(s) – removal, inspection and installation 11
Rear sprocket coupling/rubber damper – removal,
   inspection and installation 19
Rear suspension linkage (GSX600/750F models) – removal,
   inspection and installation 12
Sprockets – check, removal and installation 18
Sidestand and centrestand – check and lubrication . . . .see Chapter 1
Sidestand and centrestand – removal and installation 4
Sidestand switch – check, removal and installation . . . .see Chapter 8
Steering head bearings – check and adjustment . . . . . . .see Chapter 1
Steering head bearings – inspection and renewal 10
Steering head bearings – lubrication . . . . .see Chapter 1
Steering stem – removal and installation 9
Suspension – adjustments 13
Suspension – check . . . . .see Chapter 1
Swingarm – inspection, bearing check and renewal 15
Swingarm – removal and installation 14
Swingarm and suspension linkage bearings –
   lubrication . . . . .see Chapter 1

Degrees of difficulty

Easy, suitable for novice with little experience	**Fairly easy,** suitable for beginner with some experience	**Fairly difficult,** suitable for competent DIY mechanic	**Difficult,** suitable for experienced DIY mechanic

Very difficult, suitable for expert DIY or professional

Specifications

Front forks

Fork oil type . . . . 10W fork oil
Fork oil capacity
   GSX600F . . . . 499 cc
   GSX750F . . . . 513 cc
   GSX750 . . . . 573 cc
Fork oil level*
   GSX600F . . . . 108 mm
   GSX750F . . . . 102 mm
   GSX750 . . . . 95 mm
Fork spring free length
   GSX600F
      Standard . . . . not available
      Service limit . . . . 361 mm
   GSX750F
      Standard . . . . 367 mm
      Service limit . . . . 359 mm
   GSX750
      Standard . . . . not available
      Service limit . . . . 380 mm
Fork tube runout limit . . . . 0.2 mm
Oil level is measured from the top of the tube with the fork spring removed and the leg fully compressed.

5

Rear suspension

Swingarm pivot bolt runout (max) .... 0.3 mm

Final drive

Drive chain slack and lubricant .... see Chapter 1
Drive chain
  GSX600F
    Type RK50MFOZ1
    Length .... 118 links
  GSX750F
    Type RK50MFOZ1
    Length .... 116 links
  GSX750
    Type RK50MFOZ1
    Length .... 112 links
Sprocket sizes
  Front (engine) sprocket 15T
  Rear (wheel) sprocket
    GSX600F 47T
    GSX750F 45T
    GSX750 .... 42T

Torque settings

Brake hose banjo bolt .... 23 Nm
Brake torque arm nuts
  GSX600F .... 32 Nm
  GSX750F and GSX750 .... 35 Nm
Footrest bracket bolts – GSX750F .... 23 Nm
Fork bottom yoke fork clamp bolts .... 23 Nm
Fork damper rod bolt .... 20 Nm
Fork top bolt .... 23 Nm
Fork top yoke fork clamp bolts .... 23 Nm
Front brake master cylinder clamp bolts .... 10 Nm
Front sprocket nut .... 115 Nm
Front sprocket nut stopper bolt – GSX750 .... 11 Nm
Handlebar bracket nuts – GSX750F .... 35 Nm
Handlebar clamp bolts – GSX750 .... 23 Nm
Handlebar holder bolts – GSX750F .... 23 Nm
Handlebar positioning bolts and nuts – GSX600F .... 32 Nm
Rear sprocket nuts
  GSX750F .... 60 Nm
  GSX600F and GSX750 .... 50 Nm
Shock absorber mounting bolts/nuts
  GSX600/750F models .... 50 Nm
  GSX750 models
    Upper mounting bolts .... 23 Nm
    Lower mounting bolt nuts .... 35 Nm
Speed sensor rotor bolt
  GSX600F .... 13 Nm
  GSX750F .... 18 Nm
Steering head bearing adjuster nut preload .... 45 Nm
Steering stem nut .... 65 Nm
Suspension linkage rod and arm bolt nuts (except shock absorber mount)
  GSX600F .... 78 Nm
  GSX750F .... 100 Nm
Swingarm pivot bolt nut
  GSX600/750F .... 65 Nm
  GSX750 .... 100 Nm

1 General information

All models have a steel cradle frame with a detachable section to facilitate engine removal.

On GSX600/750F models front suspension is by a pair of 41 mm oil-damped telescopic forks which are adjustable for rebound damping. GSX750 models have non-adjustable 43 mm forks.

At the rear, on GSX600/750F models a box-section aluminium swingarm acts on a single shock absorber via a three-way linkage. The shock absorber is adjustable for spring pre-load and rebound damping on all models, and on the 750, which has a remote reservoir, for compression damping. On GSX750 models the swingarm acts on twin shock absorbers with remote reservoirs, and which are adjustable for spring pre-load.

The drive to the rear wheel is by chain and sprockets.

2 Frame –
inspection and repair

1 The frame should not require attention unless accident damage has occurred. In most cases, frame renewal is the only satisfactory remedy for such damage. A few frame specialists have the jigs and other equipment necessary for straightening the frame to the required standard of accuracy, but even then there is no simple way of assessing to what extent the frame may have been over stressed.

2 After the machine has accumulated a lot of miles, the frame should be examined closely for signs of cracking or splitting at the welded joints. Loose engine mount bolts can cause ovaling or fracturing of the mounting tabs. Minor damage can often be repaired by welding, depending on the extent and nature of the damage.

3 Remember that a frame which is out of alignment will cause handling problems. If misalignment is suspected as the result of an accident, it will be necessary to strip the machine completely so the frame can be thoroughly checked.

3 Footrests, brake pedal and gearchange lever –
removal and installation

Footrests – GSX600/750F models

1 To remove the front footrests, first unhook the return spring **(see illustration)**. Remove the E-clip and washer from the top of the pivot pin, then withdraw the pin and remove the footrest **(see illustration)**. On GSX750F models, if required separate the plate from the bottom of the footrest by undoing the two screws **(see illustration)**.

2 To remove the rear footrests, remove the E-clip from the bottom of the pivot pin, then withdraw the pin and remove the footrest, noting how the ball and spring are fitted **(see illustration)**. Take care not to let the spring and ball ping out.

3.1a Unhook the return spring (arrowed)

3.1b Remove the E-clip (arrowed) to free the pivot pin

3.1c Undo the screws (arrowed) to remove the plate

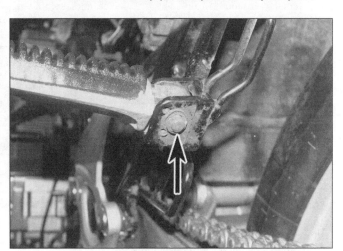

3.2 Remove the E-clip (arrowed) to free the pivot pin

5

3.9a Unscrew the bolt . . .

3.9b . . . then draw the pedal off the shaft . . .

3.9c . . . and remove the washer

3 Installation is the reverse of removal. Apply some grease to the pivot pin.

Footrests – GSX750 models

4 To remove the front footrests, remove the E-clip from the bottom of the pivot pin, then withdraw the pin and remove the footrest, noting how the return spring ends locate. Also note the collar fitted in the pivot. If required separate the footrest components by undoing the two screws.

5 To remove the rear footrests, remove the E-clip from the bottom of the pivot pin, then withdraw the pin and remove the footrest, noting how the detent plate, ball and spring are fitted. Take care not to let the spring and ball ping out.

6 Installation is the reverse of removal. Apply some grease to the pivot pin.

Brake pedal

7 Before removing the pedal, note the alignment of the punch mark on the end of the pivot shaft with the slit in the pedal clamp. If no mark is visible make your own.

8 On GSX750 models, remove the split pin and washer from the clevis pin securing the brake pedal to the master cylinder pushrod, then remove the clevis pin and separate the pedal from the pushrod.

9 Unscrew the brake pedal clamp bolt, then

draw the pedal off the shaft **(see illustrations)**. On GSX600/750F models remove the washer **(see illustration)**.

10 Installation is the reverse of removal, noting the following:

● Apply grease to the shaft.

● Align the pedal as noted on removal.

● On GSX750 models use a new split pin on the clevis pin securing the brake pedal to the master cylinder pushrod and bend the split pin ends securely.

● Check the operation of the rear brake light switch (see Chapter 1).

Gearchange lever

11 To remove the lever by itself leaving the linkage rod and arm in place, slacken the linkage rod locknuts, then unscrew the rod and separate it from the lever and the arm (the rod is reverse-threaded on one end and so will simultaneously unscrew from both lever and arm when turned in the one direction) **(see illustration)**. Note how far the rod is threaded into the lever and arm as this determines the height of the lever relative to the footrest. Now remove the circlip and washer securing the lever on its pivot, then draw the lever off.

12 To remove the lever, linkage rod and arm as an assembly, note the alignment of the punch mark on the gearchange shaft end with

the slit in the arm, then unscrew the pinch bolt **(see illustration)**. If no marks are visible make your own so that the arm can be installed in the correct position. Now remove the circlip and washer securing the lever on its pivot **(see illustration 3.11)**, then draw the lever, rod and arm off **(see illustration)**.

13 Installation is the reverse of removal, noting the following:

● If the linkage arm was removed, align the slit in the clamp with the punch mark on the end of the gearchange shaft.

● Apply grease to the gear lever pivot.

● Use a new circlip if the old one is deformed (it is best to use a new one as a matter of course).

● Adjust the gear lever height as required by screwing the linkage rod in or out of the lever and arm. Tighten the locknuts.

4 Sidestand and centrestand – removal and installation

Sidestand

Removal

1 The sidestand is attached to a bracket on the frame. Two springs ensure the stand is held in the retracted or extended position.

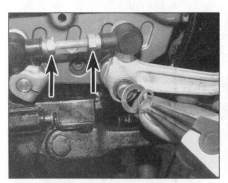

3.11 Slacken the locknuts (arrowed) and thread the rod out of the lever and arm, then remove the circlip and washer and slide the lever off

3.12a Unscrew the bolt (arrowed)

3.12b Draw the lever and linkage arm off their shafts

4.2 Unhook the springs (arrowed) . . .

4.3 . . . then unscrew the nut (A) and the pivot bolt (B)

2 Support the bike on its centrestand. Unhook the stand springs **(see illustration)**.
3 Unscrew the nut from the pivot bolt, on GSX600/750F models noting the washer, then unscrew the bolt and remove the stand **(see illustration)**.

Installation

4 Apply grease to the pivot bolt shank and tighten it. Install the nut, on GSX600/750F models with the washer, and tighten it.
5 Reconnect the springs and check that they hold the stand securely up when not in use – an accident is almost certain to occur if the stand extends while the machine is in motion. Make sure the contact tab locates against the sidestand switch plunger and actuates it correctly.

Centrestand

Removal

6 The centrestand is bolted to the frame. Springs anchored between them ensure the stand is held in the retracted position. Support the bike on the sidestand.
7 Unhook the stand springs **(see illustration)**.
8 On GSX600/750F models, unscrew the pivot bolts and remove the stand **(see illustration)**. Withdraw the spacer from each pivot.
9 On GSX750 models, unscrew the nut from the pivot bolt, then withdraw the bolt and remove the stand. Withdraw the spacer from the pivot.

Installation

10 Apply grease to the pivot bolt(s) and spacer(s). Tighten the bolts or nut.
11 Reconnect the springs and check that they hold the stand securely up when not in use – an accident is almost certain to occur if the stand extends while the machine is in motion.

5 Handlebars and levers – removal and installation

Handlebars – GSX600F models

Right handlebar removal

Note: *The handlebar can be displaced from the top yoke without having to remove the individual assemblies – follow Steps 4 and 5 only.*
1 Disconnect the wires from the brake light switch **(see illustration 5.15a)**. Unscrew the master cylinder assembly clamp bolts and position the assembly clear of the handlebar keeping it upright, making sure no strain is placed on the hydraulic hose **(see illustration 5.15b)**. Keep the master cylinder reservoir upright to prevent possible fluid leakage.
2 Unscrew the two handlebar switch housing screws and separate the halves. If required, free the throttle cable ends from the throttle

pulley, creating slack in the cable as necessary using the adjusters (see Chapter 1). To avoid having to do this, note that the throttle pulley can be slid off the end of the handlebar with the cables still attached after the handlebar has been displaced from the fork.
3 Unscrew the handlebar end-weight retaining screw, then remove the weight from the end of the handlebar **(see illustration 5.17)**. If the throttle cables have been detached, slide the twistgrip off the handlebar.
4 Free the handlebar switch wiring from its guide on the top yoke.
5 Carefully remove the handlebar positioning bolt blanking cap. Unscrew the nut on the bottom of the bolt, then unscrew the bolt. Ease the handlebar up and off the fork.
6 If required, slacken the clamp bolts securing the bar itself in the holder and slide it out, noting its alignment.

Left handlebar removal

Note: *The handlebar can be displaced from the top yoke without having to remove the individual assemblies – follow Steps 10 and 11 only.*
7 Disconnect the wires from the clutch switch **(see illustration 5.16a)**. Refer to Chapter 2 and detach the clutch cable from the lever and bracket. Slacken the clutch lever bracket clamp bolt **(see illustration 5.16b)**.
8 Refer to Chapter 3 and detach the choke cable from the lever – this procedure incorporates detaching the handlebar switch housing.
9 Unscrew the handlebar end-weight retaining screw, then remove the weight from the end of the handlebar and slide off the grip **(see illustration 5.17)**. If the grip has been glued on, you will probably have to slit it with a knife to remove it. Slide the clutch lever assembly off the handlebar.
10 Free the handlebar switch wiring from its guide on the top yoke.
11 Carefully prise the blanking cap out of the handlebar positioning bolt. Unscrew the nut on the bottom of the bolt, then unscrew the bolt. Ease the handlebar up and off the fork.
12 If required, slacken the clamp bolts securing the bar itself in the holder and slide it out, noting its alignment.

Installation

13 Installation is the reverse of removal, noting the following.
● Tighten the handlebar positioning bolt and its nut to the torque setting specified at the beginning of the Chapter.
● Apply some grease to the throttle twistgrip section of the right handlebar.
● Align the master cylinder clamp mating surfaces with the punch mark on the top of the handlebar.
● Make sure the front brake master cylinder assembly clamp is installed with the UP mark facing up **(see illustration 5.15b)**. Tighten the master cylinder clamp bolts to

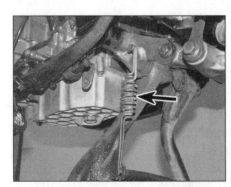

4.7 Unhook the springs (arrowed) . . .

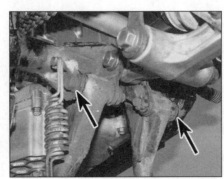

4.8 . . . then unscrew the bolts (arrowed)

5

5.15a Disconnect the wiring connectors (arrowed) . . .

5.15b . . . then unscrew the master cylinder clamp bolts (arrowed) and displace the assembly

the specified torque setting, tightening the top bolt first.
● Align the clutch lever assembly clamp mating surfaces with the punch mark on the bottom of the handlebar, and tighten the bolt.
● Make sure the pin in the top half of each switch housing locates in its hole in the handlebar (see illustration 5.22).
● When installing the handlebar end-weights, use some non-permanent thread locking

compound on the screws. If new grips are being fitted, secure them using a suitable adhesive.
● Do not forget to reconnect the front brake light switch and clutch switch wiring connectors.

Handlebars – GSX750F models

Removal

Note: The handlebar assembly can be

displaced from the top yoke without having to remove the individual assemblies – follow Steps 19 and 20 only. If you do this, cover the instrument cluster with some rag and lay the handlebar assembly on it keeping the master cylinder upright, or if the fuel tank has been removed lay the handlebar assembly on the frame behind the steering head, again using rag.

14 Refer to Chapter 3 and detach the throttle cables and choke cable – these procedures incorporate detaching the handlebar switch housings. Create slack in the throttle cables as necessary using the adjusters (see Chapter 1) to avoid having to detach the cable ends from the throttle cam on the carburettors.
15 Disconnect the wires from the brake light switch (see illustration). Unscrew the two front brake master cylinder assembly clamp bolts and position the assembly clear of the handlebar, making sure no strain is placed on the hydraulic hose (see illustration). Keep the master cylinder reservoir upright to prevent possible fluid leakage.
16 Disconnect the wires from the clutch switch (see illustration). Refer to Chapter 2 and detach the clutch cable from the lever and bracket. Slacken the clutch lever bracket clamp bolt (see illustration).
17 Unscrew the right handlebar end-weight retaining screw, then remove the weight from the end of the handlebar and slide the throttle twistgrip off the end (see illustration).
18 Unscrew the left handlebar end-weight retaining screw, then remove the weight from the end of the handlebar and slide off the grip. If the grip has been glued on, you will probably have to slit it with a knife to remove it. Slide the clutch lever assembly off the handlebar.
19 Free the handlebar switch wiring from its guide on the top yoke (see illustration).
20 Carefully prise the blanking caps out of

5.16a Disconnect the wiring connectors (arrowed) . . .

5.16b . . . then slacken the clutch bracket clamp bolt (arrowed)

5.17 Handlebar end-weight screw (arrowed)

5.19 Free the wiring from its guide (arrowed)

5.20a Prise out the blanking caps . . .

5.20b . . . then unscrew the nuts . . .

5.20c . . . withdraw the bolts . . .

5.20d . . . and remove the handlebars

5.20e Remove the dampers from the yoke . . .

5.20f . . . noting the collar

the handlebar bracket bolts **(see illustration)**. Unscrew the nuts on the bottom of the bolts, noting the washers **(see illustration)**. Support the handlebars, then withdraw the bolts and remove the handlebar assembly **(see illustrations)**. Remove the handlebar dampers and collars from the top yoke for safekeeping **(see illustration)**. Check the condition of the dampers and fit new ones if they are damaged, deformed or deteriorated.

21 If required, slacken the holder bolt securing each bar itself in the handlebar bracket and slide it out, noting its alignment.

Installation

22 Installation is the reverse of removal, noting the following.

● If slackened, tighten the holder bolt to the torque setting specified at the beginning of the Chapter.

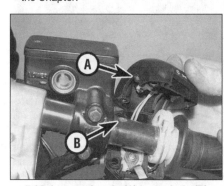

5.22 Locate the pin (A) in the hole (B)

● Tighten the handlebar bracket nuts to the torque setting specified at the beginning of the Chapter.

● Apply some grease to the throttle twistgrip section of the handlebar.

● Align the master cylinder clamp mating surfaces with the punch mark on the top of the handlebar.

● Make sure the front brake master cylinder assembly clamp is installed with the UP mark facing up **(see illustration 5.15b)**. Tighten the master cylinder clamp bolts to the specified torque setting, tightening the top bolt first.

● Align the clutch lever assembly clamp mating surfaces with the punch mark on the bottom of the handlebar, and tighten the bolt.

● Make sure the pin in the top half of each switch housing locates in its hole in the handlebar **(see illustration)**.

● When installing the handlebar end-weights, use some non-permanent thread locking compound on the screws. If new grips are being fitted, secure them using a suitable adhesive.

● Do not forget to reconnect the front brake light switch and clutch switch wiring connectors.

Handlebars – GSX750 models

Removal

Note: *The handlebars can be displaced from the top yoke without having to remove the*

individual assemblies from them – follow Step 29 only. If you do this, cover the instrument cluster with some rag and lay the handlebar assembly on it keeping the master cylinder upright, or if the fuel tank has been removed lay the handlebar assembly on the frame behind the steering head, again using rag.

23 Remove the rear view mirrors (see Chapter 7).

24 Refer to Chapter 3 and detach the throttle cables and choke cable – these procedures incorporate detaching the handlebar switch housings. Create slack in the throttle cables as necessary using the adjusters (see Chapter 1) to avoid having to detach the cable ends from the throttle cam on the carburettor.

25 Disconnect the wires from the brake light switch **(see illustration 5.15a)**. Unscrew the two front brake master cylinder assembly clamp bolts and position the assembly clear of the handlebar, making sure no strain is placed on the hydraulic hose **(see illustration 5.15b)**. Keep the master cylinder reservoir upright to prevent possible fluid leakage.

26 Disconnect the wires from the clutch switch **(see illustration 5.16a)**. Refer to Chapter 2 and detach the clutch cable from the lever and bracket. Slacken the clutch lever bracket clamp bolt **(see illustration 5.16b)**.

27 Unscrew the right handlebar end-weight retaining screw, then remove the weight from the end of the handlebar and slide the throttle twistgrip off the end **(see illustration 5.17)**.

5

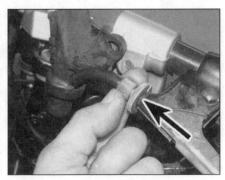

5.31a Unscrew the nut (arrowed) . . .

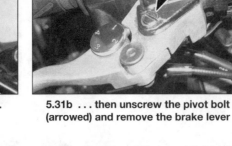

5.31b . . . then unscrew the pivot bolt (arrowed) and remove the brake lever

5.32a Slacken the ring (arrowed) and thread the adjuster in

28 Unscrew the left handlebar end-weight retaining screw, then remove the weight from the end of the handlebar and slide off the grip **(see illustration 5.17)**. If the grip has been glued on, you will probably have to slit it with a knife to remove it. Slide the clutch lever assembly off the handlebar.

29 Carefully prise the blanking caps out of the handlebar clamp bolts. Support the handlebars, then unscrew the bolts and remove the clamps and the handlebars.

Installation

30 Installation is the reverse of removal, noting the following.

● Align the punch mark on the front of the handlebar with the mating surfaces of the left handlebar holder and clamp

● Tighten the handlebar clamp bolts evenly so that the gap between holder and clamp is the same at the front and back, and tighten them to the specified torque setting.

● Apply some grease to the throttle twistgrip section of the handlebar.

● Make sure the front brake master cylinder assembly clamp is installed with the mirror mounting facing up and the clamp mating surfaces aligned with the punch mark on the bottom of the handlebar. Tighten the clamp bolts to the specified torque setting, tightening the top bolt first.

● Align the clutch lever bracket clamp mating surfaces with the punch mark on the

bottom of the handlebar, and tighten the bolt.

● Make sure the pin in the top half of each switch housing locates in its hole in the handlebar **(see illustration 5.22)**.

● When installing the handlebar end-weights, use some non-permanent thread locking compound on the screws. If new grips are being fitted, secure them using a suitable adhesive.

● Do not forget to reconnect the front brake light switch and clutch switch wiring connectors.

Handlebar levers

31 To remove the brake lever, unscrew the nut on the underside of the lever bracket **(see illustration)**. Unscrew the pivot bolt and remove the lever **(see illustration)**.

32 To remove the clutch lever, pull the rubber boot off the clutch cable adjuster. Slacken the adjuster lockring and thread the adjuster fully into the bracket to provide maximum freeplay in the cable **(see illustration)**. Unscrew the nut on the underside of the lever bracket **(see illustration)**. Unscrew the pivot bolt and remove the lever, detaching the cable end as you do so **(see illustration)**.

33 Installation of the levers is the reverse of removal. Apply grease to their pivot bolt shafts and the contact areas between the lever and its bracket. When installing the

brake lever, apply silicone grease to the tip of the master cylinder pushrod. When installing the clutch lever apply grease to the cable nipple. Adjust the clutch cable freeplay (see Chapter 1).

6 Forks – removal and installation

Removal

1 On GSX600/750F models, remove the fairing side panels (See Chapter 7). This will prevent accidental damage to the paintwork.

2 Remove the front wheel (see Chapter 6). On GSX600/750F models unscrew the bolts securing the brake hoses to the forks **(see illustration)**. Tie the front brake calipers and hoses back so that they are out of the way.

3 Remove the front mudguard and on GSX600/750F models also remove the fork brace (see Chapter 7).

4 On GSX600F models, carefully remove the handlebar positioning bolt blanking caps. Slacken the nuts on the bottom of the bolts, then slacken the bolts.

5 Working on one fork at a time, slacken the fork clamp bolt(s) in the top yoke **(see illustration 6.9b)**. If the fork is to be disassembled, or if the fork oil is being

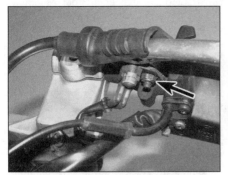

5.32b Unscrew the nut (arrowed) . . .

5.32c . . . then unscrew the pivot bolt (arrowed) and remove the clutch lever

6.2 Unscrew the bolt and detach the brake hose from the fork

6.5 If required slacken the fork top bolt

6.6a Bottom yoke fork clamp bolts (arrowed)

6.6b Draw the fork down and out of the yokes

changed, it is advisable to slacken the fork top bolt at this stage (see illustration).

6 Slacken the fork clamp bolts in the bottom yoke, and remove each fork by twisting it and pulling it downwards (see illustrations).

 HAYNES HINT *If the fork legs are seized in the yokes, spray the area with penetrating oil and allow time for it to soak in before trying again.*

Installation

7 Remove all traces of corrosion from the fork tube and the yokes. On GSX600/750F models, slide the fork up through the bottom yoke and into the top yoke and handlebar bracket or holders. On GSX750 models, slide the fork up through the bottom yoke, through the headlight assembly holders and into the top yoke. Make sure all cables, hoses and wiring are routed on the correct side of the fork.

8 Set the fork in the yokes so the top of the fork tube (not the top of the fork top bolt) is flush with the top surface of the handlebar on GSX600F models, flush with the top surface of the handlebar bracket on GSX750F models, and flush with the top surface of the top yoke on GSX750 models. Make sure it is the same on both sides. If the handlebar bracket has yet to be fitted on GSX750F models, note that the fork must be positioned so that it is 27.5 mm above the top surface of the top yoke.

9 Tighten the fork clamp bolts in the bottom yoke to the torque setting specified at the beginning of the Chapter. If the fork has been dismantled or if the fork oil was changed, tighten the fork top bolt to the specified torque setting (see illustration). Now tighten the fork clamp bolt(s) in the top yoke to the specified torque (see illustration).

10 On GSX600F models, tighten the handlebar positioning bolts and nuts to the specified torque setting.

11 Install the front mudguard, and on GSX600/750F models the fork brace (see Chapter 7), and the front wheel (see Chapter 6).

6.9a If required tighten the fork top bolt to the specified torque

On GSX600/750F models, secure the brake hoses to the forks (see illustration 6.2), and install the fairing side panels (see Chapter 7).

12 Check the operation of the front forks and brakes before taking the machine out on the road.

7 Forks – oil change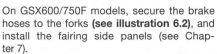

1 Remove the forks (see Section 6). Always work on the fork legs separately to avoid interchanging parts and thus causing an accelerated rate of wear.

7.2 If not already done, slacken the top bolt

6.9b Tighten the top yoke clamp bolt(s) to the specified torque

2 If the fork top bolt was not slackened with the fork in situ, carefully clamp the fork tube in a vice equipped with soft jaws, taking care not to overtighten or score its surface, and slacken the top bolt (see illustration).

3 Unscrew and remove the fork top bolt from the top of the fork tube – on GSX600/750F models the damping adjuster rod comes with the top bolt (see illustration).

⚠ *Warning: The fork spring is pressing on the fork top bolt, though not with any great pressure. Unscrew the bolt carefully, keeping a downward pressure on it and release it slowly.*

4 Slide the fork tube down into the slider and

7.3 Thread the top bolt out of the tube

7.4a Remove the spacer . . .

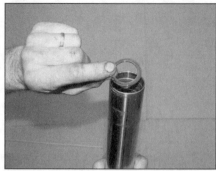

7.4b . . . then hook out the spacer seat . . .

7.4c . . . and the spring

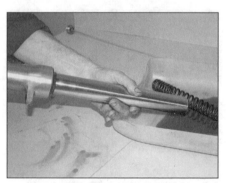

7.5 Invert the fork over a container and pump the tube to expel the oil

remove the spacer **(see illustration)**. Using a piece of wire bent over at the end as a hook if required, remove the spacer seat and the spring from the tube **(see illustrations)**.

5 Invert the fork over a suitable container and pump the fork tube vigorously to expel as much oil as possible **(see illustration)**. Support the fork upside down in the container for a while to allow as much oil as possible to drain, and pump the fork again.

6 Slowly pour in the specified quantity of the specified grade of fork oil and pump the fork at least ten times to distribute it evenly **(see**

illustration). Allow a few minutes for the oil level to settle, then fully compress the fork tube into the slider and measure the oil level, and make any adjustment by adding more or tipping some out until the oil is at the level specified at the beginning of the Chapter **(see illustration)**.

7 Clamp the slider in a soft-jawed vice using the brake caliper mounting lugs, taking care not to overtighten and damage them. Pull the fork tube out of the slider as far as possible then install the spring, on GSX600/750F models with the closer wound coils at the bottom and on GSX750 models with them at the top. Install the spacer seat and the spacer.

8 Fit a new O-ring smeared with fork oil onto the fork top bolt. On GSX600/750F models insert the damping adjuster rod and top bolt into the fork, noting that the rod must be aligned so the flat locates in the corresponding flat in the damper – as you probably won't be able to see the flat in the damper you will have to turn the top bolt until the adjuster rod is felt to locate. On all models thread the bolt into the top of the fork tube. Keep the fork tube fully extended whilst doing so. Screw the top bolt carefully into the fork tube making sure it is not cross-threaded. **Note:** *The top bolt can be tightened to the*

specified torque setting at this stage if the tube is held between the padded jaws of a vice, but do not risk distorting the tube by doing so. A better method is to tighten the top bolt when the fork has been installed in the bike and is held in the bottom yoke, but before the top yoke clamp bolt is tightened (see illustration 6.9a).

9 Install the forks (see Section 6).

 Use a ratchet-type tool when installing the fork top bolt. This makes it unnecessary to remove the tool from the bolt whilst threading it in making it easier to maintain a downward pressure on the spring.

8 Forks – disassembly, inspection and reassembly

Disassembly

1 Remove the forks (see Section 6). Always dismantle the fork legs separately to avoid interchanging parts and thus causing an

7.6a Pour the oil into the top of the tube

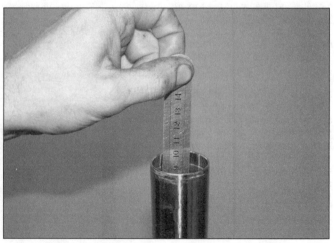

7.6b Measure the oil level and adjust if necessary

accelerated rate of wear. Store all components in separate, clearly marked containers **(see illustration)**.

2 Before dismantling the fork, slacken the damper rod bolt now as there is less chance of the damper rotating with it (due to the pressure of the spring). When working on the left-hand fork on GSX600/750F models or the right-hand fork on GSX750 models, first remove the axle spacer from the fork **(see illustration)**. Compress the fork tube in the slider so that the spring exerts maximum pressure on the damper head, then have an assistant slacken the bolt in the base of the fork slider **(see illustration)**. If the bolt does not unscrew, but merely rotates inside the fork tube, on GSX600/750F models use an impact driver or air wrench although take care not to damage the wheel axle mounting at the base of the slider. On GSX750 models the damper rod can be held as described in Step 7.

3 If the fork top bolt was not slackened with the fork in situ, carefully clamp the fork tube in a vice equipped with soft jaws, taking care not to overtighten or score its surface, and slacken the top bolt **(see illustration 7.2)**.

4 Unscrew and remove the fork top bolt from the top of the fork tube – on GSX600/750F models the damping adjuster rod comes with the top bolt **(see illustration 7.3)**.

> ⚠ **Warning: The fork spring is pressing on the fork top bolt, though not with any great pressure. Unscrew the bolt carefully, keeping a downward pressure on it and release it slowly.**

5 Slide the fork tube down into the slider and remove the spacer **(see illustration 7.4a)**. Using a piece of wire bent over at the end as a hook if required, remove the spacer seat and the spring from the tube **(see illustrations 7.4b and c)**.

6 Invert the fork over a suitable container and pump the fork tube vigorously to expel as much oil as possible **(see illustration 7.5)**.

7 Remove the previously slackened damper rod bolt and its copper sealing washer from the bottom of the slider **(see illustration)**. Discard the sealing washer as a new one must be used on reassembly. Invert the fork and tip

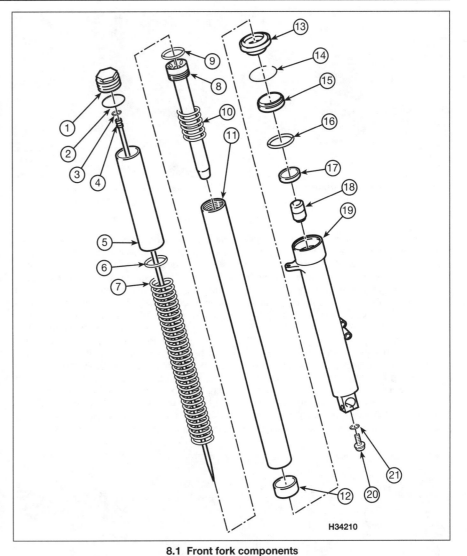

8.1 Front fork components

1 Top bolt	7 Spring	15 Oil seal
2 O-ring	8 Damper rod	16 Washer
3 O-ring – GSX600/750F models	9 Piston ring	17 Top bush
4 Damping adjuster rod – GSX600/750F models	10 Rebound spring	18 Damper rod seat
5 Spacer	11 Fork tube	19 Slider
6 Spacer seat	12 Bottom bush	20 Damper rod bolt
	13 Dust seal	21 Sealing washer
	14 Retaining clip	

8.2a Remove the axle spacer

8.2b Slacken the damper rod bolt

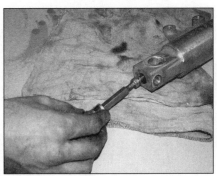

8.7a Unscrew and remove the damper rod bolt . . .

5

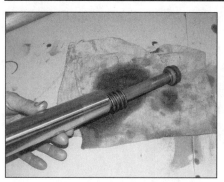

8.7b . . . then tip the damper rod out of the
fork

8.8 Prise out the dust seal using a flat-
bladed screwdriver

8.9 Prise out the retaining clip using a flat-
bladed screwdriver

the damper rod out of the top of the tube **(see illustration). Note:** *On GSX750 models if the damper rod bolt couldn't be successfully slackened, the head of the damper rod can be held by passing a holding tool down through the top of the fork tube – Suzuki produce a service tool (Pt. Nos. 09940-34520 for the handle and 09940-34531 for the adapter) for this purpose.*

8 Carefully prise out the dust seal from the top of the slider to gain access to the oil seal retaining clip **(see illustration)**. Discard the dust seal as a new one must be used.

9 Carefully remove the retaining clip, taking care not to scratch the surface of the tube **(see illustration)**. It is advisable to slide the

tube fully into the slider to keep any accidental damage above the seal area.

10 To separate the tube from the slider it is necessary to displace the oil seal and top bush. In theory the bottom bush does not pass through the top bush, and this can be used to good effect. Push the tube gently inwards until it stops against the damper seat. Take care not to do this forcibly or the seat may be damaged. Now pull the tube sharply outwards until the bottom bush strikes the top bush **(see illustration)**. Repeat this operation until the top bush and seal are tapped out of the slider. **Note:** *On the fork photographed, which contained worn bushes, it was found that the bottom bush passed through the top*

bush, leaving the top bush and the oil seal in the top of the slider. If this is the case, lever out the seal using a seal hook or screwdriver, protecting the rim of the slider as it is easily damaged, then remove the washer and bush.

11 With the tube removed, slide off the oil seal, washer and top bush, noting which way up they fit **(see illustration)**. Discard the oil seal as a new one must be used.

Caution: *Do not remove the bottom bush from the tube unless it is to be renewed.*

12 Remove the damper rod seat from the bottom of the tube, or tip it out of the slider – you may have to push it from the bottom via the damper bolt hole **(see illustration)**.

Inspection

13 Clean all parts in solvent and blow them dry with compressed air, if available. Check the fork tube for score marks, scratches, flaking of the chrome finish and excessive or abnormal wear. Look for dents in the tube and fit new tubes if any are found. Check the fork seal seat for nicks, gouges and scratches. If damage is evident, leaks will occur. Also check the oil seal washer for damage or distortion and fit a new one if necessary.

14 Check the fork tube for runout using V-blocks and a dial gauge. If the amount of runout exceeds the service limit specified, a new tube should be fitted.

⚠ **Warning:** *If the tube is bent or exceeds the runout limit, it should not be straightened; renew it.*

15 Check the springs (the main spring and the rebound spring on the damper rod) for cracks and other damage. Measure the main spring free length and compare the measurement to the service limit at the beginning of the Chapter **(see illustration)**. If it is defective or sagged below the service limit, fit new main springs in both forks. Never renew only one spring.

16 Examine the working surfaces of the two bushes; if worn or scuffed new ones must be installed. To remove the bottom bush from the fork tube, prise it apart at the slit using a flat-bladed screwdriver and slide it off **(see**

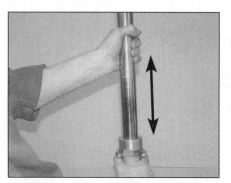

8.10 To separate the fork tube from the
slider, pull them apart firmly several times

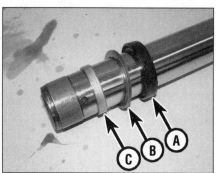

8.11 Slide the oil seal (A), washer (B) and
top bush (C) off the top of the tube

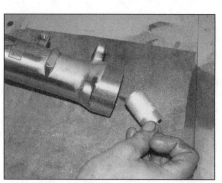

8.12 Tip the damper rod seat out of the
slider

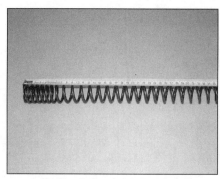

8.15 Check the spring free length

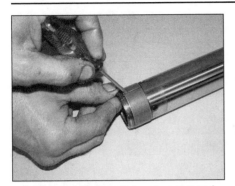

8.16 Carefully lever the ends apart and slide the bush off the fork tube

8.17 Check the damper rod, rebound spring and piston ring (arrowed)

8.18a Slide the damper rod into the tube and all the way down so that it projects from the bottom . . .

illustration). Make sure the new one seats properly.

17 Check the damper rod and its piston ring for damage and wear, and use new ones if necessary **(see illustration)**. Do not remove the ring from the top of the rod unless a new one is being fitted.

Reassembly

18 If removed, fit the piston ring into the groove in the damper rod head, then slide the rebound spring onto the rod. Insert the damper rod into the top of the fork tube and slide it down so that it projects fully from the bottom of the tube **(see illustration)**. Fit the seat onto the bottom of the damper, then push the seat and damper up into the tube **(see illustration)**.

19 Oil the fork tube and bottom bush with the specified fork oil and insert the assembly into the slider **(see illustration)**. Fit a new copper sealing washer onto the damper rod bolt and apply a few drops of a suitable non-permanent thread locking compound, then thread the bolt into the bottom of the slider **(see illustration)**. Tighten the bolt to the specified torque setting **(see illustration)**. If the damper rod rotates inside the tube, temporarily install the fork spring, spacer seat, spacer and top bolt (see Steps 26 and 27) and compress the fork to hold the damper rod. On GSX750 models the Suzuki service tool (see Step 7) or a length of wood doweling pressed hard into the damper rod head can be used. Otherwise, wait until the fork is fully reassembled before tightening the bolt.

20 Push the fork tube fully into the slider, then oil the top bush and slide it down over the tube **(see illustration)**. Press the bush squarely into its recess in the slider as far as possible, then install the oil seal washer with its flat side facing up **(see illustration)**. Use either the Suzuki service tool (Pt. No. 09940-52861), or a suitable piece of plastic tubing to tap the bush fully into place; the tubing must be slightly larger in diameter than the fork tube and slightly smaller in diameter than the bush recess in the slider. Take care not to scratch the fork tube during this operation; push the tube fully into the slider so that any accidental scratching is confined to the area above the oil seal and wind insulating tape around the exposed length of tube. A drift or punch can be used, but this does not help the bush enter

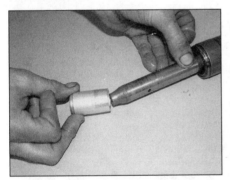

8.18b . . . then fit the seat onto the rod

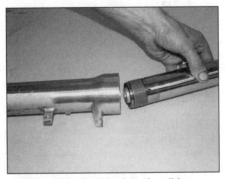

8.19a Slide the tube into the slider . . .

8.19b . . . then fit the bolt using threadlock and a new sealing washer . . .

8.19c . . . and tighten it to the specified torque

8.20a Install the top bush . . .

8.20b . . . followed by the washer

5

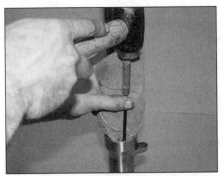

8.20c A drift can be used to tap the bush into place

8.22 Smear the new oil seal with clean fork oil then slide it down the tube

8.23 Install the retaining clip . . .

squarely, and the angle narrows as the bush gets deeper and makes it more difficult to make a good contact with a hammer **(see illustration)**. If using a drift or punch, wrap tape around it to prevent it scratching the tube.
21 Remove the washer to check the bush is seated fully and squarely in its recess in the slider, then wipe the recess clean and refit the washer.
22 Smear the lips of the new oil seal with fork oil and slide it over the tube so that its markings face upwards **(see illustration)**. Press the seal into the slider, then drive it fully into place as described in Step 20 until the retaining clip groove is visible above it.
23 Once the seal is correctly seated, fit the retaining clip, making sure it is correctly located in its groove **(see illustration)**.
24 Lubricate the lips of the new dust seal then slide it down the fork tube and press it into position **(see illustrations)**.
25 Slowly pour in the specified quantity of the specified grade of fork oil and pump the fork at least ten times to distribute it evenly **(see illustration 7.6a)**. Allow a few minutes for the oil level to settle, then fully compress the fork tube and damper rod into the slider and measure the oil level; make any adjustment by adding more or tipping some out until it is at the level specified at the beginning of the Chapter **(see illustration 7.6b)**.
26 Pull the fork tube out of the slider as far as possible then install the spring, on GSX600/750F models with the closer wound

coils at the bottom and on GSX750 models with them at the top **(see illustration 7.4c)**. Install the spacer seat and the spacer **(see illustrations 7.4b and a)**.
27 Fit a new O-ring smeared with fork oil onto the fork top bolt. On GSX600/750F models insert the damping adjuster rod and top bolt into the fork, noting that the rod must be aligned so the flat locates in the corresponding flat in the damper – as you probably won't be able to see the flat in the damper you will have to turn the top bolt until the adjuster rod is felt to locate **(see illustration 7.3)**. On all models thread the bolt into the top of the fork tube **(see illustration 7.2)**. Keep the fork tube fully extended whilst doing so. Screw the top bolt carefully into the fork tube making sure it is not cross-threaded. **Note:** *The top bolt can be tightened to the specified torque setting at this stage if the tube is held between the padded jaws of a vice, but do not risk distorting the tube by doing so. A better method is to tighten the top bolt when the fork has been installed in the bike and is held in the bottom yoke, but before the top yoke clamp bolt is tightened (see illustration 6.9a).*

TOOL TiP *Use a ratchet-type tool when installing the fork top bolt. This makes it unnecessary to remove the tool from the bolt whilst threading it in making it easier to maintain a downward pressure on the spring.*

28 If the damper rod bolt requires tightening (see Step 19), clamp the fork slider between the padded jaws of a vice and have an assistant compress the tube into the slider so that maximum spring pressure is placed on the damper rod head – tighten the damper rod bolt to the specified torque setting **(see illustration 8.19c)**. When working on the left-hand fork on GSX600/750F models or the right-hand fork on GSX750 models, fit the axle spacer into the axle bore **(see illustration 8.2a)**.
29 Install the forks (see Section 6).

9 Steering stem –
removing and installation

Removal

1 On GSX600/750F models remove the fairing side panels (See Chapter 7).
2 Remove the fuel tank (see Chapter 3). This will prevent the possibility of damage should a tool slip.
3 On GSX750 models, remove the horns, headlight assembly and instrument cluster (see Chapter 8).
4 Unscrew the bolt securing the front brake hose splitter to the bottom yoke **(see illustration)**. On GSX750 models free the speedometer cable from its guide on the bottom yoke.
5 Remove the front wheel (see Chapter 6). On

8.24a . . . followed by the dust seal . . .

8.24b . . . which can be pressed in using your fingers

9.4 Unscrew the bolt (arrowed) and displace the brake hose splitter

9.9 Disconnect the ignition switch
wiring connector (arrowed) –
GSX750F model shown

9.10a Unscrew the steering stem nut . . .

9.10b . . . then lift the top yoke up off the
steering head

GSX600/750F models unscrew the bolts
securing the brake hoses to the forks **(see
illustration 6.2)**. Tie the front brake calipers
and hoses back so that they are out of the
way.
6 Remove the front mudguard and on
GSX600/750F models also remove the fork
brace (see Chapter 7).
7 Remove the front forks (see Section 6). On
GSX750 models remove the headlight
assembly holders, noting how they locate
between the top and bottom yokes – if they
are tight fit, remove them after slackening the
steering stem nut (Step 10).
8 Displace the handlebars (see Section 5).
9 If the top yoke is being removed from the
bike rather than just being displaced, trace the
wiring from the ignition switch and disconnect
it at the connector **(see illustration)**.
10 Unscrew the steering stem nut and
remove the washer **(see illustration)**. Ease
the top yoke up and off the steering stem and
either remove it or position it clear, using a rag
to protect other components **(see
illustration)**.
11 Supporting the bottom yoke, unscrew the
adjuster nut using either a C-spanner, a peg-
spanner, or a drift located in one of the
notches **(see illustration)**. Remove the

9.11a Unscrew the adjuster nut . . .

9.11b . . . and remove the grease seal

adjuster nut and the grease seal from the
steering stem **(see illustration)**. Check the
condition of the grease seal and discard it if it
is damaged.
12 Gently lower the bottom yoke and
steering stem out of the steering head **(see
illustration)**.
13 Remove the inner race and bearing from
the top of the steering head **(see illustrations
9.15b and a)**. Remove the bearing from the
base of the steering stem **(see illustration
9.14)**. Remove all traces of old grease from
the bearings and races and check them for

wear and damage as described in Section 10.
Note: *Do not attempt to remove the outer
races from the steering head or the inner race
from the steering stem unless they are to be
renewed.*

Installation

14 Smear a liberal quantity of multi-purpose
grease onto the bearing races, and work
some grease well into both the upper and
lower bearings. Also smear the grease seal lip,
with grease. Fit the lower bearing onto the
steering stem **(see illustration)**.

9.12 Draw the bottom yoke/steering stem out of the
steering head

9.14 Fit the lower bearing onto the steering stem

5

9.15a Fit the upper bearing . . .

9.15b . . . and the inner race

9.15c Thread the adjuster nut onto the stem

9.16 Tighten the adjuster nut as described

9.17 Tighten the steering stem nut to the specified torque

Caution: Take great care not to overtighten the bearings as this will cause premature failure.

17 When the bearings are correctly adjusted, tighten the steering stem nut and the fork clamp bolts in the bottom yoke to the torque setting specified at the beginning of the Chapter (see illustration and 6.6a).

18 Install the remaining components in a reverse of the removal procedure.

19 Carry out a final check of the steering head bearing adjustment as described in Chapter 1, and if necessary re-adjust.

15 Carefully lift the steering stem/bottom yoke up through the steering head. Fit the upper bearing and its inner race into the top of the steering head (see illustrations). Fit the grease seal (see illustration 9.11b). Thread the adjuster nut onto the steering stem (see illustration).

16 If the service tool (Pt. No. 09940-14911) is available, tighten the adjuster nut to the preload torque setting specified at the beginning of the Chapter, then turn the steering stem through its full lock at least five times. Now slacken the adjuster nut by _ to _ a turn. If the service too is not available, tighten the nut using a C-spanner (or a drift) to pre-load the bearings, then slacken it off a bit, but not so much that freeplay can be felt (see illustration). Now install all remaining components (except the fuel tank, on GSX750

models the handlebars, and on GSX600/750F models the fairing panels) in a reverse of the removal procedure, referring to the relevant Sections or Chapters, but leave the steering stem nut and the bottom yoke fork clamp bolts slack, then refer to the procedure in Chapter 1 and finally adjust the bearings – setting the bearings is a lot easier and more accurate after the forks, wheel and handlebars are installed as their leverage and inertia need to be taken into account.

10 Steering head bearings – inspection and renewal

Inspection

1 Remove the steering stem (see Section 9).

2 Remove all traces of old grease from the bearings and races and check them for wear or damage.

3 The outer races should be polished and free from indentations. Inspect the bearing balls for signs of wear, damage or discoloration, and examine the ball retainer cage for signs of cracks or splits. If there are any signs of wear on any of the above components both upper and lower bearing assemblies must be renewed as a set. Only remove the outer races in the steering head and the lower bearing inner race on the steering stem if they need to be renewed – do not re-use them once they have been removed.

Renewal

4 The outer races are an interference fit in the steering head and can be tapped from position with a suitable drift (see illustration). Tap firmly and evenly around each race to ensure that it is driven out squarely. It may prove advantageous to curve the end of the drift slightly to improve access.

5 Alternatively, the races can be removed using a slide-hammer type bearing extractor; these can often be hired from tool shops.

6 The new outer races can be pressed into the head using a drawbolt arrangement (see illustration), or by using a large diameter

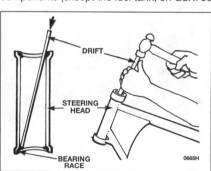

10.4 Drive the bearing races out of the steering head with a brass drift locating it as shown

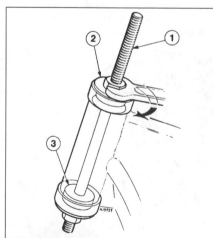

10.6 Drawbolt arrangement for fitting steering stem bearing races

1 Long bolt or threaded bar
2 Thick washer
3 Guide for lower race

10.7a Remove the lower bearing inner race (arrowed) . . .

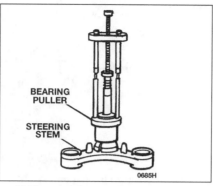

10.7b . . . using a puller if necessary

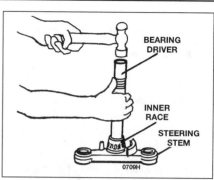

10.9 Drive the new inner race on using a suitable driver or a length of pipe that bears only against the inner edge of the race, and not on its working surface

tubular drift. Ensure that the drawbolt washer or drift (as applicable) bears only on the outer edge of the race and does not contact the working surface. Alternatively, have the races installed by a Suzuki dealer equipped with the bearing race installation tools.

 HAYNES HINT *Installation of new bearing outer races is made much easier if the races are left overnight in the freezer. This causes them to contract slightly making them a looser fit. Alternatively, use a freeze spray.*

7 The lower bearing inner race should only be removed from the steering stem if a new one is being fitted (see illustration). To remove the race, use two screwdrivers placed on opposite sides to work it free, using blocks of wood to improve leverage and protect the yoke, or tap under it using a cold chisel. If the steering stem is placed on its side on a hard surface, thread a suitable nut onto the top to prevent the threads being damaged. If the race is firmly in place it will be necessary to use a puller (see illustration). Take the steering stem to a Suzuki dealer if required.
8 Remove the dust seal from the bottom of the stem and replace it with a new one. Smear the new seal with grease.
9 Fit the new lower race onto the steering stem. A length of tubing with an internal diameter slightly larger than the steering stem

will be needed to tap the new race into position (see illustration).
10 Install the steering stem (see Section 9).

11 Rear shock absorber(s) – removal, inspection and installation

Removal
GSX600/750F models
1 Support the motorcycle on its centrestand. Position a support under the rear wheel or swingarm so that it does not drop when the shock absorber is removed, but also making sure that the weight of the machine is off the rear suspension so that the shock is not

11.3a Slacken the clamp screws (arrowed) . . .

compressed. Make a note of which side the bolts go in from, and make a note of which way round the shock absorber fits.
2 To prevent the possibility of damage remove the fairing side panels (see Chapter 7).
3 On GSX750F models remove the seat cowling (see Chapter 7). Slacken the clamps securing the shock absorber reservoir and displace it from its bracket, noting how it fits (see illustrations).
4 Unscrew the nut and withdraw the bolt securing the linkage rods to the linkage arm (see illustrations).
5 Unscrew the bolt securing the bottom of the shock absorber to the linkage arm, then swing the arm down (see illustration).

11.3b . . . and slide the reservoir out

11.4a Unscrew the nut (arrowed) . . .

11.4b . . . and withdraw the linkage rods-to-arm bolt

11.5 Remove the shock absorber lower mounting bolt and pivot the arm down

5

6 Unscrew the nut on the shock absorber upper mounting bolt **(see illustration)**. Support the shock absorber, then withdraw the bolt and manoeuvre the shock out of the bottom, on GSX750F models feeding the reservoir down with it **(see illustrations)**.

GSX750 models

7 Support the motorcycle on its centrestand. Place a support under the rear wheel or swingarm so that it does not drop when the shock absorbers are removed, but also making sure that the weight of the machine is off the rear suspension so that the shocks are not compressed.

8 Carefully prise the blanking caps out of the shock absorber upper mounting bolts.

9 Unscrew the nut and withdraw the bolt securing the bottom of the shock absorber to the swingarm, then pivot the shock back out of its mount. Note the spacers for the bolts.

10 Unscrew the shock absorber upper mounting bolt, noting the washer on each side, and remove the shock.

Inspection

11 Inspect the shock absorber(s) for obvious physical damage and the coil spring(s) for looseness, cracks or signs of fatigue.

12 Inspect the damper rod(s) for signs of bending, pitting and oil leakage.

13 Inspect the pivot hardware at the top and bottom of the shock(s) for wear or damage.

14 Individual components are not available for the shock absorber(s) – do not attempt to dismantle it/them.

Installation

15 Installation is the reverse of removal, noting the following points.

● Apply multi-purpose grease to the shock absorber pivot points and components, and on GSX600/750F models to the linkage pivots.

● On GSX750F models install the shock absorber with the threaded section for the lower mounting bolt on the right-hand side. Do not tighten the upper bolt/nut until the lower bolt is in position.

● Install all bolts and nuts finger-tight only until all components are in position. Where nuts are fitted counter-hold the bolts and tighten

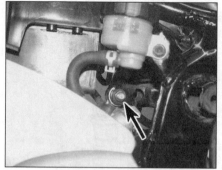

11.6a Unscrew the nut on the bolt (arrowed) . . .

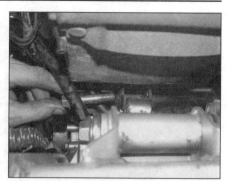

11.6b . . . then withdraw the bolt . . .

11.6c . . . and remove the shock absorber from the bottom . . .

11.6d . . . on GSX750F models bringing the reservoir with it

the nuts to the torque settings specified at the beginning of the Chapter. Otherwise tighten the bolts to the specified torque.

---

12 Rear suspension linkage (GSX600/750F models) – removal, inspection and installation

Removal

1 Support the motorcycle on its centrestand. Position a support under the rear wheel or swingarm so that it does not drop when the shock absorber lower mounting is detached, but also making sure that the weight of the machine is off the rear suspension so that the shock is not compressed. Make a note of which side the bolts go in from.

2 Mark the linkage arm and rods so that they can be installed the same way round.

3 Unscrew the nut and withdraw the bolt securing the linkage rods to the linkage arm **(see illustrations 11.4a and b)**.

4 Unscrew the bolt securing the bottom of the shock absorber to the linkage arm, then swing the arm down **(see illustration 11.5)**.

5 Unscrew the nut and withdraw the bolt securing the linkage arm to the frame and remove the arm **(see illustration)**.

6 To access the linkage rods-to-swingarm bolt, first remove the rear brake pedal (see Section 3), then unscrew the bolts securing the heel protector (GSX600F) or footrest bracket (GSX750F) and remove it **(see illustration)**. Unscrew the nut and withdraw the bolt securing the linkage rods to the swingarm and remove the rods **(see illustration)**.

12.5 Unscrew the nut then withdraw the bolt and remove the arm

12.6a Unscrew the bolts and remove the footrest bracket (GSX750F model shown) . . .

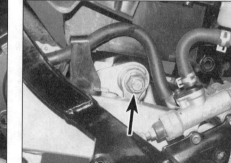

12.6b . . . to access the nut (arrowed)

12.7a **Withdraw the spacers from the linkage arm . . .**

12.7b **. . . and the linkage rod pivot in the swingarm (shown removed)**

Inspection

7 Withdraw the spacers from the linkage arm and swingarm, noting any difference in sizes **(see illustrations)**. Thoroughly clean all components, removing all traces of dirt, corrosion and grease.

8 Inspect all components closely, looking for obvious signs of wear such as heavy scoring, or for damage such as cracks or distortion. Slip each spacer back into its bearing and check that there is not an excessive amount of freeplay between the two components. Renew any components as required.

9 Check the condition of the needle roller bearings in the linkage arm and swingarm **(see illustrations 12.7a and b)**. Refer to *Tools and Workshop Tips* (Section 5) in the Reference section for more information on bearings.

10 Worn bearings can be drifted out of their bores, but note that removal will destroy them; new bearings should be obtained before work commences. The new bearings should be pressed or drawn into their bores rather than driven into position. In the absence of a press, a suitable drawbolt tool can be made up as described in *Tools and Workshop Tips* in the Reference section.

11 Lubricate the needle bearings and spacers with multi-purpose grease. Install the spacers.

Installation

12 Installation is the reverse of removal, noting the following points.

● Apply multi-purpose grease to the bearings, spacers and bolts.

● Install all bolts and nuts finger-tight only until all components are in position, then counter-hold the bolts and tighten the nuts to the torque settings specified at the beginning of the Chapter.

● On GSX750F models check the condition of the bushes in the footrest bracket mounts and fit new ones if they are damaged, deformed or deteriorated. If you do fit new ones it is worthwhile doing so on the other bracket as well. Do not omit the washers and tighten the bolts to the specified torque setting.

13 Suspension – adjustments

Front forks – GSX600/750F

1 The front forks are adjustable for rebound damping.

2 Damping is adjusted using a screwdriver on the adjuster in the fork top bolt **(see illustration)**. There are four settings, each indicated by a click. Turn the adjuster clockwise to increase damping and anti-clockwise to decrease it. To establish the current setting, turn the adjuster clockwise until it stops, counting the number of clicks as you do. To reset it turn it back out by the required number of clicks. The damping is at its hardest at the first click out, and at its softest at the fourth click out. The standard setting and the setting for dual riding is at the third click out.

3 Always set the adjuster on one of the click positions, not in between them. Do not force the adjuster beyond its limits. Always make sure both forks are set equally.

13.2 **Rebound damping adjuster screw**

Rear shock absorber

GSX600F models

4 The shock absorber is adjustable for spring pre-load and rebound damping.

5 Spring pre-load is adjusted using a suitable C-spanner (one is provided in the toolkit) on the adjuster ring on the bottom of the shock absorber **(see illustration)**. There are seven positions – the number 1 position provides minimum pre-load, and the number 7 provides the maximum. The standard setting is on number 4.

6 Rebound damping is adjusted by turning the dial on the top of the shock absorber **(see illustration)**. There are four settings, each indicated by a click and a number. The

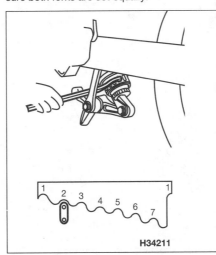

13.5 **Adjusting rear pre-load – GSX600F**

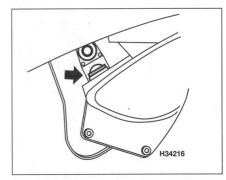

13.6 **Rebound damping adjuster – GSX600F**

5

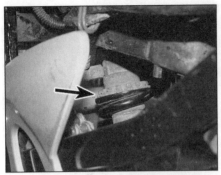

13.8 Spring pre-load adjuster (arrowed) – GSX750F

13.9 Rebound damping adjuster (arrowed) – GSX750F

13.10a Compression damping adjuster (arrowed) – GSX750F

damping is at its softest setting on the no. 1 setting and at its hardest on the no. 4 setting. The standard setting is on number 2. Always set the adjuster on one of the click positions, not in between them. Do not force the adjuster beyond its limits.

GSX750F models

7 The shock absorber is adjustable for spring pre-load, rebound damping and compression damping.

8 Spring pre-load is adjusted by turning the adjuster nut on the threads on the shock absorber body. Slacken the locknut, then turn the adjuster nut clockwise to increase pre-load and anti-clockwise to decrease it **(see illustration)**. Tighten the locknut after adjustment. Do not set the spring length to anything more than 163.5 mm or anything less than 153.5 mm on US models, or more than 165 mm or anything less than 155 mm on all other models.

9 Rebound damping is adjusted by turning the dial on the bottom of the shock absorber **(see illustration)**. There are four settings, each indicated by a click and a number. The damping is at its softest setting on the no. 1 setting and at its hardest on the no. 4 setting. Always set the adjuster on one of the click positions, not in between them. The standard setting is no. 1 for US models and no. 2 for all other models. Do not force the adjuster beyond its limits.

10 Compression damping is adjusted using a screwdriver on the adjuster on the shock

absorber reservoir **(see illustration)**. Turn the adjuster clockwise to increase damping and anti-clockwise to decrease it. The standard position is $1\frac{3}{4}$ turns anti-clockwise from the fully turned in position – at this point the punch marks should align **(see illustration)**. When adjusting the damping, do so by $\frac{1}{4}$ turn at a time and assess the difference by riding the bike.

GSX750 models

11 The shock absorbers are adjustable for spring pre-load.

12 Spring pre-load is adjusted using a suitable C-spanner (one is provided in the toolkit) on the adjuster ring on the top of the shock absorber **(see illustration)**. There are five positions – the number 1 position provides minimum pre-load, and the number 5 provides the maximum. The standard setting is on number 2. Both shock absorbers must be set on the same pre-load setting.

> **HAYNES HiNT**
> *It is important on GSX600/750F models that the front and rear suspension settings are suited to ensure good handling and comfort. Refer to the owner's manual supplied with the motorcycle for recommended settings for solo and dual riding.*

14 Swingarm – removal and installation

Removal

1 Due to the rear brake hose being routed through a closed riveted guide on the inside of the swingarm, it is necessary to detach the hose from the rear brake caliper, and then draw the hose out of the guide (see **Method 1** below). The alternative to this is to displace the rear brake master cylinder and its reservoir, and to remove the swingarm bringing the brake system with it (see **Method 2** below). Your choice will depend upon the reason for removing the swingarm.

2 **Method 1:** On GSX600/750F models, unscrew the bolt securing the closed guide to the top of the swingarm, then free the hose from the open guide. On GSX750 models, free the brake hose from its open guides on the swingarm. On all models unscrew the brake hose banjo bolt and detach the hose from the caliper, noting its alignment **(see illustration)**. Draw the hose out of the closed guide on the inside of the swingarm, taking care not to splash brake fluid around – have some rag on hand to quickly mop up any spills **(see illustration)**. Either plug the hose using another suitable short piece of hose fitted through the eye of the banjo bolt (it must be a fairly tight fit to seal it properly), clamp it using a hose clamp, or wrap a plastic bag tightly

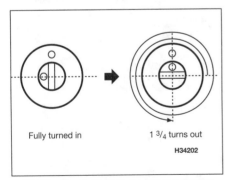

13.10b Compression damping adjuster standard setting – GSX750F

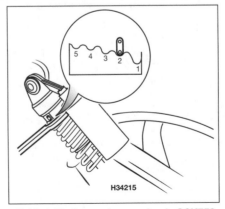

13.12 Adjusting spring pre-load– GSX750

14.2a Unscrew the banjo bolt (arrowed) and detach the hose

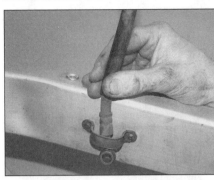

14.2b Draw the hose out of the guide

14.5 Undo the screws (arrowed) and remove the chainguard

14.6 Unscrew the nut (arrowed), withdraw the bolt and detach the torque arm

14.8a Remove the blanking cap from each side . . .

14.8b . . . then unscrew the nut

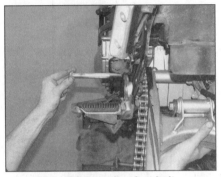

14.9a Withdraw the pivot bolt . . .

around to minimise fluid loss and prevent dirt entering the system. Discard the sealing washers as new ones must be used on installation. Note the routing of the brake hose around the swingarm.

 Warning: Brake fluid can harm your eyes and damage painted surfaces and plastic parts, so use extreme care when disconnecting the hose.

3 Method 2: Refer to Chapter 6 and remove the rear brake master cylinder and its reservoir – do not detach any of the hoses.

4 Remove the rear wheel (see Chapter 6).

5 Undo the screws securing the chainguard to the swingarm and remove the guard, noting how it locates **(see illustration).**

6 If you are following Method 1, you may want to unscrew the nut and withdraw the bolt securing the brake torque arm to the swingarm and remove it along with the brake caliper **(see illustration).**

7 On GSX600/750F models remove the rear shock absorber (see Section 11). On GSX750 models, detach the shock absorbers at their lower mounting points and pivot them up out of the way (see Section 11).

8 Remove the blanking cap from each end of

the swingarm pivot **(see illustration).** Unscrew the nut on the right-hand end of the pivot bolt **(see illustration).**

9 Support the swingarm and withdraw the pivot bolt from the left-hand side **(see illustration).** Manoeuvre the swingarm out of the frame, noting how the drive chain routes around the front **(see illustration).**

10 If required on GSX600/750F models, unscrew the nut and withdraw the bolt securing the linkage rods to the swingarm and remove them **(see illustration).**

11 Inspect all pivot components for wear or damage as described in Section 15.

14.9b . . . and manoeuvre the swingarm out

14.10 Remove the linkage rods if required

5

14.12a Remove the dust cap and thrust washer . . .

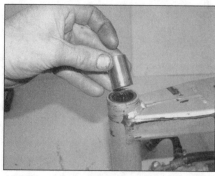

14.12b . . . then withdraw the outer spacer on each side . . .

14.12c . . . and the central spacer that fits between them

Installation

12 Remove the dust cap and thrust washer from each side of the swingarm pivot, then withdraw the spacers (see illustrations). Clean off all old grease, then lubricate the bearings, spacers, washers, caps and the pivot bolt with multi-purpose grease. Insert the spacers, then fit the washers and dust caps.

13 If removed on GSX600/750F models, fit the linkage rods onto the pivot on the swingarm (see illustration). Before tightening the nut, pass the linkage rods-to linkage arm bolt through the lower eyes on the rods so they are parallel, then tighten the nut to the torque setting specified at the beginning of the Chapter (see illustrations).

14.13a Install the linkage rods . . .

14 Offer up the swingarm and if available have an assistant hold it in place. Make sure the drive chain is looped over the front of the swingarm. Slide the pivot bolt through from the left-hand side and push it all the way through.

15 Fit the nut onto the left-hand end of the bolt. Counter-hold the head of the bolt and tighten the nut to the specified torque setting.

16 Install the shock absorber(s) (see Section 11).

17 If removed, fit the brake torque arm onto the swingarm, then install the bolt and tighten the nut to the specified torque setting (see illustration 14.6).

18 Install the rear wheel (see Chapter 6).

19 Install the chainguard (see illustration 14.5).

20 If you used **Method 1** on removal, route the brake hose through its closed guide on the inside of the swingarm (see illustration 14.2b). On GSX600/750F models fit the closed brake hose guide on to the top of the swingarm and tighten its bolt, then fit the hose into the open guide. On GSX750 models fit the hose into the two open guides. Connect the brake hose to the caliper, using new sealing washers on each side of the fitting (see illustration). Align the hose as noted on removal (see illustration 14.2a). Tighten the banjo bolt to the torque setting specified at the beginning

of the Chapter. Remove the brake hose clamp if used. Refer to Chapter 7 and bleed the brakes.

21 If you used **Method 2** on removal, install the rear brake master cylinder and reservoir (see Chapter 6).

22 Check and adjust the drive chain slack (see Chapter 1). Check the operation of the rear suspension and brake before taking the machine on the road.

15 Swingarm – inspection, bearing check and renewal

Inspection

1 Remove the swingarm (see Section 14). Remove the chain adjusters if required, noting how and which way round they fit.

2 Thoroughly clean the swingarm, removing all traces of dirt, corrosion and grease. Inspect the swingarm closely, looking for obvious signs of wear such as heavy scoring, and cracks or distortion due to accident damage. Any damaged or worn component must be replaced.

3 Inspect the chain slider on the left-hand side of the swingarm and renew it if it has become worn or damaged by the drive chain.

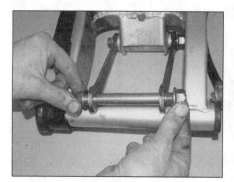

14.13b . . . then fit the bolt through the rods to keep them parallel . . .

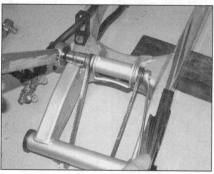

14.13c . . . and tighten the nut to the specified torque

14.20 Use a new sealing washer on each side of the union

15.3 Chain slider locates in clip and over pivot boss

The slider fits over the pivot boss and locates in a clip **(see illustration)**.

4 Check the swingarm pivot bolt for straightness by rolling it on a flat surface such as a piece of plate glass (first wipe off all old grease and remove any corrosion using wire wool). If the equipment is available, place the axle in V-blocks and measure the runout using a dial gauge. If the axle is bent or the runout exceeds the limit specified, renew it.

Bearing check and renewal

5 Remove the dust cap and thrust washer from each side of the swingarm pivot, then withdraw the spacers **(see illustrations 14.12a, b and c)**. Clean off all old grease from the spacers and bearings.
6 Check the condition of the bearings – a needle roller bearing is fitted on each side **(see illustration)**. Slip each spacer back into its bearing and check that there is not an excessive amount of freeplay between the two components. If the bearings do not run smoothly and freely or if there is excessive freeplay, they must be renewed. Refer to *Tools and Workshop Tips* (Section 5) in the Reference section for more information on bearings. Note that on GSX600/750F models it is worth checking the suspension linkage bearings in the swingarm and linkage arm at the same time (see Section 12).
7 Worn bearings can be drifted out of their bores, but note that removal will destroy them; new bearings should be obtained before work commences. The new bearings should be pressed or drawn into their bores

15.6 Check each needle bearing as described

rather than driven into position. In the absence of a press, a suitable drawbolt tool can be made up as described in *Tools and Workshop Tips* in the Reference section.
8 Check the condition of the washers and dust caps and renew them if they are damaged, deformed or have deteriorated.
9 Lubricate the bearings, spacers, washers, and caps with multi-purpose grease. Insert the spacers, then fit the washers and dust caps **(see illustrations 14.12c, b and a)**. Install the chain adjusters if removed.

16 Drive chain – removal, cleaning and installation

Note: *Inspect the drive chain to determine whether it has a soft joining link (its pin ends will be deeply centre punched rather than peened over as all other chain links). If a soft link is fitted, the chain can be split and rejoined using a new soft link – this must be done using the correct tool (see 'Chains' in the Tools and Workshop Tips section in Reference). If a soft link is not fitted, the chain is effectively endless, and can only be removed as described below.*

⚠️ **Warning: NEVER install a drive chain which uses a clip-type master (split) link.**

Removal
1 If new sprockets are being fitted, slacken the front sprocket nut before removing the

rear wheel so that the rear brake can be used to stop the sprocket turning (see Section 18).
2 Remove the swingarm (see Section 14), then remove the chain.

Cleaning
3 Soak the chain in kerosene (paraffin) for approximately five or six minutes, then clean it using a soft brush.
Caution: Don't use gasoline (petrol), solvent or other cleaning fluids which might damage its internal sealing properties. Don't use high-pressure water. Remove the chain, wipe it off, then blow dry it with compressed air immediately. The entire process shouldn't take longer than ten minutes – if it does, the O-rings in the chain rollers could be damaged.

Installation
4 Installation is the reverse of removal. On completion adjust and lubricate the chain following the procedures described in Section 1.

17 Front sprocket cover – removal and installation

Note: *If required the sprocket cover can just be displaced with the clutch cable and speed sensor (GSX600/750F only) still attached, as long as it is supported so that no strain is placed on the sensor wiring – follow Steps 1, 2 and 5 only.*

Removal
1 On GSX600/750F models remove the left-hand fairing side panel (see Chapter 7).
2 Unscrew the gearchange lever linkage arm pinch bolt and draw the arm off the shaft, noting the alignment of the punch mark on the shaft end with the slit in the linkage arm clamp (make your own alignment mark if none is visible) **(see illustration)**. On GSX600/750F models, if required remove the circlip and washer securing the gearchange lever on its pivot, then draw the lever and linkage assembly off together **(see illustrations)**.
3 On GSX600/750F models either detach the speed sensor from the cover, or leave it in

17.2a Unscrew the bolt (arrowed) and slide the arm off the shaft

17.2b Remove the circlip and washer . . .

17.2c . . . and draw the lever off with the linkage rod and arm

17.4 Pull the boot up and slacken the locknut (arrowed)

17.5 Unscrew the bolts (arrowed) and displace the cover

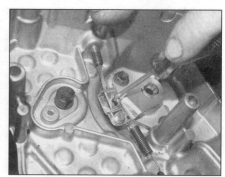

17.6a Bend back the tab . . .

place but disconnect its wiring connector (see Chapter 8).

4 If you are going to detach the clutch cable from the cover, pull up the rubber boot covering the cable adjuster on the top of the cover, then slacken the locknut on the adjuster **(see illustration)**.

5 Unscrew the bolts securing the cover and displace it – note which bolt fits where as they are of different lengths **(see illustration)**.

6 Bend back the tab securing the clutch cable end in the release mechanism arm and detach the cable **(see illustrations)**. Thread the adjuster out of the cover **(see illustration)**.

7 With the cover removed, check the operation of the release mechanism – clean it and re grease it if required (see Chapter 2).

Installation

8 Installation is the reverse of removal. Bend

up the retaining tab in the release arm to secure the cable **(see illustration)**. Make sure the clutch pushrod end locates correctly in the centre of the release mechanism **(see illustration)**.

---

18 Sprockets – check, removal and installation

Check

1 Remove the front sprocket cover (see Section 17).

2 Check the wear pattern on both sprockets (see Chapter 1, Section 1). If the sprocket teeth are worn excessively, renew the chain and both sprockets as a set. Whenever the sprockets are inspected, the drive chain

should be inspected also (see Chapter 1). If you are renewing the chain, renew the sprockets as well.

3 Adjust and lubricate the chain following the procedures described in Chapter 1.

Removal and installation

Front sprocket

4 Remove the front sprocket cover (see Section 17).

5 On GSX600/750F models, unscrew the bolt securing the speed sensor rotor to the end of the output shaft and remove the rotor **(see illustration)**. On GSX750 models unscrew the sprocket nut stopper bolt. Apply the rear brake to prevent the sprocket turning.

6 Engage first gear, then have an assistant hold the rear brake on hard. Unscrew the sprocket nut and remove the washer **(see illustration)**.

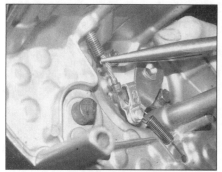

17.6b . . . then detach the cable end . . .

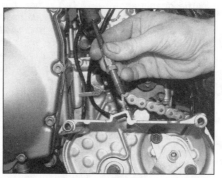

17.6c . . . and thread the cable out of the cover

17.8a Bend the tab up to secure the cable

17.8b The pushrod end locates in the hole in the release mechanism (arrowed)

18.5 Unscrew the bolt and remove the speed sensor rotor

18.6 Unscrew the nut and remove the washer

18.8 Disengage the chain and remove the front sprocket

18.10 Tighten the sprocket nut to the specified torque setting

18.14 Rear sprocket nuts (arrowed)

Check the condition of the washer and discard it if there are any cracks or if it is badly scored or deformed. Otherwise it can be reused.

7 Fully slacken the drive chain as described in Chapter 1. If the rear sprocket is being renewed as well, remove the rear wheel now to give full slack (see Chapter 6). Otherwise disengage the chain from the rear sprocket.

8 Disengage the chain from the front sprocket then slide the sprocket off the shaft **(see illustration)**.

9 Slide the new sprocket on the shaft, making sure the marked side is facing out, and fit the chain around it. Fit the chain onto the rear sprocket or install the rear wheel (see Chapter 6), then take up the slack in the chain.

10 Apply a suitable non-permanent thread locking compound to the threads on the output shaft or in the nut. Fit the nut with its washer and tighten it to the specified torque setting, holding the rear brake on to prevent the sprocket turning (if the rear sprocket is being renewed as well do that now and install

the rear wheel so that the brake can be used) **(see illustration)**.

11 On GSX600/750F models fit the speed sensor rotor and tighten its bolt to the specified torque setting. On GSX750 models fit the stopper bolt with its washer and tighten to the specified torque.

 Keep your old front sprocket as it can be used along with a holding tool to lock the transmission input shaft should you ever need to remove the clutch (see Chapter 2).

12 Install the sprocket cover (see Section 17). Adjust and lubricate the chain following the procedures described in Chapter 1.

Rear sprocket

13 Remove the rear wheel (see Chapter 6).
14 Unscrew the nuts securing the sprocket to the hub assembly **(see illustration)**.

Remove the sprocket, noting which way round it fits.

15 Fit the sprocket onto the hub with the stamped mark facing out. Install the nuts and tighten them evenly and in a criss-cross sequence to the torque setting specified at the beginning of the Chapter.

16 Install the rear wheel (see Chapter 6).

19 Rear sprocket coupling/ rubber dampers – removal, inspection and installation

1 Remove the rear wheel (see Chapter 6). *Caution: Do not lay the wheel down on the disc as it could become warped. Lay the wheel on wooden blocks so that the disc is off the ground.*

2 Lift the sprocket coupling away from the wheel leaving the rubber dampers in position **(see illustration)**. Note the spacer inside the coupling – it should be a tight fit but remove it if it is likely to drop out. Check the coupling for cracks or any obvious signs of damage. Also check the sprocket studs for wear or damage.

3 Lift the rubber damper segments from the wheel and check them for cracks, hardening and general deterioration **(see illustration)**. Renew them as a set if necessary.

4 Checking and renewal procedures for the sprocket coupling bearing are described in Chapter 6.

5 Installation is the reverse of removal. Smear some grease around the outside of the left-hand bearing housing where the sprocket coupling fits over it. Make sure the spacer is still correctly installed in the coupling, or install it if it was removed.

6 Install the rear wheel (see Chapter 6).

19.2 Lift the sprocket coupling out of the wheel noting the spacer (arrowed)

19.3 Check the rubber dampers

5

Notes

Chapter 6
Brakes, wheels and tyres

Contents

Brake discs – inspection, removal and installation 3
Brake fluid level check . . . . .see *Daily (pre-ride) checks*
Brake light switches – check and replacement . . . . . . .see Chapter 8
Brake pads – renewal 2
Brake pad wear check . . . . .see Chapter 1
Brake hoses and fittings – inspection and renewal 8
Brake system – bleeding and fluid change 9
Brake system check . . . . .see Chapter 1
Front brake calipers – removal, overhaul and installation 4
Front brake master cylinder – removal, overhaul and installation . . . 6
Front wheel – removal and installation 12

General information 1
Rear brake caliper – removal, overhaul and installation 5
Rear brake master cylinder – removal, overhaul and installation . . . 7
Rear wheel – removal and installation 13
Tyres – general information and fitting 15
Tyres – pressure, tread depth and condition . . .see *Daily (pre-ride) checks*
Wheels – general check . . . . .see Chapter 1
Wheel bearings – check . . . . .see Chapter 1
Wheel bearings – inspection and renewal 14
Wheels – alignment check 11
Wheels – inspection and repair 10

Degrees of difficulty

Easy, suitable for novice with little experience		Fairly easy, suitable for beginner with some experience		Fairly difficult, suitable for competent DIY mechanic		Difficult, suitable for experienced DIY mechanic	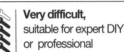	Very difficult, suitable for expert DIY or professional

Specifications

Brakes

Brake fluid type	DOT 4
Disc minimum thickness	
Front	
Standard	4.5 mm
Service limit	4.0 mm
Rear	
Standard	5.0 mm
Service limit	4.5 mm
Disc maximum runout (front and rear)	0.3 mm
Caliper bore ID	
Front	30.230 to 30.306 mm
Rear	38.180 to 38.256 mm
Caliper piston OD	
Front	30.150 to 30.200 mm
Rear	38.098 to 38.148 mm
Master cylinder bore ID	
Front	14.000 to 14.043 mm
Rear	12.700 to 12.743 mm
Master cylinder piston OD	
Front	13.957 to 13.984 mm
Rear	12.657 to 12.684 mm
Rear brake pedal height	see Chapter 1

Wheels

Maximum wheel runout (front and rear)	
Axial (side-to-side)	2.0 mm
Radial (out-of-round)	2.0 mm
Maximum axle runout (front and rear)	0.25 mm
Rim size	
Front	17 x MT3.50
Rear	
GSX600/750F	17 x MT4.50
GSX750	17 x MT5.50

6

Tyres

Tyre pressures . . . . see *Daily (pre-ride) checks*
Tyre sizes*
  Front 120/70-ZR17 58W
  Rear
    GSX600/750F 150/70-ZR17 69W
    GSX750 . . . . 170/60-ZR17 72W
Refer to the owners handbook or the tyre information label on the chainguard for approved tyre brands.

Torque settings

Brake caliper bleed valves . . . . 7.5 Nm
Brake hose banjo bolts . . . . 23 Nm
Footrest bracket bolts – GSX750F . . . . 23 Nm
Front brake master cylinder clamp bolts . . . . 10 Nm
Front brake caliper mounting bolts . . . . 39 Nm
Front brake disc bolts . . . . 23 Nm
Front wheel axle – GSX750 . . . . 100 Nm
Front wheel axle clamp bolt(s) . . . . 23 Nm
Front wheel axle nut – GSX600/750F . . . . 44 Nm
Rear brake caliper body joining bolts . . . . 30 Nm
Rear brake caliper mounting bolts . . . . 26 Nm
Rear brake disc bolts . . . . 23 Nm
Rear brake master cylinder bolts . . . . 10 Nm
Rear brake torque arm nuts
  GSX600F . . . . 32 Nm
  GSX750F and GSX750 . . . . 35 Nm
Rear wheel axle nut
  GSX600/750F . . . . 65 Nm
  GSX750 . . . . 100 Nm

1 General information

All models covered in this manual are fitted with cast alloy wheels designed for tubeless tyres only. Both front and rear brakes are hydraulically operated disc brakes.

On all models the front brakes have twin piston sliding calipers and the rear brake has a single opposed piston caliper.

Caution: Hydraulic disc brake components rarely require disassembly. Do not disassemble components unless absolutely necessary. If a hydraulic brake line is loosened, the entire system must be disassembled, drained, cleaned and then properly filled and bled upon reassembly. Do not use solvents on internal brake components. Solvents will cause the seals to swell and distort. Use only clean brake fluid or denatured alcohol for cleaning. Use care when working with brake fluid as it can injure your eyes and it will damage painted surfaces and plastic parts.

2 Brake pads – renewal

> **Warning: The dust created by the brake system may contain asbestos, which is harmful to your health. Never blow it out with compressed air and don't inhale any of it. An approved filtering mask should be worn when working on the brakes. Do not, under any circumstances, use petroleum-based solvents to clean brake parts. Use clean brake fluid, brake cleaner or denatured alcohol only.**

Front brake pads

1 If new pads are being fitted, push the brake caliper against the disc so that the pistons are forced back into the caliper to allow for the increased friction material thickness. It may be necessary to remove the master cylinder reservoir cover and diaphragm and remove some fluid (see *Daily (pre-ride) checks*). If the pistons are difficult to push back, either attach a length of clear hose to the bleed valve and place the open end in a suitable container, then open the valve and try again, or wait until the caliper has been displaced and the pads removed as it is not good to push too hard against a floating disc (see Step 7). If you open the bleed valve, take great care not to draw any air into the system **(see illustration 9.5a)**. If in doubt, bleed the brakes afterwards (see Section 9).

2 Unscrew the bolt(s) securing the brake hose clamp to the front fork **(see illustration 4.2)**. Unscrew the caliper bracket mounting bolts and slide the caliper assembly off the disc **(see illustrations)**.

3 Pull the retaining clip out of the pad pin,

2.2a Unscrew the caliper mounting bolts (arrowed) . . .

2.2b . . . and slide the caliper off the disc

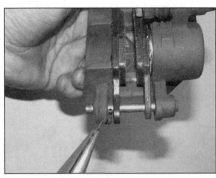

2.3a Remove the clip . . .

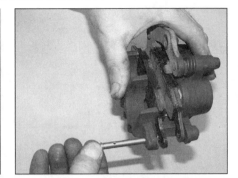

2.3b . . . and withdraw the pin

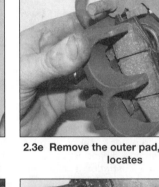

2.3c Pivot the inner pad up . . .

then withdraw the pin **(see illustrations)**. Pivot the inner pad out of the caliper until it clears the bracket then slide it sideways off its post **(see illustrations)**. Remove the outer pad, noting how it locates against the guide **(see illustration)**. Note the pad spring in the top of caliper and the pad guide on the caliper bracket and remove them if required for cleaning or renewal, noting how they fit **(see illustrations)**.

4 Inspect the surface of each pad for contamination and check whether the friction material has worn excessively (see Chapter 1). If either pad is excessively worn, is fouled with oil or grease, or is heavily scored or damaged by dirt and debris, both sets of pads must be renewed as a set. Note that it is extremely difficult to effectively degrease the friction material; if the pads are contaminated in any way new ones must be fitted.

5 If the pads are in good condition clean them carefully, using a fine wire brush which is completely free of oil and grease to remove all traces of road dirt and corrosion. Using a pointed instrument, clean out the grooves in the friction material and dig out any embedded particles of foreign matter **(see illustration)**. Spray with a dedicated brake cleaner to remove any dust. It is also worth spraying the inside of the caliper to remove any dust there, and also to spray the discs.

6 Check the condition of the brake discs (see Section 3).

7 If necessary, push the pistons back into the

2.3d . . . then slide it off its post

2.3f Note the pad spring (arrowed) . . .

2.3e Remove the outer pad, noting how it locates

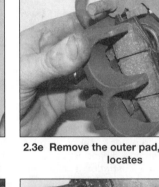

2.3g . . . and the pad guide (arrowed)

caliper to create room for the new pads – you can use your hands to do this, though a piece of wood against the pistons in conjunction with some grips and a piece of card to protect the caliper works very well, as does a proper piston-pushing tool **(see illustrations)**.

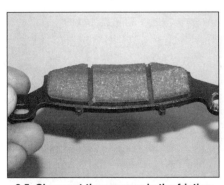

2.5 Clean out the grooves in the friction material

2.7a Push the pistons back using your fingers . . .

2.7b . . . or some grips and a piece of wood

6

2.11 Slide the caliper onto the disc and tighten the bolts to the specified torque

2.14 Remove the pad cover

2.15 Remove the retaining clip

8 Make sure that the pad spring and pad guide are correctly fitted **(see illustrations 2.3f and g)**.

9 Remove all traces of corrosion from the pad pin and check it is not bent or damaged. Smear the pin, the inner pad post, the backs of the pads and the leading and trailing edges of the backing material with copper-based grease, making sure that none gets on the friction material.

10 Fit the outer pad into the caliper so that its back is against the pistons, making sure the inner end locates correctly against the guide on the bracket **(see illustration 2.3e)**. Fit the inner pad over its post, then slide it across and pivot it down **(see illustrations 2.3d and c)**. Press the pads up against the pad spring to align the holes and insert the pad pin **(see illustration 2.3b)**. Secure the pin with the retaining clip, making sure it fits through the hole in the pin – if necessary rotate the pad pin to align the hole correctly **(see illustration 2.3a)**. Use a new clip if the old one is deformed in any way.

11 Slide the caliper assembly onto the disc making sure the pads locate on each side **(see illustration)**. Tighten the mounting bolts to the specified torque setting. Fit the brake hose clamp onto the front fork and secure it with the bolt(s) **(see illustration 4.2)**.

12 Top up the master cylinder reservoir if necessary (see *Daily (pre-ride) checks*).

13 Operate the brake lever several times to bring the pads into contact with the disc. Check the operation of the brake before riding the motorcycle. Repeat the operation on the pads in the other front brake caliper.

Rear brake pads

Note: *If the pad pins have not been previously greased and have not been removed for a while, they could well be very difficult to withdraw (see Step 16). If this is the case, they will have to be driven out from the back of the caliper. To do this you will have to remove the caliper (see Section 5), as otherwise the shock could distort the disc. If you apply penetrating fluid this will help, but make sure none gets on the pads.*

14 Prise off the brake pad cover using a flat-bladed screwdriver **(see illustration)**.

15 Pull the retaining clip out of the pad pins **(see illustration)**. Before removing the pads. Look up into the caliper and note how the pad springs fit.

16 Withdraw the pad pins from the caliper using a suitable pair of pliers and remove the pad springs **(see illustration)**. Withdraw the pads from the caliper body. If required remove the anti-chatter shim from the back of each pad, noting how they fit.

17 If new pads are being fitted, push the pistons as far back into the caliper as possible

to allow for the increased friction material thickness. Use a piece of wood as leverage, or place the old pads back in the caliper and use a metal bar or a screwdriver inserted between them, or use grips and a rag or card to protect the caliper body **(see illustrations)**. You can do this with the pads removed, but you should only use wood or your fingers so as not to damage the pistons. In both cases take care not to damage the disc. It may be necessary to remove the master cylinder reservoir cap and diaphragm and remove some fluid (see *Daily (pre-ride) checks*). If the pistons are difficult to push back, attach a length of clear hose to the bleed valve and place the open end in a suitable container, then open the valve and try again **(see illustration 9.5b)**. Take great care not to draw any air into the system. If in doubt, bleed the brake afterwards (see Section 9).

18 Refer to Steps 4, 5 and 6 above.

19 Smear the backs of the pads and the shank of each pad pin with copper-based grease, making sure that none gets on the front or sides of the pads. Fit the anti-chatter shim onto the back of each pad so that its open side will be facing forward when the pad is installed.

20 Insert the outer pad up into the caliper with the friction material facing the disc, then slide one pad pin, with its holed end on the outside, through the hole in the pad and part-

2.16 Withdraw the pad pins and remove the springs and pads

2.17a Push the pistons back using a bar as leverage . . .

2.17b . . . or grips

2.20a Insert the outer pad and slide one pin part-way through . . .

2.20b . . . then locate the end of one spring under the pin and onto the pad

2.20c Push up on the other end of the spring and slide the pin through

2.20d Fit the inner pad . . .

20.20e . . . then locate the spring end under the pin and onto the pad . . .

20.20f . . . and push the other end up and slide the pin through

way through the caliper **(see illustrations)**. Fit the pad spring, locating one end under the installed pad pin and onto the edge of the friction material, fitting the central hooked section over the bottom edge of the pad backing **(see illustration)**. Press up on the free end of the pad spring and slide the other pad pin over the spring end **(see illustration)**. Fit the inner pad up into the caliper and repeat the procedure of installing the pad spring and second pin **(see illustrations)**. Secure the pins with the retaining clip, making sure it fits through the holes in the pad pins – if necessary rotate the pad pins to align their holes correctly **(see illustration 2.15)**. Use a new clip if the old one is deformed in any way.

21 Fit the pad cover **(see illustration 2.14)**.

22 Top up the master cylinder reservoir if necessary (see *Daily (pre-ride) checks*).

23 Operate the brake pedal several times to bring the pads into contact with the disc. Check the operation of the brake before riding the motorcycle.

3 Brake discs – inspection, removal and installation

⚠️ *Warning: The dust created by the brake system may contain asbestos, which is harmful to your health. Never blow it out with compressed air and don't inhale any of it. An approved filtering mask should be worn when working on the brakes. Do not,*

under any circumstances, use petroleum-based solvents to clean brake parts. Use clean brake fluid, brake cleaner or denatured alcohol only.

Inspection

1 Visually inspect the surface of the disc for score marks and other damage. Light scratches are normal after use and won't affect brake operation, but deep grooves and heavy score marks will reduce braking efficiency and accelerate pad wear. If a disc is badly grooved it must be machined or renewed.

2 To check disc runout, position the bike on its centrestand so that the wheel being checked can be raised off the ground. Mount a dial gauge to a fork slider or on the swingarm, according to wheel, with the plunger on the gauge touching the surface of

the disc about 10 mm (1/2 in) from the outer edge. Rotate the wheel and watch the gauge needle, comparing the reading with the limit listed in the Specifications at the beginning of the Chapter. If the runout is greater than the service limit, check the wheel bearings for play (see Chapter 1). If the bearings are worn, renew them (see Section 14) and repeat this check. It is also worth removing the disc (see below) and checking for built-up corrosion (see Step 6) as this will cause runout. If the runout is still excessive, the disc must be renewed, although machining by an engineer may be possible. **Note:** *Always renew the front discs as a pair, never singly.*

3 The disc must not be machined or allowed to wear down to a thickness less than the service limit as listed in this Chapter's Specifications and as marked on the disc itself **(see illustrations)**. Check the thickness

3.3a Front disc minimum thickness markings

3.3b Rear disc minimum thickness markings

6

3.3c Checking disc thickness

3.5a Front disc bolts (arrowed)

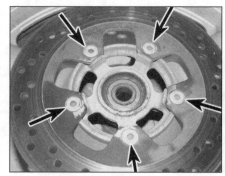

3.5b Rear disc bolts (arrowed)

of the disc using a micrometer **(see illustration)**. If the thickness of the disc is less than the service limit, it must be renewed.

Removal

4 Remove the wheel (see Section 12 or 13). *Caution: Do not lay the wheel down and allow it to rest on the disc – the disc could become warped. Set the wheel on wood blocks so the disc doesn't support the weight of the wheel.*
5 Mark the relationship of the disc to the wheel, so it can be installed in the same position and on the same side of the wheel in the case of the front discs. Unscrew the disc retaining bolts, loosening them a little at a time in a criss-cross pattern to avoid distorting the disc, then remove the disc from the wheel **(see illustrations)**.

Installation

6 Before installing the disc, make sure there is no dirt or corrosion where the disc seats on the hub, particularly right in the angle of the seat, as this will not allow the disc to sit flat when it is bolted down and it will appear to be warped when checked or when using the brake.
7 Install the disc on the wheel, making sure the directional arrow is on the outside and pointing in the direction of normal (i.e. forward) rotation. Also note any R or L marking on the front discs that denotes on which side of the wheel it must be mounted.

Align the previously applied matchmarks (if you're reinstalling the original disc).
8 Apply a suitable non-permanent thread locking compound to the threads of the disc bolts, and tighten them evenly in a criss-cross pattern to the torque setting specified at the beginning of the Chapter. Clean off all grease from the brake disc(s) using acetone or brake system cleaner. If a new brake disc has been installed, remove any protective coating from its working surfaces.
9 Install the wheel (see Section 12 or 13). Note that when installing a new disc also fit new brake pads (see Section 2).
10 Operate the brake lever or pedal (as applicable) several times to bring the pads into contact with the disc. Check the operation of the brakes carefully before riding the bike.

---

4 Front brake calipers –
removal, overhaul and installation

> **Warning: If a caliper indicates the need for an overhaul (usually due to leaking fluid or sticky operation), all old brake fluid should be flushed from the system. Also, the dust created by the brake system may contain asbestos, which is harmful to your health. Never blow it out with compressed air and don't inhale any of it. An approved**

filtering mask should be worn when working on the brakes. Do not, under any circumstances, use petroleum-based solvents to clean brake parts. Use clean brake fluid, brake cleaner or denatured alcohol only.

> **Warning: Use care when working with brake fluid as it can injure your eyes and it will damage painted surfaces and plastic parts.**

Removal

1 If the caliper is just being displaced and not completely removed or overhauled, do not disconnect the brake hose. If the caliper is being completely removed or overhauled, unscrew the brake hose banjo bolt and detach the hose, noting its alignment with the caliper **(see illustration)**. Either plug the hose using another suitable short piece of hose fitted through the eye of the banjo union (it must be a fairly tight fit to seal it properly), clamp it using a hose clamp, or wrap a plastic bag tightly around to minimise fluid loss and prevent dirt entering the system. Discard the sealing washers as new ones must be used on installation. **Note:** *If you are planning to overhaul the caliper and don't have a source of compressed air to blow out the pistons, just loosen the banjo bolt at this stage and retighten it lightly. The bike's hydraulic system can then be used to force the pistons out of the body once the pads have been removed. Disconnect the hose once the pistons have been sufficiently displaced.*
2 If required, unscrew the bolt(s) securing the brake hose clamp to the front fork **(see illustration)**.
3 Unscrew the caliper bracket mounting bolts and slide the caliper assembly off the disc **(see illustrations 2.2a and b)**.
4 If the caliper is being overhauled, remove the brake pads (see Section 2).

Overhaul

5 Separate the caliper from the bracket by sliding them apart **(see illustration)**. If required, remove the pad spring from the caliper and the guide from the bracket, noting how they fit **(see illustrations 2.3f and g)**.

4.1 Brake hose banjo bolt (arrowed)

4.2 Brake hose clamp bolt (arrowed)

4.5 Separate the caliper and bracket by sliding them apart

6 Clean the exterior of the caliper with denatured alcohol or brake system cleaner **(see illustration)**.

7 Remove the pistons from the caliper body, either by pumping them out by operating the brake lever, or by using compressed air. If the compressed air method is used, place a wad of rag over the pistons to act as a cushion, then use compressed air directed into the fluid inlet to force the pistons out of the body. Use only low pressure to ease the pistons out, and make sure they are displaced at the same time. If the air pressure is too high and the pistons are forced out, the caliper and/or pistons may be damaged.

 Warning: Never place your fingers in front of the pistons in an attempt to catch or protect them when applying compressed air, as serious injury could result. Place the caliper piston side down on a bench, with the rag between them, and let the air lift the caliper off the piston. Caution: Do not try to remove the pistons by levering them out, or by using pliers or any other grips.

8 Using a wooden or plastic tool, remove the dust seals from the caliper bore. Discard them as new ones must be used on installation. If a metal tool is being used, take great care not to damage the caliper bores.

9 Remove and discard the piston seals in the same way.

10 Clean the pistons and bores, paying attention to the seal grooves, with denatured

4.12 Remove the rubber boots

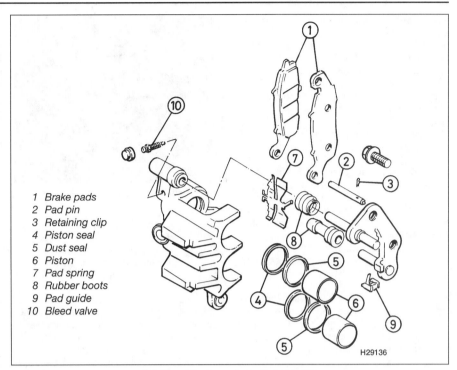

1 Brake pads
2 Pad pin
3 Retaining clip
4 Piston seal
5 Dust seal
6 Piston
7 Pad spring
8 Rubber boots
9 Pad guide
10 Bleed valve

H29136

4.6 Front brake caliper components

alcohol, clean brake fluid or brake system cleaner. If compressed air is available, use it to dry the parts thoroughly (make sure it's filtered and unlubricated).
Caution: Do not, under any circumstances, use a petroleum-based solvent to clean brake parts.

11 Inspect the caliper bores and pistons for signs of corrosion, nicks and burrs and loss of plating. If surface defects are present, the caliper and/or pistons must be renewed. If the necessary measuring equipment is available, compare the dimensions of the pistons and bores to those given in the Specifications Section of this Chapter for new components. Renew any component which is worn significantly beyond the standard dimensions. If the caliper is in bad shape the master cylinder should also be checked.

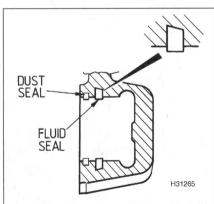

DUST SEAL

FLUID SEAL

H31265

4.13 Make sure each piston seal is fitted correctly

12 Remove the slider pin rubber boots from the caliper **(see illustration)**. Clean off all traces of corrosion and hardened grease from the boots and pins. If the rubber boots are damaged, deformed or deteriorated, fit new ones. Apply a smear of silicone based grease to the boots and fit them into their bores in the caliper.

13 Lubricate the new piston seals with clean brake fluid and fit them in their grooves in the caliper bores, with the wider side facing out **(see illustration)**.

14 Lubricate the new dust seals with clean brake fluid and fit them in their grooves in the caliper bore.

15 Lubricate the pistons with clean brake fluid and fit them closed-end first into the caliper bores. Using your thumbs, push the pistons all the way in, making sure they enter the bore squarely.

16 Make sure that the pad spring and pad guide are correctly fitted **(see illustrations 2.3f and g)**. Apply a smear of silicone based grease to the slider pins on the bracket. Slide the caliper and bracket together.

Installation

17 If the caliper has not been overhauled, separate the caliper from the bracket by sliding them apart **(see illustration 4.5)**. Remove the slider pin rubber boots from the caliper **(see illustration 4.12)**. Clean off all traces of corrosion and hardened grease from the boots and pins. If the rubber boots are damaged, deformed or deteriorated, fit new ones. Apply a smear of silicone based grease to the boots and slider pins. Fit the boots into their bores. Make sure that the pad spring and pad guide are correctly fitted **(see**

6

illustrations 2.3f and g). Slide the caliper and bracket together.

18 If the caliper has been overhauled, install the brake pads (see Section 2).

19 Slide the caliper assembly onto the disc making sure the pads locate on each side. Tighten the mounting bolts to the torque setting specified at the beginning of the Chapter.

20 If detached, connect the brake hose to the caliper, using new sealing washers on each side of the fitting. Align the hose as noted on removal **(see illustration 4.1)**. Tighten the banjo bolt to the torque setting specified at the beginning of the Chapter.

21 If removed, fit the brake hose clamp onto the front fork and secure it with the bolt(s) **(see illustration 4.2)**.

22 Fill the master cylinder reservoir with DOT 4 brake fluid (see *Daily (pre-ride) checks*) and bleed the hydraulic system as described in Section 9.

23 Operate the brake lever several times to bring the pads into contact with the disc. Check that there are no fluid leaks and thoroughly test the operation of the front brake before riding the motorcycle.

---

5 Rear brake caliper – removal, overhaul and installation

> ⚠️ *Warning: If a caliper indicates the need for an overhaul (usually due to leaking fluid or sticky operation), all old brake fluid should be flushed from the system. Also, the dust created by the brake system may contain asbestos, which is harmful to your health. Never blow it out with compressed air and don't inhale any of it. An approved filtering mask should be worn when working on the brakes. Do not, under any circumstances, use petroleum-based solvents to clean brake parts. Use clean brake fluid, brake cleaner or denatured alcohol only.*

5.1 Brake hose banjo bolt (arrowed)

> ⚠️ *Warning: Use care when working with brake fluid as it can injure your eyes and it will damage painted surfaces and plastic parts.*

Removal

1 If the caliper is just being displaced and not completely removed or overhauled, do not disconnect the brake hose. If the caliper is being completely removed or overhauled, unscrew the brake hose banjo bolt and detach the hose, noting its alignment with the caliper **(see illustration)**. Either plug the hose using another suitable short piece of hose fitted through the eye of the banjo union (it must be a tight fit to seal it properly), clamp it using a hose clamp, or wrap a plastic bag tightly around to minimise fluid loss and prevent dirt entering the system. Discard the sealing washers as new ones must be used on installation. **Note:** *If you are planning to overhaul the caliper and don't have a source of compressed air to blow out the pistons, just loosen the banjo bolt at this stage and retighten it lightly. The bike's hydraulic system can then be used to force the pistons out of the body once the pads have been removed. Disconnect the hose once the pistons have been sufficiently displaced.*

2 If the caliper is being overhauled, remove the brake pads (see Section 2). If the caliper

5.2 Caliper body joining bolts (A), caliper mounting bolts (B), torque arm bolt (C)

5.4 Unscrew the bolts and slide the caliper off the disc

body is to be split into its halves for overhaul, slacken the joining bolts now and lightly retighten them **(see illustration)**.

3 Slacken the caliper mounting bolts, but do not yet remove them. Unscrew the nut on the bolt securing the brake torque arm to the caliper. Withdraw the bolt and move the arm off the caliper.

4 Unscrew the caliper mounting bolts and slide the caliper down off the disc **(see illustration)**.

Overhaul

5 Clean the exterior of the caliper with denatured alcohol or brake system cleaner **(see illustration)**.

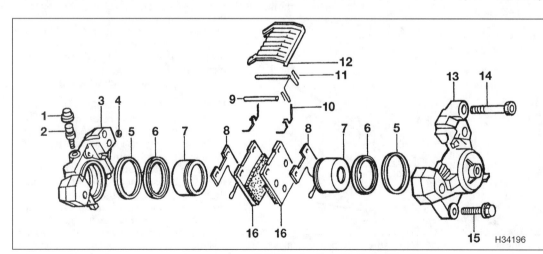

1	Bleed valve cap
2	Bleed valve
3	Caliper body half
4	Caliper seal
5	Piston seal
6	Dust seal
7	Piston
8	Anti-chatter shim
9	Pad pin
10	Pad spring
11	Retaining clip
12	Brake pad cover
13	Caliper body half
14	Caliper joining bolt
15	Caliper mounting bolt
16	Brake pads

H34196

5.5 Rear brake caliper components

5.16 Install the bolts and tighten them as described

5.20 Use a new sealing washer on each side of the union

6.3 Slacken the reservoir cover screws

6 Displace the pistons as far as possible from the caliper body, either by pumping them out by operating the rear brake pedal, or by forcing them out using compressed air – do not allow the piston heads to touch. If the compressed air method is used, place a wad of rag between the pistons to act as a cushion, then use compressed air directed into the fluid inlet to force the pistons out of the body. Use only low pressure to ease the pistons out. If the air pressure is too high and the pistons are forced out, the caliper and/or pistons may be damaged.

 Warning: Never place your fingers in front of either piston in an attempt to catch or protect it when applying compressed air, as serious injury could result.
Caution: Do not try to remove the pistons by levering them out, or by using pliers or any other grips.

7 Unscrew the caliper body joining bolts and separate the body halves. Remove the piston from each half. Mark each piston head and caliper body with a felt marker to ensure that the pistons can be matched to their original bores on reassembly. Extract the fluid seal from whichever body half it is in and discard it as a new one must be used.

8 Using a wooden or plastic tool, remove the dust seals from the caliper bores. Discard them as new ones must be used on installation. If a metal tool is being used, take great care not to damage the caliper bore.

9 Remove and discard the piston seals in the same way.

10 Clean the pistons and bores, paying attention to the seal grooves, with denatured alcohol, clean brake fluid or brake system cleaner. If compressed air is available, use it to dry the parts thoroughly (make sure it's filtered and unlubricated).
Caution: Do not, under any circumstances, use a petroleum-based solvent to clean brake parts.

11 Inspect the caliper bores and pistons for signs of corrosion, nicks and burrs and loss of plating. If surface defects are present, the caliper and/or pistons must be renewed. If the necessary measuring equipment is available, compare the dimensions of the pistons and bores to those given in the Specifications

Section of this Chapter for new components. Renew any component which is worn significantly beyond the standard dimensions. If the caliper is in bad shape the master cylinder should also be checked.

12 Lubricate the new piston seals with clean brake fluid and fit them in their grooves in the caliper bores, with the wider side facing out **(see illustration 4.13)**.

13 Lubricate the new dust seal with clean brake fluid and fit it in its groove in the caliper bore.

14 Lubricate the pistons with clean brake fluid and install each one closed-end first into its caliper bore. Using your thumbs, push the pistons all the way in, making sure they enter the bores squarely.

15 Lubricate the new caliper body fluid seal with clean brake fluid and install it into one half of the caliper body. Join the two halves of the caliper body together, making sure that the seal stays correctly seated in its recess. Install the caliper body joining bolts and tighten them to the torque setting specified at the beginning of the Chapter. If it is not possible to tighten the bolts fully at this stage, tighten them as much as possible, then tighten them fully once the caliper has been installed.

Installation

16 Slide the caliper onto the brake disc, making sure the pads sit squarely over each side of the disc if they weren't removed **(see illustration 5.4)**. Install the caliper mounting bolts, and tighten them finger-tight **(see illustration)**.

17 Fit the brake torque arm onto the caliper and secure it with its bolt **(see illustration 5.2)**. Tighten the nut to the torque setting specified at the beginning of the Chapter. Now tighten the caliper mounting bolts to the specified torque setting.

18 If the calipers were overhauled and if not already done, tighten the caliper body joining bolts to the specified torque setting **(see illustration 5.2)**.

19 If removed, install the brake pads (see Section 2).

20 If removed, connect the brake hose to the caliper, making sure it is routed through its guide on the swingarm, using new sealing washers on each side of the fitting **(see illustration)**. Align the hose as noted on

removal **(see illustration 5.1)**. Tighten the banjo bolt to the torque setting specified at the beginning of the Chapter. Top up the master cylinder reservoir with DOT 4 brake fluid (see *Daily (pre-ride) checks*) and bleed the hydraulic system as described in Section 9.

21 Operate the brake pedal several times to bring the pads into contact with the disc. Check that there are no fluid leaks and thoroughly test the operation of the rear brake before riding the motorcycle.

---

6 Front brake master cylinder
– removal, overhaul and installation

 Warning: Take care when working with brake fluid as it can injure your eyes and it will damage painted surfaces and plastic parts.

1 If the master cylinder is leaking fluid, or if the lever does not produce a firm feel when the brake is applied, and bleeding the brakes does not help (see Section 9), and the hydraulic hoses and unions are all in good condition, then master cylinder overhaul is recommended.

2 Before disassembling the master cylinder, read through the entire procedure and make sure that you have the correct rebuild kit. Also, you will need some new DOT 4 brake fluid, some clean rags and internal circlip pliers. **Note:** *To prevent damage to the paint from spilled brake fluid, always cover the fuel tank, fairing panels (GSX600/750F models) and any other painted surfaces that could be affected, when working on the master cylinder.*
Caution: Disassembly, overhaul and reassembly of the brake master cylinder must be done in a spotlessly clean work area to avoid contamination and possible failure of the brake hydraulic system components.

Removal

Note: *If the master cylinder is being displaced from the handlebar and not being removed completely or overhauled, follow Step 8 only.*

3 Loosen, but do not remove, the screws holding the reservoir cover in place **(see illustration)**.

6

6.6 Disconnect the brake light switch wiring connectors (arrowed)

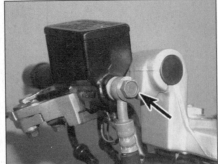

6.7 Brake hose banjo bolt (arrowed)

6.8 Master cylinder clamp bolts (arrowed)

4 Remove the front brake lever (see Chapter 5).

5 On GSX750 models, remove the rear view mirror (see Chapter 7).

6 Disconnect the electrical connectors from the brake light switch **(see illustration)**.

7 Unscrew the brake hose banjo bolt and separate the hose from the master cylinder, noting its alignment **(see illustration)**. Either plug the hose using another suitable short piece of hose fitted through the eye of the banjo union (it must be a tight fit to seal it properly), clamp it using a hose clamp, or wrap a plastic bag tightly around to minimise fluid loss and prevent dirt entering the system. Discard the sealing washers as new ones must be used on installation.

8 Unscrew the master cylinder clamp bolts, then lift the master cylinder assembly away from the handlebar, noting how the mating surfaces of the clamp align with the punch mark on the top (GSX600/750F models) or bottom (GSX750 models) of the handlebar **(see illustration)**.

Caution: Do not tip the master cylinder upside down or brake fluid will run out.

9 Remove the reservoir cover, diaphragm plate and rubber diaphragm. Drain the brake fluid from the reservoir into a suitable container. Wipe any remaining fluid out of the reservoir with a clean rag.

10 If required undo the brake light switch screw and remove the switch, noting how it fits **(see illustration)**.

6.10 Brake light switch screw (arrowed)

Overhaul

11 Carefully remove the rubber dust boot from the end of the master cylinder and from around the piston, noting how it locates **(see illustration)**.

12 Push the piston in and, using circlip pliers, remove the circlip from its groove in the master cylinder and slide out the piston assembly and the spring, noting how they fit. If they are difficult to remove, apply low pressure compressed air to the fluid outlet. Remove the seal from the piston and the cup from the spring. Lay the parts out in order as you remove them to prevent confusion during reassembly.

13 Clean all parts with clean brake fluid or denatured alcohol. If compressed air is available, use it to dry the parts thoroughly (make sure it's filtered and unlubricated).

Caution: Do not, under any circumstances, use a petroleum-based solvent to clean brake parts.

14 Check the master cylinder bore for corrosion, scratches, nicks and score marks. If the necessary measuring equipment is available, compare the dimensions of the piston and bore to those given in the

Specifications Section of this Chapter for new components. Renew any component which is worn significantly beyond the standard dimensions. If the master cylinder is in poor condition, then the calipers should be checked as well. Check that the fluid inlet and outlet ports in the master cylinder are clear.

If the necessary measuring equipment is available, compare the dimensions of the piston and bore to those given in the Specifications Section of this Chapter for new components. Renew any component which is worn significantly beyond the standard dimensions. If the caliper is in bad shape the master cylinder should also be checked.

15 The dust boot, circlip, piston, seal, cup and spring are included in the rebuild kit. Use all of the new parts, regardless of the apparent condition of the old ones. If the seal is not already on the piston, fit it according to the layout of the old one.

16 Lubricate the cup, seal and piston with clean brake fluid.

17 Locate the cup onto the narrow end of the spring with the flat side facing away. Slide the spring into the master cylinder with the wide end going in first, then slide the piston into the

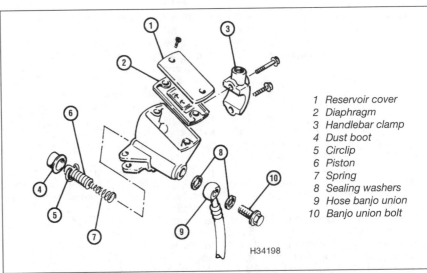

1 Reservoir cover
2 Diaphragm
3 Handlebar clamp
4 Dust boot
5 Circlip
6 Piston
7 Spring
8 Sealing washers
9 Hose banjo union
10 Banjo union bolt

H34198

6.11 Front master cylinder components

7.4 Unscrew the bolts and remove the footrest bracket –
GSX750F shown

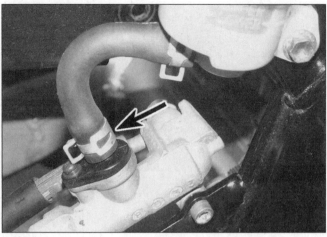

7.5 Release the clamp (arrowed), then detach the hose and drain
the reservoir

cylinder. Make sure the lips on the cup and seal do not turn inside out when they enter the bore. Depress the piston and install the new circlip, making sure that it locates in the groove in the master cylinder.

18 Apply some silicone grease to the inside of the rubber dust boot, then install it, making sure it is seated properly in the groove in the master cylinder and around the piston.

19 Inspect the reservoir rubber diaphragm and renew it if it is damaged or deteriorated.

Installation

20 If removed, locate the brake light switch on the underside of the master cylinder so that the projection on the switch fits into the hole in the master cylinder body, and secure it with the screw.

21 Attach the master cylinder to the handlebar and fit the clamp, on GSX600/750F models with its UP mark facing up and on GSX750 models with the mirror mounting facing up. Align the top (GSX600/750F models) or bottom (GSX750 models) mating surfaces of the clamp with the punch mark on the top or bottom of the handlebar, then tighten the top bolt first, then the bottom bolt, to the torque setting specified at the beginning of the Chapter.

22 Connect the brake hose to the master cylinder, using new sealing washers on each side of the union, and aligning the hose as noted on removal (see illustration 6.7). Tighten the banjo bolt to the torque setting specified at the beginning of the Chapter.

23 Install the brake lever (see Chapter 5). Connect the brake light switch wiring.

24 On GSX750 models fit the rear view mirror (see Chapter 7).

25 Fill the fluid reservoir with new DOT 4 brake fluid as described in *Daily (pre-ride) checks*. Refer to Section 9 of this Chapter and bleed the air from the system.

26 Fit the rubber diaphragm, making sure it is correctly seated, the diaphragm plate and the cover onto the reservoir.

27 Check that there are no fluid leaks and thoroughly test the operation of the front brake before riding the motorcycle. Check that the front brake light switch works correctly.

7 Rear brake master cylinder – removal, overhaul and installation

1 If the master cylinder is leaking fluid, or if the pedal does not produce a firm feel when the brake is applied, and bleeding the brake does not help (see Section 9), and the hydraulic hoses and unions are all in good condition, then master cylinder overhaul is recommended.

2 Before disassembling the master cylinder, read through the entire procedure and make sure that you have the correct rebuild kit. Also, you will need some new DOT 4 brake fluid, some clean rags and internal circlip pliers. **Note:** *To prevent damage to the paint from spilled brake fluid, always cover the surrounding components when working on the master cylinder.*

Caution: Disassembly, overhaul and reassembly of the brake master cylinder must be done in a spotlessly clean work area to avoid contamination and possible failure of the brake hydraulic system components.

⚠️ *Warning: Use care when working with brake fluid as it can injure your eyes and it will damage painted surfaces and plastic parts.*

Removal

3 On GSX600/750F models remove the right-hand fairing side panel (see Chapter 7). On GSX750 models remove the right-hand side panel (see Chapter 7).

4 On GSX600/750F models remove the rear brake pedal (see Chapter 5). Unscrew the

bolts securing the heel protector (GSX600F) or footrest bracket (GSX750F) or both (GSX750) and remove it/them **(see illustration)**.

5 Remove the reservoir cap or cover to act as a vent. Detach the hose from the union on the master cylinder and allow the fluid from the reservoir to drain into a suitable container **(see illustration)**. Refit the cover or cap afterwards.

6 Unscrew the brake hose banjo bolt and separate the hose from the master cylinder, noting its alignment **(see illustration)**. Either plug the hose using another suitable short piece of hose fitted through the eye of the banjo union (it must be a tight fit to seal it properly), clamp it using a hose clamp, or wrap a plastic bag tightly around it to minimise fluid loss and prevent dirt entering the system. Discard the two sealing washers as new ones must be used.

7 On GSX750 models remove the split pin and washer from the clevis pin securing the master cylinder pushrod to the brake pedal, then remove the clevis pin and separate the pedal from the pushrod. Unscrew the two bolts securing the master cylinder to the bracket and remove the master cylinder.

8 On GSX600/750F models unscrew the two bolts securing the master cylinder to the

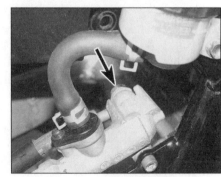

7.6 Brake hose banjo bolt (arrowed)

7.8a Master cylinder mounting bolts (arrowed)

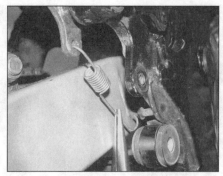

7.8b Unhook the return spring . . .

7.8c . . . then draw the shaft out of its bore . . .

bracket and displace the master cylinder **(see illustration)**. Unhook the brake pedal return spring from the arm on the pedal pivot bracket, then draw the bracket out of the frame, turning it as required to clear the swingarm **(see illustrations)**. Unhook the brake light switch spring from the arm on the bracket then remove the master cylinder assembly **(see illustration)**. If required, remove the split pin and washer from the clevis pin securing the master cylinder pushrod to the pedal pivot bracket, then remove the clevis pin and separate the pedal from the bracket **(see illustration)**.

Overhaul

9 If required, mark the position of the clevis locknut on the pushrod, then slacken the locknut and thread the clevis and its base nut off the pushrod **(see illustration 7.8e)**.
10 Dislodge the rubber dust boot from the base of the master cylinder and from around the pushrod, noting how it locates, and slide it down the pushrod **(see illustration)**.
11 Push the pushrod in and, using circlip pliers, remove the circlip from its groove in the master cylinder and slide out the piston assembly and the spring, noting how they fit. If they are difficult to remove, apply low pressure compressed air to the fluid outlet. Remove the seal from the piston and the cup from the spring. Lay the parts out in the proper order to prevent confusion during reassembly.

12 If required, remove the screw securing the fluid reservoir hose union and detach it from the master cylinder. Discard the O-ring as a new one must be used. Inspect the reservoir hose for cracks or splits and fit a new one if necessary.
13 Clean all of the parts with clean brake fluid or denatured alcohol.
Caution: Do not, under any circumstances, use a petroleum-based solvent to clean brake parts. If compressed air is available, use it to dry the parts thoroughly (make sure it's filtered and unlubricated).
14 Check the master cylinder bore for corrosion, scratches, nicks and score marks. If the necessary measuring equipment is available, compare the dimensions of the piston and bore to those given in the Specifications Section of this Chapter for new components. Renew any component which is worn significantly beyond the standard dimensions. If the master cylinder is in poor condition, then the caliper should be checked as well.
15 The dust boot, circlip, piston, seal, cup and spring are included in the rebuild kit. Use all of the new parts, regardless of the apparent condition of the old ones. Fit them according to the layout of the old ones.
16 Lubricate the cup, seal and piston with clean brake fluid. Slide the new boot onto the pushrod, making sure it is the correct way round.
17 Locate the cup onto the narrow end of the

spring with the flat side facing away. Slide the spring into the master cylinder with the wide end going in first, then slide the piston into the cylinder. Make sure the lips on the cup and seal do not turn inside out when they enter the bore. Depress the piston and install the new circlip, making sure that it locates in the groove in the master cylinder.
18 Apply some silicone grease to the end of the pushrod and fit it into the master cylinder. Depress the pushrod, then install the new circlip, making sure it is properly seated in the groove.
19 Install the rubber dust boot, making sure it is seated properly in the groove in the master cylinder and around the pushrod.
20 If removed, fit a new O-ring to the fluid reservoir hose union, then fit the union onto

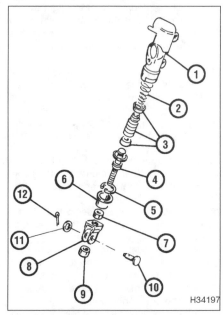

7.10 Rear master cylinder components

1	Master cylinder body	7	Locknut
2	Spring	8	Clevis
3	Piston assembly	9	Base nut
4	Pushrod	10	Clevis pin
5	Circlip	11	Washer
6	Rubber dust boot	12	Split pin

7.8d . . . and unhook the brake light switch spring

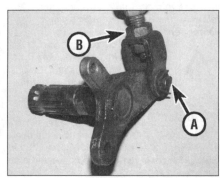

7.8e Remove the split pin and washer (A), then withdraw the pin. Clevis locknut (B)

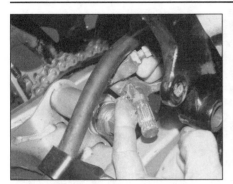

7.22a Smear some grease onto the shaft

7.22b Install the threadlocked bolts and tighten them to the specified torque

8.2 Flex the brake hoses and check for cracks, bulges and leaking fluid

the master cylinder and secure it with its screw.

21 If removed, thread the clevis locknut, the clevis and its base nut onto the master cylinder pushrod end. Position the clevis as noted on removal, then tighten the clevis locknut.

Installation

22 On GSX600/750F models, if separated align the arm on the brake pedal pivot bracket with the master cylinder pushrod clevis, then slide in the clevis pin, fit the washer and secure it using a new split pin **(see illustration 7.8e)**. Smear some grease onto the pivot section of the shaft on the bracket **(see illustration)**. Manoeuvre the master cylinder assembly into its rough position then hook the brake light switch spring onto its arm **(see illustration 7.8d)**. Align the bracket so the arms clear the swingarm, then slide the shaft into the frame **(see illustration 7.8c)**. Hook the pedal return spring onto its post **(see illustration 7.8b)**. Apply a suitable non-permanent thread locking compound to the master cylinder mounting bolts. Fit the master cylinder onto its bracket and tighten the bolts to the torque setting specified at the beginning of the Chapter **(see illustration)**.

23 On GSX750 models, apply a suitable non-permanent thread locking compound to the master cylinder mounting bolts. Fit the master cylinder onto its bracket and tighten the bolts to the torque setting specified at the beginning of the Chapter. Align the brake pedal or its arm with the master cylinder pushrod clevis, then slide in the clevis pin, fit the washer and secure it using a new split pin.

24 Connect the brake hose to the master cylinder, using new sealing washers on each side of the union. Align the hose as noted on removal and tighten the banjo bolt to the specified torque setting **(see illustration 7.6)**.

25 Connect the reservoir hose to the union on the master cylinder and secure it with the clip. Check that the hose is secure at the reservoir end as well. If the clips have weakened, use new ones.

26 Fill the fluid reservoir with new DOT 4 brake fluid (see *Daily (pre-ride) checks*) and

bleed the system following the procedure in Section 9.

27 Check that there are no fluid leaks and check the operation of the brake and brake light carefully before riding the motorcycle.

28 Install the footrest bracket and/or heel protector according to model. On GSX600/750F models install the right-hand fairing side panel (see Chapter 7). On GSX750 models install the right-hand side panel (see Chapter 7).

29 If the clevis locknut position was marked prior to disassembling the master cylinder, and the locknut subsequently returned to the original position, the brake pedal height relative to the top of the footrest, will be unchanged. If, however the locknut position was not marked or there is doubt about the pedal position, refer to Chapter 1, Section 11 to check and adjust the setting.

8 Brake hoses and fittings – inspection and renewal

Inspection

1 Brake hose condition should be checked regularly and new hoses installed at the specified interval (see Chapter 1).

2 Twist and flex the rubber hoses while looking for cracks, bulges and seeping fluid **(see illustration)**. Check extra carefully around the areas where the hoses connect with the banjo fittings, as these are common areas for hose failure.

3 Inspect the banjo union fittings connected to the brake hoses, and the hose splitter (bolted to the bottom yoke) for the front brake system. If the fittings are rusted, scratched or cracked, install new hoses.

Renewal

4 The brake hoses have banjo union fittings on each end. Cover the surrounding area with plenty of rags and unscrew the banjo bolt at each end of the hose, noting its alignment. Free the hoses from any clips or guides and remove them. Discard the sealing washers as new ones must be used.

5 Position the new hose, making sure it isn't twisted or otherwise strained, and abut the tab on the hose union with the lug on the component casting, where present. Otherwise align the hose as noted on removal. Install the hose banjo bolts using new sealing washers on both sides of the unions **(see illustration 5.20)**. Tighten the banjo bolts to the torque setting specified at the beginning of this Chapter.

6 Make sure the hoses are correctly aligned and routed clear of all moving components. Flush the old brake fluid from the system, refill with new DOT 4 brake fluid (see *Daily (pre-ride) checks*) and bleed the air from the system (see Section 9). Check the operation of the brakes carefully before riding the motorcycle.

9 Brake system – bleeding and fluid change

> **Warning: Use care when working with brake fluid as it can injure your eyes and it will damage painted surfaces and plastic parts.**

Bleeding

1 Bleeding the brakes is simply the process of removing all the air bubbles from the brake fluid reservoirs, the hoses and the brake calipers. Bleeding is necessary whenever a brake system hydraulic connection is loosened, when a component or hose is renewed, or when a master cylinder or caliper is overhauled. Leaks in the system may also allow air to enter, but leaking brake fluid will reveal their presence and warn you of the need for repair.

2 To bleed the brakes, you will need some new DOT 4 brake fluid, a length of clear vinyl or plastic tubing, a small container partially filled with clean brake fluid, some rags and a ring spanner to fit the brake caliper bleed valves.

3 Cover the fuel tank, fairing panels (GSX600/750F models), front mudguard, seat cowling and other painted components as

6

9.5a Front brake caliper bleed valve (arrowed)

9.5b Rear brake caliper outer bleed valve

9.5c To bleed the brakes, you need a spanner, a short section of clear tubing, and a container half-filled with brake fluid

required to prevent damage in the event that brake fluid is spilled.

4 Remove the reservoir cover or cap, diaphragm plate and diaphragm (see *Daily (pre-ride) checks*) and slowly pump the brake lever or pedal a few times, until no air bubbles can be seen floating up from the holes in the bottom of the reservoir. Doing this bleeds the air from the master cylinder end of the line. Loosely refit the reservoir cover.

5 Pull the dust cap off the bleed valve **(see illustrations)**. Attach one end of the clear vinyl or plastic tubing to the bleed valve and submerge the other end in the brake fluid in the container **(see illustration)**. Note that the rear caliper has two bleed valves, one on each side of the caliper.

6 Remove the reservoir cap or cover and check the fluid level (see *Daily (pre-ride) checks*). Do not allow the fluid level to drop below the lower mark during the bleeding process.

7 Carefully pump the brake lever or pedal three or four times and hold it in (front) or down (rear) while opening the caliper bleed valve. When the valve is opened, brake fluid will flow out of the caliper into the clear tubing and the lever will move toward the handlebar or the pedal will move down.

8 Retighten the bleed valve, then release the

brake lever or pedal gradually. Repeat the process until no air bubbles are visible in the brake fluid leaving the caliper and the lever or pedal is firm when applied. On completion, disconnect the bleeding equipment, then tighten the bleed valve to the torque setting specified at the beginning of the chapter and install the dust cap. When bleeding the front brake repeat the procedure on the other caliper, and when bleeding the rear brake repeat the procedure via the other bleed valve on the caliper body.

9 Install the diaphragm, plate and cover or cap assembly, wipe up any spilled brake fluid and check the entire system for leaks.

> **HAYNES HINT** *If it's not possible to produce a firm feel to the lever or pedal the fluid my be aerated. Let the brake fluid in the system stabilise for a few hours and then repeat the procedure when the tiny bubbles in the system have settled out. Also check to make sure that there are no 'high-spots' in the brake hose in which an air bubble can become trapped – this will occur most often in an incorrectly mounted hose union, but can also arise through bleeding the brakes while some of the brake system components are at such an angle to encourage this. Reversing the angle or displacing and moving the offending component around will normally dislodge any trapped air.*

Fluid change

10 Changing the brake fluid is a similar process to bleeding the brakes and requires the same materials plus a suitable tool (poultry baster) for siphoning the fluid out of the reservoir – do not siphon by mouth. Ensure that the container is large enough to take all the old fluid when it is flushed out of the system.

11 Follow Steps 3 and 5, then remove the reservoir cap or cover, diaphragm plate and diaphragm and siphon the old fluid out of the reservoir. Fill the reservoir with new brake fluid, then follow Step 7.

12 Tighten the bleed valve, then release the brake lever or pedal gradually. Keep the reservoir topped-up with new fluid to above the LOWER level at all times or air may enter the system and greatly increase the length of the task. Repeat the process until new fluid can be seen emerging from the bleed valve.

> **HAYNES HINT** *Old brake fluid is invariably much darker in colour than new fluid, making it easy to see when all old fluid has been expelled from the system.*

13 Disconnect the hose, then tighten the bleed valve to the specified torque setting and install the dust cap. If changing the fluid in the front brake system, repeat the procedure on the other front caliper, and when changing the rear brake fluid repeat the procedure via the other bleed valve on the caliper body.

14 Top-up the reservoir, install the diaphragm, diaphragm plate and cap or cover, and wipe up any spilled brake fluid. Check the entire system for fluid leaks.

15 Check the operation of the brakes before riding the motorcycle.

10 Wheels –
inspection and repair

1 Position the motorcycle on its centrestand. Support the bike so that the wheel to be checked is raised off the ground. Clean the wheels thoroughly to remove mud and dirt that may interfere with the inspection procedure or mask defects. Make a general check of the wheels (see Chapter 1) and tyres (see *Daily (pre-ride) checks*).

2 To check axial (side-to-side) runout, attach a dial gauge to the fork slider or the swingarm and position its stem against the side of the rim **(see illustration)**. Spin the wheel slowly and check the amount of runout at the rim. To accurately check radial (out of round) runout with the dial gauge, remove the wheel from the machine, and the tyre from the wheel. With the axle clamped in a vice and the dial

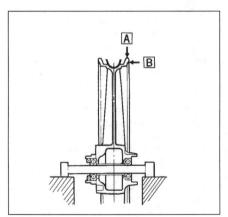

10.2 Check the wheel for radial (out-of-round) runout (A) and axial (side-to-side) runout (B)

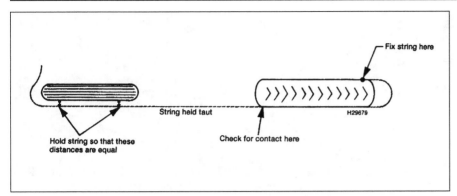

11.5 Wheel alignment check using string

gauge positioned on the top of the rim, rotate the wheel and check the runout.

3 An easier, though slightly less accurate, method is to attach a stiff wire pointer to the fork slider or the swingarm and position the end a fraction of an inch from the wheel (where the wheel and tyre join). If the wheel is true, the distance from the pointer to the rim will be constant as the wheel is rotated. **Note:** *If wheel runout is excessive, check the wheel bearings and axle very carefully before assuming the wheel to be distorted.*

4 Visually inspect the wheels for cracks, flat spots on the rim, and other damage. Look very closely for dents in the area where the tyre bead contacts the rim. Dents in this area may prevent complete sealing of the tyre against the rim, which leads to deflation of the tyre over a period of time.

5 If damage is evident, or if runout in either direction is excessive, the wheel will have to be renewed. Never attempt to repair a damaged cast alloy wheel.

11 Wheels – alignment check

1 Misalignment of the wheels, which may be due to a cocked rear wheel or a bent frame or fork yokes, can cause strange and possibly serious handling problems. If the frame or yokes are at fault, repair by a frame specialist or replacement with new parts are the only alternatives.

2 To check the alignment you will need an assistant, a length of string or a perfectly straight piece of wood and a ruler. A plumb bob or other suitable weight will also be required.

3 Place the bike on its centrestand. Measure the width of both tyres at their widest points. Subtract the smaller measurement from the larger measurement, then divide the difference by two. The result is the amount of offset that should exist between the front and rear tyres on both sides.

4 If a string is used, have your assistant hold one end of it about halfway between the floor

and the rear axle, touching the rear sidewall of the tyre.

5 Run the other end of the string forward and pull it tight so that it is roughly parallel to the floor **(see illustration)**. Slowly bring the string into contact with the front sidewall of the rear tyre, then turn the front wheel until it is parallel with the string. Measure the distance from the front tyre sidewall to the string.

6 Repeat the procedure on the other side of the motorcycle. The distance from the front tyre sidewall to the string should be equal on both sides.

7 As previously mentioned, a perfectly straight length of wood or metal bar may be substituted for the string **(see illustration)**. The procedure is the same.

8 If the distance between the string and tyre is greater on one side, or if the rear wheel appears to be cocked, refer to Chapter 1 and check that the chain adjuster markings are in the same position on each side of the swingarm.

9 If the front-to-back alignment is correct, the wheels still may be out of alignment vertically.

10 Using a plumb bob, or other suitable weight, and a length of string, check the rear wheel to make sure it is vertical. To do this, hold the string against the tyre upper sidewall and allow the weight to settle just off the floor. When the string touches both the upper and lower tyre sidewalls and is perfectly straight, the wheel is vertical. If it is not, place thin spacers under one leg of the stand until it is.

11 Once the rear wheel is vertical, check the front wheel in the same manner. If both wheels are not perfectly vertical, the frame and/or major suspension components are bent.

12 Front wheel – removal and installation

GSX600/750F models

Removal

1 Position the motorcycle on its centrestand.

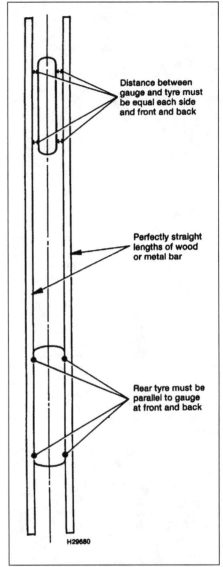

11.7 Wheel alignment check using a straight-edge

Remove the fairing side panels (see Chapter 7). Place a jack under the engine so that the front wheel is off the ground – fit a block of wood between the jack and the engine to protect the sump. Always make sure the motorcycle is properly supported.

2 Unscrew the bolt securing each brake hose clamp to the front forks **(see illustration 4.2)**. Unscrew the brake caliper bracket mounting bolts and slide the calipers off the discs **(see illustrations 2.2a and b)**. Tie the calipers back out of the way with a cable tie, string or a bungee cord so that no strain is placed on their hydraulic hoses. There is no need to disconnect the hoses from the calipers. **Note:** *Do not operate the front brake lever with the calipers removed.*

3 Slacken the axle clamp bolt on the bottom of the left-hand fork, then unscrew the nut on

12.3a Slacken the axle clamp bolt (arrowed) . . .

12.3b . . . then unscrew the nut (arrowed) and remove the washer

12.4 Withdraw the axle and remove the wheel

the right-hand end of the axle and remove the washer **(see illustrations)**.

4 Support the wheel, then withdraw the axle, using a drift to tap it out if necessary, and carefully lower the wheel **(see illustration)**.

5 Remove the spacer from each side of the wheel, noting how they fit **(see illustrations)**. Also note the axle spacer in the left-hand fork **(see illustration 12.8)**.

Caution: Don't lay the wheel down and allow it to rest on a disc – the disc could become warped. Set the wheel on wood blocks so the disc doesn't support the weight of the wheel.

6 Check the axle for straightness by rolling it on a flat surface such as a piece of plate glass (first wipe off all old grease and remove any corrosion using wire wool). If the equipment is available, place the axle in V-blocks and measure the runout using a dial gauge. If the axle is bent or the runout exceeds the limit specified, fit a new one.

7 Check the condition of the wheel bearings (see Section 14).

Installation

8 Apply a smear of grease to the inside of the axle spacer in the left-hand fork and the wheel spacers. Also apply a thin coat of grease to the axle. If removed, fit the axle spacer with its shouldered end on the inside into the left-hand fork **(see illustration)**.

9 Manoeuvre the wheel into position between the fork sliders, making sure the directional arrow points in the direction of normal rotation **(see illustration)**. Fit the double-sided spacer into the left-hand side of the wheel and the single-sided spacer into the right-hand side **(see illustrations 12.5b and a)**.

10 Lift the wheel into place making sure the spacers remain in position. Slide the axle in from the left-hand side **(see illustration 12.4)**. Fit the washer and the nut and tighten the nut to the torque setting specified at the beginning of the Chapter, counter-holding the axle head if necessary **(see illustrations)**. Check that the wheel spins freely.

11 Lower the front wheel to the ground. Slide the calipers onto their discs, make sure the pads locate on each side of the disc, and tighten them to the specified torque setting **(see illustration 2.11)**. Fit each brake hose clamp onto its fork and secure it with the bolt **(see illustration 4.2)**.

12.5a Remove the right-hand spacer . . .

12.5b . . . and the left-hand spacer, noting their difference

12.8 Do not forget the axle spacer if removed – GSX600/750F model shown with fork removed

12.9 Make sure the directional arrow is pointing the correct way

12.10a Fit the nut with its washer . . .

12.10b . . . and tighten it to the specified torque

12 Apply the front brake a few times to bring the pads back into contact with the discs. Move the motorcycle off its stand, apply the front brake and pump the front forks a few times to settle all components in position.

13 Now tighten the axle clamp bolts to the specified torque setting **(see illustration 12.3a)**.

14 Install the fairing side panels (see Chapter 7).

15 Check for correct operation of the front brake before riding the motorcycle.

GSX750 models

Removal

16 Position the motorcycle on its centrestand. Place a jack under the engine so that the front wheel is off the ground – fit a block of wood between the jack and the engine to protect the sump. Always make sure the motorcycle is properly supported.

17 Free each brake hose from the guides on the front forks. Unscrew the brake caliper bracket mounting bolts and slide the calipers off the discs. Tie the calipers back out of the way with a cable tie, string or a bungee cord so that no strain is placed on their hydraulic hoses. There is no need to disconnect the hoses from the calipers. **Note:** *Do not operate the front brake lever with the calipers removed.*

18 Slacken the axle clamp bolts in the bottom of the right-hand fork, then unscrew the axle.

19 Support the wheel, then withdraw the axle, using a drift to tap it out if necessary, and carefully lower the wheel.

20 Remove the speedometer drive housing from the left-hand side of the wheel, noting how it fits, and the spacer from the right-hand side, noting which way round it fits. Also note the axle spacer in the right-hand front fork – it is not shouldered so could come away with the axle.

Caution: Don't lay the wheel down and allow it to rest on a disc – the disc could become warped. Set the wheel on wood blocks so the disc doesn't support the weight of the wheel.

21 Check the axle for straightness by rolling it on a flat surface such as a piece of plate glass (first wipe off all old grease and remove any corrosion using wire wool). If the equipment is available, place the axle in V-blocks and measure the runout using a dial gauge. If the axle is bent or the runout exceeds the limit specified, fit a new one.

22 Check the condition of the wheel bearings (see Section 14).

Installation

23 Apply a smear of grease to the inside of the axle spacer in the right-hand fork, the wheel spacer and the speedometer drive housing. Also apply a thin coat of grease to

the axle. If removed, fit the axle spacer into the right-hand fork.

24 Manoeuvre the wheel into position between the fork sliders, making sure the directional arrow points in the direction of normal rotation. Fit the speedometer drive housing into the left-hand side of the wheel, locating its tabs into the drive plate cut-outs, and fit the spacer into the right-hand side with its shouldered end on the inside.

25 Lift the wheel into place, making sure the spacer and drive housing remain in position, and that the drive housing is positioned so that the lug on the bottom of the fork is in front of but butted against the stopper on the housing. Slide the axle in from the right-hand side. Tighten the axle to the specified torque. Check that the wheel spins freely. Rotate the speedometer drive housing if necessary so that it butts up against the back of the lug on the front fork.

26 Lower the front wheel to the ground. Slide the calipers onto their discs, make sure the pads locate on each side of the disc, and tighten them to the specified torque setting. Fit each brake hose back into its guide.

27 Apply the front brake a few times to bring the pads back into contact with the discs. Remove the jack then move the motorcycle off its stand, apply the front brake and pump the front forks a few times to settle all components in position.

28 Now tighten the axle clamp bolts to the specified torque setting.

29 Check for correct operation of the front brake before riding the motorcycle.

13 Rear wheel – removal and installation

Removal

1 Position the motorcycle on its centrestand.
2 Slacken the nut on the brake torque arm front bolt **(see illustration)**. Release the brake hose from its open guide(s) on the swingarm.
3 On US and Canada models, remove the split pin from the axle nut.
4 Unscrew the axle nut and remove the washer (GSX600/750F models) and the chain adjustment marker **(see illustration)**.
5 Support the wheel (a good way to do this is to slide your foot part way under it) then withdraw the axle along with the other adjustment marker **(see illustration)**. Gently lower the wheel to the ground, making sure no strain is placed on the brake hose as the caliper lowers with it. Disengage the chain from the sprocket, then draw the wheel back so the disc is clear of the caliper and manoeuvre the wheel out, taking care not to scratch it on the caliper **(see illustration)**. Note how the axle passes through the caliper mounting bracket.

13.2 Slacken the nut (arrowed)   **13.4 Unscrew the nut (arrowed) and remove the washer and marker**

13.5a Withdraw the axle and lower the wheel . . .

13.5b . . . and disengage the chain from the sprocket

6

13.6a Remove the spacer from the right-hand side . . .

13.6b . . . and from the left-hand side, noting their location

13.12 Fit the disc between the pads in the caliper

6 Remove the spacer from each side of the wheel, noting which fits where **(see illustrations)**.
Caution: Do not lay the wheel down and allow it to rest on the disc or the sprocket – they could become warped. Set the wheel on wood blocks so the disc or the sprocket doesn't support the weight of the wheel. Do not operate the brake pedal with the wheel removed.
7 Check the axle for straightness by rolling it on a flat surface such as a piece of plate glass (if the axle is corroded, first remove the corrosion with wire wool). If the equipment is available, place the axle in V-blocks and check the runout using a dial gauge. If the

axle is bent or the runout exceeds the limit specified at the beginning of the Chapter, renew it.
8 Check the condition of the grease seals and wheel bearings (see Section 14).

Installation

9 Apply a smear of grease to the inside of the wheel spacers, and also to the outside where they fit into the wheel. Fit the shouldered spacer into the right-hand side of the wheel, on GSX600/750F models with the flanged end innermost and on GSX750 models with the narrower end fitting into the grease seal, and the plain spacer into the left-hand side **(see illustrations 13.6b and a)**.

10 Push the pistons a little way back into the brake caliper using hand pressure or a piece of wood between the pads as leverage.
11 On GSX600/750F models the axle goes in from the left-hand side. On GSX750 models the axle goes in from the right-hand side. Slide the relevant adjustment marker onto the axle, making sure it is the correct way round.
12 Manoeuvre the wheel so that it is between the ends of the swingarm and move it forward so that the brake disc slides into the caliper, making sure the pads sit squarely on each side of the disc **(see illustration)**.
13 Engage the drive chain with the sprocket **(see illustration 13.5b)**.
14 Lift the wheel into position, bringing the caliper up with the disc, and making sure the caliper bracket is correctly aligned with the wheel and the swingarm, and the spacers remain correctly in place in the wheel **(see illustration)**. Slide the axle all the way through, making sure it passes through the caliper mounting bracket and the adjustment markers are correctly positioned **(see illustration)**. Check that everything is correctly aligned, then fit the other adjustment marker, the washer (GSX600/750F models), and the axle nut, but do not tighten it yet **(see illustration)**. If it is difficult to insert the axle due to the tension of the drive chain, back off the chain adjusters (see Chapter 1).
15 Adjust the chain slack as described in Chapter 1.
16 Tighten the axle nut to the torque setting specified at the beginning of the Chapter, counter-holding the axle head on the other side of the wheel to prevent it turning if necessary **(see illustration)**. On US and Canada models, fit a new split pin into the nut and secure its ends correctly.
17 Tighten the brake torque arm nut to the specified torque setting.
18 Operate the brake pedal several times to bring the pads into contact with the disc. Check the operation of the rear brake carefully before riding the bike.

13.14a Bring the caliper with the disc when raising the wheel

13.14b Slide the axle through the wheel

13.14c Fit the adjustment marker, the washer and the nut

13.16 Tighten the axle nut to the specified torque

14.4a Knock out the bearings using a drift . . .

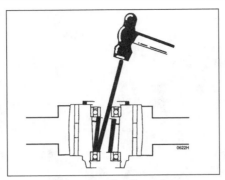

14.4b . . . locating it as shown

14.6 A socket can be used to drive in the bearing

14 Wheel bearings – inspection and renewal

Note: *Examine the wheel bearings and sprocket coupling bearing while they are installed in their housings. Once the bearings have been driven out they must never be reused. Where existing bearings have an open side facing outwards, and if new ones are not being fitted, work some grease into the bearing before installing the wheel.*

Front wheel bearings

1 Remove the wheel (see Section 12).

2 Rotate the inner race of each bearing using your fingers. If either bearing race doesn't turn smoothly, has rough spots or is noisy, fit two new bearings – never fit just one new bearing.

3 Set the wheel on blocks so as not to allow the weight to rest on either brake disc.

4 Using a metal rod (preferably a brass drift punch) inserted through the centre of the upper bearing, tap evenly around the inner race of the lower bearing to drive it from the hub **(see illustrations)**. The bearing spacer will also come out.

5 Lay the wheel on its other side so that the remaining bearing faces down. Drive the bearing out of the wheel using the same technique as above.

6 Thoroughly clean the hub area of the wheel. Install the new left-hand bearing into the

recess in the hub, with its marked (sealed) side facing outwards. Using the old bearing, a bearing driver or a socket large enough to contact the outer race of the bearing, drive it in until it's completely seated **(see illustration)**.

7 Turn the wheel over and install the bearing spacer. Drive the other new bearing into place as described above.

8 Clean off all grease from the brake discs using acetone or brake system cleaner then install the wheel (see Section 12).

Rear wheel bearings

9 Remove the rear wheel (see Section 13). Lift the sprocket coupling out of the left-hand side of the wheel, noting how it fits and its spacer **(see illustration)**.

10 Rotate the inner race of each bearing using your fingers. If either bearing race doesn't turn smoothly, has rough spots or is noisy, fit two new bearings – never fit just one new bearing.

11 Set the wheel on blocks so as not to allow the weight of the wheel to rest on the brake disc.

12 On GSX750 models, using a flat-bladed screwdriver, lever out the grease seal from the right-hand side of the wheel, using a block of wood or rag to protect the hub if necessary.

13 Using a metal rod (preferably a brass drift punch) inserted through the centre of one bearing, tap evenly around the inner race of the other bearing to drive it from the hub **(see**

illustration and 14.4b). The bearing spacer will also come out.

14 Lay the wheel on its other side so that the remaining bearing faces down. Drive the bearing out of the wheel using the same technique as above.

15 Thoroughly clean the hub area of the wheel. First install the new right-hand bearing into its recess in the hub, with its marked (sealed) side facing outwards. Using the old bearing, a bearing driver or a socket large enough to contact the outer race of the bearing, drive it in squarely until it's completely seated.

16 Turn the wheel over and install the bearing spacer. Drive the new left-hand side bearing into place as described above **(see illustration)**.

17 On GSX750 models, apply a smear of grease to the lips of the new seal, and press it into the right-hand side of the wheel, using a seal or bearing driver, a suitable socket or a flat piece of wood to drive it into place if necessary. As the seal sits flush with the top surface of their housing, using a piece of wood across the seal and housing rim will automatically set it flush without the risk of setting it too deep and having to lever it out again.

18 Clean off all grease from the brake disc using acetone or brake system cleaner. Ensure that spacer is in place in the sprocket coupling, then fit the sprocket coupling assembly onto the wheel **(see illustration 14.9)**. Install the wheel (see Section 13).

14.9 Lift the sprocket coupling out of the wheel, noting the spacer (arrowed)

14.13 Drive the bearings out as described

14.16 A socket can be used to drive in the bearing

6

14.20 Lever out the grease seal

14.23 Drive the bearing out as described

Sprocket coupling bearing

19 Remove the rear wheel (see Section 13). Lift the sprocket coupling out of the wheel, noting how it fits **(see illustration 14.9)**.

20 Using a flat-bladed screwdriver, lever out the grease seal from the outside of the coupling **(see illustration)**.

21 Remove the spacer from the inside of the coupling bearing, noting which way round it fits. The spacer could be a tight fit and may have to be driven out from the outside using a suitable socket or piece of tubing. Support the coupling on blocks of wood to do this.

22 Rotate the inner race of the bearing using your fingers. If the bearing race doesn't turn smoothly, has rough spots or is noisy, fit a new one.

23 Support the coupling on blocks of wood and drive the bearing out from the inside using a bearing driver or socket **(see illustration)**.

24 Thoroughly clean the bearing recess then fit the new bearing into the coupling, with its marked (sealed) side facing out. Using the old bearing, a bearing driver or a socket large enough to contact the outer race of the bearing, drive it in until it is completely seated **(see illustration)**. Apply grease to the bearing if necessary.

25 Fit the spacer into the inside of the coupling, making sure it is the correct way round and fits squarely into the bearing. Drive it into place if it is tight, supporting the bearing inner race on a suitable socket to prevent it from being damaged or driven out at the same time.

26 Apply a smear of grease to the lips of the new seal, and press it into the coupling, using a seal or bearing driver, a suitable socket or a flat piece of wood to drive it into place if necessary **(see illustration)**. As the seal sits flush with the top surface of their housing, using a piece of wood as shown will automatically set it flush without the risk of setting it too deep and having to lever it out again.

27 Check the sprocket coupling/rubber dampers (see Chapter 5).

28 Fit the sprocket coupling into the wheel **(see illustration 14.9)**, then install the wheel (see Section 13).

15 Tyres –
general information and fitting

General information

1 The wheels fitted to all models are designed to take tubeless tyres only. Tyre sizes are given in the Specifications at the beginning of this chapter and are displayed on a label attached to the chainguard. Tyre sizes are also given the machine's owners manual.

2 Refer to the *Daily (pre-ride) checks* listed at the beginning of this manual for tyre maintenance.

14.24 A socket can be used to drive in the bearing

14.26 Press or drive the seal into the coupling - using a piece of wood as shown automatically sets the seal flush

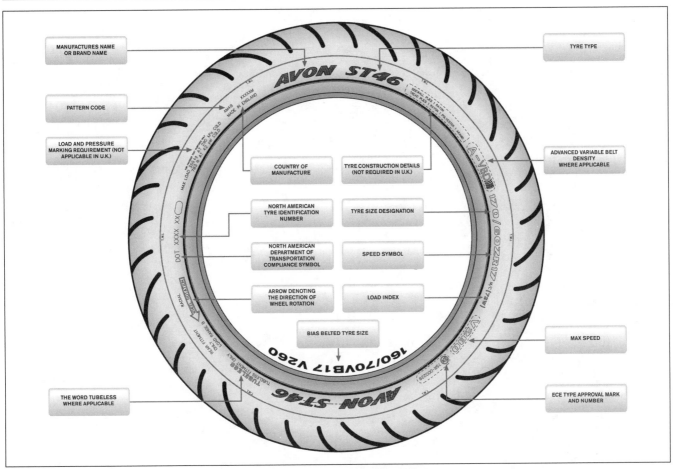

MANUFACTURES NAME OR BRAND NAME

PATTERN CODE

LOAD AND PRESSURE MARKING REQUIREMENT (NOT APPLICABLE IN U.K.)

TYRE TYPE

ADVANCED VARIABLE BELT DENSITY WHERE APPLICABLE

COUNTRY OF MANUFACTURE

TYRE CONSTRUCTION DETAILS (NOT REQUIRED IN U.K.)

NORTH AMERICAN TYRE IDENTIFICATION NUMBER

TYRE SIZE DESIGNATION

NORTH AMERICAN DEPARTMENT OF TRANSPORTATION COMPLIANCE SYMBOL

SPEED SYMBOL

ARROW DENOTING THE DIRECTION OF WHEEL ROTATION

LOAD INDEX

BIAS BELTED TYRE SIZE

MAX SPEED

THE WORD TUBELESS WHERE APPLICABLE

ECE TYPE APPROVAL MARK AND NUMBER

15.3 Common tyre sidewall markings

Fitting new tyres

3 When selecting new tyres ensure that front and rear tyre types are compatible, the correct size and correct speed rating; if necessary seek advice from a Suzuki dealer or tyre fitting specialist **(see illustration)**.

4 It is recommended that tyres are fitted by a motorcycle tyre specialist rather than attempted in the home workshop. This is particularly relevant in the case of tubeless tyres because the force required to break the seal between the wheel rim and tyre bead is substantial, and is usually beyond the capabilities of an individual working with normal tyre levers. Additionally, the specialist will be able to balance the wheels after tyre fitting.

5 Note that punctured tubeless tyres can in some cases be repaired. Repairs must only be carried out by a motorcycle tyre specialist. Suzuki advise that the motorcycle must not exceed 50 mph (80 km/h) for the first 24 hrs after the repair, and must not exceed 80 mph (130 km/h) thereafter.

6

Chapter 7
Bodywork

Contents

Fairing and body panels – removal and installation 4
Front mudguard – removal and installation 5
General information 1
Seat – removal and installation 2
Rear view mirrors – removal and installation 3

Degrees of difficulty

Easy, suitable for novice with little experience	**Fairly easy,** suitable for beginner with some experience	**Fairly difficult,** suitable for competent DIY mechanic	**Difficult,** suitable for experienced DIY mechanic	**Very difficult,** suitable for expert DIY or professional

1 General information

This Chapter covers the procedures necessary to remove and install the body parts. Since many service and repair operations require the removal of body parts, the procedures are grouped here and referred to from other Chapters.

In the case of damage to the body parts, it is usually necessary to remove the broken component and replace it with a new (or used) one. There are however companies who specialise in repair of plastic body panels and there are also a number of kits available for DIY repair.

When attempting to remove any body panel, first study it closely, noting any fasteners and associated fittings, to be sure of returning everything to its correct place on installation. In some cases the aid of an assistant will be required when removing panels, to help avoid the risk of damage to paintwork. Once the evident fasteners have been removed, try to withdraw the panel as described but DO NOT FORCE IT – if it will not release, check that all fasteners have been removed and try again. Where a panel engages another by means of tabs, be careful not to break the tab or its mating slot or to damage the paintwork. Remember that a few moments of patience at this stage will save you a lot of money in replacing broken fairing panels!

When installing a body panel, first study it closely, noting any fasteners and associated fittings removed with it, to be sure of returning everything to its correct place. Check that all fasteners are in good condition, including all trim nuts or clips and damping/rubber mounts; any of these must be renewed if faulty before the panel is reassembled. Check also that all mounting brackets are straight and repair or renew them if necessary before attempting to install the panel. Where assistance was required to remove a panel, make sure your assistant is on hand to install it. Be careful not to overtighten any of the fasteners or the panel may break (not always immediately) due to the uneven stress.

 Note that a small amount of lubricant (liquid soap or similar) applied to the mounting rubber grommets of the fairing side panels on GSX600/750F models and the side panels on GSX750 models will assist the lugs to engage without the need for undue pressure.

7

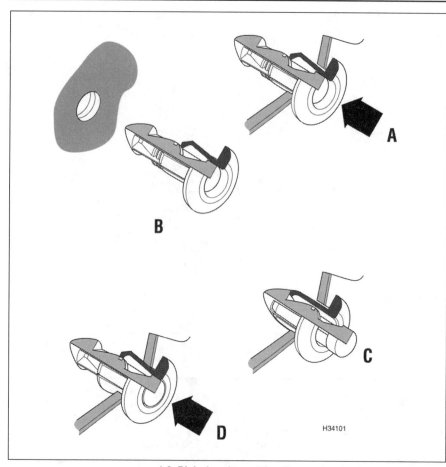

H34101

1.0 Plain-head type trim clip

To remove, push the centre in (A) to allow the clip body to be withdrawn from the panel (B).
To install, depress the clips pawls to extend the centre and insert it into the panel (C), then
press the centre in flush with the body of the clip to lock it in place (D)

Trim clips

There are two types of trim clip used on the bodywork, a plain-head type and a Phillips-head type.

To release the plain-head type, push the centre into the body, then carefully withdraw the body from the panel **(see illustration)**. Reset the clip by withdrawing the centre from the body, then install it by inserting the body into the panel then pressing the centre into the body.

To release the Phillips-head type, unscrew the centre from the body, then carefully withdraw the body from the panel. Install it by inserting the body into the panel then pressing the centre into the body.

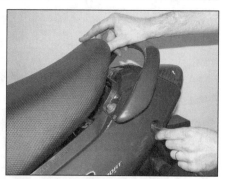

2.1 Unlock the seat, lift it up at the rear and remove it

2 Seat – removal and installation

1 Insert the ignition key into the seat lock located on the left-hand side and turn it clockwise to unlock the seat **(see illustration)**. Remove the seat by lifting it at the rear and drawing it back, noting how the tab at the front locates under the fuel tank bracket.
2 Installation is the reverse of removal. Make sure the tab locates correctly under the tank bracket **(see illustration)**. Push down on the rear of the seat to engage the latch.

3 Rear view mirrors – removal and installation

GSX600/750F models

1 Pull the rubber boot up off the base of the mirror **(see illustration)**.
2 Unscrew the two bolts and remove the mirror **(see illustration)**.
3 Installation is the reverse of removal.

GSX750 models

4 The mirrors simply screw into the handlebar mounting – slacken the locknut on the base of the stem then unscrew the mirror.

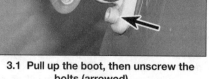

2.2 The tab (arrowed) locates under the tank bracket

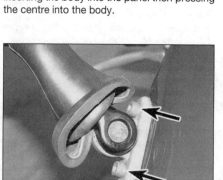

3.1 Pull up the boot, then unscrew the bolts (arrowed) . . .

3.2 . . . and remove the mirror

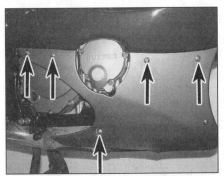

4.1a Unscrew the bolts (arrowed) . . .

4.1b . . . and manoeuvre the lower fairing out

4.7a Undo the screws (arrowed) . . .

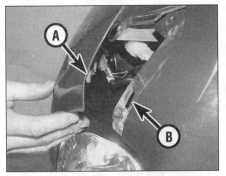

4.7b . . . then lift the panel to disengage each hook (A) from its slot (B) . . .

4.7c . . . and disconnect the wiring connector

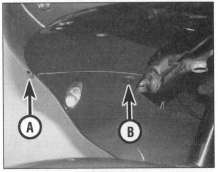

4.8 Undo the screw (A) and release the trim clip (B)

5 Installation is the reverse of removal. The position of the mirror can be adjusted by slackening the locknut, moving the mirror as required, then retightening the locknut.

4 Fairing and body panels – removal and installation

Note: *Refer to Section 1 for information on releasing and installing trim clips.*

GSX600/750F models

Lower fairing

1 Unscrew the five bolts securing each side of the lower fairing and remove it as one piece (see illustrations). Note the difference in the bottom rear bolt on each side.

2 If required the lower fairing can be separated into its three component parts by undoing the two bolts on the underside and the four screws securing the centre section, but note that the two bolts are likely to have seized; apply some penetrating fluid to these bolts before attempting to undo them.

3 Installation is the reverse of removal.

Fairing side panels

4 Remove the seat (see Section 2).
5 Remove the lower fairing (see above).
6 Remove the rear view mirrors (see Section 3).
7 Undo the two screws securing the centre panel above the headlight (see illustration). Lift the panel to disengage the hooks from the slot in each fairing side panel, then disconnect the sidelight wiring connector and remove the panel (see illustrations).

8 Undo the screw and release the trim clip securing the side panel to the centre panel below the headlight (see illustration).

9 Undo the screw securing the side panel to the top of the cockpit trim panel, and the screw securing the top of the side panel to the windshield (see illustration).

10 Undo the three screws securing the panel to the frame (see illustration). Carefully pull the side of the panel away to release the three pegs from the grommets (see illustration). Disengage the panel from the lower centre

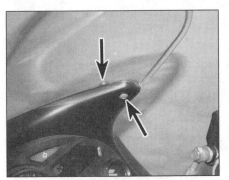

4.9 Undo the screws (arrowed)

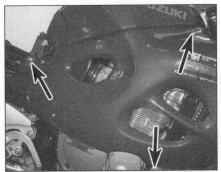

4.10a Undo the screws (arrowed) . . .

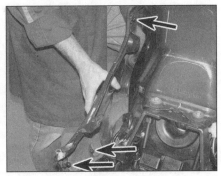

4.10b . . . then pull the panel away to release the pegs (arrowed) from the grommets

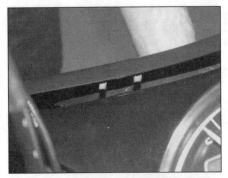

4.10c Note how the panel engages with the cockpit trim panel

4.15 Release the trim clip and remove the windshield

4.18 Release the bulb holder from the tail light

panel and the cockpit trim panel, noting how it fits, and disconnect the turn signal wiring connector when accessible **(see illustration)**.
11 If both fairing side panels have been removed, it is best to release the remaining trim clip securing the windshield and to remove it to prevent the possibility of damage **(see illustration 4.15)**.
12 Installation is the reverse of removal.

Windshield

13 Undo the two screws securing the centre panel above the headlight **(see illustration 4.7a)**. Lift the panel to disengage the hooks from the slot in each fairing side panel, then disconnect the sidelight wiring connector and remove the panel **(see illustrations 4.7b and c)**.
14 Undo the screw securing the side panel to

the top of the cockpit trim panel **(see illustration 4.9)**. Undo the screw securing the side panel to the windshield, noting the washer. Withdraw the rubber wellnuts.
15 Release the trim clip securing the bottom of the windshield and carefully withdraw it from the fairing, noting how it fits **(see illustration)**.
16 Installation is the reverse of removal.

Seat cowling

17 Remove the seat (see Section 2).
18 Twist the tail light bulb holder anticlockwise and withdraw it **(see illustration)**.
19 Detach the seat lock cable from the release mechanism on the latch **(see illustration)**.
20 Undo the screw securing the fairing side

panel to the fuel tank bracket **(see illustration 4.10a)**. Carefully pull the side of each panel away to release the pegs from the grommets in the seat cowling **(see illustration 4.10b)**.
21 Undo the two screws on the underside of the cowling **(see illustration)**.
22 Undo the two passenger grab-rail bolts, noting the washers, and remove the grab-rail **(see illustration)**.
23 Undo the screws securing the top of the cowling to the rear sub-frame **(see illustration)**.
24 Carefully pull each side away at the front to release the pegs from the grommets **(see illustration)**. Carefully draw the cowling back and off the rear sub-frame **(see illustration)**.
25 Installation is the reverse of removal.

4.19 Detach the set lock cable

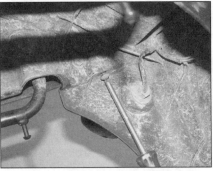

4.21 Undo the screw on each side

4.22 Unscrew the bolts and remove the grab-rail

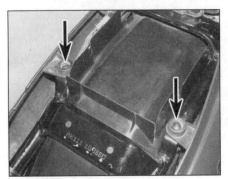

4.23 Undo the screws (arrowed) . . .

4.24a . . . then pull each side away to release the peg from the grommet . . .

4.24b . . . and remove the cowling

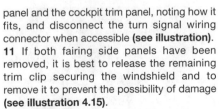

GSX750 models

Side panels

26 Remove the seat (see Section 2).
27 Undo the screw, noting the collar, then carefully pull the panel away to release the pegs from the grommets.
28 Installation is the reverse of removal.

Seat cowling

29 Remove the seat (see Section 2).
30 Disconnect the tail light wiring connector.
31 Detach the seat lock cable from the release mechanism on the latch.
32 Undo the four screws on the underside of the cowling.
33 Undo the two passenger grab-rail bolts, noting the washers, and remove the grab-rail.
34 Undo the screws securing the cowling to the rear sub-frame.

35 Carefully draw the cowling back and off the rear sub-frame.
36 Installation is the reverse of removal.

5 Front mudguard –
removal and installation

GSX600/750F models

1 Undo the four screws securing the mudguard to the fork brace, and the four screws securing the fork brace to the forks **(see illustration)**. Remove the brace and the mudguard, noting how they fit.
2 Installation is the reverse of removal.

GSX750 models

3 Unscrew the two bolts on each side, noting how they secure the brake hose and

5.1 Undo the eight screws and remove the fork brace and mudguard

speedometer guide brackets to the inside of the mudguard.
4 Draw the mudguard forwards and remove it from between the forks.
5 Installation is the reverse of removal.

Notes

Chapter 8
Electrical system

Contents

Alternator/regulator/rectifier – check, removal, overhaul
  and installation 33
Battery – charging 4
Battery – removal, installation, inspection and maintenance 3
Brake light switches – check and renewal 14
Brake/tail light bulb and licence plate light bulb – renewal 9
Carburettor fan (California models) – check, removal
  and installation 34
Charging system – leakage and output test 32
Charging system testing – general information and
  precautions 31
Clutch switch – check, removal and installation 25
Diodes – check and renewal 26
Electrical system – fault finding 2
Fuses – check and renewal 5
General information 1
Handlebar switches – check 21
Handlebar switches – removal and installation 22
Headlight aim – check and adjustment .... see Chapter 1
Headlight bulb(s) and sidelight bulb – renewal 7
Headlight assembly – removal and installation 8
Horn(s) – check, removal and installation 27
Ignition (main) switch – check, removal and installation 20
Ignition system components .... see Chapter 4
Instrument and warning light bulbs – renewal 17
Instrument cluster – removal and installation 15
Instruments – check and renewal 16
Lighting system – check 6
Neutral switch – check, removal and installation 23
Oil pressure switch – check, removal and installation 19
Sidestand switch and relay – check and renewal 24
Speed sensor (GSX600/750F models) – check, removal and
  installation 18
Speedometer cable (GSX750 models) – removal and
  installation 18
Starter motor – disassembly, inspection and reassembly 30
Starter motor – removal and installation 29
Starter relay – check and renewal 28
Tail light assembly – removal and installation 10
Turn signal bulbs – renewal 12
Turn signal assemblies – removal and installation 13
Turn signal circuit – check 11

Degrees of difficulty

Easy, suitable for novice with little experience		Fairly easy, suitable for beginner with some experience		Fairly difficult, suitable for competent DIY mechanic		Difficult, suitable for experienced DIY mechanic		Very difficult, suitable for expert DIY or professional	

Specifications

Battery

Type	
GSX600F and GSX750	YTX9-BS
GSX750F	FTX9-BS
Capacity	12 V, 8 Ah
Voltage	
Fully charged	12.0 to 12.5 V
Uncharged	below 12.0 V
Charging rate	
Normal	0.9 A for 5 to 10 hrs
Quick	4.0 A for 1.0 hr

Charging system

Current leakage	0.1 mA (max)
Regulated voltage output	13.6 to 14.4 V @ 5000 rpm
Alternator output (max)	approx. 550 W @ 5000 rpm
Alternator slip ring shaft OD (min)	14.0 mm
Alternator brush length (min)	4.5 mm

Starter relay

Coil resistance	3 to 6 ohms

Fuses

Main	30A
Headlight	15A x 2
Signal	15A
Ignition	10A
Tail light and instrument lights (clock on GSX600/750F-Y, F-K1, F-K2 models)	10A

Bulbs

Headlight	
GSX600F and GSX750F	
UK, Canada, Australia and all US models	12V, 60/55W x 2
All other models	12V, 55W x 2
GSX750	12V, 60/55W
Sidelight	12V, 5W
Licence plate light	12V, 5W
Brake/tail light	12V, 21/5W
Turn signal lights	12V, 21W x 4
Instrument illumination lights	12V, 1.7W
Low fuel level warning light – GSX750	12V, 3W
Turn signal indicator light	
GSX600/750F	12V, 1.4W x 2
GSX750	12V, 1.7W x 2
High beam indicator light	
GSX600/750F	12V, 1.4W
GSX750	12V, 1.7W
Neutral indicator light	
GSX600/750F	12V, 1.4W
GSX750	12V, 1.7W
Oil pressure warning light	
GSX600/750F	12V, 1.4W
GSX750	12V, 1.7W

Torque settings

Alternator bearing cover screws	2.5 Nm
Alternator driven gear nut	60 Nm
Alternator mounting bolts	25 Nm
Alternator rear cover nuts	4.5 Nm
Oil pressure switch	14 Nm
Speed sensor rotor bolt	
GSX600F	13 Nm
GSX750F	18 Nm
Starter motor mounting bolts	6 Nm

1 General information

All models have a 12-volt electrical system charged by a three-phase alternator with integral regulator/rectifier.

The regulator maintains the charging system output within the specified range to prevent overcharging, and the rectifier converts the ac (alternating current) output of the alternator to dc (direct current) to power the lights and other components and to charge the battery. The alternator is mounted on the top of the crankcase behind the cylinder block and is gear driven off the clutch housing.

The starter motor is also mounted on the top of the crankcase behind the cylinder block. The starting system includes the motor, the battery, the relay and the various wiring and switches, and a starter safety interlock system. If the engine kill switch is in the RUN position, the ignition (main) switch is ON and the clutch lever is pulled in, the system prevents the engine from being started if the sidestand is down and the engine is in gear – the engine can be started with the transmission in gear if the sidestand is up.

Note: *Keep in mind that electrical parts, once purchased, often cannot be returned. To avoid unnecessary expense, make very sure the faulty component has been positively identified before buying a new part.*

2 Electrical system – fault finding

Warning: To prevent the risk of short circuits, the ignition (main) switch must always be OFF and the battery negative (–ve)

terminal should be disconnected before any of the bike's other electrical components are disturbed. Don't forget to reconnect the terminal securely once work is finished or if battery power is needed for circuit testing.

1 A typical electrical circuit consists of an electrical component, the switches, relays, etc. related to that component and the wiring and connectors that link the component to the battery and the frame. To aid in locating a problem in any electrical circuit, and to guide you with the wiring colour codes and connectors, refer to the *Wiring Diagrams* at the end of this Chapter.

2 Before tackling any troublesome electrical circuit, first study the wiring diagram (see end of Chapter) thoroughly to get a complete picture of what makes up that individual circuit. Trouble spots, for instance, can often be narrowed down by noting if other components related to that circuit are operating properly or not. If several components or circuits fail at one

time, chances are the fault lies in the fuse or earth (ground) connection, as several circuits often are routed through the same fuse and earth (ground) connections.

3 Electrical problems often stem from simple causes, such as loose or corroded connections or a blown fuse. Prior to any electrical fault finding, always visually check the condition of the fuse, wires and connections in the problem circuit. Intermittent failures can be especially frustrating, since you can't always duplicate the failure when it's convenient to test. In such situations, a good practice is to clean all connections in the affected circuit, whether or not they appear to be good. All of the connections and wires should also be wiggled to check for looseness which can cause intermittent failure.

4 If testing instruments are going to be utilised, use the wiring diagram to plan where you will make the necessary connections in order to accurately pinpoint the trouble spot.

5 The basic tools needed for electrical fault finding include a battery and bulb test circuit or a continuity tester, a test light, and a jumper wire. A multimeter capable of reading volts, ohms and amps is a very useful alternative and performs the functions of all of the above, and is necessary for performing more extensive tests and checks where specific voltage, current or resistance values are needed.

 Refer to Fault Finding Equipment in the Reference section for details of how to use electrical test equipment.

3 Battery – removal, installation, inspection and maintenance

Caution: Be extremely careful when handling or working around the battery. The electrolyte is very caustic and an explosive gas (hydrogen) is given off when the battery is charging.

Removal and installation

1 Make sure the ignition is switched OFF. Remove the seat (see Chapter 7).

2 On GSX600/750F models remove the seat cowling (see Chapter 7), then unscrew the two bolts securing the fusebox and relay/diode unit bracket and lay it aside **(see illustrations)**.

3 On GSX750 models remove the document tray.

4 Unscrew the negative (–ve) terminal bolt first and disconnect the lead from the battery **(see illustration)**. Lift up the red insulating cover to access the positive (+ve) terminal, then unscrew the bolt and disconnect the lead.

5 Lift the battery out of its box and remove it **(see illustration)**.

6 On installation, clean the battery terminals and lead ends with a wire brush or knife and emery paper. When reconnecting the leads, connecting the positive (+ve) terminal first.

 Battery corrosion can be kept to a minimum by applying a layer of petroleum jelly to the terminals after the cables have been connected. There are also dedicated sprays commercially available.

Inspection and maintenance

7 The battery is of the maintenance free (sealed) type, therefore requiring no scheduled maintenance. However, the following checks should still be regularly performed.

8 Check the battery terminals and leads for tightness and corrosion. If corrosion is evident, unscrew the terminal bolts and disconnect the leads from the battery, disconnecting the negative (–ve) terminal first, and clean the terminals and lead ends with a wire brush or knife and emery paper. Reconnect the leads, connecting the negative (–ve) terminal last, and apply a thin coat of petroleum jelly to the connections to slow further corrosion.

9 Keep the battery case clean to prevent current leakage, which can discharge the battery over a period of time (especially when it sits unused). Wash the outside of the case with a solution of baking soda and water. Rinse the battery thoroughly, then dry it.

10 Look for cracks in the case and replace the battery with a new one if any are found. If acid has been spilled on the frame or battery box, neutralise it with a baking soda and water solution, dry it thoroughly, then touch up any damaged paint.

11 If the motorcycle sits unused for long periods of time, disconnect the cables from the battery terminals, negative (–ve) terminal first. Refer to Section 4 and charge the battery once every month to six weeks.

12 Check the condition of the battery by measuring the voltage present at the battery terminals. Connect the voltmeter positive (+ve) probe to the battery positive (+ve) terminal, and the negative (–ve) probe to the battery negative (–ve) terminal. When fully charged there should be 12.0 to 12.5 volts present. If the voltage falls below 12.0 volts the battery must be removed, disconnecting the negative (–ve) terminal first, and recharged as described in Section 4.

4 Battery – charging

Caution: Be extremely careful when handling or working around the battery. The electrolyte is very caustic and an explosive gas (hydrogen) is given off when the battery is charging.

3.2a Unscrew the bolts (arrowed) . . .

3.2b . . . and lift the fusebox bracket off the battery

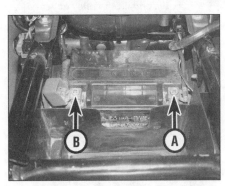
3.4 Disconnect the negative lead (A) first then lift the terminal cover and disconnect the positive lead (B)

3.5 Lift the battery out of its box

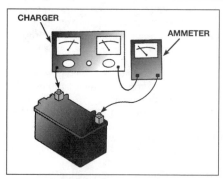

4.2 If the charger doesn't have an ammeter built in, connect one in series as shown. DO NOT connect the ammeter between the battery terminals or it will be ruined

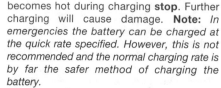

5.2a Remove the seat to access the fusebox (arrowed) on GSX600/750F models

5.2b Unclip the lid to access the fuses

1 Remove the battery (see Section 3). Connect the charger to the battery, making sure that the positive (+ve) lead on the charger is connected to the positive (+ve) terminal on the battery, and the negative (–ve) lead is connected to the negative (–ve) terminal.
2 Suzuki recommend that the battery is charged at the normal rate specified at the beginning of the Chapter. Exceeding this figure can cause the battery to overheat, buckling the plates and rendering it useless. Few owners will have access to an expensive current controlled charger, so if a normal domestic charger is used check that after a possible initial peak, the charge rate falls to a safe level **(see illustration)**. If the battery

becomes hot during charging **stop**. Further charging will cause damage. **Note:** *In emergencies the battery can be charged at the quick rate specified. However, this is not recommended and the normal charging rate is by far the safer method of charging the battery.*
3 If the recharged battery discharges rapidly if left disconnected it is likely that an internal short caused by physical damage or sulphation has occurred. A new battery will be required. A good battery will tend to lose its charge at about 1% per day.
4 Install the battery (see Section 3).
5 If the motorcycle sits unused for long periods of time, leave the battery disconnected and charge it once every month to six weeks.

5 Fuses – check and renewal

1 The electrical system is protected by fuses of different ratings. All except the main fuse are housed in the fusebox. The main fuse is housed in the starter relay.
2 To access the fusebox fuses, on GSX600/750F models remove the seat, and on GSX750 models remove the left-hand side panel (see Chapter 7), then unclip the fusebox lid **(see illustrations)**.
3 To access the main fuse, on GSX600/750F models remove the left-hand fairing side panel, and on GSX750 models remove the right-hand side panel (see Chapter 7), then disconnect the wiring connector and remove the starter relay cover **(see illustrations)**.
4 The fuses can be removed and checked visually **(see illustration)**. If you can't pull the fuse out with your fingertips, use a pair of suitable pliers. A blown fuse is easily identified by a break in the element **(see illustration)**. Each fuse is clearly marked with its rating and must only be replaced by a fuse of the correct rating. A spare fuse of each rating except the main fuse is housed in the fusebox, and a spare main fuse is housed with the starter relay **(see illustration 5.3c)**. If a spare fuse is used, always renew it so that a spare of each rating is carried on the bike at all times.

5.3a Disconnect the wiring connector . . .

5.3b . . . and lift the relay cover . . .

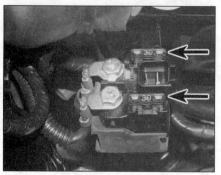

5.3c . . . to access the main fuse and its spare (arrowed)

5.4a Remove the fuse and check it visually

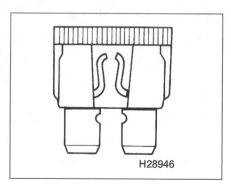

H28946

5.4b A blown fuse can be identified by a break in its element

Warning: Never put in a fuse of a higher rating or bridge the terminals with any other substitute, however temporary it may be. Serious damage may be done to the circuit, or a fire may start.

5 If a fuse blows, be sure to check the wiring circuit very carefully for evidence of a short-circuit. Look for bare wires and chafed, melted or burned insulation. If the fuse is renewed before the cause is located, the new fuse will blow immediately.

6 Occasionally a fuse will blow or cause an open-circuit for no obvious reason. Corrosion of the fuse ends and fusebox terminals may occur and cause poor fuse contact. If this happens, remove the corrosion with a wire brush or emery paper, then spray the fuse ends and terminals with electrical contact cleaner.

6 Lighting system – check

1 The battery provides power for operation of the headlight, tail light, brake light and instrument cluster lights. If none of the lights operate, check the battery first, making sure its terminals are clean and secure and the voltage level is sufficient. Low battery voltage indicates either a neglected or faulty battery or a defective charging system. Refer to Section 3 for battery checks and Sections 31 and 32 for charging system tests. Also, check the fuses. Note that if there is more than one problem at the same time, it is likely to be a fault relating to a multi-function component, such as one of the fuses governing more than one circuit, or the ignition switch.

Headlight

2 If a headlight beam fails to work, first check the high or low headlight fuse, as applicable (see Section 5), and then the bulb(s) (see Section 7). If the bulb is good the problem lies in the wiring or connectors, or the switches in the circuit. Refer to Section 21 for the switch testing procedures, and also to the wiring diagrams at the end of this Chapter.

3 If the low beam does not work, check for battery voltage at the white wire terminal on the headlight wiring connector with the ignition ON, the light switch ON (where applicable) and the dimmer switch set to LO. If voltage is present, check for continuity to earth (ground) in the black/white wire from the wiring connector. Repair or renew the wiring or connectors as necessary. If there is no voltage, check the wiring, connectors and switches.

4 If the high beam does not work, check for battery voltage at the yellow wire terminal on the headlight wiring connector with the ignition ON, the light switch ON (where

applicable) and the dimmer switch set to HI. If voltage is present, check for continuity to earth (ground) in the black/white wire from the wiring connector. Repair or renew the wiring or connectors as necessary. If there is no voltage, check the wiring, connectors and switches.

5 When checking the headlights on GSX600/750F models, note that the lighting arrangement differs depending on the country of use. On models with twin filament bulbs, both headlights will come on in the HI or LO switch positions. Where asymmetrical lighting is used, the right-hand headlight will come on in the HI position and the left-hand headlight in the LO position.

Sidelight, tail light, licence plate light

6 First check the tail light/instrument circuit fuse (see Section 5), and then the bulbs (see Section 7 and/or 9). If the bulb is good the problem lies in the wiring or connectors, or the switches in the circuit. Refer to Section 21 for the switch testing procedures, and also to the wiring diagrams at the end of this Chapter.

7 Check for battery voltage at the brown wire terminal on the light wiring connectors with the ignition switch ON. If voltage is present, check for continuity to earth (ground) in the black/white wire from the wiring connector. If no voltage is indicated, check the wiring and connectors between the light unit and the ignition switch, via the fusebox and the handlebar switch, then check the ignition switch itself (see Section 20).

Brake light

8 If the brake lights fail to work, first check the signal circuit fuse (see Section 5), and then the bulb (see Section 9). If the bulb is good the problem lies in the wiring or connectors, or the switches in the circuit.

9 Check for battery voltage at the white/black wire terminal on the tail light wiring connector, first with the front brake lever on, then with the rear brake pedal on. If voltage is present with one brake on but not the other, then the switch or its wiring is faulty. If voltage is present in both cases, check for continuity to

earth (ground) in the black/white wire from the bulb wiring connector. If no voltage is indicated, check the wiring and connectors between the brake light and the brake switches, then between the switches and the fusebox. Next check the switches themselves (see Section 14).

Instrument and warning lights

10 See Section 17 for instrument and warning light bulb renewal.

Turn signals

11 See Section 11 for turn signal circuit check.

7 Headlight bulb(s) and sidelight bulb – renewal

Caution: Quartz-halogen headlight bulb – do not touch the bulb glass as skin acids will shorten the bulb's service life. If the bulb is accidentally touched, it should be wiped carefully when cold with a rag soaked in alcohol or soapy water and dried before fitting.

Warning: Allow the bulb time to cool before removing it if the headlight has just been on.

Headlight – GSX600/750F models

Note: *The lighting arrangement differs depending on the country of use. On models with twin filament bulbs, both headlights will come on in the HI or LO switch positions. Where asymmetrical lighting is used, the right-hand headlight will come on in the Hi beam position and the left-hand headlight in the LO beam position.*

1 Remove the relevant fairing side panel (see Chapter 7).

2 Disconnect the wiring connector from the back of the headlight **(see illustration)**. Remove the rubber dust cover, noting how it fits **(see illustration)**. Release the bulb

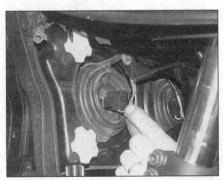

7.2a Disconnect the wiring connector . . .

7.2b . . . then remove the dust cover

8

7.2c Release the clip . . .

7.2d . . . and remove the bulb

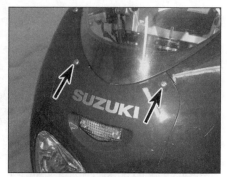

7.14a Undo the screws (arrowed) . . .

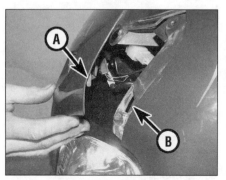

7.14b . . . then lift the panel to disengage each hook (A) from its slot (B) . . .

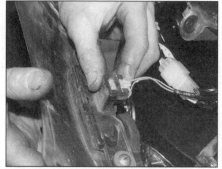

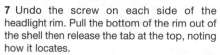

7.14c . . . and disconnect the wiring connector

11 Install the dust cover, making sure it is correctly seated and with the 'TOP' mark at the top. Connect the wiring connector. Connect the sidelight wiring connector.
12 Check the operation of the headlight.
13 Locate the tab on the top of the headlight rim behind the protrusion on the shell, then push the bottom of the rim in. Make sure it is correctly seated all the way round then install the screws.

> **HAYNES HiNT** *Always use a paper towel or dry cloth when handling new bulbs to prevent injury if the bulb should break and to increase bulb life.*

retaining clip, noting how it fits, then remove the bulb **(see illustrations)**. Where asymmetric headlights are fitted, separate the bulb from its adapter.
3 Where asymmetric headlights are fitted, fit the new bulb onto its adapter. On all models fit the new bulb into the headlight, bearing in mind the information in the **Caution** above. Make sure the tabs on the bulb fit correctly in the slots in the bulb housing, and secure it in position with the retaining clip.
4 Install the dust cover, making sure it is correctly seated and with the 'TOP' mark at the top, and connect the wiring connector.
5 Check the operation of the headlights.
6 Install the fairing side panel (see Chapter 7).

Headlight – GSX750 models

7 Undo the screw on each side of the headlight rim. Pull the bottom of the rim out of the shell then release the tab at the top, noting how it locates.
8 Disconnect the headlight and sidelight wiring connectors.
9 Remove the rubber dust cover, noting how it fits. Release the bulb retaining clip, noting how it fits, then remove the bulb.
10 Fit the new bulb, bearing in mind the information in the **Caution** above. Make sure the tabs on the bulb fit correctly in the slots in the bulb housing, and secure it in position with the retaining clip.

Sidelight – GSX600/750F models

14 Undo the two screws securing the fairing centre panel above the headlight **(see illustration)**. Lift the panel to disengage the hooks from the slot in each fairing side panel, then disconnect the sidelight wiring connector and remove the panel **(see illustrations)**.
15 Undo the two screws securing the sidelight assembly to the panel and remove it **(see illustration)**. Note the washers and the collars in the rubber mounts **(see illustration)**.
16 Undo the two screws securing the

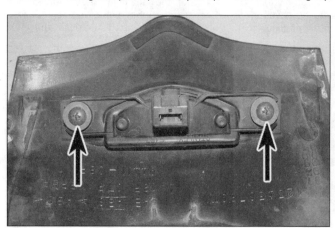

7.15a Undo the screws (arrowed) . . .

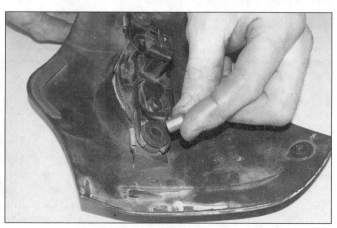

7.15b . . . noting the collars

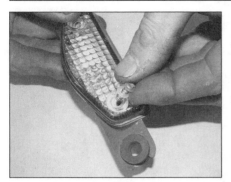
7.16a Undo the screws . . .

7.16b . . . and detach the lens

7.17 Pull the bulb out of the holder

sidelight lens and remove it **(see illustrations)**.

17 Carefully pull the old bulb out of its socket **(see illustration)**. Fit the new bulb.

18 Fit the lens, making sure it is correctly seated, and secure it with the screws. Fit the sidelight onto the fairing panel, then install the panel.

Sidelight – GSX750 models

19 Undo the screw on each side of the headlight rim. Pull the bottom of the rim out of the shell then release the tab at the top, noting how it locates.

20 Disconnect the headlight and sidelight wiring connectors.

21 Pull the sidelight bulbholder out of the headlight, then remove the bulb. Fit the new bulb in the bulbholder, then fit the bulbholder into the headlight, making sure it correctly seated. Check the operation of the sidelight.

22 Connect the headlight and sidelight wiring connectors.

23 Locate the tab on the top of the headlight rim behind the protrusion on the shell, then push the bottom of the rim in. Make sure it is correctly seated all the way round then install the screws.

8 Headlight assembly – removal and installation

GSX600/750F models

1 Remove the fairing side panels and the windshield (see Chapter 7). For best access, also remove the instrument cluster (see Section 15).

2 Disconnect the headlight wiring connectors **(see illustration 7.2a)**.

3 Undo the four screws and remove the washers securing the headlight assembly to the bracket **(see illustration)**. Draw the top of the headlight forwards to free the top mounting lugs from the grommets, then lift the headlight to free the bottom lugs **(see illustrations)**.

4 Check the rubber mounting grommets in the bracket for damage, deformation and deterioration and renew them if necessary.

5 Installation is the reverse of removal. Make sure all the wiring is correctly connected and secured. Check the operation of the headlights. Check the headlight aim (see Chapter 1).

GSX750 models

6 Undo the screw on each side of the headlight rim. Pull the bottom of the rim out of the shell then release the tab at the top, noting how it locates.

7 Disconnect the headlight and sidelight wiring connectors.

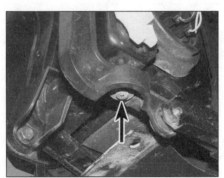
8.3a Undo the screw (arrowed) on each bottom corner . . .

8.3c Draw the top forwards out of the grommets . . .

8 Make a note of the routing of all the wiring in the headlight shell and the location of the wiring connectors. Release the wiring from the clips and disconnect the connectors, then feed the wiring out of the back of the shell.

9 Unscrew the headlight adjuster clamp bolt. Support the shell, then either unscrew the two nuts, withdraw the bolts and remove the shell from between the brackets, or unscrew the bracket bolts and remove the shell with them attached.

10 Installation is the reverse of removal. Make sure all the wiring is correctly connected and secured. Check the operation of the headlight and sidelight. Check the headlight aim (see Chapter 1).

8.3b . . . and the two on the top

8.3d . . . then lift the unit out of the bottom grommets and remove it

8

9.2 Twist the bulbholder anti-clockwise and withdraw it from the tail light

9.3 Carefully push the bulb in slightly and twist it anti-clockwise to release it

9.7a Unscrew the nuts (arrowed) . . .

9.7b . . . and remove the cover

9.8 Pull the bulb out of its socket

9 Brake/tail light bulb and licence plate light bulb – renewal

Brake/tail light

Note: *The pins on the bulbs are offset so that the bulbs can only be installed one way. It is a good idea to use a paper towel or dry cloth when handling a new bulb to prevent injury if it breaks, and to increase bulb life.*

1 Remove the seat (See Chapter 7).
2 Twist the bulbholder anti-clockwise and withdraw it from the tail light **(see illustration)**.
3 Carefully push the bulb in slightly and twist it anti-clockwise to release it **(see illustration)**.
4 Check the socket terminals for corrosion and clean them if necessary.

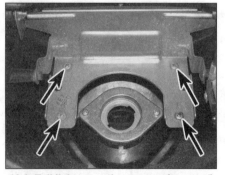

10.2 Tail light mounting screws (arrowed) – GSX600/750F model shown

5 Install the new bulb by aligning its pins with the correct cut-outs, then pushing it into the socket and twisting it clockwise.
6 Fit the bulbholder into the tail light and turn it clockwise to secure it.

Licence plate light (GSX600/750F models)

7 Unscrew the two nuts on the inside of the rear mudguard, then draw the licence plate light cover off the bulb housing **(see illustrations)**.
8 Carefully pull the bulb out of its socket **(see illustration)**.
9 Check the socket terminals for corrosion and clean them if necessary.
10 Install the new bulb by pushing it into the socket – it can be installed either way round.
11 Fit the cover and secure it with the nuts.

11.2 Relay/diode unit (arrowed)

10 Tail light assembly – removal and installation

Removal

1 Remove the seat cowling (see Chapter 7).
2 Undo the screws securing the tail light assembly and withdraw it from the cowling **(see illustration)**.
3 If required, remove the tail light bracket by undoing its screws.

Installation

4 Installation is the reverse of removal. Check the operation of the tail light and brake light.

11 Turn signal circuit – check

1 Most turn signal problems are the result of a burned out bulb or corroded socket. This is especially true when the turn signals function properly in one direction, but fail to flash in the other direction. If this is the case, first check the bulbs, the sockets and the wiring connectors. If all the turn signals fail to work, first check the signal fuse (see Section 5), and then the wiring and connectors, and the switch. Refer to Section 21 for the switch testing procedures, and also to the wiring diagrams at the end of this Chapter.
2 If all the above are good, then the relay (flasher unit) is probably faulty. The turn signal relay is integrated in one component with the sidestand relay and diode circuit. Suzuki provide no test details for the turn signal function of the relay, so the best way to determine whether it is faulty is to substitute it with one that is known to be good. If the turn signals then work, the relay is faulty. To access the relay/diode unit, remove the seat, and on GSX750 models remove the left-hand side panel (see Chapter 7). The unit is next to the fusebox and plugs into a socket in the tray **(see illustration)**. Pull the relay/diode unit out of its socket and fit the new one.

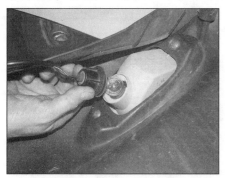

12.2 Release the bulbholder . . .

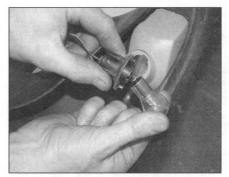

12.3 . . . and remove the bulb

12.8a Undo the screw . . .

3 If a substitute is not available, or if it does not solve the problem, pull the relay/diode unit out of its socket. Check for battery voltage at terminal G (the orange/green wire terminal) in the socket with the ignition ON (see illustration 24.7). Turn the ignition OFF when the check is complete. If no voltage was present, check the wiring from the socket to the ignition (main) switch (via the fusebox) for voltage and continuity. If voltage was present, check the light blue wire from the socket to the switch for continuity. Continue to check the wiring right through to the bulbs, referring to the appropriate wiring diagram at the end of this Chapter. Repair or renew the wiring or connectors as necessary.

12.8b . . . and remove the lens assembly

12.9 Release the bulbholder . . .

12 Turn signal bulbs – renewal

Note: *It is a good idea to use a paper towel or dry cloth when handling the new bulb to prevent injury if the bulb should break and to increase bulb life.*

Front – GSX600/750F models

1 It may be possible to access the bulbholder from above after turning the steering to full lock the other side, or from below by reaching up past the forks, though this depends on the size of your hands and your dexterity. If access is difficult or to negate the possibility of damaging either the bike or yourself, remove the inner panel from the fairing side panel (it is secured by three screws and a trim clip), or remove the fairing side panel itself (see Chapter 7).
2 Turn the bulbholder anti-clockwise and withdraw it from the lens (see illustration).
3 Push the bulb into the holder and twist it anti-clockwise to remove it (see illustration).
4 Check the socket terminals for corrosion and clean them if necessary.
5 Line up the pins of the new bulb with the slots in the socket, then push the bulb in and turn it clockwise until it locks into place.
6 Fit the bulbholder into the lens and turn it clockwise to secure it.

7 Install the fairing side panel or inner panel if removed.

Front – GSX750 models, rear – all models

8 Undo the screw securing the lens assembly and detach it from the housing, noting how it fits (see illustrations).
9 Turn the bulbholder anti-clockwise and withdraw it from the lens (see illustration).
10 Push the bulb into the holder and twist it anti-clockwise to remove it (see illustration).
11 Check the socket terminals for corrosion and clean them if necessary.
12 Line up the pins of the new bulb with the slots in the socket, then push the bulb in and turn it clockwise until it locks into place.
13 Fit the bulbholder into the lens and turn it clockwise to secure it.

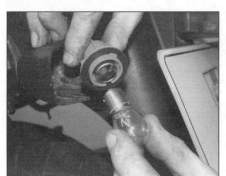

12.10 . . . and remove the bulb

14 Fit the lens assembly into the housing, making sure the tab on the inner end locates correctly, and install the screw (see illustration). Do not overtighten the screw as it is easy to strip the threads or crack the lens. Check that the turn signal works correctly.

13 Turn signal assemblies – removal and installation

Front turn signals – GSX600/750F models

1 Remove the fairing side panel (see Chapter 8). If required, turn the bulbholder anti-clockwise and withdraw it (see illustration 12.2).

12.14 Make sure the tab locates correctly

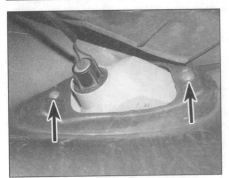

13.2 Turn signal screws (arrowed)

13.9 Turn signal wiring connectors (arrowed) – GSX600/750F model shown

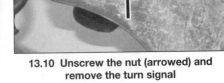

13.10 Unscrew the nut (arrowed) and remove the turn signal

2 Undo the two screws securing the turn signal to the inside of the panel and remove it from the outside **(see illustration)**.
3 Installation is the reverse of removal. Check the operation of the turn signals.

Front turn signals – GSX750 models

4 Refer to Section 8, Steps 6 and 7 and remove the headlight from the shell.
5 Trace the wiring from the turn signal and disconnect it at the connector. Feed the wiring out the back of the headlight shell and through to the turn signal, noting its routing.
6 Support the turn signal, then unscrew the nut on the inside of the bracket. Draw the nut off the wiring, then remove the turn signal, taking care not to snag the connector as you draw it through the bracket.
7 Installation is the reverse of removal. Check the operation of the turn signals.

Rear turn signals – all models

8 Remove the seat, and if necessary to access the wiring connector also remove the seat cowling (see Chapter 7).
9 Trace the wiring from the turn signal and disconnect the wiring connector **(see illustration)**. Free the wiring from any ties and carefully draw it through to the stem, taking care not to snag it.
10 Unscrew the nut securing the stem, and remove the washer **(see illustration)**. Remove the turn signal, again taking care as you draw

the wiring through. Note the mounting spacer and remove it if loose, noting how it fits.
11 Installation is the reverse of removal. Check the operation of the turn signals.

14 Brake light switches – check and renewal

Circuit check

1 Before checking the switches, and if not already done, check the brake light circuit (see Section 6, Steps 8 and 9).
2 The front brake light switch is mounted on the underside of the brake master cylinder. Disconnect the wiring connectors from the switch **(see illustration)**. Using a continuity tester, connect the probes to the terminals of the switch. With the brake lever at rest, there should be no continuity. With the brake lever applied, there should be continuity. If the switch does not behave as described, replace it with a new one.
3 The rear brake light switch is mounted on the inside of the frame, near the brake pedal **(see illustration)**. On GSX600/750F models disconnect the wiring connector from the switch. On GSX750 models trace the wiring from the switch and disconnect it at the connector. Using a continuity tester, connect the probes to the terminals on the switch side or on the switch side of the wiring connector. With the brake pedal at rest, there should be no

continuity. With the brake pedal applied, there should be continuity. If the switch does not behave as described, and you have already tried adjusting the switch (see Step 10), replace it with a new one.
4 If the switches are good, check for voltage at the black/red (front) or orange/green (rear) wire on the connector with the ignition switched ON – there should be battery voltage. If there's no voltage present, check the wiring between the switch and the ignition switch via the fusebox (see the *Wiring Diagrams* at the end of this Chapter). If voltage is present, check the black and white/black (front) or white/black (rear) wire for continuity to the brake light bulb wiring connector, referring to the relevant *Wiring Diagram*. Repair or renew the wiring as necessary.

Renewal

Front brake switch

5 The switch is mounted on the underside of the brake master cylinder. Disconnect the wiring connectors from the switch **(see illustration 14.2)**.
6 Undo the single screw securing the switch to the master cylinder and remove it, noting how it fits **(see illustration)**.
7 Locate the brake light switch on the underside of the master cylinder so that the projection on the switch fits into the hole in the master cylinder body, and secure it with the screw. Reconnect the wiring, and test the operation of the switch.

14.2 Front brake switch wiring connectors (arrowed)

14.3 Rear brake light switch (arrowed) – viewed with seat removed

14.6 Front brake light switch screw (arrowed)

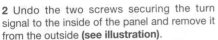

Rear brake switch

8 The rear brake light switch is mounted on the inside of the frame, near the brake pedal **(see illustration 14.3)**. On GSX600/750F models disconnect the wiring connector from the switch. On GSX750 models trace the wiring from the switch and disconnect it at the connector.

9 Detach the lower end of the switch spring from the brake pedal arm, then either release the switch with its adjustment nut from the mounting by squeezing the tabs on the underside of the nut, or thread the switch itself out of the nut, leaving the nut in the mounting.

10 Installation is the reverse of removal. Make sure the brake light is activated just before the rear brake pedal takes effect. If

adjustment is necessary, hold the switch body and turn the adjustment nut as required (either raising or lowering the switch) until the brake light is activated correctly.

15 Instrument cluster – removal and installation

GSX600/750F models

1 Remove the fairing side panels and the windshield (see Chapter 7).

2 Release the four trim clips securing the cockpit trim panel **(see illustrations)**. To release the clips, push the centre into the body, then carefully withdraw the body from the panel **(see illustrations)**.

3 Undo the two screws securing the trim panel, then displace the instrument cluster and cockpit trim panel assembly and disconnect the wiring connector when accessible, then remove the assembly **(see illustrations)**.

4 If required, unscrew the three nuts securing the instrument cluster in the trim panel and separate them, noting the washers **(see illustrations)**.

5 Installation is the reverse of removal. Check the rubber grommets in the trim panel for damage, deformation and deterioration and replace them with new ones if necessary. Make sure that the wiring connector is correctly routed and secured. Reset the trim clips by withdrawing the centre from the body, then install them by inserting the body into the panel then pressing the centre into the body.

15.2a Release the two trim clips (arrowed) at the front . . .

15.2b . . . and the two (arrowed) at the back

15.2c Push the centre in . . .

15.2d . . . then draw the body out

15.3a Undo the screws (arrowed) . . .

15.3b . . . then displace the assembly, disconnect the wiring connector . . .

15.3c . . . and remove the instrument cluster with the trim panel

15.4a Unscrew the nuts (arrowed) . . .

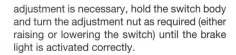
15.4b . . . and lift the instrument cluster out

8

GSX750 models

6 Refer to Section 8, Steps 6 and 7 and remove the headlight from the shell.

7 Trace the wiring from the instrument cluster and disconnect it at the connectors.

8 Unscrew the knurled ring securing the speedometer cable and detach it.

9 Unscrew the nuts securing the cluster and lift it off the top yoke, drawing the wiring out the back of the shell as you do. Note the arrangement of the mounting rubbers and collar and remove them from the top yoke if required. Replace the rubbers with new ones if they are damaged, deformed or deteriorated.

10 Installation is the reverse of removal.

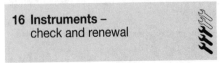

16 Instruments –
check and renewal

Circuit check

1 On GSX600/750F models, remove the instrument cluster (see Section 15).

2 On GSX750 models, remove the headlight from its shell (see Section 8). Trace the wiring from the instrument cluster and disconnect it at the connector.

3 If there has been a total loss of power to all instruments and bulbs, first check for battery voltage at the orange/green wire terminal on the loom side of the wiring connector with the ignition ON. If no voltage is present, refer to the relevant wiring diagram at the end of the Chapter and trace the fault.

4 To test the individual circuits and functions, using a multimeter or continuity tester, refer to the relevant diagram for your model and perform the continuity checks between the indicated terminals on the instrument cluster wiring connector socket (GSX600/750F models) or the connector on the sub-loom coming out of the instrument cluster **(see illustrations)**. If any test reveals no continuity, first remove, check and renew if necessary the relevant bulb (see Section 17).

5 On GSX600/750F models, if there is still no continuity in that circuit, remove the instrument and circuit board from the housing, then remove the fuel gauge and, where fitted, the clock (see Steps 10 to 13 below) and replace the instrument and circuit board with a new one.

6 On GSX750 models, if there is still no continuity in that circuit, remove the bulbholders from the cluster (see Section 17) and check for continuity in the individual wires between the connectors and the bulb sockets, and then from the socket back to the connectors, to isolate the fault, then repair the wire if possible. Otherwise fit a new wiring sub-loom.

7 If the above checks reveal no faults, then the problem will lie in the relevant switch (i.e. neutral switch, oil pressure switch, turn signal

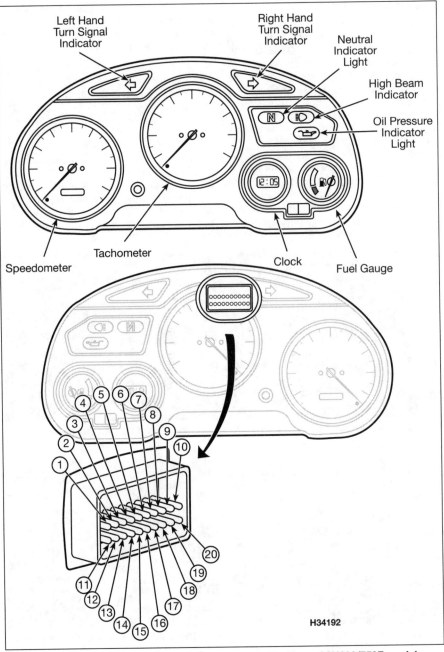

16.4a Instrument cluster tests and terminal identification – GSX600/750F models

1 Ignition
2 Meter illumination +ve
3 Speedometer
4 Speedometer
5 Earth (ground)
6 Blank
7 Blank
8 Blank
9 Neutral light –ve
10 High beam light +ve
11 Turn signal light left
12 Turn signal light right
13 Blank
14 Tachometer
15 Oil pressure light
16 Fuel gauge
17 Blank
18 Blank
19 Blank
20 Blank

Test connections	+ve probe	–ve probe
Meter illumination	2	5
Turn signal light right	12	5
Turn signal light left	11	5
Neutral light	1	9
High beam light	10	5
Oil pressure light	1	15

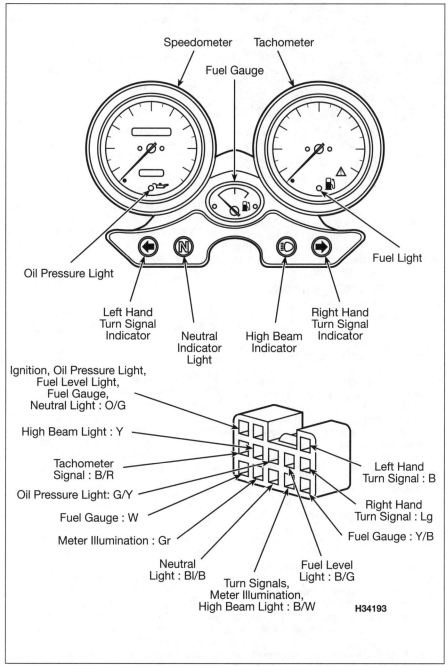

16.4b Instrument cluster tests and terminal identification – GSX750 models

B	Black	Bl/B	Blue and black	O/G	Orange and green
B/G	Black and green	G/Y	Green and yellow	W	White
B/R	Black and red	Gr	Grey	Y	Yellow
B/W	Black and white	Lg	Light green	Y/B	Yellow and black

Test connections	+ve probe	–ve probe
Meter illumination	Gr	B/W
Turn signal light right	Lg	B/W
Turn signal light left	B	B/W
Neutral light	O/G	Bl/B
High beam light	Y	B/W
Oil pressure light	O/G	G/Y
Fuel level light	O/G	B/G

switch, lighting switch or dimmer switch, fuel level sender or warning light sensor), or its circuit – refer to the relevant Section in this Chapter or in Chapter 3 for checks on those switches, and to the wiring diagrams at the end of this Chapter for the connecting circuits.

Speedometer

Check

8 On GSX600/750F models, first check the speed sensor (see Section 18). If the sensor is proved good and the wiring between the sensor and speedometer is unbroken the speedometer is likely to be faulty. The speedometer is part of the instrument circuit board and is not available separately.

9 On GSX750 models, first make sure that any fault is not due to a detached or broken cable or faulty drive gear, either at the front wheel or at the instruments. If they are good, the speedometer is probably faulty, in which case it must be replaced with a new one, though it may be worth checking with an instrument specialist whether a repair is possible.

Renewal – GSX600/750F models

10 Remove the instrument cluster and separate it from the trim panel (see Section 15).
11 Undo the screws on the back of the housing and lift the housing off the front cover **(see illustrations)**.

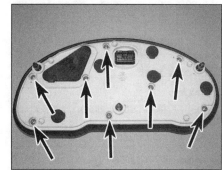

16.11a Undo the screws (arrowed) . . .

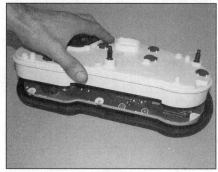

16.11b . . . and remove the housing

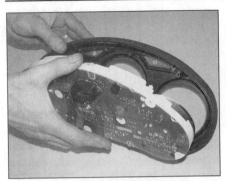

16.12 Separate the instrument and circuit board from the front cover

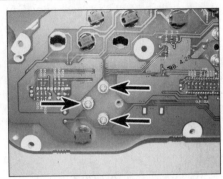

16.13 Fuel gauge screws (arrowed)

12 Carefully separate the instrument and circuit board from the front cover **(see illustration)**.

13 Undo the screws securing the fuel gauge, and where fitted the clock, and remove them **(see illustration)**.

14 Installation is the reverse of removal.

Renewal – GSX750 models

15 Remove the instrument cluster (see Section 15).

16 Undo the instrument shell screws and remove the shells.

17 Undo the rear cover screws and remove the cover.

18 Unscrew the mounting bracket nuts, then remove the bracket.

19 Undo the front cover screws on the back of the housing and lift off the front cover.

20 Undo the screws securing the speedometer and remove it from the housing, noting how it fits.

21 Installation is the reverse of removal.

Tachometer

Check

22 On GSX600/750F models, remove the seat cowling and the fairing centre panel above the headlight (see Chapter 7). Disconnect the ignition control unit wiring connector(s) and the instrument cluster wiring connector. Check for continuity in the black/yellow wire between the connectors, and check the connectors themselves for loose terminals. If the wiring and connectors are good, either the tachometer or the ignition control unit are faulty. No individual test details for either are available, so it is best to seek advice from a Suzuki dealer. The tachometer is part of the instrument circuit board and is not available separately.

23 On GSX750 models, remove the right-hand side panel (see Chapter 7), then disconnect the ignition control unit wiring connector(s). Remove the headlight from its shell (see Section 8). Trace the wiring from the instrument cluster and disconnect it at the connector. Check for continuity in the black/red wire between the connectors, and check the connectors themselves for loose

terminals. If the wiring and connectors are good, either the tachometer or the ignition control unit are faulty. No individual test details for either are available, so it is best to seek advice from a Suzuki dealer.

Renewal – GSX600/750F models

24 Remove the instrument cluster and separate it from the trim panel (see Section 15).

25 Undo the screws on the back of the housing and lift the housing off the front cover **(see illustrations 16.11a and b)**.

26 Carefully separate the instrument and circuit board from the front cover **(see illustration 16.12)**.

27 Undo the screws securing the fuel gauge, and where fitted the clock, and remove them **(see illustration 16.13)**.

28 Installation is the reverse of removal.

Renewal – GSX750 models

29 Remove the instrument cluster (see Section 15).

30 Undo the instrument shell screws and remove the shells.

31 Undo the rear cover screws and remove the cover.

32 Unscrew the mounting bracket nuts, then remove the bracket.

33 Undo the front cover screws on the back of the housing and lift off the front cover.

34 Undo the screws securing the wiring terminals and detach them, noting which fits where.

35 Undo the screws securing the tachometer and remove it from the housing, noting how it fits.

36 Installation is the reverse of removal.

Fuel gauge

Check

37 See Chapter 3.

Renewal – GSX600/750F models

38 Remove the instrument cluster and separate it from the trim panel (see Section 15).

39 Undo the screws on the back of the housing and lift the housing off the front cover **(see illustrations 16.11a and b)**.

40 Carefully separate the instrument and circuit board from the front cover **(see illustration 16.12)**.

41 Undo the screws securing the fuel gauge and remove it **(see illustration 16.13)**.

42 Installation is the reverse of removal.

Renewal – GSX750 models

43 Remove the instrument cluster (see Section 15).

44 Undo the instrument shell screws and remove the shells.

45 Undo the rear cover screws and remove the cover.

46 Unscrew the mounting bracket nuts, then remove the bracket.

47 Undo the front cover screws on the back of the housing and lift off the front cover.

48 Undo the screws securing the fuel gauge and its wiring terminals and remove it from the housing, noting which wire fits where.

49 Installation is the reverse of removal.

Clock – GSX600/750F-Y, F-K1 and F-K2 (2000 to 2002) models

Check

50 Refer to the wiring diagram at the end of this chapter and identify the fuse which supplies the clock circuit (red/yellow wire). If the fuse is good, check for battery voltage at the red/yellow wire terminal on the loom side of the instrument wiring connector. If no voltage is present, check for a break in the red/yellow wire between the instruments and the fusebox.

51 If the fuse and wiring are good, the clock is faulty and should be renewed.

Renewal

52 Remove the instrument cluster and separate it from the trim panel (see Section 15).

53 Undo the screws on the back of the housing and lift the housing off the front cover **(see illustrations 16.11a and b)**.

54 Carefully separate the instrument and circuit board from the front cover **(see illustration 16.12)**.

55 Undo the screws securing the clock and remove it.

56 Installation is the reverse of removal.

---

17 Instrument and warning light bulbs – renewal

GSX600/750F models

1 Remove the instrument cluster and separate it from the trim panel (see Section 15). The meter illumination bulbs are behind the small rubber covers, and the warning light bulbs are behind the large cover

17.1a Remove the small panels to access the illumination bulbs

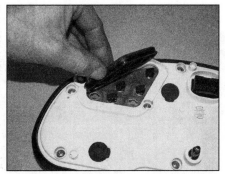

17.1b Remove the large panel to access the warning light bulbs

17.2a Carefully remove the bulbholder from the instrument cluster . . .

17.2b . . . using thin-nosed pliers to grip the illumination bulb holders . . .

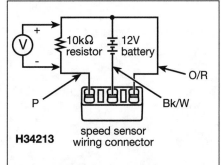

17.2c . . . then pull the bulb out of the holder

8 Make sure the new bulb is of the correct wattage (see Specifications). Carefully fit the new bulb into the holder, then fit the holder into the housing.

9 Assemble and install the instrument cluster in a reverse of the disassembly and removal procedure.

18 Speed sensor or speedometer cable – check, removal and installation

Speed sensor – GSX600/750F models

Check

Note: *To check the sensor you need a 12 volt battery, a 10 K-ohm resistor, a voltmeter, some wire to make a circuit, and some small crocodile clips.*

1 Remove the seat (see Chapter 7). You may be able to access the speed sensor wiring connector from there – it is a black 3-pin connector inside the rubber boot on the left-hand end of the fuel tank mounting bracket **(see illustration)**. If you can't access it, remove the left-hand fairing side panel (see Chapter 7).

2 Place the motorcycle on its centrestand.

3 Rig up the battery, resistor and voltmeter (see **Note** above) as shown in the circuit, and connect to the speed sensor wiring connector **(see illustration)**.

4 Turn the rear wheel in its normal direction of rotation and observe the voltmeter. The reading should alternate between zero and 12.0 volts as the wheel spins. If it doesn't, and the sensor wiring and connectors are good, replace the sensor with a new one (see below).

Removal and installation

5 Remove the seat (see Chapter 7). You may be able to access the speed sensor wiring connector from there – it is a black 3-pin connector inside the rubber boot on the left-hand end of the fuel tank mounting bracket **(see illustration 18.1)**. If you can't access it, remove the left-hand fairing side panel (see Chapter 7). Feed the wiring down to the sprocket cover, freeing it from any ties and noting its routing.

(see illustrations). Remove the panel(s) as required.

2 Turn the bulbholder anti-clockwise and draw it out of the circuit board **(see illustration)**. Use a pair of thin-nosed pliers to get at the illumination bulbholders **(see illustration)**. Pull the bulb out of the holder **(see illustration)**. If the socket contacts are dirty or corroded, scrape them clean and spray with electrical contact cleaner before a new bulb is installed.

3 Make sure the new bulb is of the correct wattage (see Specifications). Carefully fit the new bulb into the holder, then fit the holder into the housing and turn it clockwise to secure it in place.

4 Fit the rubber panel(s), then install the instrument cluster.

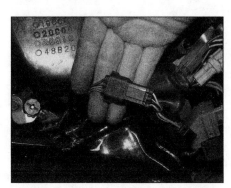

18.1 Speed sensor wiring connector

GSX750 models

5 Remove the instrument cluster (see Section 15).

6 Undo the instrument shell screws and remove the shells – the meter illumination bulbs are now accessible. To access the warning light bulbs, go on to undo the rear cover screws and remove the cover. If required unscrew the mounting bracket nuts and remove the washers, then remove the bracket.

7 Carefully pull the bulbholder out of the instrument cluster, then pull the bulb out of the bulbholder. If the socket contacts are dirty or corroded, scrape them clean and spray with electrical contact cleaner before a new bulb is installed.

H34213

18.3 Speed sensor test set-up

Bk/W Black and white
O/R Orange and red
P Pink

18.6 Speed sensor bolt (arrowed)

18.8 Unscrew the bolt and remove the rotor

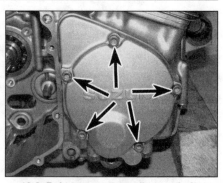

19.8 Pulse generator coil cover bolts (arrowed)

6 Unscrew the bolt securing the speed sensor in the front sprocket cover and draw it out **(see illustration)**.

7 Installation is the reverse of removal.

8 To remove the speed sensor rotor, remove the front sprocket cover (see Chapter 5). Unscrew the bolt securing the rotor on the end of the output shaft and remove it **(see illustration)**. Apply the rear brake to prevent the sprocket turning. On installation tighten the rotor bolt to the specified torque setting.

Speedometer cable – GSX750 models

9 Undo the screw securing the speedometer cable to the drive housing on the front wheel and detach it, noting how it locates.

10 Unscrew the knurled ring securing the speedometer cable to the speedometer and detach it.

11 Withdraw the cable, noting its routing.

12 Installation is the reverse of removal. Unless a new cable is being fitted, refer to Chapter 1 and lubricate it before installation. Make sure the cable is correctly routed.

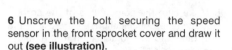

19 Oil pressure switch – check, removal and installation

Check

1 The oil pressure warning light should come on when the ignition (main) switch is turned

ON and extinguish a few seconds after the engine is started. If the oil pressure warning light comes on whilst the engine is running, stop the engine immediately and check the oil level (see *Daily (pre-ride) checks*), and if the level is correct, carry out an oil pressure check (see Chapter 1).

2 If the oil pressure warning light does not come on when the ignition is turned on, check the bulb (see Section 17), signal fuse (see Section 5), and the instrument cluster circuit (see Section 16).

3 The oil pressure switch is screwed into the crankcase on the right-hand side, below the timing rotor. Remove the pulse generator coil cover and detach the wiring connector from the switch (see Steps 6 to 9 below). With the ignition switched ON, earth (ground) the connector on the crankcase and check that the warning light comes on. If the light comes on, the switch is defective and must be replaced with a new one.

4 If the light still does not come on, check for voltage at the wire terminal with the ignition ON. If there is no voltage present, check the wire between the switch, the instrument cluster and fusebox for continuity (see the *wiring diagrams* at the end of this Chapter).

5 If the warning light comes on whilst the engine is running, yet the oil pressure is satisfactory, remove the wire from the oil pressure switch. With the wire detached and the ignition switched ON the light should be out. If it is illuminated, the wire between the

switch and instrument cluster must be earthed (grounded) at some point. If the wiring is good, the switch must be assumed faulty and replaced with a new one.

Removal

6 On GSX600/750F models remove the fairing right-hand side panel (see Chapter 7).

7 Drain the engine oil (see Chapter 1).

8 Unscrew the five bolts securing the pulse generator coil cover to the right-hand side of the engine **(see illustration)**. Note the sealing washer with the top bolt – discard the washer as a new one should be used. Lift the cover away from the engine, being prepared to catch any residual oil. Remove the gasket and discard it.

9 Undo the screw securing the wiring connector to the switch and detach it **(see illustration)**.

10 Unscrew the switch and withdraw it from the crankcase **(see illustration)**.

Installation

11 Apply a suitable sealant (such as Suzuki Bond 1207B or equivalent) to the upper portion of the switch threads near the switch body, leaving the bottom half of thread clean **(see illustration)**. Install the switch and tighten it to the torque setting specified at the beginning of the Chapter.

12 Attach the wiring connector and secure it with the screw.

13 Apply sealant around the crankcase joints

19.9 Undo the terminal screw and detach the wiring . . .

19.10 . . . then unscrew the switch

19.11 Apply sealant to the threads as described

19.13a Smear some sealant around the joints (arrowed)

19.13b Fit the cover using a new gasket . . .

19.13c . . . and do not forget the sealing washer

as shown **(see illustration)**. Install the pulse generator cover using a new gasket and a suitable non-permanent thread lock on the bolts, and fit a new sealing washer with the top bolt **(see illustrations)**.

14 Replenish the engine with oil (see Chapter 1). Run the engine and check that the switch operates correctly.

15 On GSX600/750F models install the fairing right-hand side panel (see Chapter 7).

20 Ignition (main) switch –
check, removal and installation

⚠ *Warning: To prevent the risk of short circuits, disconnect the battery negative (–ve) lead before making any ignition (main) switch checks.*

Check

1 On GSX600/750F models, remove the fuel tank (see Chapter 3). Trace the wiring from the ignition switch and disconnect it at the connector **(see illustration)**.

2 On GSX750 models, refer to Section 8, Steps 6 and 7 and remove the headlight from the shell. Trace the wiring from the ignition switch and disconnect it at the connector.

3 Using an ohmmeter or a continuity tester, check the continuity of the connector terminal pairs (see the *Wiring Diagrams* at the end of this Chapter). Continuity should exist between the terminals connected by a solid line on the

diagram when the switch is in the indicated position.

4 If the switch fails any of the tests, replace it with a new one.

Removal

Note: *The ignition switch bolts are a special type of Torx bolt with a raised pip in their centres for security. Unfortunately this means that a special Torx bit (available from any good tool shop) is needed to unscrew them.*

5 Remove the seat and disconnect the battery negative (–ve) lead (see Section 3).

6 On GSX600/750F models, remove the fuel tank (see Chapter 3). Trace the wiring from the ignition switch and disconnect it at the connector **(see illustration 20.1)**. Release the wiring from any clips or ties and feed it through to the switch. Remove the instrument cluster (see Section 15), and if required for best access also remove the headlight (see Section 8).

7 On GSX750 models, remove the headlight assembly (see Section 8), and if required for best access also remove the instrument cluster.

8 Unscrew the two Torx bolts securing the switch and withdraw it from the top yoke **(see illustration)**.

Installation

9 Installation is the reverse of removal. If reusing the old Torx bolts, apply a suitable non-permanent thread locking compound to their threads and tighten them. Note that new bolts are already pre-treated with thread locking compound. Make sure the wiring connectors are securely connected and correctly routed. Reconnect the battery negative (–ve) lead.

21 Handlebar switches –
check

1 Generally speaking, the switches are reliable and trouble-free. Most troubles, when they do occur, are caused by dirty or corroded contacts, but wear and breakage of internal parts is a possibility that should not be overlooked. If breakage does occur, the entire switch and related wiring harness will have to be replaced with a new one, as individual parts are not available.

2 The switches can be checked for continuity using an ohmmeter or a continuity test light. Always disconnect the battery negative (–ve) lead, which will prevent the possibility of a short circuit, before making the checks.

3 On GSX600/750F models, remove the fairing centre panel above the headlight (see Chapter 7). You may be able to access the switch wiring connectors, located above the right-hand end of the headlight assembly, from there, but if you have large hands or there is the slightest possibility of damaging either yourself or the fairing when disconnecting them, also remove the fairing right-hand side panel (see Chapter 7). Disconnect the connector for the switch being tested – the 9-pin black connector is for the right-hand switch housing and the 11-pin yellow connector is for the left-hand one **(see illustration)**.

4 On GSX750 models, refer to Section 8,

20.1 Ignition switch wiring connector (arrowed) – GSX600/750F models

20.8 Ignition switch bolts (arrowed) – yoke shown displaced for clarity

21.3 Handlebar switch wiring connectors – GSX600/750F models

Steps 6 and 7 and remove the headlight from the shell. Trace the wiring from the switch housing being tested and disconnect it at the connector.

5 Check for continuity between the terminals of the switch connector with the switch in the various positions (i.e. switch off – no continuity, switch on – continuity) – see the *Wiring Diagrams* at the end of this Chapter. Continuity should exist between the terminals connected by a solid line on the diagram when the switch is in the indicated position.

6 If the continuity check indicates a problem exists, refer to Section 22, displace the switch housing and spray the switch contacts with electrical contact cleaner (there is no need to remove the switch completely). If they are accessible, the contacts can be scraped clean with a knife or polished with crocus cloth. If switch components are damaged or broken, it should be obvious when the switch is disassembled. If no problems are found, then there is a break in the wiring between the connector and the switch, or there is a loose wire in the connector – trace and repair the problem, or replace the switch housing with a new one – it comes with its loom.

22 Handlebar switches – removal and installation

Removal

1 On GSX600/750F models, if the switch is to be removed from the bike, rather than just displaced from the handlebar, remove the fairing centre panel above the headlight (see Chapter 7). You may be able to access the switch wiring connectors, located above the right-hand end of the headlight assembly, from there, but if you have large hands or there is the slightest possibility of damaging either yourself or the fairing when disconnecting them, also remove the fairing right-hand side panel (see Chapter 7). Disconnect the connector for the switch being removed – the 9-pin black connector is for the right-hand switch housing and the 11-pin yellow connector is for the left-hand one **(see illustration 21.3)**. Work back along the harness, freeing it from any clips and ties, noting its correct routing.

2 On GSX750 models, if the switch is to be removed from the bike, rather than just displaced from the handlebar, refer to Section 8, Steps 6 and 7 and remove the headlight from the shell. Trace the wiring from the switch housing being tested and disconnect it at the connector. Work back along the harness, freeing it from any clips and ties, noting its correct routing.

3 Disconnect the wiring from the brake light switch (if removing the right-hand switch) or the clutch switch (if removing the left-hand switch) **(see illustration 14.2 or 25.2)**.

4 To remove the right-hand switch, refer to Chapter 3 for throttle cable removal and to

remove the left-hand switch, refer to Chapter 3 for choke cable removal. Note in each case you do not need to detach the cables from the carburettors, though in the case of the throttle cables you may need to access the adjusters at the carburettor end to create enough slack to detach them from the twistgrip.

Installation

5 Installation is the reverse of removal. Make sure the locating pin in the switch housing locates in the hole in the handlebar.

23 Neutral switch – check, removal and installation

Check

1 The switch does not only illuminate the neutral light in the instrument cluster, but is also part of the safety interlock circuit, which will cut the ignition if the sidestand is extended whilst the engine is running and in gear (with the clutch pulled in), or if a gear is selected whilst the engine is running and the sidestand is down. It also prevents the engine from being started if the sidestand is down and the engine is in gear even though the clutch is held in . The engine can only be started on the sidestand with the transmission in neutral and the clutch lever pulled in, or, if the transmission is in gear, if the sidestand is up and the clutch lever is pulled in.. Before checking the electrical circuit, check the bulb (see Section 17), signal fuse (see Section 5), and the instrument cluster circuit (see Section 16).

2 The switch is located in the left-hand side of the crankcase below the front sprocket. Make sure the transmission is in neutral.

3 On GSX600/750F models remove the seat (see Chapter 7). You may be able to access the neutral switch wiring connectors from there – they are a white 2-pin connector and a white 1-pin connector inside the rubber boot on the left-hand end of the fuel tank mounting bracket **(see illustration)**. If you can't access them, remove the fairing left-hand side panel (see Chapter 7). Disconnect the 1-pin connector with the blue wire.

4 On GSX750 models remove the fuel tank (see Chapter 3). Trace the wiring from the

neutral switch and disconnect it at the white 1-pin connector with the blue wire.

5 With the connector disconnected, the transmission in neutral and the ignition switch ON, the neutral light should be out. If not, the blue wire between the connector and the relay/diode unit (next to the fusebox), or the blue/black wire between the relay/diode unit and the instrument cluster must be earthed (grounded) at some point.

6 Check for continuity between the blue wire terminal on the switch side of the 1-pin connector and the crankcase. With the transmission in neutral, there should be continuity. With the transmission in gear, there should be no continuity. If the tests prove otherwise, then the switch is faulty.

7 If the continuity tests prove the switch is good, check for voltage at the blue wire terminal on the loom side of the 1-pin connector with the ignition switch ON. If there's no voltage present, check the wire between the switch, and the instrument cluster via the diodes (see the *Wiring Diagrams* at the end of this Chapter). If no faults are found check the diodes (see Section 26).

Removal

8 The switch is located in the left-hand side of the crankcase below the front sprocket. Drain the engine oil (see Chapter 1). Remove the front sprocket cover (see Chapter 5).

9 On GSX600/750F models remove the seat (see Chapter 7). You may be able to access the neutral switch wiring connectors from there – they are a white 2-pin connector and a white 1-pin connector inside the rubber boot on the left-hand end of the fuel tank mounting bracket **(see illustration 23.3)**. If you can't access them, remove the fairing left-hand side panel (see Chapter 7). Free the wiring from any guides or ties and feed it down to the switch, noting its routing.

10 On GSX750 models remove the fuel tank (see Chapter 3). Trace the wiring from the neutral switch and disconnect it at the white 2-pin and white 1-pin connectors. Free the wiring from any guides or ties and feed it down to the switch, noting its routing.

11 Clean all chain grease and road dirt from the switch area. Undo the switch screws and withdraw it from the crankcase **(see illustration)**. Discard the O-ring as a new one

23.3 Neutral switch wiring connectors

23.11a Undo the screws and remove the switch

23.11b Remove the plunger and spring for safekeeping

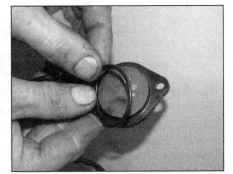

23.12a Fit a new O-ring onto the switch . . .

23.12b . . . and fit it into the crankcase

should be used. Note the contact plunger in the end of the selector drum and remove it with its spring for safekeeping if required **(see illustration)**.

Installation

12 If removed, fit the spring and contact plunger into its bore in the end of the selector drum. Install the switch using a new O-ring smeared with grease and tighten the screws **(see illustrations)**.
13 Route the wiring as noted on removal and connect the wiring connectors. Check the operation of the neutral light.
14 Replenish the engine oil (see Chapter 1). Install the sprocket cover (see Chapter 5) and any other removed components.

24 Sidestand switch and relay – check and renewal

1 The sidestand switch is mounted on the frame in front of the sidestand. The switch is part of the safety interlock circuit, which will cut the ignition if the sidestand is extended whilst the engine is running and in gear (with the clutch pulled in), or if a gear is selected whilst the engine is running and the sidestand is down. It also prevents the engine from being started if the sidestand is down and the engine is in gear even though the clutch is held in. The engine can only be started on the sidestand with the transmission in neutral and the clutch lever pulled in, or, if the transmission is in gear, if the sidestand is up and the clutch lever is pulled in. The sidestand switch relay is integrated into one component with the turn signal relay and diode circuit.

Check

2 Before checking the electrical circuit, check the ignition fuse (see Section 5).
3 On GSX600/750F models remove the seat (see Chapter 7). You may be able to access the sidestand switch wiring connector from there – it is a green 2-pin connector inside the rubber boot on the left-hand end of the fuel tank mounting bracket **(see illustration)**. If you can't access it, remove the fairing left-

hand side panel (see Chapter 7). Disconnect the connector.
4 On GSX750 models remove the fuel tank (see Chapter 3). Trace the wiring from the sidestand switch and disconnect it at the green 2-pin connector.
5 To check the switch, connect an ohmmeter or continuity tester between the terminals on the switch side of the wiring connector. With the sidestand up there should be continuity (zero resistance) between the terminals, and with the stand down there should be no continuity (infinite resistance). If the switch does not perform as expected, it is faulty and must be replaced with a new one.
6 The switch incorporates a diode. To test this, with the sidestand up, check that there is continuity when the positive (+ve) probe is connected to the green wire terminal on the switch side of the connector, and the negative (–ve) probe is connected to the black/white wire terminal. Now reverse the probes, whereupon there should be no continuity. If your test meter incorporates a diode tester function set it to that. With the probes connected as stated, there should be 0.4 to 0.6 volts with the sidestand up, and 1.4 to 1.5 volts with the stand down.
7 To check the relay/diode unit, on GSX600/750F models remove the seat, and on GSX750 models remove the left-hand side panel (see Chapter 7). The relay/diode unit is next to the fusebox and plugs into a socket in the tray **(see illustration 11.2)**. Pull the relay/diode unit out of its socket. Set a

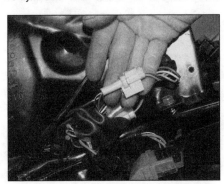

24.3 Sidestand switch wiring connector

multimeter to the ohms x 1 scale and connect it across the relay's D and E terminals as shown **(see illustration)**. There should be no continuity. Using a fully-charged 12 volt battery and two insulated jumper wires, connect the positive (+ve) terminal of the battery to terminal D on the relay/diode unit, and the negative (–ve) terminal to terminal C on the relay/diode unit. At this point the relay should be heard to click and the multimeter read 0 ohms (continuity). If this is the case the relay/diode unit is proved good. If the relay does not click when battery voltage is applied and indicates no continuity (infinite resistance) across its terminals, it is faulty and a new one must be installed.

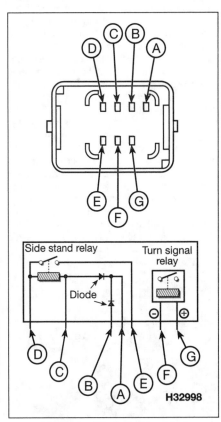

24.7 Relay/diode unit terminal identification and circuit diagram

8 If the switch and relay/diode unit are good, check for battery voltage at terminal D in the relay socket with the ignition ON, the transmission in neutral and the engine STOP switch in the RUN position **(see illustration 24.7)**. Turn the ignition OFF when the check is complete. If no voltage was present, check the wiring from the socket to the ignition (main) switch (via the fusebox) for voltage and continuity. If the voltage is good, check the wiring and connectors between the various components in the starter safety circuit using a continuity tester, and check the other components themselves (see the *Wiring Diagrams* at the end of this book). If no faults can be found, the ignition control unit may be faulty (see Chapter 4).

Renewal

9 The sidestand switch is mounted on the frame ahead of the sidestand.
10 On GSX600/750F models remove the seat (see Chapter 7). You may be able to access the sidestand switch wiring connector from there – it is a green 2-pin connector inside the rubber boot on the left-hand end of the fuel tank mounting bracket **(see illustration 24.3)**. If you can't access it, remove the fairing left-hand side panel (see Chapter 7). Disconnect the connector. Work back along the switch wiring, freeing it from any clips and ties, noting its routing.
11 On GSX750 models remove the fuel tank (see Chapter 3). Trace the wiring from the sidestand switch and disconnect it at the green 2-pin connector. Work back along the switch wiring, freeing it from any clips and ties, noting its routing.
12 Unscrew the two bolts securing the switch and remove it, noting how it fits **(see illustration)**. Fit the new switch onto the bracket, making sure the plunger locates correctly against the sidestand when it is raised. Secure the switch with the bolts and tighten them. Make sure the wiring is correctly routed up to the connector and retained by any clips and ties, then reconnect the wiring connector.
13 To access the relay, on GSX600/750F models remove the seat, and on GSX750 models remove the left-hand side panel (see Chapter 7). The relay is integrated into one component with the turn signal relay and diode circuit and is next to the fusebox and plugs into

a socket in the tray **(see illustration 11.2)**. Pull the relay/diode unit out of its socket and replace it with a new one.
14 Check the operation of the switch and relay.

25 Clutch switch –
check and renewal

Check

1 The clutch switch is mounted on the clutch lever bracket. The switch is part of the safety interlock circuit, which will cut the ignition if the sidestand is extended whilst the engine is running and in gear (with the clutch pulled in), or if a gear is selected whilst the engine is running and the sidestand is down. It also prevents the engine from being started if the sidestand is down and the engine is in gear even though the clutch is held in . The engine can only be started on the sidestand with the transmission in neutral and the clutch lever pulled in, or, if the transmission is in gear, if the sidestand is up and the clutch lever is pulled in.
2 To check the switch, disconnect the wiring connectors from it **(see illustration)**. Connect the probes of an ohmmeter or a continuity tester to the two switch terminals. With the clutch lever pulled in, there should be continuity (zero resistance). With the clutch lever out, there should be no continuity (infinite resistance).
3 If the switch is good, check the other components in the starter circuit as described in the relevant sections of this Chapter. If all components are good, check the wiring and connectors between the various components (see the *wiring diagrams* at the end of this book). If no faults can be found, the ignition control unit may be faulty (see Chapter 4).

Renewal

4 The clutch switch is mounted on the clutch lever bracket.
5 Disconnect the wiring connectors from the switch. Undo the screws securing the switch to the bracket and remove the switch, noting how it fits.
6 Installation is the reverse of removal.

26 Diodes –
check and renewal

1 The diodes are part of the starter safety interlock system (see Section 1). A diode allows current flow in one direction only. The diodes are integrated with the turn signal relay and sidestand relay in one component, which plugs into a socket next to the fusebox **(see illustration 11.2)**. Refer to the relevant wiring diagram at the end of the Chapter for details.
2 To test the diode circuit, on GSX600/750F models remove the seat, and on GSX750 models remove the left-hand side panel (see Chapter 7), and pull the unit out of its socket. Connect the positive (+ve) probe of an ohmmeter or continuity tester to the B terminal on the diode as shown and the negative (-ve) probe to the A terminal **(see illustration 24.7)**. There should be continuity. Now reverse the probes. There should be no continuity. Repeat the tests between the other C terminal and the A terminal. The same results should be achieved. If it doesn't behave as stated, install a new diode/relay unit.
3 If your test meter incorporates a diode tester function set it to that. With the probes connected as stated above, there should be 0.4 to 0.6 volts with the first test, and 1.4 to 1.5 volts with the probes reversed.
4 If the diodes are good, check the other components in the starter circuit as described in the relevant sections of this Chapter. If all components are good, check the wiring between the various components (see the *Wiring Diagrams* at the end of this book). If no faults can be found, the ignition control unit may be faulty (see Chapter 4).

27 Horn(s) – check,
removal and installation

Check

1 On GSX600/750F models the horn is mounted in front of the oil cooler. On GSX750 models, the horns are mounted below the headlight.
2 Unplug the wiring connectors from the horn **(see illustration)**. Using two jumper wires,

24.12 Sidestand switch bolts (arrowed)

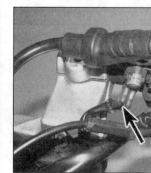

25.2 Clutch switch wiring connectors (arrowed)

27.2 Horn wiring connectors (arrowed)

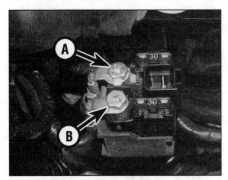

28.4 Starter relay battery lead (A) and starter motor lead (B)

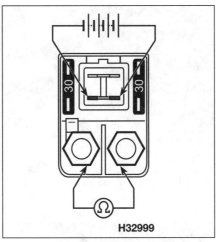

H32999

28.5 Starter relay test set-up

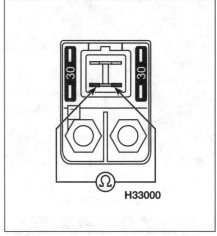

H33000

28.6 Measuring the relay coil resistance

apply battery voltage directly to the terminals on the horn. If the horn sounds, check the switch (see Section 21). Also check for voltage at the orange/green (GSX600/750F) or black/orange (GSX750) wire connector with the ignition ON. If voltage is present, check the black/blue wire for continuity to earth with the horn button pressed. If no voltage was present, check the orange/green wire or black/orange wire, as applicable, and the connectors for faults (see the *Wiring Diagrams* at the end of this Chapter). If no continuity was present, locate the fault by systematically working along the circuit (use the wiring diagrams) checking where the continuity breaks down.

3 If the horn doesn't sound, install a new one.

Removal and installation

4 On GSX600/750F models the horn is mounted in front of the oil cooler. On GSX750 models, the horns are mounted below the headlight.

5 Unplug the wiring connectors from the horn. Unscrew the bolt securing the horn to its bracket and remove it.

6 Install the horn and tighten the bolt. Connect the wiring to the horn. Check that it works.

28 Starter relay – check and renewal

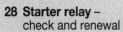

Check

1 If the starter circuit is faulty, first check the ignition fuse (see Section 5).

2 The starter relay is behind the fairing left-hand side panel on GSX600/750F models, and behind the right-hand side panel on GSX750 models. Remove the panel for access (see Chapter 7).

3 Disconnect the battery negative (–ve) terminal (see Section 3).

4 Disconnect the wiring connector and lift

the insulating cover off the relay **(see illustrations 5.3a and b)**. Unscrew the bolts securing the starter motor and battery leads to the relay and detach the leads, noting which fits where **(see illustration)**. Move the relay to the bench for testing.

5 Connect a multimeter set to the ohms scale across the relay's starter motor and battery terminals – no continuity should be shown. Now connect a 12V battery across the relay's coil terminals (the two nearest the starter motor and battery terminals) – continuity should now be shown on the meter and the relay should be heard to click **(see illustration)**.

Caution: Do not connect the battery for more than five seconds or the relay coil may be damaged.

6 If no continuity is shown in the test described above, connect a multimeter set to the ohms x 1 scale across the relay's coil terminals (the two nearest the starter motor and battery terminals) **(see illustration)**. The coil resistance should be as specified at the beginning of this Chapter. If no continuity (infinite resistance) is shown, the relay is confirmed faulty and should be renewed.

7 If the relay is good, check for continuity in the main lead from the battery to the relay. Also check that the terminals and connectors at each end of the lead are tight and corrosion-free. Next check the wiring between the relay wiring connector and the other components in the starter circuit, including the starter button in the right-hand handlebar switch, as described in the relevant sections of this Chapter. If all components are good, check the wiring and connectors between the various components (see the *wiring diagrams* at the end of this book).

Renewal

8 The starter relay is behind the left-hand fairing side panel on GSX600/750F models, and behind the right-hand side panel on

GSX750 models. Remove the panel for access (see Chapter 7).

9 Disconnect the battery negative (–ve) terminal (see Section 3).

10 Disconnect the wiring connector and lift the insulating cover off the relay **(see illustrations 5.3a and b)**. Unscrew the bolts securing the starter motor and battery leads to the relay and detach the leads **(see illustration 28.4)**. Remove the relay with its rubber sleeve from its mounting lug on the frame. If a new relay is being installed, remove the main and spare fuses, and remove the relay from its sleeve.

11 Installation is the reverse of removal. Make sure the terminal bolts are securely tightened – the red lead from the battery connects to the inner terminal, and the black lead to the starter motor connects to the outer terminal. Do not forget to fit the main and spare fuses into the relay, if removed. Connect the negative (–ve) lead last when reconnecting the battery.

29 Starter motor – removal and installation

Removal

1 Disconnect the battery negative (–ve) lead (see Section 3). On GSX600/750F models remove the fairing left-hand side panel (see Chapter 7). The starter motor is mounted on the crankcase behind the cylinder block. For improved access displace or remove the carburettors (see Chapter 3). Access to the front bolt is quite restricted, and depending on the tools you have available you may have to remove the alternator as well (see Section 33).

2 Peel back the rubber terminal cover on the starter motor. Unscrew the bolt (GSX600/750F models) or nut (GSX750

29.2 Pull back the terminal cover then unscrew the bolt or nut and detach the lead – GSX600/750F shown

29.3a Unscrew the two bolts (arrowed) . . .

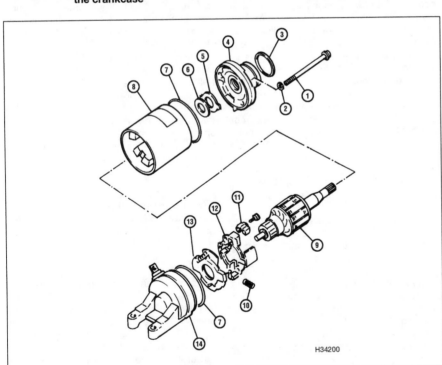

29.3b . . . and slide the starter motor out of the crankcase

29.5 Fit a new O-ring smeared with grease

30.1 Starter motor components – GSX600/750F models

1 Long bolt
2 O-ring
3 O-ring
4 Front cover
5 Tabbed washer
6 Shim
7 Sealing ring
8 Main housing
9 Armature
10 Brush spring
11 Brush
12 Upper brush plate
13 Lower brush plate
14 Rear cover

H34200

models) securing the starter lead to the motor and detach the lead (see illustration).

3 Unscrew the two bolts securing the starter motor to the crankcase (see illustration). Slide the starter motor out and remove it (see illustration)

4 Remove the O-ring on the end of the starter motor and discard it as a new one must be used.

Installation

5 Fit a new O-ring smeared with grease onto the end of the starter motor, making sure it is seated in its groove (see illustration).

6 Manoeuvre the motor into position and slide it into the crankcase. Ensure that the starter motor teeth mesh correctly with those of the starter drive gear. Install the mounting bolts and tighten them, to the torque setting specified at the beginning of the Chapter if you have the correct tools (access is restricted).

7 Connect the starter lead to the motor and secure it with the bolt or nut. Fit the rubber cover over the terminal.

8 Reconnect the battery negative (–ve) lead. On GSX600/750F models remove the fairing left-hand side panel (see Chapter 7).

---

30 Starter motor – disassembly, inspection and reassembly

GSX600/750F models

Disassembly

1 Remove the starter motor (see Section 29) (see illustration).

2 Note the alignment marks between the main housing and the front and rear covers, or make your own if they aren't clear (see illustration). Wrap some insulating tape around the teeth on the end of the starter motor shaft – this will protect the oil seal from damage as the front cover is removed.

3 Unscrew the two long bolts, noting the O-rings, then remove the front cover from the motor, noting the sealing ring (see

30.2 Note the alignment marks, or make your own

illustrations). Remove the tabbed washer from the cover and the shim from the front end of the armature (see illustrations).

4 Remove the rear cover from the motor, noting the sealing ring. The brushes are under spring pressure and will probably pop out when the armature is removed – take care not to lose the springs.

5 Withdraw the armature from the main housing, noting that it is held by the attraction of the magnets.

Inspection

6 The parts of the starter motor that are most likely to require attention are the brushes. Suzuki give no specifications for the minimum length of the brushes, however if they are obviously worn down and are close to the wire, cracked, chipped, or otherwise damaged, new ones should be installed. Draw all the brushes out of their holders and remove the springs (see illustration). Remove the two screws securing the upper brush plate and remove it, noting how it fits, then remove the lower brush plate. The top brushes can be replaced individually, the lower brushes come with the lower brush plate. Locate the lower brush plate into the rear cover, then fit the upper brush plate, making sure the lower brushes are correctly located, then secure them with the two screws.

7 Inspect the commutator bars on the armature for scoring, scratches and discoloration. The commutator can be cleaned and polished with crocus cloth, but do not use sandpaper or emery paper. After cleaning, wipe away any residue with a cloth soaked in electrical system cleaner or denatured alcohol. Also check that the insulation between each bar is not close to the level of the bars. If it is, scrape some away.

8 Using an ohmmeter or a continuity test light, check for continuity between the commutator bars (see illustration). Continuity should exist between each bar and all of the others. Also, check for continuity between the commutator bars and the armature shaft (see illustration). There should be no continuity (infinite resistance) between the commutator and the shaft. If the checks indicate otherwise, the armature is defective.

9 Check the end of the starter shaft for worn, cracked, chipped and broken teeth. If they are

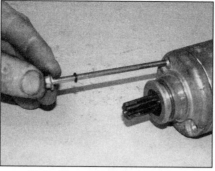
30.3a Unscrew and remove the two bolts . . .

30.3c Remove the tabbed washer . . .

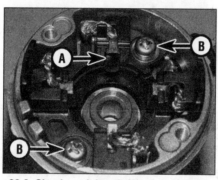
30.6 Check each brush (A) as described. Brushplate screws (B)

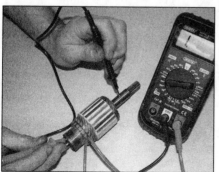
30.8b There should be no continuity between the bars and the shaft

30.3b . . . then remove the front cover and sealing ring (arrowed)

30.3d . . . and the shim (arrowed)

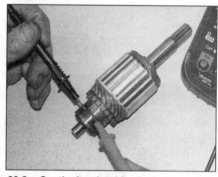
30.8a Continuity should exist between the commutator bars

30.10a Check the seal and needle bearing in the front cover . . .

30.10b . . . and the bush (arrowed) in the rear cover

damaged or worn, renew the starter motor – the armature is not available separately.

10 Inspect the end covers for signs of cracks or wear. Check the needle bearing and oil seal

in the front cover and the bush in the rear cover for wear and damage (see illustrations). The seal is available separately but if the bearing is worn a new front cover must be

30.13 Locate the armature in the rear cover

30.14 Carefully slide the housing over the armature

fitted. Inspect the magnets in the main housing and the housing itself for cracks.

11 Inspect the housing sealing rings for signs of damage, deformation and deterioration and fit new ones if necessary.

Reassembly

12 Fit the sealing ring onto the rear cover. Slide the springs and brushes back into their holders. To make it easy to install the armature, it is necessary to draw the brushes as far back as possible in the holders and secure them there to provide clearance (if you are lucky they may hold themselves in place if the wire is shaped around the guide as shown in illustration 30.6). An alternative way is to cut up a cable tie into four sections, then use one for each brush, locating them between the wire and the guide.

13 Apply a smear of molybdenum disulphide grease to the armature shaft rear end. Insert the armature in the rear cover, then remove the cable tie pieces (if used) and locate the brushes on the commutator bars **(see illustration)**. Check that each brush is securely pressed against the commutator by its spring and is free to move easily in its holder.

14 Grasp both the armature and the rear cover in one hand and hold them together – this will prevent the armature being drawn out by the magnets in the housing. Note however that you should take care not to let the housing be drawn forcibly onto the armature by the magnets. Carefully allow the housing to be drawn onto the armature, aligning the marks between the cover and housing **(see illustration)**.

15 Apply a smear of grease to the lips of the front cover oil seal and armature shaft and fit a new sealing ring onto the cover. Fit the shim onto the shaft and the special washer onto the front cover, making sure that its tabs locate correctly in the cover cut-outs **(see illustrations 30.3d and c)**. Install the cover, aligning the marks **(see illustration 30.3b)**. Remove the protective tape from the shaft end.

16 Check the condition of the O-rings on the long bolts and fit new ones if necessary. Apply a smear of suitable non-permanent thread locking compound to their threads and tighten them **(see illustration 30.3a)**.

17 Install the starter motor (see Section 29).

GSX750 models

Disassembly

18 Remove the starter motor (see Section 29) **(see illustration)**.

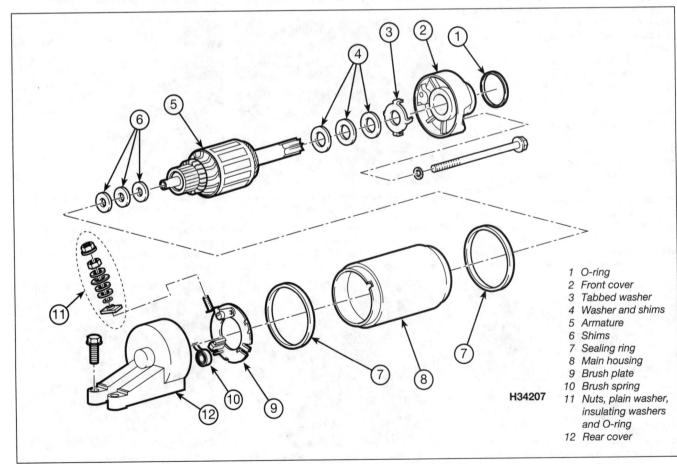

1 O-ring
2 Front cover
3 Tabbed washer
4 Washer and shims
5 Armature
6 Shims
7 Sealing ring
8 Main housing
9 Brush plate
10 Brush spring
11 Nuts, plain washer, insulating washers and O-ring
12 Rear cover

H34207

30.18 Starter motor components – GSX750 models

19 Note the alignment marks between the main housing and the front and rear covers, or make your own if they aren't clear. Wrap some insulating tape around the teeth on the end of the starter motor shaft – this will protect the oil seal from damage as the front cover is removed.

20 Unscrew the two long bolts, noting the O-rings, then remove the front cover from the motor along with its sealing ring. Remove the tabbed washer from the cover and slide the insulating washer and shims from the front end of the armature, noting their order.

21 Remove the rear cover from the motor along with its sealing ring. Remove the shims from the rear end of the armature noting their order.

22 Withdraw the armature from the main housing, noting that it will be held by the pull of the magnets.

23 Unscrew the nut from the terminal bolt and remove the plain washer, the one large and two small insulating washers and the rubber O-ring. Remove the brushplate assembly and terminal bolt from the rear cover, noting how it locates, and recover the insulator.

24 Move each brush spring end off its brush and slide the brushes out.

Inspection

25 The parts of the starter motor that are most likely to require attention are the brushes. Suzuki give no specifications for the minimum length of the brushes, however if they are obviously worn down and are close to the wire, cracked, chipped, or otherwise damaged, renew the brushplate assembly.

26 Inspect the commutator bars on the armature for scoring, scratches and discoloration. The commutator can be cleaned and polished with crocus cloth, but do not use sandpaper or emery paper. After cleaning, wipe away any residue with a cloth soaked in electrical system cleaner or denatured alcohol. Make sure the insulating mica that separates the bars is not level with their outer surface. If it is, scrape out the mica using a pointed instrument or hacksaw blade.

27 Using an ohmmeter or a continuity tester, check for continuity between the commutator bars **(see illustration 30.8a)**. Continuity should exist between each bar and all of the others. Also, check for continuity between the commutator bars and the armature shaft **(see illustration 30.8b)**. There should be no continuity (infinite resistance) between the commutator and the shaft. If the checks indicate otherwise, the armature is defective.

28 Check for continuity between the terminal bolt and the brush it connects to. There should be continuity (zero resistance). Check for continuity between the terminal bolt and the brushplate. There should be no continuity (infinite resistance). Also check for continuity between the other brush wire and the brushplate. There should be continuity (zero resistance). If there is no continuity when

there should be or vice versa, identify the faulty component and renew it.

29 Check the starter shaft gear for worn, cracked, chipped and broken teeth. If they are damaged or worn, renew the starter motor – the armature is not available separately.

30 Inspect the end covers for signs of cracks or wear. Check the needle bearing and oil seal in the front cover and the bush in the rear cover for wear and damage. Inspect the magnets in the main housing and the housing itself for cracks.

31 Inspect the terminal bolt insulating washers and O-ring, and the housing sealing rings, for signs of damage, deformation and deterioration and fit new ones if necessary.

Reassembly

32 Slide the brushes back into position in their housings and locate the spring ends onto the outer ends of the brushes.

33 Fit the insulator into the rear cover. Insert the terminal bolt through the insulator and the cover and locate the brushplate, making sure its tab is correctly located in the housing slot. Slide the rubber O-ring and small insulating washers onto the terminal bolt, followed by the large insulating washer and the plain washer. Fit the nut onto the terminal bolt and tighten it.

35 Fit the shims onto the rear of the armature shaft. Apply a smear of molybdenum grease to the end of the shaft. Insert the armature into the brushplate at an angle so that the brushes locate against the commutator, then straighten the armature, pushing the brushes back into their housings against the springs, and insert it into the rear cover so that the shaft end locates in the bush.

36 Fit the sealing ring onto the rear of the main housing. Grasp both the armature and the rear cover in one hand and hold them together – this will prevent the armature being drawn out by the magnets in the housing. Note however that you should take care not to let the housing be drawn forcibly onto the armature by the magnets. Carefully allow the housing to be drawn onto the armature, making sure the end with the cut-out faces the rear cover and aligns with the brushplate outer tab (aligning the marks between the cover and housing (Step 2) will help).

37 Apply a smear of grease to the front cover oil seal lip. Fit the tabbed washer into the cover so that its teeth are correctly located with the cover ribs.

38 Slide the shims onto the front end of the armature shaft then fit the insulating washer. Fit the sealing ring onto the front of the housing. Slide the front cover into position, aligning the marks made on removal.

39 Check the alignment marks made on removal are correctly aligned. Apply a smear of grease to the long bolt O-rings, using new ones if the old ones are damaged, deformed or deteriorated. Apply a small amount of a suitable non-permanent thread locking compound to the bolts, then install and tighten them.

40 Install the starter motor (see Section 29).

31 Charging system testing – general information and precautions

1 If the performance of the charging system is suspect, the system as a whole should be checked first, followed by testing of the individual components. **Note:** *Before beginning the checks, make sure the battery is fully charged and that all system connections are clean and tight.*

2 Checking the output of the charging system and the performance of the various components within the charging system requires the use of a multimeter (with voltage, current and resistance checking facilities).

3 When making the checks, follow the procedures carefully to prevent incorrect connections or short circuits, as irreparable damage to electrical system components may result if short circuits occur.

4 If a multimeter is not available, the job of checking the charging system should be left to a Suzuki dealer.

32 Charging system – leakage and output test

1 If the charging system of the machine is thought to be faulty, perform the following checks.

Leakage test

2 Turn the ignition switch OFF and disconnect the lead from the battery negative (–ve) terminal (see Section 3).

3 Set a multimeter to the Amps function and connect its negative (–ve) probe to the battery negative (–ve) terminal, and positive (+ve) probe to the disconnected negative (–ve) lead **(see illustration)**. Always set the meter to a high amps range initially and then bring it down to the mA (milli Amps) range; if there is a

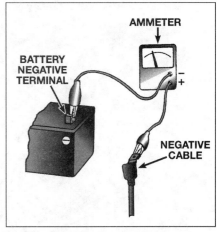

32.3 Checking the charging system leakage rate – connect the meter as shown

8

high current flow in the circuit it may blow the meter's fuse.

Caution: Always connect an ammeter in series, never in parallel with the battery, otherwise it will be damaged. Do not turn the ignition ON or operate the starter motor when the ammeter is connected – a sudden surge in current will blow the meter's fuse.

4 If the current leakage indicated exceeds the amount specified at the beginning of the Chapter, there is probably a short circuit in the wiring. Use the wiring diagrams at the end of this book and systematically disconnect individual electrical components until the source is identified.

5 Disconnect the meter and reconnect the negative (–ve) lead to the battery.

 If an alarm or immobiliser is fitted, its current drain should be taken into account when checking for current leakage.

Output test

6 Start the engine and allow it to warm up.
7 To check the regulated voltage output, connect a multimeter set to the 0 to 20 volts DC scale (voltmeter) across the terminals of the battery (positive (+ve) lead to battery positive (+ve) terminal, negative (–ve) lead to battery negative (–ve) terminal) **(see illustration 3.4)**. Turn the lighting switch on (where fitted) and turn the dimmer switch to the HI position. Slowly increase the engine speed to 5000 rpm and note the reading obtained. The regulated voltage output should be as specified at the beginning of the Chapter. If not, check the alternator/regulator/rectifier (see Section 33).

 Clues to a faulty regulator are constantly blowing bulbs, with brightness varying considerably with engine speed, and battery overheating.

33 Alternator/regulator/rectifier – check, removal, overhaul and installation

Check

1 On GSX600/750F models remove the fairing left-hand side panel (see Chapter 7).
2 Peel back the rubber terminal cover on the alternator **(see illustration)**. Unscrew the outer nut securing the lead and detach it. Also disconnect the wiring connector. Unscrew the inner nut on the terminal and remove the shouldered rubber insulator **(see illustration)**. Undo the alternator end cover screws and remove the cover **(see illustration)**.
3 Undo the screws securing the brush holder and remove the holder, noting how it fits **(see illustrations)**. Inspect the holder for any signs of damage. Measure the length of the brushes and compare the results to the service limit in this Chapter's Specifications. Push the brushes into the holder and check they move freely. Set a multimeter to the ohms x 1 (ohmmeter) scale and check for continuity between each brush and the mounting plate – there should be continuity (zero resistance) **(see illustration)**. If the brushes are not worn excessively, nor cracked, chipped, or otherwise damaged, they may be re-used. Otherwise, replace the holder assembly with a new one – the brushes are not available separately. Clean the slip rings (the rings on the shaft which contact the brushes) with a rag moistened with some solvent.

33.2a Peel back the cover, then unscrew the nut and detach the lead, then disconnect the wiring connector (arrowed)

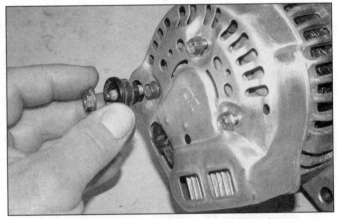

33.2b Unscrew the nut and remove the insulator

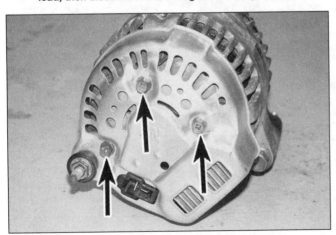

33.2c Undo the screws (arrowed) and remove the cover

33.3a Undo the screws (arrowed) . . .

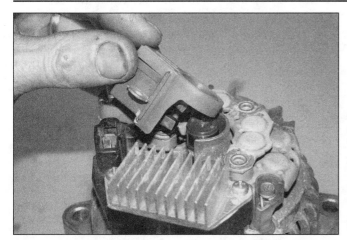

33.3b ... and remove the brush holder

33.3c Check for continuity between each brush and the mounting plate

4 To check the rotor coil continuity, first remove the brush holder (see above), then set a multimeter to the ohms x 1 (ohmmeter) scale and check for continuity between the slip rings **(see illustration)**. There should be continuity (zero resistance). If not, replace the rotor with a new one. Also check for continuity between each ring and the alternator housing

– there should be no continuity (infinite resistance) **(see illustration)**.
5 To check the stator coil, set a multimeter to the ohms x 1 (ohmmeter) scale and check for continuity between each wire terminal screw in turn, then check between each one and the housing **(see illustration)**. There should be continuity (zero resistance) between each

wire, and no continuity (infinite resistance) between the wires and the housing (infinite resistance). If not, the stator coil assembly is faulty and must be replaced with a new one.
6 To check the regulator, first remove the brush holder (see above), then undo the three screws securing the regulator to the alternator and remove it **(see illustration)**. Set a

33.4a Check for continuity between the slip rings

33.4b There should be no continuity between either slip ring and the housing

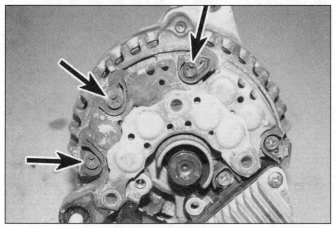

33.5 Check the stator coil terminals (arrowed) as described

33.6a Undo the screws (arrowed) and remove the regulator

8

multimeter to the ohms x 1 (ohmmeter) scale
and check for continuity between the two
terminals as shown, then reverse the probes
on the terminals and check again for
continuity **(see illustration)**. There should be
continuity (zero resistance) in one direction
and no continuity (infinite resistance) in the
other direction. If not, replace the regulator
with a new one.

7 To test the rectifier, first remove the
regulator (see above), then undo the four
screws, carefully straighten the wire ends, and
draw the rectifier off **(see illustration)**. Note
the insulating washers on the base of the
rectifier or on the alternator. With the rectifier
removed, use a multimeter set to the ohms x 1
scale and check between the terminals as
shown **(see illustration)**. Each pair of
terminals is checked in both directions by
reversing the meter probes. Continuity
should exist in one direction only; if no
continuity is shown in both directions, or
continuity is shown in both directions, the
particular diode is faulty and a new rectifier
must be installed.

1 to 2	2 to 1
1 to P1	P1 to 1
1 to P2	P2 to 1
1 to P3	P3 to 1
1 to P4	P4 to 1
2 to P1	P1 to 2
2 to P2	P2 to 2
2 to P3	P3 to 2
2 to P4	P4 to 2

Removal

8 Remove the seat (see Chapter 7) and
disconnect the battery negative (–ve) lead (see
Section 3).
9 Remove the carburettors (see Chapter 3).
10 Peel back the rubber terminal cover on

the alternator **(see illustration 33.2a)**.
Unscrew the nut securing the lead and
detach it. Also disconnect the wiring
connector.
11 Unscrew the three bolts securing the
alternator assembly to the crankcase and
withdraw it **(see illustrations)**. Discard the
O-ring as a new one must be used.

Overhaul

12 Unscrew the nut on the terminal and
remove the shouldered rubber insulator **(see
illustration 33.2b)**. Undo the alternator end
cover screws and remove the cover **(see
illustration 33.2c)**.
13 Undo the screws securing the brush
holder and remove the holder, noting how it
fits **(see illustrations 33.3a and b)**.
14 To remove the regulator undo the three
screws securing it to the alternator and
remove it **(see illustration 33.6a)**.
15 To remove the rectifier undo the four
screws, carefully straighten the wire ends, and
draw the rectifier off **(see illustration 33.7a)**.
Note the insulating washers on the base of the
rectifier or on the alternator.

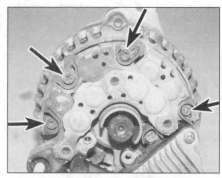
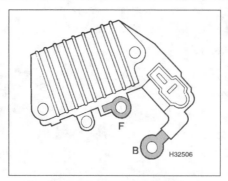

33.6b Test the regulator as described

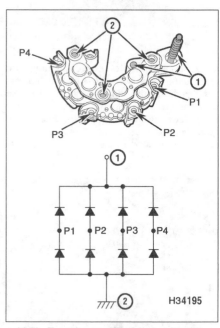

33.7a Undo the screws (arrowed) and remove the rectifier

33.7b Test the rectifier by checking for continuity between terminals 1 and 2

33.11a Unscrew the bolts (arrowed) . . .

33.11b . . . and remove the alternator

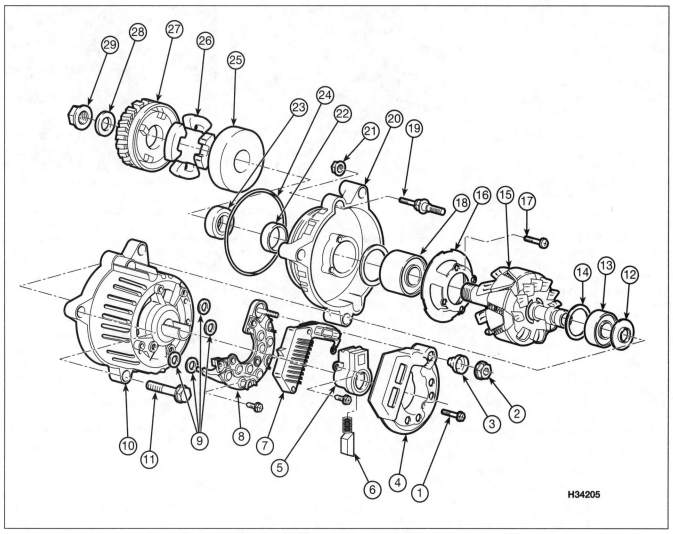

33.16a Alternator components

1 Cover bolts	9 Insulating washers	16 Bearing retainer	23 Oil seal
2 Terminal nut	10 Main housing	17 Retainer screws	24 O-ring
3 Insulator	11 Mounting bolts	18 Bearing	25 Damper housing
4 End cover	12 Bearing cover	19 Studs	26 Rubber dampers
5 Brush holder	13 Bearing	20 Rear cover	27 Driven gear
6 Brush and spring	14 Bearing cover	21 Nuts	28 Washer
7 Regulator	15 Rotor	22 Spacer	29 Nut
8 Rectifier			

16 Place the alternator driven gear in a vice with two pieces of wood to protect the gear teeth – do not clamp the damper housing behind the gear otherwise it will distort. Remove the nut and washer from the shaft end, followed by the driven gear **(see illustrations)**. Inspect the rubber dampers for damage or deterioration and replace them with new ones if necessary. Use a puller to draw the damper housing off if necessary.

17 To access the rotor assembly and bearings, unscrew the two nuts securing the rear cover and remove the cover. Draw the rotor out of the main housing/stator assembly, but note that you will probably need a press to do this. To access the bearing in the rear

cover undo the four screws and remove the bearing cover. The other bearing will either be on the end of the rotor or in the main housing. Refer to *Tools and Workshop Tips* in the Reference Section for information on bearing checks and removal and installation methods. Discard the oil seal in the rear cover as a new one must be fitted. Apply grease to its lips. Note that when installing the bearing for the slip ring end of the shaft, turn the expander ring to align its lug with the centre of the chamfered edge of the bearing outer race.

18 Reassemble the alternator in a reverse of the above procedure. Apply a thread locking compound to the bearing cover screws and tighten them to the specified torque setting.

33.16b Unscrew the nut (arrowed) as described

8

Also tighten the rear cover nuts and the driven gear nut to the specified torque settings. Fit the shouldered rubber insulator over the terminal before tightening the end cover screws.

Installation

19 Installation is the reverse of removal. Use a new O-ring smeared with grease **(see illustration)**. Tighten the alternator bolts to the torque setting specified at the beginning of the Chapter.

33.19 Fit a new O-ring into the groove

34.1 Carburettor cooling fan – US models

---

34 Carburettor cooling fan –
check, removal and installation

1 California GSX600/750F models have a cooling fan mounted on the frame above the front sprocket cover **(see illustration)**. The fan blows cooling air over the carburettors for thirty seconds after the engine is shut off to prevent the fuel in the float chambers getting too hot. The fan does not operate if the ignition switch is ON for less than three seconds.

Check

2 Remove the fairing left-hand side panel (see Chapter 7).
3 Trace the wiring from the fan and disconnect it at the connector.
4 Connect a fully charged 12 volt battery directly to the connector terminals on the fan side of the connector using some auxiliary wiring and connectors – connect the positive (+ve) wire from the battery to the red wire terminal on the connector, and the negative (–ve) wire to the black/red terminal. The fan should run. If it doesn't, and the connections and battery are good, replace the fan with a new one.
5 If the fan is good, but does not function as described, check for battery voltage at the red wire on the loom side of the wiring connector. There should be voltage with the ignition OFF. If not, check the wiring for faults (refer to the Wiring Diagrams at the end of the Chapter).
6 If the voltage is good, check the black/red wire between the fan and the timer for continuity, then check for continuity to earth (ground) in the black/white wire from the timer. If that is good, check for battery voltage at the red wire to the timer with the ignition OFF, and in the orange/white wire to the timer with the ignition ON. If all the wiring and voltage is good, then the timer itself is probably faulty. Substitute a new or known good second-hand one and check the operation of the fan. If it now works the timer is faulty.

Removal and installation

7 Remove the fairing left-hand side panel (See Chapter 7).
8 Trace the wiring from the fan and disconnect it at the connector.
9 Undo the screws securing the fan and remove it.
10 Installation is the reverse of removal.

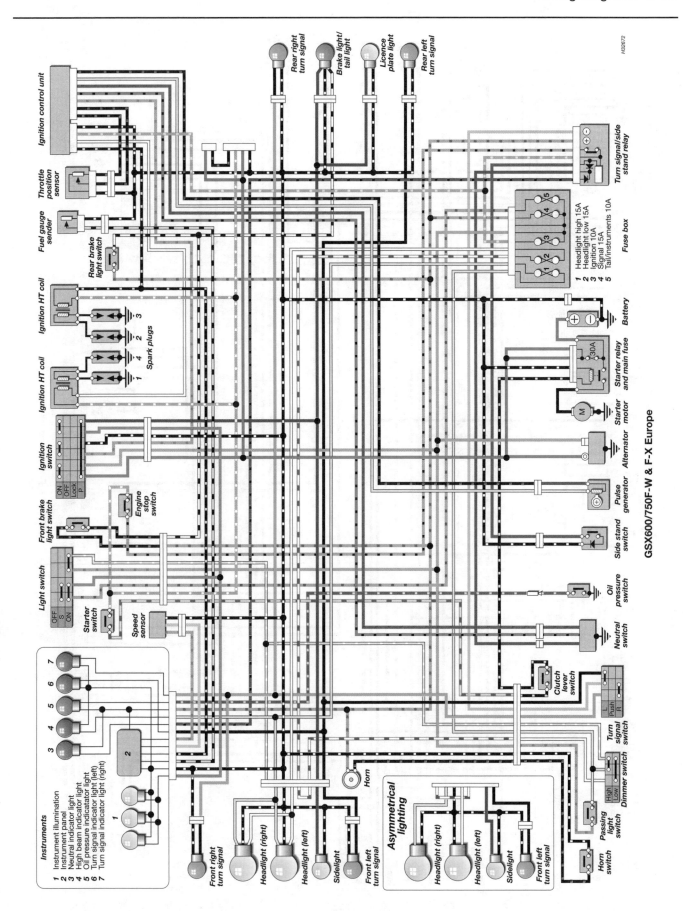

GSX600/750F-W & F-X Europe

H32672

8

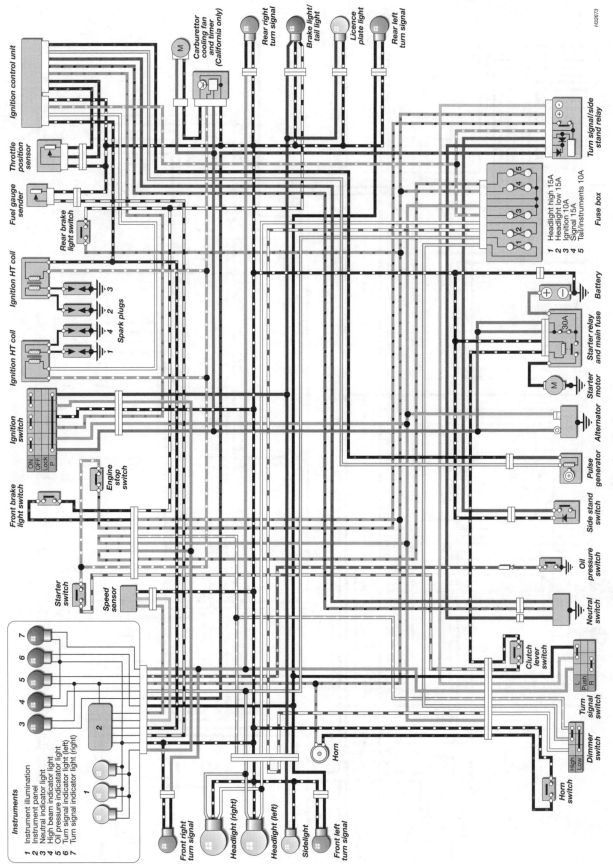

Carburettor cooling fan and timer (California only)

Rear right turn signal

Brake light/tail light

Licence plate light

Rear left turn signal

Ignition control unit

Throttle position sensor

Turn signal/side stand relay

Fuel gauge sender

Rear brake light switch

	Fuse box
1	Headlight high 15A
2	Headlight low 15A
3	Ignition 10A
4	Signal 15A
5	Tail/instruments 10A

Ignition HT coil

Spark plugs

Ignition HT coil

Battery

Starter relay and main fuse 30A

Starter motor

Ignition switch

ON
OFF
Lock
P

Alternator

Engine stop switch

Pulse generator

Front brake light switch

Side stand switch

Oil pressure switch

Starter switch

Speed sensor

Neutral switch

Clutch lever switch

Turn signal switch

L Push R

Dimmer switch

High Low

Horn

Horn switch

Instruments
1 Instrument illumination
2 Instrument panel
3 Neutral indicator light
4 High beam indicator light
5 Oil pressure indicator light
6 Turn signal indicator light (left)
7 Turn signal indicator light (right)

Front right turn signal

Headlight (right)

Headlight (left)

Sidelight

Front left turn signal

GSX600/750F-W & F-X US and Canada

H32673

H32674

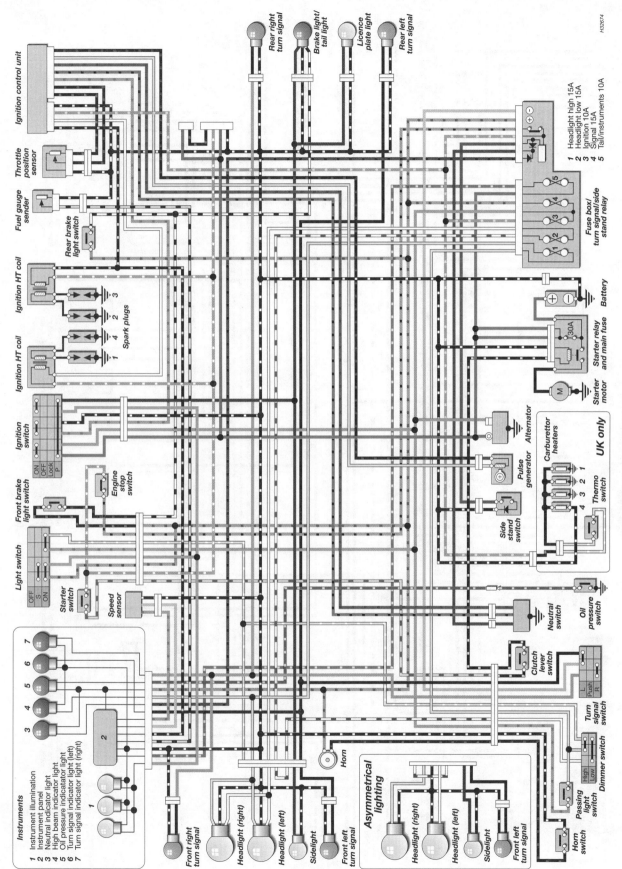

Ignition control unit

Throttle position sensor

Fuel gauge sender

Rear brake light switch

Ignition HT coil

Ignition HT coil

Spark plugs

Ignition switch

ON
OFF
Lock
P

Front brake light switch

Engine stop switch

Light switch

OFF
S
ON

Starter switch

Speed sensor

Rear right turn signal

Brake light/ tail light

Licence plate light

Rear left turn signal

1 Headlight high 15A
2 Headlight low 15A
3 Ignition 10A
4 Signal 15A
5 Tail/instruments 10A

Fuse box/ turn signal/side stand relay

Battery

30A

Starter relay and main fuse

M **Starter motor**

Alternator

Pulse generator

UK only

Carburettor heaters

Thermo switch

Side stand switch

Neutral switch

Oil pressure switch

Clutch lever switch

Turn signal switch

L Push R

GSX600/750F-Y & F-K1 Europe

Instruments
1 Instrument illumination
2 Instrument panel
3 Neutral indicator light
4 High beam indicator light
5 Oil pressure indicator light
6 Turn signal indicator light (left)
7 Turn signal indicator light (right)

Horn

Asymmetrical lighting

Headlight (right)

Headlight (left)

Sidelight

Front left turn signal

Passing light switch

Dimmer switch

High Low

Horn switch

Front right turn signal

Headlight (right)

Headlight (left)

Sidelight

Front left turn signal

8

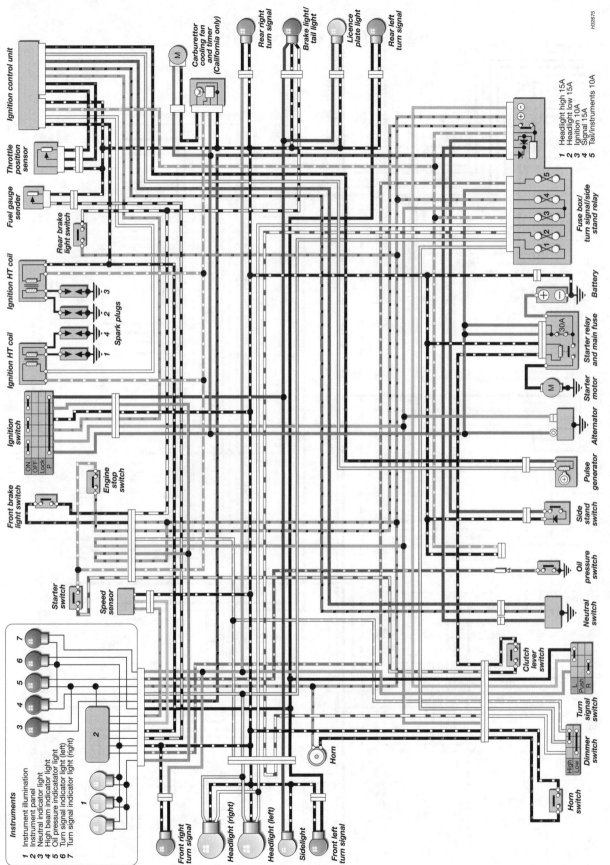

GSX600/750F-Y & F-K1 US and Canada

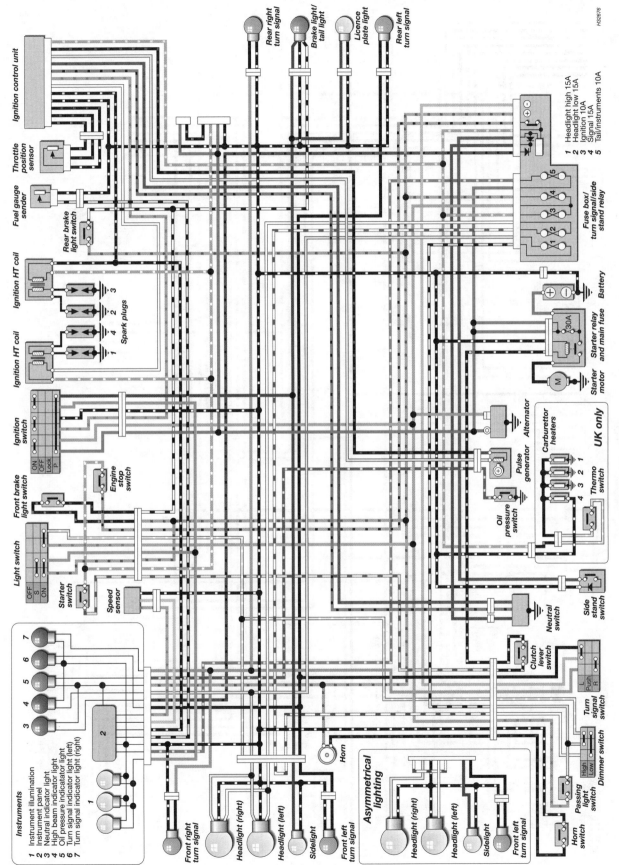

Ignition control unit

Throttle position sensor

Fuel gauge sender

Rear brake light switch

Ignition HT coil

Ignition HT coil

Spark plugs

Ignition switch

ON
OFF
Lock
P

Engine stop switch

Front brake light switch

Light switch

OFF
S
ON

Starter switch

Speed sensor

Instruments
1 Instrument illumination
2 Instrument panel
3 Neutral indicator light
4 High beam indicator light
5 Oil pressure indicator light
6 Turn signal indicator light (left)
7 Turn signal indicator light (right)

Rear right turn signal

Brake light/ tail light

Licence plate light

Rear left turn signal

1 Headlight high 15A
2 Headlight low 15A
3 Ignition 10A
4 Signal 15A
5 Tail/instruments 10A

Fuse box/ turn signal/side stand relay

Battery

Starter relay and main fuse

30A

Starter motor

M

Alternator

Carburettor heaters

Pulse generator

Thermo switch

Oil pressure switch

UK only

GSX600/750F-K2 Europe

Neutral switch

Side stand switch

Clutch lever switch

Turn signal switch

Horn

Asymmetrical lighting

Headlight (right)

Headlight (left)

Sidelight

Front left turn signal

Dimmer switch

High
LOW

Passing light switch

Horn switch

Front right turn signal

Headlight (right)

Headlight (left)

Sidelight

Front left turn signal

8

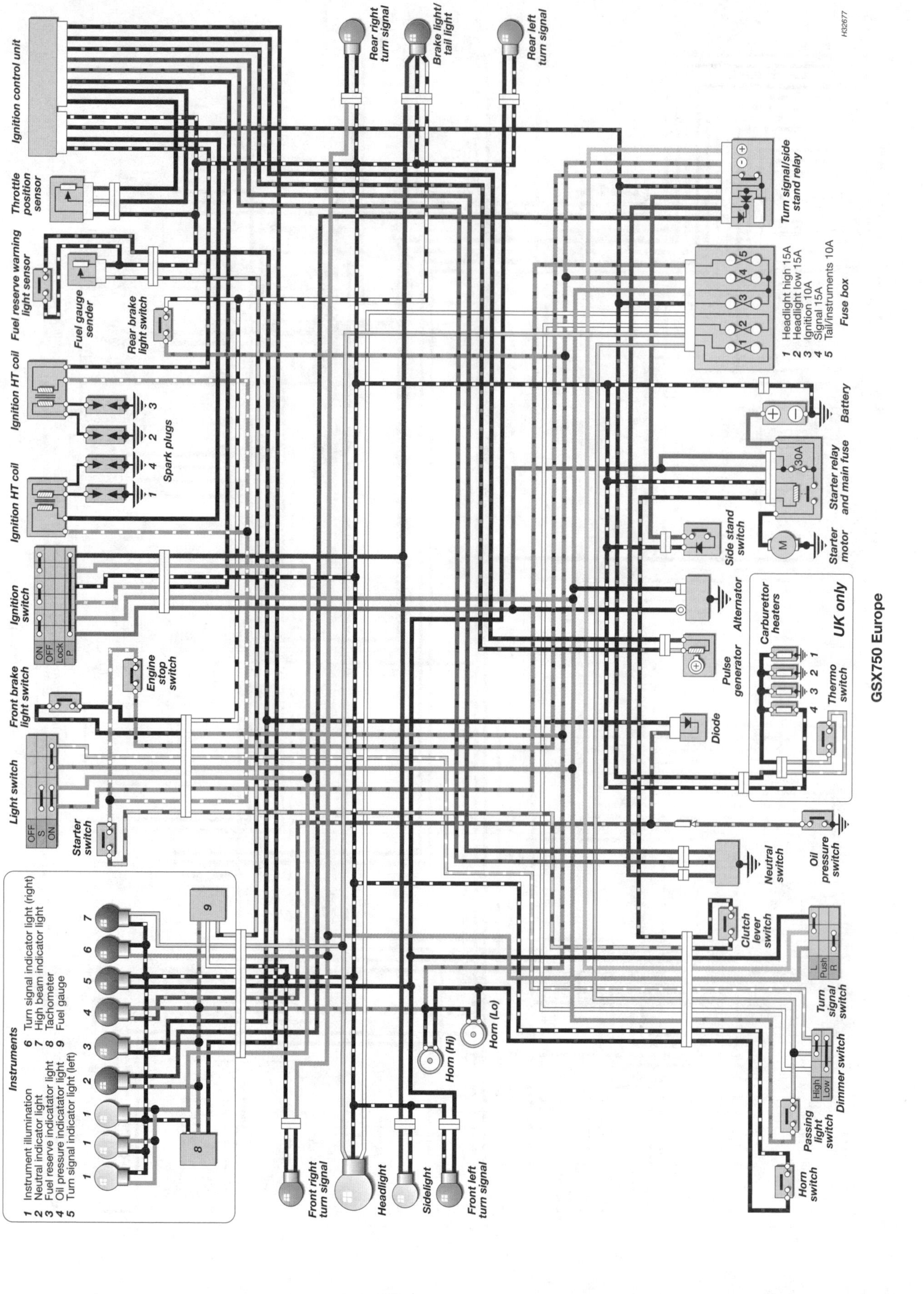

H32677

Ignition control unit

Rear right turn signal

Brake light/ tail light

Rear left turn signal

Throttle position sensor

Turn signal/side stand relay

Fuel reserve warning light sensor

Fuel gauge sender

Rear brake light switch

5	
4	Headlight high 15A
3	Headlight low 15A
2	Ignition 10A
1	Signal 15A
	Tail/instruments 10A

Fuse box

Ignition HT coil

Spark plugs

Battery

Ignition HT coil

30A

Starter relay and main fuse

Side stand switch

Starter motor

Ignition switch

ON	
OFF	
Lock	
P	

Alternator

Carburettor heaters

UK only

Front brake light switch

Engine stop switch

Pulse generator

Thermo switch

4 3 2 1

Diode

Light switch

OFF	
S	
ON	

Starter switch

Neutral switch

Oil pressure switch

Clutch lever switch

| L | Push | R |

Instruments
1 Instrument illumination
2 Neutral indicator light
3 Fuel reserve indicatator light
4 Oil pressure indicator light
5 Turn signal indicator light (left)
6 Turn signal indicator light (right)
7 High beam indicator light
8 Tachometer
9 Fuel gauge

Turn signal switch

Dimmer switch

| High |
| Low |

Passing light switch

Horn switch

Front right turn signal

Headlight

Sidelight

Front left turn signal

Horn (Hi)

Horn (Lo)

GSX750 Europe

Reference

Tools and Workshop Tips

● Building up a tool kit and equipping your workshop ● Using tools ● Understanding bearing, seal, fastener and chain sizes and markings ● Repair techniques

Security

● Locks and chains ● U-locks ● Disc locks ● Alarms and immobilisers ● Security marking systems ● Tips on how to prevent bike theft

Lubricants and fluids `REF•23`

● Engine oils ● Transmission (gear) oils ● Coolant/anti-freeze ● Fork oils and suspension fluids ● Brake/clutch fluids ● Spray lubes, degreasers and solvents

Conversion Factors `REF•26`

$$34 \ Nm \times 0.738$$
$$= 25 \ lbf \ ft$$

● Formulae for conversion of the metric (SI) units used throughout the manual into Imperial measures

MOT Test Checks `REF•27`

● A guide to the UK MOT test ● Which items are tested ● How to prepare your motorcycle for the test and perform a pre-test check

Storage `REF•32`

● How to prepare your motorcycle for going into storage and protect essential systems ● How to get the motorcycle back on the road

Fault Finding `REF•35`

● Common faults and their likely causes ● How to check engine cylinder compression ● How to make electrical tests and use test meters

Technical Terms Explained `REF•48`

● Component names, technical terms and common abbreviations explained

Index `REF•52`

Buying tools

A toolkit is a fundamental requirement for servicing and repairing a motorcycle. Although there will be an initial expense in building up enough tools for servicing, this will soon be offset by the savings made by doing the job yourself. As experience and confidence grow, additional tools can be added to enable the repair and overhaul of the motorcycle. Many of the specialist tools are expensive and not often used so it may be preferable to hire them, or for a group of friends or motorcycle club to join in the purchase.

As a rule, it is better to buy more expensive, good quality tools. Cheaper tools are likely to wear out faster and need to be renewed more often, nullifying the original saving.

> ⚠️ **Warning: To avoid the risk of a poor quality tool breaking in use, causing injury or damage to the component being worked on, always aim to purchase tools which meet the relevant national safety standards.**

The following lists of tools do not represent the manufacturer's service tools, but serve as a guide to help the owner decide which tools are needed for this level of work. In addition, items such as an electric drill, hacksaw, files, soldering iron and a workbench equipped with a vice, may be needed. Although not classed as tools, a selection of bolts, screws, nuts, washers and pieces of tubing always come in useful.

For more information about tools, refer to the Haynes *Motorcycle Workshop Practice TechBook* (Bk. No. 3470).

Manufacturer's service tools

Inevitably certain tasks require the use of a service tool. Where possible an alternative tool or method of approach is recommended, but sometimes there is no option if personal injury or damage to the component is to be avoided. Where required, service tools are referred to in the relevant procedure.

Service tools can usually only be purchased from a motorcycle dealer and are identified by a part number. Some of the commonly-used tools, such as rotor pullers, are available in aftermarket form from mail-order motorcycle tool and accessory suppliers.

Maintenance and minor repair tools

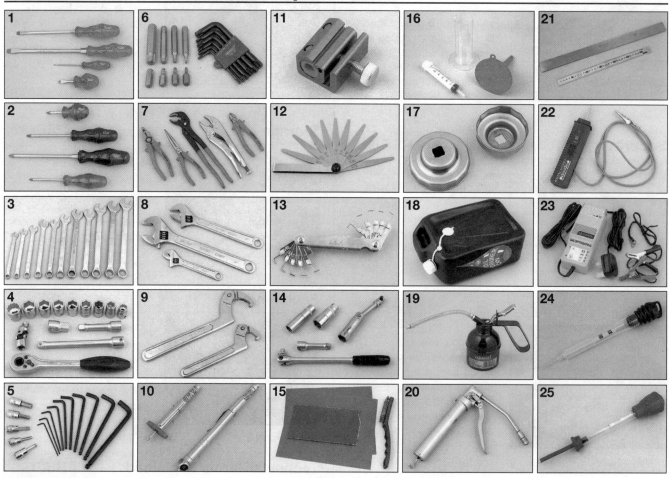

1 Set of flat-bladed screwdrivers
2 Set of Phillips head screwdrivers
3 Combination open-end and ring spanners
4 Socket set (3/8 inch or 1/2 inch drive)
5 Set of Allen keys or bits

6 Set of Torx keys or bits
7 Pliers, cutters and self-locking grips (Mole grips)
8 Adjustable spanners
9 C-spanners
10 Tread depth gauge and tyre pressure gauge

11 Cable oiler clamp
12 Feeler gauges
13 Spark plug gap measuring tool
14 Spark plug spanner or deep plug sockets
15 Wire brush and emery paper

16 Calibrated syringe, measuring vessel and funnel
17 Oil filter adapters
18 Oil drainer can or tray
19 Pump type oil can
20 Grease gun

21 Straight-edge and steel rule
22 Continuity tester
23 Battery charger
24 Hydrometer (for battery specific gravity check)
25 Anti-freeze tester (for liquid-cooled engines)

Repair and overhaul tools

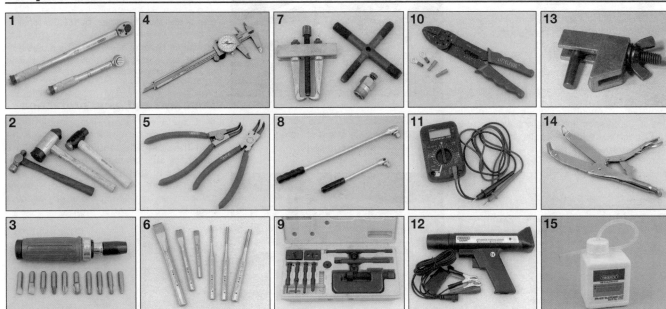

1 Torque wrench
   (small and mid-ranges)
2 Conventional, plastic or
   soft-faced hammers
3 Impact driver set

4 Vernier gauge
5 Circlip pliers (internal and
   external, or combination)
6 Set of cold chisels
   and punches

7 Selection of pullers
8 Breaker bars
9 Chain breaking/
   riveting tool set

10 Wire stripper and
   crimper tool
11 Multimeter (measures
   amps, volts and ohms)
12 Stroboscope (for
   dynamic timing checks)

13 Hose clamp
   (wingnut type shown)
14 Clutch holding tool
15 One-man brake/clutch
   bleeder kit

Specialist tools

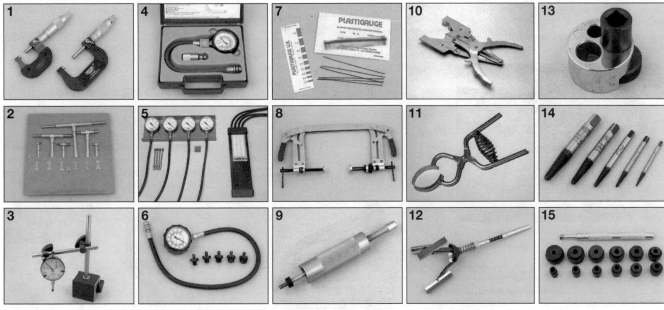

1 Micrometers
   (external type)
2 Telescoping gauges
3 Dial gauge

4 Cylinder
   compression gauge
5 Vacuum gauges (left) or
   manometer (right)
6 Oil pressure gauge

7 Plastigauge kit
8 Valve spring compressor
   (4-stroke engines)
9 Piston pin drawbolt tool

10 Piston ring removal and
   installation tool
11 Piston ring clamp
12 Cylinder bore hone
   (stone type shown)

13 Stud extractor
14 Screw extractor set
15 Bearing driver set

1 Workshop equipment and facilities

The workbench

● Work is made much easier by raising the bike up on a ramp - components are much more accessible if raised to waist level. The hydraulic or pneumatic types seen in the dealer's workshop are a sound investment if you undertake a lot of repairs or overhauls **(see illustration 1.1)**.

1.1 Hydraulic motorcycle ramp

● If raised off ground level, the bike must be supported on the ramp to avoid it falling. Most ramps incorporate a front wheel locating clamp which can be adjusted to suit different diameter wheels. When tightening the clamp, take care not to mark the wheel rim or damage the tyre - use wood blocks on each side to prevent this.
● Secure the bike to the ramp using tie-downs **(see illustration 1.2)**. If the bike has only a sidestand, and hence leans at a dangerous angle when raised, support the bike on an auxiliary stand.

1.2 Tie-downs are used around the passenger footrests to secure the bike

● Auxiliary (paddock) stands are widely available from mail order companies or motorcycle dealers and attach either to the wheel axle or swingarm pivot **(see illustration 1.3)**. If the motorcycle has a centrestand, you can support it under the crankcase to prevent it toppling whilst either wheel is removed **(see illustration 1.4)**.

1.3 This auxiliary stand attaches to the swingarm pivot

1.4 Always use a block of wood between the engine and jack head when supporting the engine in this way

Fumes and fire

● Refer to the Safety first! page at the beginning of the manual for full details. Make sure your workshop is equipped with a fire extinguisher suitable for fuel-related fires (Class B fire - flammable liquids) - it is not sufficient to have a water-filled extinguisher.
● Always ensure adequate ventilation is available. Unless an exhaust gas extraction system is available for use, ensure that the engine is run outside of the workshop.
● If working on the fuel system, make sure the workshop is ventilated to avoid a build-up of fumes. This applies equally to fume build-up when charging a battery. Do not smoke or allow anyone else to smoke in the workshop.

Fluids

● If you need to drain fuel from the tank, store it in an approved container marked as suitable for the storage of petrol (gasoline) **(see illustration 1.5)**. Do not store fuel in glass jars or bottles.

1.5 Use an approved can only for storing petrol (gasoline)

● Use proprietary engine degreasers or solvents which have a high flash-point, such as paraffin (kerosene), for cleaning off oil, grease and dirt - never use petrol (gasoline) for cleaning. Wear rubber gloves when handling solvent and engine degreaser. The fumes from certain solvents can be dangerous - always work in a well-ventilated area.

Dust, eye and hand protection

● Protect your lungs from inhalation of dust particles by wearing a filtering mask over the nose and mouth. Many frictional materials still contain asbestos which is dangerous to your health. Protect your eyes from spouts of liquid and sprung components by wearing a pair of protective goggles **(see illustration 1.6)**.

1.6 A fire extinguisher, goggles, mask and protective gloves should be at hand in the workshop

● Protect your hands from contact with solvents, fuel and oils by wearing rubber gloves. Alternatively apply a barrier cream to your hands before starting work. If handling hot components or fluids, wear suitable gloves to protect your hands from scalding and burns.

What to do with old fluids

● Old cleaning solvent, fuel, coolant and oils should not be poured down domestic drains or onto the ground. Package the fluid up in old oil containers, label it accordingly, and take it to a garage or disposal facility. Contact your local authority for location of such sites or ring the oil care hotline.

OIL CARE
FOLLOW THE CODE
OIL BANK LINE
0800 66 33 66
www.oilbankline.org.uk

Note: It is antisocial and illegal to dump oil down the drain. To find the location of your local oil recycling bank, call this number free.

In the USA, note that any oil supplier must accept used oil for recycling.

2 Fasteners -
screws, bolts and nuts

Fastener types and applications

Bolts and screws

● Fastener head types are either of hexagonal, Torx or splined design, with internal and external versions of each type **(see illustrations 2.1 and 2.2)**; splined head fasteners are not in common use on motorcycles. The conventional slotted or Phillips head design is used for certain screws. Bolt or screw length is always measured from the underside of the head to the end of the item **(see illustration 2.11)**.

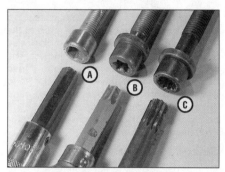

2.1 Internal hexagon/Allen (A), Torx (B) and splined (C) fasteners, with corresponding bits

2.2 External Torx (A), splined (B) and hexagon (C) fasteners, with corresponding sockets

● Certain fasteners on the motorcycle have a tensile marking on their heads, the higher the marking the stronger the fastener. High tensile fasteners generally carry a 10 or higher marking. Never replace a high tensile fastener with one of a lower tensile strength.

Washers **(see illustration 2.3)**

● Plain washers are used between a fastener head and a component to prevent damage to the component or to spread the load when torque is applied. Plain washers can also be used as spacers or shims in certain assemblies. Copper or aluminium plain washers are often used as sealing washers on drain plugs.

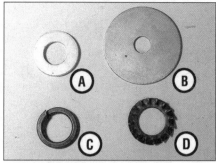

2.3 Plain washer (A), penny washer (B), spring washer (C) and serrated washer (D)

● The split-ring spring washer works by applying axial tension between the fastener head and component. If flattened, it is fatigued and must be renewed. If a plain (flat) washer is used on the fastener, position the spring washer between the fastener and the plain washer.

● Serrated star type washers dig into the fastener and component faces, preventing loosening. They are often used on electrical earth (ground) connections to the frame.

● Cone type washers (sometimes called Belleville) are conical and when tightened apply axial tension between the fastener head and component. They must be installed with the dished side against the component and often carry an OUTSIDE marking on their outer face. If flattened, they are fatigued and must be renewed.

● Tab washers are used to lock plain nuts or bolts on a shaft. A portion of the tab washer is bent up hard against one flat of the nut or bolt to prevent it loosening. Due to the tab washer being deformed in use, a new tab washer should be used every time it is disturbed.

● Wave washers are used to take up endfloat on a shaft. They provide light springing and prevent excessive side-to-side play of a component. Can be found on rocker arm shafts.

Nuts and split pins

● Conventional plain nuts are usually six-sided **(see illustration 2.4)**. They are sized by thread diameter and pitch. High tensile nuts carry a number on one end to denote their tensile strength.

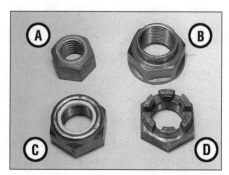

2.4 Plain nut (A), shouldered locknut (B), nylon insert nut (C) and castellated nut (D)

● Self-locking nuts either have a nylon insert, or two spring metal tabs, or a shoulder which is staked into a groove in the shaft - their advantage over conventional plain nuts is a resistance to loosening due to vibration. The nylon insert type can be used a number of times, but must be renewed when the friction of the nylon insert is reduced, ie when the nut spins freely on the shaft. The spring tab type can be reused unless the tabs are damaged. The shouldered type must be renewed every time it is disturbed.

● Split pins (cotter pins) are used to lock a castellated nut to a shaft or to prevent slackening of a plain nut. Common applications are wheel axles and brake torque arms. Because the split pin arms are deformed to lock around the nut a new split pin must always be used on installation - always fit the correct size split pin which will fit snugly in the shaft hole. Make sure the split pin arms are correctly located around the nut **(see illustrations 2.5 and 2.6)**.

2.5 Bend split pin (cotter pin) arms as shown (arrows) to secure a castellated nut

2.6 Bend split pin (cotter pin) arms as shown to secure a plain nut

> *Caution: If the castellated nut slots do not align with the shaft hole after tightening to the torque setting, tighten the nut until the next slot aligns with the hole - never slacken the nut to align its slot.*

● R-pins (shaped like the letter R), or slip pins as they are sometimes called, are sprung and can be reused if they are otherwise in good condition. Always install R-pins with their closed end facing forwards **(see illustration 2.7)**.

2.7 Correct fitting of R-pin. Arrow indicates forward direction

Circlips (see illustration 2.8)

● Circlips (sometimes called snap-rings) are used to retain components on a shaft or in a housing and have corresponding external or internal ears to permit removal. Parallel-sided (machined) circlips can be installed either way round in their groove, whereas stamped circlips (which have a chamfered edge on one face) must be installed with the chamfer facing away from the direction of thrust load **(see illustration 2.9)**.

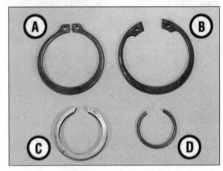

2.8 External stamped circlip (A), internal stamped circlip (B), machined circlip (C) and wire circlip (D)

● Always use circlip pliers to remove and install circlips; expand or compress them just enough to remove them. After installation, rotate the circlip in its groove to ensure it is securely seated. If installing a circlip on a splined shaft, always align its opening with a shaft channel to ensure the circlip ends are well supported and unlikely to catch **(see illustration 2.10)**.

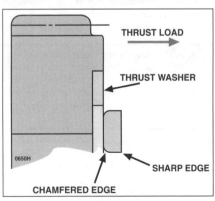

2.9 Correct fitting of a stamped circlip

THRUST LOAD

THRUST WASHER

SHARP EDGE

CHAMFERED EDGE

0650H

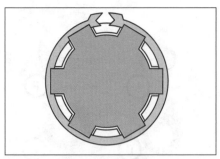

2.10 Align circlip opening with shaft channel

● Circlips can wear due to the thrust of components and become loose in their grooves, with the subsequent danger of becoming dislodged in operation. For this reason, renewal is advised every time a circlip is disturbed.

● Wire circlips are commonly used as piston pin retaining clips. If a removal tang is provided, long-nosed pliers can be used to dislodge them, otherwise careful use of a small flat-bladed screwdriver is necessary. Wire circlips should be renewed every time they are disturbed.

Thread diameter and pitch

● Diameter of a male thread (screw, bolt or stud) is the outside diameter of the threaded portion **(see illustration 2.11)**. Most motorcycle manufacturers use the ISO (International Standards Organisation) metric system expressed in millimetres, eg M6 refers to a 6 mm diameter thread. Sizing is the same for nuts, except that the thread diameter is measured across the valleys of the nut.

● Pitch is the distance between the peaks of the thread **(see illustration 2.11)**. It is expressed in millimetres, thus a common bolt size may be expressed as 6.0 x 1.0 mm (6 mm thread diameter and 1 mm pitch). Generally pitch increases in proportion to thread diameter, although there are always exceptions.

● Thread diameter and pitch are related for conventional fastener applications and the accompanying table can be used as a guide. Additionally, the AF (Across Flats), spanner or socket size dimension of the bolt or nut **(see illustration 2.11)** is linked to thread and pitch specification. Thread pitch can be measured with a thread gauge **(see illustration 2.12)**.

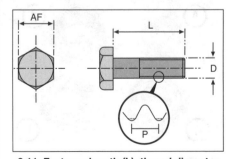

2.11 Fastener length (L), thread diameter (D), thread pitch (P) and head size (AF)

2.12 Using a thread gauge to measure pitch

AF size	Thread diameter x pitch (mm)
8 mm	M5 x 0.8
8 mm	M6 x 1.0
10 mm	M6 x 1.0
12 mm	M8 x 1.25
14 mm	M10 x 1.25
17 mm	M12 x 1.25

● The threads of most fasteners are of the right-hand type, ie they are turned clockwise to tighten and anti-clockwise to loosen. The reverse situation applies to left-hand thread fasteners, which are turned anti-clockwise to tighten and clockwise to loosen. Left-hand threads are used where rotation of a component might loosen a conventional right-hand thread fastener.

Seized fasteners

● Corrosion of external fasteners due to water or reaction between two dissimilar metals can occur over a period of time. It will build up sooner in wet conditions or in countries where salt is used on the roads during the winter. If a fastener is severely corroded it is likely that normal methods of removal will fail and result in its head being ruined. When you attempt removal, the fastener thread should be heard to crack free and unscrew easily - if it doesn't, stop there before damaging something.

● A smart tap on the head of the fastener will often succeed in breaking free corrosion which has occurred in the threads **(see illustration 2.13)**.

● An aerosol penetrating fluid (such as WD-40) applied the night beforehand may work its way down into the thread and ease removal. Depending on the location, you may be able to make up a Plasticine well around the fastener head and fill it with penetrating fluid.

2.13 A sharp tap on the head of a fastener will often break free a corroded thread

● If you are working on an engine internal component, corrosion will most likely not be a problem due to the well lubricated environment. However, components can be very tight and an impact driver is a useful tool in freeing them (see illustration 2.14).

2.14 Using an impact driver to free a fastener

● Where corrosion has occurred between dissimilar metals (eg steel and aluminium alloy), the application of heat to the fastener head will create a disproportionate expansion rate between the two metals and break the seizure caused by the corrosion. Whether heat can be applied depends on the location of the fastener - any surrounding components likely to be damaged must first be removed (see illustration 2.15). Heat can be applied using a paint stripper heat gun or clothes iron, or by immersing the component in boiling water - wear protective gloves to prevent scalding or burns to the hands.

2.15 Using heat to free a seized fastener

● As a last resort, it is possible to use a hammer and cold chisel to work the fastener head unscrewed (see illustration 2.16). This will damage the fastener, but more importantly extreme care must be taken not to damage the surrounding component.

Caution: Remember that the component being secured is generally of more value than the bolt, nut or screw - when the fastener is freed, do not unscrew it with force, instead work the fastener back and forth when resistance is felt to prevent thread damage.

2.16 Using a hammer and chisel to free a seized fastener

Broken fasteners and damaged heads

● If the shank of a broken bolt or screw is accessible you can grip it with self-locking grips. The knurled wheel type stud extractor tool or self-gripping stud puller tool is particularly useful for removing the long studs which screw into the cylinder mouth surface of the crankcase or bolts and screws from which the head has broken off (see illustration 2.17). Studs can also be removed by locking two nuts together on the threaded end of the stud and using a spanner on the lower nut (see illustration 2.18).

2.17 Using a stud extractor tool to remove a broken crankcase stud

2.18 Two nuts can be locked together to unscrew a stud from a component

● A bolt or screw which has broken off below or level with the casing must be extracted using a screw extractor set. Centre punch the fastener to centralise the drill bit, then drill a hole in the fastener (see illustration 2.19). Select a drill bit which is approximately half to three-quarters the

2.19 When using a screw extractor, first drill a hole in the fastener . . .

diameter of the fastener and drill to a depth which will accommodate the extractor. Use the largest size extractor possible, but avoid leaving too small a wall thickness otherwise the extractor will merely force the fastener walls outwards wedging it in the casing thread.

● If a spiral type extractor is used, thread it anti-clockwise into the fastener. As it is screwed in, it will grip the fastener and unscrew it from the casing (see illustration 2.20).

2.20 . . . then thread the extractor anti-clockwise into the fastener

● If a taper type extractor is used, tap it into the fastener so that it is firmly wedged in place. Unscrew the extractor (anti-clockwise) to draw the fastener out.

⚠ *Warning: Stud extractors are very hard and may break off in the fastener if care is not taken - ask an engineer about spark erosion if this happens.*

● Alternatively, the broken bolt/screw can be drilled out and the hole retapped for an oversize bolt/screw or a diamond-section thread insert. It is essential that the drilling is carried out squarely and to the correct depth, otherwise the casing may be ruined - if in doubt, entrust the work to an engineer.

● Bolts and nuts with rounded corners cause the correct size spanner or socket to slip when force is applied. Of the types of spanner/socket available always use a six-point type rather than an eight or twelve-point type - better grip

2.21 Comparison of surface drive ring spanner (left) with 12-point type (right)

is obtained. Surface drive spanners grip the middle of the hex flats, rather than the corners, and are thus good in cases of damaged heads **(see illustration 2.21)**.

● Slotted-head or Phillips-head screws are often damaged by the use of the wrong size screwdriver. Allen-head and Torx-head screws are much less likely to sustain damage. If enough of the screw head is exposed you can use a hacksaw to cut a slot in its head and then use a conventional flat-bladed screwdriver to remove it. Alternatively use a hammer and cold chisel to tap the head of the fastener around to slacken it. Always replace damaged fasteners with new ones, preferably Torx or Allen-head type.

A dab of valve grinding compound between the screw head and screwdriver tip will often give a good grip.

Thread repair

● Threads (particularly those in aluminium alloy components) can be damaged by overtightening, being assembled with dirt in the threads, or from a component working loose and vibrating. Eventually the thread will fail completely, and it will be impossible to tighten the fastener.

● If a thread is damaged or clogged with old locking compound it can be renovated with a thread repair tool (thread chaser) **(see illustrations 2.22 and 2.23)**; special thread

2.22 A thread repair tool being used to correct an internal thread

2.23 A thread repair tool being used to correct an external thread

chasers are available for spark plug hole threads. The tool will not cut a new thread, but clean and true the original thread. Make sure that you use the correct diameter and pitch tool. Similarly, external threads can be cleaned up with a die or a thread restorer file **(see illustration 2.24)**.

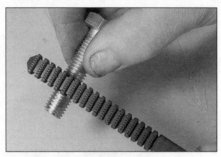

2.24 Using a thread restorer file

● It is possible to drill out the old thread and retap the component to the next thread size. This will work where there is enough surrounding material and a new bolt or screw can be obtained. Sometimes, however, this is not possible - such as where the bolt/screw passes through another component which must also be suitably modified, also in cases where a spark plug or oil drain plug cannot be obtained in a larger diameter thread size.

● The diamond-section thread insert (often known by its popular trade name of Heli-Coil) is a simple and effective method of renewing the thread and retaining the original size. A kit can be purchased which contains the tap, insert and installing tool **(see illustration 2.25)**. Drill out the damaged thread with the size drill specified **(see illustration 2.26)**. Carefully retap the thread **(see illustration 2.27)**. Install the

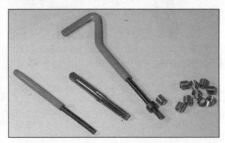

2.25 Obtain a thread insert kit to suit the thread diameter and pitch required

2.26 To install a thread insert, first drill out the original thread . . .

2.27 . . . tap a new thread . . .

2.28 . . . fit insert on the installing tool . . .

2.29 . . . and thread into the component . . .

2.30 . . . break off the tang when complete

insert on the installing tool and thread it slowly into place using a light downward pressure **(see illustrations 2.28 and 2.29)**. When positioned between a 1/4 and 1/2 turn below the surface withdraw the installing tool and use the break-off tool to press down on the tang, breaking it off **(see illustration 2.30)**.

● There are epoxy thread repair kits on the market which can rebuild stripped internal threads, although this repair should not be used on high load-bearing components.

Thread locking and sealing compounds

● Locking compounds are used in locations where the fastener is prone to loosening due to vibration or on important safety-related items which might cause loss of control of the motorcycle if they fail. It is also used where important fasteners cannot be secured by other means such as lockwashers or split pins.

● Before applying locking compound, make sure that the threads (internal and external) are clean and dry with all old compound removed. Select a compound to suit the component being secured - a non-permanent general locking and sealing type is suitable for most applications, but a high strength type is needed for permanent fixing of studs in castings. Apply a drop or two of the compound to the first few threads of the fastener, then thread it into place and tighten to the specified torque. Do not apply excessive thread locking compound otherwise the thread may be damaged on subsequent removal.

● Certain fasteners are impregnated with a dry film type coating of locking compound on their threads. Always renew this type of fastener if disturbed.

● Anti-seize compounds, such as copper-based greases, can be applied to protect threads from seizure due to extreme heat and corrosion. A common instance is spark plug threads and exhaust system fasteners.

3 Measuring tools and gauges

Feeler gauges

● Feeler gauges (or blades) are used for measuring small gaps and clearances (see illustration 3.1). They can also be used to measure endfloat (sideplay) of a component on a shaft where access is not possible with a dial gauge.

● Feeler gauge sets should be treated with care and not bent or damaged. They are etched with their size on one face. Keep them clean and very lightly oiled to prevent corrosion build-up.

3.1 Feeler gauges are used for measuring small gaps and clearances - thickness is marked on one face of gauge

● When measuring a clearance, select a gauge which is a light sliding fit between the two components. You may need to use two gauges together to measure the clearance accurately.

Micrometers

● A micrometer is a precision tool capable of measuring to 0.01 or 0.001 of a millimetre. It should always be stored in its case and not in the general toolbox. It must be kept clean and never dropped, otherwise its frame or measuring anvils could be distorted resulting in inaccurate readings.

● External micrometers are used for measuring outside diameters of components and have many more applications than internal micrometers. Micrometers are available in different size ranges, eg 0 to 25 mm, 25 to 50 mm, and upwards in 25 mm steps; some large micrometers have interchangeable anvils to allow a range of measurements to be taken. Generally the largest precision measurement you are likely to take on a motorcycle is the piston diameter.

● Internal micrometers (or bore micrometers) are used for measuring inside diameters, such as valve guides and cylinder bores. Telescoping gauges and small hole gauges are used in conjunction with an external micrometer, whereas the more expensive internal micrometers have their own measuring device.

External micrometer

Note: *The conventional analogue type instrument is described. Although much easier to read, digital micrometers are considerably more expensive.*

● Always check the calibration of the micrometer before use. With the anvils closed (0 to 25 mm type) or set over a test gauge (for

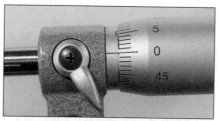

3.2 Check micrometer calibration before use

the larger types) the scale should read zero **(see illustration 3.2)**; make sure that the anvils (and test piece) are clean first. Any discrepancy can be adjusted by referring to the instructions supplied with the tool. Remember that the micrometer is a precision measuring tool - don't force the anvils closed, use the ratchet (4) on the end of the micrometer to close it. In this way, a measured force is always applied.

● To use, first make sure that the item being measured is clean. Place the anvil of the micrometer (1) against the item and use the thimble (2) to bring the spindle (3) lightly into contact with the other side of the item **(see illustration 3.3)**. Don't tighten the thimble down because this will damage the micrometer - instead use the ratchet (4) on the end of the micrometer. The ratchet mechanism applies a measured force preventing damage to the instrument.

● The micrometer is read by referring to the linear scale on the sleeve and the annular scale on the thimble. Read off the sleeve first to obtain the base measurement, then add the fine measurement from the thimble to obtain the overall reading. The linear scale on the sleeve represents the measuring range of the micrometer (eg 0 to 25 mm). The annular scale

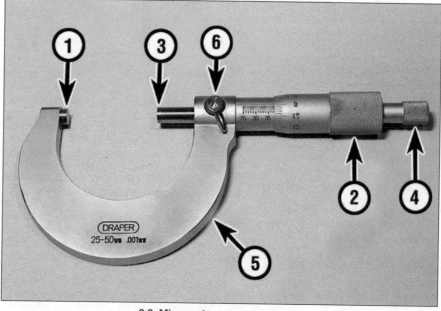

3.3 Micrometer component parts

1 Anvil	3 Spindle	5 Frame
2 Thimble	4 Ratchet	6 Locking lever

on the thimble will be in graduations of 0.01 mm (or as marked on the frame) - one full revolution of the thimble will move 0.5 mm on the linear scale. Take the reading where the datum line on the sleeve intersects the thimble's scale. Always position the eye directly above the scale otherwise an inaccurate reading will result.

In the example shown the item measures 2.95 mm **(see illustration 3.4)**:

Linear scale	2.00 mm
Linear scale	0.50 mm
Annular scale	0.45 mm
Total figure	**2.95 mm**

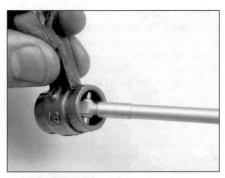

3.5 Micrometer reading of 46.99 mm on linear and annular scales . . .

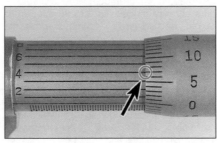

3.6 . . . and 0.004 mm on vernier scale

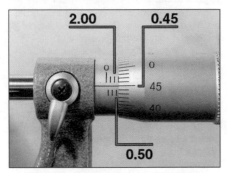

3.4 Micrometer reading of 2.95 mm

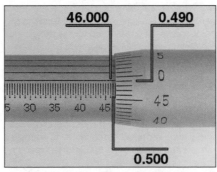

3.7 Expand the telescoping gauge in the bore, lock its position . . .

3.8 . . . then measure the gauge with a micrometer

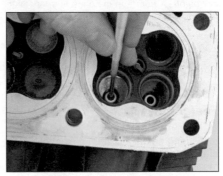

3.9 Expand the small hole gauge in the bore, lock its position . . .

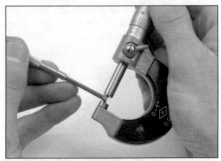

3.10 . . . then measure the gauge with a micrometer

Most micrometers have a locking lever (6) on the frame to hold the setting in place, allowing the item to be removed from the micrometer.
● Some micrometers have a vernier scale on their sleeve, providing an even finer measurement to be taken, in 0.001 increments of a millimetre. Take the sleeve and thimble measurement as described above, then check which graduation on the vernier scale aligns with that of the annular scale on the thimble **Note:** *The eye must be perpendicular to the scale when taking the vernier reading - if necessary rotate the body of the micrometer to ensure this.* Multiply the vernier scale figure by 0.001 and add it to the base and fine measurement figures.

In the example shown the item measures 46.994 mm **(see illustrations 3.5 and 3.6)**:

Linear scale (base)	46.000 mm
Linear scale (base)	00.500 mm
Annular scale (fine)	00.490 mm
Vernier scale	00.004 mm
Total figure	**46.994 mm**

Internal micrometer

● Internal micrometers are available for measuring bore diameters, but are expensive and unlikely to be available for home use. It is suggested that a set of telescoping gauges and small hole gauges, both of which must be used with an external micrometer, will suffice for taking internal measurements on a motorcycle.
● Telescoping gauges can be used to

measure internal diameters of components. Select a gauge with the correct size range, make sure its ends are clean and insert it into the bore. Expand the gauge, then lock its position and withdraw it from the bore **(see illustration 3.7)**. Measure across the gauge ends with a micrometer **(see illustration 3.8)**.
● Very small diameter bores (such as valve guides) are measured with a small hole gauge. Once adjusted to a slip-fit inside the component, its position is locked and the gauge withdrawn for measurement with a micrometer **(see illustrations 3.9 and 3.10)**.

Vernier caliper

Note: *The conventional linear and dial gauge type instruments are described. Digital types are easier to read, but are far more expensive.*
● The vernier caliper does not provide the precision of a micrometer, but is versatile in being able to measure internal and external diameters. Some types also incorporate a depth gauge. It is ideal for measuring clutch plate friction material and spring free lengths.
● To use the conventional linear scale vernier, slacken off the vernier clamp screws (1) and set its jaws over (2), or inside (3), the item to be measured **(see illustration 3.11)**. Slide the jaw into contact, using the thumbwheel (4) for fine movement of the sliding scale (5) then tighten the clamp screws (1). Read off the main scale (6) where the zero on the sliding scale (5) intersects it, taking the whole number to the left of the zero; this provides the base measurement. View along the sliding scale and select the division which

lines up exactly with any of the divisions on the main scale, noting that the divisions usually represents 0.02 of a millimetre. Add this fine measurement to the base measurement to obtain the total reading.

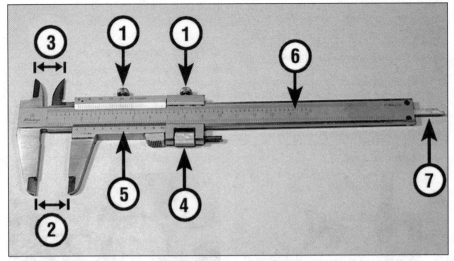

3.11 Vernier component parts (linear gauge)

1 Clamp screws	3 Internal jaws	5 Sliding scale	7 Depth gauge
2 External jaws	4 Thumbwheel	6 Main scale	

In the example shown the item measures 55.92 mm **(see illustration 3.12)**:

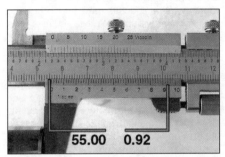

3.12 Vernier gauge reading of 55.92 mm

3.13 Vernier component parts (dial gauge)

1 Clamp screw   5 Main scale
2 External jaws   6 Sliding scale
3 Internal jaws   7 Dial gauge
4 Thumbwheel

Base measurement	55.00 mm
Fine measurement	00.92 mm
Total figure	**55.92 mm**

● Some vernier calipers are equipped with a dial gauge for fine measurement. Before use, check that the jaws are clean, then close them fully and check that the dial gauge reads zero. If necessary adjust the gauge ring accordingly. Slacken the vernier clamp screw (1) and set its jaws over (2), or inside (3), the item to be measured **(see illustration 3.13)**. Slide the jaws into contact, using the thumbwheel (4) for fine movement. Read off the main scale (5) where the edge of the sliding scale (6) intersects it, taking the whole number to the left of the zero; this provides the base measurement. Read off the needle position on the dial gauge (7) scale to provide the fine measurement; each division represents 0.05 of a millimetre. Add this fine measurement to the base measurement to obtain the total reading.

In the example shown the item measures 55.95 mm **(see illustration 3.14)**:

Base measurement	55.00 mm
Fine measurement	00.95 mm
Total figure	**55.95 mm**

3.14 Vernier gauge reading of 55.95 mm

Plastigauge

● Plastigauge is a plastic material which can be compressed between two surfaces to measure the oil clearance between them. The width of the compressed Plastigauge is measured against a calibrated scale to determine the clearance.

● Common uses of Plastigauge are for measuring the clearance between crankshaft journal and main bearing inserts, between crankshaft journal and big-end bearing inserts, and between camshaft and bearing surfaces. The following example describes big-end oil clearance measurement.

● Handle the Plastigauge material carefully to prevent distortion. Using a sharp knife, cut a length which corresponds with the width of the bearing being measured and place it carefully across the journal so that it is parallel with the shaft **(see illustration 3.15)**. Carefully install both bearing shells and the connecting rod. Without rotating the rod on the journal tighten its bolts or nuts (as applicable) to the specified torque. The connecting rod and bearings are then disassembled and the crushed Plastigauge examined.

3.15 Plastigauge placed across shaft journal

● Using the scale provided in the Plastigauge kit, measure the width of the material to determine the oil clearance **(see illustration 3.16)**. Always remove all traces of Plastigauge after use using your fingernails.

Caution: Arriving at the correct clearance demands that the assembly is torqued correctly, according to the settings and sequence (where applicable) provided by the motorcycle manufacturer.

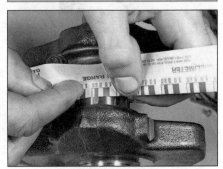

3.16 Measuring the width of the crushed Plastigauge

Dial gauge or DTI (Dial Test Indicator)

● A dial gauge can be used to accurately measure small amounts of movement. Typical uses are measuring shaft runout or shaft endfloat (sideplay) and setting piston position for ignition timing on two-strokes. A dial gauge set usually comes with a range of different probes and adapters and mounting equipment.

● The gauge needle must point to zero when at rest. Rotate the ring around its periphery to zero the gauge.

● Check that the gauge is capable of reading the extent of movement in the work. Most gauges have a small dial set in the face which records whole millimetres of movement as well as the fine scale around the face periphery which is calibrated in 0.01 mm divisions. Read off the small dial first to obtain the base measurement, then add the measurement from the fine scale to obtain the total reading.

In the example shown the gauge reads 1.48 mm (see illustration 3.17):

Base measurement	1.00 mm
Fine measurement	0.48 mm
Total figure	**1.48 mm**

3.17 Dial gauge reading of 1.48 mm

● If measuring shaft runout, the shaft must be supported in vee-blocks and the gauge mounted on a stand perpendicular to the shaft. Rest the tip of the gauge against the centre of the shaft and rotate the shaft slowly whilst watching the gauge reading (see illustration 3.18). Take several measurements along the length of the shaft and record the

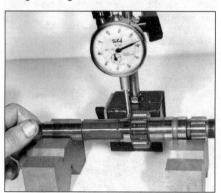

3.18 Using a dial gauge to measure shaft runout

maximum gauge reading as the amount of runout in the shaft. **Note:** *The reading obtained will be total runout at that point - some manufacturers specify that the runout figure is halved to compare with their specified runout limit.*

● Endfloat (sideplay) measurement requires that the gauge is mounted securely to the surrounding component with its probe touching the end of the shaft. Using hand pressure, push and pull on the shaft noting the maximum endfloat recorded on the gauge (see illustration 3.19).

3.19 Using a dial gauge to measure shaft endfloat

● A dial gauge with suitable adapters can be used to determine piston position BTDC on two-stroke engines for the purposes of ignition timing. The gauge, adapter and suitable length probe are installed in the place of the spark plug and the gauge zeroed at TDC. If the piston position is specified as 1.14 mm BTDC, rotate the engine back to 2.00 mm BTDC, then slowly forwards to 1.14 mm BTDC.

Cylinder compression gauges

● A compression gauge is used for measuring cylinder compression. Either the rubber-cone type or the threaded adapter type can be used. The latter is preferred to ensure a perfect seal against the cylinder head. A 0 to 300 psi (0 to 20 Bar) type gauge (for petrol/gasoline engines) will be suitable for motorcycles.

● The spark plug is removed and the gauge either held hard against the cylinder head (cone type) or the gauge adapter screwed into the cylinder head (threaded type) (see illustration 3.20). Cylinder compression is measured with the engine turning over, but not running - carry out the compression test as described in

3.20 Using a rubber-cone type cylinder compression gauge

Fault Finding Equipment. The gauge will hold the reading until manually released.

Oil pressure gauge

● An oil pressure gauge is used for measuring engine oil pressure. Most gauges come with a set of adapters to fit the thread of the take-off point (see illustration 3.21). If the take-off point specified by the motorcycle manufacturer is an external oil pipe union, make sure that the specified replacement union is used to prevent oil starvation.

3.21 Oil pressure gauge and take-off point adapter (arrow)

● Oil pressure is measured with the engine running (at a specific rpm) and often the manufacturer will specify pressure limits for a cold and hot engine.

Straight-edge and surface plate

● If checking the gasket face of a component for warpage, place a steel rule or precision straight-edge across the gasket face and measure any gap between the straight-edge and component with feeler gauges (see illustration 3.22). Check diagonally across the component and between mounting holes (see illustration 3.23).

3.22 Use a straight-edge and feeler gauges to check for warpage

3.23 Check for warpage in these directions

● Checking individual components for warpage, such as clutch plain (metal) plates, requires a perfectly flat plate or piece or plate glass and feeler gauges.

4 Torque and leverage

What is torque?

● Torque describes the twisting force about a shaft. The amount of torque applied is determined by the distance from the centre of the shaft to the end of the lever and the amount of force being applied to the end of the lever; distance multiplied by force equals torque.
● The manufacturer applies a measured torque to a bolt or nut to ensure that it will not slacken in use and to hold two components securely together without movement in the joint. The actual torque setting depends on the thread size, bolt or nut material and the composition of the components being held.
● Too little torque may cause the fastener to loosen due to vibration, whereas too much torque will distort the joint faces of the component or cause the fastener to shear off. Always stick to the specified torque setting.

Using a torque wrench

● Check the calibration of the torque wrench and make sure it has a suitable range for the job. Torque wrenches are available in Nm (Newton-metres), kgf m (kilograms-force metre), lbf ft (pounds-feet), lbf in (inch-pounds). Do not confuse lbf ft with lbf in.
● Adjust the tool to the desired torque on the scale (see illustration 4.1). If your torque wrench is not calibrated in the units specified, carefully convert the figure (see Conversion Factors). A manufacturer sometimes gives a torque setting as a range (8 to 10 Nm) rather than a single figure - in this case set the tool midway between the two settings. The same torque may be expressed as 9 Nm ± 1 Nm. Some torque wrenches have a method of locking the setting so that it isn't inadvertently altered during use.

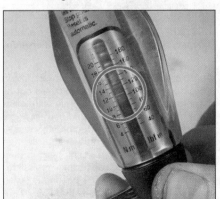

4.1 Set the torque wrench index mark to the setting required, in this case 12 Nm

● Install the bolts/nuts in their correct location and secure them lightly. Their threads must be clean and free of any old locking compound. Unless specified the threads and flange should be dry - oiled threads are necessary in certain circumstances and the manufacturer will take this into account in the specified torque figure. Similarly, the manufacturer may also specify the application of thread-locking compound.
● Tighten the fasteners in the specified sequence until the torque wrench clicks, indicating that the torque setting has been reached. Apply the torque again to double-check the setting. Where different thread diameter fasteners secure the component, as a rule tighten the larger diameter ones first.
● When the torque wrench has been finished with, release the lock (where applicable) and fully back off its setting to zero - do not leave the torque wrench tensioned. Also, do not use a torque wrench for slackening a fastener.

Angle-tightening

● Manufacturers often specify a figure in degrees for final tightening of a fastener. This usually follows tightening to a specific torque setting.
● A degree disc can be set and attached to the socket (see illustration 4.2) or a protractor can be used to mark the angle of movement on the bolt/nut head and the surrounding casting (see illustration 4.3).

4.2 Angle tightening can be accomplished with a torque-angle gauge . . .

4.3 . . . or by marking the angle on the surrounding component

Loosening sequences

● Where more than one bolt/nut secures a component, loosen each fastener evenly a little at a time. In this way, not all the stress of the joint is held by one fastener and the components are not likely to distort.
● If a tightening sequence is provided, work in the REVERSE of this, but if not, work from the outside in, in a criss-cross sequence (see illustration 4.4).

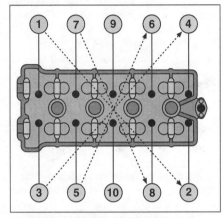

4.4 When slackening, work from the outside inwards

Tightening sequences

● If a component is held by more than one fastener it is important that the retaining bolts/nuts are tightened evenly to prevent uneven stress build-up and distortion of sealing faces. This is especially important on high-compression joints such as the cylinder head.
● A sequence is usually provided by the manufacturer, either in a diagram or actually marked in the casting. If not, always start in the centre and work outwards in a criss-cross pattern (see illustration 4.5). Start off by securing all bolts/nuts finger-tight, then set the torque wrench and tighten each fastener by a small amount in sequence until the final torque is reached. By following this practice,

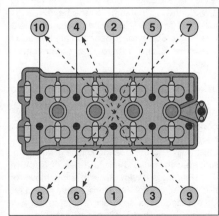

4.5 When tightening, work from the inside outwards

the joint will be held evenly and will not be distorted. Important joints, such as the cylinder head and big-end fasteners often have two- or three-stage torque settings.

Applying leverage

● Use tools at the correct angle. Position a socket wrench or spanner on the bolt/nut so that you pull it towards you when loosening. If this can't be done, push the spanner without curling your fingers around it **(see illustration 4.6)** - the spanner may slip or the fastener loosen suddenly, resulting in your fingers being crushed against a component.

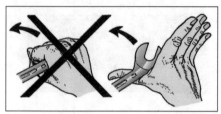

4.6 If you can't pull on the spanner to loosen a fastener, push with your hand open

● Additional leverage is gained by extending the length of the lever. The best way to do this is to use a breaker bar instead of the regular length tool, or to slip a length of tubing over the end of the spanner or socket wrench.
● If additional leverage will not work, the fastener head is either damaged or firmly corroded in place (see *Fasteners*).

5   Bearings

Bearing removal and installation

Drivers and sockets

● Before removing a bearing, always inspect the casing to see which way it must be driven out - some casings will have retaining plates or a cast step. Also check for any identifying markings on the bearing and if installed to a certain depth, measure this at this stage. Some roller bearings are sealed on one side - take note of the original fitted position.
● Bearings can be driven out of a casing using a bearing driver tool (with the correct size head) or a socket of the correct diameter. Select the driver head or socket so that it contacts the outer race of the bearing, not the balls/rollers or inner race. Always support the casing around the bearing housing with wood blocks, otherwise there is a risk of fracture. The bearing is driven out with a few blows on the driver or socket from a heavy mallet. Unless access is severely restricted (as with wheel bearings), a pin-punch is not recommended unless it is moved around the bearing to keep it square in its housing.

● The same equipment can be used to install bearings. Make sure the bearing housing is supported on wood blocks and line up the bearing in its housing. Fit the bearing as noted on removal - generally they are installed with their marked side facing outwards. Tap the bearing squarely into its housing using a driver or socket which bears only on the bearing's outer race - contact with the bearing balls/rollers or inner race will destroy it **(see illustrations 5.1 and 5.2)**.
● Check that the bearing inner race and balls/rollers rotate freely.

5.1 Using a bearing driver against the bearing's outer race

5.2 Using a large socket against the bearing's outer race

Pullers and slide-hammers

● Where a bearing is pressed on a shaft a puller will be required to extract it **(see illustration 5.3).** Make sure that the puller clamp or legs fit securely behind the bearing and are unlikely to slip out. If pulling a bearing

5.3 This bearing puller clamps behind the bearing and pressure is applied to the shaft end to draw the bearing off

off a gear shaft for example, you may have to locate the puller behind a gear pinion if there is no access to the race and draw the gear pinion off the shaft as well **(see illustration 5.4)**.

> *Caution: Ensure that the puller's centre bolt locates securely against the end of the shaft and will not slip when pressure is applied. Also ensure that puller does not damage the shaft end.*

5.4 Where no access is available to the rear of the bearing, it is sometimes possible to draw off the adjacent component

● Operate the puller so that its centre bolt exerts pressure on the shaft end and draws the bearing off the shaft.
● When installing the bearing on the shaft, tap only on the bearing's inner race - contact with the balls/rollers or outer race with destroy the bearing. Use a socket or length of tubing as a drift which fits over the shaft end **(see illustration 5.5)**.

5.5 When installing a bearing on a shaft use a piece of tubing which bears only on the bearing's inner race

● Where a bearing locates in a blind hole in a casing, it cannot be driven or pulled out as described above. A slide-hammer with knife-edged bearing puller attachment will be required. The puller attachment passes through the bearing and when tightened expands to fit firmly behind the bearing **(see illustration 5.6)**. By operating the slide-hammer part of the tool the bearing is jarred out of its housing **(see illustration 5.7)**.
● It is possible, if the bearing is of reasonable weight, for it to drop out of its housing if the casing is heated as described opposite. If this

5.6 Expand the bearing puller so that it locks behind the bearing . . .

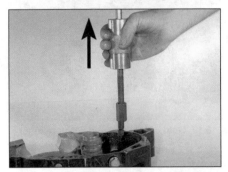

5.7 . . . attach the slide hammer to the bearing puller

method is attempted, first prepare a work surface which will enable the casing to be tapped face down to help dislodge the bearing - a wood surface is ideal since it will not damage the casing's gasket surface. Wearing protective gloves, tap the heated casing several times against the work surface to dislodge the bearing under its own weight **(see illustration 5.8)**.

5.8 Tapping a casing face down on wood blocks can often dislodge a bearing

● Bearings can be installed in blind holes using the driver or socket method described above.

Drawbolts

● Where a bearing or bush is set in the eye of a component, such as a suspension linkage arm or connecting rod small-end, removal by drift may damage the component. Furthermore, a rubber bushing in a shock absorber eye cannot successfully be driven out of position. If access is available to a engineering press, the task is straightforward. If not, a drawbolt can be fabricated to extract the bearing or bush.

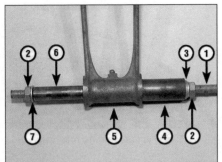

5.9 Drawbolt component parts assembled on a suspension arm

1 Bolt or length of threaded bar
2 Nuts
3 Washer (external diameter greater than tubing internal diameter)
4 Tubing (internal diameter sufficient to accommodate bearing)
5 Suspension arm with bearing
6 Tubing (external diameter slightly smaller than bearing)
7 Washer (external diameter slightly smaller than bearing)

5.10 Drawing the bearing out of the suspension arm

● To extract the bearing/bush you will need a long bolt with nut (or piece of threaded bar with two nuts), a piece of tubing which has an internal diameter larger than the bearing/bush, another piece of tubing which has an external diameter slightly smaller than the bearing/bush, and a selection of washers **(see illustrations 5.9 and 5.10)**. Note that the pieces of tubing must be of the same length, or longer, than the bearing/bush.
● The same kit (without the pieces of tubing) can be used to draw the new bearing/bush back into place **(see illustration 5.11)**.

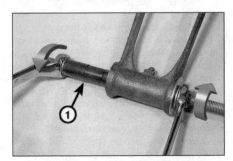

5.11 Installing a new bearing (1) in the suspension arm

Temperature change

● If the bearing's outer race is a tight fit in the casing, the aluminium casing can be heated to release its grip on the bearing. Aluminium will expand at a greater rate than the steel bearing outer race. There are several ways to do this, but avoid any localised extreme heat (such as a blow torch) - aluminium alloy has a low melting point.
● Approved methods of heating a casing are using a domestic oven (heated to 100°C) or immersing the casing in boiling water **(see illustration 5.12)**. Low temperature range localised heat sources such as a paint stripper heat gun or clothes iron can also be used **(see illustration 5.13)**. Alternatively, soak a rag in boiling water, wring it out and wrap it around the bearing housing.

> ⚠️ **Warning: All of these methods require care in use to prevent scalding and burns to the hands. Wear protective gloves when handling hot components.**

5.12 A casing can be immersed in a sink of boiling water to aid bearing removal

5.13 Using a localised heat source to aid bearing removal

● If heating the whole casing note that plastic components, such as the neutral switch, may suffer - remove them beforehand.
● After heating, remove the bearing as described above. You may find that the expansion is sufficient for the bearing to fall out of the casing under its own weight or with a light tap on the driver or socket.
● If necessary, the casing can be heated to aid bearing installation, and this is sometimes the recommended procedure if the motorcycle manufacturer has designed the housing and bearing fit with this intention.

● Installation of bearings can be eased by placing them in a freezer the night before installation. The steel bearing will contract slightly, allowing easy insertion in its housing. This is often useful when installing steering head outer races in the frame.

Bearing types and markings

● Plain shell bearings, ball bearings, needle roller bearings and tapered roller bearings will all be found on motorcycles (see illustrations 5.14 and 5.15). The ball and roller types are usually caged between an inner and outer race, but uncaged variations may be found.

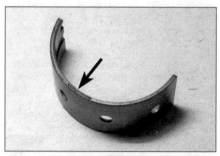

5.14 Shell bearings are either plain or grooved. They are usually identified by colour code (arrow)

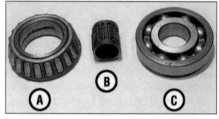

5.15 Tapered roller bearing (A), needle roller bearing (B) and ball journal bearing (C)

● Shell bearings (often called inserts) are usually found at the crankshaft main and connecting rod big-end where they are good at coping with high loads. They are made of a phosphor-bronze material and are impregnated with self-lubricating properties.
● Ball bearings and needle roller bearings consist of a steel inner and outer race with the balls or rollers between the races. They require constant lubrication by oil or grease and are good at coping with axial loads. Taper roller bearings consist of rollers set in a tapered cage set on the inner race; the outer race is separate. They are good at coping with axial loads and prevent movement along the shaft - a typical application is in the steering head.
● Bearing manufacturers produce bearings to ISO size standards and stamp one face of the bearing to indicate its internal and external diameter, load capacity and type (see illustration 5.16).
● Metal bushes are usually of phosphor-bronze material. Rubber bushes are used in suspension mounting eyes. Fibre bushes have also been used in suspension pivots.

5.16 Typical bearing marking

Bearing fault finding

● If a bearing outer race has spun in its housing, the housing material will be damaged. You can use a bearing locking compound to bond the outer race in place if damage is not too severe.
● Shell bearings will fail due to damage of their working surface, as a result of lack of lubrication, corrosion or abrasive particles in the oil (see illustration 5.17). Small particles of dirt in the oil may embed in the bearing material whereas larger particles will score the bearing and shaft journal. If a number of short journeys are made, insufficient heat will be generated to drive off condensation which has built up on the bearings.

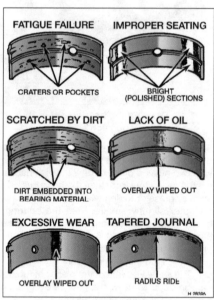

5.17 Typical bearing failures

● Ball and roller bearings will fail due to lack of lubrication or damage to the balls or rollers. Tapered-roller bearings can be damaged by overloading them. Unless the bearing is sealed on both sides, wash it in paraffin (kerosene) to remove all old grease then allow it to dry. Make a visual inspection looking to dented balls or rollers, damaged cages and worn or pitted races (see illustration 5.18).
● A ball bearing can be checked for wear by listening to it when spun. Apply a film of light oil to the bearing and hold it close to the ear - hold the outer race with one hand and spin the inner

5.18 Example of ball journal bearing with damaged balls and cages

5.19 Hold outer race and listen to inner race when spun

race with the other hand (see illustration 5.19). The bearing should be almost silent when spun; if it grates or rattles it is worn.

6 Oil seals

Oil seal removal and installation

● Oil seals should be renewed every time a component is dismantled. This is because the seal lips will become set to the sealing surface and will not necessarily reseal.
● Oil seals can be prised out of position using a large flat-bladed screwdriver (see illustration 6.1). In the case of crankcase seals, check first that the seal is not lipped on the inside, preventing its removal with the crankcases joined.

6.1 Prise out oil seals with a large flat-bladed screwdriver

● New seals are usually installed with their marked face (containing the seal reference code) outwards and the spring side towards the fluid being retained. In certain cases, such as a two-stroke engine crankshaft seal, a double lipped seal may be used due to there being fluid or gas on each side of the joint.

● Use a bearing driver or socket which bears only on the outer hard edge of the seal to install it in the casing - tapping on the inner edge will damage the sealing lip.

Oil seal types and markings

● Oil seals are usually of the single-lipped type. Double-lipped seals are found where a liquid or gas is on both sides of the joint.
● Oil seals can harden and lose their sealing ability if the motorcycle has been in storage for a long period - renewal is the only solution.
● Oil seal manufacturers also conform to the ISO markings for seal size - these are moulded into the outer face of the seal (see illustration 6.2).

6.2 These oil seal markings indicate inside diameter, outside diameter and seal thickness

7 Gaskets and sealants

Types of gasket and sealant

● Gaskets are used to seal the mating surfaces between components and keep lubricants, fluids, vacuum or pressure contained within the assembly. Aluminium gaskets are sometimes found at the cylinder joints, but most gaskets are paper-based. If the mating surfaces of the components being joined are undamaged the gasket can be installed dry, although a dab of sealant or grease will be useful to hold it in place during assembly.
● RTV (Room Temperature Vulcanising) silicone rubber sealants cure when exposed to moisture in the atmosphere. These sealants are good at filling pits or irregular gasket faces, but will tend to be forced out of the joint under very high torque. They can be used to replace a paper gasket, but first make sure that the width of the paper gasket is not essential to the shimming of internal components. RTV sealants should not be used on components containing petrol (gasoline).
● Non-hardening, semi-hardening and hard setting liquid gasket compounds can be used with a gasket or between a metal-to-metal joint. Select the sealant to suit the application: universal non-hardening sealant can be used on virtually all joints; semi-hardening on joint faces which are rough or damaged; hard setting sealant on joints which require a permanent bond and are subjected to high temperature and pressure. **Note:** *Check first if the paper gasket has a bead of sealant*

impregnated in its surface before applying additional sealant.
● When choosing a sealant, make sure it is suitable for the application, particularly if being applied in a high-temperature area or in the vicinity of fuel. Certain manufacturers produce sealants in either clear, silver or black colours to match the finish of the engine. This has a particular application on motorcycles where much of the engine is exposed.
● Do not over-apply sealant. That which is squeezed out on the outside of the joint can be wiped off, whereas an excess of sealant on the inside can break off and clog oilways.

Breaking a sealed joint

● Age, heat, pressure and the use of hard setting sealant can cause two components to stick together so tightly that they are difficult to separate using finger pressure alone. Do not resort to using levers unless there is a pry point provided for this purpose (see illustration 7.1) or else the gasket surfaces will be damaged.
● Use a soft-faced hammer (see illustration 7.2) or a wood block and conventional hammer to strike the component near the mating surface. Avoid hammering against cast extremities since they may break off. If this method fails, try using a wood wedge between the two components.

Caution: If the joint will not separate, double-check that you have removed all the fasteners.

7.1 If a pry point is provided, apply gently pressure with a flat-bladed screwdriver

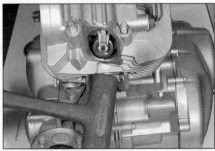

7.2 Tap around the joint with a soft-faced mallet if necessary - don't strike cooling fins

Removal of old gasket and sealant

● Paper gaskets will most likely come away complete, leaving only a few traces stuck on

HAYNES HiNT

Most components have one or two hollow locating dowels between the two gasket faces. If a dowel cannot be removed, do not resort to gripping it with pliers - it will almost certainly be distorted. Install a close-fitting socket or Phillips screwdriver into the dowel and then grip the outer edge of the dowel to free it.

the sealing faces of the components. It is imperative that all traces are removed to ensure correct sealing of the new gasket.
● Very carefully scrape all traces of gasket away making sure that the sealing surfaces are not gouged or scored by the scraper (see illustrations 7.3, 7.4 and 7.5). Stubborn deposits can be removed by spraying with an aerosol gasket remover. Final preparation of

7.3 Paper gaskets can be scraped off with a gasket scraper tool . . .

7.4 . . . a knife blade . . .

7.5 . . . or a household scraper

7.6 Fine abrasive paper is wrapped around a flat file to clean up the gasket face

7.7 A kitchen scourer can be used on stubborn deposits

the gasket surface can be made with very fine abrasive paper or a plastic kitchen scourer **(see illustrations 7.6 and 7.7)**.
● Old sealant can be scraped or peeled off components, depending on the type originally used. Note that gasket removal compounds are available to avoid scraping the components clean; make sure the gasket remover suits the type of sealant used.

8 Chains

Breaking and joining final drive chains

● Drive chains for all but small bikes are continuous and do not have a clip-type connecting link. The chain must be broken using a chain breaker tool and the new chain securely riveted together using a new soft rivet-type link. Never use a clip-type connecting link instead of a rivet-type link, except in an emergency. Various chain breaking and riveting tools are available, either as separate tools or combined as illustrated in the accompanying photographs - read the instructions supplied with the tool carefully.

> **Warning: The need to rivet the new link pins correctly cannot be overstressed - loss of control of the motorcycle is very likely to result if the chain breaks in use.**

● Rotate the chain and look for the soft link. The soft link pins look like they have been

8.1 Tighten the chain breaker to push the pin out of the link . . .

8.2 . . . withdraw the pin, remove the tool . . .

8.3 . . . and separate the chain link

deeply centre-punched instead of peened over like all the other pins **(see illustration 8.9)** and its sideplate may be a different colour. Position the soft link midway between the sprockets and assemble the chain breaker tool over one of the soft link pins **(see illustration 8.1)**. Operate the tool to push the pin out through the chain **(see illustration 8.2)**. On an O-ring chain, remove the O-rings **(see illustration 8.3)**. Carry out the same procedure on the other soft link pin.

> **Caution: Certain soft link pins (particularly on the larger chains) may require their ends to be filed or ground off before they can be pressed out using the tool.**

● Check that you have the correct size and strength (standard or heavy duty) new soft link - do not reuse the old link. Look for the size marking on the chain sideplates **(see illustration 8.10)**.
● Position the chain ends so that they are engaged over the rear sprocket. On an O-ring

8.4 Insert the new soft link, with O-rings, through the chain ends . . .

8.5 . . . install the O-rings over the pin ends . . .

8.6 . . . followed by the sideplate

chain, install a new O-ring over each pin of the link and insert the link through the two chain ends **(see illustration 8.4)**. Install a new O-ring over the end of each pin, followed by the sideplate (with the chain manufacturer's marking facing outwards) **(see illustrations 8.5 and 8.6)**. On an unsealed chain, insert the link through the two chain ends, then install the sideplate with the chain manufacturer's marking facing outwards.
● Note that it may not be possible to install the sideplate using finger pressure alone. If using a joining tool, assemble it so that the plates of the tool clamp the link and press the sideplate over the pins **(see illustration 8.7)**. Otherwise, use two small sockets placed over

8.7 Push the sideplate into position using a clamp

8.8 Assemble the chain riveting tool over one pin at a time and tighten it fully

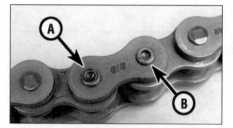

8.9 Pin end correctly riveted (A), pin end unriveted (B)

the rivet ends and two pieces of the wood between a G-clamp. Operate the clamp to press the sideplate over the pins.

● Assemble the joining tool over one pin (following the maker's instructions) and tighten the tool down to spread the pin end securely **(see illustrations 8.8 and 8.9)**. Do the same on the other pin.

> ⚠️ **Warning: Check that the pin ends are secure and that there is no danger of the sideplate coming loose. If the pin ends are cracked the soft link must be renewed.**

Final drive chain sizing

● Chains are sized using a three digit number, followed by a suffix to denote the chain type **(see illustration 8.10)**. Chain type is either standard or heavy duty (thicker sideplates), and also unsealed or O-ring/X-ring type.

● The first digit of the number relates to the pitch of the chain, ie the distance from the centre of one pin to the centre of the next pin **(see illustration 8.11)**. Pitch is expressed in eighths of an inch, as follows:

8.10 Typical chain size and type marking

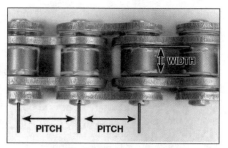

8.11 Chain dimensions

Sizes commencing with a 4 (eg 428) have a pitch of 1/2 inch (12.7 mm)

Sizes commencing with a 5 (eg 520) have a pitch of 5/8 inch (15.9 mm)

Sizes commencing with a 6 (eg 630) have a pitch of 3/4 inch (19.1 mm)

● The second and third digits of the chain size relate to the width of the rollers, again in imperial units, eg the 525 shown has 5/16 inch (7.94 mm) rollers **(see illustration 8.11)**.

9 Hoses

Clamping to prevent flow

● Small-bore flexible hoses can be clamped to prevent fluid flow whilst a component is worked on. Whichever method is used, ensure that the hose material is not permanently distorted or damaged by the clamp.

a) A brake hose clamp available from auto accessory shops **(see illustration 9.1)**.
b) A wingnut type hose clamp **(see illustration 9.2)**.

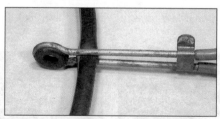

9.1 Hoses can be clamped with an automotive brake hose clamp . . .

9.2 . . . a wingnut type hose clamp . . .

c) Two sockets placed each side of the hose and held with straight-jawed self-locking grips **(see illustration 9.3)**.
d) Thick card each side of the hose held between straight-jawed self-locking grips **(see illustration 9.4)**.

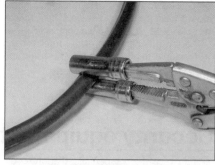

9.3 . . . two sockets and a pair of self-locking grips . . .

9.4 . . . or thick card and self-locking grips

Freeing and fitting hoses

● Always make sure the hose clamp is moved well clear of the hose end. Grip the hose with your hand and rotate it whilst pulling it off the union. If the hose has hardened due to age and will not move, slit it with a sharp knife and peel its ends off the union **(see illustration 9.5)**.

● Resist the temptation to use grease or soap on the unions to aid installation; although it helps the hose slip over the union it will equally aid the escape of fluid from the joint. It is preferable to soften the hose ends in hot water and wet the inside surface of the hose with water or a fluid which will evaporate.

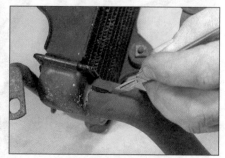

9.5 Cutting a coolant hose free with a sharp knife

Introduction

In less time than it takes to read this introduction, a thief could steal your motorcycle. Returning only to find your bike has gone is one of the worst feelings in the world. Even if the motorcycle is insured against theft, once you've got over the initial shock, you will have the inconvenience of dealing with the police and your insurance company.

The motorcycle is an easy target for the professional thief and the joyrider alike and the official figures on motorcycle theft make for depressing reading; on average a motorcycle is stolen every 16 minutes in the UK!

Motorcycle thefts fall into two categories, those stolen 'to order' and those taken by opportunists. The thief stealing to order will be on the look out for a specific make and model and will go to extraordinary lengths to obtain that motorcycle. The opportunist thief on the other hand will look for easy targets which can be stolen with the minimum of effort and risk.

Whilst it is never going to be possible to make your machine 100% secure, it is estimated that around half of all stolen motorcycles are taken by opportunist thieves. Remember that the opportunist thief is always on the look out for the easy option: if there are two similar motorcycles parked side-by-side, they will target the one with the lowest level of security. By taking a few precautions, you can reduce the chances of your motorcycle being stolen.

Security equipment

There are many specialised motorcycle security devices available and the following text summarises their applications and their good and bad points.

Once you have decided on the type of security equipment which best suits your needs, we recommended that you read one of the many equipment tests regularly carried out by the motorcycle press. These tests compare the products from all the major manufacturers and give impartial ratings on their effectiveness, value-for-money and ease of use.

No one item of security equipment can provide complete protection. It is highly recommended that two or more of the items described below are combined to increase the security of your motorcycle (a lock and chain plus an alarm system is just about ideal). The more security measures fitted to the bike, the less likely it is to be stolen.

Pass the chain through the bike's frame, rather than just through a wheel . . .

Lock and chain

Pros: *Very flexible to use; can be used to secure the motorcycle to almost any immovable object. On some locks and chains, the lock can be used on its own as a disc lock (see below).*

Cons: *Can be very heavy and awkward to carry on the motorcycle, although some types will be supplied with a carry bag which can be strapped to the pillion seat.*

● Heavy-duty chains and locks are an excellent security measure **(see illustration 1)**. Whenever the motorcycle is parked, use the lock and chain to secure the machine to a solid, immovable object such as a post or railings. This will prevent the machine from being ridden away or being lifted into the back of a van.

● When fitting the chain, always ensure the chain is routed around the motorcycle frame or swingarm **(see illustrations 2 and 3)**. Never merely pass the chain around one of the wheel rims; a thief may unbolt the wheel and lift the rest of the machine into a van, leaving you with just the wheel! Try to avoid having excess chain free, thus making it difficult to use cutting tools, and keep the chain and lock off the ground to prevent thieves attacking it with a cold chisel. Position the lock so that its lock barrel is facing downwards; this will make it harder for the thief to attack the lock mechanism.

Ensure the lock and chain you buy is of good quality and long enough to shackle your bike to a solid object

. . . and loop it around a solid object

U-locks

Pros: *Highly effective deterrent which can be used to secure the bike to a post or railings. Most U-locks come with a carrier which allows the lock to be easily carried on the bike.*

Cons: *Not as flexible to use as a lock and chain.*

● These are solid locks which are similar in use to a lock and chain. U-locks are lighter than a lock and chain but not so flexible to use. The length and shape of the lock shackle limit the objects to which the bike can be secured **(see illustration 4)**.

Disc locks

Pros: *Small, light and very easy to carry; most can be stored underneath the seat.*

Cons: *Does not prevent the motorcycle being lifted into a van. Can be very embarrassing if you*

U-locks can be used to secure the bike to a solid object – ensure you purchase one which is long enough

forget to remove the lock before attempting to ride off!

● Disc locks are designed to be attached to the front brake disc. The lock passes through one of the holes in the disc and prevents the wheel rotating by jamming against the fork/brake caliper **(see illustration 5)**. Some are equipped with an alarm siren which sounds if the disc lock is moved; this not only acts as a theft deterrent but also as a handy reminder if you try to move the bike with the lock still fitted.

● Combining the disc lock with a length of cable which can be looped around a post or railings provides an additional measure of security **(see illustration 6)**.

Alarms and immobilisers

Pros: *Once installed it is completely hassle-free to use. If the system is 'Thatcham' or 'Sold Secure-approved', insurance companies may give you a discount.*

Cons: *Can be expensive to buy and complex to install. No system will prevent the motorcycle from being lifted into a van and taken away.*

● Electronic alarms and immobilisers are available to suit a variety of budgets. There are three different types of system available: pure alarms, pure immobilisers, and the more expensive systems which are combined alarm/immobilisers **(see illustration 7)**.

● An alarm system is designed to emit an audible warning if the motorcycle is being tampered with.

● An immobiliser prevents the motorcycle being started and ridden away by disabling its electrical systems.

● When purchasing an alarm/immobiliser system, check the cost of installing the system unless you are able to do it yourself. If the motorcycle is not used regularly, another consideration is the current drain of the system. All alarm/immobiliser systems are powered by the motorcycle's battery; purchasing a system with a very low current drain could prevent the battery losing its charge whilst the motorcycle is not being used.

A typical disc lock attached through one of the holes in the disc

A disc lock combined with a security cable provides additional protection

A typical alarm/immobiliser system

Indelible markings can be applied to most areas of the bike – always apply the manufacturer's sticker to warn off thieves

Chemically-etched code numbers can be applied to main body panels . . .

. . . again, always ensure that the kit manufacturer's sticker is applied in a prominent position

Security marking kits

Pros: *Very cheap and effective deterrent. Many insurance companies will give you a discount on your insurance premium if a recognised security marking kit is used on your motorcycle.*

Cons: *Does not prevent the motorcycle being stolen by joyriders.*

● There are many different types of security marking kits available. The idea is to mark as many parts of the motorcycle as possible with a unique security number **(see illustrations 8, 9 and 10)**. A form will be included with the kit to register your personal details and those of the motorcycle with the kit manufacturer. This register is made available to the police to help them trace the rightful owner of any motorcycle or components which they recover should all other forms of identification have been removed. Always apply the warning stickers provided with the kit to deter thieves.

Ground anchors, wheel clamps and security posts

Pros: *An excellent form of security which will deter all but the most determined of thieves.*

Cons: *Awkward to install and can be expensive.*

● Whilst the motorcycle is at home, it is a good idea to attach it securely to the floor or a solid wall, even if it is kept in a securely locked garage. Various types of ground anchors, security posts and wheel clamps are available for this purpose **(see illustration 11)**. These security devices are either bolted to a solid concrete or brick structure or can be cemented into the ground.

![Ground anchor securing front wheel]

Permanent ground anchors provide an excellent level of security when the bike is at home

Security at home

A high percentage of motorcycle thefts are from the owner's home. Here are some things to consider whenever your motorcycle is at home:

✔ Where possible, always keep the motorcycle in a securely locked garage. Never rely solely on the standard lock on the garage door, these are usual hopelessly inadequate. Fit an additional locking mechanism to the door and consider having the garage alarmed. A security light, activated by a movement sensor, is also a good investment.

✔ Always secure the motorcycle to the ground or a wall, even if it is inside a securely locked garage.
✔ Do not regularly leave the motorcycle outside your home, try to keep it out of sight wherever possible. If a garage is not available, fit a motorcycle cover over the bike to disguise its true identity.
✔ It is not uncommon for thieves to follow a motorcyclist home to find out where the bike is kept. They will then return at a later date. Be aware of this whenever you are returning

home on your motorcycle. If you suspect you are being followed, do not return home, instead ride to a garage or shop and stop as a precaution.
✔ When selling a motorcycle, do not provide your home address or the location where the bike is normally kept. Arrange to meet the buyer at a location away from your home. Thieves have been known to pose as potential buyers to find out where motorcycles are kept and then return later to steal them.

Security away from the home

As well as fitting security equipment to your motorcycle here are a few general rules to follow whenever you park your motorcycle.
✔ Park in a busy, public place.
✔ Use car parks which incorporate security features, such as CCTV.

✔ At night, park in a well-lit area, preferably directly underneath a street light.
✔ Engage the steering lock.
✔ Secure the motorcycle to a solid, immovable object such as a post or railings with an additional lock. If this is not possible,

secure the bike to a friend's motorcycle. Some public parking places provide security loops for motorcycles.
✔ Never leave your helmet or luggage attached to the motorcycle. Take them with you at all times.

Lubricants and fluids

A wide range of lubricants, fluids and cleaning agents is available for motor-cycles. This is a guide as to what is available, its applications and properties.

Four-stroke engine oil

● Engine oil is without doubt the most important component of any four-stroke engine. Modern motorcycle engines place a lot of demands on their oil and choosing the right type is essential. Using an unsuitable oil will lead to an increased rate of engine wear and could result in serious engine damage. Before purchasing oil, always check the recommended oil specification given by the manufacturer. The manufacturer will state a recommended 'type or classification' and also a specific 'viscosity' range for engine oil.

● The oil 'type or classification' is identified by its API (American Petroleum Institute) rating. The API rating will be in the form of two letters, e.g. SG. The S identifies the oil as being suitable for use in a petrol (gasoline) engine (S stands for spark ignition) and the second letter, ranging from A to J, identifies the oil's performance rating. The later this letter, the higher the specification of the oil; for example API SG oil exceeds the requirements of API SF oil. **Note:** *On some oils there may also be a second rating consisting of another two letters, the first letter being C, e.g. API SF/CD. This rating indicates the oil is also suitable for use in a diesel engines (the C stands for compression ignition) and is thus of no relevance for motorcycle use.*

● The 'viscosity' of the oil is identified by its SAE (Society of Automotive Engineers) rating. All modern engines require multigrade oils and the SAE rating will consist of two numbers, the first followed by a W, e.g.

10W/40. The first number indicates the viscosity rating of the oil at low temperatures (W stands for winter – tested at –20°C) and the second number represents the viscosity of the oil at high temperatures (tested at 100°C). The lower the number, the thinner the oil. For example an oil with an SAE 10W/40 rating will give better cold starting and running than an SAE 15W/40 oil.

● As well as ensuring the 'type' and 'viscosity' of the oil match the recommendations, another consideration to make when buying engine oil is whether to purchase a standard mineral-based oil, a semi-synthetic oil (also known as a synthetic blend or synthetic-based oil) or a fully-synthetic oil. Although all oils will have a similar rating and viscosity, their cost will vary considerably; mineral-based oils are the cheapest, the fully-synthetic oils the most expensive with the semi-synthetic oils falling somewhere in-between. This decision is very much up to the owner, but it should be noted that modern synthetic oils have far better lubricating and cleaning qualities than traditional mineral-based oils and tend to retain these properties for far longer. Bearing in mind the operating conditions inside a modern, high-revving motorcycle engine it is highly recommended that a fully synthetic oil is used. The extra expense at each service could save you money in the long term by preventing premature engine wear.

● As a final note always ensure that the oil is specifically designed for use in motorcycle engines. Engine oils designed primarily for use in car engines sometimes contain additives or friction modifiers which could cause clutch slip on a motorcycle fitted with a wet-clutch.

Two-stroke engine oil

● Modern two-stroke engines, with their high power outputs, place high demands on their oil. If engine seizure is to be avoided it is essential that a high-quality oil is used. Two-stroke oils differ hugely from four-stroke oils. The oil lubricates only the crankshaft and piston(s) (the transmission has its own lubricating oil) and is used on a total-loss basis where it is burnt completely during the combustion process.

● The Japanese have recently introduced a classification system for two-stroke oils, the JASO rating. This rating is in the form of two letters, either FA, FB or FC – FA is the lowest classification and FC the highest. Ensure the oil being used meets or exceeds the recommended rating specified by the manufacturer.

● As well as ensuring the oil rating matches the recommendation, another consideration to make when buying engine oil is whether to purchase a standard mineral-based oil, a semi-synthetic oil (also known as a synthetic blend or synthetic-based oil) or a fully-synthetic oil. The cost of each type of oil varies considerably; mineral-based oils are the cheapest, the fully-synthetic oils the most expensive with the semi-synthetic oils falling somewhere in-between. This decision is very much up to the owner, but it should be noted that modern synthetic oils have far better lubricating properties and burn cleaner than traditional mineral-based oils. It is therefore recommended that a fully synthetic oil is used. The extra expense could save you money in the long term by preventing premature engine wear, engine performance will be improved, carbon deposits and exhaust smoke will be reduced.

● Always ensure that the oil is specifically designed for use in an injector system. Many high quality two-stroke oils are designed for competition use and need to be pre-mixed with fuel. These oils are of a much higher viscosity and are not designed to flow through the injector pumps used on road-going two-stroke motorcycles.

Transmission (gear) oil

● On a two-stroke engine, the transmission and clutch are lubricated by their own separate oil bath which must be changed in accordance with the Maintenance Schedule.
● Although the engine and transmission units of most four-strokes use a common lubrication supply, there are some exceptions where the engine and gearbox have separate oil reservoirs and a dry clutch is used.
● Motorcycle manufacturers will either recommend a monograde transmission oil or a four-stroke multigrade engine oil to lubricate the transmission.
● Transmission oils, or gear oils as they are often called, are designed specifically for use in transmission systems. The viscosity of these oils is represented by an SAE number, but the scale of measurement applied is different to that used to grade engine oils. As a rough guide a SAE90 gear oil will be of the same viscosity as an SAE50 engine oil.

Shaft drive oil

● On models equipped with shaft final drive, the shaft drive gears are will have their own oil supply. The manufacturer will state a recommended 'type or classification' and also a specific 'viscosity' range in the same manner as for four-stroke engine oil.
● Gear oil classification is given by the number which follows the API GL (GL standing for gear lubricant) rating, the higher the number, the higher the specification of the oil, e.g. API GL5 oil is a higher specification than API GL4 oil. Ensure the oil meets or

exceeds the classification specified and is of the correct viscosity. The viscosity of gear oils is also represented by an SAE number but the scale of measurement used is different to that used to grade engine oils. As a rough guide an SAE90 gear oil will be of the same viscosity as an SAE50 engine oil.
● If the use of an EP (Extreme Pressure) gear oil is specified, ensure the oil purchased is suitable.

Fork oil and suspension fluid

● Conventional telescopic front forks are hydraulic and require fork oil to work. To ensure the forks function correctly, the fork oil must be changed in accordance with the Maintenance Schedule.
● Fork oil is available in a variety of viscosities, identified by their SAE rating; fork oil ratings vary from light (SAE 5) to heavy (SAE 30). When purchasing fork oil, ensure the viscosity rating matches that specified by the manufacturer.
● Some lubricant manufacturers also produce a range of high-quality suspension fluids which are very similar to fork oil but are designed mainly for competition use. These fluids may have a different viscosity rating system which is not to be confused with the SAE rating of normal fork oil. Refer to the manufacturer's instructions if in any doubt.

Brake and clutch fluid

● All disc brake systems and some clutch systems are hydraulically operated. To ensure correct operation, the hydraulic fluid must be changed in accordance with the Maintenance Schedule.
● Brake and clutch fluid is classified by its DOT rating with most motorcycle manufacturers specifying DOT 3 or 4 fluid. Both fluid types are glycol-based and can be mixed together without adverse effect; DOT 4 fluid exceeds the requirements of DOT 3

fluid. Although it is safe to use DOT 4 fluid in a system designed for use with DOT 3 fluid, never use DOT 3 fluid in a system which specifies the use of DOT 4 as this will adversely affect the system's performance. The type required for the system will be marked on the fluid reservoir cap.
● Some manufacturers also produce a DOT 5 hydraulic fluid. DOT 5 hydraulic fluid is silicone-based and is not compatible with the glycol-based DOT 3 and 4 fluids. Never mix DOT 5 fluid with DOT 3 or 4 fluid as this will seriously affect the performance of the hydraulic system.

Coolant/antifreeze

● When purchasing coolant/antifreeze, always ensure it is suitable for use in an aluminium engine and contains corrosion inhibitors to prevent possible blockages of the internal coolant passages of the system. As a general rule, most coolants are designed to be used neat and should not be diluted whereas antifreeze can be mixed with distilled water to provide a coolant solution of the required strength. Refer to the manufacturer's instructions on the bottle.
● Ensure the coolant is changed in accordance with the Maintenance Schedule.

Chain lube

● Chain lube is an aerosol-type spray lubricant specifically designed for use on motorcycle final drive chains. Chain lube has two functions, to minimise friction between the final drive chain and sprockets and to prevent corrosion of the chain. Regular use of a good-quality chain lube will extend the life of the drive chain and sprockets and thus maximise the power being transmitted from the transmission to the rear wheel.
● When using chain lube, always allow some time for the solvents in the lube to evaporate before riding the motorcycle. This will minimise the amount of lube which will

'fling' off from the chain when the motorcycle is used. If the motorcycle is equipped with an 'O-ring' chain, ensure the chain lube is labelled as being suitable for use on 'O-ring' chains.

Degreasers and solvents

● There are many different types of solvents and degreasers available to remove the grime and grease which accumulate around the motorcycle during normal use. Degreasers and solvents are usually available as an aerosol-type spray or as a liquid which you apply with a brush. Always closely follow the manufacturer's instructions and wear eye protection during use. Be aware that many solvents are flammable and may give off noxious fumes; take adequate precautions when using them (see Safety First!).

● For general cleaning, use one of the many solvents or degreasers available from most motorcycle accessory shops. These solvents are usually applied then left for a certain time before being washed off with water.

Brake cleaner is a solvent specifically designed to remove all traces of oil, grease and dust from braking system components. Brake cleaner is designed to evaporate quickly and leaves behind no residue.

Carburettor cleaner is an aerosol-type solvent specifically designed to clear carburettor blockages and break down the hard deposits and gum often found inside carburettors during overhaul.

Contact cleaner is an aerosol-type solvent designed for cleaning electrical components. The cleaner will remove all traces of oil and dirt from components such as switch contacts or fouled spark plugs and then dry, leaving behind no residue.

Gasket remover is an aerosol-type solvent designed for removing stubborn gaskets from engine components during overhaul. Gasket remover will minimise the amount of scraping required to remove the gasket and therefore reduce the risk of damage to the mating surface.

Spray lubricants

● Aerosol-based spray lubricants are widely available and are excellent for lubricating lever pivots and exposed cables and switches. Try to use a lubricant which is of the dry-film type as the fluid evaporates, leaving behind a dry-film of lubricant. Lubricants which leave behind an oily residue will attract dust and dirt which will increase the rate of wear of the cable/lever.

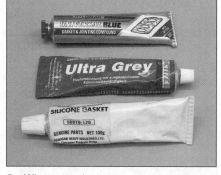

● Most lubricants also act as a moisture dispersant and a penetrating fluid. This means they can also be used to 'dry out' electrical components such as wiring connectors or switches as well as helping to free seized fasteners.

Greases

● Grease is used to lubricate many of the pivot-points. A good-quality multi-purpose grease is suitable for most applications but some manufacturers will specify the use of specialist greases for use on components such as swingarm and suspension linkage bushes. These specialist greases can be purchased from most motorcycle (or car) accessory shops; commonly specified types include molybdenum disulphide grease, lithium-based grease, graphite-based grease, silicone-based grease and high-temperature copper-based grease.

Gasket sealing compounds

● Gasket sealing compounds can be used in conjunction with gaskets, to improve their sealing capabilities, or on their own to seal metal-to-metal joints. Depending on their type, sealing compounds either set hard or stay relatively soft and pliable.

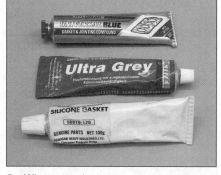

● When purchasing a gasket sealing compound, ensure that it is designed specifically for use on an internal combustion engine. General multi-purpose sealants available from DIY stores may appear visibly similar but they are not designed to withstand the extreme heat or contact with fuel and oil encountered when used on an engine (see 'Tools and Workshop Tips' for further information).

Thread locking compound

● Thread locking compounds are used to secure certain threaded fasteners in position to prevent them from loosening due to vibration. Thread locking compounds can be purchased from most motorcycle (and car) accessory shops. Ensure the threads of the both components are completely clean and dry before sparingly applying the locking compound (see 'Tools and Workshop Tips' for further information).

Fuel additives

● Fuel additives which protect and clean the fuel system components are widely available. These additives are designed to remove all traces of deposits that build up on the carburettors/injectors and prevent wear, helping the fuel system to operate more efficiently. If a fuel additive is being used, check that it is suitable for use with your motorcycle, especially if your motorcycle is equipped with a catalytic converter.

● Octane boosters are also available. These additives are designed to improve the performance of highly-tuned engines being run on normal pump-fuel and are of no real use on standard motorcycles.

Length (distance)

Inches (in)	x 25.4	= Millimetres (mm)	x 0.0394 =	Inches (in)
Feet (ft)	x 0.305	= Metres (m)	x 3.281 =	Feet (ft)
Miles	x 1.609	= Kilometres (km)	x 0.621 =	Miles

Volume (capacity)

Cubic inches (cu in; in³)	x 16.387	= Cubic centimetres (cc; cm³)	x 0.061 =	Cubic inches (cu in; in³)
Imperial pints (Imp pt)	x 0.568	= Litres (l)	x 1.76 =	Imperial pints (Imp pt)
Imperial quarts (Imp qt)	x 1.137	= Litres (l)	x 0.88 =	Imperial quarts (Imp qt)
Imperial quarts (Imp qt)	x 1.201	= US quarts (US qt)	x 0.833 =	Imperial quarts (Imp qt)
US quarts (US qt)	x 0.946	= Litres (l)	x 1.057 =	US quarts (US qt)
Imperial gallons (Imp gal)	x 4.546	= Litres (l)	x 0.22 =	Imperial gallons (Imp gal)
Imperial gallons (Imp gal)	x 1.201	= US gallons (US gal)	x 0.833 =	Imperial gallons (Imp gal)
US gallons (US gal)	x 3.785	= Litres (l)	x 0.264 =	US gallons (US gal)

Mass (weight)

Ounces (oz)	x 28.35	= Grams (g)	x 0.035 =	Ounces (oz)
Pounds (lb)	x 0.454	= Kilograms (kg)	x 2.205 =	Pounds (lb)

Force

Ounces-force (ozf; oz)	x 0.278	= Newtons (N)	x 3.6 =	Ounces-force (ozf; oz)
Pounds-force (lbf; lb)	x 4.448	= Newtons (N)	x 0.225 =	Pounds-force (lbf; lb)
Newtons (N)	x 0.1	= Kilograms-force (kgf; kg)	x 9.81 =	Newtons (N)

Pressure

Pounds-force per square inch (psi; lbf/in²; lb/in²)	x 0.070	= Kilograms-force per square centimetre (kgf/cm²; kg/cm²)	x 14.223 =	Pounds-force per square inch (psi; lbf/in²; lb/in²)
Pounds-force per square inch (psi; lbf/in²; lb/in²)	x 0.068	= Atmospheres (atm)	x 14.696 =	Pounds-force per square inch (psi; lbf/in²; lb/in²)
Pounds-force per square inch (psi; lbf/in²; lb/in²)	x 0.069	= Bars	x 14.5 =	Pounds-force per square inch (psi; lbf/in²; lb/in²)
Pounds-force per square inch (psi; lbf/in²; lb/in²)	x 6.895	= Kilopascals (kPa)	x 0.145 =	Pounds-force per square inch (psi; lbf/in²; lb/in²)
Kilopascals (kPa)	x 0.01	= Kilograms-force per square centimetre (kgf/cm²; kg/cm²)	x 98.1 =	Kilopascals (kPa)
Millibar (mbar)	x 100	= Pascals (Pa)	x 0.01 =	Millibar (mbar)
Millibar (mbar)	x 0.0145	= Pounds-force per square inch (psi; lbf/in²; lb/in²)	x 68.947 =	Millibar (mbar)
Millibar (mbar)	x 0.75	= Millimetres of mercury (mmHg)	x 1.333 =	Millibar (mbar)
Millibar (mbar)	x 0.401	= Inches of water (inH₂O)	x 2.491 =	Millibar (mbar)
Millimetres of mercury (mmHg)	x 0.535	= Inches of water (inH₂O)	x 1.868 =	Millimetres of mercury (mmHg)
Inches of water (inH₂O)	x 0.036	= Pounds-force per square inch (psi; lbf/in²; lb/in²)	x 27.68 =	Inches of water (inH₂O)

Torque (moment of force)

Pounds-force inches (lbf in; lb in)	x 1.152	= Kilograms-force centimetre (kgf cm; kg cm)	x 0.868 =	Pounds-force inches (lbf in; lb in)
Pounds-force inches (lbf in; lb in)	x 0.113	= Newton metres (Nm)	x 8.85 =	Pounds-force inches (lbf in; lb in)
Pounds-force inches (lbf in; lb in)	x 0.083	= Pounds-force feet (lbf ft; lb ft)	x 12 =	Pounds-force inches (lbf in; lb in)
Pounds-force feet (lbf ft; lb ft)	x 0.138	= Kilograms-force metres (kgf m; kg m)	x 7.233 =	Pounds-force feet (lbf ft; lb ft)
Pounds-force feet (lbf ft; lb ft)	x 1.356	= Newton metres (Nm)	x 0.738 =	Pounds-force feet (lbf ft; lb ft)
Newton metres (Nm)	x 0.102	= Kilograms-force metres (kgf m; kg m)	x 9.804 =	Newton metres (Nm)

Power

Horsepower (hp)	x 745.7	= Watts (W)	x 0.0013 =	Horsepower (hp)

Velocity (speed)

Miles per hour (miles/hr; mph)	x 1.609	= Kilometres per hour (km/hr; kph)	x 0.621 =	Miles per hour (miles/hr; mph)

Fuel consumption*

Miles per gallon (mpg)	x 0.354	= Kilometres per litre (km/l)	x 2.825 =	Miles per gallon (mpg)

Temperature

Degrees Fahrenheit = (°C x 1.8) + 32   Degrees Celsius (Degrees Centigrade; °C) = (°F - 32) x 0.56

It is common practice to convert from miles per gallon (mpg) to litres/100 kilometres (l/100km), where mpg x l/100 km = 282

About the MOT Test

In the UK, all vehicles more than three years old are subject to an annual test to ensure that they meet minimum safety requirements. A current test certificate must be issued before a machine can be used on public roads, and is required before a road fund licence can be issued. Riding without a current test certificate will also invalidate your insurance.

For most owners, the MOT test is an annual cause for anxiety, and this is largely due to owners not being sure what needs to be checked prior to submitting the motorcycle for testing. The simple answer is that a fully roadworthy motorcycle will have no difficulty in passing the test.

This is a guide to getting your motorcycle through the MOT test. Obviously it will not be possible to examine the motorcycle to the same standard as the professional MOT tester, particularly in view of the equipment required for some of the checks. However, working through the following procedures will enable you to identify any problem areas before submitting the motorcycle for the test.

It has only been possible to summarise the test requirements here, based on the regulations in force at the time of printing. Test standards are becoming increasingly stringent, although there are some exemptions for older vehicles. More information about the MOT test can be obtained from the TSO publications, *How Safe is your Motorcycle* and *The MOT Inspection Manual for Motorcycle Testing*.

Many of the checks require that one of the wheels is raised off the ground. If the motorcycle doesn't have a centre stand, note that an auxiliary stand will be required. Additionally, the help of an assistant may prove useful.

Certain exceptions apply to machines under 50 cc, machines without a lighting system, and Classic bikes - if in doubt about any of the requirements listed below seek confirmation from an MOT tester prior to submitting the motorcycle for the test.

Check that the frame number is clearly visible.

> **HAYNES HiNT** *If a component is in borderline condition, the tester has discretion in deciding whether to pass or fail it. If the motorcycle presented is clean and evidently well cared for, the tester may be more inclined to pass a borderline component than if the motorcycle is scruffy and apparently neglected.*

Electrical System

Lights, turn signals, horn and reflector

✔ With the ignition on, check the operation of the following electrical components. **Note:** *The electrical components on certain small-capacity machines are powered by the generator, requiring that the engine is run for this check.*

a) *Headlight and tail light. Check that both illuminate in the low and high beam switch positions.*

b) *Position lights. Check that the front position light (or sidelight) and tail light illuminate in this switch position.*

c) *Turn signals. Check that all flash at the correct rate, and that the warning light(s) function correctly. Check that the turn signal switch works correctly.*

d) *Hazard warning system (where fitted). Check that all four turn signals flash in this switch position.*

e) *Brake stop light. Check that the light comes on when the front and rear brakes are independently applied. Models first used on or after 1st April 1986 must have a brake light switch on each brake.*

f) *Horn. Check that the sound is continuous and of reasonable volume.*

✔ Check that there is a red reflector on the rear of the machine, either mounted separately or as part of the tail light lens.

✔ Check the condition of the headlight, tail light and turn signal lenses.

Headlight beam height

✔ The MOT tester will perform a headlight beam height check using specialised beam setting equipment **(see illustration 1)**. This equipment will not be available to the home mechanic, but if you suspect that the headlight is incorrectly set or may have been maladjusted in the past, you can perform a rough test as follows.

✔ Position the bike in a straight line facing a brick wall. The bike must be off its stand, upright and with a rider seated. Measure the height from the ground to the centre of the headlight and mark a horizontal line on the wall at this height. Position the motorcycle 3.8 metres from the wall and draw a vertical

Headlight beam height checking equipment

line up the wall central to the centreline of the motorcycle. Switch to dipped beam and check that the beam pattern falls slightly lower than the horizontal line and to the left of the vertical line **(see illustration 2)**.

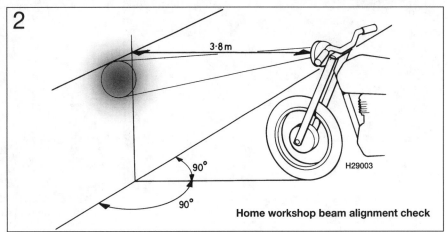

3·8 m

90°

90°

H29003

Home workshop beam alignment check

Exhaust System and Final Drive

Exhaust

✔ Check that the exhaust mountings are secure and that the system does not foul any of the rear suspension components.
✔ Start the motorcycle. When the revs are increased, check that the exhaust is neither holed nor leaking from any of its joints. On a linked system, check that the collector box is not leaking due to corrosion.

✔ Note that the exhaust decibel level ("loudness" of the exhaust) is assessed at the discretion of the tester. If the motorcycle was first used on or after 1st January 1985 the silencer must carry the BSAU 193 stamp, or a marking relating to its make and model, or be of OE (original equipment) manufacture. If the silencer is marked NOT FOR ROAD USE, RACING USE ONLY or similar, it will fail the MOT.

Final drive

✔ On chain or belt drive machines, check that the chain/belt is in good condition and does not have excessive slack. Also check that the sprocket is securely mounted on the rear wheel hub. Check that the chain/belt guard is in place.
✔ On shaft drive bikes, check for oil leaking from the drive unit and fouling the rear tyre.

Steering and Suspension

Steering

✔ With the front wheel raised off the ground, rotate the steering from lock to lock. The handlebar or switches must not contact the fuel tank or be close enough to trap the rider's hand. Problems can be caused by damaged lock stops on the lower yoke and frame, or by the fitting of non-standard handlebars.
✔ When performing the lock to lock check, also ensure that the steering moves freely without drag or notchiness. Steering movement can be impaired by poorly routed cables, or by overtight head bearings or worn bearings. The tester will perform a check of the steering head bearing lower race by mounting the front wheel on a surface plate, then performing a lock to

lock check with the weight of the machine on the lower bearing (see illustration 3).
✔ Grasp the fork sliders (lower legs) and attempt to push and pull on the forks (see

Front wheel mounted on a surface plate for steering head bearing lower race check

illustration 4). Any play in the steering head bearings will be felt. Note that in extreme cases, wear of the front fork bushes can be misinterpreted for head bearing play.
✔ Check that the handlebars are securely mounted.
✔ Check that the handlebar grip rubbers are secure. They should by bonded to the bar left end and to the throttle cable pulley on the right end.

Front suspension

✔ With the motorcycle off the stand, hold the front brake on and pump the front forks up and down (see illustration 5). Check that they are adequately damped.

Checking the steering head bearings for freeplay

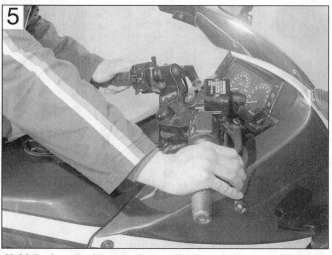

Hold the front brake on and pump the front forks up and down to check operation

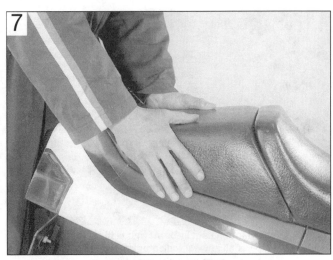

Inspect the area around the fork dust seal for oil
leakage (arrow)

Bounce the rear of the motorcycle to check rear
suspension operation

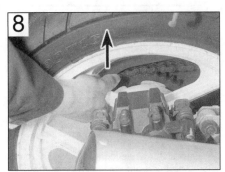

Checking for rear suspension linkage play

✔ Inspect the area above and around the
front fork oil seals **(see illustration 6)**. There
should be no sign of oil on the fork tube
(stanchion) nor leaking down the slider (lower
leg). On models so equipped, check that there
is no oil leaking from the anti-dive units.
✔ On models with swingarm front
suspension, check that there is no freeplay in
the linkage when moved from side to side.

Rear suspension

✔ With the motorcycle off the stand and an
assistant supporting the motorcycle by its
handlebars, bounce the rear suspension **(see
illustration 7)**. Check that the suspension
components do not foul on any of the cycle
parts and check that the shock absorber(s)
provide adequate damping.
✔ Visually inspect the shock absorber(s) and
check that there is no sign of oil leakage from
its damper. This is somewhat restricted on
certain single shock models due to the
location of the shock absorber.
✔ With the rear wheel raised off the
ground, grasp the wheel at the highest point
and attempt to pull it up **(see illustration 8)**.
Any play in the swingarm pivot or suspension
linkage bearings will be felt as movement.
Note: *Do not confuse play with actual
suspension movement.* Failure to lubricate
suspension linkage bearings can lead to
bearing failure **(see illustration 9)**.
✔ With the rear wheel raised off the ground,
grasp the swingarm ends and attempt to
move the swingarm from side to side and
forwards and backwards - any play indicates
wear of the swingarm pivot bearings **(see
illustration 10)**.

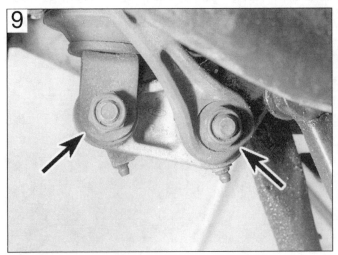

Worn suspension linkage pivots (arrows) are usually the cause of
play in the rear suspension

Grasp the swingarm at the ends to check for play in its pivot
bearings

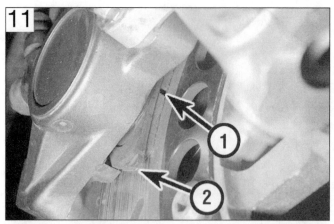

Brake pad wear can usually be viewed without removing the caliper. Most pads have wear indicator grooves (1) and some also have indicator tangs (2)

On drum brakes, check the angle of the operating lever with the brake fully applied. Most drum brakes have a wear indicator pointer and scale.

Brakes, Wheels and Tyres

Brakes

✔ With the wheel raised off the ground, apply the brake then free it off, and check that the wheel is about to revolve freely without brake drag.

✔ On disc brakes, examine the disc itself. Check that it is securely mounted and not cracked.

✔ On disc brakes, view the pad material through the caliper mouth and check that the pads are not worn down beyond the limit **(see illustration 11)**.

✔ On drum brakes, check that when the brake is applied the angle between the operating lever and cable or rod is not too great **(see illustration 12)**. Check also that the operating lever doesn't foul any other components.

✔ On disc brakes, examine the flexible hoses from top to bottom. Have an assistant hold the brake on so that the fluid in the hose is under pressure, and check that there is no sign of fluid leakage, bulges or cracking. If there are any metal brake pipes or unions, check that these are free from corrosion and damage. Where a brake-linked anti-dive system is fitted, check the hoses to the anti-dive in a similar manner.

✔ Check that the rear brake torque arm is secure and that its fasteners are secured by self-locking nuts or castellated nuts with split-pins or R-pins **(see illustration 13)**.

✔ On models with ABS, check that the self-check warning light in the instrument panel works.

✔ The MOT tester will perform a test of the motorcycle's braking efficiency based on a calculation of rider and motorcycle weight. Although this cannot be carried out at home, you can at least ensure that the braking systems are properly maintained. For hydraulic disc brakes, check the fluid level, lever/pedal feel (bleed of air if its spongy) and pad material. For drum brakes, check adjustment, cable or rod operation and shoe lining thickness.

Wheels and tyres

✔ Check the wheel condition. Cast wheels should be free from cracks and if of the built-up design, all fasteners should be secure. Spoked wheels should be checked for broken, corroded, loose or bent spokes.

✔ With the wheel raised off the ground, spin the wheel and visually check that the tyre and wheel run true. Check that the tyre does not foul the suspension or mudguards.

✔ With the wheel raised off the ground, grasp the wheel and attempt to move it about the axle (spindle) **(see illustration 14)**. Any play felt here indicates wheel bearing failure.

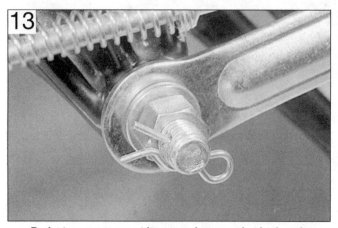

Brake torque arm must be properly secured at both ends

Check for wheel bearing play by trying to move the wheel about the axle (spindle)

Checking the tyre tread depth

Tyre direction of rotation arrow can be found on tyre sidewall

Castellated type wheel axle (spindle) nut must be secured by a split pin or R-pin

Two straightedges are used to check wheel alignment

✔ Check the tyre tread depth, tread condition and sidewall condition **(see illustration 15)**.
✔ Check the tyre type. Front and rear tyre types must be compatible and be suitable for road use. Tyres marked NOT FOR ROAD USE, COMPETITION USE ONLY or similar, will fail the MOT.

✔ If the tyre sidewall carries a direction of rotation arrow, this must be pointing in the direction of normal wheel rotation **(see illustration 16)**.
✔ Check that the wheel axle (spindle) nuts (where applicable) are properly secured. A self-locking nut or castellated nut with a split-pin or R-pin can be used **(see illustration 17)**.
✔ Wheel alignment is checked with the motorcycle off the stand and a rider seated. With the front wheel pointing straight ahead, two perfectly straight lengths of metal or wood and placed against the sidewalls of both tyres **(see illustration 18)**. The gap each side of the front tyre must be equidistant on both sides. Incorrect wheel alignment may be due to a cocked rear wheel (often as the result of poor chain adjustment) or in extreme cases, a bent frame.

General checks and condition

✔ Check the security of all major fasteners, bodypanels, seat, fairings (where fitted) and mudguards.

✔ Check that the rider and pillion footrests, handlebar levers and brake pedal are securely mounted.

✔ Check for corrosion on the frame or any load-bearing components. If severe, this may affect the structure, particularly under stress.

Sidecars

A motorcycle fitted with a sidecar requires additional checks relating to the stability of the machine and security of attachment and swivel joints, plus specific wheel alignment (toe-in) requirements. Additionally, tyre and lighting requirements differ from conventional motorcycle use. Owners are advised to check MOT test requirements with an official test centre.

Preparing for storage

Before you start

If repairs or an overhaul is needed, see that this is carried out now rather than left until you want to ride the bike again.

Give the bike a good wash and scrub all dirt from its underside. Make sure the bike dries completely before preparing for storage.

Engine

● Remove the spark plug(s) and lubricate the cylinder bores with approximately a teaspoon of motor oil using a spout-type oil can **(see illustration 1)**. Reinstall the spark plug(s). Crank the engine over a couple of times to coat the piston rings and bores with oil. If the bike has a kickstart, use this to turn the engine over. If not, flick the kill switch to the OFF position and crank the engine over on the starter **(see illustration 2)**. If the nature on the ignition system prevents the starter operating with the kill switch in the OFF position,

remove the spark plugs and fit them back in their caps; ensure that the plugs are earthed (grounded) against the cylinder head when the starter is operated **(see illustration 3)**.

 Warning: It is important that the plugs are earthed (grounded) away from the spark plug holes otherwise there is a risk of atomised fuel from the cylinders igniting.

 HAYNES HINT *On a single cylinder four-stroke engine, you can seal the combustion chamber completely by positioning the piston at TDC on the compression stroke.*

● Drain the carburettor(s) otherwise there is a risk of jets becoming blocked by gum deposits from the fuel **(see illustration 4)**.

● If the bike is going into long-term storage, consider adding a fuel stabiliser to the fuel in the tank. If the tank is drained completely, corrosion of its internal surfaces may occur if left unprotected for a long period. The tank can be treated with a rust preventative especially for this purpose. Alternatively, remove the tank and pour half a litre of motor oil into it, install the filler cap and shake the tank to coat its internals with oil before draining off the excess. The same effect can also be achieved by spraying WD40 or a similar water-dispersant around the inside of the tank via its flexible nozzle.

● Make sure the cooling system contains the correct mix of antifreeze. Antifreeze also contains important corrosion inhibitors.

● The air intakes and exhaust can be sealed off by covering or plugging the openings. Ensure that you do not seal in any condensation; run the engine until it is hot,

Squirt a drop of motor oil into each cylinder

Flick the kill switch to OFF . . .

. . . and ensure that the metal bodies of the plugs (arrows) are earthed against the cylinder head

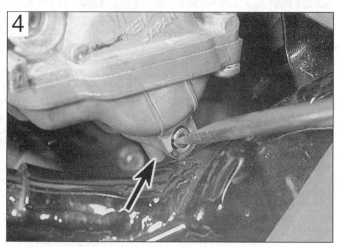

Connect a hose to the carburettor float chamber drain stub (arrow) and unscrew the drain screw

Exhausts can be sealed off with a plastic bag

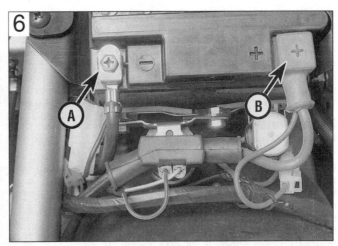

Disconnect the negative lead (A) first, followed by the positive lead (B)

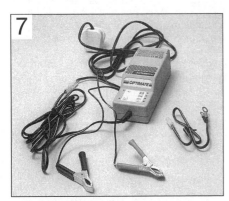

Use a suitable battery charger - this kit also assess battery condition

then switch off and allow to cool. Tape a piece of thick plastic over the silencer end(s) **(see illustration 5)**. Note that some advocate pouring a tablespoon of motor oil into the silencer(s) before sealing them off.

Battery

● Remove it from the bike - in extreme cases of cold the battery may freeze and crack its case **(see illustration 6)**.

● Check the electrolyte level and top up if necessary (conventional refillable batteries). Clean the terminals.
● Store the battery off the motorcycle and away from any sources of fire. Position a wooden block under the battery if it is to sit on the ground.
● Give the battery a trickle charge for a few hours every month **(see illustration 7)**.

Tyres

● Place the bike on its centrestand or an auxiliary stand which will support the motorcycle in an upright position. Position wood blocks under the tyres to keep them off the ground and to provide insulation from damp. If the bike is being put into long-term storage, ideally both tyres should be off the ground; not only will this protect the tyres, but will also ensure that no load is placed on the steering head or wheel bearings.
● Deflate each tyre by 5 to 10 psi, no more or the beads may unseat from the rim, making subsequent inflation difficult on tubeless tyres.

Pivots and controls

● Lubricate all lever, pedal, stand and

footrest pivot points. If grease nipples are fitted to the rear suspension components, apply lubricant to the pivots.
● Lubricate all control cables.

Cycle components

● Apply a wax protectant to all painted and plastic components. Wipe off any excess, but don't polish to a shine. Where fitted, clean the screen with soap and water.
● Coat metal parts with Vaseline (petroleum jelly). When applying this to the fork tubes, do not compress the forks otherwise the seals will rot from contact with the Vaseline.
● Apply a vinyl cleaner to the seat.

Storage conditions

● Aim to store the bike in a shed or garage which does not leak and is free from damp.
● Drape an old blanket or bedspread over the bike to protect it from dust and direct contact with sunlight (which will fade paint). This also hides the bike from prying eyes. Beware of tight-fitting plastic covers which may allow condensation to form and settle on the bike.

Getting back on the road

Engine and transmission

● Change the oil and replace the oil filter. If this was done prior to storage, check that the oil hasn't emulsified - a thick whitish substance which occurs through condensation.
● Remove the spark plugs. Using a spout-type oil can, squirt a few drops of oil into the cylinder(s). This will provide initial lubrication as the piston rings and bores comes back into contact. Service the spark plugs, or fit new ones, and install them in the engine.

● Check that the clutch isn't stuck on. The plates can stick together if left standing for some time, preventing clutch operation. Engage a gear and try rocking the bike back and forth with the clutch lever held against the handlebar. If this doesn't work on cable-operated clutches, hold the clutch lever back against the handlebar with a strong elastic band or cable tie for a couple of hours **(see illustration 8)**.
● If the air intakes or silencer end(s) were blocked off, remove the bung or cover used.
● If the fuel tank was coated with a rust

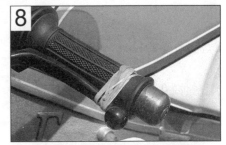

Hold clutch lever back against the handlebar with elastic bands or a cable tie

preventative, oil or a stabiliser added to the fuel, drain and flush the tank and dispose of the fuel sensibly. If no action was taken with the fuel tank prior to storage, it is advised that the old fuel is disposed of since it will go off over a period of time. Refill the fuel tank with fresh fuel.

Frame and running gear

● Oil all pivot points and cables.
● Check the tyre pressures. They will definitely need inflating if pressures were reduced for storage.
● Lubricate the final drive chain (where applicable).
● Remove any protective coating applied to the fork tubes (stanchions) since this may well destroy the fork seals. If the fork tubes weren't protected and have picked up rust spots, remove them with very fine abrasive paper and refinish with metal polish.
● Check that both brakes operate correctly. Apply each brake hard and check that it's not possible to move the motorcycle forwards, then check that the brake frees off again once released. Brake caliper pistons can stick due to corrosion around the piston head, or on the sliding caliper types, due to corrosion of the slider pins. If the brake doesn't free after repeated operation, take the caliper off for examination. Similarly drum brakes can stick

due to a seized operating cam, cable or rod linkage.
● If the motorcycle has been in long-term storage, renew the brake fluid and clutch fluid (where applicable).
● Depending on where the bike has been stored, the wiring, cables and hoses may have been nibbled by rodents. Make a visual check and investigate disturbed wiring loom tape.

Battery

● If the battery has been previously removal and given top up charges it can simply be reconnected. Remember to connect the positive cable first and the negative cable last.
● On conventional refillable batteries, if the battery has not received any attention, remove it from the motorcycle and check its electrolyte level. Top up if necessary then charge the battery. If the battery fails to hold a charge and a visual checks show heavy white sulphation of the plates, the battery is probably defective and must be renewed. This is particularly likely if the battery is old. Confirm battery condition with a specific gravity check.
● On sealed (MF) batteries, if the battery has not received any attention, remove it from the motorcycle and charge it according to the information on the battery case - if the battery fails to hold a charge it must be renewed.

Starting procedure

● If a kickstart is fitted, turn the engine over a couple of times with the ignition OFF to distribute oil around the engine. If no kickstart is fitted, flick the engine kill switch OFF and the ignition ON and crank the engine over a couple of times to work oil around the upper cylinder components. If the nature of the ignition system is such that the starter won't work with the kill switch OFF, remove the spark plugs, fit them back into their caps and earth (ground) their bodies on the cylinder head. Reinstall the spark plugs afterwards.
● Switch the kill switch to RUN, operate the choke and start the engine. If the engine won't start don't continue cranking the engine - not only will this flatten the battery, but the starter motor will overheat. Switch the ignition off and try again later. If the engine refuses to start, go through the fault finding procedures in this manual. **Note:** *If the bike has been in storage for a long time, old fuel or a carburettor blockage may be the problem. Gum deposits in carburettors can block jets - if a carburettor cleaner doesn't prove successful the carburettors must be dismantled for cleaning.*
● Once the engine has started, check that the lights, turn signals and horn work properly.
● Treat the bike gently for the first ride and check all fluid levels on completion. Settle the bike back into the maintenance schedule.

This Section provides an easy reference-guide to the more common faults that are likely to afflict your machine. Obviously, the opportunities are almost limitless for faults to occur as a result of obscure failures, and to try and cover all eventualities would require a book. Indeed, a number have been written on the subject.

Successful troubleshooting is not a mysterious 'black art' but the application of a bit of knowledge combined with a systematic and logical approach to the problem. Approach any troubleshooting by first accurately identifying the symptom and then checking through the list of possible causes, starting with the simplest or most obvious and progressing in stages to the most complex.

Take nothing for granted, but above all apply liberal quantities of common sense.

The main symptom of a fault is given in the text as a major heading below which are listed the various systems or areas which may contain the fault. Details of each possible cause for a fault and the remedial action to be taken are given, in brief, in the paragraphs below each heading. Further information should be sought in the relevant Chapter.

1 Engine doesn't start or is difficult to start

Starter motor doesn't rotate
Starter motor rotates but engine does not turn over
Starter works but engine won't turn over (seized)
No fuel flow
Engine flooded
No spark or weak spark
Compression low
Stalls after starting
Rough idle

2 Poor running at low speed

Spark weak
Fuel/air mixture incorrect
Compression low
Poor acceleration

3 Poor running or no power at high speed

Firing incorrect
Fuel/air mixture incorrect
Compression low
Knocking or pinking
Miscellaneous causes

4 Overheating

Engine overheats
Firing incorrect
Fuel/air mixture incorrect
Compression too high
Engine load excessive
Lubrication inadequate
Miscellaneous causes

5 Clutch problems

Clutch slipping
Clutch not disengaging completely

6 Gearchange problems

Doesn't go into gear, or lever doesn't return
Jumps out of gear
Overselects

7 Abnormal engine noise

Knocking or pinking
Piston slap or rattling
Valve noise
Other noise

8 Abnormal driveline noise

Clutch noise
Transmission noise
Final drive noise

9 Abnormal frame and suspension noise

Front end noise
Shock absorber noise
Brake noise

10 Oil pressure low

Engine lubrication system

11 Excessive exhaust smoke

White smoke
Black smoke
Brown smoke

12 Poor handling or stability

Handlebar hard to turn
Handlebar shakes or vibrates excessively
Handlebar pulls to one side
Poor shock absorbing qualities

13 Braking problems

Brakes are spongy, don't hold
Brake lever or pedal pulsates
Brakes drag

14 Electrical problems

Battery dead or weak
Battery overcharged

1 Engine doesn't start or is difficult to start

Starter motor doesn't rotate

- ☐ Engine kill switch OFF.
- ☐ Fuse blown. Check main fuse and ignition circuit fuse (Chapter 8).
- ☐ Battery voltage low. Check and recharge battery (Chapter 8).
- ☐ Starter motor defective. Make sure the wiring to the starter is secure. Make sure the starter relay clicks when the start button is pushed. If the relay clicks, then the fault is in the wiring or motor.
- ☐ Starter relay faulty. Check it according to the procedure in Chapter 8.
- ☐ Starter button not contacting. The contacts could be wet, corroded or dirty. Disassemble and clean the switch (Chapter 8).
- ☐ Wiring open or shorted. Check all wiring connections and harnesses to make sure that they are dry, tight and not corroded. Also check for broken or frayed wires that can cause a short to ground (earth) (see wiring diagram, Chapter 8).
- ☐ Ignition (main) switch defective. Check the switch according to the procedure in Chapter 8. Replace the switch with a new one if it is defective.
- ☐ Engine kill switch defective. Check for wet, dirty or corroded contacts. Disassemble and clean the switch (Chapter 8).
- ☐ Faulty neutral, side stand or clutch switch, or diodes. Check the wiring to each switch and the switch itself according to the procedures in Chapter 8, and check the diodes.

Starter motor rotates but engine does not turn over

- ☐ Starter clutch defective. Inspect and repair or renew (Chapter 2).
- ☐ Damaged idler or starter gears. Inspect and renew the damaged parts (Chapter 2).

Starter works but engine won't turn over (seized)

- ☐ Seized engine caused by one or more internally damaged components. Failure due to wear, abuse or lack of lubrication. Damage can include seized valves, rockers, camshafts, pistons, crankshaft, connecting rod bearings, or transmission gears or bearings. Refer to Chapter 2 for engine disassembly.

No fuel flow

- ☐ No fuel in tank.
- ☐ Fuel tank breather hose obstructed.
- ☐ Fuel tap filter clogged. Remove the tap and clean it and the filter (Chapter 3). On GSX600/750F models also check the in-line filter.
- ☐ Fuel tap vacuum hose split or detached. Check the hose.
- ☐ Fuel tap diaphragm split. Remove the tap and check the diaphragm (Chapter 3).
- ☐ Fuel line clogged. Pull the fuel line loose and carefully blow through it.
- ☐ Float needle valve clogged. For all of the valves to be clogged, either a very bad batch of fuel with an unusual additive has been used, or some other foreign material has entered the tank. Many times after a machine has been stored for many months without running, the fuel turns to a varnish-like liquid and forms deposits on the inlet needle valves and jets. The carburettors should be removed and overhauled if draining the float chambers doesn't solve the problem.

Engine flooded

- ☐ Float height too high. Check as described in Chapter 3.
- ☐ Float needle valve worn or stuck open. A piece of dirt, rust or other debris can cause the valve to seat improperly, causing excess fuel to be admitted to the float chamber. In this case, the float chamber should be cleaned and the needle valve and seat inspected. If the needle and seat are worn, then the leaking will persist and the parts should be replaced with new ones (Chapter 3).
- ☐ Starting technique incorrect. Under normal circumstances (i.e., if all the carburettor functions are sound) the machine should start with little or no throttle. When the engine is cold, the choke should be operated and the engine started without opening the throttle. When the engine is at operating temperature, only a very slight amount of throttle should be necessary. If the engine is flooded, disconnect the vacuum hose (see Chapter 3) and hold the throttle open while cranking the engine. This will allow additional air to reach the cylinders. Remember to reconnect the vacuum hose.

No spark or weak spark

- ☐ Ignition switch OFF.
- ☐ Engine kill switch turned to the OFF position.
- ☐ Battery voltage low. Check and recharge the battery as necessary (Chapter 8).
- ☐ Spark plugs dirty, defective or worn out. Locate reason for fouled plugs using spark plug condition chart and follow the plug maintenance procedures (Chapter 1).
- ☐ Spark plug caps or secondary (HT) wiring faulty. Check condition. Renew either or both components if cracks or deterioration are evident (Chapter 4).
- ☐ Spark plug caps not making good contact. Make sure that the plug caps fit snugly over the plug ends.
- ☐ Ignition control unit defective. Check the unit (Chapter 4).
- ☐ Pulse generator coil defective. Check the unit (Chapter 4).
- ☐ Ignition HT coils defective. Check the coils (Chapter 4).
- ☐ Ignition or kill switch shorted. This is usually caused by water, corrosion, damage or excessive wear. The switches can be disassembled and cleaned with electrical contact cleaner. If cleaning does not help, renew the switches (Chapter 8).
- ☐ Wiring shorted or broken between:
  - a) Ignition (main) switch and engine kill switch (or blown ignition fuse)
  - b) Ignition control unit and engine kill switch
  - c) Ignition control unit and ignition HT coils
  - d) Ignition HT coils and spark plugs
  - e) Ignition control unit and pulse generator coil
- ☐ Make sure that all wiring connections are clean, dry and tight. Look for chafed and broken wires (Chapters 4 and 8).

Compression low

- ☐ Spark plugs loose. Remove the plugs and inspect their threads. Reinstall and tighten to the specified torque (Chapter 1).
- ☐ Cylinder head not sufficiently tightened down. If the cylinder head is suspected of being loose, then there's a chance that the gasket or head is damaged if the problem has persisted for any length of time. The head nuts should be tightened to the proper torque in the correct sequence (Chapter 2).
- ☐ Improper valve clearance. This means that the valve is not closing completely and compression pressure is leaking past the valve. Check and adjust the valve clearances (Chapter 1).
- ☐ Cylinder and/or piston worn. Excessive wear will cause compression pressure to leak past the rings. This is usually accompanied by worn rings as well. A top-end overhaul is necessary (Chapter 2).
- ☐ Piston rings worn, weak, broken, or sticking. Broken or sticking piston rings usually indicate a lubrication or carburation problem that causes excess carbon deposits or seizures to form on the pistons and rings. Top-end overhaul is necessary (Chapter 2).
- ☐ Piston ring-to-groove clearance excessive. This is caused by excessive wear of the piston ring lands. Piston renewal is necessary (Chapter 2).
- ☐ Cylinder head gasket damaged. If the head is allowed to become loose, or if excessive carbon build-up on the piston crown and combustion chamber causes extremely high compression, the head gasket may leak. Re-torquing the head is not always sufficient to restore the seal, so gasket renewal is necessary (Chapter 2).

1 Engine doesn't start or is difficult to start (continued)

- ☐ Cylinder head warped. This is caused by overheating or improperly tightened head nuts. Machine shop resurfacing or head renewal is necessary (Chapter 2).
- ☐ Valve spring broken or weak. Caused by component failure or wear; the springs must be renewed (Chapter 2).
- ☐ Valve not seating properly. This is caused by a bent valve (from over-revving or improper valve adjustment), burned valve or seat (improper carburation) or an accumulation of carbon deposits on the seat (from carburation or lubrication problems). The valves must be cleaned and/or renewed and the seats serviced if possible (Chapter 2).

Stalls after starting

- ☐ Improper choke action. Make sure the choke linkage shaft is getting a full stroke and staying in the out position (Chapter 3).
- ☐ Ignition malfunction (Chapter 4).
- ☐ Carburettor malfunction (Chapter 3).
- ☐ Fuel contaminated. The fuel can be contaminated with either dirt or water, or can change chemically if the machine is allowed to sit for several months or more. Drain the tank and float chambers (Chapter 3).

- ☐ Intake air leak. Check for loose carburettor-to-intake manifold connections, loose or missing vacuum gauge adapter screws or hoses, or loose carburettor tops (Chapter 3).
- ☐ Engine idle speed incorrect. Turn idle adjusting screw until the engine idles at the specified rpm (Chapter 1).

Rough idle

- ☐ Ignition malfunction (Chapter 4).
- ☐ Idle speed incorrect (Chapter 1).
- ☐ Carburettors not synchronised. Adjust carburettors with vacuum gauge or manometer set as described in Chapter 1.
- ☐ Carburettor malfunction (Chapter 3).
- ☐ Fuel contaminated. The fuel can be contaminated with either dirt or water, or can change chemically if the machine is allowed to sit for several months or more. Drain the tank and float chambers (Chapter 3).
- ☐ Intake air leak. Check for loose carburettor-to-intake manifold connections, loose or missing vacuum gauge adapter screws or hoses, or loose carburettor tops (Chapter 3).
- ☐ Air filter clogged. Clean the air filter element or replace it with a new one (Chapter 1).

2 Poor running at low speeds

Spark weak

- ☐ Battery voltage low. Check and recharge battery (Chapter 8).
- ☐ Spark plugs fouled, defective or worn out. Refer to Chapter 1 for spark plug maintenance.
- ☐ Spark plug cap or HT wiring defective. Refer to Chapters 1 and 4 for details on the ignition system.
- ☐ Spark plug caps not making contact. Make sure they are securely pushed on to the plugs.
- ☐ Incorrect spark plugs. Wrong type, heat range or cap configuration. Check and install correct plugs listed in Chapter 1.
- ☐ Ignition control unit defective (Chapter 4).
- ☐ Pulse generator coil defective (Chapter 4).
- ☐ Ignition HT coils defective (Chapter 4).

Fuel/air mixture incorrect

- ☐ Pilot screws out of adjustment (Chapter 3).
- ☐ Pilot jet or air passage clogged, or incorrect pilot jet size. Remove and overhaul the carburettors (Chapter 3).
- ☐ Incorrect jet needle, or needle set too high or low (see Chapter 3).
- ☐ Air bleed holes clogged. Remove carburettor and blow out all passages (Chapter 3).
- ☐ Air filter clogged, poorly sealed or missing (Chapter 1).
- ☐ Air filter housing poorly sealed. Look for cracks, holes or loose clamps and renew or repair defective parts.
- ☐ Fuel level too high or too low. Check the level or float height (Chapter 3).
- ☐ Fuel tank breather hose obstructed.
- ☐ Carburettor intake manifolds loose. Check for cracks, breaks, tears or loose clamps. Renew the rubber intake manifold joints if split or perished.

Compression low

- ☐ Spark plugs loose. Remove the plugs and inspect their threads. Reinstall and tighten to the specified torque (Chapter 1).
- ☐ Cylinder head not sufficiently tightened down. If the cylinder head is suspected of being loose, then there's a chance that the gasket and head are damaged if the problem has persisted for any length of time. The head nuts should be tightened to the proper torque in the correct sequence (Chapter 2).
- ☐ Improper valve clearance. This means that the valve is not closing completely and compression pressure is leaking past the valve. Check and adjust the valve clearances (Chapter 1).

- ☐ Cylinder and/or piston worn. Excessive wear will cause compression pressure to leak past the rings. This is usually accompanied by worn rings as well. A top end overhaul is necessary (Chapter 2).
- ☐ Piston rings worn, weak, broken, or sticking. Broken or sticking piston rings usually indicate a lubrication or carburation problem that causes excess carbon deposits or seizures to form on the pistons and rings. Top-end overhaul is necessary (Chapter 2).
- ☐ Piston ring-to-groove clearance excessive. This is caused by excessive wear of the piston ring lands. Piston renewal is necessary (Chapter 2).
- ☐ Cylinder head gasket damaged. If the head is allowed to become loose, or if excessive carbon build-up on the piston crown and combustion chamber causes extremely high compression, the head gasket may leak. Retorquing the head is not always sufficient to restore the seal, so gasket renewal is necessary (Chapter 2).
- ☐ Cylinder head warped. This is caused by overheating or improperly tightened head nuts. Machine shop resurfacing or head renewal is necessary (Chapter 2).
- ☐ Valve spring broken or weak. Caused by component failure or wear; the springs must be renewed (Chapter 2).
- ☐ Valve not seating properly. This is caused by a bent valve (from over-revving or improper valve adjustment), burned valve or seat (improper carburation) or an accumulation of carbon deposits on the seat (from carburation, lubrication problems). The valves must be cleaned and/or renewed and the seats serviced if possible (Chapter 2).

Poor acceleration

- ☐ Carburettors leaking or dirty. Overhaul the carburettors (Chapter 3).
- ☐ Timing not advancing. The pulse generator coil or the ignition control unit may be defective. If so, they must be replaced with new ones, as they can't be repaired.
- ☐ Carburettors not synchronised. Adjust them with a vacuum gauge set or manometer (Chapter 1).
- ☐ Engine oil viscosity too high. Using a heavier oil than that recommended in Chapter 1 can damage the oil pump or lubrication system and cause drag on the engine.
- ☐ Brakes dragging. Usually caused by debris which has entered the brake piston seals, or from a warped disc or bent axle. Repair as necessary (Chapter 6).
- ☐ Fuel flow rate insufficient. Check the filter(s) (Chapter 1).

3 Poor running or no power at high speed

Firing incorrect

- [ ] Air filter restricted. Clean or renew filter (Chapter 1).
- [ ] Spark plugs fouled, defective or worn out. See Chapter 1 for spark plug maintenance.
- [ ] Spark plug caps or HT wiring defective. See Chapters 1 and 4 for details of the ignition system.
- [ ] Spark plug caps not in good contact (Chapter 4).
- [ ] Incorrect spark plugs. Wrong type, heat range or cap configuration. Check and install correct plugs listed in Chapter 1.
- [ ] Ignition control unit defective (Chapter 4).
- [ ] Ignition HT coils defective (Chapter 4).

Fuel/air mixture incorrect

- [ ] Incorrect jet needle, or needle set too high or low (see Chapter 3).
- [ ] Main jet clogged. Dirt, water or other contaminants can clog the main jets. Clean the fuel tap filter, the in-line filter (GSX600/750F models), the float chamber area, and the jets and carburettor orifices (Chapter 3).
- [ ] Main jet wrong size. The standard jetting is for sea level atmospheric pressure and oxygen content.
- [ ] Throttle shaft-to-carburettor body clearance excessive. Refer to Chapter 3 for inspection and part renewal procedures.
- [ ] Air bleed holes clogged. Remove and overhaul carburettors (Chapter 3).
- [ ] Air filter clogged, poorly sealed, or missing (Chapter 1).
- [ ] Air filter housing poorly sealed. Look for cracks, holes or loose clamps, and renew or repair defective parts.
- [ ] Fuel level too high or too low. Check the level or float height (Chapter 3).
- [ ] Fuel tank breather hose obstructed.
- [ ] Carburettor intake manifolds loose. Check for cracks, breaks, tears or loose clamps. Renew the rubber intake manifolds if they are split or perished (Chapter 3).

Compression low

- [ ] Spark plugs loose. Remove the plugs and inspect their threads. Reinstall and tighten to the specified torque (Chapter 1).
- [ ] Cylinder head not sufficiently tightened down. If the cylinder head is suspected of being loose, then there's a chance that the gasket and head are damaged if the problem has persisted for any length of time. The head nuts should be tightened to the proper torque in the correct sequence (Chapter 2).
- [ ] Improper valve clearance. This means that the valve is not closing completely and compression pressure is leaking past the valve. Check and adjust the valve clearances (Chapter 1).
- [ ] Cylinder and/or piston worn. Excessive wear will cause compression pressure to leak past the rings. This is usually accompanied by worn rings as well. A top-end overhaul is necessary (Chapter 2).
- [ ] Piston rings worn, weak, broken, or sticking. Broken or sticking piston rings usually indicate a lubrication or carburation problem that causes excess carbon deposits or seizures to form on the pistons and rings. Top-end overhaul is necessary (Chapter 2).

- [ ] Piston ring-to-groove clearance excessive. This is caused by excessive wear of the piston ring lands. Piston renewal is necessary (Chapter 2).
- [ ] Cylinder head gasket damaged. If the head is allowed to become loose, or if excessive carbon build-up on the piston crown and combustion chamber causes extremely high compression, the head gasket may leak. Retorquing the head is not always sufficient to restore the seal, so gasket renewal is necessary (Chapter 2).
- [ ] Cylinder head warped. This is caused by overheating or improperly tightened head nuts. Machine shop resurfacing or head renewal is necessary (Chapter 2).
- [ ] Valve spring broken or weak. Caused by component failure or wear; the springs must be renewed (Chapter 2).
- [ ] Valve not seating properly. This is caused by a bent valve (from over-revving or improper valve adjustment), burned valve or seat (improper carburation) or an accumulation of carbon deposits on the seat (from carburation or lubrication problems). The valves must be cleaned and/or renewed and the seats serviced if possible (Chapter 2).

Knocking or pinking

- [ ] Carbon build-up in combustion chamber. Use of a fuel additive that will dissolve the adhesive bonding the carbon particles to the crown and chamber is the easiest way to remove the build-up. Otherwise, the cylinder head will have to be removed and decarbonised (Chapter 2).
- [ ] Incorrect or poor quality fuel. Old or improper grades of fuel can cause detonation. This causes the piston to rattle, thus the knocking or pinking sound. Drain old fuel and always use the recommended fuel grade.
- [ ] Spark plug heat range incorrect. Uncontrolled detonation indicates the plug heat range is too hot. The plug in effect becomes a glow plug, raising cylinder temperatures. Install the proper heat range plug (Chapter 1).
- [ ] Improper air/fuel mixture. This will cause the cylinders to run hot, which leads to detonation. Clogged jets or an air leak can cause this imbalance. See Chapter 3.

Miscellaneous causes

- [ ] Throttle valve doesn't open fully. Adjust the throttle grip freeplay (Chapter 1).
- [ ] Clutch slipping. May be caused by loose or worn clutch components. Refer to Chapter 2 for clutch overhaul procedures. Also check the cable and release mechanism adjustment (Chapter 1).
- [ ] Timing not advancing.
- [ ] Engine oil viscosity too high. Using a heavier oil than the one recommended in Chapter 1 can damage the oil pump or lubrication system and cause drag on the engine.
- [ ] Brakes dragging. Usually caused by debris which has entered the brake piston seals, or from a warped disc or bent axle. Repair as necessary.
- [ ] Fuel flow rate insufficient. Check the filter(s) (Chapter 1).

4 Overheating

Firing incorrect

☐ Spark plugs fouled, defective or worn out. See Chapter 1 for spark plug maintenance.
☐ Incorrect spark plugs.
☐ Ignition control unit defective (Chapter 4).
☐ Faulty ignition HT coils (Chapter 4).

Fuel/air mixture incorrect

☐ Incorrect jet needle, or needle set too low (see Chapter 3).
☐ Main jet clogged. Dirt, water and other contaminants can clog the main jets. Clean the fuel tap filter, the in-line filter (GSX600/750F models), the float chamber area and the jets and carburettor orifices (Chapter 3).
☐ Main jet wrong size. The standard jetting is for sea level atmospheric pressure and oxygen content.
☐ Air filter clogged, poorly sealed or missing (Chapter 1).
☐ Air filter housing poorly sealed. Look for cracks, holes or loose clamps and renew or repair.
☐ Fuel level too low. Check the level (Chapter 3).
☐ Fuel tank breather hose obstructed.
☐ Carburettor intake manifolds loose. Check for cracks, breaks, tears or loose clamps. Renew the rubber intake manifold joints if split or perished.

Compression too high

☐ Carbon build-up in combustion chamber. Use of a fuel additive that will dissolve the adhesive bonding the carbon particles to the piston crown and chamber is the easiest way to remove the build-up. Otherwise, the cylinder head will have to be removed and decarbonised (Chapter 2).
☐ Improperly machined head surface or installation of incorrect gasket during engine assembly.

Engine load excessive

☐ Clutch slipping. Can be caused by damaged, loose or worn clutch components. Refer to Chapter 2 for overhaul procedures. Also check the cable and release mechanism adjustment (Chapter 1).
☐ Engine oil level too high. The addition of too much oil will cause pressurisation of the crankcase and inefficient engine operation. Check Specifications and drain to proper level (Daily (pre-ride) checks).
☐ Engine oil viscosity too high. Using a heavier oil than the one recommended in Chapter 1 can damage the oil pump or lubrication system as well as cause drag on the engine.
☐ Brakes dragging. Usually caused by debris which has entered the brake piston seals, or from a warped disc or bent axle. Repair as necessary.

Lubrication inadequate

☐ Engine oil level too low. Friction caused by intermittent lack of lubrication or from oil that is overworked can cause overheating. The oil provides a definite cooling function in the engine. Check the oil level (Daily (pre-ride) checks).
☐ Poor quality engine oil or incorrect viscosity or type. Oil is rated not only according to viscosity but also according to type. Some oils are not rated high enough for use in this engine. Check the Specifications section and change to the correct oil (Daily (pre-ride) checks).

Miscellaneous causes

☐ Modification to exhaust system. Most aftermarket exhaust systems cause the engine to run leaner, which make them run hotter. When installing an accessory exhaust system, always rejet the carburettors.

5 Clutch problems

Clutch slipping

☐ Clutch cable or release mechanism incorrectly adjusted (see Chapter 1).
☐ Friction plates worn or warped. Overhaul the clutch assembly (Chapter 2).
☐ Plain plates warped (Chapter 2).
☐ Clutch springs broken or weak. Old or heat-damaged (from slipping clutch) springs should be replaced with new ones (Chapter 2).
☐ Clutch release mechanism defective. Replace any defective parts (Chapter 2).
☐ Clutch centre or housing unevenly worn. This causes improper engagement of the plates. Replace the damaged or worn parts (Chapter 2).

Clutch not disengaging completely

☐ Clutch cable or release mechanism incorrectly adjusted (see Chapter 1) or faulty. The inner cable could be seizing in outer cable, caused by dirt, kinks or incorrect routing. Check the cable and renew if necessary (see Chapter 2).

☐ Clutch plates warped or damaged. This will cause clutch drag, which in turn will cause the machine to creep. Overhaul the clutch assembly (Chapter 2).
☐ Clutch spring tension uneven. Usually caused by a sagged or broken spring. Check and replace the springs as a set (Chapter 2).
☐ Engine oil deteriorated. Old, thin, worn out oil will not provide proper lubrication for the plates, causing the clutch to drag. Replace the oil and filter (Chapter 1).
☐ Engine oil viscosity too high. Using a heavier oil than recommended in Chapter 1 can cause the plates to stick together, putting a drag on the engine. Change to the correct weight oil (Chapter 1).
☐ Clutch needle roller bearing and spacer seized on input shaft. Lack of lubrication, severe wear or damage can cause the guide to seize on the shaft. Overhaul of the clutch, and perhaps transmission, may be necessary to repair the damage (Chapter 2).
☐ Clutch release mechanism defective. Overhaul the components in the clutch cover (Chapter 2).
☐ Loose clutch centre nut. Causes housing and centre misalignment putting a drag on the engine. Engagement adjustment continually varies. Overhaul the clutch assembly (Chapter 2).

6 Gearchange problems

Doesn't go into gear or lever doesn't return

- ☐ Clutch not disengaging. See above.
- ☐ Selector fork(s) bent or seized. Often caused by dropping the machine or from lack of lubrication. Overhaul the transmission (Chapter 2).
- ☐ Gear(s) stuck on shaft. Most often caused by a lack of lubrication or excessive wear in transmission bearings and bushes. Overhaul the transmission (Chapter 2).
- ☐ Selector drum binding. Caused by lubrication failure or excessive wear. Renew the drum and bearing (Chapter 2).
- ☐ Gearchange shaft centralising spring weak or broken (Chapter 2).
- ☐ Gearchange lever or linkage broken. Splines stripped out of lever or shaft, caused by allowing the lever to get loose or from dropping the machine. Renew necessary parts (Chapter 2).
- ☐ Worn pawl mechanism (Chapter 2).

Jumps out of gear

- ☐ Selector fork(s) worn. Overhaul the transmission (Chapter 2).
- ☐ Gear groove(s) worn. Overhaul the transmission (Chapter 2).
- ☐ Gear dogs or dog slots worn or damaged. The gears should be inspected and renewed. No attempt should be made to service the worn parts.
- ☐ Worn pawl mechanism, pawl lifter plate or holder guide plate (Chapter 2).

Overselects

- ☐ Worn pawl mechanism, pawl lifter plate or holder guide plate (Chapter 2).
- ☐ Gearchange shaft centralising spring locating pin broken or distorted (Chapter 2).

7 Abnormal engine noise

Knocking or pinking

- ☐ Carbon build-up in combustion chamber. Use of a fuel additive that will dissolve the adhesive bonding the carbon particles to the piston crown and chamber is the easiest way to remove the build-up. Otherwise, the cylinder head will have to be removed and decarbonised (Chapter 2).
- ☐ Incorrect or poor quality fuel. Old or improper fuel can cause detonation. This causes the pistons to rattle, thus the knocking or pinking sound. Drain the old fuel and always use the recommended grade fuel (Chapter 3).
- ☐ Spark plug heat range incorrect. Uncontrolled detonation indicates that the plug heat range is too hot. The plug in effect becomes a glow plug, raising cylinder temperatures. Install the proper heat range plugs (Chapter 1).
- ☐ Improper air/fuel mixture. This will cause the cylinders to run hot and lead to detonation. Clogged jets or an air leak can cause this imbalance. See Chapter 3.

Piston slap or rattling

- ☐ Cylinder-to-piston clearance excessive. Caused by improper assembly. Inspect and overhaul top-end parts (Chapter 2).
- ☐ Connecting rod bent. Caused by over-revving, trying to start a badly flooded engine or from ingesting a foreign object into the combustion chamber. Renew the damaged parts (Chapter 2).
- ☐ Piston pin or piston pin bore worn or seized from wear or lack of lubrication. Renew damaged parts (Chapter 2).
- ☐ Piston ring(s) worn, broken or sticking. Overhaul the top-end (Chapter 2).
- ☐ Piston seizure damage. Usually from lack of lubrication or overheating. Fit oversize pistons and rebore the cylinder block (Chapter 2).

- ☐ Connecting rod upper or lower end clearance excessive. Caused by excessive wear or lack of lubrication. Renew worn parts with new ones.

Valve noise

- ☐ Incorrect valve clearances. Adjust the clearances by referring to Chapter 1.
- ☐ Valve spring broken or weak. Check and renew weak valve springs (Chapter 2).
- ☐ Rocker arms or shafts worn, or thrust spring broken. Check and renew (Chapter 2).
- ☐ Camshafts or cylinder head worn or damaged. Lack of lubrication at high rpm is usually the cause of damage. Insufficient oil or failure to change the oil at the recommended intervals are the chief causes. Since there are no renewable bearings in the head, the head itself will have to be renewed if there is excessive wear or damage (Chapter 2).

Other noise

- ☐ Cylinder head gasket leaking.
- ☐ Exhaust pipe leaking at cylinder head connection. Caused by improper fit of pipe(s) or loose exhaust flange. All exhaust fasteners should be tightened evenly and carefully. Failure to do this will lead to a leak.
- ☐ Crankshaft runout excessive. Caused by a bent crankshaft (from over-revving) or damage from an upper cylinder component failure.
- ☐ Engine mounting bolts or frame cradle bolts loose, or damping rubbers worn. Inspect the damping rubbers and tighten all engine and frame mounting bolts (Chapter 2).
- ☐ Crankshaft bearings worn (Chapter 2).
- ☐ Cam chain worn or tensioner faulty. Check according to the procedure in Chapter 2.

8 Abnormal driveline noise

Clutch noise

☐ Clutch outer drum/friction plate clearance excessive (Chapter 2).
☐ Loose or damaged clutch pressure plate and/or bolts (Chapter 2).

Transmission noise

☐ Bearings worn. Also includes the possibility that the shafts are worn. Overhaul the transmission (Chapter 2).
☐ Gears worn or chipped (Chapter 2).
☐ Metal chips jammed in gear teeth. Probably pieces from a broken clutch, gear or selector mechanism that were picked up by the gears. This will cause early bearing failure (Chapter 2).

☐ Engine oil level too low. Causes a howl from transmission. Also affects engine power and clutch operation (Daily (pre-ride) checks).

Final drive noise

☐ Chain not adjusted properly (Chapter 1).
☐ Front or rear sprocket loose. Tighten fasteners (Chapter 5).
☐ Sprockets worn. Renew sprockets (Chapter 5).
☐ Rear sprocket warped. Renew sprockets (Chapter 5).
☐ Loose or worn rear wheel or sprocket coupling bearings. Check and renew as needed (Chapter 6).

9 Abnormal frame and suspension noise

Front end noise

☐ Low fork oil level or improper viscosity oil. This can sound like spurting and is usually accompanied by irregular fork action (Chapter 5).
☐ Spring weak or broken. Makes a clicking or scraping sound. Fork oil, when drained, will have a lot of metal particles in it (Chapter 5).
☐ Steering head bearings loose or damaged. Clicks when braking. Check and adjust or renew as necessary (Chapters 1 and 5).
☐ Fork yokes loose. Make sure all clamp bolts are tightened to the specified torque (Chapter 5).
☐ Fork tube bent. Good possibility if machine has been dropped. Renew the tubes in both fork legs (Chapter 5).
☐ Front axle bolt or axle clamp bolt loose. Tighten them to the specified torque (Chapter 6).
☐ Loose or worn wheel bearings. Check and renew as needed (Chapter 6).

Shock absorber noise

☐ Fluid level incorrect. Indicates a leak caused by defective seal. Shock will be covered with oil. Renew shock or seek advice on repair from a Suzuki dealer or suspension specialist (Chapter 5).
☐ Defective shock absorber with internal damage. This is in the body of the shock and can't be remedied. The shock must be renewed (Chapter 5).
☐ Bent or damaged shock body. Renew the shock (Chapter 5). On GSX750 models the shocks must be renewed as a pair.

☐ Loose or worn suspension linkage components (GSX600/750F models). Check and renew as necessary (Chapter 6).
☐ Loose or worn suspension mounts. Check and tighten as necessary (Chapter 5).

Brake noise

☐ Squeal caused by pad shim not installed or positioned correctly (rear pads only) (Chapter 6).
☐ Squeal caused by dust on brake pads. Usually found in combination with glazed pads. Clean using brake cleaning solvent (Chapter 6).
☐ Contamination of brake pads. Oil, brake fluid or dirt causing brake to chatter or squeal. Clean or renew pads (Chapter 6).
☐ Pads glazed. Caused by excessive heat from prolonged use or from contamination. Do not use sandpaper, emery cloth, carborundum cloth or any other abrasive to roughen the pad surfaces as abrasives will stay in the pad material and damage the disc. A very fine flat file can be used, but pad renewal is suggested as a cure (Chapter 6).
☐ Disc warped. Can cause a chattering, clicking or intermittent squeal. Usually accompanied by a pulsating lever/pedal and uneven braking. Renew the disc (Chapter 6). In the case of the front discs always renew the discs as a pair.
☐ Loose caliper mounting bolts – tighten them to the specified torque setting (Chapter 6).
☐ Loose or worn wheel bearings. Check and renew as needed (Chapter 6).

10 Oil pressure low

Engine lubrication system

☐ Engine oil level low. Inspect for leak or other problem causing low oil level and add recommended oil (Daily (pre-ride) checks).
☐ Engine oil viscosity too low. Very old, thin oil or an improper weight of oil used in the engine. Change to correct oil (Chapter 1).
☐ Engine oil pump defective, blocked oil strainer gauze or failed pressure relief valve. Carry out oil pressure check (Chapter 1).

☐ Camshaft or journals worn. Excessive wear causing drop in oil pressure. Renew camshafts and/or cylinder head. Abnormal wear could be caused by oil starvation at high rpm from low oil level or improper weight or type of oil (Chapter 1).
☐ Crankshaft and/or bearings worn. Same problems as above. Check and renew crankshaft and/or bearings (Chapter 2).

11 Excessive exhaust smoke

White smoke

☐ Piston oil ring worn. The ring may be broken or damaged, causing oil from the crankcase to be pulled past the piston into the combustion chamber. Renew the rings (Chapter 2).

☐ Cylinders worn, cracked, or scored. Caused by overheating or oil starvation. Check the cylinder block and lubrication system (see Chapter 2).

☐ Valve oil seal damaged or worn. Renew the oil seals on all valves (Chapter 2).

☐ Valve guide worn. Perform a complete valve job (Chapter 2).

☐ Engine oil level too high, which causes the oil to be forced past the rings. Drain oil to the proper level (Daily (pre-ride) checks).

☐ Head gasket broken between oil return and cylinder. Causes oil to be pulled into the combustion chamber. Renew the head gasket and check the head for warpage (Chapter 2).

☐ Abnormal crankcase pressurisation, which forces oil past the rings. Clogged breather is usually the cause.

Black smoke

☐ Air filter clogged. Clean or renew the element (Chapter 1).

☐ Incorrect jet needle, or needle set too high (see Chapter 3).

☐ Main jet too large or loose. Compare the jet size to the Specifications (Chapter 3).

☐ Choke cable or linkage shaft stuck, causing fuel to be pulled through choke circuit (Chapter 3).

☐ Fuel level too high. Check and adjust the float height(s) as necessary (Chapter 3).

☐ Float needle valve held off needle seat. Clean the float chambers and fuel line and renew the needles and seats if necessary (Chapter 3).

Brown smoke

☐ Incorrect jet needle, or needle set too low (see Chapter 3).

☐ Main jet too small or clogged. Lean condition caused by wrong size main jet or by a restricted orifice. Clean float chambers and jets and compare jet size to Specifications (Chapter 3).

☐ Fuel flow insufficient – float needle valve stuck closed due to chemical reaction with old fuel; fuel level incorrect; restricted fuel line, blocked filter (Chapters 1 and 3).

☐ Carburettor intake manifold clamps loose (Chapter 3).

☐ Air filter poorly sealed or not installed (Chapter 1).

12 Poor handling or stability

Handlebar hard to turn

☐ Steering head bearing adjuster nut too tight. Check adjustment as described in Chapter 1.

☐ Bearings damaged. Roughness can be felt as the bars are turned from side-to-side. Renew bearings and races (Chapter 5).

☐ Races dented or worn. Denting results from wear in only one position (e.g., straight ahead), from a collision or hitting a pothole or from dropping the machine. Renew races and bearings (Chapter 5)

☐ Steering stem lubrication inadequate. Causes are grease getting hard from age or being washed out by high pressure jet washes. Disassemble steering head and repack bearings (Chapter 5).

☐ Steering stem bent. Caused by a collision, hitting a pothole or by dropping the machine. Renew damaged part. Don't try to straighten the steering stem (Chapter 5).

☐ Front tyre air pressure too low (Daily (pre-ride) checks).

Handlebar shakes or vibrates excessively

☐ Tyres worn or out of balance (Chapter 6).

☐ Swingarm bearings worn. Renew worn bearings (Chapter 5).

☐ Wheel rim(s) warped or damaged. Inspect wheels for runout (Chapter 6).

☐ Wheel bearings worn. Worn front or rear wheel bearings can cause poor tracking. Worn front bearings will cause wobble (Chapter 6).

☐ Handlebar clamp bolts loose (Chapter 5).

☐ Fork yoke bolts loose. Tighten them to the specified torque (Chapter 5).

☐ Engine mounting bolts loose or rubber dampers in front mountings worn. Will cause excessive vibration with increased engine rpm (Chapter 2).

Handlebar pulls to one side

☐ Frame bent. Definitely suspect this if the machine has been dropped. May or may not be accompanied by cracking near the bend. Renew the frame (Chapter 5).

☐ Wheels out of alignment. Caused by incorrect alignment of rear wheel during chain adjustment, improper location of axle spacers or from bent steering stem or frame (Chapter 6).

☐ Swingarm bent or twisted. Caused by age (metal fatigue) or impact damage. Renew the arm (Chapter 5).

☐ Steering stem bent. Caused by impact damage or by dropping the motorcycle. Renew the steering stem (Chapter 5).

☐ Fork tube bent. Disassemble the forks and renew the damaged parts (Chapter 5). Always renew the fork tubes as a pair.

☐ Fork oil level uneven. Check and add or drain as necessary (Chapter 5).

Poor shock absorbing qualities

☐ Too hard:
  a) *Fork oil level excessive (Chapter 5).*
  b) *Fork oil viscosity too high. Use a lighter oil (see the Specifications in Chapter 5).*
  c) *Fork tube bent. Causes a harsh, sticking feeling (Chapter 5).*
  d) *Fork internal damage (Chapter 5).*
  e) *Shock shaft or body bent or damaged (Chapter 5).*
  f) *Shock internal damage.*
  g) *Tyre pressure too high (Daily (pre-ride) checks).*

Too soft:
  a) *Fork or shock oil insufficient and/or leaking (Chapter 5).*
  b) *Fork oil level too low (Chapter 5).*
  c) *Fork oil viscosity too light (Chapter 5).*
  d) *Fork springs weak or broken (Chapter 5).*
  e) *Shock internal damage or leakage (Chapter 5).*

13 Braking problems

Brakes are spongy, don't hold

- [ ] Air in brake line. Caused by inattention to master cylinder fluid level or by leakage. Locate problem and bleed brakes (Chapter 6).
- [ ] Pad or disc worn (Chapters 1 and 6).
- [ ] Brake fluid leak. See paragraph 1.
- [ ] Contaminated pads. Caused by contamination with oil, grease, brake fluid, etc. Renew pads. Clean disc thoroughly with brake cleaner (Chapter 6).
- [ ] Brake fluid deteriorated. Fluid is old or contaminated. Drain system, replenish with new fluid and bleed the system (Chapter 6).
- [ ] Master cylinder internal parts worn or damaged causing fluid to bypass (Chapter 6).
- [ ] Master cylinder bore scratched by foreign material or broken spring. Repair or renew master cylinder (Chapter 6).
- [ ] Disc warped. Renew disc (Chapter 6).

Brake lever or pedal pulsates

- [ ] Disc warped. Renew disc (Chapter 6).
- [ ] Axle bent. Renew axle (Chapter 6).

- [ ] Brake caliper bolts loose (Chapter 6).
- [ ] Brake caliper sliders damaged or sticking (front calipers), causing caliper to bind. Lubricate the sliders or renew them if they are corroded or bent (Chapter 6).
- [ ] Wheel warped or otherwise damaged (Chapter 6).
- [ ] Wheel bearings damaged or worn (Chapter 6).

Brakes drag

- [ ] Master cylinder piston seized. Caused by wear or damage to piston or cylinder bore (Chapter 6).
- [ ] Lever balky or stuck. Check pivot and lubricate (Chapter 6).
- [ ] Brake caliper binds. Caused by inadequate lubrication or damage to caliper slider pins – front calipers (Chapter 6).
- [ ] Brake caliper piston seized in bore. Caused by wear or ingestion of dirt past deteriorated seal (Chapter 6).
- [ ] Brake pad damaged. Pad material separated from backing plate. Usually caused by faulty manufacturing process or from contact with chemicals. Renew pads (Chapter 6).
- [ ] Pads improperly installed (Chapter 6).

14 Electrical problems

Battery dead or weak

- [ ] Battery faulty. Caused by sulphated plates which are shorted through sedimentation. Also, broken battery terminal making only occasional contact (Chapter 8).
- [ ] Battery cables making poor contact (Chapter 8).
- [ ] Load excessive. Caused by addition of high wattage lights or other electrical accessories.
- [ ] Ignition (main) switch defective. Switch either grounds (earths) internally or fails to shut off system. Renew the switch (Chapter 8).
- [ ] Regulator/rectifier defective (Chapter 8).
- [ ] Alternator stator coil open or shorted (Chapter 8).

- [ ] Wiring faulty. Wiring grounded (earthed) or connections loose in ignition, charging or lighting circuits (Chapter 8).

Battery overcharged

- [ ] Regulator/rectifier defective. Overcharging is noticed when battery gets excessively warm (Chapter 8). Constantly blowing bulbs are a sign of a faulty regulator.
- [ ] Battery defective. Renew battery with a new one (Chapter 8).
- [ ] Battery amperage too low, wrong type or size. Install manufacturer's specified amp-hour battery to handle charging load (Chapter 8).

Checking engine compression

● Low compression will result in exhaust smoke, heavy oil consumption, poor starting and poor performance. A compression test will provide useful information about an engine's condition and if performed regularly, can give warning of trouble before any other symptoms become apparent.

● A compression gauge will be required, along with an adapter to suit the spark plug hole thread size. Note that the screw-in type gauge/adapter set up is preferable to the rubber cone type.

● Before carrying out the test, first check the valve clearances as described in Chapter 1.

1 Run the engine until it reaches normal operating temperature, then stop it and remove the spark plug(s), taking care not to scald your hands on the hot components.

2 Install the gauge adapter and compression gauge in No. 1 cylinder spark plug hole (see illustration 1).

Screw the compression gauge adapter into the spark plug hole, then screw the gauge into the adapter

3 On kickstart-equipped motorcycles, make sure the ignition switch is OFF, then open the throttle fully and kick the engine over a couple of times until the gauge reading stabilises.

4 On motorcycles with electric start only, the procedure will differ depending on the nature of the ignition system. Flick the engine kill switch (engine stop switch) to OFF and turn the ignition switch ON; open the throttle fully and crank the engine over on the starter motor for a couple of revolutions until the gauge reading stabilises. If the starter will not operate with the kill switch OFF, turn the ignition switch OFF and refer to the next paragraph.

5 Install the plugs back in their caps and arrange the plug electrodes so that their metal bodies are earthed (grounded) against the cylinder head; this is essential to prevent damage to the ignition system (see illustration 2). Position the plugs well away from the plug holes otherwise there is a risk of

All spark plugs must be earthed (grounded) against the cylinder head

atomised fuel escaping from the plug holes and igniting. As a safety precaution, cover the cylinder head with rag. Turn the ignition switch and kill switch ON, pull in the clutch lever, open the throttle fully and crank the engine over on the starter motor for a couple of revolutions until the gauge reading stabilises.

6 After one or two revolutions the pressure should build up to a maximum figure and then stabilise. Take a note of this reading and on multi-cylinder engines repeat the test on the remaining cylinders.

7 The correct pressures are given in Chapter 1 Specifications. If the results fall within the specified range and on multi-cylinder engines all are relatively equal, the engine is in good condition. If there is a marked difference between the readings, or if the readings are lower than specified,

inspection of the top-end components will be required.

8 Low compression pressure may be due to worn cylinder bores, pistons or rings, failure of the cylinder head gasket, worn valve seals, or poor valve seating.

9 To distinguish between cylinder/piston wear and valve leakage, pour a small quantity of oil into the bore to temporarily seal the piston rings, then repeat the compression tests (see illustration 3). If the readings show

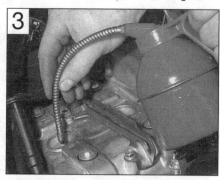

Bores can be temporarily sealed with a squirt of motor oil

a noticeable increase in pressure this confirms that the cylinder bore, piston, or rings are worn. If, however, no change is indicated, the cylinder head gasket or valves should be examined.

10 High compression pressure indicates excessive carbon build-up in the combustion chamber and on the piston crown. If this is the case the cylinder head should be removed and the deposits removed. Note that excessive carbon build-up is less likely with the used on modern fuels.

Checking battery open-circuit voltage

 Warning: The gases produced by the battery are explosive - never smoke or create any sparks in the vicinity of the battery. Never allow the electrolyte to contact your skin or clothing - if it does, wash it off and seek immediate medical attention.

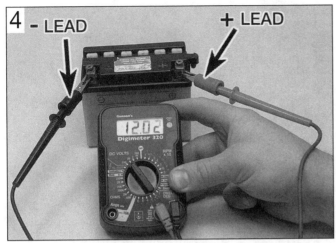

Measuring open-circuit battery voltage

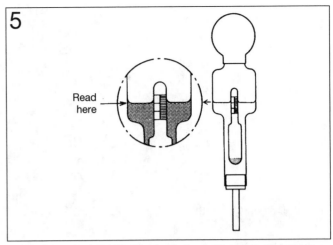

Read here

Float-type hydrometer for measuring battery specific gravity

● Before any electrical fault is investigated the battery should be checked.

● You'll need a dc voltmeter or multimeter to check battery voltage. Check that the leads are inserted in the correct terminals on the meter, red lead to positive (+ve), black lead to negative (-ve). Incorrect connections can damage the meter.

● A sound fully-charged 12 volt battery should produce between 12.3 and 12.6 volts across its terminals (12.8 volts for a maintenance-free battery). On machines with a 6 volt battery, voltage should be between 6.1 and 6.3 volts.

1 Set a multimeter to the 0 to 20 volts dc range and connect its probes across the battery terminals. Connect the meter's positive (+ve) probe, usually red, to the battery positive (+ve) terminal, followed by the meter's negative (-ve) probe, usually black, to the battery negative terminal (-ve) **(see illustration 4)**.

2 If battery voltage is low (below 10 volts on a 12 volt battery or below 4 volts on a six volt battery), charge the battery and test the voltage again. If the battery repeatedly goes flat, investigate the motorcycle's charging system.

Checking battery specific gravity (SG)

 Warning: The gases produced by the battery are explosive - never smoke or create any sparks in the vicinity of the battery. Never allow the electrolyte to contact your skin or clothing - if it does, wash it off and seek immediate medical attention.

● The specific gravity check gives an indication of a battery's state of charge.

● A hydrometer is used for measuring specific gravity. Make sure you purchase one

which has a small enough hose to insert in the aperture of a motorcycle battery.

● Specific gravity is simply a measure of the electrolyte's density compared with that of water. Water has an SG of 1.000 and fully-charged battery electrolyte is about 26% heavier, at 1.260.

● Specific gravity checks are not possible on maintenance-free batteries. Testing the open-circuit voltage is the only means of determining their state of charge.

1 To measure SG, remove the battery from the motorcycle and remove the first cell cap. Draw

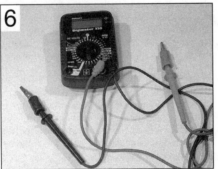

Digital multimeter can be used for all electrical tests

some electrolyte into the hydrometer and note the reading **(see illustration 5)**. Return the electrolyte to the cell and install the cap.

2 The reading should be in the region of 1.260 to 1.280. If SG is below 1.200 the battery needs charging. Note that SG will vary with temperature; it should be measured at 20°C (68°F). Add 0.007 to the reading for every 10°C above 20°C, and subtract 0.007 from the reading for every 10°C below 20°C. Add 0.004 to the reading for every 10°F above 68°F, and subtract 0.004 from the reading for every 10°F below 68°F.

3 When the check is complete, rinse the hydrometer thoroughly with clean water.

Checking for continuity

● The term continuity describes the uninterrupted flow of electricity through an electrical circuit. A continuity check will determine whether an **open-circuit** situation exists.

● Continuity can be checked with an ohmmeter, multimeter, continuity tester or battery and bulb test circuit **(see illustrations 6, 7 and 8)**.

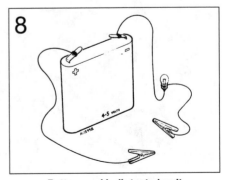

Battery and bulb test circuit

Battery-powered continuity tester

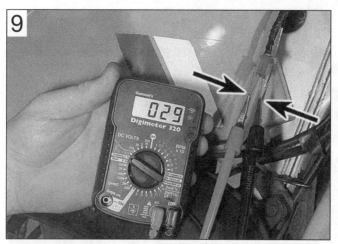

Continuity check of front brake light switch using a meter - note split pins used to access connector terminals

Continuity check of rear brake light switch using a continuity tester

● All of these instruments are self-powered by a battery, therefore the checks are made with the ignition OFF.

● As a safety precaution, always disconnect the battery negative (-ve) lead before making checks, particularly if ignition switch checks are being made.

● If using a meter, select the appropriate ohms scale and check that the meter reads infinity (∞). Touch the meter probes together and check that meter reads zero; where necessary adjust the meter so that it reads zero.

● After using a meter, always switch it OFF to conserve its battery.

Switch checks

1 If a switch is at fault, trace its wiring up to the wiring connectors. Separate the wire connectors and inspect them for security and condition. A build-up of dirt or corrosion here will most likely be the cause of the problem - clean up and apply a water dispersant such as WD40.

2 If using a test meter, set the meter to the ohms x 10 scale and connect its probes across the wires from the switch (see illustration 9). Simple ON/OFF type switches, such as brake light switches, only have two

wires whereas combination switches, like the ignition switch, have many internal links. Study the wiring diagram to ensure that you are connecting across the correct pair of wires. Continuity (low or no measurable resistance - 0 ohms) should be indicated with the switch ON and no continuity (high resistance) with it OFF.

3 Note that the polarity of the test probes doesn't matter for continuity checks, although care should be taken to follow specific test procedures if a diode or solid-state component is being checked.

4 A continuity tester or battery and bulb circuit can be used in the same way. Connect its probes as described above (see illustration 10). The light should come on to indicate continuity in the ON switch position, but should extinguish in the OFF position.

Wiring checks

● Many electrical faults are caused by damaged wiring, often due to incorrect routing or chaffing on frame components.

● Loose, wet or corroded wire connectors can also be the cause of electrical problems, especially in exposed locations.

1 A continuity check can be made on a single length of wire by disconnecting it at each end

and connecting a meter or continuity tester across both ends of the wire (see illustration 11).

2 Continuity (low or no resistance - 0 ohms) should be indicated if the wire is good. If no continuity (high resistance) is shown, suspect a broken wire.

Checking for voltage

● A voltage check can determine whether current is reaching a component.

● Voltage can be checked with a dc voltmeter, multimeter set on the dc volts scale, test light or buzzer (see illustrations 12 and 13). A meter has the advantage of being able to measure actual voltage.

● When using a meter, check that its leads are inserted in the correct terminals on the meter, red to positive (+ve), black to negative (-ve). Incorrect connections can damage the meter.

● A voltmeter (or multimeter set to the dc volts scale) should always be connected in parallel (across the load). Connecting it in series will destroy the meter.

● Voltage checks are made with the ignition ON.

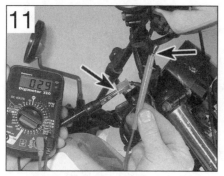

Continuity check of front brake light switch sub-harness

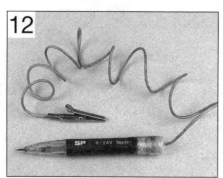

A simple test light can be used for voltage checks

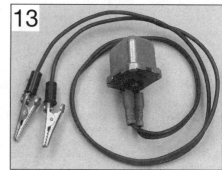

A buzzer is useful for voltage checks

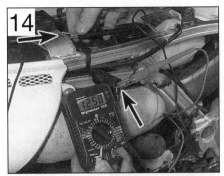

Checking for voltage at the rear brake light power supply wire using a meter . . .

1 First identify the relevant wiring circuit by referring to the wiring diagram at the end of this manual. If other electrical components share the same power supply (ie are fed from the same fuse), take note whether they are working correctly - this is useful information in deciding where to start checking the circuit.

2 If using a meter, check first that the meter leads are plugged into the correct terminals on the meter (see above). Set the meter to the dc volts function, at a range suitable for the battery voltage. Connect the meter red probe (+ve) to the power supply wire and the black probe to a good metal earth (ground) on the motorcycle's frame or directly to the battery negative (-ve) terminal **(see illustration 14)**. Battery voltage should be shown on the meter

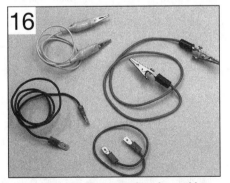

A selection of jumper wires for making earth (ground) checks

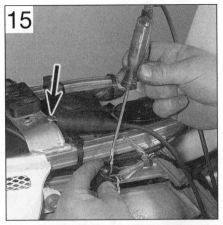

. . . or a test light - note the earth connection to the frame (arrow)

with the ignition switched ON.

3 If using a test light or buzzer, connect its positive (+ve) probe to the power supply terminal and its negative (-ve) probe to a good earth (ground) on the motorcycle's frame or directly to the battery negative (-ve) terminal **(see illustration 15)**. With the ignition ON, the test light should illuminate or the buzzer sound.

4 If no voltage is indicated, work back towards the fuse continuing to check for voltage. When you reach a point where there is voltage, you know the problem lies between that point and your last check point.

Checking the earth (ground)

● Earth connections are made either directly to the engine or frame (such as sensors, neutral switch etc. which only have a positive feed) or by a separate wire into the earth circuit of the wiring harness. Alternatively a short earth wire is sometimes run directly from the component to the motorcycle's frame.
● Corrosion is often the cause of a poor earth connection.
● If total failure is experienced, check the security of the main earth lead from the

negative (-ve) terminal of the battery and also the main earth (ground) point on the wiring harness. If corroded, dismantle the connection and clean all surfaces back to bare metal.

1 To check the earth on a component, use an insulated jumper wire to temporarily bypass its earth connection **(see illustration 16)**. Connect one end of the jumper wire between the earth terminal or metal body of the component and the other end to the motorcycle's frame.

2 If the circuit works with the jumper wire installed, the original earth circuit is faulty. Check the wiring for open-circuits or poor connections. Clean up direct earth connections, removing all traces of corrosion and remake the joint. Apply petroleum jelly to the joint to prevent future corrosion.

Tracing a short-circuit

● A short-circuit occurs where current shorts to earth (ground) bypassing the circuit components. This usually results in a blown fuse.

● A short-circuit is most likely to occur where the insulation has worn through due to wiring chafing on a component, allowing a direct path to earth (ground) on the frame.

1 Remove any bodypanels necessary to access the circuit wiring.

2 Check that all electrical switches in the circuit are OFF, then remove the circuit fuse and connect a test light, buzzer or voltmeter (set to the dc scale) across the fuse terminals. No voltage should be shown.

3 Move the wiring from side to side whilst observing the test light or meter. When the test light comes on, buzzer sounds or meter shows voltage, you have found the cause of the short. It will usually shown up as damaged or burned insulation.

4 Note that the same test can be performed on each component in the circuit, even the switch.

A

ABS (Anti-lock braking system) A system, usually electronically controlled, that senses incipient wheel lockup during braking and relieves hydraulic pressure at wheel which is about to skid.

Aftermarket Components suitable for the motorcycle, but not produced by the motorcycle manufacturer.

Allen key A hexagonal wrench which fits into a recessed hexagonal hole.

Alternating current (ac) Current produced by an alternator. Requires converting to direct current by a rectifier for charging purposes.

Alternator Converts mechanical energy from the engine into electrical energy to charge the battery and power the electrical system.

Ampere (amp) A unit of measurement for the flow of electrical current. Current = Volts ÷ Ohms.

Ampere-hour (Ah) Measure of battery capacity.

Angle-tightening A torque expressed in degrees. Often follows a conventional tightening torque for cylinder head or main bearing fasteners **(see illustration)**.

Angle-tightening cylinder head bolts

Antifreeze A substance (usually ethylene glycol) mixed with water, and added to the cooling system, to prevent freezing of the coolant in winter. Antifreeze also contains chemicals to inhibit corrosion and the formation of rust and other deposits that would tend to clog the radiator and coolant passages and reduce cooling efficiency.

Anti-dive System attached to the fork lower leg (slider) to prevent fork dive when braking hard.

Anti-seize compound A coating that reduces the risk of seizing on fasteners that are subjected to high temperatures, such as exhaust clamp bolts and nuts.

API American Petroleum Institute. A quality standard for 4-stroke motor oils.

Asbestos A natural fibrous mineral with great heat resistance, commonly used in the composition of brake friction materials. Asbestos is a health hazard and the dust created by brake systems should never be inhaled or ingested.

ATF Automatic Transmission Fluid. Often used in front forks.

ATU Automatic Timing Unit. Mechanical device for advancing the ignition timing on early engines.

ATV All Terrain Vehicle. Often called a Quad.

Axial play Side-to-side movement.

Axle A shaft on which a wheel revolves. Also known as a spindle.

B

Backlash The amount of movement between meshed components when one component is held still. Usually applies to gear teeth.

Ball bearing A bearing consisting of a hardened inner and outer race with hardened steel balls between the two races.

Bearings Used between two working surfaces to prevent wear of the components and a build-up of heat. Four types of bearing are commonly used on motorcycles: plain shell bearings, ball bearings, tapered roller bearings and needle roller bearings.

Bevel gears Used to turn the drive through 90°. Typical applications are shaft final drive and camshaft drive **(see illustration)**.

Bevel gears are used to turn the drive through 90°

BHP Brake Horsepower. The British measurement for engine power output. Power output is now usually expressed in kilowatts (kW).

Bias-belted tyre Similar construction to radial tyre, but with outer belt running at an angle to the wheel rim.

Big-end bearing The bearing in the end of the connecting rod that's attached to the crankshaft.

Bleeding The process of removing air from an hydraulic system via a bleed nipple or bleed screw.

Bottom-end A description of an engine's crankcase components and all components contained there-in.

BTDC Before Top Dead Centre in terms of piston position. Ignition timing is often expressed in terms of degrees or millimetres BTDC.

Bush A cylindrical metal or rubber component used between two moving parts.

Burr Rough edge left on a component after machining or as a result of excessive wear.

C

Cam chain The chain which takes drive from the crankshaft to the camshaft(s).

Canister The main component in an evaporative emission control system (California market only); contains activated charcoal granules to trap vapours from the fuel system rather than allowing them to vent to the atmosphere.

Castellated Resembling the parapets along the top of a castle wall. For example, a castellated wheel axle or spindle nut.

Catalytic converter A device in the exhaust system of some machines which converts certain pollutants in the exhaust gases into less harmful substances.

Charging system Description of the components which charge the battery, ie the alternator, rectifier and regulator.

Circlip A ring-shaped clip used to prevent endwise movement of cylindrical parts and shafts. An internal circlip is installed in a groove in a housing; an external circlip fits into a groove on the outside of a cylindrical piece such as a shaft. Also known as a snap-ring.

Clearance The amount of space between two parts. For example, between a piston and a cylinder, between a bearing and a journal, etc.

Coil spring A spiral of elastic steel found in various sizes throughout a vehicle, for example as a springing medium in the suspension and in the valve train.

Compression Reduction in volume, and increase in pressure and temperature, of a gas, caused by squeezing it into a smaller space.

Compression damping Controls the speed the suspension compresses when hitting a bump.

Compression ratio The relationship between cylinder volume when the piston is at top dead centre and cylinder volume when the piston is at bottom dead centre.

Continuity The uninterrupted path in the flow of electricity. Little or no measurable resistance.

Continuity tester Self-powered bleeper or test light which indicates continuity.

Cp Candlepower. Bulb rating commonly found on US motorcycles.

Crossply tyre Tyre plies arranged in a criss-cross pattern. Usually four or six plies used, hence 4PR or 6PR in tyre size codes.

Cush drive Rubber damper segments fitted between the rear wheel and final drive sprocket to absorb transmission shocks **(see illustration)**.

Cush drive rubbers dampen out transmission shocks

D

Degree disc Calibrated disc for measuring piston position. Expressed in degrees.

Dial gauge Clock-type gauge with adapters for measuring runout and piston position. Expressed in mm or inches.

Diaphragm The rubber membrane in a master cylinder or carburettor which seals the upper chamber.

Diaphragm spring A single sprung plate often used in clutches.

Direct current (dc) Current produced by a dc generator.

Decarbonisation The process of removing carbon deposits - typically from the combustion chamber, valves and exhaust port/system.

Detonation Destructive and damaging explosion of fuel/air mixture in combustion chamber instead of controlled burning.

Diode An electrical valve which only allows current to flow in one direction. Commonly used in rectifiers and starter interlock systems.

Disc valve (or rotary valve) A induction system used on some two-stroke engines.

Double-overhead camshaft (DOHC) An engine that uses two overhead camshafts, one for the intake valves and one for the exhaust valves.

Drivebelt A toothed belt used to transmit drive to the rear wheel on some motorcycles. A drivebelt has also been used to drive the camshafts. Drivebelts are usually made of Kevlar.

Driveshaft Any shaft used to transmit motion. Commonly used when referring to the final driveshaft on shaft drive motorcycles.

E

Earth return The return path of an electrical circuit, utilising the motorcycle's frame.

ECU (Electronic Control Unit) A computer which controls (for instance) an ignition system, or an anti-lock braking system.

EGO Exhaust Gas Oxygen sensor. Sometimes called a Lambda sensor.

Electrolyte The fluid in a lead-acid battery.

EMS (Engine Management System) A computer controlled system which manages the fuel injection and the ignition systems in an integrated fashion.

Endfloat The amount of lengthways movement between two parts. As applied to a crankshaft, the distance that the crankshaft can move side-to-side in the crankcase.

Endless chain A chain having no joining link. Common use for cam chains and final drive chains.

EP (Extreme Pressure) Oil type used in locations where high loads are applied, such as between gear teeth.

Evaporative emission control system Describes a charcoal filled canister which stores fuel vapours from the tank rather than allowing them to vent to the atmosphere. Usually only fitted to California models and referred to as an EVAP system.

Expansion chamber Section of two-stroke engine exhaust system so designed to improve engine efficiency and boost power.

F

Feeler blade or gauge A thin strip or blade of hardened steel, ground to an exact thickness, used to check or measure clearances between parts.

Final drive Description of the drive from the transmission to the rear wheel. Usually by chain or shaft, but sometimes by belt.

Firing order The order in which the engine cylinders fire, or deliver their power strokes, beginning with the number one cylinder.

Flooding Term used to describe a high fuel level in the carburettor float chambers, leading to fuel overflow. Also refers to excess fuel in the combustion chamber due to incorrect starting technique.

Free length The no-load state of a component when measured. Clutch, valve and fork spring lengths are measured at rest, without any preload.

Freeplay The amount of travel before any action takes place. The looseness in a linkage, or an assembly of parts, between the initial application of force and actual movement. For example, the distance the rear brake pedal moves before the rear brake is actuated.

Fuel injection The fuel/air mixture is metered electronically and directed into the engine intake ports (indirect injection) or into the cylinders (direct injection). Sensors supply information on engine speed and conditions.

Fuel/air mixture The charge of fuel and air going into the engine. See **Stoichiometric ratio**.

Fuse An electrical device which protects a circuit against accidental overload. The typical fuse contains a soft piece of metal which is calibrated to melt at a predetermined current flow (expressed as amps) and break the circuit.

G

Gap The distance the spark must travel in jumping from the centre electrode to the side electrode in a spark plug. Also refers to the distance between the ignition rotor and the pickup coil in an electronic ignition system.

Gasket Any thin, soft material - usually cork, cardboard, asbestos or soft metal - installed between two metal surfaces to ensure a good seal. For instance, the cylinder head gasket seals the joint between the block and the cylinder head.

Gauge An instrument panel display used to monitor engine conditions. A gauge with a movable pointer on a dial or a fixed scale is an analogue gauge. A gauge with a numerical readout is called a digital gauge.

Gear ratios The drive ratio of a pair of gears in a gearbox, calculated on their number of teeth.

Glaze-busting see **Honing**

Grinding Process for renovating the valve face and valve seat contact area in the cylinder head.

Gudgeon pin The shaft which connects the connecting rod small-end with the piston. Often called a piston pin or wrist pin.

H

Helical gears Gear teeth are slightly curved and produce less gear noise that straight-cut gears. Often used for primary drives.

Installing a Helicoil thread insert in a cylinder head

Helicoil A thread insert repair system. Commonly used as a repair for stripped spark plug threads **(see illustration)**.

Honing A process used to break down the glaze on a cylinder bore (also called glaze-busting). Can also be carried out to roughen a rebored cylinder to aid ring bedding-in.

HT (High Tension) Description of the electrical circuit from the secondary winding of the ignition coil to the spark plug.

Hydraulic A liquid filled system used to transmit pressure from one component to another. Common uses on motorcycles are brakes and clutches.

Hydrometer An instrument for measuring the specific gravity of a lead-acid battery.

Hygroscopic Water absorbing. In motorcycle applications, braking efficiency will be reduced if DOT 3 or 4 hydraulic fluid absorbs water from the air - care must be taken to keep new brake fluid in tightly sealed containers.

I

lbf ft Pounds-force feet. An imperial unit of torque. Sometimes written as ft-lbs.

lbf in Pound-force inch. An imperial unit of torque, applied to components where a very low torque is required. Sometimes written as in-lbs.

IC Abbreviation for Integrated Circuit.

Ignition advance Means of increasing the timing of the spark at higher engine speeds. Done by mechanical means (ATU) on early engines or electronically by the ignition control unit on later engines.

Ignition timing The moment at which the spark plug fires, expressed in the number of crankshaft degrees before the piston reaches the top of its stroke, or in the number of millimetres before the piston reaches the top of its stroke.

Infinity (∞) Description of an open-circuit electrical state, where no continuity exists.

Inverted forks (upside down forks) The sliders or lower legs are held in the yokes and the fork tubes or stanchions are connected to the wheel axle (spindle). Less unsprung weight and stiffer construction than conventional forks.

J

JASO Quality standard for 2-stroke oils.

Joule The unit of electrical energy.

Journal The bearing surface of a shaft.

K

Kickstart Mechanical means of turning the engine over for starting purposes. Only usually fitted to mopeds, small capacity motorcycles and off-road motorcycles.

Kill switch Handebar-mounted switch for emergency ignition cut-out. Cuts the ignition circuit on all models, and additionally prevent starter motor operation on others.

km Symbol for kilometre.

kmh Abbreviation for kilometres per hour.

L

Lambda (λ) sensor A sensor fitted in the exhaust system to measure the exhaust gas oxygen content (excess air factor).

Lapping see **Grinding**.
LCD Abbreviation for Liquid Crystal Display.
LED Abbreviation for Light Emitting Diode.
Liner A steel cylinder liner inserted in a aluminium alloy cylinder block.
Locknut A nut used to lock an adjustment nut, or other threaded component, in place.
Lockstops The lugs on the lower triple clamp (yoke) which abut those on the frame, preventing handlebar-to-fuel tank contact.
Lockwasher A form of washer designed to prevent an attaching nut from working loose.
LT Low Tension Description of the electrical circuit from the power supply to the primary winding of the ignition coil.

M

Main bearings The bearings between the crankshaft and crankcase.
Maintenance-free (MF) battery A sealed battery which cannot be topped up.
Manometer Mercury-filled calibrated tubes used to measure intake tract vacuum. Used to synchronise carburettors on multi-cylinder engines.
Micrometer A precision measuring instrument that measures component outside diameters **(see illustration)**.

Tappet shims are measured with a micrometer

MON (Motor Octane Number) A measure of a fuel's resistance to knock.
Monograde oil An oil with a single viscosity, eg SAE80W.
Monoshock A single suspension unit linking the swingarm or suspension linkage to the frame.
mph Abbreviation for miles per hour.
Multigrade oil Having a wide viscosity range (eg 10W40). The W stands for Winter, thus the viscosity ranges from SAE10 when cold to SAE40 when hot.
Multimeter An electrical test instrument with the capability to measure voltage, current and resistance. Some meters also incorporate a continuity tester and buzzer.

N

Needle roller bearing Inner race of caged needle rollers and hardened outer race. Examples of uncaged needle rollers can be found on some engines. Commonly used in rear suspension applications and in two-stroke engines.
Nm Newton metres.
NOx Oxides of Nitrogen. A common toxic pollutant emitted by petrol engines at higher temperatures.

O

Octane The measure of a fuel's resistance to knock.
OE (Original Equipment) Relates to components fitted to a motorcycle as standard or replacement parts supplied by the motorcycle manufacturer.
Ohm The unit of electrical resistance. Ohms = Volts ÷ Current.
Ohmmeter An instrument for measuring electrical resistance.
Oil cooler System for diverting engine oil outside of the engine to a radiator for cooling purposes.
Oil injection A system of two-stroke engine lubrication where oil is pump-fed to the engine in accordance with throttle position.
Open-circuit An electrical condition where there is a break in the flow of electricity - no continuity (high resistance).
O-ring A type of sealing ring made of a special rubber-like material; in use, the O-ring is compressed into a groove to provide the sealing action.
Oversize (OS) Term used for piston and ring size options fitted to a rebored cylinder.
Overhead cam (sohc) engine An engine with single camshaft located on top of the cylinder head.
Overhead valve (ohv) engine An engine with the valves located in the cylinder head, but with the camshaft located in the engine block or crankcase.
Oxygen sensor A device installed in the exhaust system which senses the oxygen content in the exhaust and converts this information into an electric current. Also called a Lambda sensor.

P

Plastigauge A thin strip of plastic thread, available in different sizes, used for measuring clearances. For example, a strip of Plastigauge is laid across a bearing journal. The parts are assembled and dismantled; the width of the crushed strip indicates the clearance between journal and bearing.
Polarity Either negative or positive earth (ground), determined by which battery lead is connected to the frame (earth return). Modern motorcycles are usually negative earth.
Pre-ignition A situation where the fuel/air mixture ignites before the spark plug fires. Often due to a hot spot in the combustion chamber caused by carbon build-up. Engine has a tendency to 'run-on'.
Pre-load (suspension) The amount a spring is compressed when in the unloaded state. Preload can be applied by gas, spacer or mechanical adjuster.
Premix The method of engine lubrication on older two-stroke engines. Engine oil is mixed with the petrol in the fuel tank in a specific ratio. The fuel/oil mix is sometimes referred to as "petroil".
Primary drive Description of the drive from the crankshaft to the clutch. Usually by gear or chain.
PS Pfedestärke - a German interpretation of BHP.
PSI Pounds-force per square inch. Imperial measurement of tyre pressure and cylinder pressure measurement.
PTFE Polytetrafluroethylene. A low friction substance.

Pulse secondary air injection system A process of promoting the burning of excess fuel present in the exhaust gases by routing fresh air into the exhaust ports.

Q

Quartz halogen bulb Tungsten filament surrounded by a halogen gas. Typically used for the headlight **(see illustration)**.

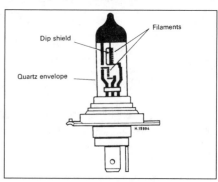

Quartz halogen headlight bulb construction

R

Rack-and-pinion A pinion gear on the end of a shaft that mates with a rack (think of a geared wheel opened up and laid flat). Sometimes used in clutch operating systems.
Radial play Up and down movement about a shaft.
Radial ply tyres Tyre plies run across the tyre (from bead to bead) and around the circumference of the tyre. Less resistant to tread distortion than other tyre types.
Radiator A liquid-to-air heat transfer device designed to reduce the temperature of the coolant in a liquid cooled engine.
Rake A feature of steering geometry - the angle of the steering head in relation to the vertical **(see illustration)**.

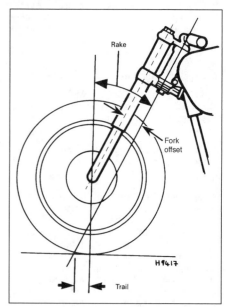

Steering geometry

Rebore Providing a new working surface to the cylinder bore by boring out the old surface. Necessitates the use of oversize piston and rings.

Rebound damping A means of controlling the oscillation of a suspension unit spring after it has been compressed. Resists the spring's natural tendency to bounce back after being compressed.

Rectifier Device for converting the ac output of an alternator into dc for battery charging.

Reed valve An induction system commonly used on two-stroke engines.

Regulator Device for maintaining the charging voltage from the generator or alternator within a specified range.

Relay A electrical device used to switch heavy current on and off by using a low current auxiliary circuit.

Resistance Measured in ohms. An electrical component's ability to pass electrical current.

RON (Research Octane Number) A measure of a fuel's resistance to knock.

rpm revolutions per minute.

Runout The amount of wobble (in-and-out movement) of a wheel or shaft as it's rotated. The amount a shaft rotates `out-of-true'. The out-of-round condition of a rotating part.

S

SAE (Society of Automotive Engineers) A standard for the viscosity of a fluid.

Sealant A liquid or paste used to prevent leakage at a joint. Sometimes used in conjunction with a gasket.

Service limit Term for the point where a component is no longer useable and must be renewed.

Shaft drive A method of transmitting drive from the transmission to the rear wheel.

Shell bearings Plain bearings consisting of two shell halves. Most often used as big-end and main bearings in a four-stroke engine. Often called bearing inserts.

Shim Thin spacer, commonly used to adjust the clearance or relative positions between two parts. For example, shims inserted into or under tappets or followers to control valve clearances. Clearance is adjusted by changing the thickness of the shim.

Short-circuit An electrical condition where current shorts to earth (ground) bypassing the circuit components.

Skimming Process to correct warpage or repair a damaged surface, eg on brake discs or drums.

Slide-hammer A special puller that screws into or hooks onto a component such as a shaft or bearing; a heavy sliding handle on the shaft bottoms against the end of the shaft to knock the component free.

Small-end bearing The bearing in the upper end of the connecting rod at its joint with the gudgeon pin.

Spalling Damage to camshaft lobes or bearing journals shown as pitting of the working surface.

Specific gravity (SG) The state of charge of the electrolyte in a lead-acid battery. A measure of the electrolyte's density compared with water.

Straight-cut gears Common type gear used on gearbox shafts and for oil pump and water pump drives.

Stanchion The inner sliding part of the front forks, held by the yokes. Often called a fork tube.

Stoichiometric ratio The optimum chemical air/fuel ratio for a petrol engine, said to be 14.7 parts of air to 1 part of fuel.

Sulphuric acid The liquid (electrolyte) used in a lead-acid battery. Poisonous and extremely corrosive.

Surface grinding (lapping) Process to correct a warped gasket face, commonly used on cylinder heads.

T

Tapered-roller bearing Tapered inner race of caged needle rollers and separate tapered outer race. Examples of taper roller bearings can be found on steering heads.

Tappet A cylindrical component which transmits motion from the cam to the valve stem, either directly or via a pushrod and rocker arm. Also called a cam follower.

TCS Traction Control System. An electronically-controlled system which senses wheel spin and reduces engine speed accordingly.

TDC Top Dead Centre denotes that the piston is at its highest point in the cylinder.

Thread-locking compound Solution applied to fastener threads to prevent slackening. Select type to suit application.

Thrust washer A washer positioned between two moving components on a shaft. For example, between gear pinions on gearshaft.

Timing chain See **Cam Chain**.

Timing light Stroboscopic lamp for carrying out ignition timing checks with the engine running.

Top-end A description of an engine's cylinder block, head and valve gear components.

Torque Turning or twisting force about a shaft.

Torque setting A prescribed tightness specified by the motorcycle manufacturer to ensure that the bolt or nut is secured correctly. Undertightening can result in the bolt or nut coming loose or a surface not being sealed. Overtightening can result in stripped threads, distortion or damage to the component being retained.

Torx key A six-point wrench.

Tracer A stripe of a second colour applied to a wire insulator to distinguish that wire from another one with the same colour insulator. For example, Br/W is often used to denote a brown insulator with a white tracer.

Trail A feature of steering geometry. Distance from the steering head axis to the tyre's central contact point.

Triple clamps The cast components which extend from the steering head and support the fork stanchions or tubes. Often called fork yokes.

Turbocharger A centrifugal device, driven by exhaust gases, that pressurises the intake air. Normally used to increase the power output from a given engine displacement.

TWI Abbreviation for Tyre Wear Indicator. Indicates the location of the tread depth indicator bars on tyres.

U

Universal joint or U-joint (UJ) A double-pivoted connection for transmitting power from a driving to a driven shaft through an angle. Typically found in shaft drive assemblies.

Unsprung weight Anything not supported by the bike's suspension (ie the wheel, tyres, brakes, final drive and bottom (moving) part of the suspension).

V

Vacuum gauges Clock-type gauges for measuring intake tract vacuum. Used for carburettor synchronisation on multi-cylinder engines.

Valve A device through which the flow of liquid, gas or vacuum may be stopped, started or regulated by a moveable part that opens, shuts or partially obstructs one or more ports or passageways. The intake and exhaust valves in the cylinder head are of the poppet type.

Valve clearance The clearance between the valve tip (the end of the valve stem) and the rocker arm or tappet/follower. The valve clearance is measured when the valve is closed. The correct clearance is important - if too small the valve won't close fully and will burn out, whereas if too large noisy operation will result.

Valve lift The amount a valve is lifted off its seat by the camshaft lobe.

Valve timing The exact setting for the opening and closing of the valves in relation to piston position.

Vernier caliper A precision measuring instrument that measures inside and outside dimensions. Not quite as accurate as a micrometer, but more convenient.

VIN Vehicle Identification Number. Term for the bike's engine and frame numbers.

Viscosity The thickness of a liquid or its resistance to flow.

Volt A unit for expressing electrical "pressure" in a circuit. Volts = current x ohms.

W

Water pump A mechanically-driven device for moving coolant around the engine.

Watt A unit for expressing electrical power. Watts = volts x current.

Wear limit see **Service limit**

Wet liner A liquid-cooled engine design where the pistons run in liners which are directly surrounded by coolant **(see illustration)**.

Wet liner arrangement

Wheelbase Distance from the centre of the front wheel to the centre of the rear wheel.

Wiring harness or loom Describes the electrical wires running the length of the motorcycle and enclosed in tape or plastic sheathing. Wiring coming off the main harness is usually referred to as a sub harness.

Woodruff key A key of semi-circular or square section used to locate a gear to a shaft. Often used to locate the alternator rotor on the crankshaft.

Wrist pin Another name for gudgeon or piston pin.

Note: *References throughout this index are in the form - "Chapter number" • "Page number"*

A

Air filter – 1•7, 1•20
Air filter housing – 3•5
Air/fuel mixture adjustment – 3•6
Alignment (wheel) – 6•15
Alternator – 8•26

B

Battery
  charging – 8•3
  check – 1•22, REF•44, REF•45
  removal and installation – 8•3
  specifications – 8•1
Bodywork – 7•1 *et seq*
Brake
  bleeding – 6•13
  calipers – 1•22, 6•6, 6•8
  discs – 6•5
  fault finding – REF•43
  fluid change – 0•21, 6•14
  fluid level check – 0•15
  hoses – 1•21, 6•13
  lever – 5•8
  master cylinders – 1•22, 6•9, 6•11
  pads – 1•13, 6•2
  pedal – 5•4
  specifications – 6•1
  system check – 1•14
Brake light – 8•2, 8•8
Brake light switches – 1•14, 8•10
Bulbs
  brake/tail light – 8•8
  headlight – 8•5
  instrument/warning lights – 8•14
  licence plate light – 8•8
  sidelight – 8•6, 8•7
  turn signal lights – 8•9
  wattages – 8•2

C

Cables
  choke – 1•12, 3•17
  clutch – 1•12, 2•40
  lubrication – 1•15
  throttle – 1•11, 3•15
Calipers (brake) – 6•6, 6•8
Cam chain and tensioner blade – 2•16
Cam chain tensioner and guide blades – 2•15
Camshafts – 2•17
Carburettors
  cooling fan – 8•30
  disassembly, cleaning and inspection – 3•7
  heater system – 3•14
  overhaul advice – 3•6
  reassembly and float height check – 3•12
  removal and installation – 3•6
  separation and joining – 3•11
  specifications – 3•1
  synchronisation – 1•17
Centrestand – 1•22, 5•5
Chain (cam) – 2•16
Chain (drive) – 0•14, 1•6, 1•7, 5•2, 5•23
Charging system
  alternator/regulator/rectifier – 8•26
  specifications – 8•1
  testing – 8•25
Choke cable – 1•12, 3•17
Clock – 8•14
Clutch
  cable – 2•40
  check and adjustment – 1•12
  lever – 5•8
  removal, inspection and installation – 2•33
  specifications – 2•3, 2•7
Clutch switch – 8•20
Connecting rods – 2•56
Control unit (ignition) – 4•4
Cooling fan (carburettor) – 8•30
Conversion factors – REF•26
Crankcase – 2•48, 2•52
Crankshaft and main bearings – 2•53
Cylinder block – 2•28
Cylinder compression check – 1•21, REF•44
Cylinder head – 2•22, 2•24

D

Dimensions – 0•10
Diodes – 8•20
Drive chain
 adjustment – 1•6
 check – 0•14, 1•6
 cleaning and lubrication – 1•7
 removal, cleaning and installation – 5•23
 sizes – 5•2
 wear and stretch check – 1•13

E

Electrical system
 battery – 1•22, 8•3
 brake/tail light – 8•8
 diodes – 8•20
 fault finding – 8•2, REF•43
 fuses – 8•4
 headlight – 1•22, 8•5, 8•7
 horn – 8•20
 instruments – 8•12, 8•13
 licence plate light – 8•8
 lighting system – 8•5
 specifications – 8•1
 starter motor – 8•21, 8•22
 switches – 8•16 to 8•20
 turn signals – 8•8, 8•9
 wiring diagrams – 8•31 *et seq*
Engine
 cam chain and tensioner blade – 2•16
 cam chain tensioner and guide blades – 2•15
 camshafts – 2•17
 connecting rods – 2•56
 crankcase – 2•48, 2•52
 crankshaft and main bearings – 2•53
 cylinder block – 2•28
 cylinder compression check – 1•21, REF•44
 cylinder head – 2•22, 2•24
 fault finding – REF•36
 front sprocket cover – 5•23
 idle speed – 1•11
 ignition timing rotor – 2•45
 main and connecting rod bearings – 2•53
 oil and filter change – 1•20
 oil change – 1•10
 oil cooler – 2•13
 oil level check – 0•14
 oil pressure check – 1•21
 oil pressure switch – 8•16
 oil pump – 2•72
 oil sump, pressure regulator and strainer – 2•46
 pistons and rings – 2•30, 2•32
 removal and installation – 2•10
 rocker arms – 2•21
 running-in – 2•73
 selector drum and forks – 2•58
 specifications – 0•10, 1•1, 2•1, 2•5
 starter clutch and idle/reduction gear – 2•42
 valve clearances – 1•15
 valve cover – 2•14
 valves – 2•24
Engine number – 0•13
EVAP system – 3•21
Exhaust system – 3•18

F

Fairing – 7•3
Fault finding – 4•2, 8•2, REF•35
Fault finding equipment – REF•44
Filter
 air – 1•7, 1•20
 fuel – 1•9, 1•18
 oil – 1•20
Final drive
 chain – 0•14, 1•6, 1•7, 5•2, 5•23
 specifications – 5•1
 sprockets – 1•6, 5•2, 5•24
Footrests – 5•3, 5•4
Frame – 5•3
Frame number – 0•13
Front brake
 calipers – 6•6
 discs – 6•5
 fluid level check – 0•15
 master cylinder – 6•9
 pads – 1•13, 6•2
Front forks
 adjustment – 5•19
 oil change – 1•22, 5•9
 disassembly, inspection and reassembly – 5•10
 removal and installation – 5•8
 specifications – 5•1
Front mudguard – 7•5
Front wheel
 bearings – 1•22, 6•19
 removal and installation – 6•15
Fuel system
 carburettors – 1•17, 3•6
 check – 1•9
 fault finding – REF• 37
 filter and strainer – 1•9, 1•18
 gauge – 8•14
 hoses – 1•21
 level sender and warning light switch – 3•18
 tank – 3•3
 tap – 3•4
Fuses – 8•2, 8•4

G

Gearchange
 fault finding – REF•40
 lever – 5•4
 mechanism – 2•41
 selector drum and forks – 2•58
Gearshafts – 2•61, 2•62

H

Handlebar levers – 5•8
Handlebar switches – 8•17, 8•18
Handlebars – 5•5, 5•6, 5•7
Headlight
 aim – 1•22
 bulb – 8•2, 8•5
 unit – 8•7
Heater system (carburettor) – 3•14
Horn – 8•20
HT coils – 4•3

I

Identification numbers – 0•13
Idle speed – 1•11
Ignition (main) switch – 8•17
Ignition system
    check – 4•2
    fault finding – REF•37
    HT coils – 4•3
    ignition control unit (ICU) – 4•4
    pulse generator coil – 4•4
    spark plugs – 1•8, 1•15
    specifications – 4•1
    throttle position sensor – 4•5
    timing – 4•5
    timing rotor – 2•45
Instruments – 8•11, 8•12, 8•14

L

Legal checks – 0•16
Licence plate light – 8•2, 8•8
Lighting system – 8•5
Lubricants (recommended) – 1•2
Lubricants and fluids (general) – REF•23
Lubrication (stands, levers and cables) – 1•15

M

Main bearings – 2•53
Maintenance (routine) – 1•1 *et seq*
Master cylinders (brake) – 6•9, 6•11
Mirrors – 7•2
MOT test checks – REF•27
Mudguard – 7•5

N

Neutral switch – 8•18

O

Oil (engine/transmission)
    change – 1•10
    level check – 0•14
    specification – 1•2
Oil (front forks)
    change – 1•22, 5•9
    specification – 5•1
Oil cooler – 2•13
Oil filter (engine/transmission) – 1•20
Oil pressure check – 1•21
Oil pressure switch – 8•16
Oil pump – 2•72
Oil sump, pressure regulator and strainer – 2•46

P

PAIR system – 3•20
Pistons and rings – 2•30, 2•32
Pulse generator coil – 4•4
Pump (oil) – 2•72

R

Rear brake
    caliper – 6•8
    disc – 6•5
    fluid level check – 0•15
    master cylinder – 6•11
    pads – 1•13, 6•4
Rear shock absorber(s)
    adjustment – 5•19
    removal and installation – 5•17
Rear sprocket coupling (rubber dampers) – 5•25
Rear suspension linkage (GSX600/750F models)
    bearings – 1•19, 1•22
    removal, inspection and installation – 5•18
Rear view mirrors – 7•2
Rear wheel
    bearings – 1•22, 6•19
    removal and installation – 6•17
Rectifier – 8•26
Regulator – 8•26
Relay
    sidestand – 8•19
    starter – 8•21
    turn signal – 8•8
Rings (piston) – 2•32
Rocker arms – 2•21
Routine maintenance – 1•1 *et seq*

S

Safety precautions – 0•12, 0•16, 3•3, 4•2
Seat – 7•2
Seat cowling – 7•4, 7•5
Security – REF•20
Service schedule – 1•3
Side panels – 7•5
Sidelight – 8•2, 8•6, 8•7
Sidestand – 1•22, 5•4
Sidestand switch – 8•19
Spare parts buying – 0•13
Spark plugs – 1•8, 1•15
Specifications
    brakes – 6•1
    clutch – 2•3, 2•7
    electrical system – 8•1
    engine – 0•10, 1•1, 2•1, 2•5
    final drive – 5•1
    fuel system – 3•1
    general – 0•10
    ignition system – 4•1
    routine maintenance – 1•1
    suspension – 5•1
    transmission – 2•4, 2•8
    tyres – 6•2
    wheels – 6•1
Speed sensor – 8•15
Speedometer – 8•13
Speedometer cable – 8•16
Sprocket
    check – 1•6
    coupling bearing – 6•20
    coupling rubber dampers – 5•25
    removal and installation – 5•24
    sizes – 5•2

Sprocket cover – 5•23
Starter clutch and idle/reduction gear – 2•42
Starter motor – 8•21, 8•22
Starter relay – 8•21
Steering
  check – 0•14
  head bearings – 1•18, 1•22, 5•16
  stem – 5•14
Storage – REF•32
Swingarm
  bearings – 1•19, 1•22, 5•22
  removal and installation – 5•20
Suspension
  adjustments – 5•19
  check – 0•14, 1•19
  fault finding – REF•41, REF•42
  front forks – 1•22, 5•8, 5•9, 5•10
  rear shock absorber(s) – 5•17
  rear suspension linkage – 1•22, 5•18
  swingarm – 1•22, 5•20, 5•22

T

Tachometer – 8•14
Tail light – 8•2, 8•8
Tank (fuel) – 3•3
Tap (fuel) – 3•4
Throttle cables
  check and adjustment – 1•11
  removal and installation – 3•15
Throttle position sensor – 4•5
Timing (ignition) – 4•5
Timing (valve) – 2•20
Tools – REF•2
Torque settings – 1•2, 2•4, 2•8, 3•2, 5•2, 6•2, 8•2

Transmission
  fault finding – REF•40
  gearchange mechanism – 2•41, 2•58
  gearshafts – 2•61, 2•62
  specifications – 2•4, 2•8
Turn signals – 8•2, 8•8, 8•9
Tyres
  checks and pressures – 0•16
  general information and fitting – 6•20
  sizes – 6•2

V

Valve clearances – 1•15
Valve cover – 2•14
Valve timing – 2•20
Valves – 2•24

W

Warning lights – 8•2, 8•14
Weights – 0•10
Wheels
  alignment – 6•15
  bearings – 1•22
  check – 1•14
  inspection and repair – 6•14
  removal and installation – 6•15, 6•17
  specifications – 6•1
  sprocket coupling bearing – 6•20
  sprocket coupling rubber dampers – 5•25
Windshield – 7•4
Wiring diagrams – 8•31 *et seq*
Workshop tips – REF•2

Haynes Motorcycle Manuals – The Complete List

Title	Book No
BMW 2-valve Twins (70 - 96)	◆ 0249
BMW K100 & 75 2-valve Models (83 - 96)	◆ 1373
BMW R850 & R1100 4-valve Twins (93 - 97)	◆ 3466
BSA Bantam (48 - 71)	0117
BSA Unit Singles (58 - 72)	0127
BSA Pre-unit Singles (54 - 61)	0326
BSA A7 & A10 Twins (47 - 62)	0121
BSA A50 & A65 Twins (62 - 73)	0155
DUCATI MK III & Desmo Singles (69 - 76)	◇ 0445
Ducati 600, 750 & 900 2-valve V-Twins (91 - 96)	◆ 3290
Ducati 748, 916 & 996 4-valve V-Twins (94 - 01)	◆ 3756
GILERA Runner, DNA, Stalker & Ice (97 - 04)	4163
HARLEY-DAVIDSON Sportsters (70 - 01)	0702
Harley-Davidson Big Twins (70 - 99)	0703
Harley-Davidson Twin Cam 88 (99 - 03)	◆ 2478
HONDA NB, ND, NP & NS50 Melody (81 - 85)	◇ 0622
Honda NE/NB50 Vision & SA50 Vision Met-in (85 - 95)	◇ 1278
Honda MB, MBX, MT & MTX50 (80 - 93)	0731
Honda C50, C70 & C90 (67 - 99)	0324
Honda XR80R & XR100R (85 - 96)	2218
Honda XL/XR 80, 100, 125, 185 & 200 2-valve Models (78 - 87)	0566
Honda H100 & H100S Singles (80 - 92)	◇ 0734
Honda CB/CD125T & CM125C Twins (77 - 88)	◇ 0571
Honda CG125 (76 - 00)	◇ 0433
Honda NS125 (86 - 93)	◇ 3056
Honda MBX/MTX125 & MTX200 (83 - 93)	◇ 1132
Honda CD/CM185 200T & CM250C 2-valve Twins (77 - 85)	0572
Honda XL/XR 250 & 500 (78 - 84)	0567
Honda XR250L, XR250R & XR400R (86 - 03)	2219
Honda CB250 & CB400N Super Dreams (78 - 84)	◇ 0540
Honda CR Motocross Bikes (86 - 01)	2222
Honda CBR400RR Fours (88 - 99)	◇ ◆ 3552
Honda VFR400 (NC30) & RVF400 (NC35) V-Fours (89 - 98)	◇ ◆ 3496
Honda CB500 (93 - 01)	◇ ◆ 3753
Honda CB400 & CB550 Fours (73 - 77)	0262
Honda CX/GL500 & 650 V-Twins (78 - 86)	0442
Honda CBX550 Four (82 - 86)	◇ 0940
Honda XL600R & XR600R (83 - 00)	2183
Honda XL600/650V Transalp & XRV750 Africa Twin (87 - 02)	◇ ◆ 3919
Honda CBR600F1 & 1000F Fours (87 - 96)	◆ 1730
Honda CBR600F2 & F3 Fours (91 - 98)	◆ 2070
Honda CBR600F4 (99 - 02)	◆ 3911
Honda CB600F Hornet (98 - 02)	◇ ◆ 3915
Honda CB650 sohc Fours (78 - 84)	◆ 0665
Honda NTV600 Revere, NTV650, NT650V Deauville & Bros (88 - 01)	◇ ◆ 3243
Honda Shadow VT600 & 750 (USA) (88 - 03)	2312
Honda CB750 sohc Four (69 - 79)	0131
Honda V45/65 Sabre & Magna (82 - 88)	0820
Honda VFR750 & 700 V-Fours (86 - 97)	◆ 2101
Honda VFR800 V-Fours (97 - 01)	◆ 3703
Honda VTR1000 (FireStorm, Super Hawk) & XL1000V (Varadero) (97 - 00)	◆ 3744
Honda CB750 & CB900 dohc Fours (78 - 84)	0535
Honda CBR900RR FireBlade (92 - 99)	◆ 2161
Honda CBR900RR FireBlade (00 - 03)	◆ 4060
Honda CBR1100XX Super Blackbird (97 - 02)	◆ 3901
Honda ST1100 Pan European V-Fours (90 - 01)	◆ 3384
Honda Shadow VT1100 (USA) (85 - 98)	2313
Honda GL1000 Gold Wing (75 - 79)	0309
Honda GL1100 Gold Wing (79 - 81)	0669
Honda Gold Wing 1200 (USA) (84 - 87)	2199
Honda Gold Wing 1500 (USA) (88 - 00)	2225

Title	Book No
KAWASAKI AE/AR 50 & 80 (81 - 95)	1007
Kawasaki KC, KE & KH100 (75 - 99)	1371
Kawasaki KMX125 & 200 (86 - 02)	◇ 3046
Kawasaki 250, 350 & 400 Triples (72 - 79)	0134
Kawasaki 400 & 440 Twins (74 - 81)	0281
Kawasaki 400, 500 & 550 Fours (79 - 91)	0910
Kawasaki EN450 & 500 Twins (Ltd/Vulcan) (85 - 93)	2053
Kawasaki EX & ER500 (GPZ500S & ER-5) Twins (87 - 99)	◆ 2052
Kawasaki ZX600 (Ninja ZX-6, ZZ-R600) Fours (90 - 00)	◆ 2146
Kawasaki ZX-6R Ninja Fours (95 - 02)	◆ 3541
Kawasaki ZX600 (GPZ600R, GPX600R, Ninja 600R & RX) & ZX750 (GPX750R, Ninja 750R) Fours (85 - 97)	◆ 1780
Kawasaki 650 Four (76 - 78)	0373
Kawasaki Vulcan 700/750 & 800 (85 - 01)	◆ 2457
Kawasaki 750 Air-cooled Fours (80 - 91)	0574
Kawasaki ZR550 & 750 Zephyr Fours (90 - 97)	◆ 3382
Kawasaki ZX750 (Ninja ZX-7 & ZXR750) Fours (89 - 96)	◆ 2054
Kawasaki Ninja ZX-7R & ZX-9R (ZX750P, ZX900B/C/D/E) (94 - 00)	◆ 3721
Kawasaki 900 & 1000 Fours (73 - 77)	0222
Kawasaki ZX900, 1000 & 1100 Liquid-cooled Fours (83 - 97)	◆ 1681
MOTO GUZZI 750, 850 & 1000 V-Twins (74 - 78)	0339
MZ ETZ Models (81 - 95)	◇ 1680
NORTON 500, 600, 650 & 750 Twins (57 - 70)	0187
Norton Commando (68 - 77)	0125
PEUGEOT Speedfight, Trekker & Vivacity Scooters (96 - 02)	◇ 3920
Piaggio (Vespa) Scooters (91 - 98)	◇ 3492
SUZUKI GT, ZR & TS50 (77 - 90)	◇ 0799
Suzuki TS50X (84 - 00)	◇ 1599
Suzuki 100, 125, 185 & 250 Air-cooled Trail bikes (79 - 89)	0797
Suzuki GP100 & 125 Singles (78 - 93)	◇ 0576
Suzuki GS, GN, GZ & DR125 Singles (82 - 99)	◇ 0888
Suzuki 250 & 350 Twins (68 - 78)	0120
Suzuki GT250X7, GT200X5 & SB200 Twins (78 - 83)	◇ 0469
Suzuki GS/GSX250, 400 & 450 Twins (79 - 85)	0736
Suzuki GS500 Twin (89 - 02)	◆ 3238
Suzuki GS550 (77 - 82) & GS750 Fours (76 - 79)	0363
Suzuki GS/GSX550 4-valve Fours (83 - 88)	1133
Suzuki SV650 (99 - 02)	◆ 3912
Suzuki GSX-R600 & 750 (96 - 00)	◆ 3553
Suzuki GSX-R600 (01 - 02), GSX-R750 (00 - 02) & GSX-R1000 (01 - 02)	◆ 3986
Suzuki GSF600 & 1200 Bandit Fours (95 - 01)	◆ 3367
Suzuki GS850 Fours (78 - 88)	0536
Suzuki GS1000 Four (77 - 79)	0484
Suzuki GSX-R750, GSX-R1100 (85 - 92), GSX600F, GSX750F, GSX1100F (Katana) Fours (88 - 96)	◆ 2055
Suzuki GSX600/750F & GSX750 (98 - 02)	◆ 3987
Suzuki GS/GSX1000, 1100 & 1150 4-valve Fours (79 - 88)	0737
Suzuki TL1000S/R & DL1000 (97 - 03)	◆ 4083
TRIUMPH Tiger Cub & Terrier (52 - 68)	0414
Triumph 350 & 500 Unit Twins (58 - 73)	0137
Triumph Pre-Unit Twins (47 - 62)	0251
Triumph 650 & 750 2-valve Unit Twins (63 - 83)	0122
Triumph Trident & BSA Rocket 3 (69 - 75)	0136
Triumph Fuel Injected Triples (97 - 00)	◆ 3755
Triumph Triples & Fours (carburettor engines) (91 - 99)	◆ 2162
VESPA P/PX125, 150 & 200 Scooters (78 - 03)	0707
Vespa Scooters (59 - 78)	0126
YAMAHA DT50 & 80 Trail Bikes (78 - 95)	◇ 0800
Yamaha T50 & 80 Townmate (83 - 95)	◇ 1247

Title	Book No
Yamaha YB100 Singles (73 - 91)	◇ 0474
Yamaha RS/RXS100 & 125 Singles (74 - 95)	0331
Yamaha RD & DT125LC (82 - 87)	◇ 0887
Yamaha TZR125 (87 - 93) & DT125R (88 - 02)	◇ 1655
Yamaha TY50, 80, 125 & 175 (74 - 84)	◇ 0464
Yamaha XT & SR125 (82 - 02)	◇ 1021
Yamaha Trail Bikes (81 - 00)	2350
Yamaha 250 & 350 Twins (70 - 79)	0040
Yamaha XS250, 360 & 400 sohc Twins (75 - 84)	0378
Yamaha RD250 & 350LC Twins (80 - 82)	0803
Yamaha RD350 YPVS Twins (83 - 95)	1158
Yamaha RD400 Twin (75 - 79)	0333
Yamaha XT, TT & SR500 Singles (75 - 83)	0342
Yamaha XZ550 Vision V-Twins (82 - 85)	0821
Yamaha FJ, FZ, XJ & YX600 Radian (84 - 92)	2100
Yamaha XJ600S (Diversion, Seca II) & XJ600N Fours (92 - 99)	◆ 2145
Yamaha YZF600R Thundercat & FZS600 Fazer (96 - 01)	◆ 3702
Yamaha YZF-R6 (98 - 02)	◆ 3900
Yamaha 650 Twins (70 - 83)	0341
Yamaha XJ650 & 750 Fours (80 - 84)	0738
Yamaha XS750 & 850 Triples (76 - 85)	0340
Yamaha TDM850, TRX850 & XTZ750 (89 - 99)	◇ ◆ 3540
Yamaha YZF750R & YZF1000R Thunderace (93 - 00)	◆ 3720
Yamaha FZR600, 750 & 1000 Fours (87 - 96)	◆ 2056
Yamaha XV (Virago) V-Twins (81 - 03)	◆ 0802
Yamaha XJ900F Fours (83 - 94)	◆ 3239
Yamaha XJ900S Diversion (94 - 01)	◆ 3739
Yamaha YZF-R1 (98 - 01)	◆ 3754
Yamaha FJ1100 & 1200 Fours (84 - 96)	◆ 2057
Yamaha XJR1200 & 1300 (95 - 03)	◆ 3981
Yamaha V-Max (85 - 03)	◆ 4072
ATVs	
Honda ATC70, 90, 110, 185 & 200 (71 - 85)	0565
Honda TRX300 Shaft Drive ATVs (88 - 00)	2125
Honda TRX300EX & TRX400EX ATVs (93 - 99)	2318
Honda Foreman 400 and 450 ATVs (95 - 02)	2465
Kawasaki Bayou 220/250/300 & Prairie 300 ATVs (86 - 03)	2351
Polaris ATVs (85 - 97)	2302
Polaris ATVs (98 - 03)	2508
Yamaha YFS200 Blaster ATV (88 - 98)	2317
Yamaha YFB250 Timberwolf ATVs (92 - 00)	2217
Yamaha YFM350 & YFM400 (ER and Big Bear) ATVs (87 - 03)	2126
Yamaha Banshee and Warrior ATVs (87 - 03)	2314
ATV Basics	10450
TECHBOOK SERIES	
Motorcycle Basics TechBook (2nd Edition)	3515
Motorcycle Electrical TechBook (3rd Edition)	3471
Motorcycle Fuel Systems TechBook	3514
Motorcycle Workshop Practice TechBook (2nd Edition)	3470
GENERAL MANUALS	
Motorcycle Service and Repair Techniques	4071
Twist and Go (automatic transmission) Scooters Service and Repair Manual	4082

◇ = not available in the USA   ◆ = Superbike

The manuals on this page are available through good motorcycle dealers and accessory shops. In case of difficulty, contact: **Haynes Publishing**
(UK) **+44 1963 442030**   (USA) **+1 805 498 6703**
(FR) **+33 1 47 17 66 29**   (SV) **+46 18 124016**
(Australia/New Zealand) **+61 3 9763 8100**

MCL16.03/04

Preserving Our Motoring Heritage

< The Model J Duesenberg Derham Tourster. Only eight of these magnificent cars were ever built – this is the only example to be found outside the United States of America

Almost every car you've ever loved, loathed or desired is gathered under one roof at the Haynes Motor Museum. Over 300 immaculately presented cars and motorbikes represent every aspect of our motoring heritage, from elegant reminders of bygone days, such as the superb Model J Duesenberg to curiosities like the bug-eyed BMW Isetta. There are also many old friends and flames. Perhaps you remember the 1959 Ford Popular that you did your courting in? The magnificent 'Red Collection' is a spectacle of classic sports cars including AC, Alfa Romeo, Austin Healey, Ferrari, Lamborghini, Maserati, MG, Riley, Porsche and Triumph.

A Perfect Day Out

Each and every vehicle at the Haynes Motor Museum has played its part in the history and culture of Motoring. Today, they make a wonderful spectacle and a great day out for all the family. Bring the kids, bring Mum and Dad, but above all bring your camera to capture those golden memories for ever. You will also find an impressive array of motoring memorabilia, a comfortable 70 seat video cinema and one of the most extensive transport book shops in Britain. The Pit Stop Cafe serves everything from a cup of tea to wholesome, home-made meals or, if you prefer, you can enjoy the large picnic area nestled in the beautiful rural surroundings of Somerset.

John Haynes O.B.E., Founder and Chairman of the museum at the wheel of a Haynes Light 12. >

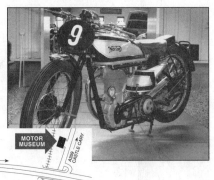

< The 1936 490cc sohc-engined International Norton – well known for its racing success

The Museum is situated on the A359 Yeovil to Frome road at Sparkford, just off the A303 in Somerset. It is about 40 miles south of Bristol, and 25 minutes drive from the M5 intersection at Taunton.

Open 9.30am - 5.30pm (10.00am - 4.00pm Winter) 7 days a week, except Christmas Day, Boxing Day and New Years Day

Special rates available for schools, coach parties and outings Charitable Trust No. 292048